I0825457

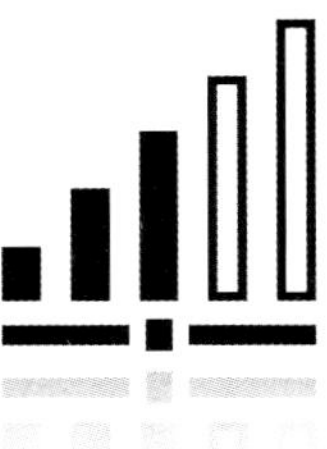

# ON RECORD 1996 G. BROWN

# CONTENTS

*ON RECORD* ENTRIES ARE NOT ORDERED ALPHABETICALLY, BUT ORGANIZED INTUITIVELY—A MIXTURE OF SEGUES BY MUSICAL GENRE OR STYLE.

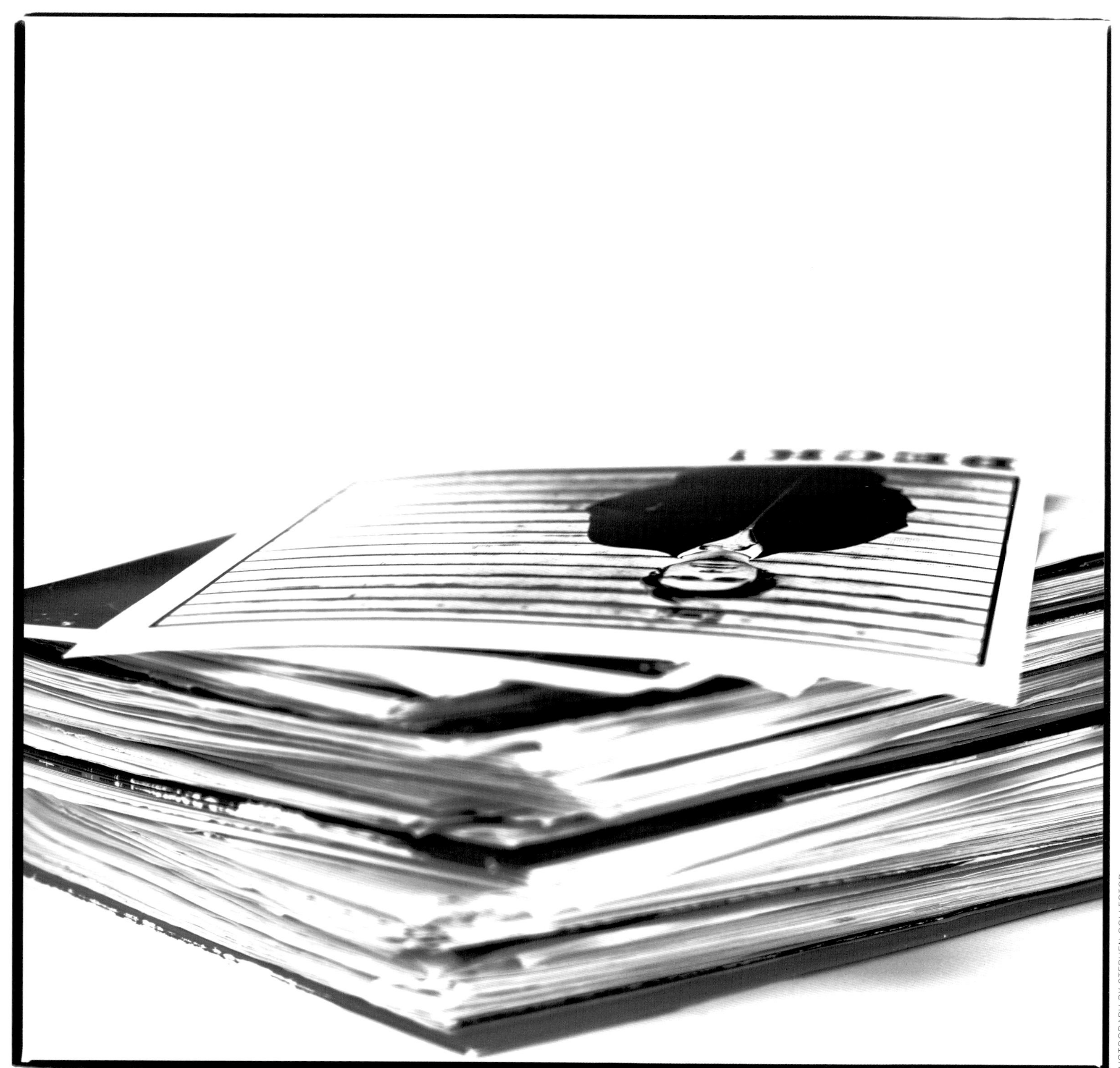

PHOTOGRAPH BY STEPHEN COLLECTOR

# ON RECORD VOL. 12 1996

**WHEN IT** started in 1987, South by Southwest seemed more like an easygoing jamboree in Texas Hill Country than serious business, as Austin became the capital of hip, with righteous Mexican food, barbecue and free-flowing Shiner Bock beer. But by 1996, SXSW had morphed into the largest and most boisterous music convention in the country, attracting 5,500 label talent scouts, musicians and writers. It was also where 12,000 fans bought $51 wristbands for admission to clubs, yet many got nothing but three nights of standing in line.

Your veteran music scribe navigated the maze of events and possibilities, from slick schmoozing (deals were made, parties were thrown) to three days of panel discussions (windbags bloviating about such topics as "Were the Grateful Dead Really Any Good?") to workshops, mentor sessions, demo critiques and a massive trade show. But predominantly, SXSW showcased Austin's love of live music. Squeezing into clubs late at night was a helluva lot of fun, with more than 600 bands performing at 39 venues.

Once a regional festival for indie bands, SXSW now saw major labels hosting their own showcases with big-name headliners and unsanctioned private performances. Thousands of fans crammed the streets, balconies and rooftops around the Outdoor Stage for free concerts. Bare-chested and writhing, punk icon Iggy Pop put on a forceful show. Joan Osborne gave a taste of her qawwali singing, which she had recently studied in India.

Krist Novoselic spoke at the opening session of the conference—the ex-Nirvana bassist was now an activist entering the political fray to fight censorship. Legendary songwriter Randy Newman, my personal hero, was the chosen spokesman for Microsoft's multimedia showcase. His ambitious modern opera version of Goethe's *Faust* was coming out on an enhanced CD—"the best thing anyone ever did for me with my clothes on," he said—and he performed part of *Faust* at the Austin Music Hall.

But he opened with his Oscar-nominated "You've Got a Friend in Me" from his film soundtrack for *Toy Story*. Afterwards, an earnest young lady asked him about the difference between his own work and work for hire. "Ah, I've been nominated eight times, and always I lose out to a singing lobster of something," he said about his luck at the Academy Awards. "When I write my diseased love songs for my own albums, it's hard work. But when I get an assignment from Disney, it's easy—I'll sell out in a second. 'You've Got a Friend in Me'? You don't got a fucking friend in me."

What we did get in 1996 was an eclectic mix of music. Four albums changed rap forever—OutKast's *ATLiens*, Fugees' *The Score*, Jay-Z's *Reasonable Doubt* and Tupac Shakur's *All Eyez on Me*. Beck, Weezer, Sublime and Rage Against the Machine released legacy-defining records, and Wilco and Fiona Apple emerged from the rock underground. Spice Girls brought pop music back to the charts with "Wannabe," and "Macarena" shrinked the world just a little bit with its corresponding goofy, easy-to-master dance. Even with two left feet, I got to interview artists, listen to all the records, go to all the concerts and pore over press kits. I was and am a lucky boy. Please allow me to share.. — **G. Brown**

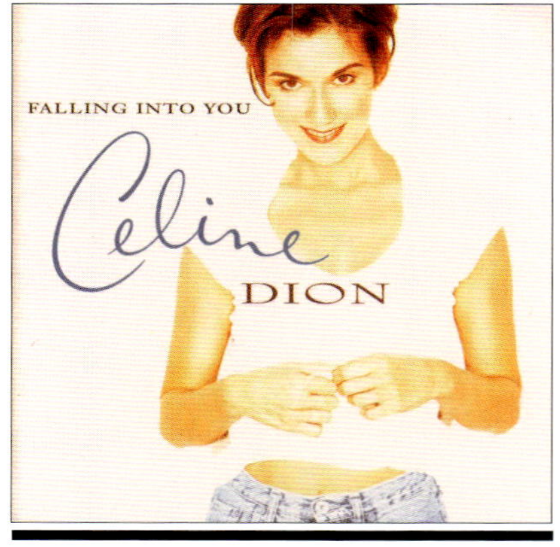


*Billboard* 200: *Falling into You* (No. 1)
*Billboard* Hot 100: "Because You Loved Me" (No. 1);
"It's All Coming Back to Me Now" (#2); "All by Myself" (#4)

## Céline Dion achieved worldwide renown releasing *Falling into You*, her fourth album of English-language songs.

**CAST AS** the next queen of all chanteuses, Céline Dion gradually become one of the world's best-selling recording artists. But the French-Canadian singer, a polished powerhouse with a rapturous five-octave soprano, never took her multinational stardom for granted. She grew up in a tiny village east of Montreal, the youngest of 14 children in a working-class musical family.

"My brothers and sisters all wanted to be singers, and each one is a part of me—growing up and hearing music every day gave me all the tools," she explained. "I'm not the most talented, but people were generous helping me get to where I am today. The rest of my family didn't have the timing, the record company support, maybe the dreams." When she turned 12, Dion came to the attention of producer René Angélil, who managed her career ever since (when Dion hit her 20s, they got married). She soon became the darling of the province—*la p'tite Québécoise*, the little Quebecker. At 18, with seven French albums to her credit, it was time to introduce her to the rest of the world. But there was a problem—she hardly spoke a word of English.

"To me, an international career meant doing whatever had to be done to sing for as many people as possible," Dion said. "So I went to school for two months and learned English—because I wanted to, not because I had to. And here I am."

In 1991, Disney chose Dion to sing the theme from *Beauty and the Beast* with a duet partner, Peabo Bryson. The song picked up a Grammy and an Oscar. Then came her first No. 1 single, "The Power of Love." Such hits as "When I Fall in Love" (from the film *Sleepless in Seattle*), "The Colour of My Love" and "If You Asked Me To" followed.

Dion's *Falling into You* album got its biggest boost from the No. 1 hit "Because You Loved Me" (the theme song to the film *Up Close and Personal*), one of three tracks produced by David Foster. The single "It's All Coming Back to Me Now," produced by former Meat Loaf partner Jim Steinman, was seven minutes of bombastic balladry. There was also a striking cover of Eric Carmen's "All by Myself."

Dion performed worldwide for over a year. Often compared to Whitney Houston and Mariah Carey, she separated from the divas with her sincere, openhearted style.

"When you're in the studio, you can always start again and do better until you're happy," she explained. "But you close your eyes, you try to deliver the song with feeling—and there's nobody in front of you. There's thick glass, you put on these big headphones, and the sound engineer doesn't even look at you while you're singing.

"But when you're onstage, you can sing other people's songs, you can move and dance with the audience. All year long I get told what to do—don't talk about this or that, don't forget to mention the new single. But onstage, nobody's telling me what to do. I can be myself, I can make mistakes—I'm just having a good time." ■

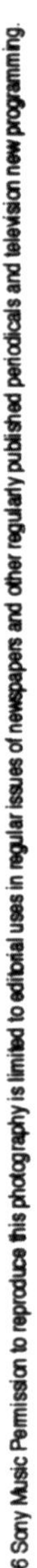

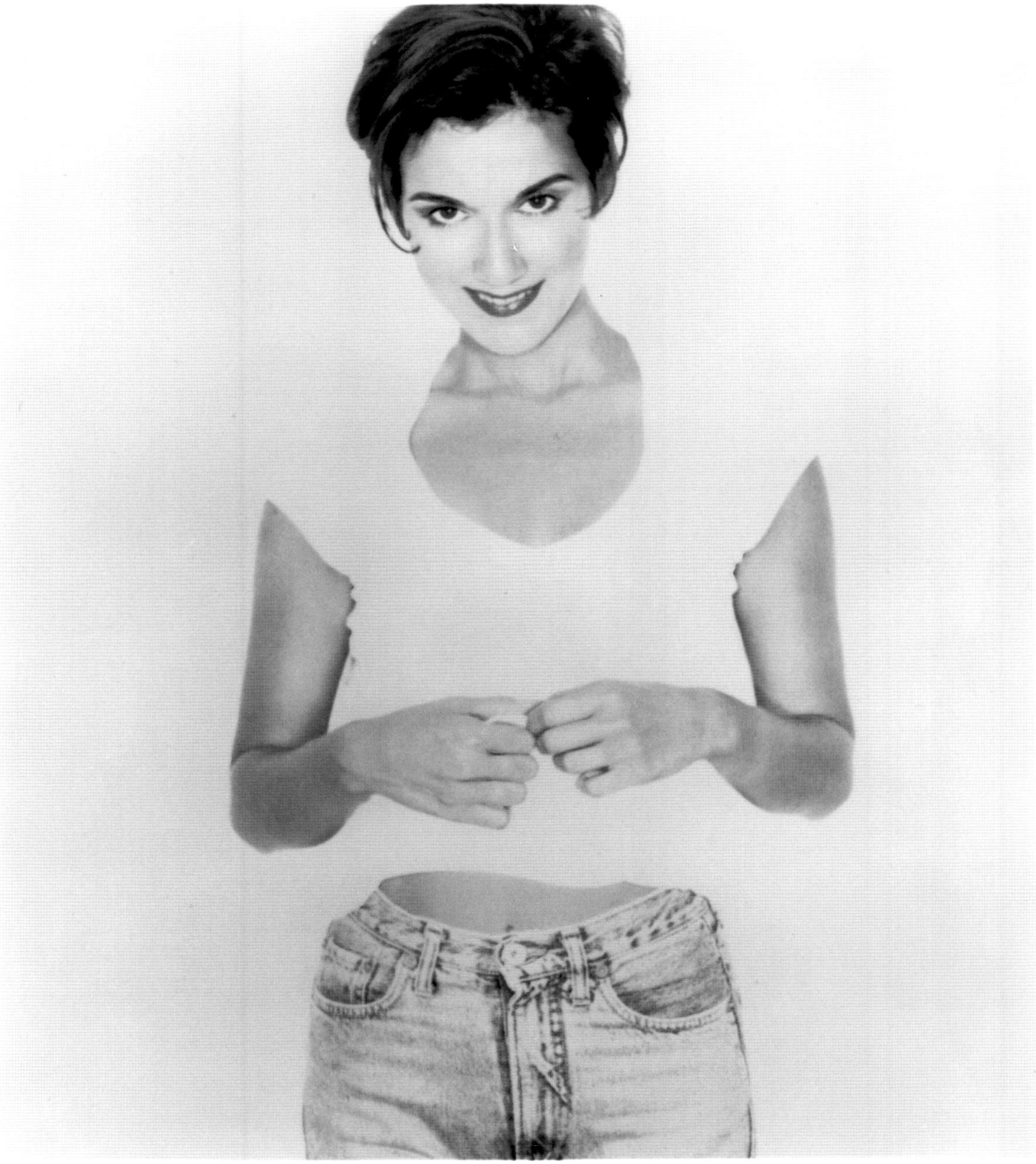

PHOTO CREDIT: RANDEE ST NICHOLAS

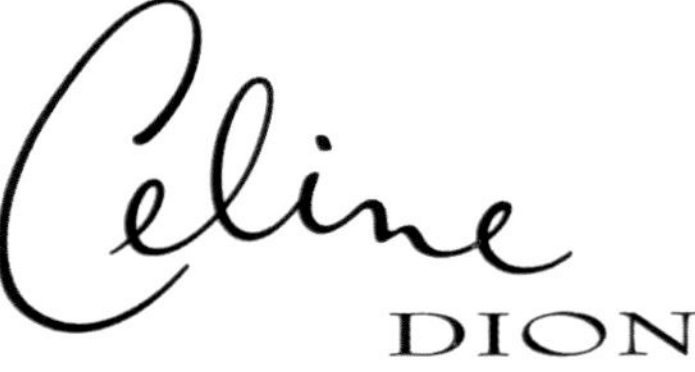


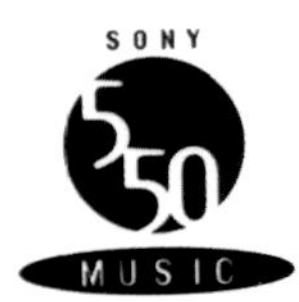

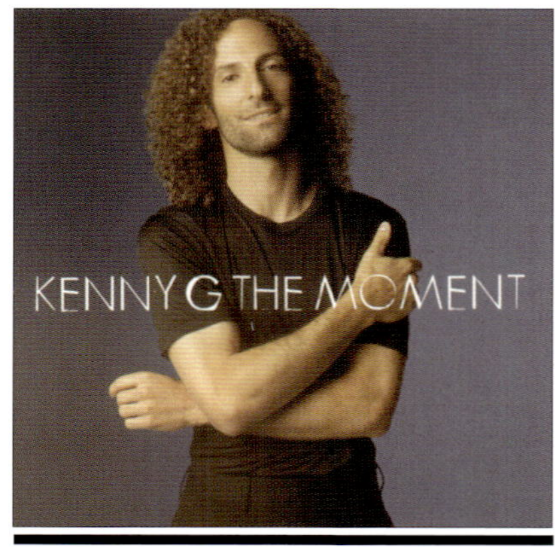


*Billboard* 200: *The Moment* (#2)
*Billboard* Hot 100: "The Moment" (#63); "Havana" (#66)

## Reaching No. 1 on the contemporary-jazz charts, *The Moment* upheld saxophonist **Kenny G**'s massive success.

**HE WAS** the best-selling instrumentalist ever—more than 40 million albums over the course of a 14-year recording career. Yet criticism of Kenny G's comforting, emotive style was significant—the musical range and depth of his records were portrayed as a fill-in for dental anesthesia in the film *Wayne's World 2*.

He said *The Moment,* his first studio album in four years, was his finest work to date. "As humbly as I can say it, I did a really good job," he assured. "I couldn't have made a better record—the sonics, the choice of songs, the playing, the diversity. When I started, I was hoping that I'd feel this way about it, and I'm glad I do."

Kenny G opened up his smooth jazz-pop sound to include tinges of Latin soul on "Havana"—a remix went to No. 1 on the dance-club charts. The title track was a pop, R&B and adult-contemporary hit—according to his publicity, Kenny G had his "moment" when he was 10 years old watching a sax player on *The Ed Sullivan Show.*

"Actually, I wanted to call the album *Moments.* My wife told me she didn't like that one, and she came up with *The Moment.* The same thing happened on my last album. I wanted to call it *One Breath.* She went, 'Nope, that's not gonna work—call it *Breathless.* So I usually come close, and my wife finishes it off. She has all the good ideas in the family."

*The Moment* contained Kenny G's finest vocal collaboration yet—Grammy award-winner Babyface wrote and sang "Everytime I Close My Eyes." "I'm proud of that piece because I normally don't participate in the songwriting and producing of the vocals on my records—I stay out of it and play my solos, work on my instrumentals," he explained. "But to see my name next to Babyface's, that makes me feel good. When we're working together, it doesn't seem like a big deal. It's just natural—we have a common way of looking at music, by feel."

Without changing his approach, Kenny G won new fans. "I'm actually a very independent guy," he said. "I don't know the other musicians in Seattle. I just hang out with my family and my seaplane-pilot friends." ■

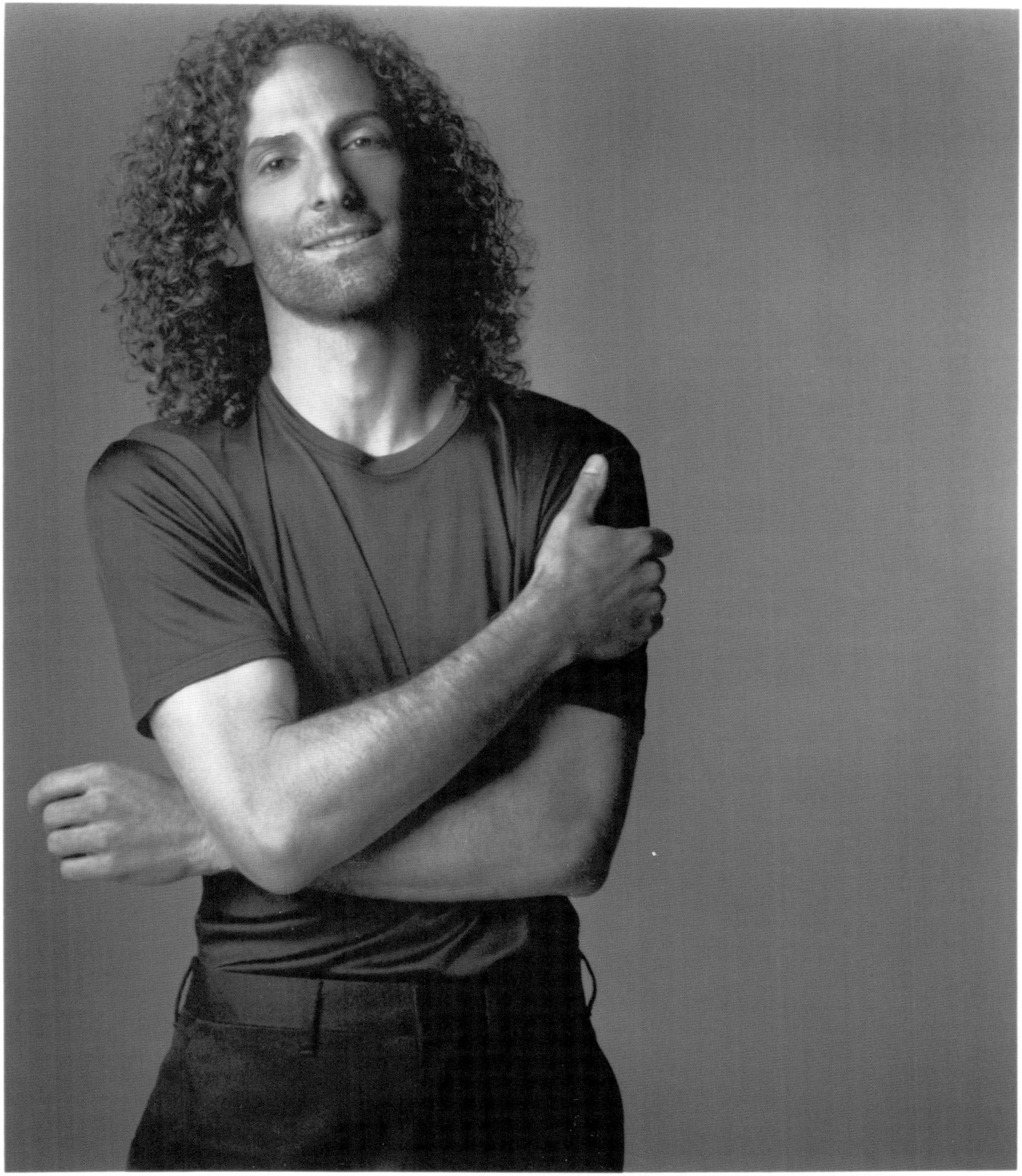

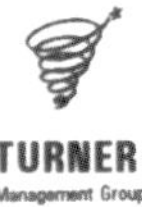


# KENNY G

ARISTA

PHOTO: MATTHEW ROLSTON

Billboard 200: *Tennessee Moon* (#14)

## Neil Diamond staged a comeback, heading for Nashville to work on an album of new material, *Tennessee Moon*.

**NEARLY 40** years since he figured out that writing songs was "a cool thing to do," Neil Diamond was one of the dominant forces in pop history—worldwide sales of 110 million albums and huge arena shows that sold out in minutes.

"I'm not prone to introversion or self-doubt," Diamond said. "I have some talent and the desire to work hard to hone that talent. I'll just keep producing music and see what happens. I hope there is a value to it beyond my own life—only time will tell. I feel like I'm part of a bigger plan, and I'm just playing my little part as best I can."

Diamond continued to enchant his fans and defy his critics when *Tennessee Moon* was acclaimed as his most exhilarating work of the past decade. His first collection of new songs since 1991 was written and recorded in Nashville with the city's greats (Waylon Jennings, Chet Atkins, the Mavericks' Raul Malo). It was country-flavored—the first time he'd had fiddle and pedal steel guitar songs on an album—but it also marked a return to his early guitar-based pop, including a remake of his 1967 hit "Kentucky Woman."

"It was a great experience," he enthused. "I got to meet a lot of creative people, to work in a brand-new situation. I was welcomed down there with open arms, and it's helpful to have fun when you're doing a project that requires a full year, day in and day out. It keeps your spirits up."

Diamond admitted to a four-year bout of writer's block before he re-emerged. "This was at a time when Columbia Records wanted some Christmas albums, a Brill Building album—the kinds of albums that I've always dreamed about doing in my career. But there was no need to write—and I didn't. I didn't have that deadline hanging over my head."

With the breakup of his 25-year marriage, Diamond threw himself into songwriting with the Nashville artists. "Certainly, there are elements that reflect my own personal feelings about my marriage," he said. "That's part of what makes a good album—exposing yourself and trying to deal with reality and truth. These are things that only inspire a writer. It's the hard way to do it, but a lot of these songs are very cathartic for me." ■

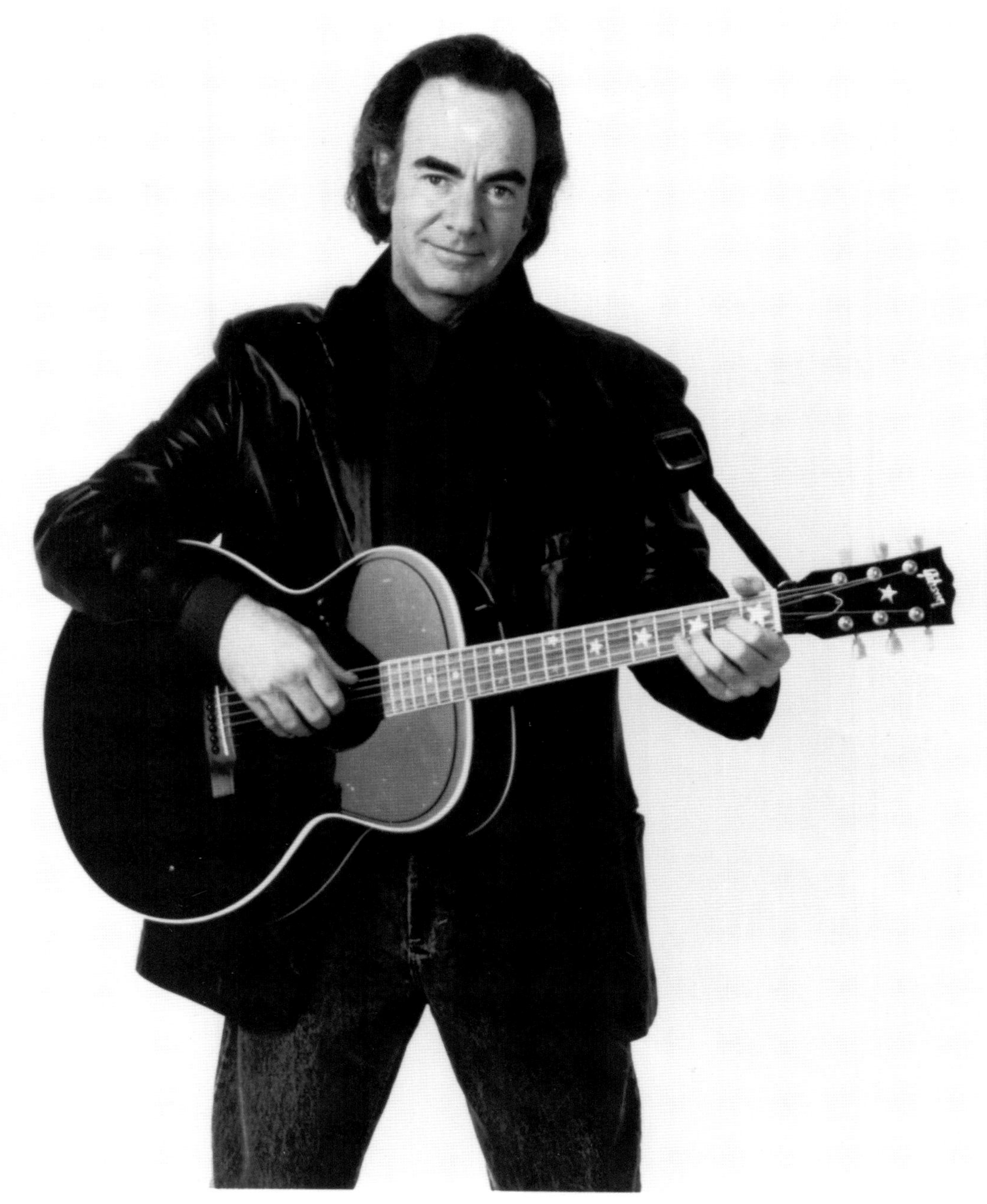



PHOTOGRAPH: NEAL PRESTON

**NEIL DIAMOND**

COLUMBIA
9601

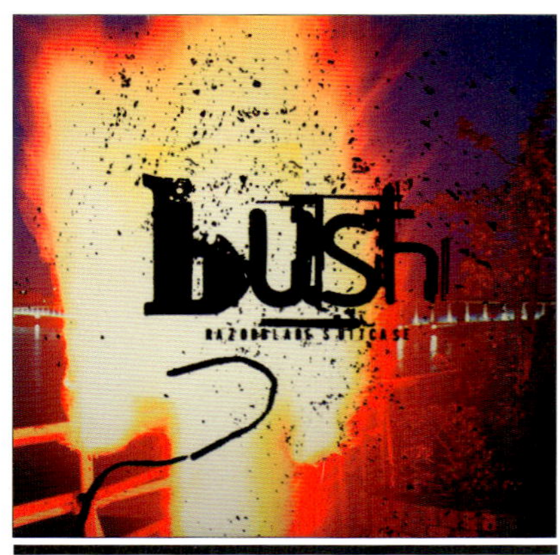


*Billboard* 200: *Razorblade Suitcase* (No. 1)

## Bush's fortunes in America blossomed when *Razorblade Suitcase* did a stretch at the top of the album charts.

**DEBUTING AT** the end of 1994 with the release of the album *Sixteen Stone*, Bush exploded on the American music scene behind monster modern-rock hits—"Everything Zen," "Little Things," "Comedown," "Glycerine" and "Machinehead"—and headline gigs across the country. Yet the British band's following had been built without a shred of homeland hype. In fact, when Bush was signed by Los Angeles-based executives, the band, co-created by vocalist Gavin Rossdale and guitarist Nigel Pulsford, had never been approached by a British label. *Sixteen Stone* had sold 3 million copies, but it wasn't even released in the UK until it broke in America.

"At the time, a lot of record companies in England didn't know what to do with bands because it was more geared toward dance music, ready-made packages of one guy doing all the music and a girl singing," Pulsford said. "Nigel and I realized we liked similar sorts of music," Rossdale added. "We wanted to have a band that entertained, that put more passion and energy into it, as a reaction against the introspective 'shoe-gazing' stuff that was coming out. Everything was in the shadow of the Smiths."

*Razorblade Suitcase* was a record to be reckoned with, another collision of swarming guitar buzz and Rossdale's dramatic, intense singing. The band worked with noted producer Steve Albini.

"It sounds less produced and more dynamic," Pulsford said. "Albini was one of my heroes for years, from Big Black on to his work with the Pixies, the Breeders' first album PJ Harvey and Nirvana. So many bands try to fit into a formula. They lose at that because they compromise their direction. We'd built up such a good base that we could afford to take risks. We tried to block out the consequences of what we'd done and make the record for ourselves."

"Swallowed" and "Greedy Fly" caught the ears of the grunge crowd, but the sudden success had resulted in alternative music snobs ridiculing Bush. The strikes against the London-based quartet? From sounding like a passionless Pearl Jam or Nirvana to Rossdale's pretty face. "It's inevitable," Rossdale said. "There are lots of easy shots to be taken—and everyone's taking them." ■

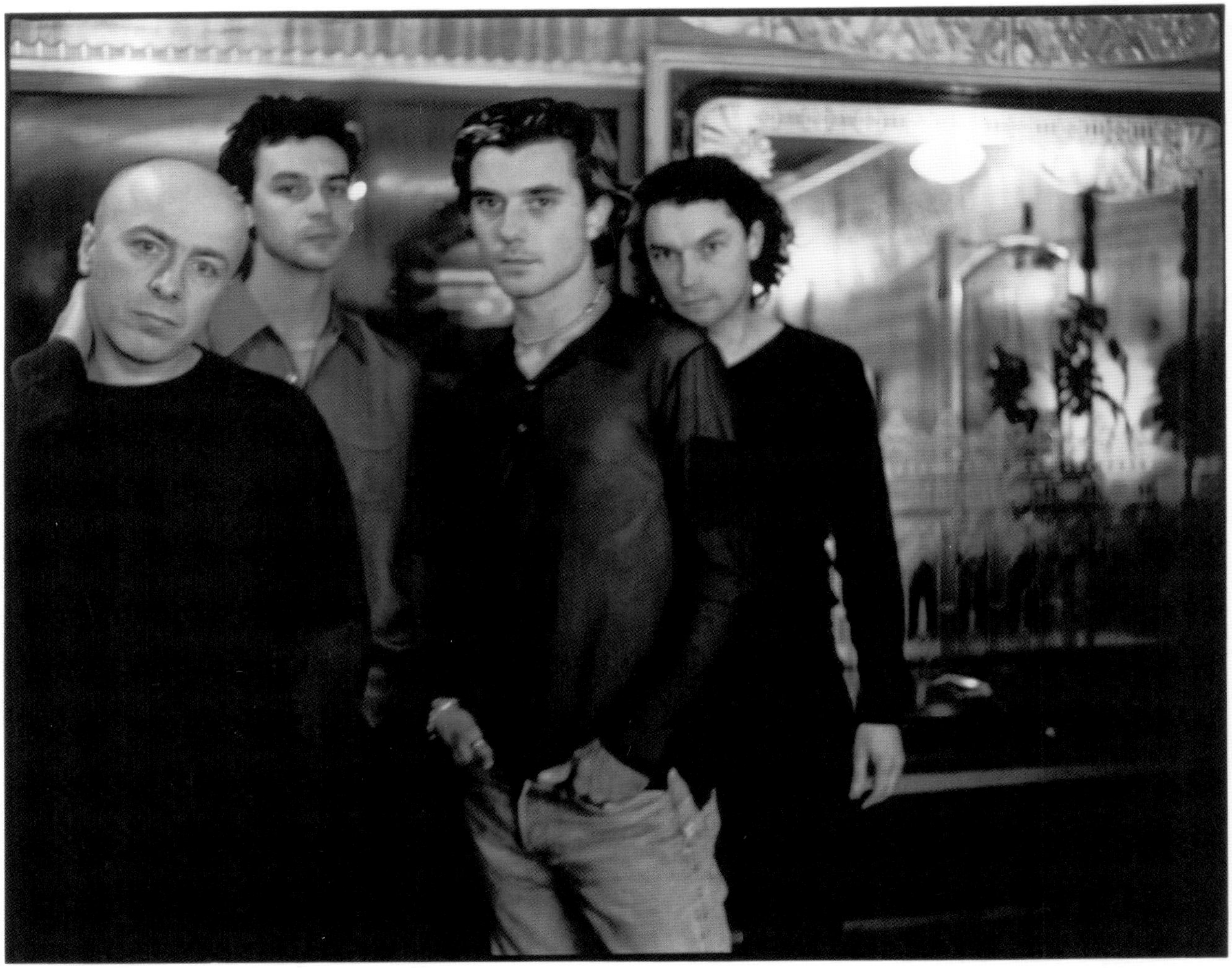

Photo credit: Glen Luchford

Nigel Pulsford Dave Parsons Gavin Rossdale Robin Goodridge

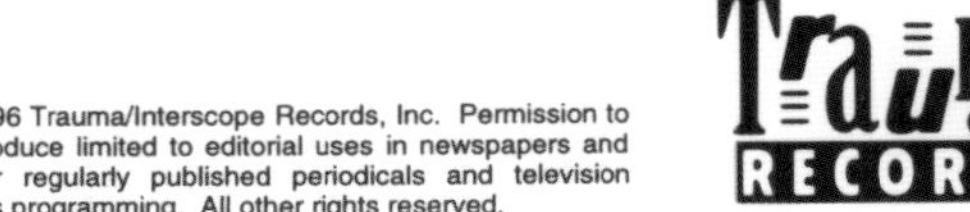


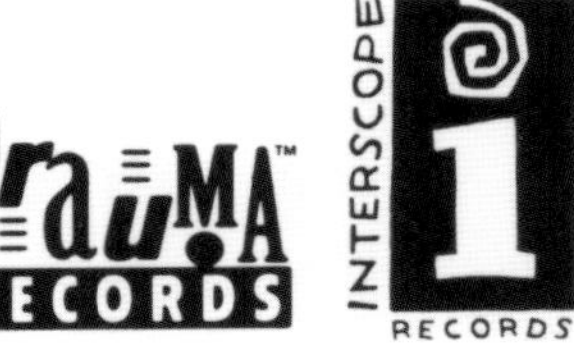

*Billboard* 200: *Tiny Music...Songs from the Vatican Gift Shop* (#4)

## *Tiny Music...Songs from the Vatican Gift Shop* was hampered by the inability of Stone Temple Pilots to tour.

**IN 1992**, *Core* made Stone Temple Pilots alterna-icons, and 1994's *Purple* debuted at No. 1 on the album charts. So when *Tiny Music... Songs from the Vatican Gift Shop* was released, the band blocked out a huge summer tour to support the album. But STP went missing in action, abandoning the plans because of singer Scott Weiland's court-ordered rehab program.

*Tiny Music*... deserved more. Collaborating with producer Brendan O'Brien (Pearl Jam, Rage Against the Machine), the California-based quartet—Weiland, Dean DeLeo, Robert DeLeo and Eric Kretz—carved out tuneful and creative musical terrain, blending metallic riffs, psychedelic experimentation, punk energy and pop melodies. "Big Bang Baby," "Trippin' on a Hole in a Paper Heart" and "Lady Picture Show" were the tight, canny hits.

Some lyrical content was used as an index of Weiland's angst. "Pop's Love Suicide," a clever, meandering tune with agitated guitar from Dean DeLeo, had a descending vocal from Weiland, who dove right into the song's references to "pop star homicide." In "Tumble in the Rough," he insisted that he was "not looking for a new way to die."

Stone Temple Pilot began a fall/winter tour. The gossip-column fodder? Weiland, fresh from one of the most trying periods of his life, was traveling with a counselor who offered a voice of constancy and reason. After gigs, all four members hung out and greeted fans and contest winners. Weiland smiled a lot and appeared upbeat—he autographed everything that was put in front of him.

"It really means a lot to play again with this band," he said. "The love and music we have between us outweigh all the personal problems." But Weiland's drug use continued. The final tour dates had to be cancelled for him to return to rehab. ■

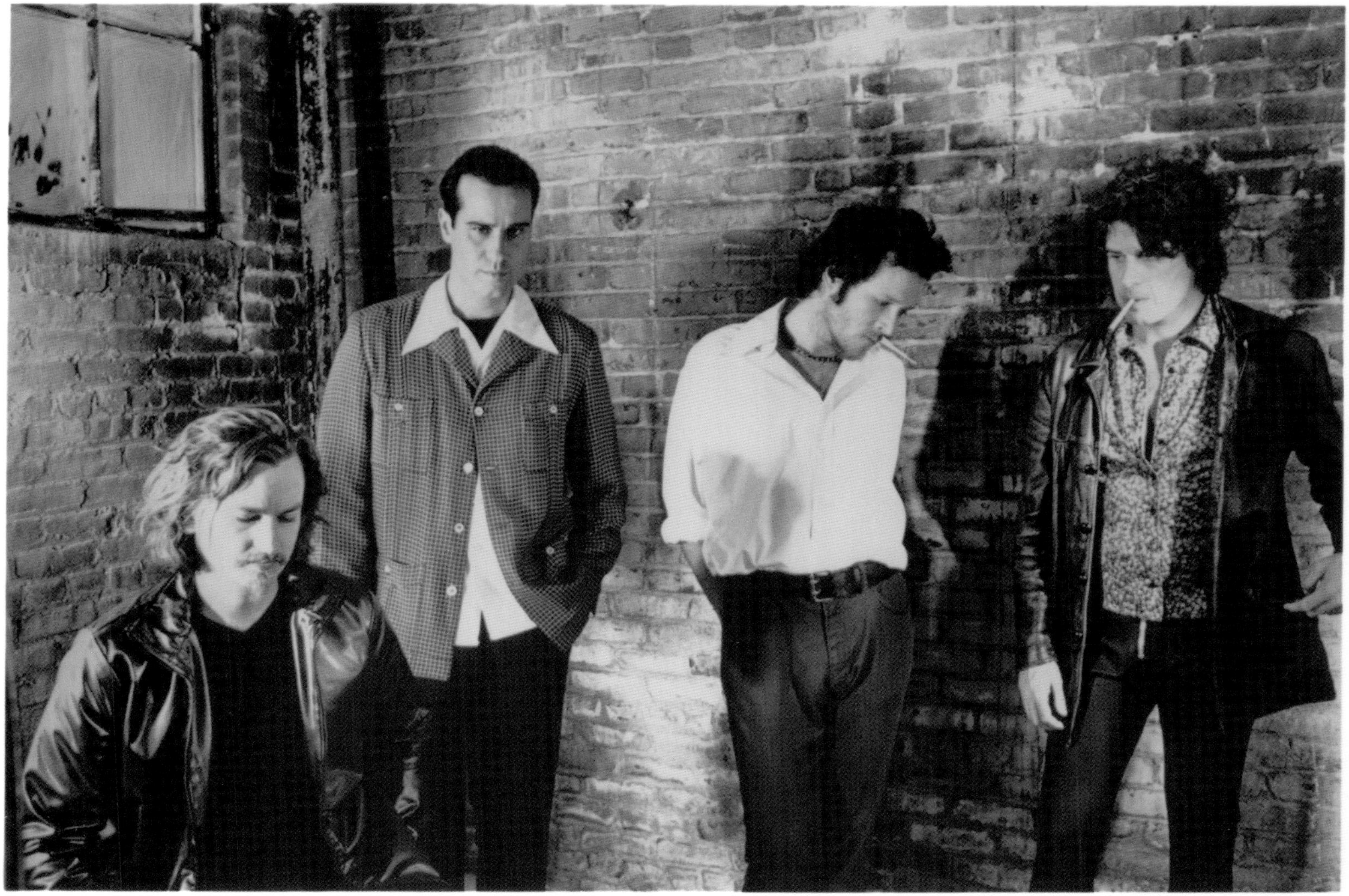

Photo credit: John Eder

Eric Kretz Robert DeLeo Scott Weiland Dean DeLeo

*Stone Temple Pilots*

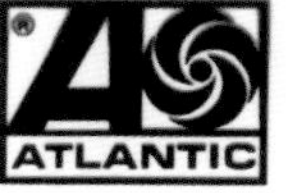

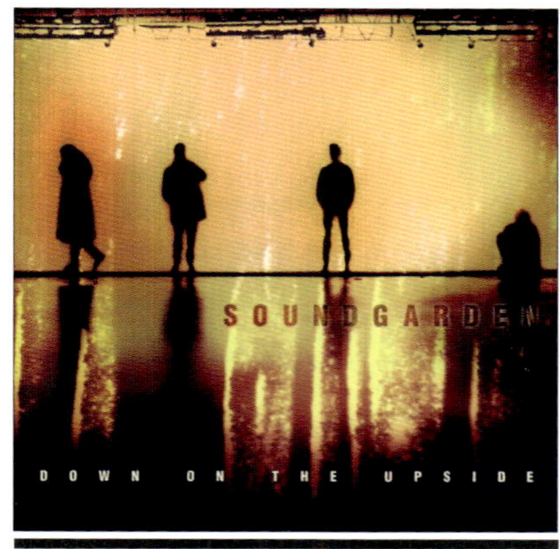


*Billboard* 200: *Down on the Upside* (#2)

## Soundgarden deviated from its heavy grunge pedigree, investigating disparate sounds on *Down on the Upside*.

**BEFORE THE** multiplatinum album *Superunknown* and the smash single "Black Hole Sun" cemented Soundgarden's position as one of Seattle's leading acts, the group was pretty much left alone to persevere, evolve and never compromise. But being a 10-year overnight success story had taken its toll.

"With fad and hype, record sales don't make any sense—10 million people can't possibly be fans of your band," vocalist Chris Cornell said. "Then you put out another record and you realize they weren't. They responded to your product just like they would respond to a commercial for a chicken sandwich—they went out and got it, it's as simple as that. Advertising does sell. "But it's not a realistic perception in music, where it becomes way too important sometimes, or people will love you or hate you for the wrong reasons. That was the biggest thing that worried me during the 'Black Hole Sun' period—I've never wanted anyone to buy a Soundgarden record who wasn't going to like it."

Returning with *Down on the Upside*, Soundgarden didn't disappoint. The band's members produced the album themselves, keeping overdubs to a minimum and granting it a more raw, gritty, spontaneous sound than the previous effort.

"We've always been trying to get that 'live' feeling," Cornell explained. "There's motion in it, like you're in a room listening to a band—as opposed to a lot of music in the late Eighties, where everything was so deep and wide sonically that it sounded like surgery. We went through years of the wall-of-sound approach to recording, where you have an assault of giant, heavy sound coming through the speakers at you.

"But certain songs can be heavier emotionally with just a fucked-up acoustic guitar playing by itself. We wanted to get into a less-is-more dynamic, hearing a guy's voice and fingers on his guitar. A lot of songs on *Superunknown* were difficult to transform live—some of the better ones never really relaxed. It feels more natural playing the new material right away."

There was a blend of tempos and styles, of delicacy and power—the lumbering swagger of "Pretty Noose" (with Kim Thayil's guitar crunches behind Cornell's throaty wail), the bluesy, acoustic-based "Burden in My Hand," and Cornell's whisper-to-a-scream tactic on "Blow Up the Outside World." Cornell wickedly spat out the chorus of "Ty Cobb"—"Hard headed fuck you all."

What Led Zeppelin was to classic rock, Soundgarden was to alternative rock—pigeon-holed as a metal/hard-rock band when they'd really gained a mature style, deftly manipulating guitar-god elements and melodic content. "Everyone's seen us now on TV a million times, and that's not going to bring in any new people coming to see another band from Seattle or sizing us up with another band from Seattle or any other reason," Cornell said. "It's just fans now." ■

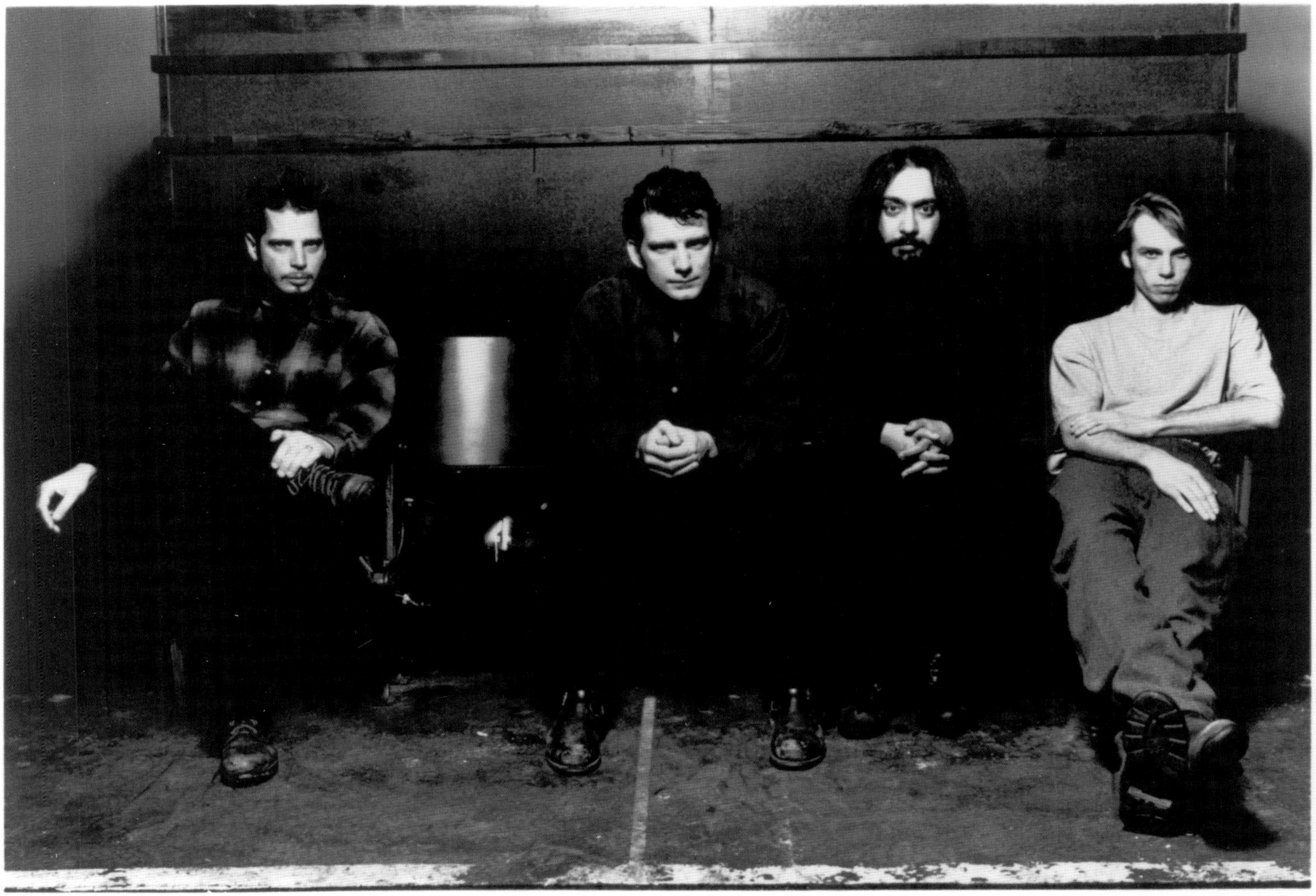

Photo: Kevin Westenberg 5/96

Chris Cornell Ben Shepherd Kim Thayil Matt Cameron

# SOUNDGARDEN

*Susan Silver Management*

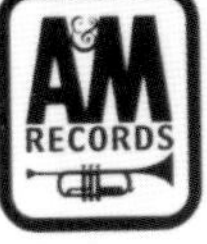

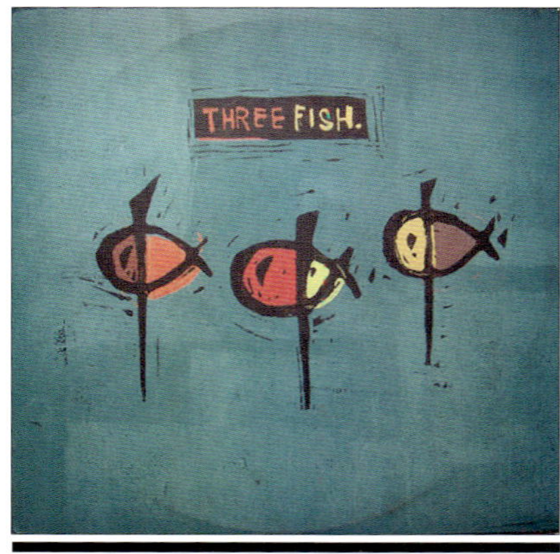


## A window of opportunity to dabble in different music than usual led Pearl Jam bassist Jeff Ament to Three Fish.

**WHEN SUCCESS** overwhelmed Jeff Ament, a founding member of a pioneering grunge band, he resorted to a side project. "It happened so fast for Pearl Jam—a lot of touring and hard work and not being centered, people constantly in our faces wanting us to come here and go there," the bassist said. "With Three Fish, I am reminded of a peaceful side again—confidence as a songwriter, playing music in small venues."

The undertaking began in 1992 when Pearl Jam toured with Tribe After Tribe, an outfit that played self-described "African acid rock." Ament struck up a friendship with guitarist and lead vocalist Robbi Robb, a native of South Africa. "Jeff and I hung out on camping trips and in hot tubs," Robb said. "We became fax warriors with our poetry, shared a lot of common interests," Ament added. "By the time we got together in Seattle and ran tape, it manifested itself in the music."

*Three Fish* resounded with melancholy hippie-rock. To create the album, Ament played 12-string and fretless bass, 12-string guitar and djembe, a West African hand drum. Robb provided the mysticism. "Each song was written a recorded in less than an hour," Robb enthused. "We picked up our instruments and started noodling. In seven days, we made 35 pieces of music. There's still a lot laying around. I had to go back to a couple of songs and figure out what I'd sung. There was a real sense of discovery—'What was that about?'"

The trio was inspired by the 13th century Persian poet Jalaluddin Rumi. "Rumi popped up in the studio, came whirling in," Robb laughed. "I found one poem Robbi had missed, the story of the three fish," Ament explained. "And while he was reading it, I was playing acoustic guitar. We got an idea—why not do a children's album, find all sorts of spiritual parables and put them to music?"

The transcendent sound of *Three Fish* was sculpted with a Middle Eastern dynamic ebb and flow familiar to fans of Led Zeppelin. "In order to be healthy, anybody interested in integrating different parts of their own psyche would have to end up in the East at some point," Robb said. "The thing I love about Jeff is that he's genuine in the way he approaches those subjects. He doesn't exploit it; he wants to learn."

Three Fish—Ament, Robb and drummer Richard Stuverud—showcased the songs on a club tour. Ament hoped to carry the energy over to Pearl Jam's fourth album, *No Code*. "I grew up on a monastery for a while, even took monk vows, so that's the way we approach the tour," Robb said. "There's no alcohol in our rider. Before we go onstage, we do lustral chants, we muse and pray to get on the same plane. There are even things we do that can nourish Jeff's relationship with his wife." ■

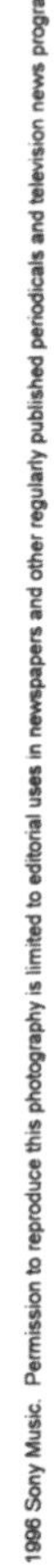

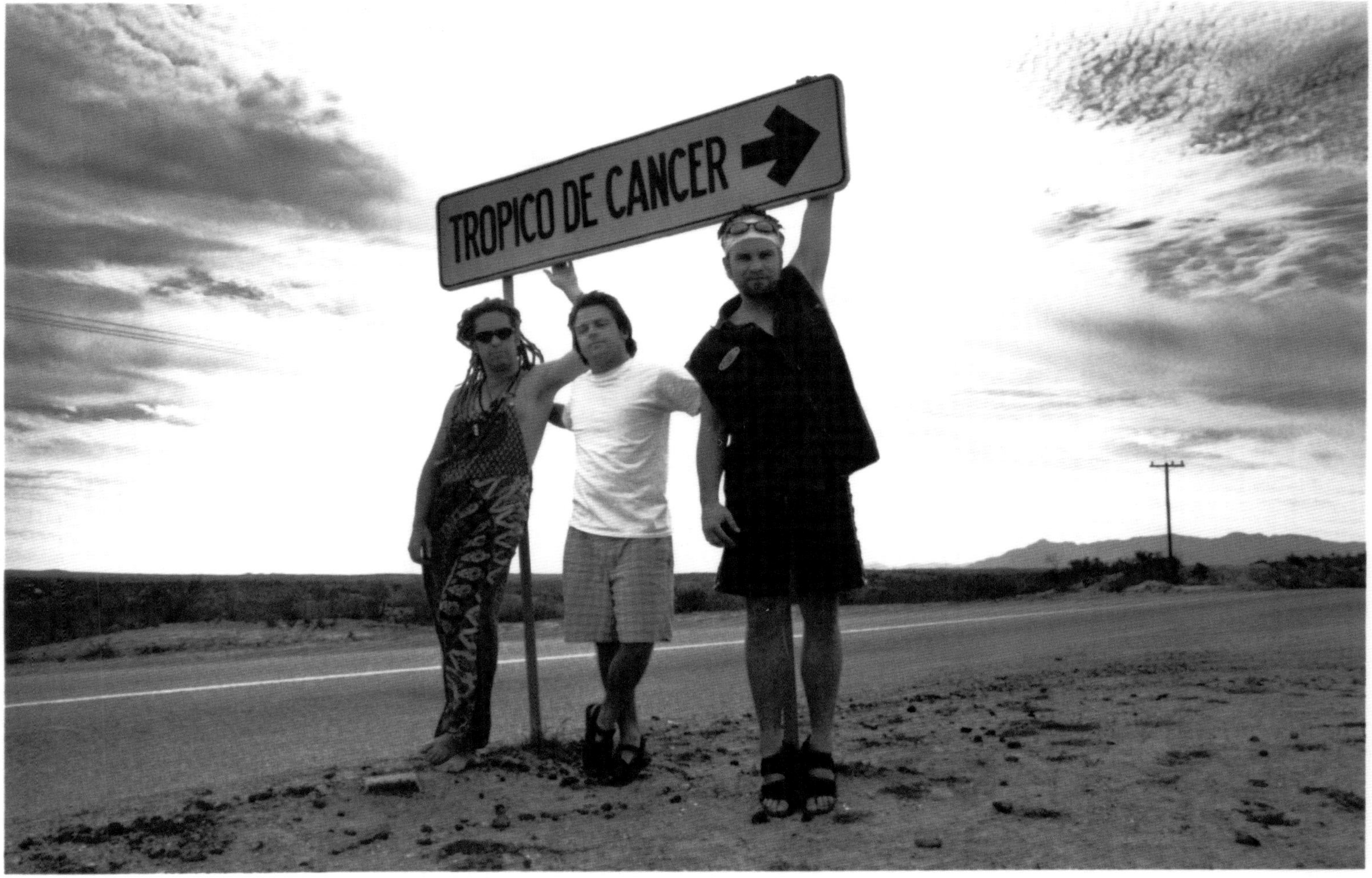

L - R : ROBBI ROBB, RICHARD STUVERUD, JEFF AMENT

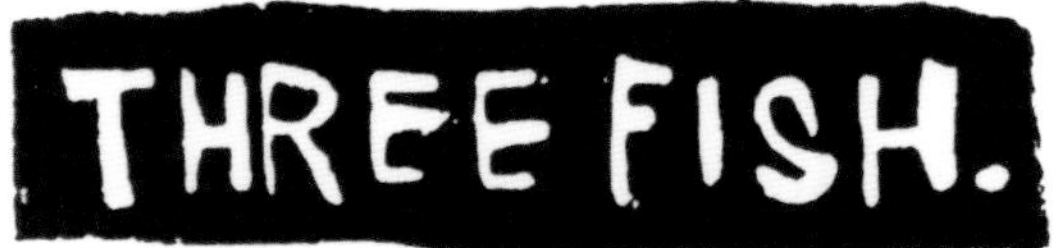

9604

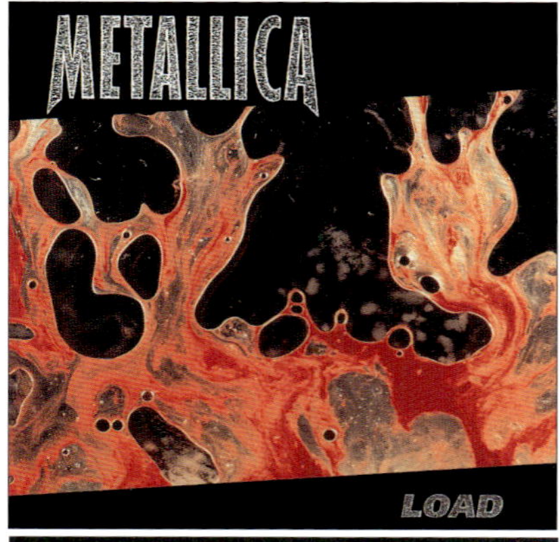


*Billboard* 200: *Load* (No. 1)
*Billboard* Hot 100: "Until It Sleeps" (#10); "Hero of the Day" (#60); "King Nothing" (#90)

# Marking a change in musical direction, the album *Load* drew fire from some of Metallica's diehard supporters.

**THE MEMBERS** of Metallica had watched the world of music change in the years since 1991's *Metallica*—colloquially known as *The Black Album*—had sold more than 12 million albums worldwide. It made for an anticipated and ballyhooed follow-up. *Load* was still undeniably heavy, but with a more accessible, somewhat scaled-down sound. The mad-dog staccato attack of yore had been displaced by a more retro hard-rock feel, with acoustic and slide guitar breaks and enriched vocal references.

The changes didn't thrill the speed-metal pundits who felt Metallica had peaked with thrashier declarations of attitude like 1986's *Master of Puppets*. They seemed aghast that the band might have matured between the ages of 20 and 30. But the Beavises and Buttheads needed to settle down. It wasn't that Metallica had gone soft, just that the band had diversified.

"People try to hate us—and it's fun," frontman James Hetfield said. "There's never any big plan. It's just natural to want to do some things. Some bands don't feel it, or they get a little safe in their older age—'Well, that's worked for us, let's keep doing it.' That has never been on Metallica's menu. We go with our hearts. Growth has always been a part of it."

*Load*, which debuted at No. 1 on the album charts, had something for everyone—the thunderous, crunchy "Ain't My Bitch," the pulsing "Hero of the Day" and "King Nothing," even country licks on "Mama Said." "Until It Sleeps" was an intimate disclosure about Hetfield's recent ordeal—his father had died after a two-year battle with cancer. In contrast to his trademark bellowing vocals, he sang the nuanced power ballad with a smooth presence.

"There are a few people out there in the crowd that really don't like that song, and they try to make it known to me. They'll follow me around flipping me off—that gives me an extra bit of fuel," Hetfield said. "Hey, you get older—fuck them. These lyrics mean a whole shitload to me, and if they can't understand it, then too bad. I know as a group those guys can't think for themselves, and they have to go with what their little leader says. They can't tell you why they don't like it."

One other thing threw Metallica loyalists into a dither—the foursome's newly shorn locks. Hetfield got a haircut when he was drunk. "My dad always told me, 'You're not gonna get hurt unless you let it get to you,' and we really do laugh along with this silly stuff that gets said. They're wasting their time. Music is the main thing, no doubt. All the songs on *Load* are completely pure and heartfelt. We can't go wrong." ■

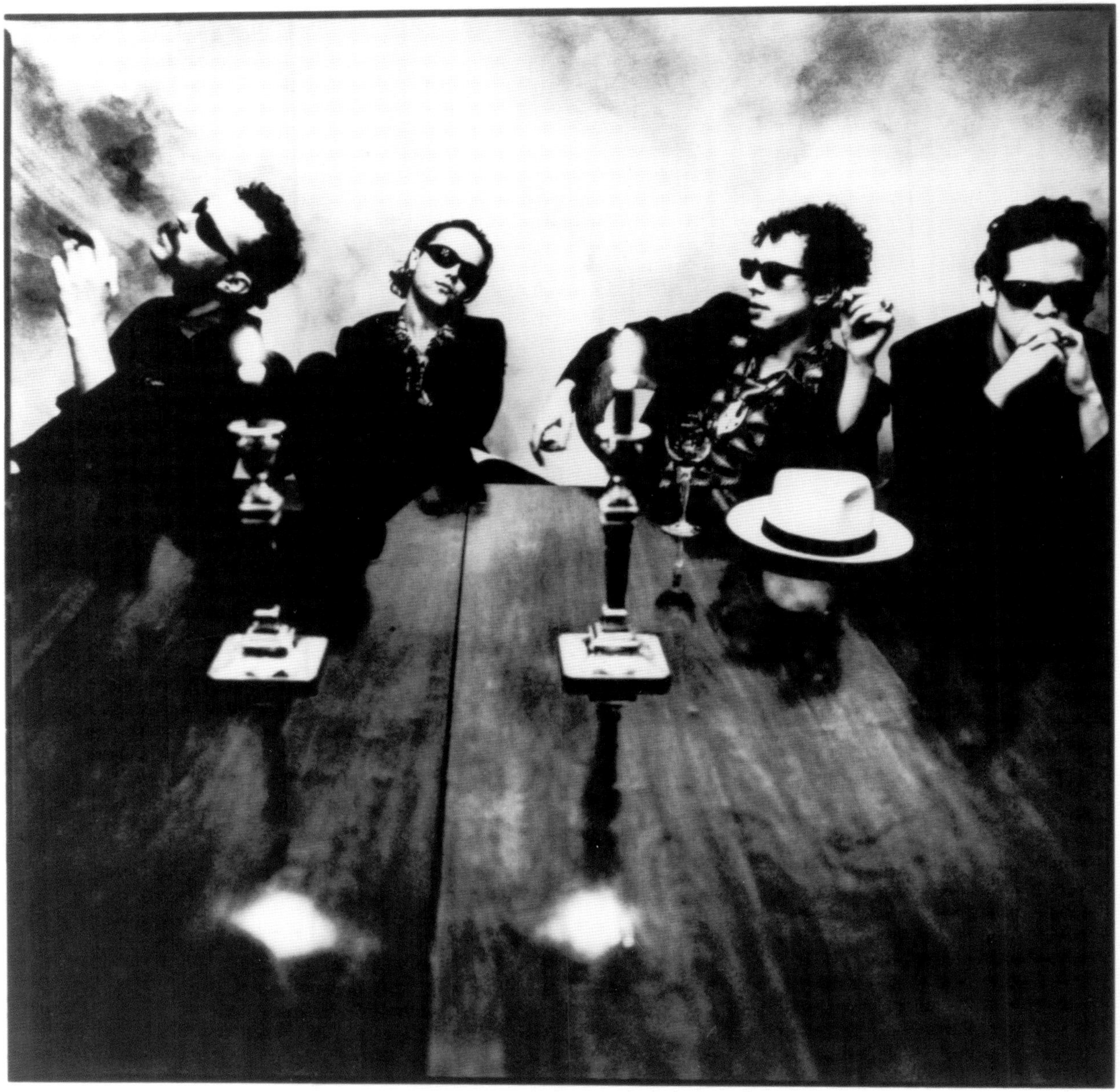

PHOTO CREDIT ANTON CORBIJN / 1996

L R : JAMES HETFIELD, LARS ULRICH, KIRK HAMMETT JASON NEWSTED

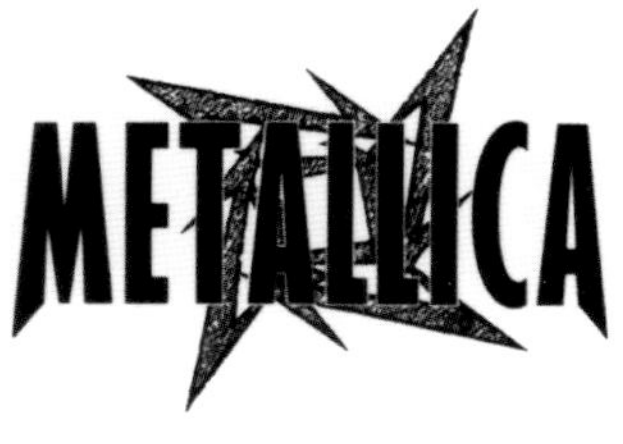


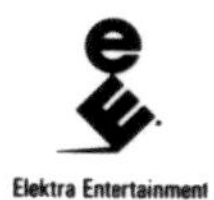

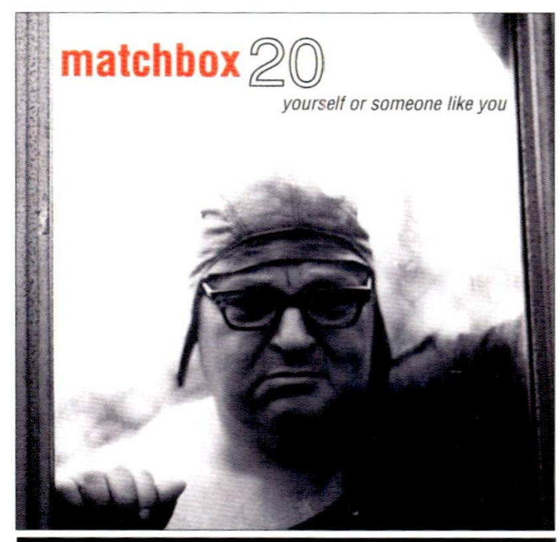


*Billboard* 200: *Yourself or Someone Like You* (#5)
*Billboard* Hot 100: "Real World" (#38); "Back 2 Good" (#24)

## The monster debut *Yourself or Someone Like You* established Florida's Matchbox 20 as a bona fide "it band."

**WITH SO** much product in the marketplace, being a new band was a dismaying prospect. But Matchbox 20 pressed on, and *Yourself or Someone Like You*, the Florida outfit's debut album, went Top 10 and multiplatinum. Leader Rob Thomas proved a savvy and successful craftsman of breakthrough radio hits—"Push," "Real World" and "3 A.M." clogged the airwaves.

"First you're in a local band, and everybody says, 'Yeah, you're good, but you have to get signed,'" Thomas said. "Then you get signed and everybody says, 'Yeah, but that doesn't mean you're going to get any radio play.' You get radio play and everybody says, 'Yeah, but that's not like selling records.' Then you sell some records and everybody says, 'Well, now you're a one-hit wonder.' Then you come out with a couple more songs, and everybody says, 'Well, this album's a hit, but you'll never be able to pull it off again.' They draw a line, you step over it, and they draw another one. Maybe it keeps your creativity up."

Producer Matt Serletic (Collective Soul) was credited for bringing Thomas, drummer Paul Doucette and bassist Brian Yale together with guitarists Adam Gaynor and Kyle Cook, the group that became Matchbox 20. Thomas was blessed with a knack for emotionally charged tunes, and fans connected with them.

"3 A.M." examined the dealings between Thomas and his young, single mother. He ran away from home in Orlando at age 15 and "stayed gone," drifting around to understand his family problems. Every night in concert, Thomas told audiences that "3 A.M." was "a drinking song about my mama." "I don't want people to get the wrong idea, that it's another woman-that-left-me song," he explained. "That's one that has been around for years."

Thomas made no secret of the fact that the theme of "Push," a No. 1 modern-rock track, was "emotional violence, about how I let myself be manipulated in a relationship." But the band received a fair amount of flak from people who took the song the wrong way, faulting the band for extolling domestic abuse. "You make a record and you sit around wondering what people are going to think, and that never popped up," Thomas said. "We didn't realize that *Time* magazine was going to call us 'the misogynistic rockers of the Nineties.'"

According to Thomas, "Push" was written from three points of view, including that of one of the women it was about. When the hit was nominated for a Grammy, Thomas was contacted by an old girlfriend who asked for royalties, claiming she inspired it. The only trouble was, it wasn't her, it was someone like her. "You can't sue someone for their thoughts and feelings," Thomas said. "Glen (Phillips) of Toad the Wet Sprocket pulled me aside and asked, 'Is that really happening? No? Phew. Every songwriter in the world didn't want that precedent to get set.'" ■

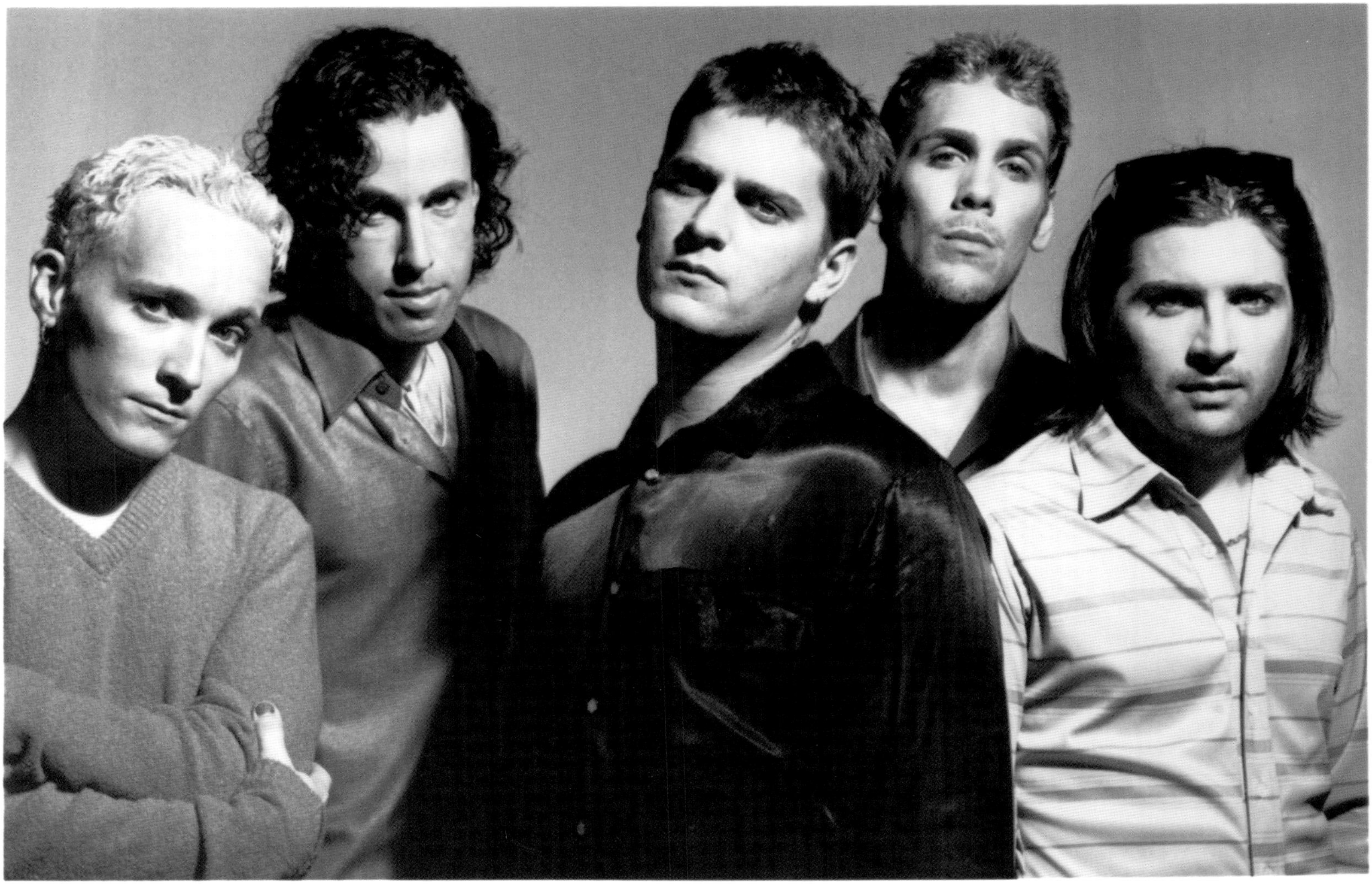

Paul Doucette

Adam Gaynor

Rob Thomas

Kyle Cook

Brian Yale

**matchbox** 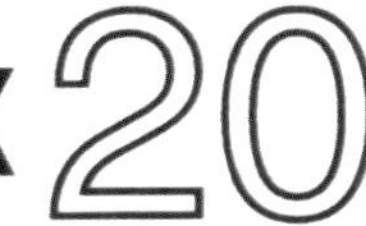


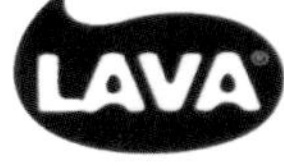


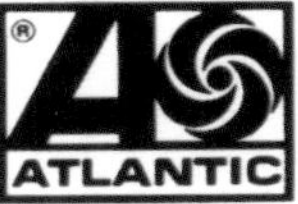

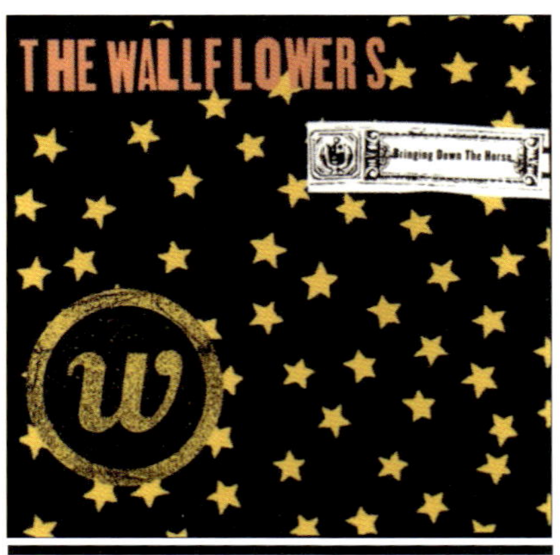


*Billboard* 200: *Bringing Down the Horse* (#4)

## The Wallflowers, guided by rock scion Jakob Dylan, stepped out of the shadows with *Bringing Down the Horse*.

**THE YOUNGEST** of Bob Dylan's five children, Jakob Dylan asked for his first electric guitar at age 12 after seeing the Clash in concert during the "Combat Rock" tour. When he formed the Wallflowers in the early Nineties, he was determined to make it without depending on his famous family connections. The Los Angeles band began introducing their rootsy, soulful intentions, finding a particularly congenial haven at the Kibitz Room of Canter's Deli, one of the town's more fabled hangouts.

Yet the first album's "retro" rock wasn't in style, as grunge had a stranglehold on the airwaves. "After just one record, we were dropped from our label," Dylan said. "At that point, we were perceived as damaged goods—the band couldn't get a new deal, and I was Bob's son. People didn't want to talk to me or work with me—they weren't responding at all. There was *nothing* going on."

But Dylan soon found himself answering fewer questions about having a rock-star relative and more about being a rock star. After switching record companies and a series of personnel changes, the Wallflowers fought their way back into the game. Produced by T-Bone Burnett, the album *Bringing Down the Horse* yielded two career-making hits—"One Headlight" slyly interwove funky organ and dobro, and "6th Avenue Heartache" offered soaring glide guitar. "I was not tempted to jump on any bandwagon and add rap or metal," Dylan said with a laugh. "I stayed with my instincts, which means using real instruments and actually playing them. I'm not strictly a traditionalist, but much of what I hear today seems temporary, a novelty, a shortcut."

The Wallflowers' sound honored such classic groups as the Band and Tom Petty & the Heartbreakers—but with dynamics for a new generation. Keyboardist Rami Jaffe (with Dylan, the only original Wallflower) delivered rich Hammond B-3 improvisations, and guitarist Michael Ward (from John Hiatt's old band) spiced things up with his lively riffing. *Bringing Down the Horse* was certified quadruple-platinum, and "One Headlight" earned Grammy Awards in the Best Rock Song and Best Rock Performance (Group) categories. ■

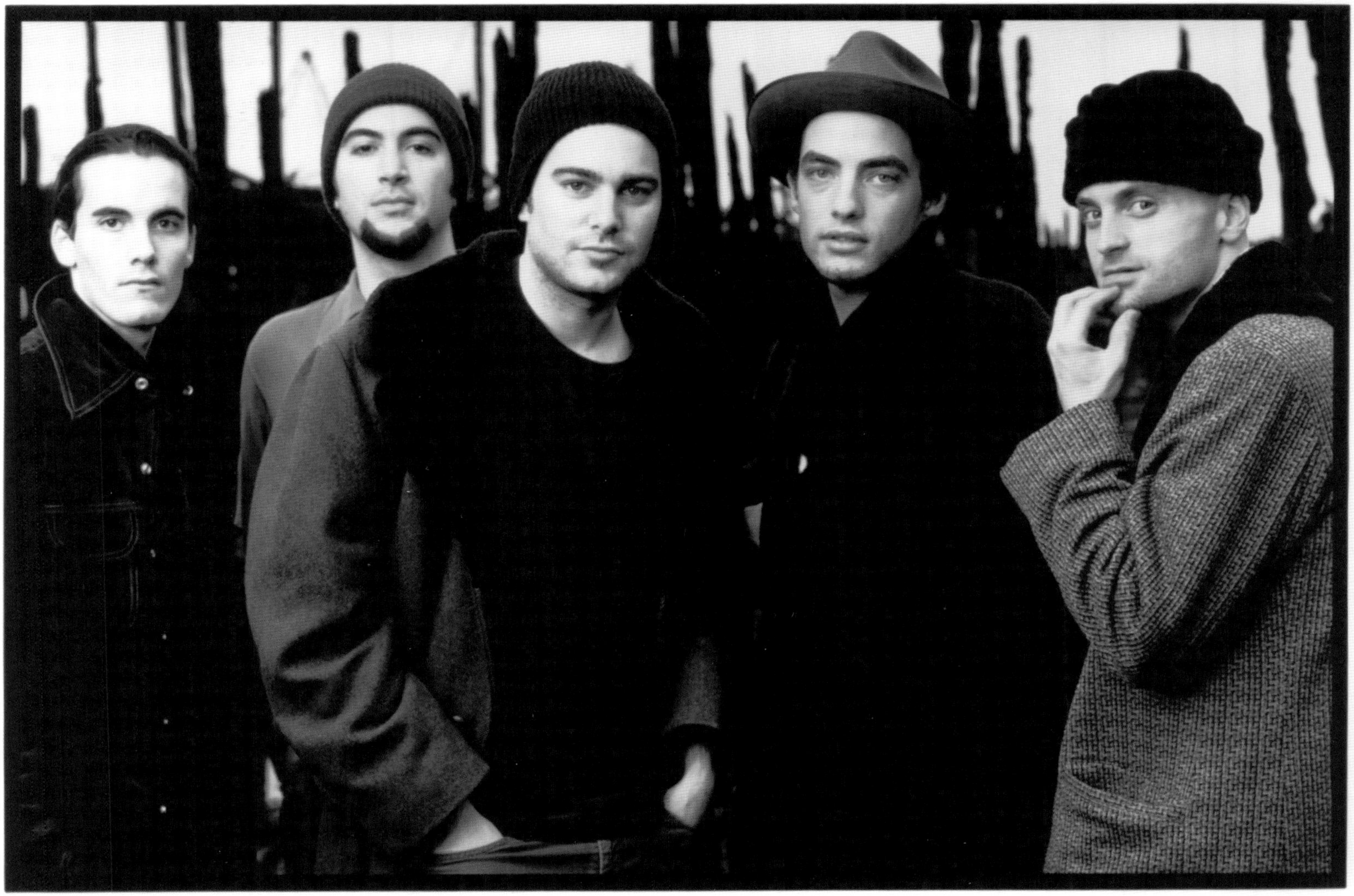

Photo credit: Mark Seliger

Mario Calire | Rami Jaffe | Greg Richling | Jakob Dylan | Michael Ward

# The Wallflowers



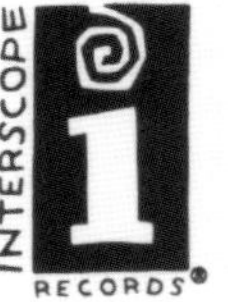

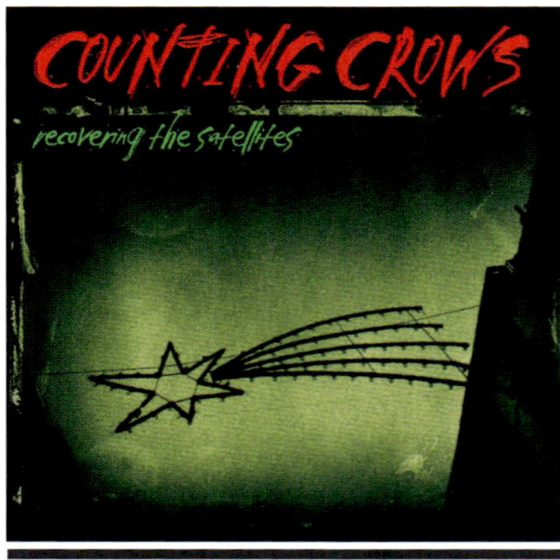


*Billboard* 200: *Recovering the Satellites* (No. 1)

## Counting Crows issued *Recovering the Satellites* three years after their debut album had launched them to fame.

**A FIRST** album of thoughtful, mature folk-flavored rock, Counting Crows' *August and Everything After* sold nearly 5 million copies in the US and drew comparisons to the Band and Van Morrison. But many critics ridiculed Adam Duritz, the lead singer and principal songwriter, for everything from copping ready-made classic rock to being a whiny enigmatic poet. Duritz was not as angst-ridden as his lyrics might have implied. He simply made painfully autobiographical records about the things that tormented him.

"That's the kind of mopey little S.O.B. I am," he said with a chuckle. "I only write songs that come, and what comes is autobiographical. I'm never going to be a protest writer, because I don't write about subjects. I only write about me, which for some people is self-absorbed, and I would entirely agree. I'm not interested in telling you what to do with your life—I want to tell you about mine. I want it to be true and vulnerable. I don't care about exposing myself. The more naked I can make it, the better it is."

After Counting Crows' rise to stardom, the dreadlocked Duritz found himself in turmoil. He wasn't prepared for the fallout of sudden stardom, and he fretted about writer's block. But the Crows second album, *Recovering the Satellites*, debuted at No. 1 on the charts. Structured as two album sides, it recounted Duritz's sometimes painful and confusing adjustment in emotional detail.

"To me, the album happened in two specific sections—when I say 'suites,' everyone jumps on me for being full of myself, but fuck 'em," Duritz said. "The first one concerns the frustration at not having any idea what to do. The second part isn't so much a howl of anger as it is letting it out, the light at the end of a dark tunnel. 'A Long December' is about taking time to grasp that even though things can be hard, they're not completely lost as long as you remember them. Which is what I have all these songs for."

*Recovering the Satellites* was more ambitious and challenging than its direct, melodic predecessor. The rest of the Crows—guitarists David Bryson and Dan Vickrey, bassist Matt Malley, keyboardist Charlie Cunningham and drummer Ben Mize—were fine players, and Duritz's rushing, rolling, quavering and anguished vocals interpreted how change can be a blessing and a threat at the same time.

Duritz still dwelled on his struggle to hold onto an identity in the wake of fame. "There were huge voids that success filled, fears about what the hell I was going to do with my life and whether I was going to end up doing a job that might be fine for someone else but would be a disappointment to me. A lot of my friends are still struggling or have given up on the music. I don't have to face that ending.

"But I don't want to spend my life writing about things I've lost, bleeding it out onto records. You can get in that trap where you start to justify all the suffering by saying, 'Well, hey, it's 10 songs every two years.' I want to make sure that I learn not to just survive this life—I've done that—but to live it, too. That's my only worry. I haven't figured that part out yet. I'm learning to do that as I go." ■

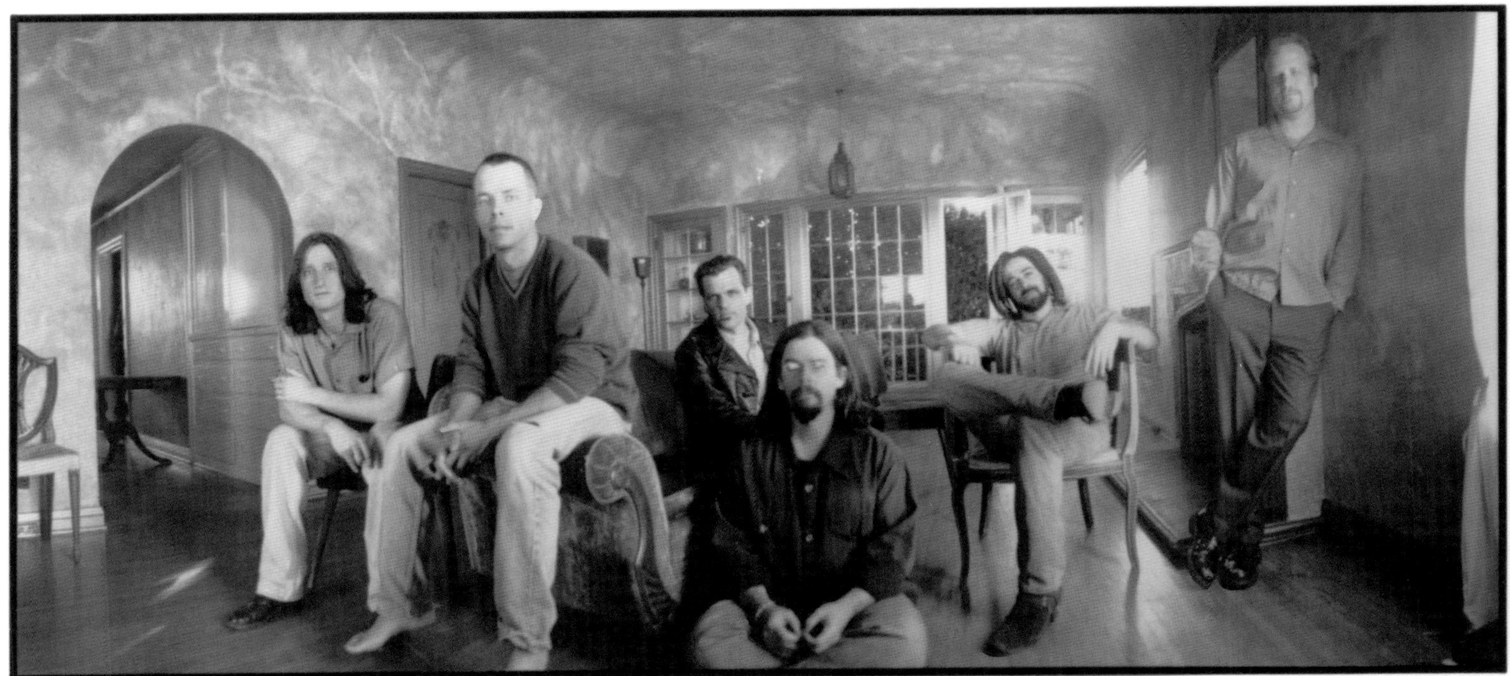

Photo Credit: Dennis Keeley

Ben Mize David Bryson Charles Gillingham Matt Malley Adam Duritz Dan Vickery

COUNTING CROWS

GEFFEN RECORDS, INC.

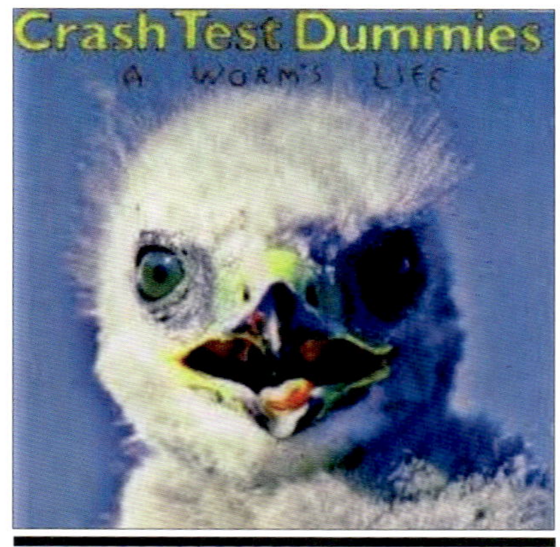


*Billboard* 200: *A Worm's Life* (#78)

# In the wake of an oddball hit, Crash Test Dummies continued to creep into the mainstream with *A Worm's Life*.

**IN 1993**, Crash Test Dummies scored an unlikely alternative and pop smash with "Mmm Mmm Mmm Mmm," a No. 1 song in 18 countries. It fueled the album *God Shuffled His Feet*, garnering a variety of international awards and generating sales of more than 5 million units worldwide, but the Canadian band found itself mostly recognized for the enigmatic hit single.

"You are stuck with the fact that people are going to strongly identify you with one song to a certain extent," lead singer and songwriter Brad Roberts said. "Well, I'd rather be stuck with that than making records that just go down the toilet into oblivion. I know some artists start to get really irritated after a while, and I suppose if I was Bob Dylan and 20 years later people were still yelling for 'Mr. Tambourine Man,' I might start to get irritated too. But so far it hasn't been too much of a problem."

*A Worm's Life* was the follow-up album from Crash Test Dummies. The appeal was the contrast in the rock band's folk-tinged sound, anchored by Roberts' ultra-deep vocals and his unmistakably twisted, literate lyrics. His funny, simple world view drove "My Enemies"—"I try to picture them dressed up as furry little bunnies"—and "He Likes to Feel It," the bizarre tale of a boy who enjoys yanking out his own teeth.

"I was sitting around one day noticing that my teeth were pretty firmly lodged in my skull, and it just seemed strange to me that there could have ever been a part of me that at one time was loosening up and falling out like rain," Roberts said. "I started thinking about when I was little and pulling my teeth out. I used to be running around waving them and wearing them and talking about the tooth fairy and getting all kinds of attention from my parents. It seemed something could be milked from that experience."

The song's slightly gruesome video clip gained attention from the powers at standards committees—as if some closeups of the youngster's teeth were going to make kids afraid to go to the dentist. "It takes the cartoon-like violence of the lyrics a step further," Roberts allowed. "Basically, the kid ends up trying to pull out his teeth by doing all kinds of extreme things, like tying it to a crane, which then hauls him up over the New York City skyline. It's absolutely absurd, extremely funny—but it is graphically violent, and in the climate of the times I knew that, even though it was clearly meant with a sense of humor, a handful of politically correct programmers would raise a few objections."

*A Worm's Life* had a slightly moodier pop feel than previous albums, but the dryly witty Roberts wasn't worried about having another hit. "I don't let that stuff bother me too much," he said. "There's always going to be a core of fans who are listening to the whole record." ■

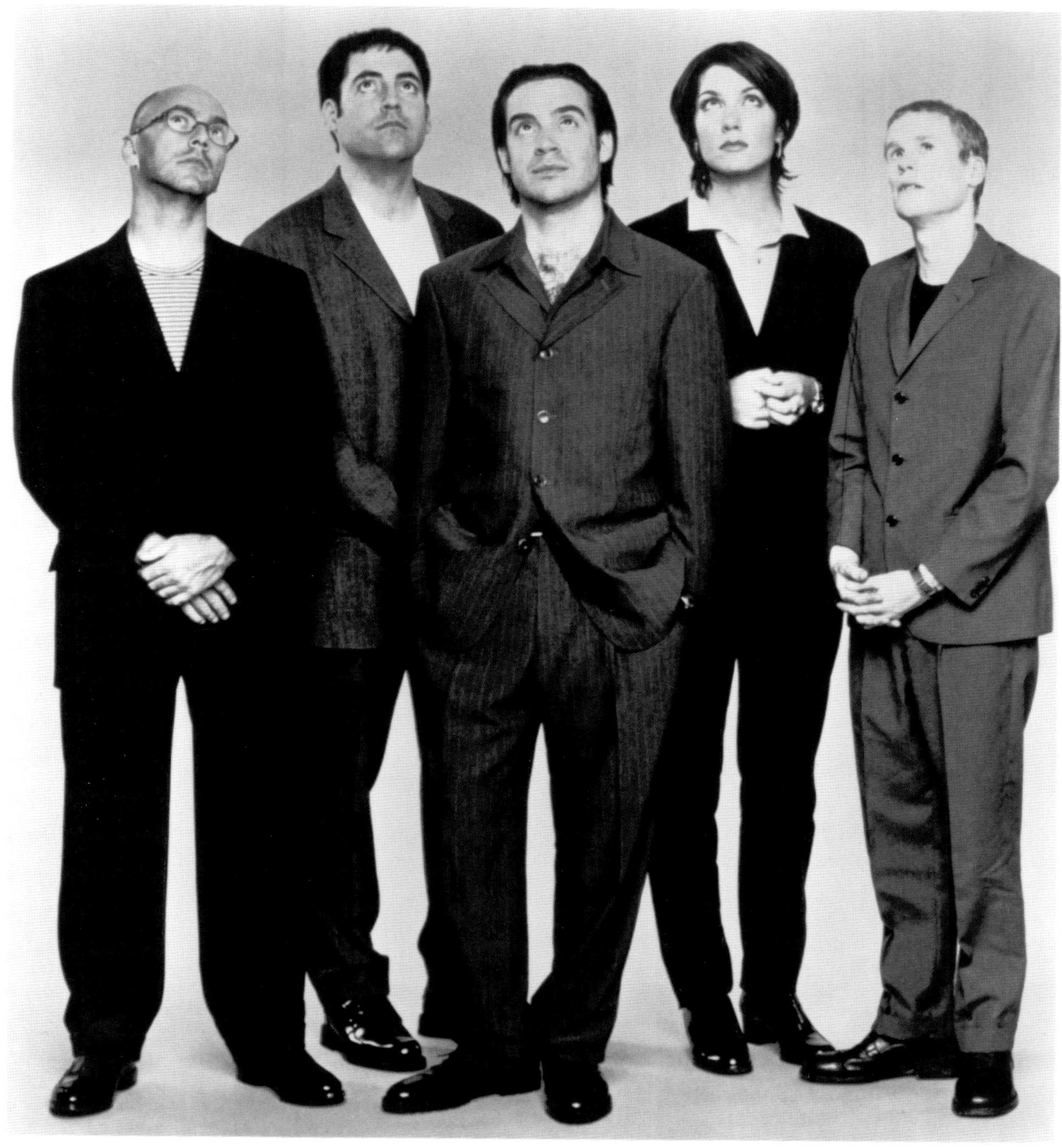

Left to Right: MITCH DORGE DAN ROBERTS BRAD ROBERTS ELLEN REID BEN DARVILL

Crash Test Dummies

ARISTA

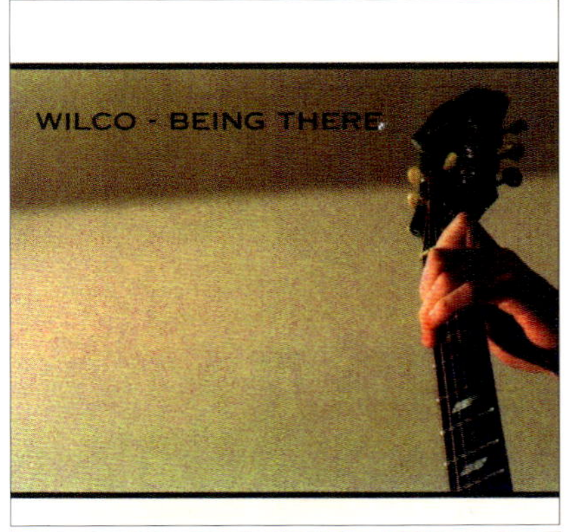


*Billboard* 200: *Being There* (#73)

## A qualified success, *Being There*, a sprawling two-disc set, presented Wilco with a wide variety of possibilities.

**CRITICS AND** fans alike claimed Uncle Tupelo helped define a hip hybrid of country, punk and rock in the early Nineties. Co-founder and co-frontman Jeff Tweedy would contribute a half-dozen songs to one of the band's alt-country albums. Bandmate Jay Farrar penned the rest.

From the painful breakup of the cult favorite in 1994, Tweedy formed Wilco with a lineup containing other former Uncle Tupelo members. Now the leader, Tweedy became an ambitious songwriting machine. *Being There*, the Chicago quintet's second album, was a double record containing 19 tracks—from a band with no substantial commercial base.

It was, as Tweedy put it, the soundtrack to a period in his life, "a look at the emotional experience of songwriting from the inside out. I had a lot to say. I became a father, and it made making a record the second-most-important thing in my life."

Tweedy's beliefs were so sanguine that Wilco agreed to take a cut in royalties in order to price *Being There* as a single disc. The album neatly combined elements of acoustic, country, working-class rock and classic pop. "I think it's more immediate and accessible than any of the albums Uncle Tupelo released," Tweedy said. "I wanted our influences to be right on the surface on this one, because I don't hear many people doing that anymore. I wanted it to be, 'Wilco quotes from their, or maybe your, record collection.'"

The hit "Outtasite (Outta Mind)" recalled the Replacements. Perhaps the most forbearing and revealing part of *Being There* was the second version that appeared—the chirpy, Beach Boys-inflected "Outta Mind (Outta Sight)."

"We had the idea of recording a lot of material," bassist John Stirratt explained. "A lot of it was totally off the cuff. Somebody put on the Phil Spector box set, and we thought it might be fun to reference that—build a track, some sort of 'wall of sound.' We cut 'Outta Mind (Outta Sight)' with two pianos, drums and guitar initially and just kept adding on timpani and things like that. It's not quite a wall of sound—it's a partition of sound." ■

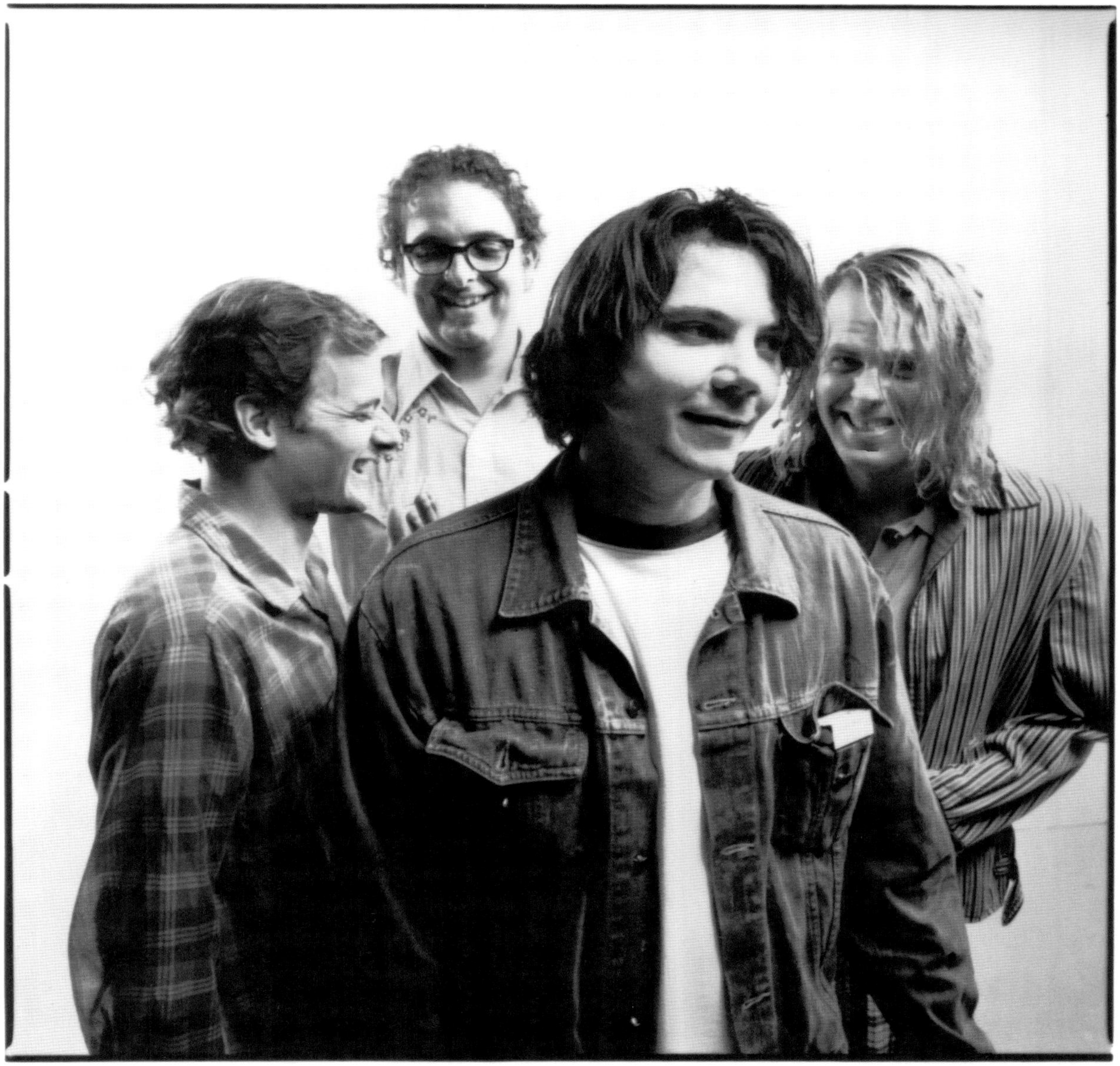

PHOTO CREDIT: Marina Chavez

# Wilco

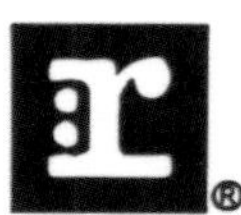

*Billboard* 200: *Fairweather Johnson* (No. 1)
*Billboard* Hot 100: "Old Man & Me (When I Get to Heaven)" (#13); "Tucker's Town" (#38)

# Hootie & the Blowfish tried to repeat the success of their debut with the assured *Fairweather Johnson* album.

**FOURTEEN MILLION** fans had plunked down their hard-earned cash and made Hootie & the Blowfish a household name. *Cracked Rear View* was 1995's top-selling album and the second best-selling debut of all time (behind only *Boston*), and Hootie-mania swept the country—two Grammys, a string of hits ("Hold My Hand," "Only Wanna Be with You") and Best New Artist winners at the MTV Video Music Awards.

But the mellow, untrendy quartet from South Carolina couldn't quiet the detractors—the most popular band around was simultaneously the most despised. The band members admitted that they played Southern frat-rock and liked to party, but the rock press had gladly torn down the guys and their music, labeling them too bland, too nice.

"The way I've managed to handle the backlash of success is upbringing," lead singer Darius Rucker said. "I really enjoyed who I was before this all happened. I thought I was a cool guy who liked to have fun—I liked being with myself. I sat down and went, 'Why do I have to be an asshole now, to change, when I wasn't that bad before? People bought our record and there's money in the bank—so what? I still want to be Darius.

"The funny thing that's helped us is meeting Gene Simmons of Kiss. A lot of what he says is so valid. If a critic says you suck and you sell 14 million records, is America that stupid? The bashing was rough, especially in the beginning when you get great underground reviews and then the record takes off and everybody hates you. But you read it, you get your feelings hurt and you go on with your day."

Naturally, expectations ran high for the group's next album. Hootie sounded determined to be taken seriously on *Fairweather Johnson*, produced by Don Gehman. The music was more complex and textured—higher energy, tougher guitars, fuller harmonies. And Rucker's singing was gruffer. "We went from a pretty long tour straight into the studio," he explained. "My voice is more controlled. Last record, I wanted to hit that high note on every song. This record, I realized you don't have to do that to make it good. It's maturity more than anything."

"Tucker's Town" featured a passionate Rucker vocal, and Hootie put a soulful pop spin on "Old Man & Me (When I Get to Heaven)," a remake of a song found on the band's 1993 indie release *Kootchypop*. Friends from Toad the Wet Sprocket and singer Nanci Griffith ended up on the album.

"I was listening to a lot of Bonnie Raitt's *Home Plate* record from '75, and there's Tom Waits and Jackson Browne singing on a song called 'Your Sweet and Shiny Eyes,'" Rucker noted. "Back in those days, music wasn't so much a competition—they all just wanted to write good songs and make good records. I wanted that feel—to have friends sing in the studio. In the mainstream, you have all these bands that want to talk shit about each other and be jerks. I hate people who say, 'You blew that guy off the stage.' It should be about music—but the Nineties are the years of the angst, so everybody's got to hate." ■

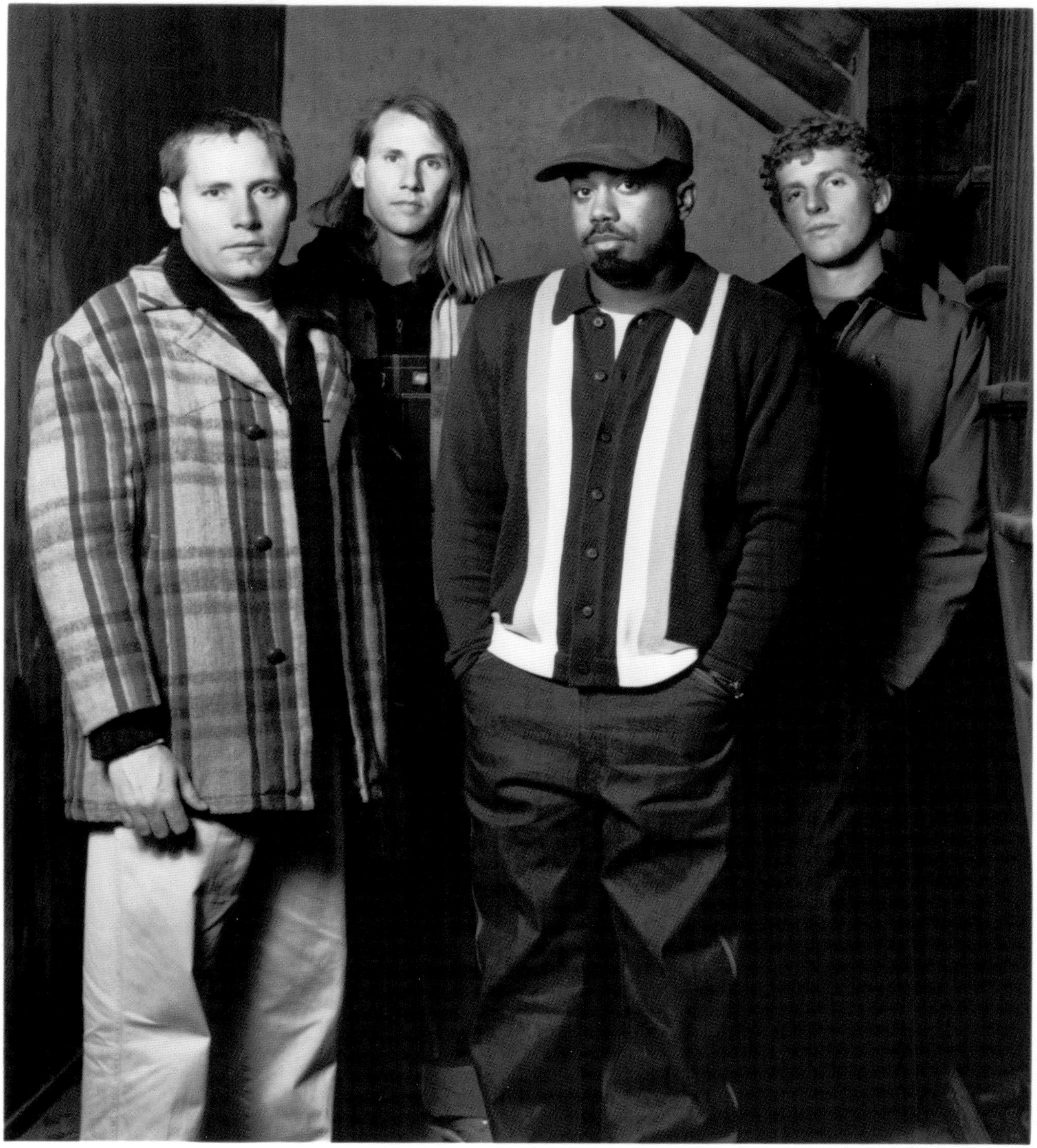

©ETHAN HILL

DEAN FELBER JIM (SONI) SONEFELD DARIUS RUCKER MARK BRYAN

# Hootie & the Blowfish

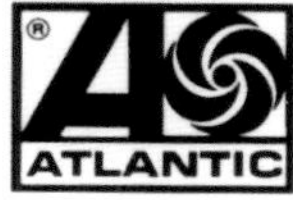

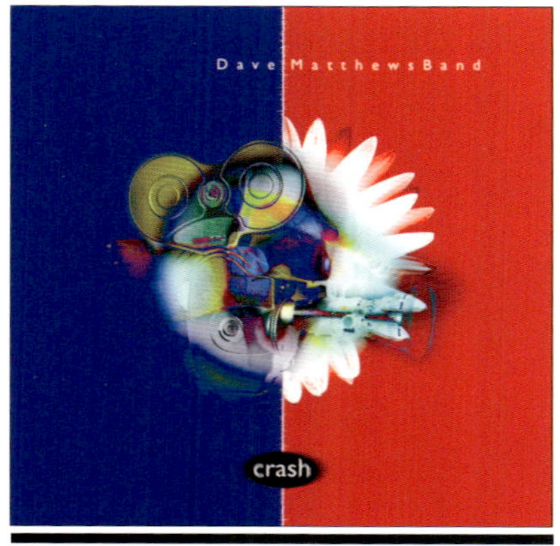


*Billboard* 200: *Crash* (#2)

## The seasoned players in Dave Matthews Band took chances on *Crash*, a beguiling fusion of folk, jazz and rock.

**WITH A** combination of steadfastness and smart, gimmick-free music, Dave Matthews Band had built a loyal worldwide following. Which came as a surprise to Matthews, a self-described square peg.

"This is the first band I've been in—with guys in high school, we drank beer and put the distortion on our instruments, but I don't think we ever finished or learned a song," the unassuming Matthews said. "The name is for lack of a name. It's a misconception that it's me and a backup band. I'm the leader because I initiated getting together around the songs I'd written, but it's five guys with 20 percent each."

During its formative years, the Virginia-based quintet toured and won fans one club at a time. "I'm lucky because I'm a pathetic businessman," Matthews admitted. "I'd go into fits trying to divide up $75. But I'm good at delegating. In Charlottesville, we had devoted people offering their help from the beginning. Our manager is our biggest fan, and the clarity of running the machine comes from him. There's not a lot of hiring and firing, only hiring."

DMB's previous album, *Under the Table and Dreaming*, was still on the charts after almost two years when *Crash* was released. The intensity of the melodic, quirky tunes distinguished it from the gracefully flowing pop textures of the last record. Matthews' jazzy acoustic guitar riffs, Boyd Tinsley's nimble fiddling and LeRoi Moore's twisting sax solos were draped over the piercing drumming of Carter Beauford and bassist Stefan Lessard's rock-steady rhythms.

"When we listened to the final mixes, I thought, 'I'm really comfortable with this'—that I could be involved in something so beautiful even though it had a pretty big sister. The first album was a little safer in that we had a list of songs and we just recorded them boom-boom-boom. This one, there was much more stopping—let's try fast, let's try slow, let's change the arrangements and instrumentation and words.

"I'm no poet," Matthews continued. "I'm always flattered when people pay attention to my lyrics. I spend a lot of time on them because I have to sing them, but I don't think I'm saying great things. It's the sound of the words, not the content."

*Crash* yielded radio hits with the urgent funk of "Too Much," the horn-driven, jazzy "So Much to Say," the balladry of "Two Step," "Tripping Billies" and "Crash Into Me." Some early Seventies groups had attempted a similar mix of earthy yet progressive elements.

"I've heard many comparisons to different kinds of music, Fairport Convention and things like that," Matthews noted. "But I haven't really listened to any of them. I'm sort of rolling along a hill, and sometimes things stick to me and sometimes not. What unifies it is just the mixture of people that get together in a similar way and play whatever. That's where we come from. The thing that ties the music together is our personalities." ■

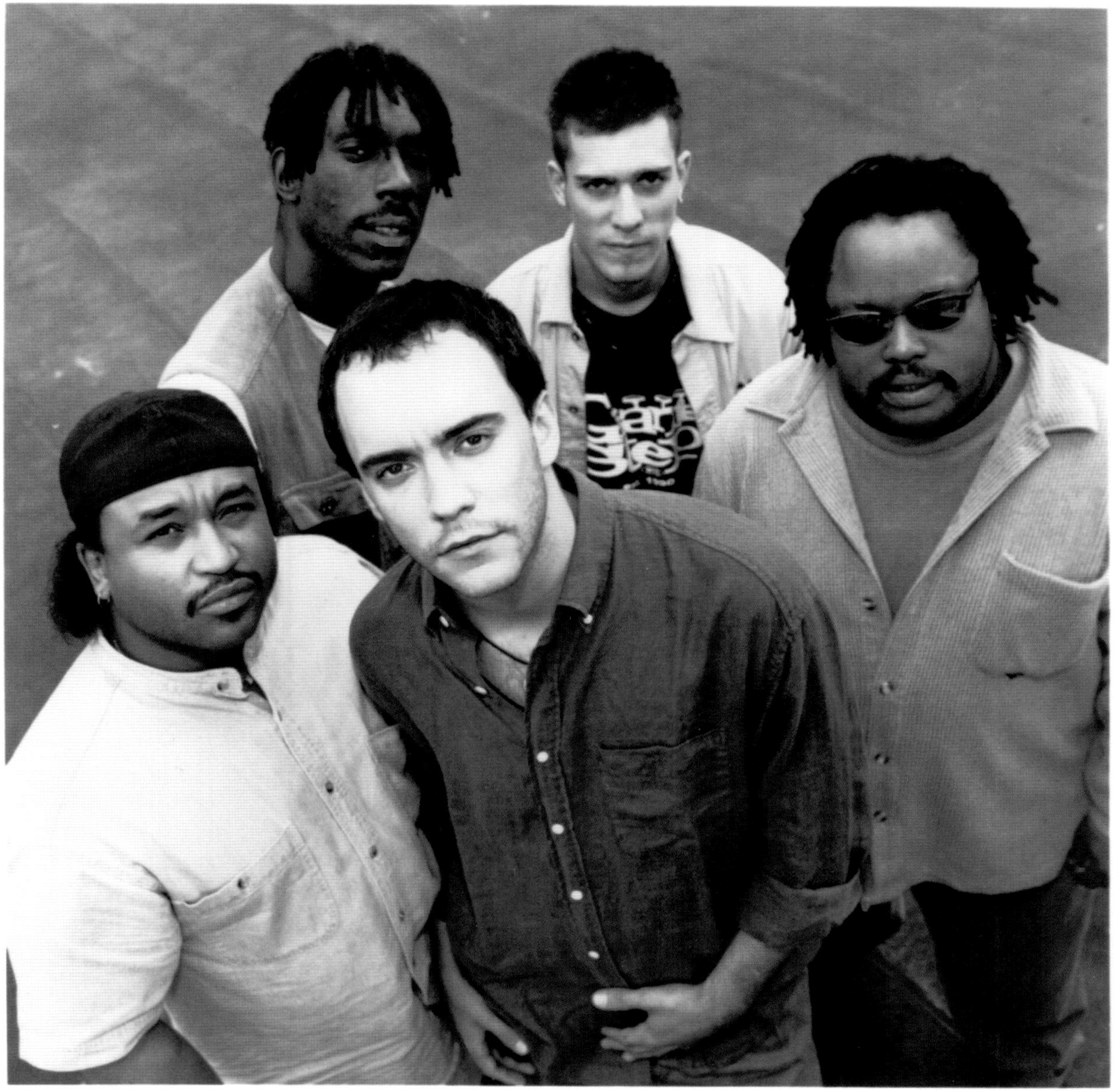

Carter Beauford  Boyd Tinsley  Dave Matthews  Stefan Lessard  LeRoi Moore

Photo Credit: Sam Erickson

# Dave Matthews Band

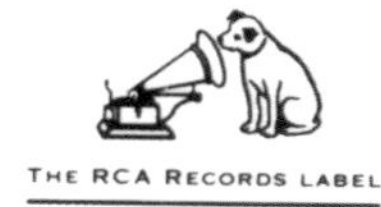

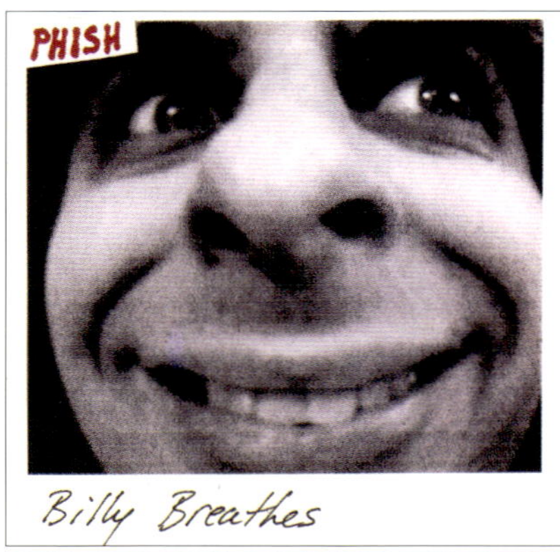


*Billboard* 200: *Billy Breathes* (#7)

## On *Billy Breathes*, Phish attempted to recreate in the recording studio the open-ended magic it attained onstage.

**ONE OF** the biggest concert draws in America, Phish was the left field success story of the decade. The virtuoso jam band, known for free-wheeling, improvisational live performances, was beloved by an army of noodle-dancing, sandal-wearing, tie-dyed nomads for its musical and social environment. Not since the demise of the Grateful Dead had a similarly devoted fan base emerged.

But Phish—guitarist Trey Anastasio, keyboardist Page McConnell, bass player Mike Gordon and drummer Jon Fishman—had never sold records the way it sold concert tickets. The determinedly eccentric Vermont quartet took a run at the mainstream with *Billy Breathes*, produced by Steve Lillywhite.

"We've always gone our own path," McConnell said. "I don't think you can draw a lot of parallels between our career and any bands that are our peers. People often compare us to the Dead for obvious, legitimate reasons—they weren't a huge album-selling band, they made their mark as a live band. We enjoy playing live music, and that's why people keep coming to see us. We've always believed in that. Now we believe that we can also make a good studio record. That's what we're trying to do."

In past practice sessions, self-devised communication exercises were rehearsed to improve the band's collective improvisation. "The listening exercises that we developed over the years were to train our ears to listen to each other. They developed different skills—sometimes it involved imitation, sometimes it involved repetition," McConnell explained. "At this point in our career we don't really do them anymore per se. The influence they had is still filtering through, but hopefully we will continue to listen and internalize those kinds of exercises."

"Free" became Phish's most successful song on the charts. "It's going to be interesting to see where the jamming in the studio goes from here, because as of now we've probably got about 30 hours of tape that's going to come down to maybe only five minutes that makes it onto the next album. Sometimes I think the jamming is too close to the exercises—I'd like it to be even more free. We're more apt to try to create a sense of openness rather than focusing on detailed listening to each other. But there's definitely a lot that we like from this process." ■

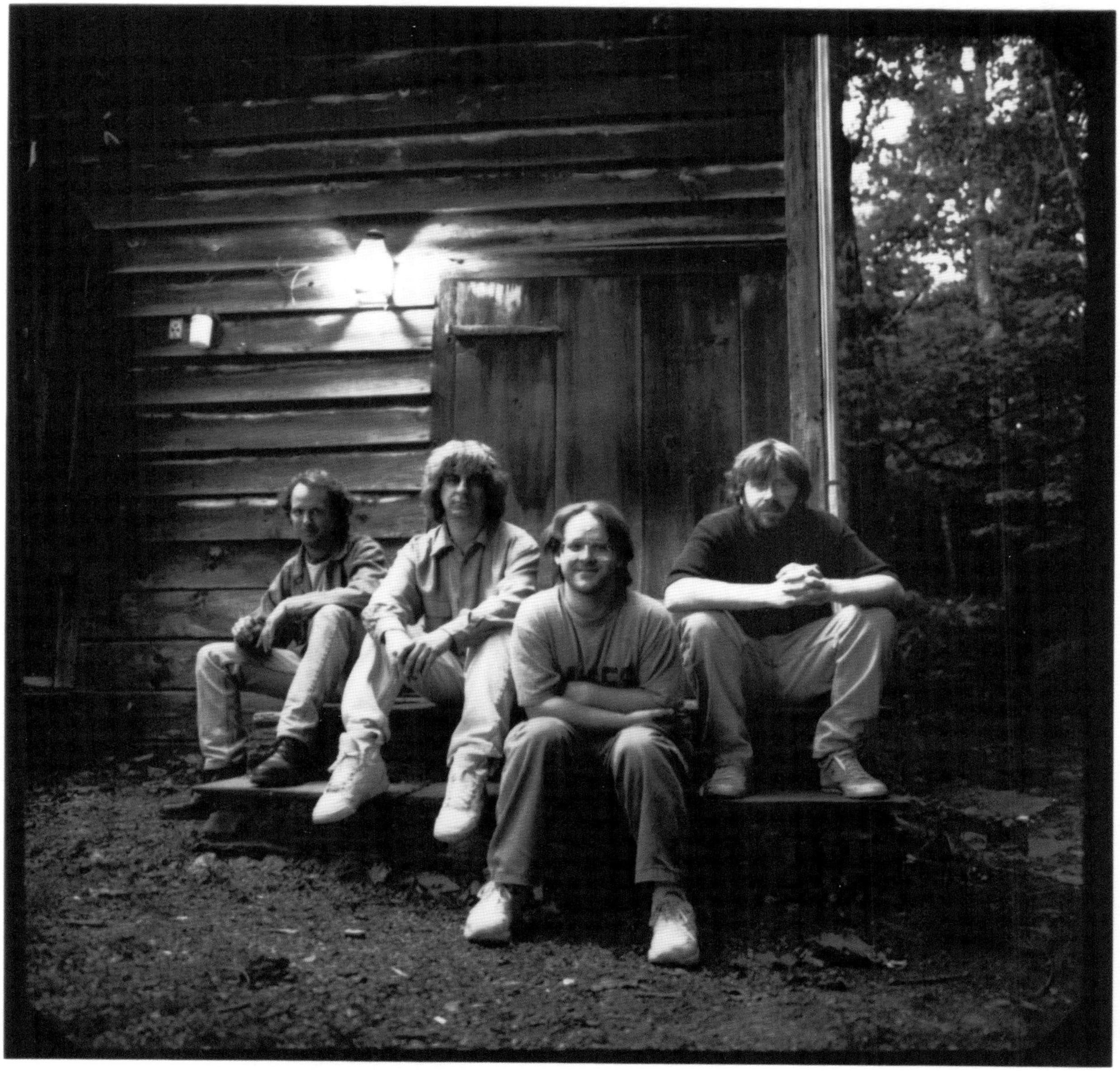

PHOTO CREDIT DANNY CLINCH

L R : PAGE McCONNELL, MIKE GORDON, JON FISHMAN, TREY ANASTASIO

# PHISH

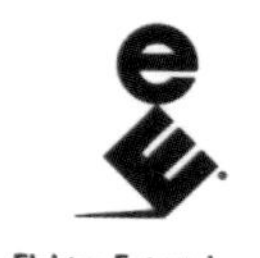

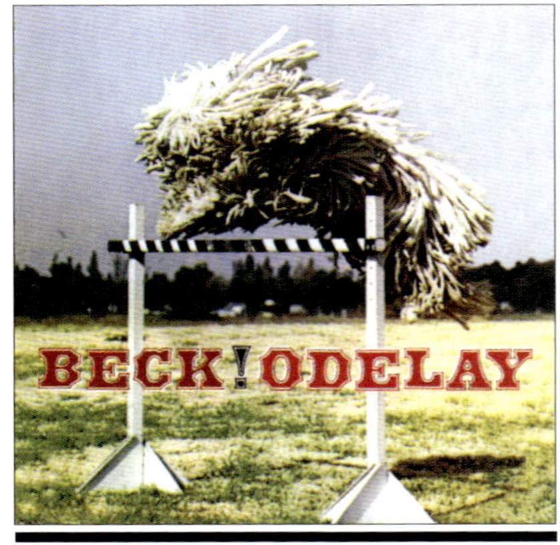


*Billboard* 200: *Odelay* (#16)
*Billboard* Hot 100: "Where It's At" (#61); "Devils Haircut" (#94); "The New Pollution" (#78); "Jack-Ass" (#73)

# Shaking the one-hit wonder label, the genre-hopping Beck cemented his free-spirited reputation with *Odelay*.

**HE WAS** smart, funny and a little weird. Beck got that way by cutting his musical teeth on blues and folk songs he heard on records owned by his bohemian parents and their friends. While in the ninth grade, Beck quit school. At 16, he got himself a guitar and started discovering the diverse cultures on the streets of Los Angeles. In 1989, he took a bus to New York and spent a year gigging around the Lower East Side before returning to L.A. and performing regularly at local punk dives.

In the early Nineties, he recorded an avant folk-based hip-hop tune called "Loser" in the living room of a local producer's home. A year later, a tiny indie label released it as a single. What followed was nothing short of a miracle. Modern rock stations began playing "Loser," the song became a runaway success—"*Soy un perdedor*/I'm a loser, baby/So why don't you kill me?" was the unforgettable chorus—and major labels set upon Beck.

His life did a 180, and a question followed: Could he survive one-hit novelty status, the albatross around his neck? The tag of "motivation-deficient slacker nincompoop/spokesman" was imposed on him, and boors wrote things like "I have two words for this kid: Tommy Tutone."

But Beck's ambitious *Odelay* showed the 26-year-old boy wonder to be one of the decade's most innovative artists. The inspired album resulted from 18 months of feverish recording, cutting, pasting, layering, dubbing and sampling. Beck enlisted the Dust Brothers, the producers responsible for the kitchen-sink approach on the Beastie Boys' seminal *Paul's Boutique*.

How did Beck make such a huge leap in artistic prowess? "I spent some time thinking about what I wanted to do and where I wanted to take it," he said in his slow, measured way. "By a chain of coincidences, I made a substantial record. It worked."

The songs that Beck stitched together were crammed full of his encyclopedic knowledge of musical genres. On the hit singles "Where It's At," "Devils Haircut" and "The New Pollution," he crafted a world of sonic shifts and hairpin stylistic turns, from Delta blues, twangy country licks, hip-hop beats, surrealistic folk, old-school rap, fuzzed-out garage rock and an esoteric list of samples. Beck wanted *Odelay* to be "the kind of album they made in the Sixties, when people experimented with whatever they felt like."

That fruitful period, he said, "had to do with the interchange between R&B and soul music with the white rock world. A lot of that came out of the folk revival, where white kids were starting to get into the traditional forms of blues and country. It manifested itself in bands like the Rolling Stones. That friction of the two approaches, the distinct cultures coming together, made the music healthy and vibrant somehow. It's sad now, but once alternative music embraces hip-hop and R&B, it'll have much more vitality." ■

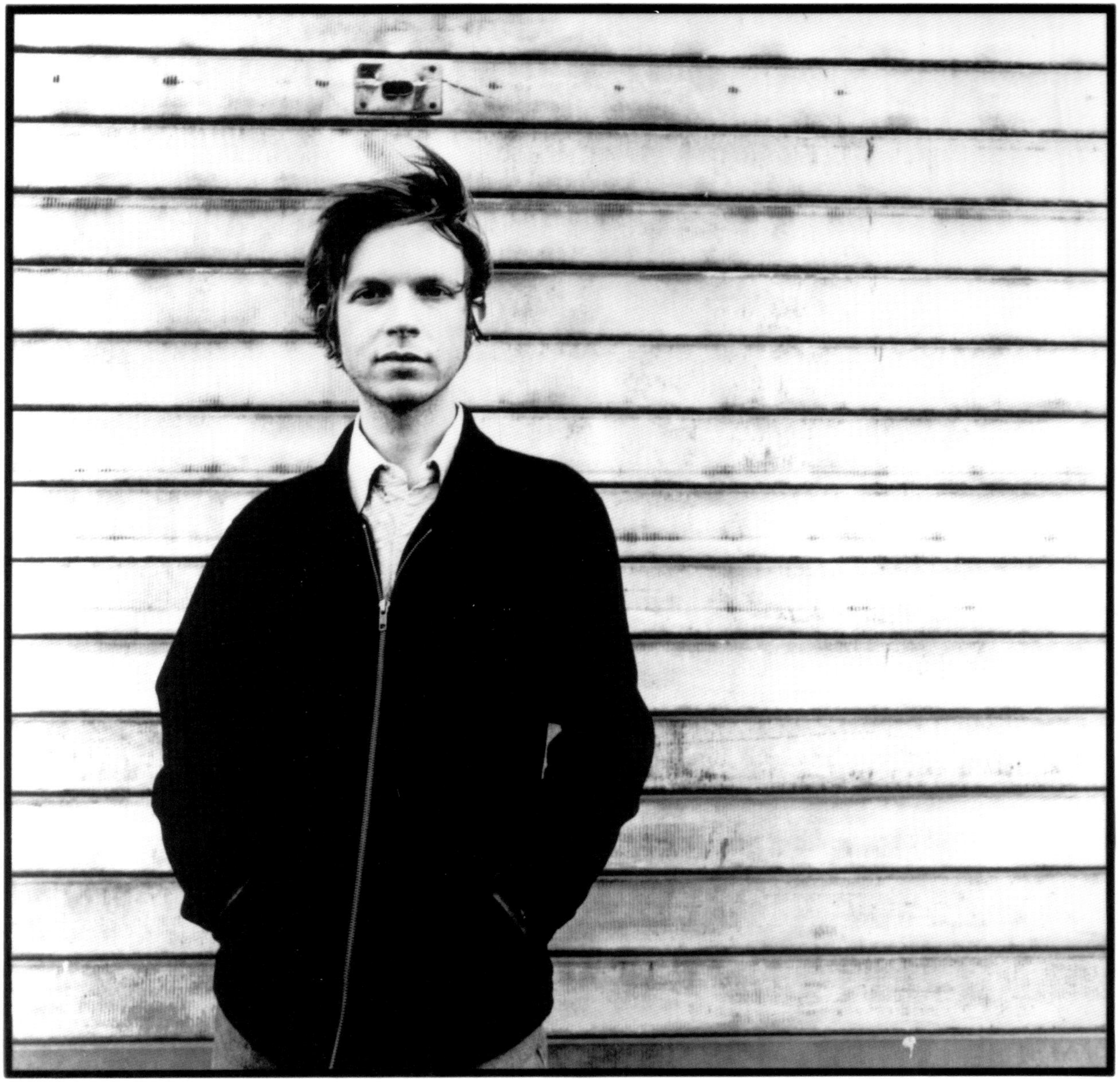

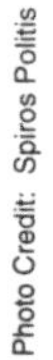


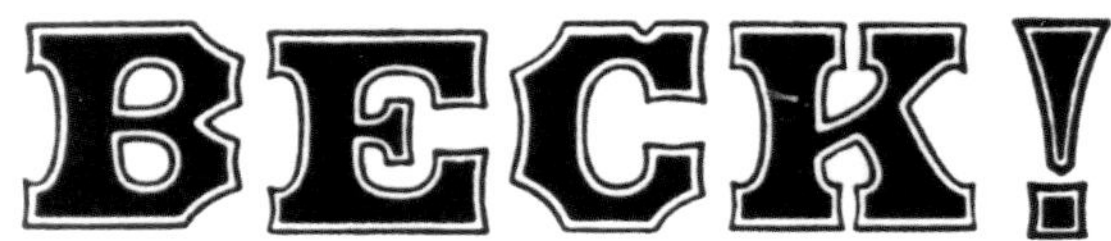

GEFFEN RECORDS, INC.

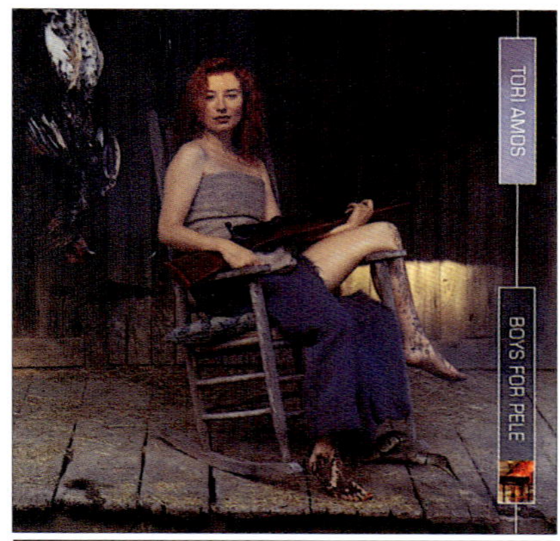


*Billboard* 200: *Boys for Pele* (#2)
*Billboard* Hot 100: "Caught a Lite Sneeze" (#60)

## With the thought-provoking *Boys for Pele*, Tori Amos strengthened her complex confessionals and resolute determination.

**DESCRIBED AS** "offbeat" and "flaky," she admitted to flirting with gods and talking to fairies. She'd been lauded as a champion of the bruised but emboldened female spirit and condemned as a new-age loon with a blunt, defiant brazenness. Tori Amos was some bundle of contradictions, and she found a way to make it work on *Boys for Pele*, her most musically adventurous collection.

"When I turned this record in, everybody at the record company had a very hard time," Amos said. "But I'm quite a fierce lioness when it comes to protecting the cubs. The piano and my songs became my allies—it became about standing by what I believe in as a musician. I felt like an outcast, living on the fringe like in *Blade Runner*. You don't get invited to the parties and you don't have that credit card that gets you in everywhere. But there is a sense of knowing why you're doing what you're doing."

Her willingness to confront painful extremes is what separated the North Carolina-born Amos from most singer-songwriters. A minister's daughter, she was a child-prodigy pianist who later trained at a music conservatory, and then abandoned the instrument and headed for Hollywood in her late teens. She hooked up with an ill-fated hard-rock band, Y Kant Tori Read, and suffered "a near nervous breakdown." She retreated to England, where she reacquainted herself with the piano and found her voice as a solo performer.

Amos emerged in 1991 with *Little Earthquakes*, an album full of detailed disclosures, and her career gained momentum with the release of 1994's *Under the Pink*. The center of *Boys for Pele* was her passionate but intimate multi-octave singing—every breath and groan could be heard—with songs couched in quirkily sophisticated settings. It marked her first use of the harpsichord, which she played on "Professional Widow" and other tracks, and the dramatic, masterful sound of the long-lined melodies was striking.

"My live engineers said to me, 'Why don't you flesh out early keyboards, really go and learn to play the things and bring them into the 20th century?' I looked at them sideways and said, 'Hmm, it is the bloodline of the piano.' I was fascinated with the bloodlines of Christian women in mythology at the time, and how they weren't passed down correctly. So I purchased a harpsichord and started to get very humbled by how difficult it is."

Full of dizzy metaphors and elliptical imagery, *Boys for Pele* was about men who were seminal to Amos, and a kind of offering to Pele, the Hawaiian volcano goddess. Fans lauded it as evocative and mysterious. Detractors called it oblique and nonsensical. Amos was unfazed. Her work had long had an almost metaphysical appeal that inspired such kindred spirits as dark fantasy comic-book author Neil Gaiman, who partially based his character Delerium, an immortal shade in *The Sandman* series, on Amos.

"Neil said, 'I find it interesting that, when critics are talking about your music, it's completely word-oriented—I've come to the opinion that most of them are music-illiterate.' That gets a little frustrating, because most of what I'm trying to say is in the music. When people don't choose to open themselves up to that language, the words don't make sense." ■

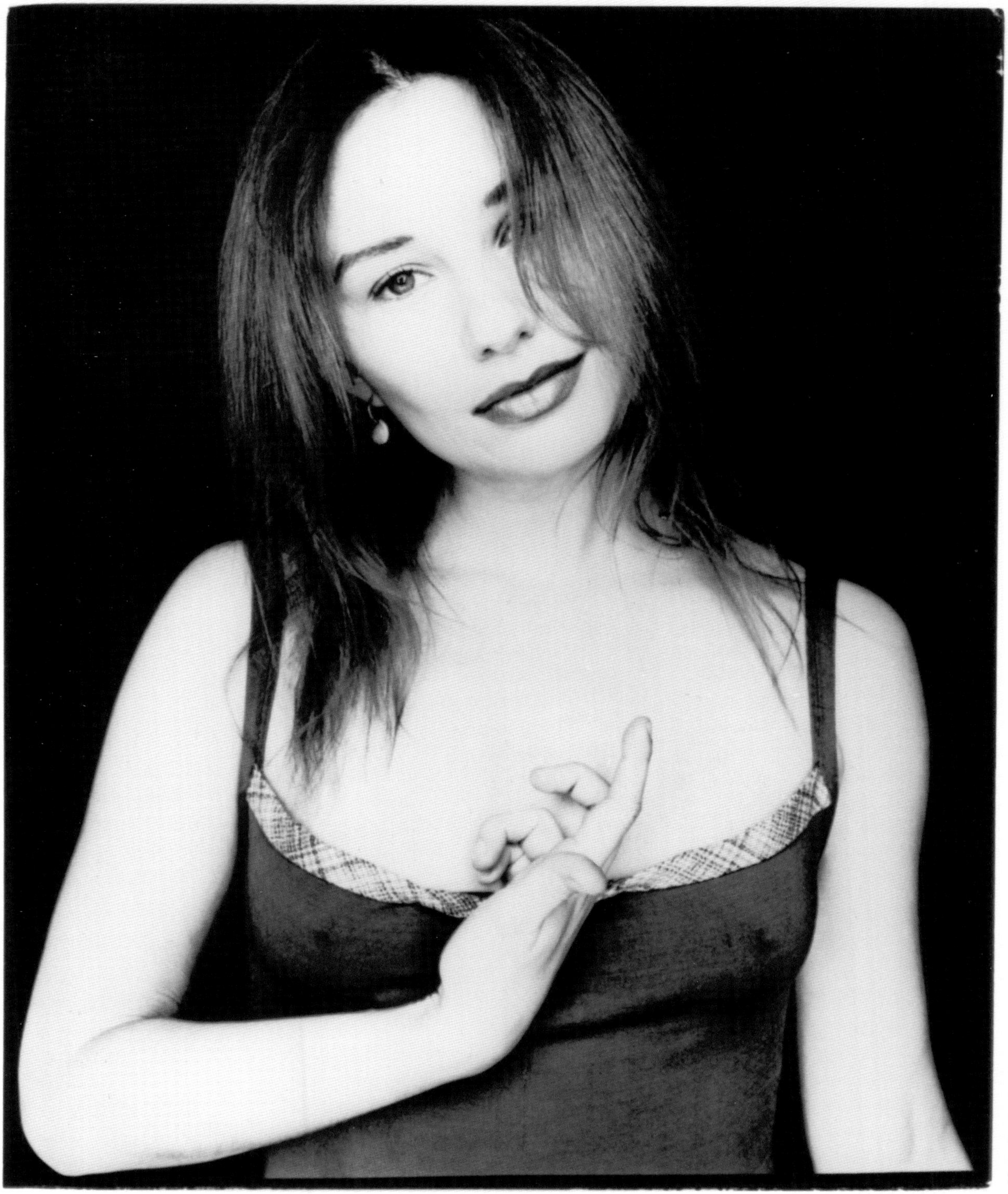

Photo Credit: Rankin

TORI AMOS

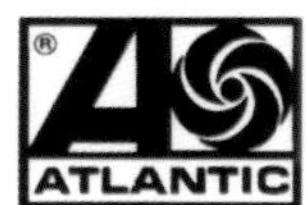

Paula Cole

This Fire

*Billboard* 200: *This Time* (#20)
*Billboard* Hot 100: "Where Have All the Cowboys Gone?" (#8); "I Don't Want to Wait" (#11); "Me" (#35)

# With *This Fire* and "Where Have All the Cowboys Gone?," Paula Cole effectuated independence from her past.

**AN UP-AND-COMING** star, Paula Cole appealed to an intelligent adult-rock audience with her passionate, uncompromising music and beautiful voice. That talent had inspired comparisons to Tori Amos (the uninhibited singing) and Joni Mitchell (the smart, excruciatingly intimate writing). Growing up in a small town in Massachusetts, Cole had attended the Berklee College of Music in Boston, where she studied jazz vocal technique and improvisation.

"But my family was my greatest artistic influence—we were always making music and singing," she said. "When I went to school and started interacting with other people, they knew all this music that I didn't know at all, stuff that you take for granted. I truly didn't discover the Beatles until a couple of years ago. Which, in a way, is beautiful. I treasure my naïveté—it's allowed me to make music in a more original way, from within."

Peter Gabriel heard Cole's debut release *Harbinger* and asked her to join his 1993 "Secret World Tour" (she backed him at the WOMAD festival and Woodstock '94). Since then, Cole had taken considerable steps. "Personal things happened," she explained. "I had a relationship dissolve on me, and he was also in my band, so it was gone. I started to make the next record with the producer from the first album, a dear friend of mine, and I had to part ways with him—I wanted this record to be performance-driven, in one or two takes, and it wasn't manifesting. I knew deep down in my heart that I wanted to do it myself, but I lacked the courage.

"Finally, I just stood up for what I believed in—I regrouped myself and looked for an engineer and did it. I was bound down to the limitations in my mind. We are what we think—that's what the Buddhists say, and it's so true. My actions were diffident because that's what I was believing myself to be. But I'm not that, and by producing this record I really discovered a lot of myself. It's a flowering for me, a maturation."

Indeed, *This Fire* was striking, from the hopeful "I Don't Want to Wait" to "Me," about the darkly emotional times that turn out to be the greatest teachers in life. The breakthrough hit, "Where Have All the Cowboys Gone?," was a playful satire of machismo in which a disenchanted Cole pleaded for her John Wayne ("I will wash the dishes/ While you go have a beer"). She rapidly changed from a yearning voice to an alluring rap.

"I wrote it back in '92," the strong-jawed, coltish singer said. "I was listening to XTC at the time and I enjoyed their wit and cleverness and sarcasm, and maybe that motivated me to put it in more of a woman's point of view. I shelved it—it was musically boring to me. But lyrically and melodically, somehow it stayed with me and it popped out in my consciousness several years later. I conceived of some production aesthetics that lifted the song—the background vocals and the chorus, the hooky little 'do-doot-de-do-doot.' So it was born again. It's important not to overlook your old work, not always to believe that your newest song is your best song." ■

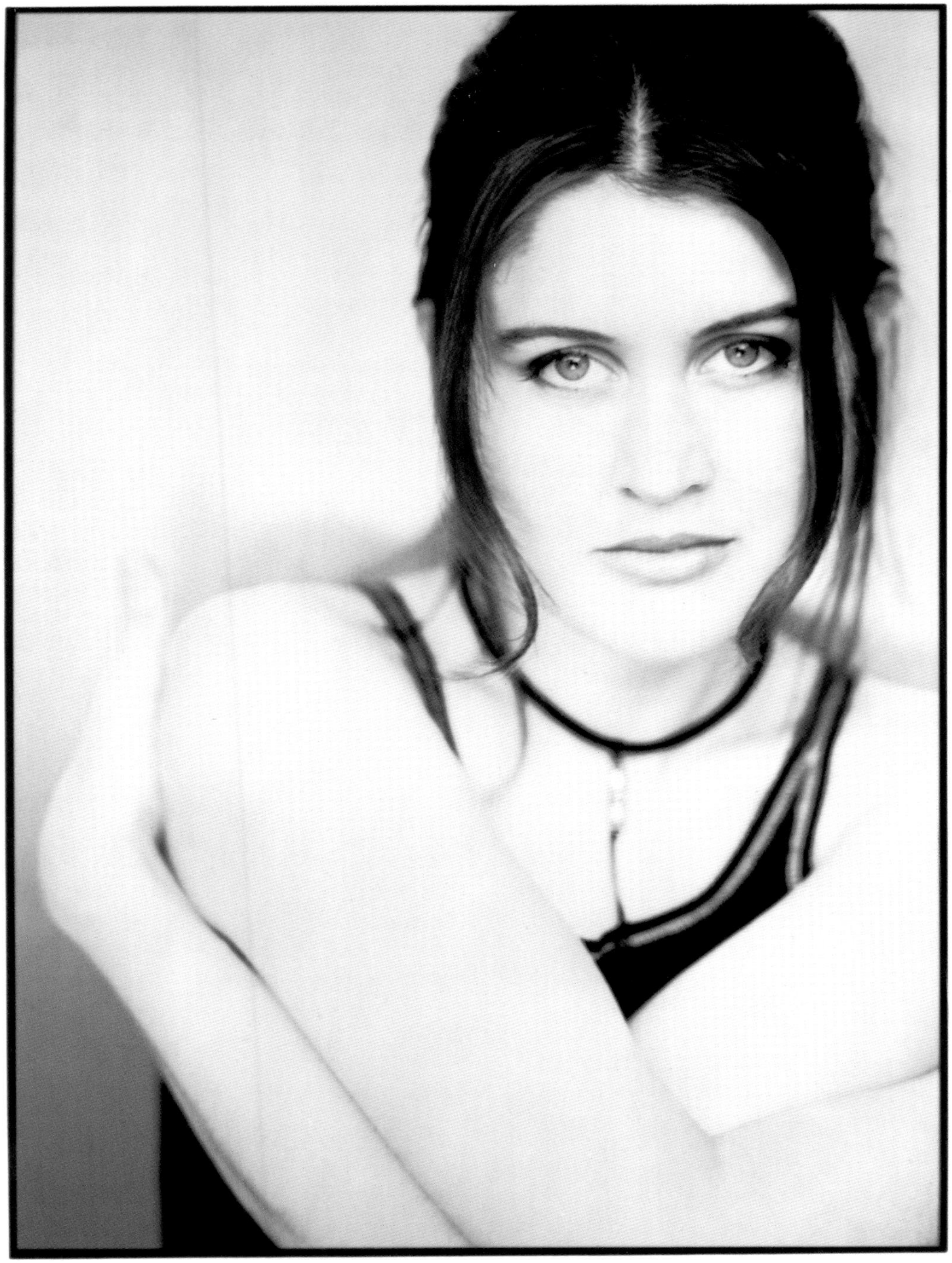

Paula Cole

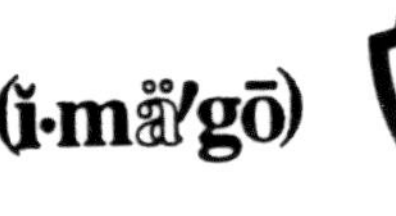


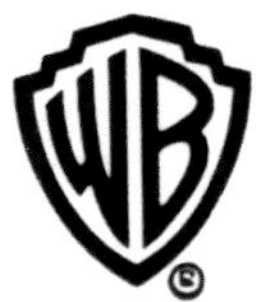

Photo Credit: Frank Ockenfels III

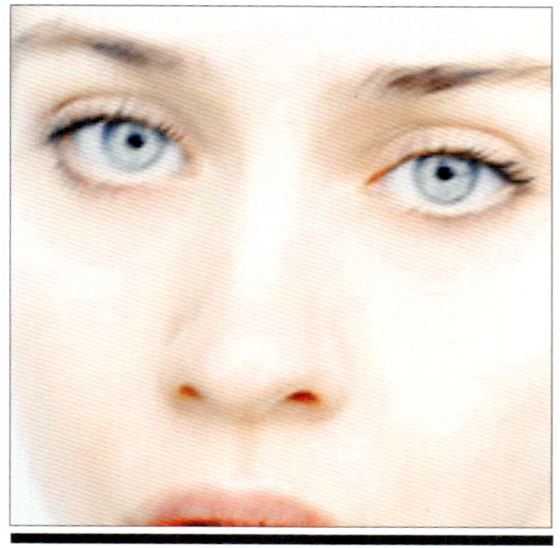

*Billboard* 200: *Tidal* (#15)
*Billboard* Hot 100: "Criminal" (#21)

# Out of nowhere, Fiona Apple established herself as a visionary singer and songwriter with the unfiltered *Tidal*.

**SHE WAS** a kid in New York who had never performed in public. A year later, Fiona Apple had gone from being a complete unknown to reaping critical and commercial success.

"I've spent so much time in my life not being listened to and not being taken seriously," the 19-year-old Apple said. "I wanted to put myself in a situation where people would be forced to listen to me. Writing songs and being able to sing how I feel about things has enabled me to get up on a stage in a spotlight and have a bunch of people come in and sit down and give me a certain level of satisfaction. That's what my psyche needs to be fed by. That's what makes it into song."

Apple's childhood years were awkward and traumatic. There was classroom teasing, and she was sent into therapy because her teachers thought she was antisocial. She was sexually assaulted by a stranger at age 12. But she held Maya Angelou's poetry close to her heart, and her interest in songwriting gave her an outlet to express her emotions. Her meteoric rise began with a simple three-song demo tape.

"I wasn't like, 'Oh, this is my dream, this is what I'm going to do for the rest of my life.' I just figured, 'Well, this is the only thing that I could probably do.' I wasn't going to be like those bands that play for nine years in clubs and wait for some A&R guy to come by and sign them. I just decided that I'd give it a try, and it worked. I didn't expect it to."

*Tidal*, Apple's debut album, was an intense piece of introspection with themes of loneliness and rejection. "I'd never worked with any other musicians," she explained. "I wrote everything on piano, so it was a tough job to figure out what the rest of the music should be on *Tidal*. We went through so many versions of things before we could find something."

Apple's lyrical maturity and vocal talents belied her tender age. With gems like "Sleep to Dream" ("I'm not confused about the guy in that song—he's a fucker!") and "Shadowboxer," she found herself at the vanguard of contemporary pop. The rocking "Criminal" became a chart hit and a fixture on MTV—Apple received a Grammy Award for Best Female Vocal Rock Performance, and *Tidal* was certified gold. The events affected her lifestyle.

"I've thought, 'God, if everyone's going to know who I am, I should always look my best and think about what I'm saying.' But I can't live my entire life that way, so I'm not going to start now. I'm just going to be myself no matter where I am. It's a much bigger problem to put on a façade—I'm not into that." ■

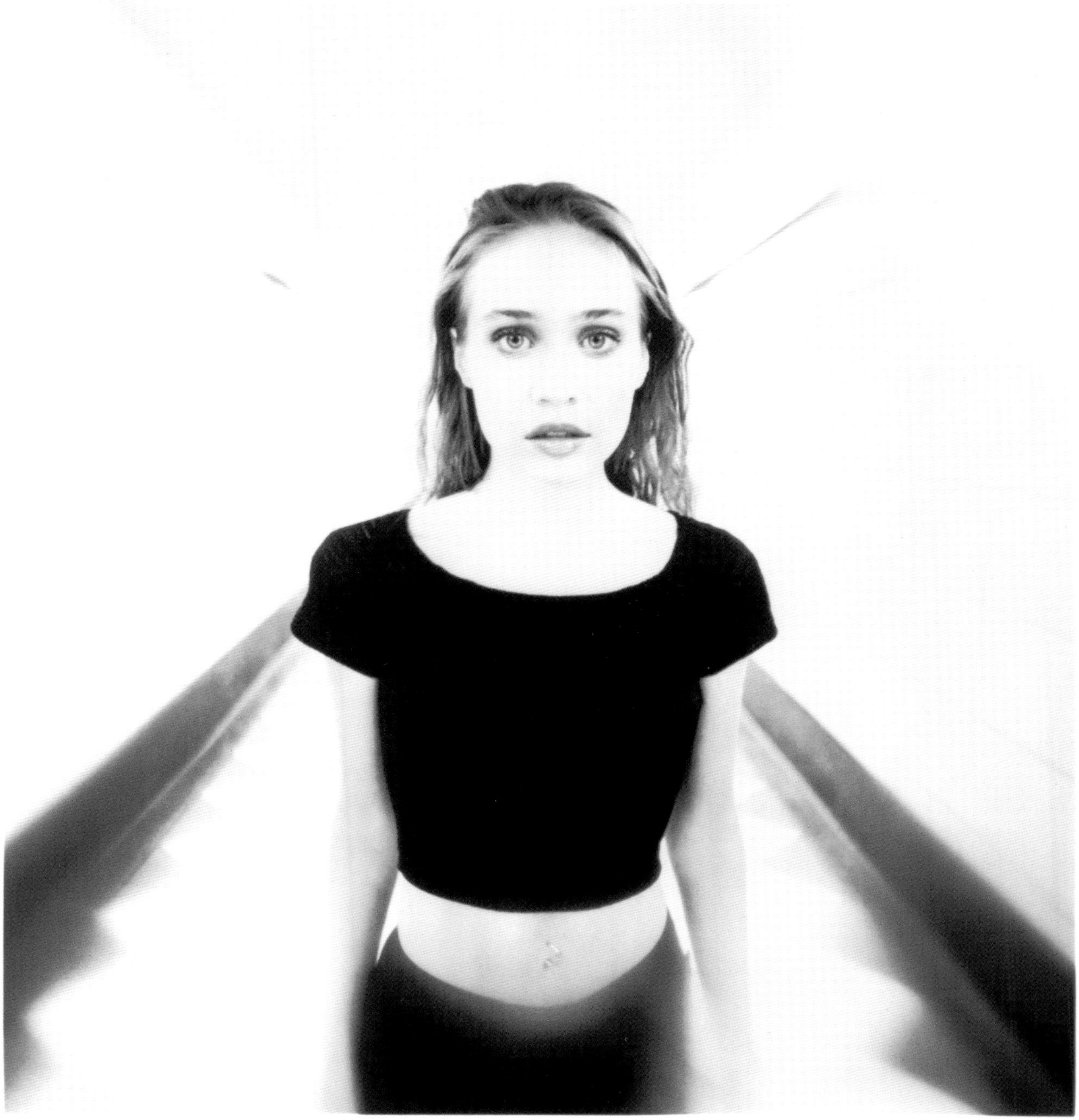

Photo Credit: Stephane Sednaoui

**WORK**

# FIONA APPLE

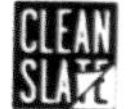

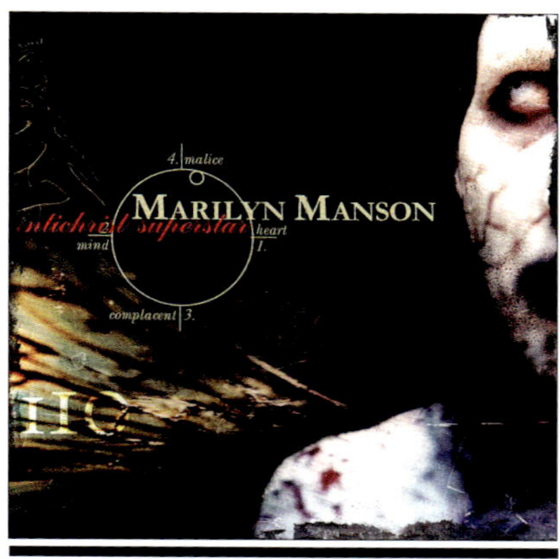


*Billboard* 200: *Antichrist Superstar* (#3)

# As Marilyn Manson's popularity grew, so did widespread attacks from right-wing Christian and political groups.

**"I'M NOT** trying to be a lightning rod for all their hatred," Marilyn Manson said of his critics. "I just want to inspire other people to have an opinion, to be an individual, to maybe question things once in a while. What I say represents the people who are never being listened to, the anger of growing up in a world that takes advantage of you. I'm lucky—I can put all of my anger into a song. Other people can't."

The only child in a middle-class family, the controversial shock rocker—born Brian Warner—was raised in Ohio and Florida. He didn't have a complaint of neglect or child abuse by his parents, a furniture salesman and a nurse. In fact, they sent him to a private Christian school for ten tears. "They weren't all that religious, but they wanted me to have the best education possible," Manson said. "And they thought I'd get it there."

But when the school warned the young Manson of rock's wickedness, it intrigued him. "They would say, 'This is what you shouldn't listen to'—so I immediately went out and bought Black Sabbath and Kiss. It's just common psychology. I've grown up to become the same thing that led me down the path of evil, as they would see it. Music was just an escape, my way of dealing with the world that I felt I didn't fit into."

Manson made his move into ghoulish, theatrical rock and set out from the beginning to push buttons as a contentious antihero. His music, videos and stage shows dealt with a large dose of sex, violence and diabolism, integrating the influence of pornography and horror films. He wasn't the first to wring fame and fortune out of portraying himself as a symptom of American pop culture, but with a few sharp songs, some inflammatory imagery and reckless performances—he sold souvenir T-shirts proclaiming "Kill God...Kill Your Mom and Dad...Kill Yourself"—he mined adolescent fantasy in ways no mainstream act could match, cementing his reputation as the bane of folks preserving family values in entertainment.

A concept album of industrial metal, *Antichrist Superstar* was a commercial success, and "The Beautiful People" reached the top of the modern-rock charts. During the tour in support of the album came reports that Manson ripped pages from the Bible onstage. The religious right dreamed up more—they wrongly accused him of everything from handing out drugs to bestiality to sacrificing virgins. There were pickets, cancelled concerts and death threats.

Manson didn't go out of his way to settle the furor. "There's a real slander campaign going on from some religious groups," he said. "When they call in bomb scares on a daily basis, it becomes a war to me. Tearing up the Bible was obviously a provocative thing to do. At the same time, I like symbolism. It's a book, made of paper. Why do you have to put your hand on it to swear to tell the truth? It's what's in your heart that counts." ■

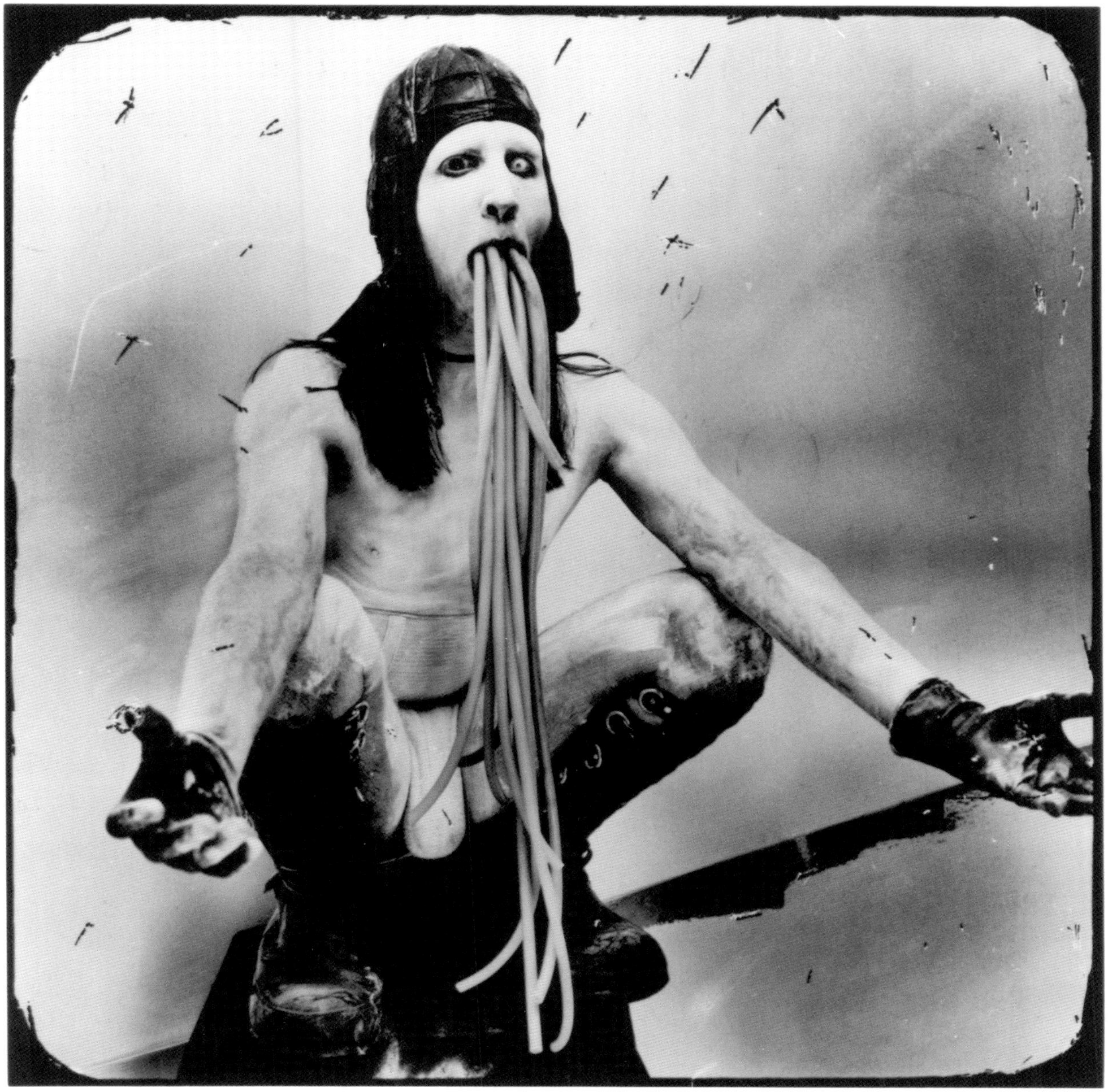

Photo credit: Joseph Cultice

MARILYN MANSON

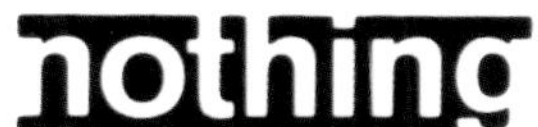

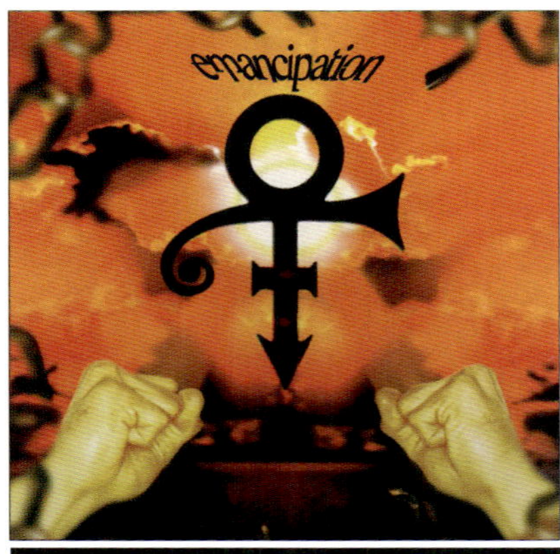


*Billboard* 200: *Emancipation* (#11)

**The Artist Formerly Known as Prince** titled *Emancipation* in regard to his freedom from contractual obligations.

**HE WAS** a chronic overachiever, one of pop music's most creative forces. He was also a major pain whose indulgences and weirdness had made him a punch line. Now Prince—who let it known that he could be addressed simply as the Artist, a shortened alternative for the Artist Formerly Known as Prince—severed his 18-year connection with Warner Bros. Records. The corporate giant had distributed his records, but he was unhappy with his last lucrative contract, primarily because the label wanted to restrict his productivity, effectively promoting a new album only every year or two.

Matters deteriorated to the point where, in 1994, he disowned the work he had recorded as Prince, announcing that he would fulfill his contract by releasing relatively weak music from countless studio tapes. He set up another label, arranged independent distribution and promptly scored a told-you-so hit with the "The Most Beautiful Girl in the World."

And he tore up his identity and started again. Prince apparently expired, only to be reincarnated with a wave of his publicist's hand—on his 35th birthday, he adopted a new, unpronounceable glyph combining the symbols for male and female. He scrawled the word "slave" on his face, his summation of his relationship with Warner Bros.

After getting freed from the deal, the Artist Formerly Known as Prince proudly called his first three-disc-long album *Emancipation* and released it on his own NPG Records. He also signed a worldwide manufacturing and distribution deal with EMI Records.

"Humans r capable of anything they put their minds 2. But 1st they must break free from the 'slave mentality.' They must learn 2 Do 4 Self," the normally reticent musician said in an idiosyncratically spelled written exchange. "All of mankind should be in control of their own destiny. Control freak is a compliment."

On *Emancipation*, the Artist set groins to grinding with the New Power Generation, the superb ensemble that pushed his creative energy buttons. The first single was "Betcha By Golly Wow!," his version of a 1972 hit by the Stylistics. "The Holy River" referenced his marriage to Mayte, a member of NPG and his "Friend, Lover, Sister, Mother/Wife," as he put it in the album credits.

"The people around me understand that our paths r interconnected now 4 a reason. So they r here by their own choice. They r control freaks 2. I am just a willing participant in their dreams and vice versa." ■

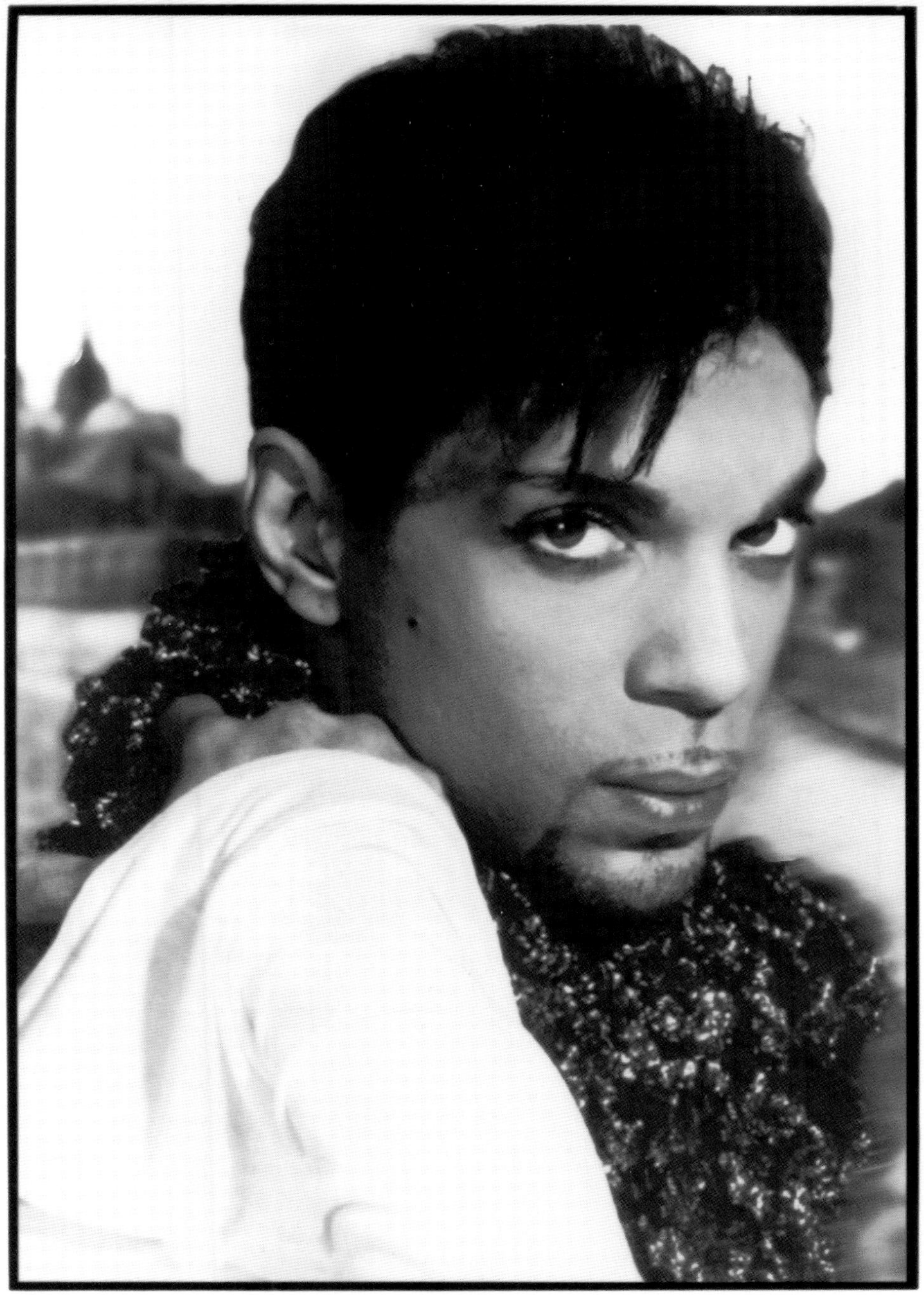

Photo credit: Jeff Katz

The freedom train will roll...
The Artist Formerly Known As Prince will celebrate the launch of Emancipation at his NPG Records/Paisley Park Studios in Minneapolis with a private party and worldwide satellite broadcast. The video for the first single "Betcha By Golly Wow," as well as an unprecedented live performance will be digitally downloaded on November 12th at midnight to radio and television alike (E.S.T.). The three disc/36 track CD will be available in stores November 19th-Emancipation Day.

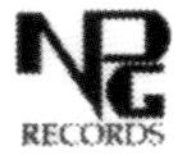

Contact: Frances Pennington
(212)492-1810

Contact: On the Scene Productions
Jim Bowling (213)930-1030

EMI Records
EMI

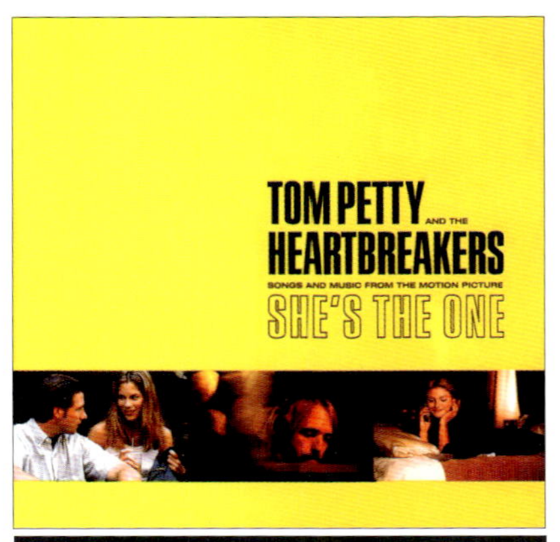


*Billboard* 200: *Songs and Music from* She's the One (#15)
*Billboard* Hot 100: "Walls (Circus)" (#69)

## Tom Petty & the Heartbreakers dished out an atypical soundtrack for an Edward Burns movie, *She's the One*.

**IN THE** modern world, movie soundtrack albums were rarely in sync with the on-screen action. Enter Tom Petty. "I hate soundtrack albums," he said. "They're just marketing ploys, really—14 incongruous acts that probably aren't in the movie, stringing up a bunch of songs that they wouldn't put on their own albums. They're crap and should be beaten out of existence. I didn't like the notion that I'd be a part of that. So I said I'd do it all."

Tom Petty & the Heartbreakers' album was billed as music from the film *She's the One*, a motion picture from the writer/director/star Edward Burns. It started as Petty contributing a new song to the wry romantic comedy about rocky relationships. Then Petty couldn't stop writing, and he and producer Rick Rubin entered the studio.

Everyone else who was going to be on the soundtrack wound up getting 86ed, because what developed was a full album. It followed *Wildflowers*, Petty's 1994 triple-platinum solo effort, and *Playback*, 1995's gold-certified boxed set. The album was also Petty's first with the Heartbreakers since 1991's *Into the Great Wide Open*.

"It's humorous to me that the word 'soundtrack' throws people into such a state of confusion," Petty said. "They really wonder where all the other bands are—it's hard for them to see it's just us. But I enjoy films that have music there for a reason."

Backed by the Heartbreakers—guitarist Mike Campbell, keyboardist Benmont Tench and bassist Howie Epstein—Petty perceived the possibilities of the project. *She's the One* was a more experimental album than *Wildflowers*, and it rocked harder than anything he'd done in years.

"Walls (Circus)" featured a light-hearted California vibe—Lindsay Buckingham's guest background vocals shot from left to right in counterpoint, and the ringing Rickenbacker guitars came right out of the Sixties. There was the scrappy "Climb That Hill" and a cover of Lucinda Williams' dismissive "Change the Locks." It was a companion piece that truly jibed with the film—10 of the 15 selections were featured in *She's the One*. Most of the soundtrack was full songs, but there was a bit of Petty's score.

"I'd never written music expressly for a movie before, but I took it on because it was different. I did it with a guitar. I didn't use computers or any sort of digital equipment—I just think it's much quicker to go in and play rather than deal with all those keyboards. I didn't take it that seriously. I just wanted the music to fit the scenes. I'm really not concerned with being that good at anything."

*She's the One* proved Petty was still at the top of his game, extending his streak of creative growth and critical acclaim. "I really don't have anything else to do," he said with a sly grin. "I'm just gonna see where the wind takes me—go hang around the mall or something." ■

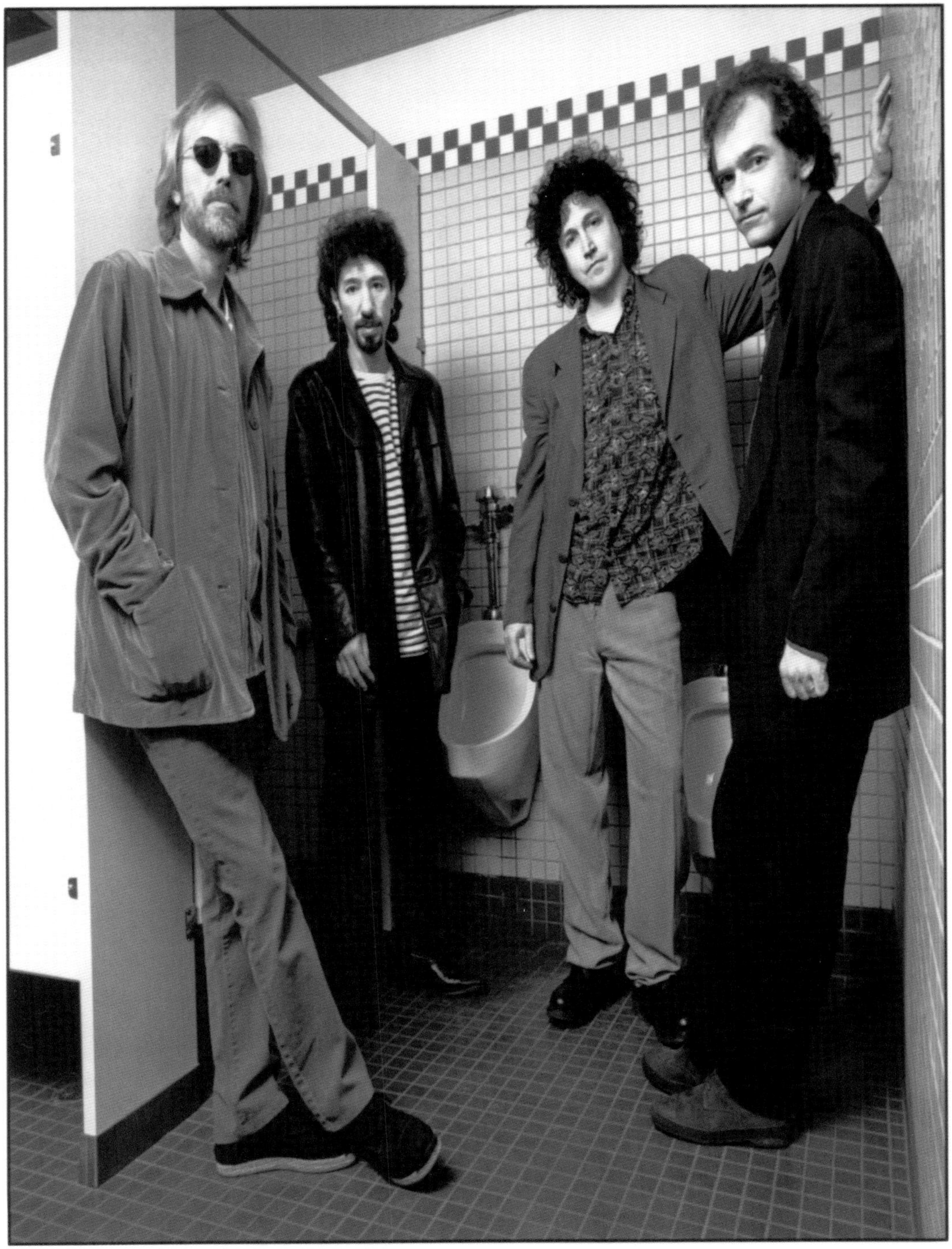

PHOTO CREDIT: Robert Sebree

Tom Petty Howie Epstein Mike Campbell Benmont Tench

tom Petty & The Heartbreakers

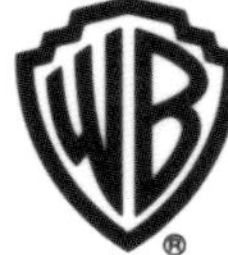

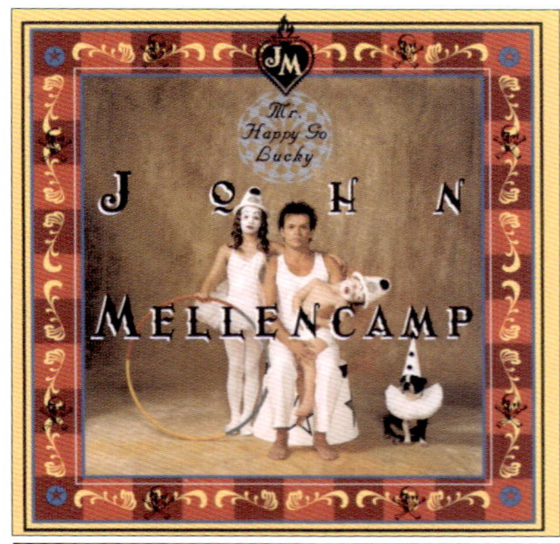


*Billboard* 200: *Mr. Happy Go Lucky* (#9)
*Billboard* Hot 100: "Key West Intermezzo (I Saw You First)" (#14); "Just Another Day" (#46)

# An investigation of dance influences, *Mr. Happy Go Lucky* suggested John Mellencamp at his most ambitious.

**"YOU KNOW** it's going to be the year 2000 pretty soon? There's nothing better for me than to know that people are going to be dancing and throwing Frisbees and screwing to my songs in 2000. What else could a guy want as a songwriter? I don't care if they remember John Mellencamp, but they sure remember, 'Oh yeah, life goes on…'"

Mellencamp knew the demands of redefining his heartland rock 'n' roll before he started his 14th album, *Mr. Happy Go Lucky*, at his studio in Bloomington, Indiana. He bolstered the violins, accordions, pedal steel guitars and dulcimers that had surfaced in his guitar-based style in the Eighties with enchanting dance beats and unusual keyboards. New York club DJ-turned-producer Junior Vasquez, known for his work with Janet Jackson and Madonna, served as musical adviser.

The combination raised eyebrows. "So many people were like, 'Well, Mellencamp's going to danceland.' Ah, fuck you. You must be out of your mind. I knew that I didn't want to make another big drums/guitar/voice record again. I'd had it with that, and if I'm bored, I have to assume the people who buy my records are going, 'Oh, God, this sounds like the last one.'

"If you talk to a guy like Junior who makes dance or hip-hop records, the first thing he starts with is the beat—everything is built around the loop, and nothing treads on that. With us, we always start with little, teeny folk songs, and sometimes the rhythm was the last thing that was added, which is completely ass-backwards. People who make dance records would go, 'Goddamn, why would you do that?' We didn't care. We were trying make their tools work inside of what we do.

"That's what was great about Junior and I working together. In the Seventies, I was in a bar band playing rock songs, but Junior was dancing in those discos in New York. What did we have in common? We both liked rhythm. So even though it seems like two guys on the other side of the world from each other, when we got down to talking music, we were right together—what is it that makes people move?"

The result was Mellencamp's most adventurous music to date. There was a fresh quality to "Key West Intermezzo (I Saw You First)," and the album's sequencing was fueled by drop-in discussions and instrumental interludes. The lyric on "Just Another Day" was more reflective, which wasn't surprising—while out on tour for his last offering, 1994's *Dance Naked*, Mellencamp suffered a minor heart attack. He said he was in better physical shape than he'd ever been—as he exhaled a puff of cigarette smoke.

"I work out, I lift weights, I run. I don't eat like I used to, I don't stay up all night like I used to, I don't smoke pot, I don't take drugs, I don't drink—all that shit's out of my life. I just smoke cigarettes. I'd quit if I knew I was gonna go to jail, so the biggest favor that could be done for me is if they would just outlaw the damn things. But if they do, everybody that doesn't smoke better head for the hills, because the guys that do smoke would lose their fucking minds. This is the toughest thing I've had to tackle in my life." ■

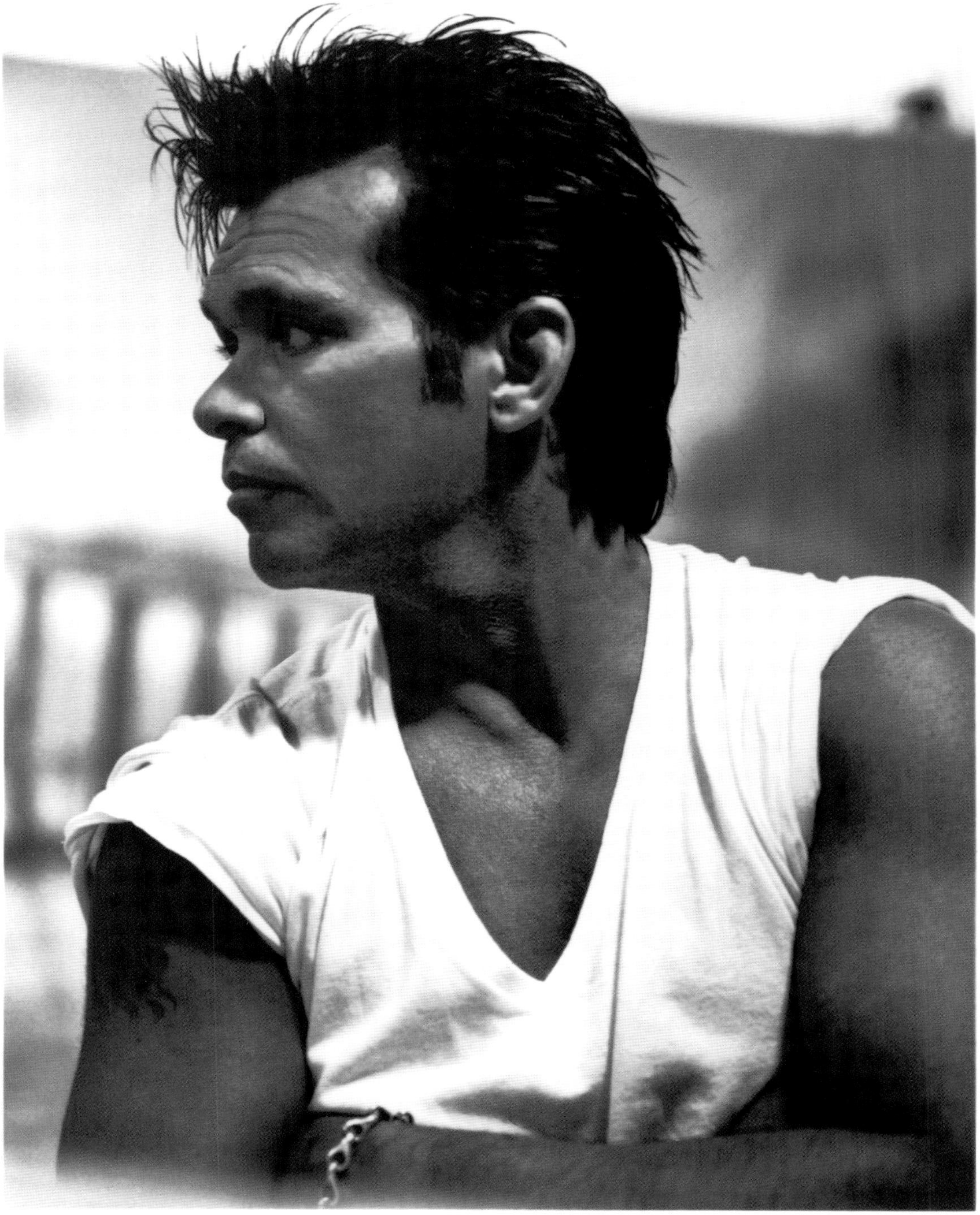

PHOTO CREDIT SAMUEL BAYER

JOHN MELLENCAMP

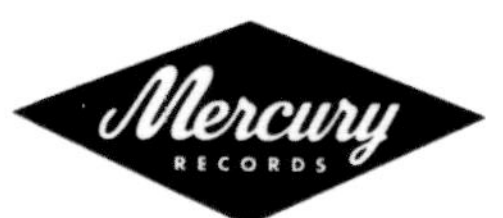

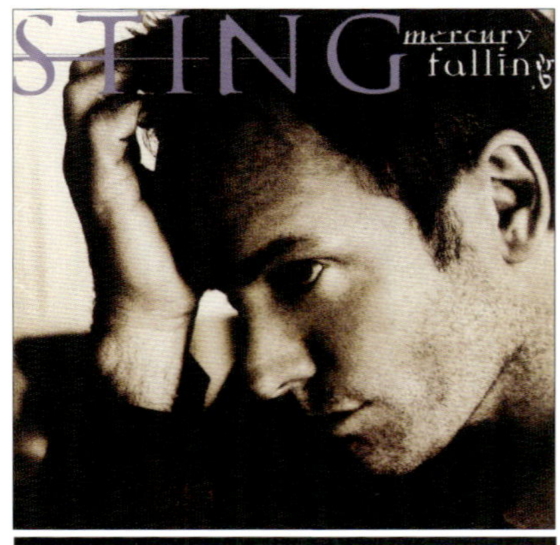


*Billboard* 200: *Mercury Falling* (#5)
*Billboard* Hot 100: "Let Your Soul Be Your Pilot" (#86); "You Still Touch Me" (#60); "I'm So Happy I Can't Stop Crying" (#94)

## *Mercury Falling* reflected Sting's changing attitudes about life, family and the musical community around him.

**BY THE** early Eighties, the Police were one of the top bands in the world, regularly hitting the top of the charts. However, the demands of fame and achievement strained the band members' relationship.

"The most successful period of my life was the most unhappy period of my life," Sting, the frontman, songwriter and bassist, said. "I had gallons of money, success and adulation, and yet my life was crumbling around me—it was a terrible paradox. This was what we had been working for all these years. Now we had it and it meant nothing."

In the 12 years since the Police disbanded, Sting had embarked on a solo career, exploring new styles in music and songwriting. He'd developed into a thoughtful, literate, innovative artist, creating a sound that merged pop, jazz and soul. He was one lucky rock star, happy and fulfilled in his personal life—married (to actress and film producer Trudy Styler), father of four (and two more by a previous marriage). On his summer tour of more than 50 cities, he commuted to most gigs in a Learjet so that he could be with his family the mornings after.

The tracks on *Mercury Falling*, Sting's sixth solo album, were written and recorded at his 16th-century country house on 800 acres near Stonehenge. "The title is a good indication of its intent. Mercury was the god of theft—and here I've stolen from every genre. I see all music, after all, as a single language."

The gorgeous "Let Your Soul Be Your Pilot," described by Sting as "a gospel ballad," featured a 70-voice choir. The clever "I Hung My Head," written in avant-garde 9/8 time, told an unsettling tale of a shooting. The gentle "You Still Touch Me" took a flier at Stax R&B ("I'm not really producing a homage—I'm putting an ironic, objective view on it"). "I'm So Happy I Can't Stop Crying," a country-flavored lament about a divorced man whose custody battle has unraveled, had an incongruous bounciness, moving from bitterness to epiphany.

Sting attributed the somber tone to the album to the fact he was still sorting out the meanings of the songs. "I write unconsciously," he said. "It's only when I finish a song that I look at it and say, 'What is this about?' In a way, it's my cheap form of therapy. On tour, I discover new things every night. I think the songs are about acceptance of things you simply can't change. Like getting old, dying—mortality, really. Those larger issues are a new acquisition for me."

How large of an issue was the failure of *Mercury Falling* to produce a significant hit single? "In my 20s all I wanted was to make No. 1 records," Sting said. "Now, I make music that I like. I like selling a lot of records, I like being a popular artist. But I can't be a pop star all of my life. I want to move—probably away from the popular arena and no one will hear it except the dog." ■

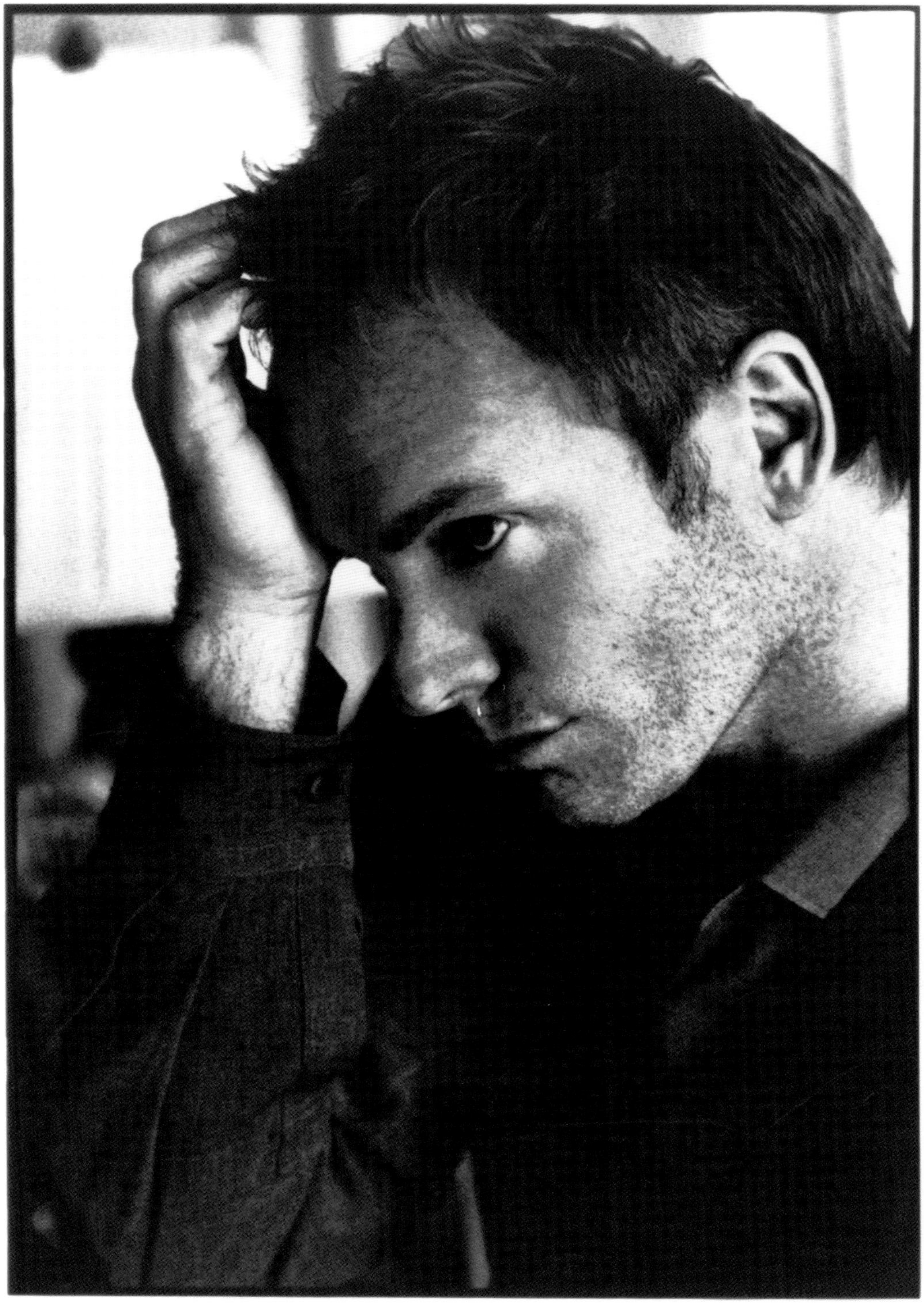

STING

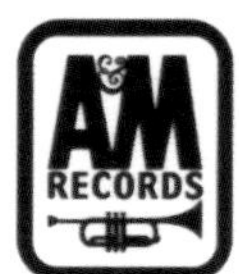


William Claxton 3/96

NO TALKING JUST HEAD

New songs from The Heads
DAMAGE I'VE DONE
with Johnette Napolitano
THE KING IS GONE
with Michael Hutchence
NO TALKING JUST HEAD
with Debbie Harry
NEVER MIND
with Richard Hell
NO BIG BANG
with Maria McKee
DON'T TAKE MY KINDNESS FOR WEAKNESS
with Shaun Ryder
NO MORE LONELY NIGHTS
with Malin Anneteg
INDIE HAIR
with Ed Kowalczyk
PUNK LOLITA
with Debbie Harry, Johnette Napolitano, & Tina Weymouth
ONLY THE LONELY
with Gordon Gano
PAPERSNOW
with Andy Partridge
BLUE BLUE MOON
with Gavin Friday

## The Heads—the original Talking Heads lineup without David Byrne—recorded with an assortment of vocalists.

**JERRY HARRISON**, Tina Weymouth and Chris Frantz comprised three-quarters of Talking Heads, one of the seminal bands to emerge out of New York's late-Seventies scene. During the eight years since *Naked*, the last Talking Heads album, they'd attempted to woo erstwhile frontman David Byrne back to the fold. They then opted to re-form as the Heads and release *No Talking Just Head*.

"Up to a point, we hadn't thought of doing this—we were really feeling that we were still in an in-between phase with Talking Heads," keyboardist and guitarist Harrison said. "But the hope of us re-forming slowly died. There was never any formal meeting, like 'Well, I guess it's over.' It was more like, 'What are we going to do this year?' 'Well, I'm really busy.'

"We try very hard to make people know where we're coming from. Chris and Tina and I have played together for 20 years, yet we weren't trying to appropriate Talking Heads. I think that the title of the album, in a humorous way, makes you understand the difference—'Oh, David's not there, there's no talking.'"

Byrne was hard to replace—the Heads teamed up with a guitarist named Blast and delegated lead vocal duties to not one, but 12 well-known guests on their album. The roster ranged from old friends like Deborah Harry, Richard Hell and XTC's Andy Partridge to alternative types like Shaun Ryder, Gavin Friday and Live's Ed Kowalczyk. Former Concrete Blonde singer Johnette Napolitano put in an intense delivery on "Damage I've Done," and she was the Heads' vocalist as they toured.

"Because of the different singers, the record has an amazing variety to it—and yet because all the songs began with Blast, Chris and Tina and I writing together and playing on them, there's a consistency as well," Harrison said. "It's like a perfectly programmed radio station."

A lawsuit Byrne filed against the band for, among other things, using the name the Heads was settled. But the fact that the Heads had decided to roll on without Byrne had sparked some skepticism. Harrison hadn't been sitting around idly waiting for Byrne; he'd made a name for himself as a record producer (Live, Crash Test Dummies, the Verve Pipe). "There are some people who feel that we're messing with history," Harrison acknowledged. "So we've gotten some very nasty reviews. You try not to get bothered by them." ■

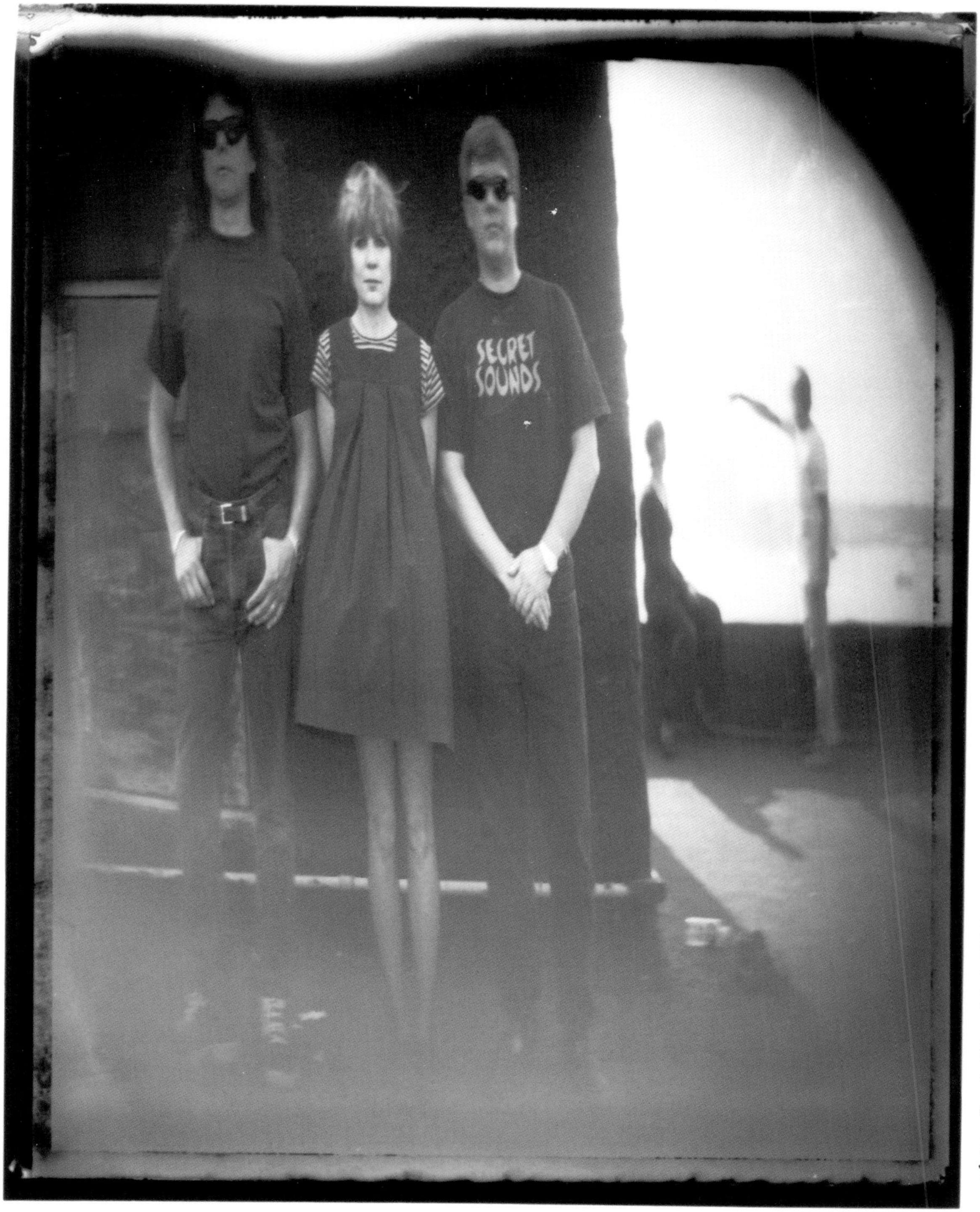

photo: Frank Ockenfels 3 9/96

JERRY HARRISON TINA WEYMOUTH CHRIS FRANTZ

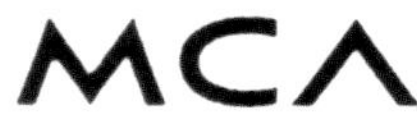


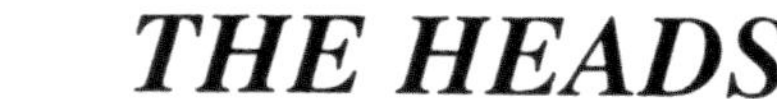


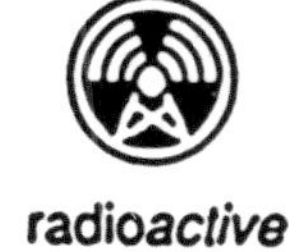

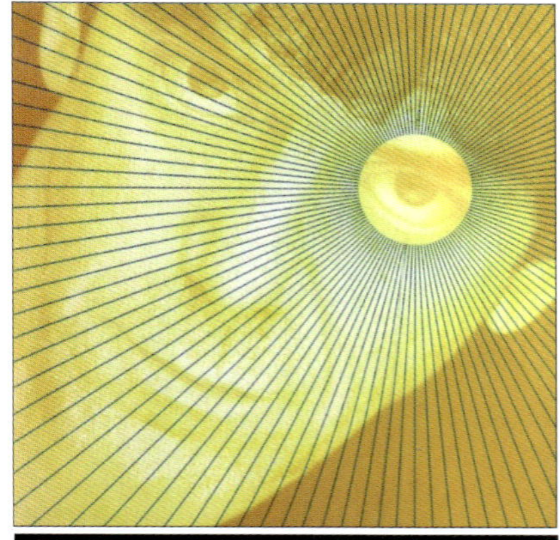

*Billboard* 200: *Set the Twilight Reeling* (#110)

## Fans were stoked to hear Lou Reed cranking up his guitar and having a good time on *Set the Twilight Reeling*.

**ROCK'S ORIGINAL** tough guy, Lou Reed started as a studied outsider set on making white-bread America safe for black nail polish. But more than 30 years had passed since he'd co-founded the Velvet Underground, the influential New York band that was inducted into the Rock and Roll Hall of Fame that year, and Reed was in love (with multimedia artist Laurie Anderson) and feeling exuberant over making music. "And happy is not the limit," he said.

A solo artist since 1970, Reed had portrayed his fascination with his city (1989's *New York*), death and the human spirit (1992's *Magic and Loss*) and patron Andy Warhol (*Songs for Drella*). He returned with *Set the Twilight Reeling*, an intense, uptempo rock album. The most time-consuming part was developing the sound. It was recorded in "The Roof," his downtown New York City studio, and involved his collection of guitars and amps.

"I didn't want to go back into making a record until I could solve certain problems, because I wasn't satisfied with what I was getting out of the recording experience," he explained. "With me, the sound drives everything else. It had a lot to do with the right technological time and space, so to speak. It's digital from start to finish. I never thought I would be the person doing that—it's counter to what I believed a couple of years ago. But things changed. The goal of this album is simple—I wanted you to hear what was really there. I think those guitar sounds are amazing."

Reed cited his dynamic, visceral work on "HookyWooky," a goofy love song. "If you go through all that to get an awesome sound in the studio, and you don't hear it on the record, you feel like you might as well just shoot yourself—what is the point? But I knew I could get these sounds recorded and played back."

The opening "Egg Cream," a three-chord paean to "some U-bet's chocolate syrup, seltzer water mixed with milk," provided the album's theme of renewal. "That's the classic way" to make the drink, Reed insisted, laughing. "Although somebody told me something weird—had I thought about putting it in the freezer and making the milk really cold so that it crystallized? And the answer is no, I've never heard that one. But why not?"

"Sex with Your Parents (Motherfucker) Part II," a live recording, glibly condemned extreme conservatives like Rush Limbaugh ("Rush Rambo"). Reed expressed the view that the reason so many of them were uptight is that they had illegal congress with their mommas. "I don't expect to hear from them," he said. "I mean, look at who's out there right now. How could I have left Pat Buchanan out? I guess I assumed he was dead." ■

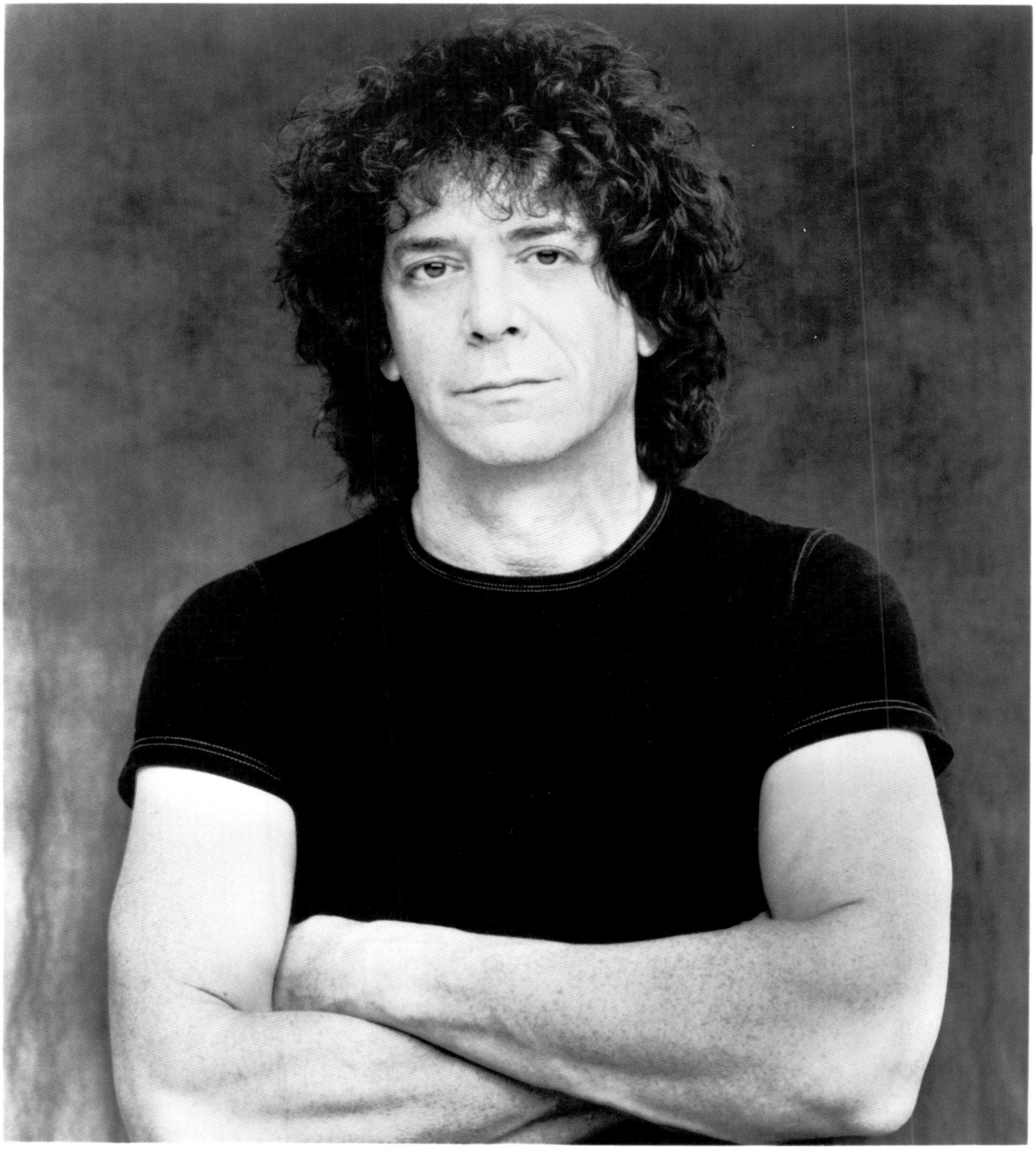

Photo Credit Timothy Greenfield-Sanders

# LOU REED

Billboard 200: *I Feel Alright* (#106)

## The intractable Steve Earle bounced back in better health, coming to grips with his misdeeds on *I Feel Alright*.

**WHEN HE** first hit the national scene in the mid-Eighties, Steve Earle seemed poised to become the Bruce Springsteen of Nashville. Straddling the borders of rural music and hard rock, he made several classic albums, including the celebrated *Guitar Town*. But Earle's once-promising career got lost in a haze of heroin addition, countless arrests and jailings. He was so strung out during his lost years that he didn't even own a guitar. He knocked around a Nashville ghetto and hit bottom after a 1994 crack bust.

Then a prison term set him straight. Earle returned claiming to be clean and sober—and the guy could still write trenchant songs. "I'm having more fun making records and touring than I ever have, so I'm pretty happy with what's happened in the last two years," he said. "But that doesn't surprise me much. I always knew that if I lived to be 40—I'm 41 now—that this part of my life would be pretty productive. My habit just took up so much space it was hard to do anything. So taking that away, it's amazing how much time, energy and money you have."

1995's *Train a Comin'* renewed Earle, paying respect to Texas troubadours like Townes Van Zandt and Guy Clark—he grew up in San Antonio spellbound by the talented, reckless country outlaws. His struggles inspired the gritty, powerful country-rock songs on *I Feel Alright*. The opening "Feel Alright" soared with tough-guy attitude, not self-pity. But the tour de force was the bluesy "CCKMP" ("Cocaine Cannot Kill My Pain"), which conveyed a junkie's desperation.

"I thought about not recording it, and I thought about not including it after I recorded it, which is something I never do—there aren't a bunch of Steve Earle outtakes sitting around," Earle said. "But there are some issues involved. 'Cocaine' was written before the other songs, before I got clean. Shortly after that followed a period when I didn't write at all for four years—it was a last gasp. I'm not real comfortable with that song sometimes, because I was dying when I wrote it. But I'm proud of it."

Earle said drugs came with his rootless loner lifestyle—he first tried heroin when he was 13 and never really stopped until he was locked up and the Nashville mainstream had left him for dead, "Everybody's got a Steve Earle story," he shared. "Some of the ones that aren't true, I made up. I'd get loaded and get on the road—I knew a girl with a really big mouth who I could call and plant a rumor about myself just to see what it became by the time I got back to town. Which is a dangerous game to play, but I was on dope—what do you expect?"

Now Earle's drug of choice was work. "People like to get their pictures taken with me a lot more than they used to," he said with a laugh. "And there's a bunch of people that genuinely care about me, that really are friends of mine, and that's gratifying. They supported me even when I was gone, and I do appreciate that. I don't think I could do much that would throw the fans I've established, as long as I write good songs." ■

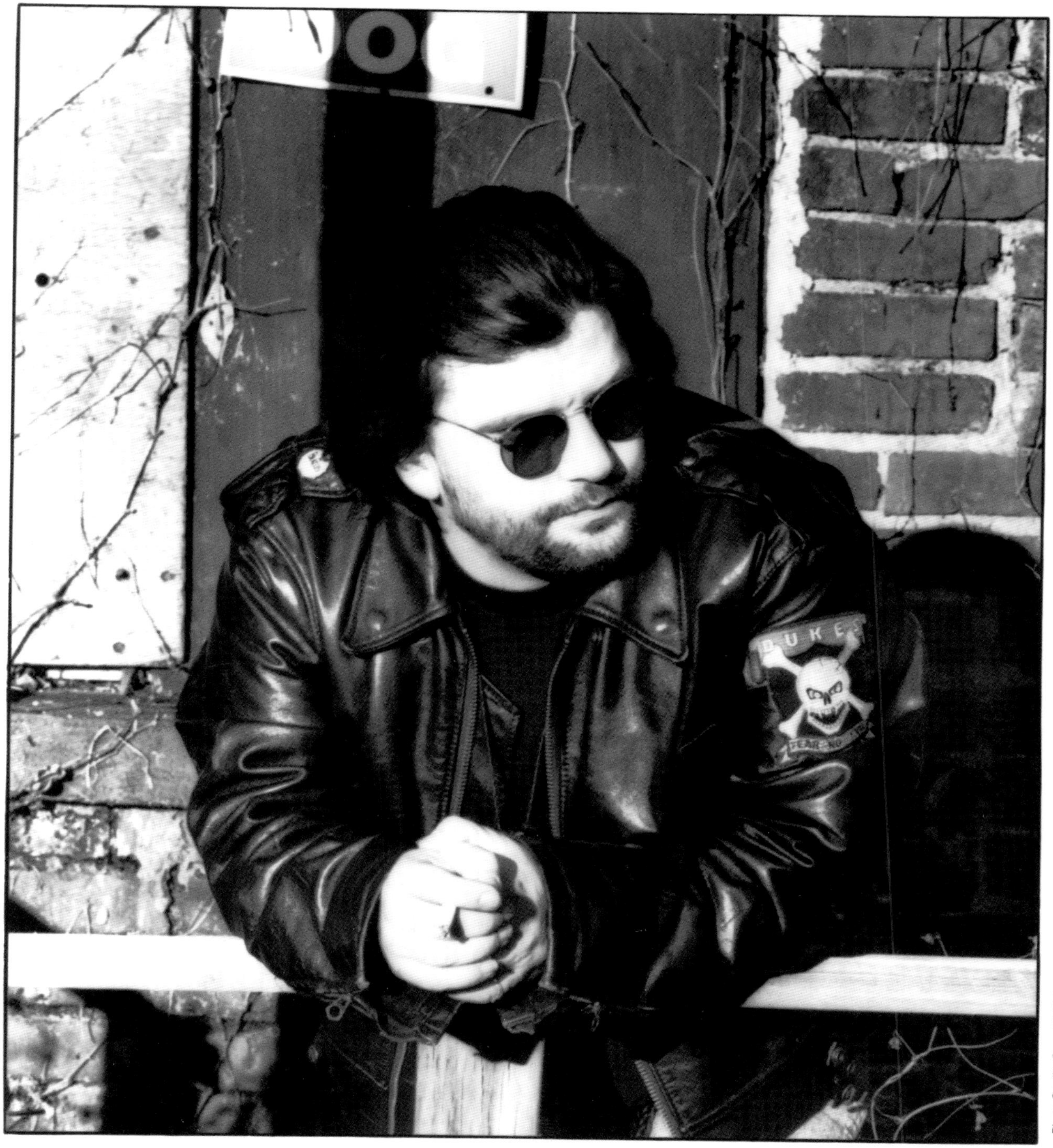

Photo Credit: Senor McGuire

# STEVE EARLE

*Billboard* 200: *The Road to Ensenada* (#24)

## The gentlemanly Lyle Lovett averred there were no references to his failed marriage in *The Road to Ensenada*.

**ON HIS** engaging sixth album, Lyle Lovett never sounded better. *The Road to Ensenada* teemed with everything that had come to be expected from him—laid-back charm, oddball humor and illuminating ruminations. But it also marked Lovett's first record since the dissolution of his tabloid-tracked marriage to film actress Julia Roberts. Enquiring minds were bound to scrutinize the album for clues to the widely publicized split.

Lovett handled the topic gracefully and articulately. "You have to expect people to look into the songs that way—I'd feel silly if I was offended by it or took exception to it, because it's just a natural thing," Lovett said. "Julia was always really supportive of my songs. I did write some of these while we were married, and she gave me the confidence to sing about feelings that I had. But in none of the narratives am I telling stories about anything that actually happened in my life. Nobody would be able to piece together something by listening."

*The Road to Ensenada* was a song cycle about impossible love—and, yes, a couple of songs mentioned a girl from Georgia (Roberts' home state)—but the album's truth went much deeper than a literal chronicle of Lovett the Hollywood husband. In the past, critics had accused him of masking his feelings behind causticity and a flaky façade. But the strongest virtue of *The Road to Ensenada* was its emotional urgency.

"Going back to my first album, I asked Guy Clark about what songs to put on it, and he looked at me and said, 'Well, what are your 10 best songs?' Every time I go in the studio, I try to take that advice. You know, I still haven't ever sat down and written an album as a whole piece. For me, it's just the next batch of songs."

The moral of the sprightly "Private Conversation" was "I guess it's easier said than done/To look at what you've been through/And to see what you've become." The opener, "Don't Touch My Hat," found Lovett giving up his woman more readily than his John B. Stetson. The acerbic "Christmas Morning," meanwhile, pondered loneliness.

Three songs dealt with "that whole Texas bravado." "That's Right (You're Not from Texas)"—dedicated to Lovett's old songwriting pal, the late Walter Hyatt—was a western swing number. In the samba "Her First Mistake," Lovett concluded, "I just keep on running faster/Chasing the happily/I am ever after." And the sessions shaped up to allow Lovett to record a wry remake of "Long Tall Texan" with Randy Newman. Jackson Browne, Shawn Colvin and others also joined in the recording of the album.

"It's just like in any kind of job, in the normal way anybody meets anybody and you make friends. That's the fun of it. It's a great thrill for me. When you admire somebody's music, you just appreciate it—you don't feel competitive with them, you just stand there and go, 'Wow!'" ■

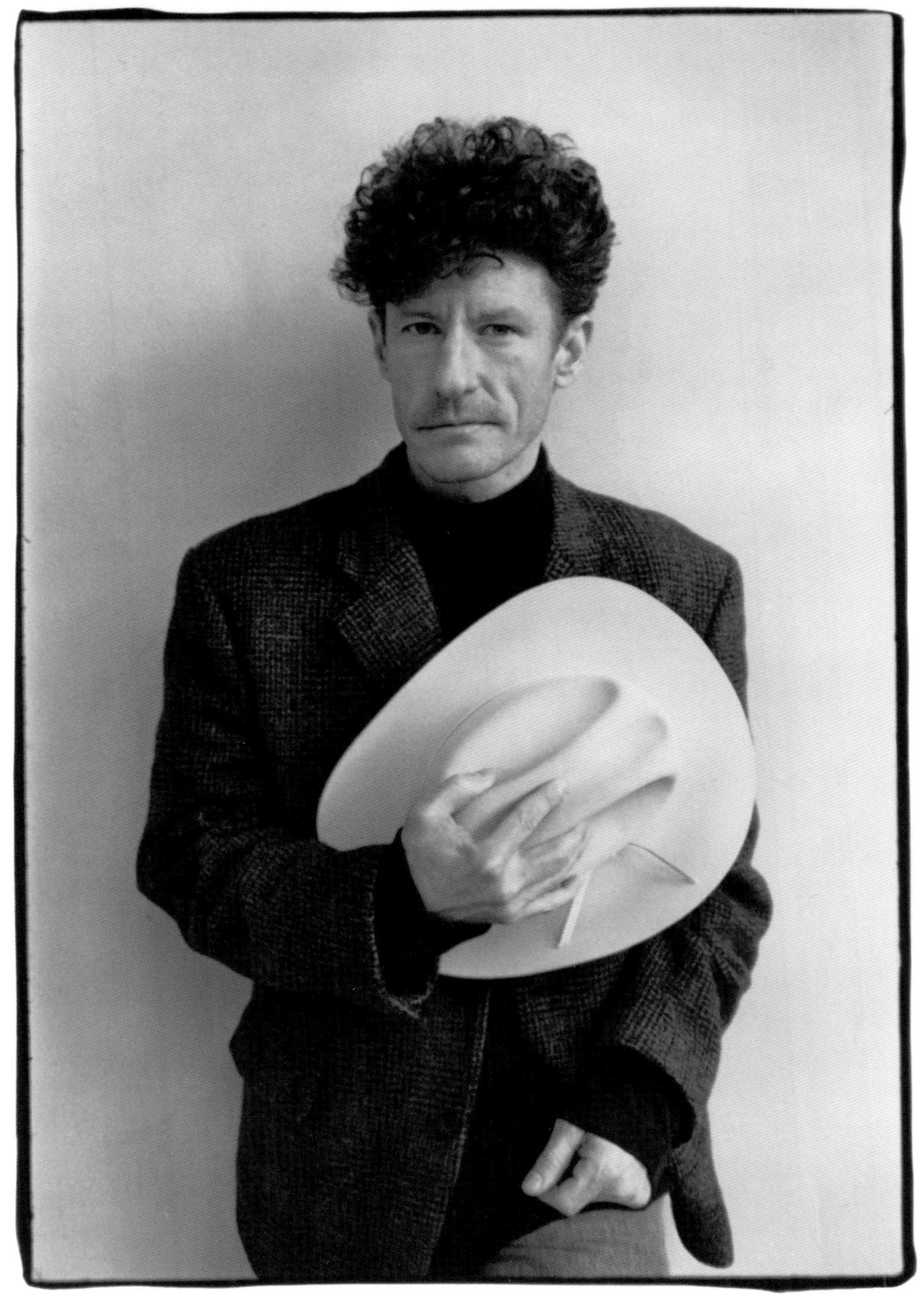

Photo Credit: Michael Wilson

5/96

# Lyle Lovett

CURB.
MCA.

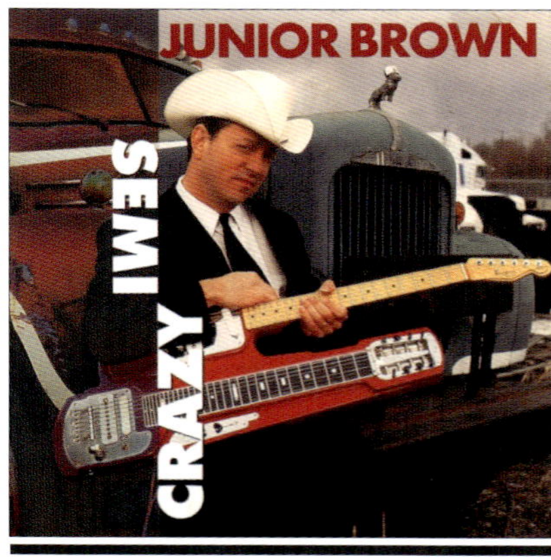


A true original, Junior Brown returned with *Semi Crazy*, another fine showcase for his marvelous guitar skills.

**WITH A** penchant for wearing old-time Western hats and suits, and a disarming baritone that sounded as if he were asking for your license and registration, Junior Brown seemed to be the one artist in country music who wasn't the result of market research. But the Austinite appealed to younger alternative rockers as well as traditional country fans. He played fiery licks on his own self-designed contraption, the hybrid "guit-steel," and it was no gimmick—something like the intersection of Ernest Tubb and Jimi Hendrix. "More than anything else, I hear people tell me they don't like country music, but they like what I'm doing," Brown said.

*Semi Crazy*, Brown's first album in three years, was fun as usual. It included such dryly self-deprecating lyrics as "Gotta get up every morning/Just to say goodnight to you" (about a partying spouse), in addition to stunning fretboard acrobatics ("I Hung It Up") and "Surf Medley," a seven-minute instrumental built around "Pipeline" and "Walk Don't Run."

"Joe the Singing Janitor," a tribute to maintenance work, supported Red Simpson's "Highway Patrol" from 1993's *Guit with It*. It was a novelty song that was serious at the same time, about a man asking for dignity and respect: "I can't carry a tune in a bucket, but I carry that bucket with pride." "People liked 'Highway Patrol' because it's a common-man subject that doesn't get a lot of attention," Brown said. "I thought, well, janitors are the same kind of thing. The song's got a funny meaning, but it's also a guy saying, 'Pay some attention to me.'"

Brown had made his living with a blue-collar day job now and then. "I know what it feels like to push that broom around, you bet. I started playing rock in the teen clubs in 1965; then in '69 I started playing in the country honky-tonks. It was a question of how I could make my bread and butter rather than what I was interested in." He spent a decade as a sideman and a guitar teacher. He switched between electric guitar and steel guitar onstage so often that he combined the two instruments into a single body.

"I'm not the most motivated guy sometimes," he said with a laugh. "I thought it up and said, 'This would be great someday if…' Eventually I did and called it the 'guit-steel.' It was trial and error—the guitar maker and I didn't know what it would be like until we finished it."

Then Brown developed his reputation as a bandleader. "I didn't pursue a solo career until I could add writing as a part of the singing and guitar-playing package. I got enthusiastic in the early Eighties, and that was the turning point. I call those turns of phrase 'catchy country.' As every writer knows, you do a lot of lousy ones and a few good ones, but the good ones spur you on."

Brown had doggedly stuck with his devotion to old country music, and at last he was receiving Grammy nominations. "For so many years, it seemed that mostly musicians liked what I did and very few other people noticed," he observed. "It's nice that it's paid off." ■

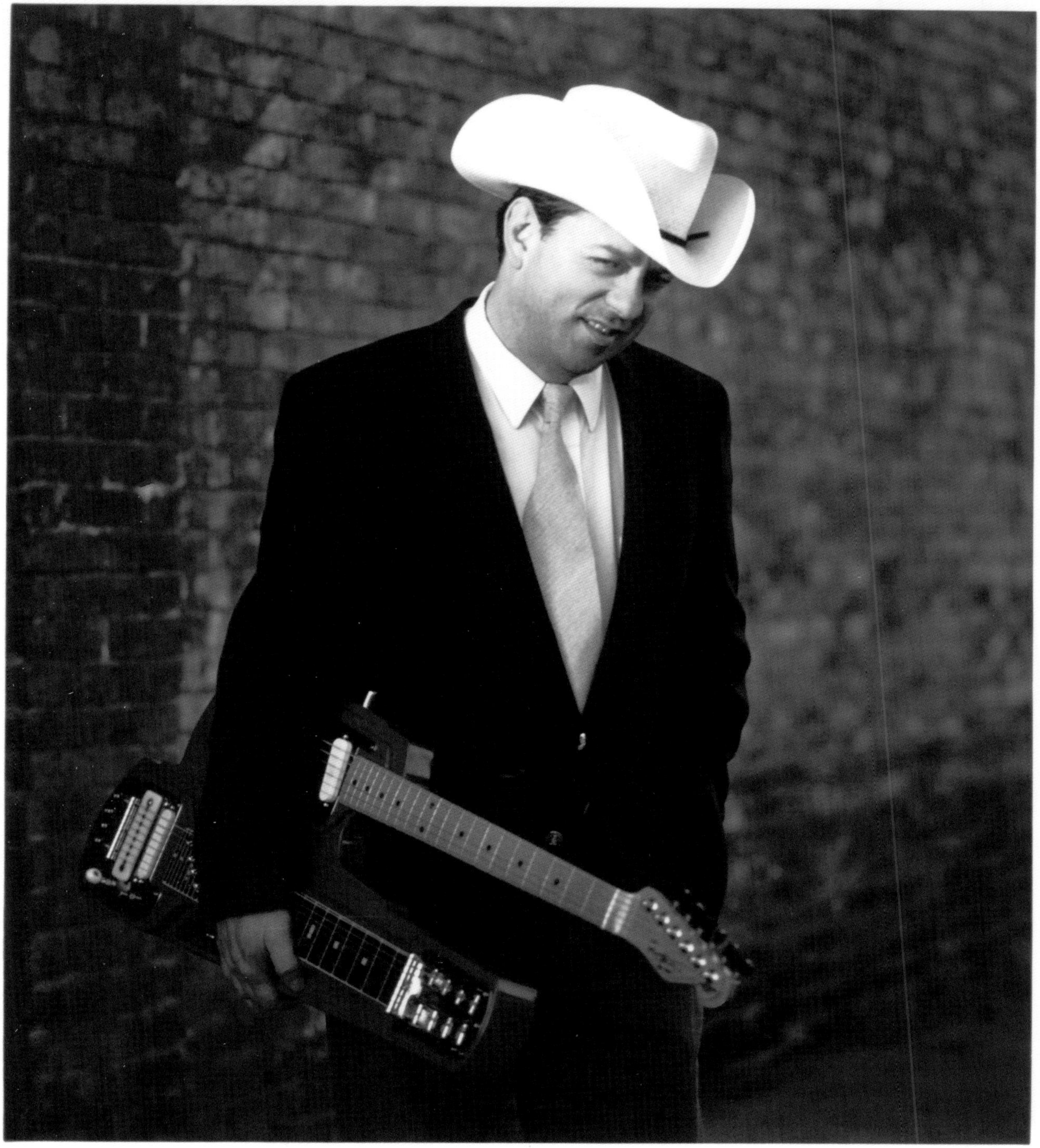

photo: Señor McGuire

FORCE
816 19th Avenue South
Nashville, TN 37203
615.321.0999 fax 615.321.9640

# JUNIOR BROWN

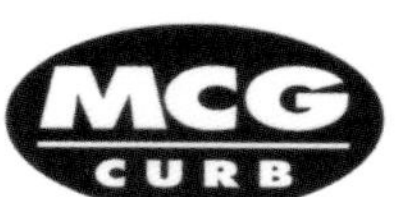


Junior Brown Fan Club
P.O. Box 180763
Utica, MI 48318

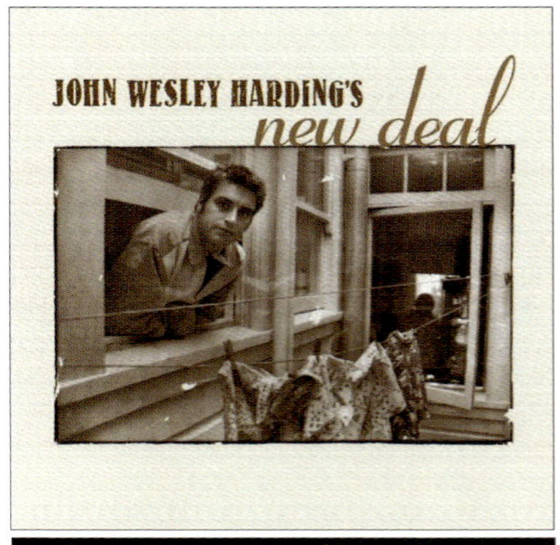


## John Wesley Harding deepened his contemplative, no-frills folk rock through *John Wesley Harding's New Deal.*

**BASED ON** his discerning wit and knack for biting pop melodies, John Wesley Harding quickly developed a reputation as one of the best new troubadours of the early Nineties. He put out a handful of albums, starting with *Here Comes the Groom*, and artists like Bruce Springsteen, the Band, Los Lobos and Joan Baez handpicked him to be their opening act. Harding, who was born in England and resided in San Francisco, re-emerged with his most stripped-down record, *John Wesley Harding's New Deal.*

"I've been singing about pop culture, and I wanted to divest myself of all those influences," the folk rebel explained. "I basically stopped watching telly and listening to the radio and reading magazines the last three years. I didn't want to get annoyed about the O.J. Simpson trial enough to write a song. I don't think the world needs that anymore.

"Acoustic music is more deeply out of fashion than ever, mainly because there's this ersatz explosion of it floating around. People say, 'What about *MTV Unplugged*? That's just a good way to resell old catalog—there's nothing at all to do with acoustic music as far as I can see. That realization has people in their marketing ghettos. Beck is the slacker singer-songwriter, Matthew Sweet is the power-pop singer-songwriter, John Gorka is the folk singer-songwriter. I wanted to make a pure singer-songwriter record."

So Harding went back to the Seventies for his offering. "I listened to loads of early Al Stewart, Cat Stevens, Gordon Lightfoot, Tim Hardin and Jim Croce," he said. "Because however wimpy or bland you think their lyrics are, you can put an orchestra or marching band or ethnic percussion or anything on those records and never lose the acoustic guitar and voice. They're so well done."

The instrumentation gave *John Wesley Harding's New Deal* a rich, uncluttered feel, and the lyrics captured the dangers and victories of modern-day life. Fans were obsessed with "Kiss Me, Miss Liberty" and "The Triumph of Trash," with the line "Trash needs nostalgia to breathe." "People say, 'The reference is too clever,' but that's what songwriting is about to me. They want you to fill in the work that you've put into making what could have been a magazine article into a five-word phrase.

"I'm still largely unknown, which I suppose is a massive problem. I'm not going to sell hundreds of thousands of records. But by the same token, I'm able to keep doing what I like to do. My trick is to write and play songs about important things without them seeming that important. I take that very seriously. The rest is just a joke." ■

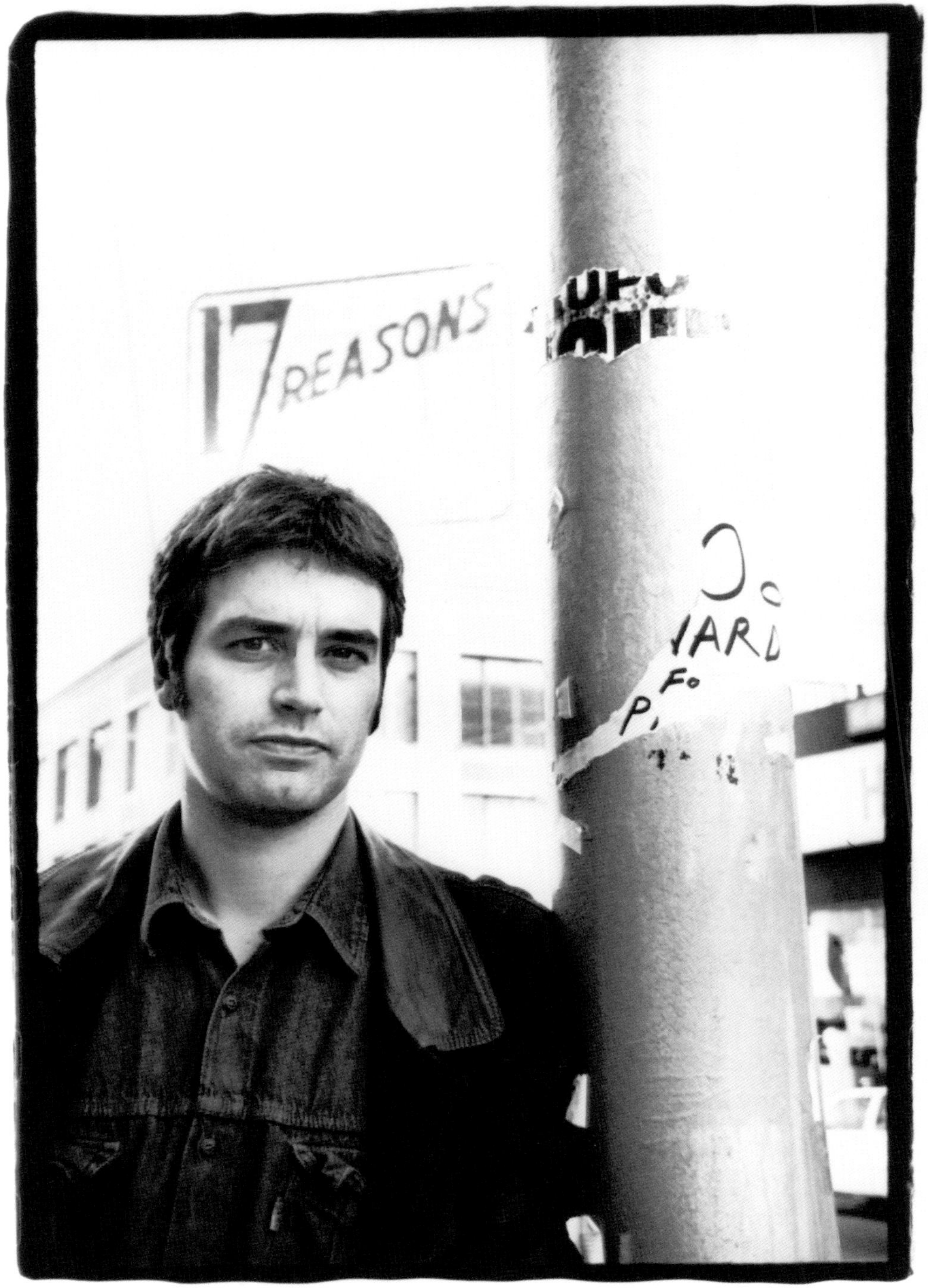

photo: David Dorn

# JOHN WESLEY HARDING

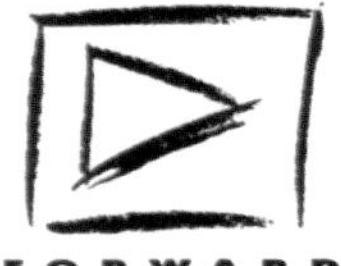

FORWARD


*FORWARD* publicity
10635 Santa Monica Blvd.
Los Angeles, CA 90025
1 (800) 827-4466•(310) 474-4778

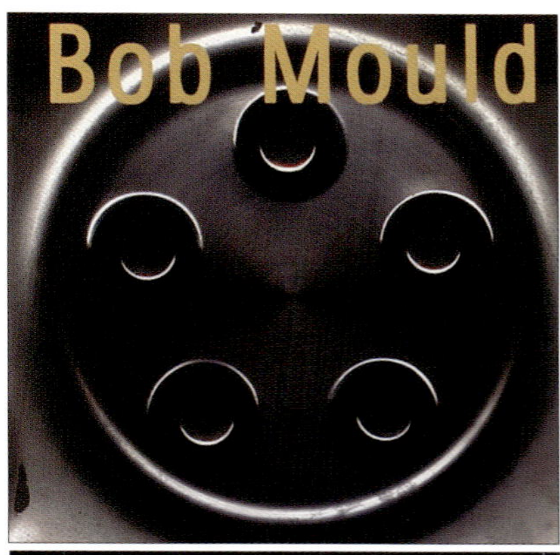


*Billboard* 200: *Bob Mould* (#101)

## A re-energized Bob Mould returned to solo recording, manning all the instruments himself on a self-titled work.

**AS THE** frontman for Hüsker Dü in the Eighties and Sugar in the Nineties, Bob Mould defined noise-pop before the alternative-rock windfall began. After filling the years between those two bands with two solo albums, Mould found himself on his own once again, as Sugar disbanded in the spring of 1996, ruined by "that quest for success"—and he released the most deeply personal record of his career.

*Bob Mould* was accompanied by a "no tours, no interviews" statement: "I have no desire to talk about myself every day for the next three months, nor do I feel any great need to perform these songs 100 times in the four months after the talking stops." But Mould's passion was rekindled when Pete Townshend invited him to open a show in New York. Conveying that passion in concert wasn't a problem for the accomplished singer-songwriter, even with an acoustic Yamaha 12-string.

"I've started to find a much calmer spot to play from, which is actually more musical—not being so anxious, not to feel like I have to convince everybody within three minutes that this is a life-or-death thing," Mould said. "I've had a bit of an awakening about relaxing, letting the music go where it's going to go as opposed to trying to force something. I feel much better about it."

Mould wrote and recorded every sound on *Bob Mould*, referred to by fans as "the hubcap album" for its cover art, with a dedication in the sleeve notes reading "This one is for me." Highlights included the damning "I Hate Alternative Rock" ("I knew you when/You had something to say") and the singles "Egøverride" and "Fort Knox, King Solomon." Mould continued to record for Rykodisc, an independent label.

"I know how the game works," he said. "The writing process is such a weird, unconscious act. When I get done with a song, I think I know what its chances are, but as far as sitting down and going, 'I really wish this one would be a hit,' I not sure I'm the kind of person who can do that."

An October 1994 *Spin* feature about his coming out had made Mould reluctant to do interviews. "I started to see the futility of trying to explain anything in great length and having it chopped down to the stuff that sells magazines," he explained. "I've been doing it long enough. I should have known better." ■

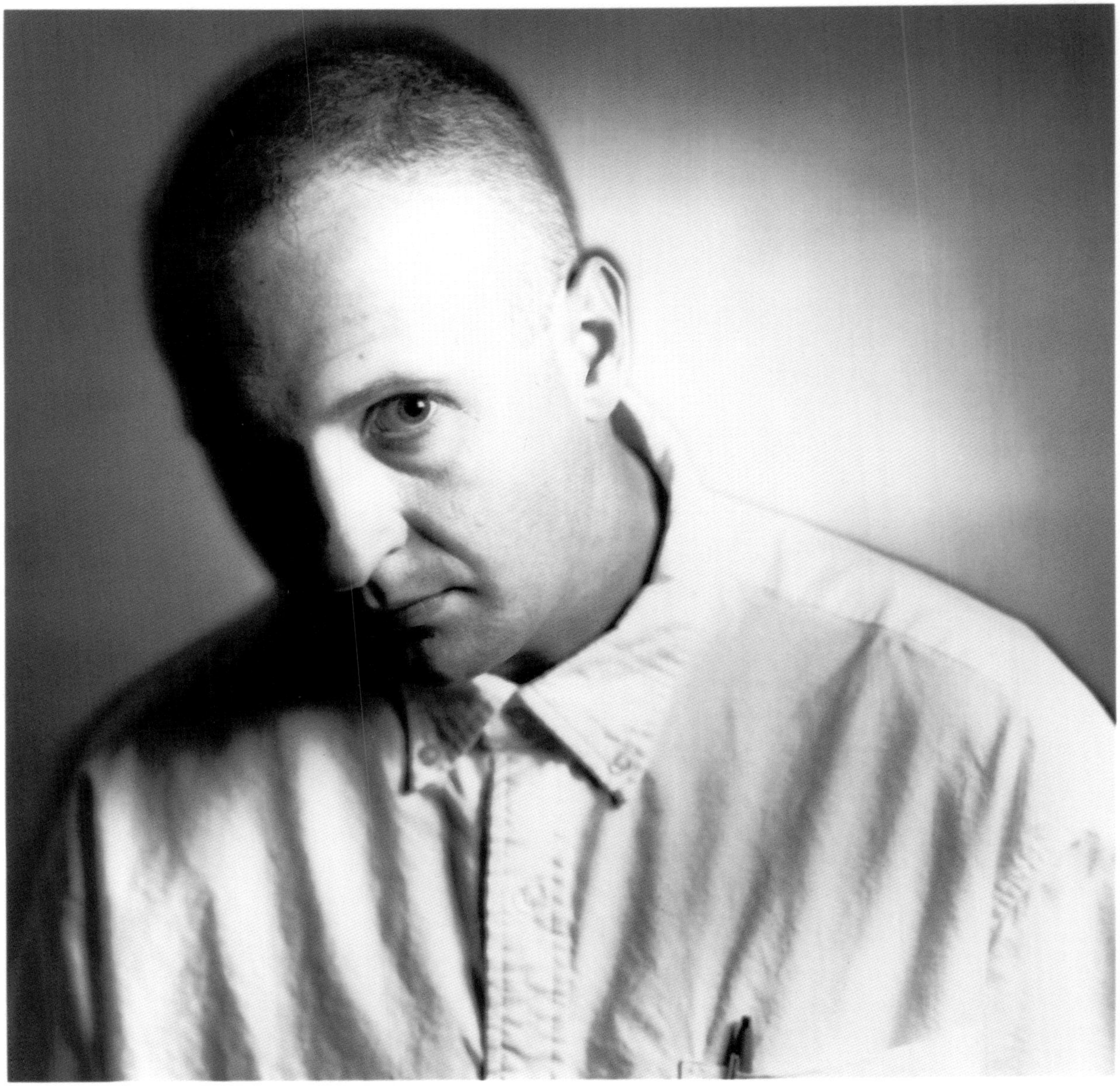

Credit: Andrew Yates

# BOB MOULD

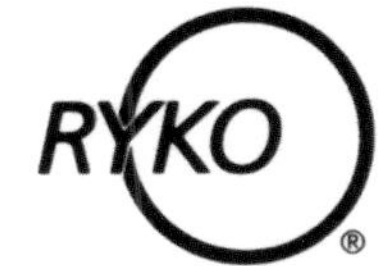

Billboard 200: The Cult of Ray (#127)

## For his album *The Cult of Ray*, erstwhile Pixies bossman Frank Black opted for an unvarnished plan of attack.

**AS A** member of the Pixies, Frank Black made some of the most inspiring guitar-fueled music of the late Eighties. "And now," Black declared, "people ask, 'Well, what do you think now that alternative music is so big and mainstream?' What do I say—that I have created the blandest monster ever?

"I'm flattered when artists cite me as an influence, regardless of whether I like their music. But it's the stuff that gets marketed that takes off. Top 40 isn't really any different than it ever was—the really good records and the really bad records seem to stick around and get played. When a handful of massive corporations go out and buy up all the rock radio stations and format them to death so that it's the same damn 20 songs everywhere around the country...alright, I'm a little cynical. I'm not saying there should be a law against that, but there used to be more variety. It's all turning into Applebee's."

In life after the Pixies, instead of trying to match the achievements of his old band, Black had gotten more eccentric. 1994's *Teenager of the Year*, his last solo album, had a lot of studio ornamentation. *The Cult of Ray* found him going back to guitar-bass-drums basics.

"It's like having Thai food twice last week—now I'm ready to go out for Italian or Mexican," Black said. "This record comes off starker, rawer, but I'm not emphasizing that as if it's a great accomplishment. If people like it, great, but I'm not trying to appease them—'I've seen the light, forget all the times I had keyboards on my albums, now I sound rock.' It's the pendulum swinging around. There's the rocking side and the dreamy side. There's Little Richard and there's Alan Parsons.

"Certainly, I think I do the simple, naïve, arty punk thing better. I don't mind that people prefer the stripped-down rock guitar situation—I have those kinds of preferences about other artists. What bothers me is when people miss out on the vibe, even if it's one they don't like. That's not thoughtful."

*The Cult of Ray* included the catchy, chugging "Men in Black" and "I Don't Want to Hurt You (Every Single Time)," a fractured romantic number. "My girlfriend's mother said, 'How about *Less Is More* for an album title?' In a way, she hit it on the head. Don't overembellish, don't overorchestrate, don't overproduce. Just keep it simple. That's all we did, with loving care."

Black, a UFO enthusiast, coined the title for *The Cult of Ray* to honor Ray Bradbury, the sci-fi scribe who penned *Fahrenheit 451* and the classic collection *The Martian Chronicles*. "I observe the genre on the fringe," he mused. "I check out the movies and get disappointed. You don't see really great science-fiction films like *2001* and *Silent Running* being made these days." ■

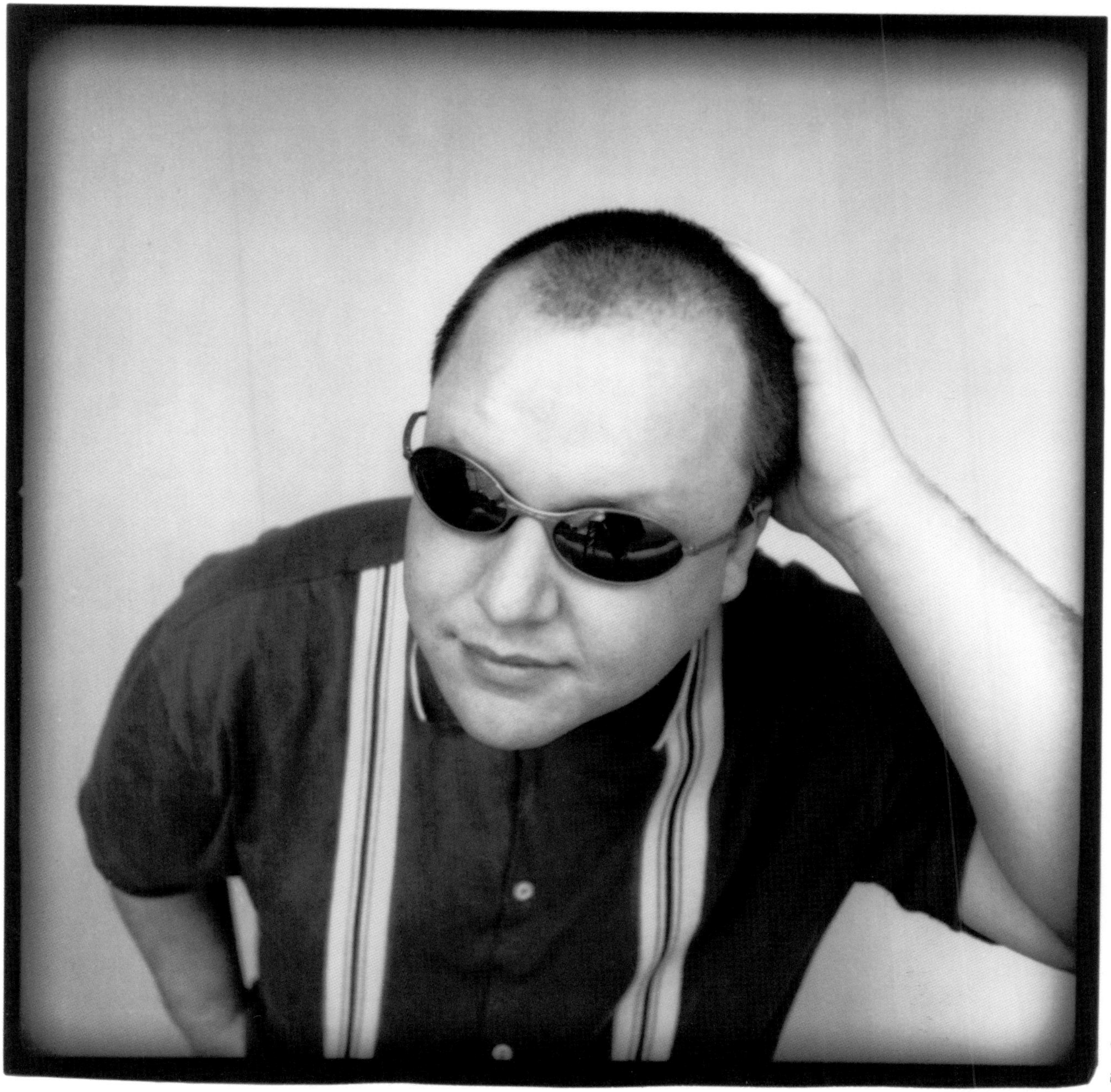

Photo Credit American Recordings

# Frank Black

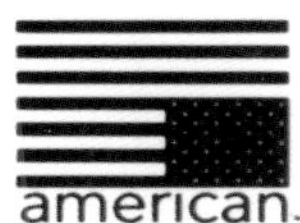

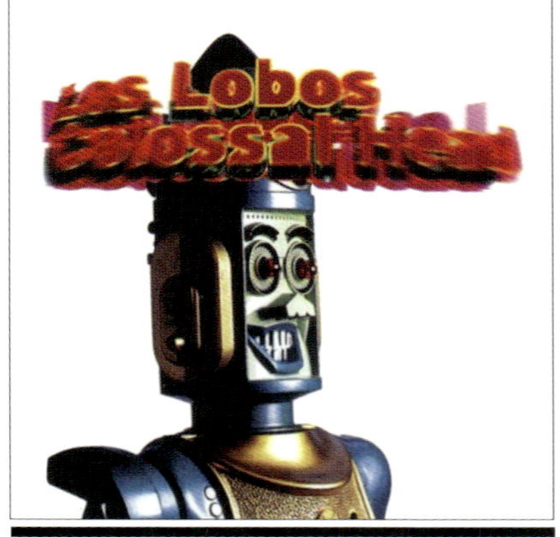


*Billboard* 200: *Colossal Head* (#81)

## Los Lobos' inspired, wide-ranging musical vision managed to be more daring and diversified on *Colossal Head*.

**IN AN** era of radio formats and market niches, it took a courageous band to follow a melting-pop strategy with certainty. The members of Los Lobos had earned their status as uncompromising innovators of American roots-rock. Drummer Louie Perez co-wrote most of the band's songs with vocalist and multi-instrumentalist David Hildago.

"We don't have the time to buy into the rock-star thing," Perez said. "A lot of that has to do with how we conduct business, do the creative thing. We don't talk about what the next step is, we don't conceptualize—we don't even do schedules very well. It drives management and record companies crazy, everybody who relies on things put down on a piece of paper. There's a certain degree of struggle, doing things on our own terms. Our lives are okay. We're making a living."

In the late Seventies, Los Lobos built a loyal following in East Los Angeles by performing acoustic Mexican folk music at weddings and dances. After getting caught up in the Hollywood club scene's power and resourcefulness, the band switched to rock and started drawing attention outside its home base. Then in the summer of 1987, the soundtrack for *La Bamba*, the hit movie about Fifties rock star Ritchie Valens, shot to the top of the pop album charts. It was powered by Los Lobos, who contributed eight songs to the album—all remakes of Valens hits, including the title track, which also reached No 1.

Choosing to escape the shadow of *La Bamba*, the band explored unusual sounds and arrangement ideas on 1992's award-winning *Kiko* and *Latin Playboys* (Perez and Hildago's 1994 side project), two of the decade's most critically heralded albums. Los Lobos' *Colossal Head* encompassed blistering guitar, straight ahead rock 'n' roll, R&B grooves, experimental art-pop and traditional flavors.

"Going into the studio without too much preparation is a good thing, like Zen recording," Perez explained. "A lot of times, the things that end up on record are the first take, maybe just a pass at getting the sound. You're assaulted with all this technology and you think, 'Well, I've gotta go in there and do it 15 times.' We've gotten over that. It's become a process of nonprocess."

The distinctive style of collaboration with producer Mitchell Froom and engineer Tchad Blake was pivotal. "What Mitchell and Tchad do is similar to a painter who shows you the medium, rather than tricking you with super-realism where it looks like a photograph. You can see the paint, the reworking of it. It makes it more human."

Airplay and sales were limited, but Los Lobos' trip to the studio was justly celebrated. "I don't know how the sense of discovery is intact—what we do is what we've been doing for the past 21 years," Perez admitted. "It's been progressive. It's hard to explain, but I really treasure that we can be excited and enthusiastic after this many years. As soon as you figure it out, it goes away." ■

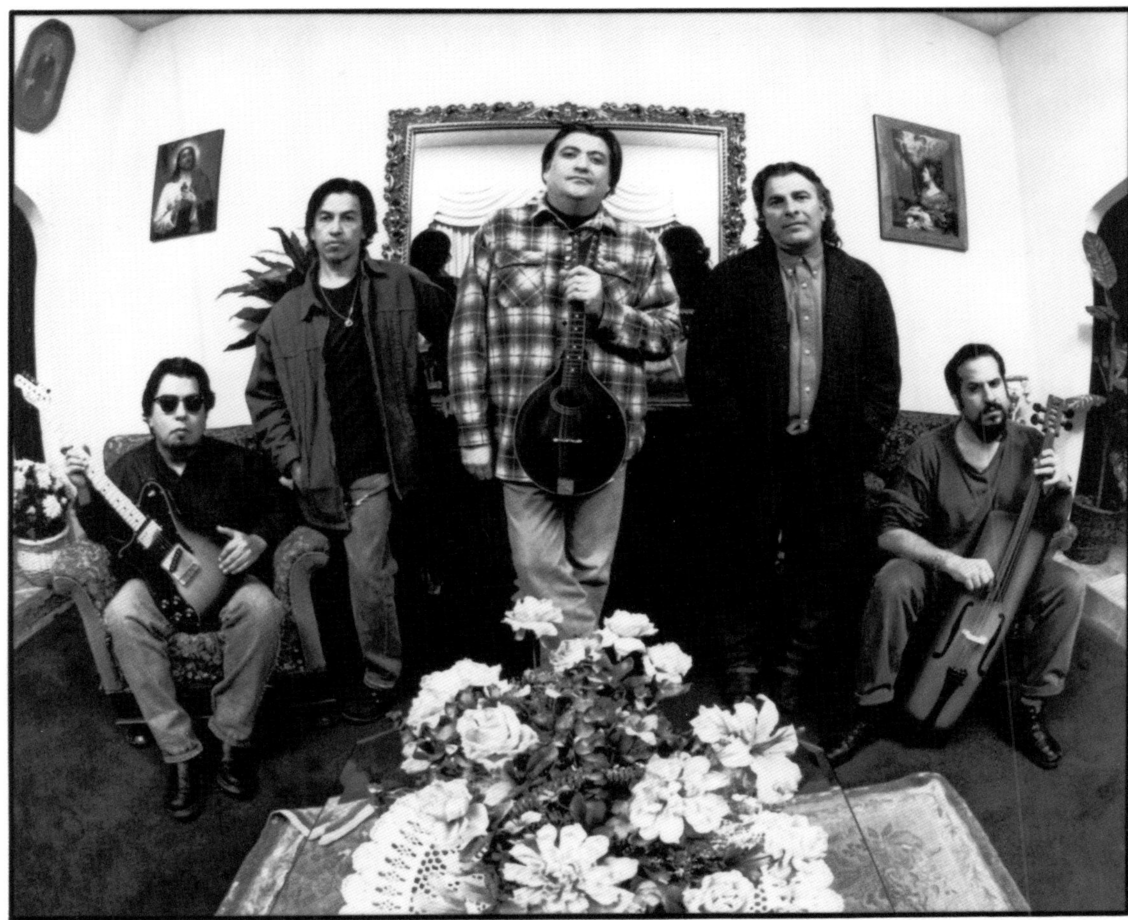

PHOTO CREDIT: Robert Sebree

Cesar Rosas Louie Perez David Hidalgo Conrad Lozano Steve Berlin

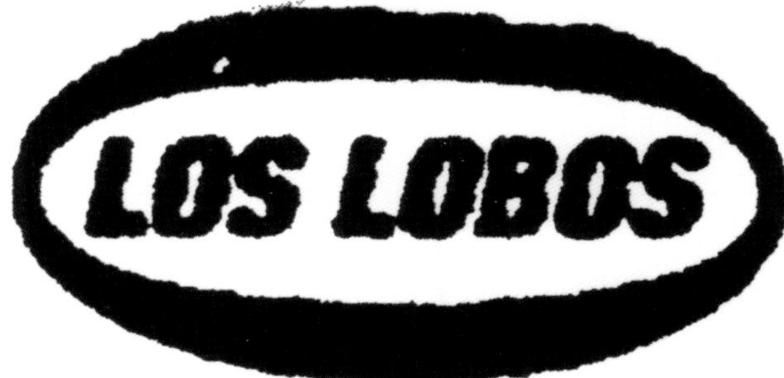


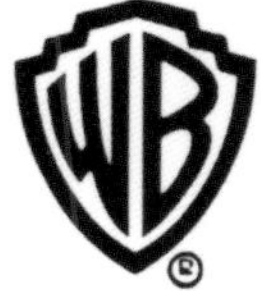

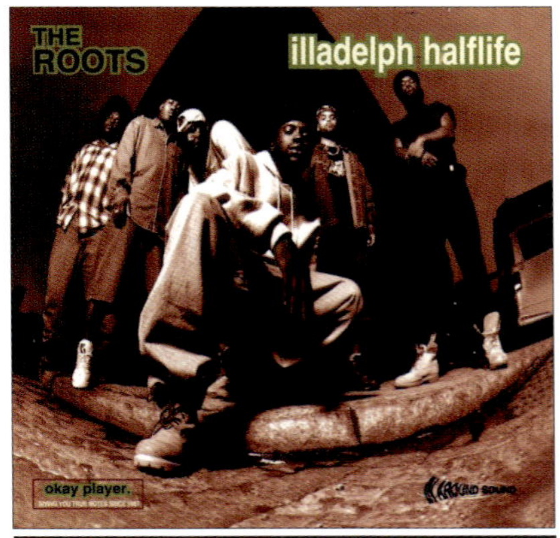


*Billboard* 200: *Illadelph Halflife* (#21)
*Billboard* Hot 100: "What They Do" (#34)

## The Roots, one of rap's most unfailingly organic groups, added some technical foundations to *Illadelph Halflife*.

**FOR A** generation weaned on groups that stepped onstage and asked the soundman to "play the tape machine," rap music had needed a fresh direction. The Roots, from the streets of Philadelphia, made the grooves come alive. The acclaimed members were funky emcees, vocal manipulators and beatmakers—but they were also impressive musicians who played real instruments. They weren't the first hip-hoppers to eschew turntables, samplers and DATs, but they were certainly in an anomalous position.

The Roots were led by drummer ?uestlove, a large, imposing man with a big Afro. In concert, his sound was that of an electronic drum machine, but the backbeats were courtesy of his sticks. "All I have to do is hit that drum roll and the crowd goes wild," he said.

Black Thought freestyled and went off rhyming, and bassist Hub's playing evoked the best of Bootsy Collins. Rahzel the Godfather of Noise did an explosive human-beat-box routine, punctuating the proceedings with his dope skills—oral sounds of scratching turntables, percussion, sampled trumpets and flawless impersonations of other deejays.

Touring was the Roots' bread and butter—they spent more than 200 nights a year on the road. "But at the end of the day, I gotta do what I do best, which is make our records," ?uestlove said. "Sometimes it's hard making art-based records while trying to get on the playlists and all that."

Continuing to groove to the infectious beat of a vastly different drummer, *Illadelph Halflife* represented an excursion into sampling. The Roots called upon an army of heavyweights from the hip-hop world and beyond. Raphael Saadiq from Tony Toni Tone appeared on "What They Do," which hit the pop charts.

"Even though 95 percent of the instruments used were live, we sampled ourselves—when we have jam sessions, we tape them and whatever sounds dope, we loop up," ?uestlove explained. "We're challenging people to believe that, with technology, you can make anything sound like anything."

Black Thought was aware of the aesthetic disparity between the Roots and the gangstas within the rap scene. "I try to block that out, because there's not too many people that's really in it for any artistic value at all. People are sayin' shit in their rhymes like, 'Fuck hip-hop, fuck rap—it's just about loot.' So if that's how they feel, fuck them. I'm on some straight hip-hop shit."

?uestlove counted himself as a hip-hop history buff. "I can't afford not to be," he mused. "We're the kind of rap group that often gets labeled alternative. All the Roots want to do is present the thinking man's rap music in a context that's acceptable to hip-hop purists. If I'm going to represent us, I'd better know every nook and cranny of hip-hop." ■

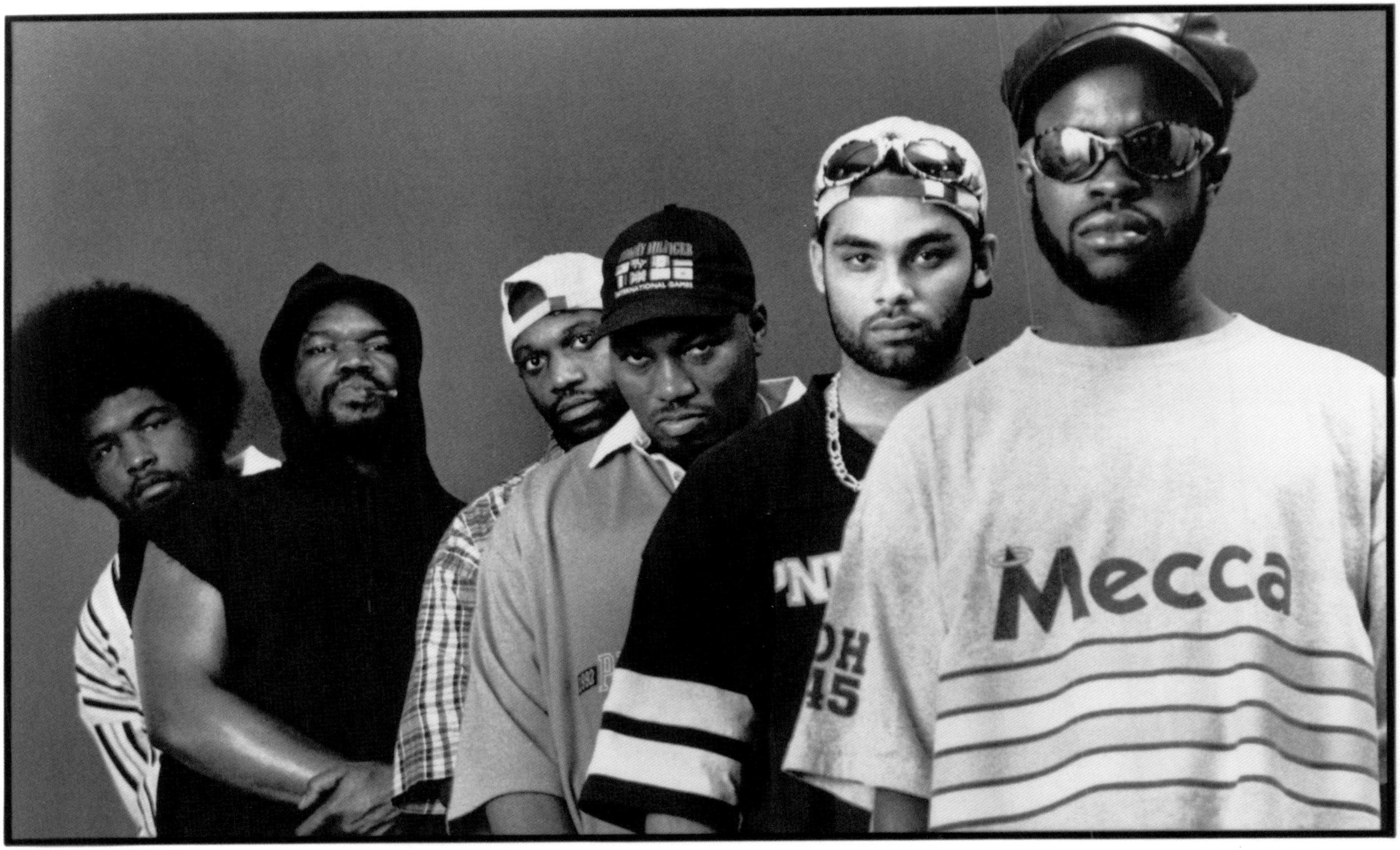

?uestlove Hub Malik B Rahzel the Godfather of Noyze Kamal Black Thought

Photo Credit: Michael Levine

# THE ROOTS

GEFFEN RECORDS, INC.

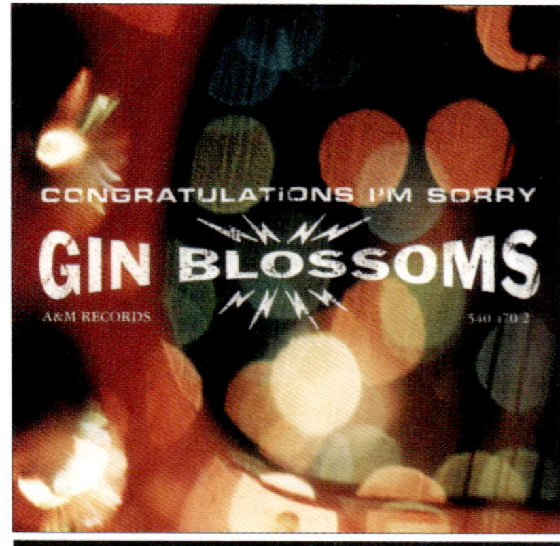


*Billboard* 200: *Congratulations I'm Sorry* (#10)
*Billboard* Hot 100: "Follow You Down" (#9);
"As Long as It Matters" (#75)

## Referencing success and a former bandmate's suicide, Gin Blossoms came up with *Congratulations I'm Sorry*.

**THE BREAKTHROUGH** of Gin Blossoms' *New Miserable Experience* was amazing and unlikely. The harmonies and energy of the double-platinum debut didn't take off commercially for nearly a year after its 1992 release, but the Arizona-based quintet's relentless touring resulted in the album finding a mass audience.

Then came the tragic death of Doug Hopkins, the band's former guitarist who had penned the two big smashes that were all over the radio, "Hey Jealousy" and "Found Out About You." He killed himself just before Christmas in 1993. Many fans wondered if the songwriting would suffer.

"'Til I Hear It from You" squelched those concerns. The cut, contributed for the *Empire Records* soundtrack, vaulted into the Top 10. "For marketing reasons, it was good to bridge album projects," singer Robin Wilson said. "On a personal level, we got to write a song with Marshall Crenshaw—and that's a real thrill for a bunch of punks from Tempe."

For *Congratulations I'm Sorry*, their sophomore effort, all five band members combined their resources to cowrite material. "It's a job," Wilson said. "Some days it's easy and natural and inspired, and sometimes you slave over it for weeks and ask other people to come up with ideas and end up scrapping it. It's a precarious thing, to bet your future on the fact that you'll have this ability for years to come. But I don't think I could live any other way right now."

The band's signature sound remained intact—not so much alternative rock as softer, more melodic pop that showcased Wilson's clear, unaffected voice and the crunching and jangly guitars of Jesse Valenzuela and Scott Johnson. "Follow You Down," a Top 10 single, was as vital as its predecessors.

Gin Blossoms went back on tour, building on their guileless reputation. "Here it comes again," Wilson laughed. "We're not going to take it for granted that there are 2 million people waiting for us to come out on the road again. Because we've done so much in the past, we're more comfortable and in tune with the traveling life. We're prepared—we've all got cool luggage, and we know if we're gonna bring a chessboard, it's gotta be magnetic, otherwise it won't work on the bus.

"The first time I looked at the record, I realized, 'Okay, this is the product, and like a trained monkey, I'm going to dance around the world trying to sell it.' It's a strange thought, facing the reality that this will last for the next two years. It's a weird life—but it's really, really good work if you can get it." ■

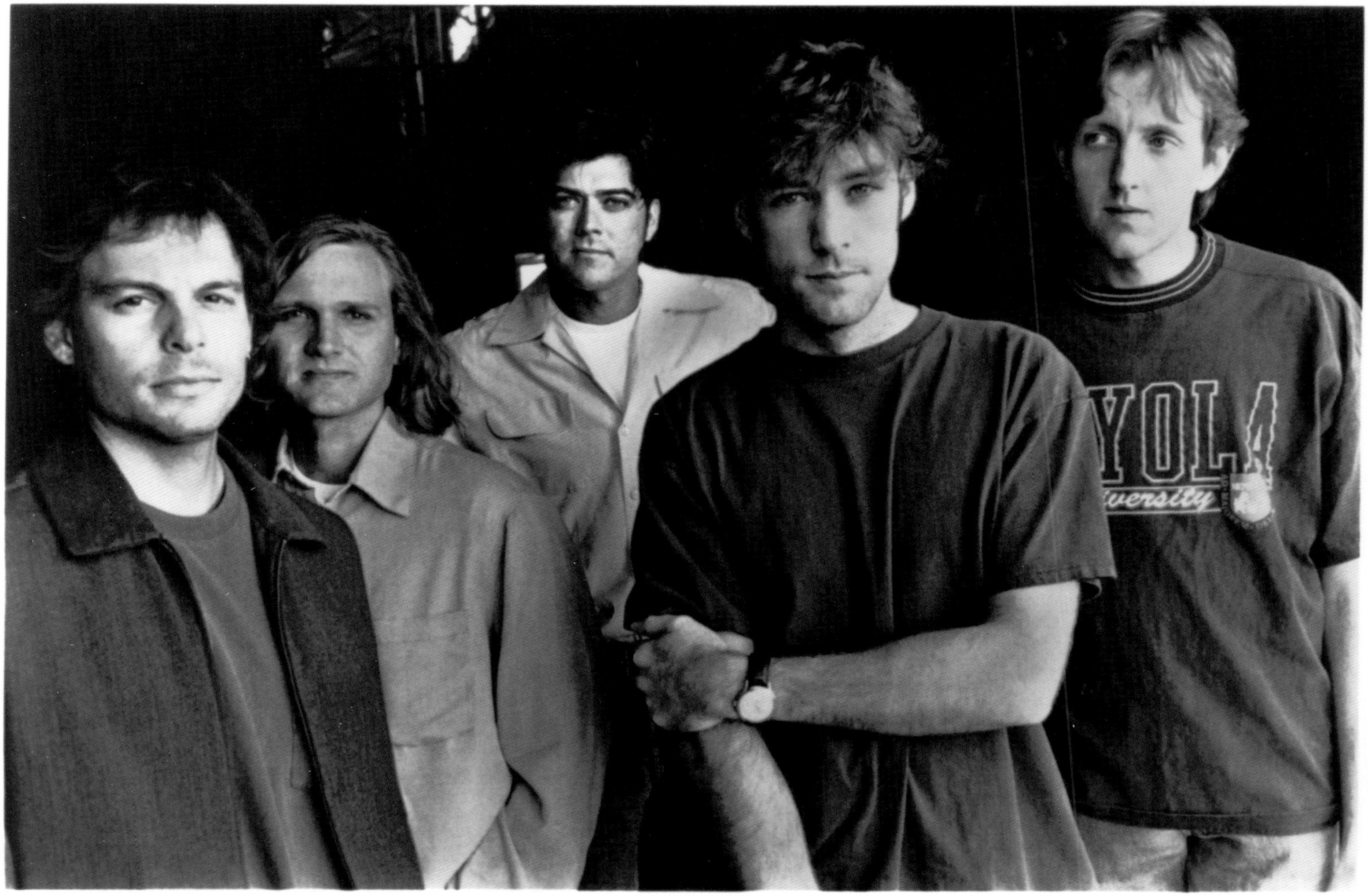

Photo: Danny Clinch 1/96

Robin Wilson    Scott Johnson    Jesse Valenzuela    Philip Rhodes    Bill Leen

# GIN BLOSSOMS

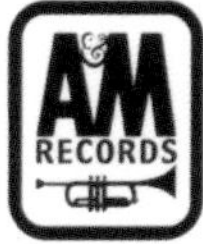

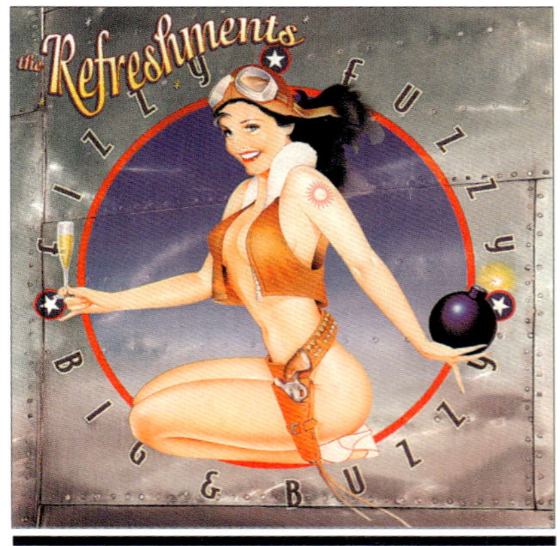


**The Refreshments had something to say without the depression that routinely filled the alternative airwaves.**

**MOSTLY CONCERNED** with serving up melody and harmony to college boys, the Refreshments had torn up the bar scene in Tempe, Arizona. "We're a fun band, we try not to be too pretentious," vocalist and guitarist Roger Clyne said. "It can be bothersome to think that people are only recognizing you as a swing of the pendulum in the opposite direction. I hope that we can have staying power, that we're not an antidote to grunge.

"At the same time, we're just a rock 'n' roll band. If it works for us right now, then I certainly welcome it. We live in a time and place, and if we're gonna get noticed as a 'refreshing' post-angst sound, I'll take it."

The good-time quartet released debut album *Fizzy Fuzzy Big & Buzzy*, a major-label debut album, and audiences got off on the straight-ahead pop-rock sound—twangy guitars, driving beats and clever lyrics. "We were influenced by the Gin Blossoms," Clyne admitted. "The first time we got together in Tempe, we drank some beers and banged around on our instruments, played some covers that we all know. After we got gigs, there was a demand for us, and we had to write more songs. We always wanted them to get better."

The Refreshments' best tune was the single "Banditos," which was on the mainstream-rock and modern-rock charts. The quirky video—a jaunt through the Southwestern desert that brought to mind *A Hard Day's Night* or a classic Monkees episode—was added to MTV's playlist. "That's one of the very first songs I wrote in this band," Clyne said. "It was a couple of years ago when we were all living pretty lean lifestyles. We were fantasizing one evening about robbing a bank for beer money. We were just not criminal or devious enough to pull it off, so we did it through music." ■

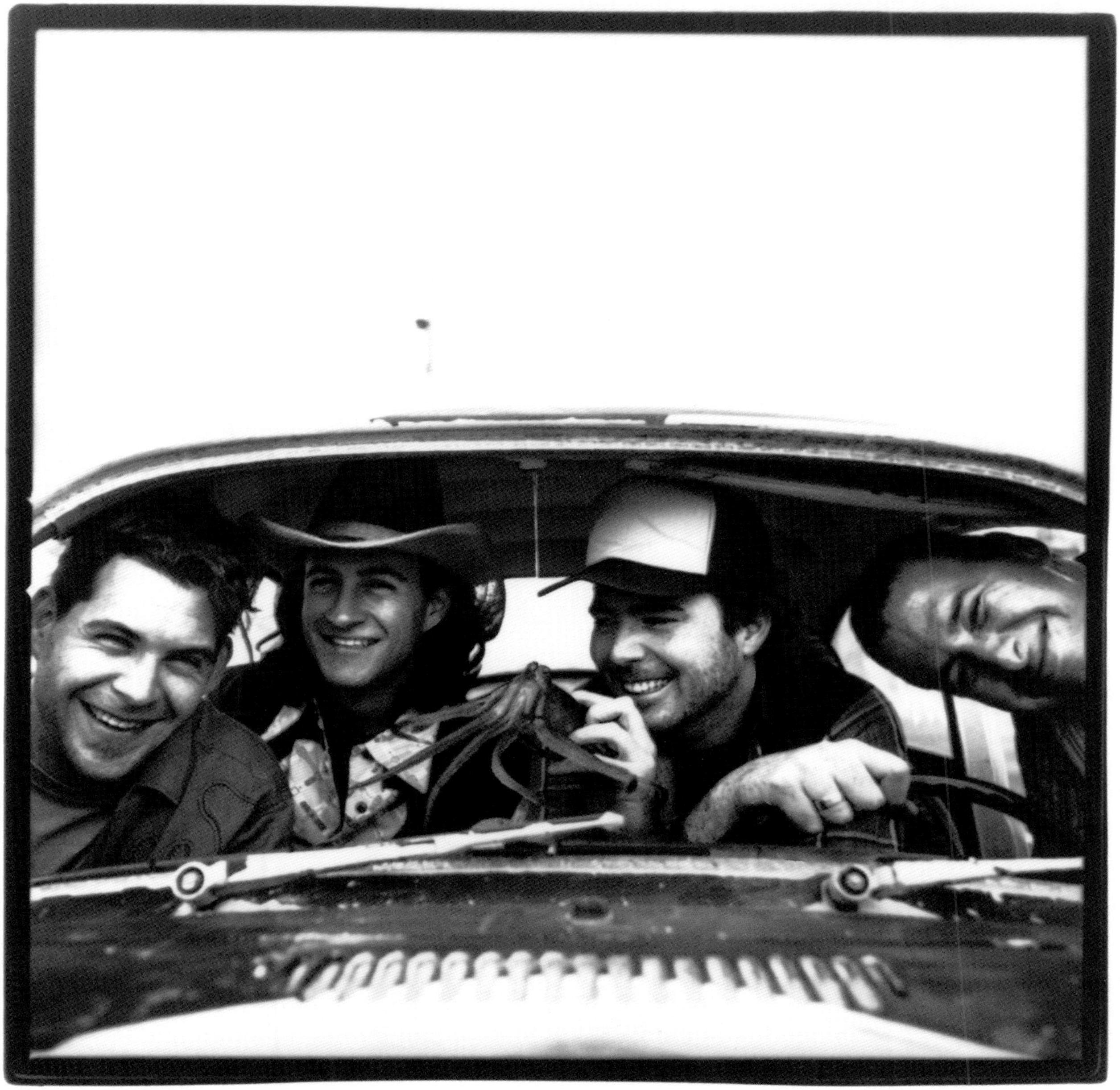

PHOTO CREDIT DANNY CLINCH

L - R : P.H. NAFFAH, ROGER CLYNE, BRIAN BLUSH, BUDDY EDWARDS

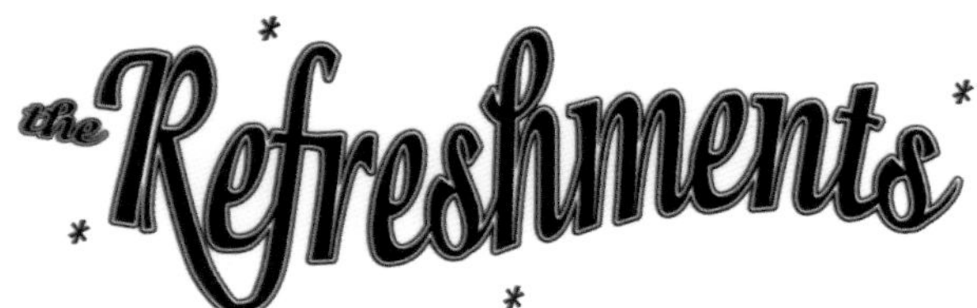


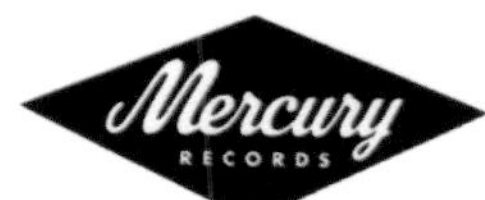

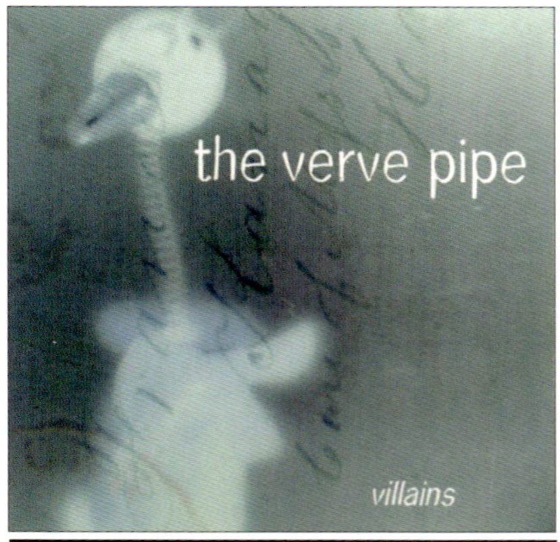


*Billboard* 200: *Villains* (#24)
*Billboard* Hot 100: "Photograph" (#53); "The Freshmen" (#5)

## The Verve Pipe graduated to the ranks of hottest up-and-coming acts with a stone-cold hit, "The Freshmen."

**AN UNSETTLING** hit single that exploded onto alternative, adult rock and even Top 40 radio, "The Freshmen" evoked a tidal wave of emotion. The Verve Pipe's tale of regret described two men and the death of a woman both had known in college. She commits suicide by taking "a week's worth of Valium." Lead vocalist and guitarist Brian Vander Ark wrote the rueful sentiment back when the Verve Pipe found a home playing the fraternity circuit in the Michigan area.

"I overheard a conversation at a drunken party. The gist of it was these guys were just passing this girl back and forth—'Oh, remember this about her?' I didn't know the girl, I don't really have a picture of her in my head, but I saw the callous way that they were treating someone. What if something happened? How would they feel 20 years from now? Making myself one of the characters was a great idea—it was the only way to tell the story. 'They were merely freshmen' instead of 'We were merely freshmen' would have been too Harry Chapin. As a writer, I like to become that person, to get inside his head.

"But 'The Freshmen' has been a bit of a nightmare. I've gotten hate mail about the way that the girl in the song is treated. People come up to me and say, 'Hey, you're an asshole for what you did to her.' People interpret the song the way they want to. I make no apologies for writing it in first person."

"The Freshmen" appeared on the first of two albums on the Verve Pipe's own indie label. *Villains*, the band's major-label debut, featured a rendition produced by former Talking Head Jerry Harrison (Live, Crash Test Dummies). "We threw the song on our first album, but it was just me and an acoustic guitar, like a demo," Vander Ark explained. "So all the old fans in Michigan considered it to be a hit from the beginning. I still get shit for changing it around on *Villains*. You know how it is, people hear something one way and they don't want to hear it any other way. People told me they started crying when they heard it, like a bad horror movie—'No-o-o-o-o!'"

Then the quintet decided to update the tune again before releasing it as a single. "I like Jerry's version—it's sexy and laid-back—but it wasn't as radio-friendly as it could have been, and not everybody in the band played on it. We wanted to make it different, to go in and record it the way we play it live. It turned out we touched a nerve in some way."

*Villains* had an admirable sense of dynamics, a merger of big guitar power chords and Vander Ark's emotionally charged vocals. "We all love music," Vander Ark said. "I love listening to the indie stuff, and I grew up listening to classic rock, too. I liked Tom Waits, Harry Chapin—they wrote self-contained songs with a beginning, middle and end. My songs start out as short stories, but I'm lazy—I'd rather describe something writing one line than a paragraph." ■

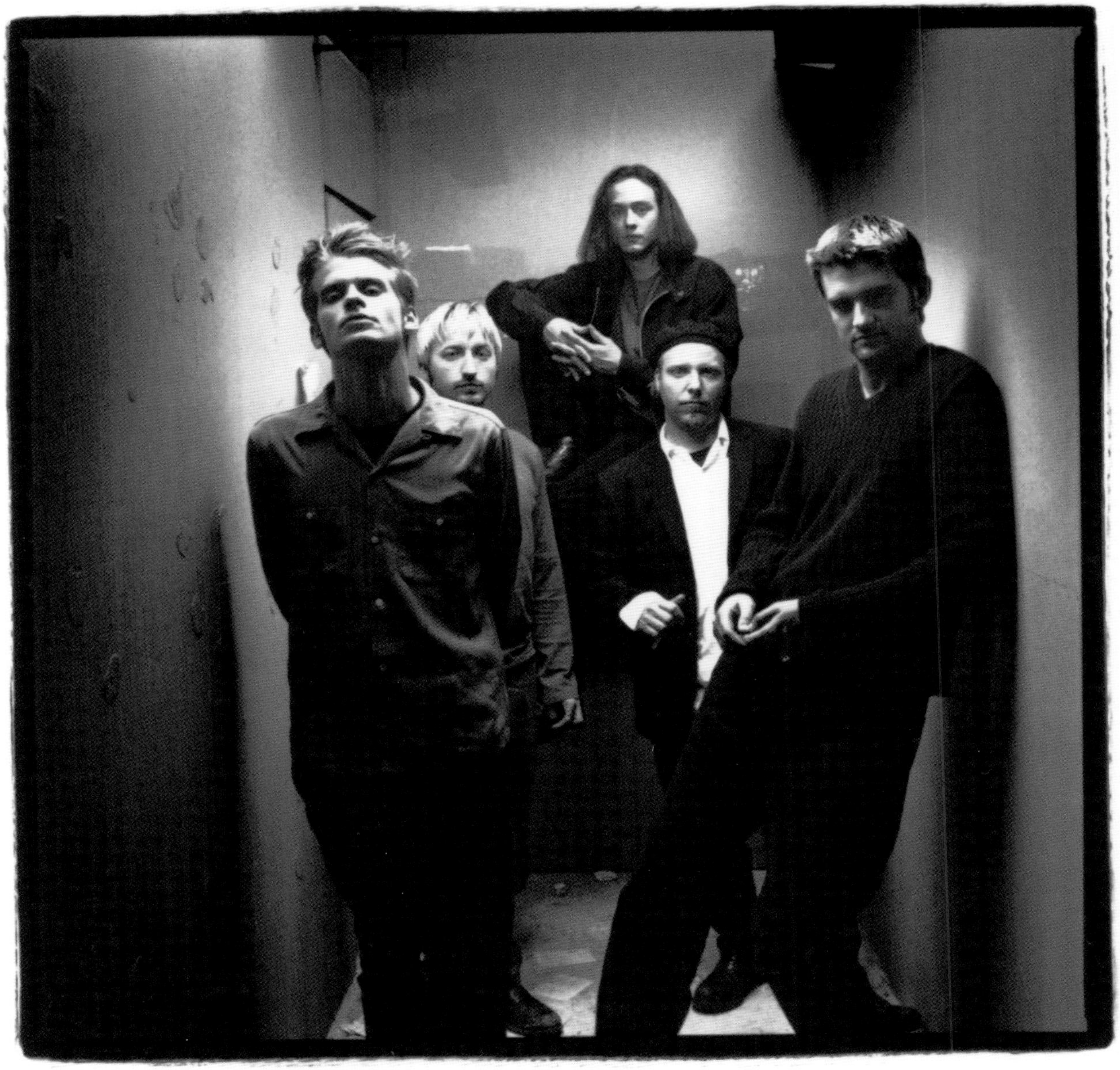

Photo Credit: Aldo Mauro

the verve pipe

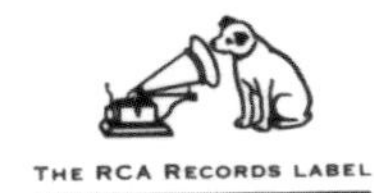

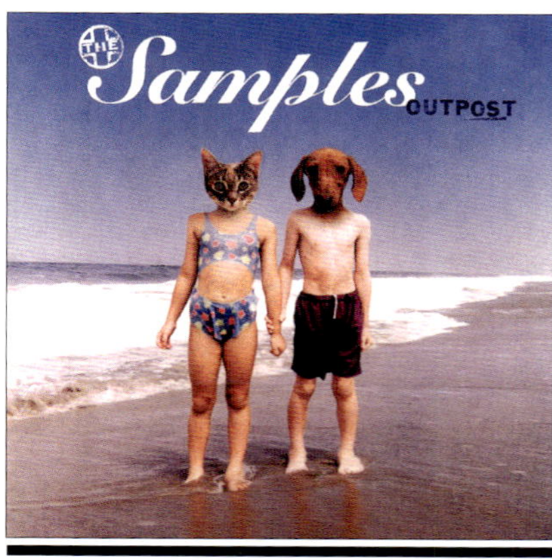


## The Samples' *Outpost* was marked by discordance within the group and an administrative lack of certitude.

**AT THE** beginning of their career, they survived on free samples cadged from the local grocer. But the Samples had gone on to a meaty future. Following five releases on the independent W.A.R.? label, the Colorado quartet signed with MCA Records and got the backing of a big-time record company.

*Outpost* was recorded "live off the studio floor," lead vocalist and guitarist Sean Kelly said. "That's the difference with this album from most of our others, having the financial backing to do four or five takes on a song and decide which was the best. We had the freedom not to have to worry too much about going over budget."

The group delivered the musical goods with a pleasing single, "The Lost Children (A Slow Motion Crash)," written by Kelly. "I thought it was a metaphor using adults—there's so much growing we need to do. If we're looked at on a grand scale, we're all just like 'the lost children.' Then it switched over to another vibe—I don't know what the song is about. Sometimes it comes later."

*Outpost* also contained new versions of old Samples favorites. "We already knew that 'Did You Ever Look So Nice' and 'Birth of Words' were tunes that worked well live, that pinpoint our sound," Kelly said. "So, we redid them. It's a cool way to bridge where we're at, because we're expecting a little more exposure than what we're used to."

*Outpost* could have taken the Samples to the next level of mainstream acceptance, but the album failed to make a commercial impact. MCA didn't tend to the band—a changing of the executive guard at the label didn't help matters. "They gave up on this one," Kelly allowed. "They're looking for their miracle—their Alanis Morissette, their Hootie & the Blowfish. I wish they knew what they already have. It's a little disappointing to the guys in the band. But success has many parents and failure is an orphan. Once again, it's back to the Samples to make it happen. Which is fine—I'd rather be in the driver's seat."

Keyboardist Al Laughlin battled a substance abuse problem—he was arrested and charged with burglarizing an apartment. Then MCA paid off the Samples' contract, and Laughlin and drummer Jeep MacNichol departed the band. Soured on recording for a major label, Kelly formed a brand-new lineup, managing as the Samples always had from a combination of tenacious touring and record sales promoted by fan volunteers. "Deserts are beautiful," Kelly insisted with a boyish spark in his eyes. "You just have to wear snake boots." ■

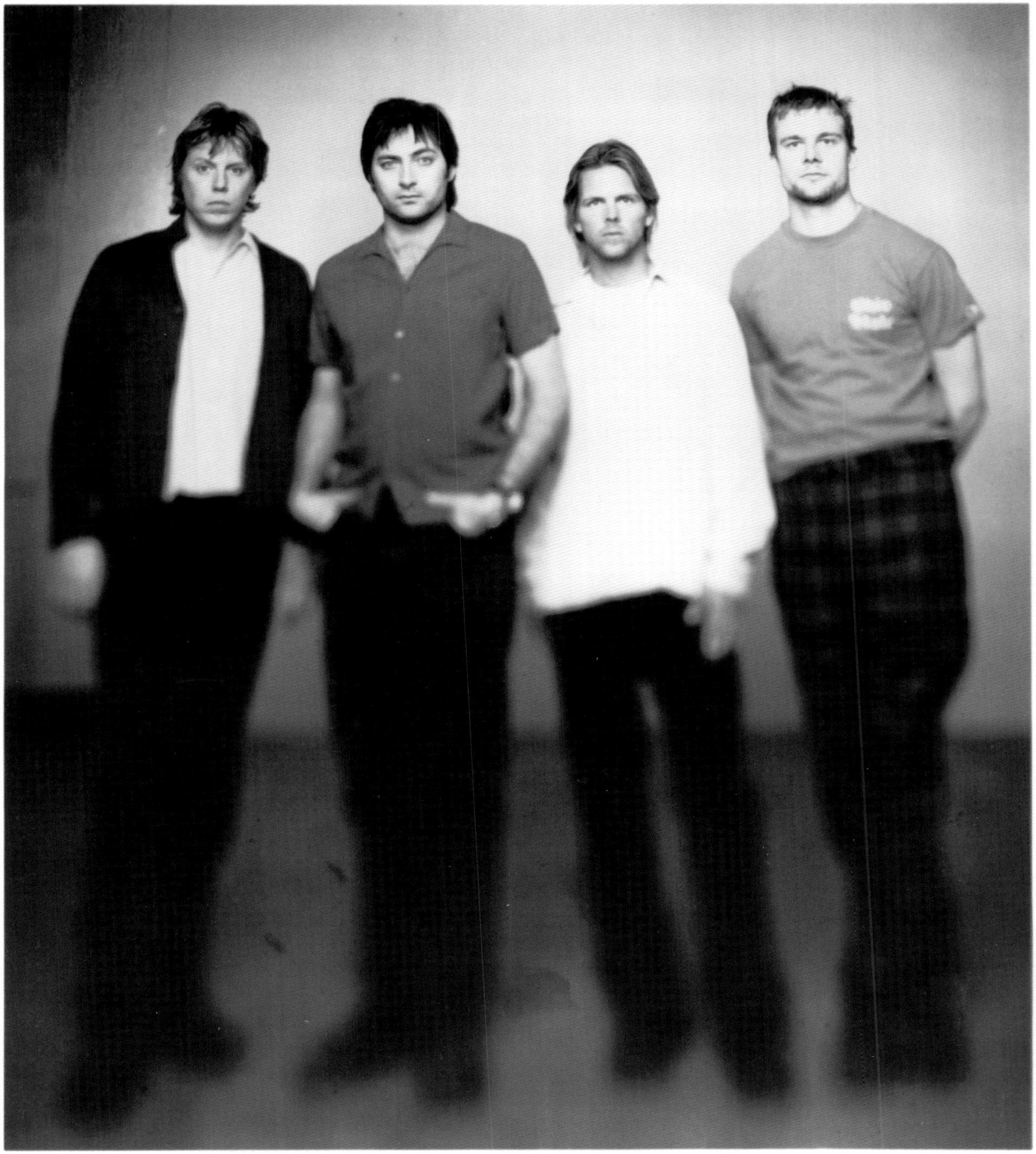

Photo Credit: Ralf Strathman

Andy Sheldon | Sean Kelly | Al Laughlin | Jeep MacNichol

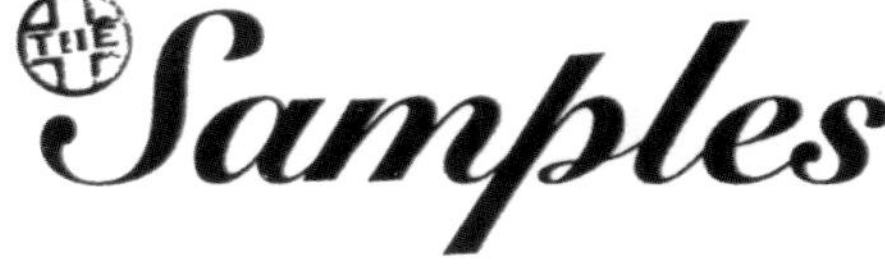


7/96

MCA.

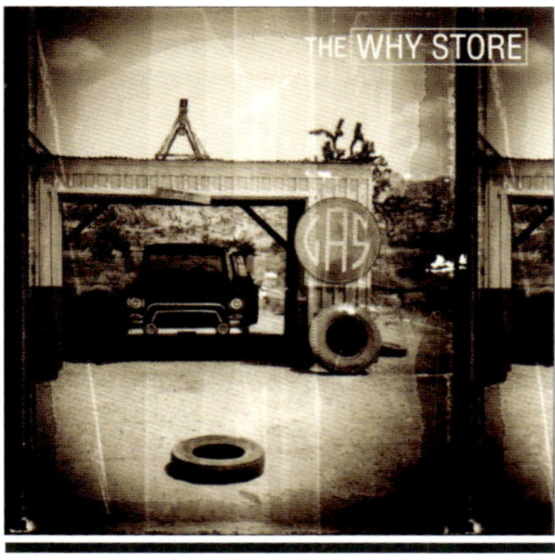


## The Why Store won attention in the Midwest before "Lack of Water" took the band to the national spotlight.

**A LOOSE** "jammy" approach to live shows earned the Why Store a neo-hippie tag typical of a H.O.R.D.E. group. Like Hootie & the Blowfish and Dave Matthews Band, the group developed a huge regional fan base by touring nonstop and releasing two independent albums.

"I feel lucky to be part of the music of the Nineties," vocalist and guitarist Chris Shaffer said. "There's a lot of alternative stuff, but the songwriters are starting to come back. You always have the Big Head Todds, the Blues Travelers and the Widespread Panics of the world. That's where we come from."

The Why Store had been self-sustaining for three years. Two CDs released on the band's own label sold more than 30,000 units, and a merchandising operation was built. The Why Store finally got the backing of a major label, MCA Records. The album *The Why Store* was produced by Mike Wanchic (longtime guitarist for John Mellencamp), who captured the band's sound, melodic rock with a rural twist.

"Lack of Water" received steady airplay on alternative radio and reached the top of the new adult alternative album (AAA or Triple A) charts. The hit originally appeared on the band's second indie album. "I was reluctant to put it on this record," Shaffer explained. "It had already been released to the world on my own little label, and I didn't really want to change it. I was willing to compromise, but I wasn't going to put it at the beginning of the record, or in the middle—it had to go on the end."

People compared Shaffer's raspy voice to Eddie Vedder and Cat Stevens, and *The Why Store* recruited new "Whomheads," the nickname for dedicated fans. "We were playing some bars around Indianapolis," Shaffer recalled. "One night a friend came up to me out of the blue and said, 'I've got a great idea—we've got these Whomheads and they belong to the what club and we don't know why!' I said, 'Hey, we've got to use that.' It just stuck."

Shaffer was prone to publicity ideas—he had graduated from Ball State University with a marketing/sales promotion degree. "It's something I don't really put forward too much, but I'm very proud of it," he said. "To this day, I use it. I'm very involved with the business end of everything." ■

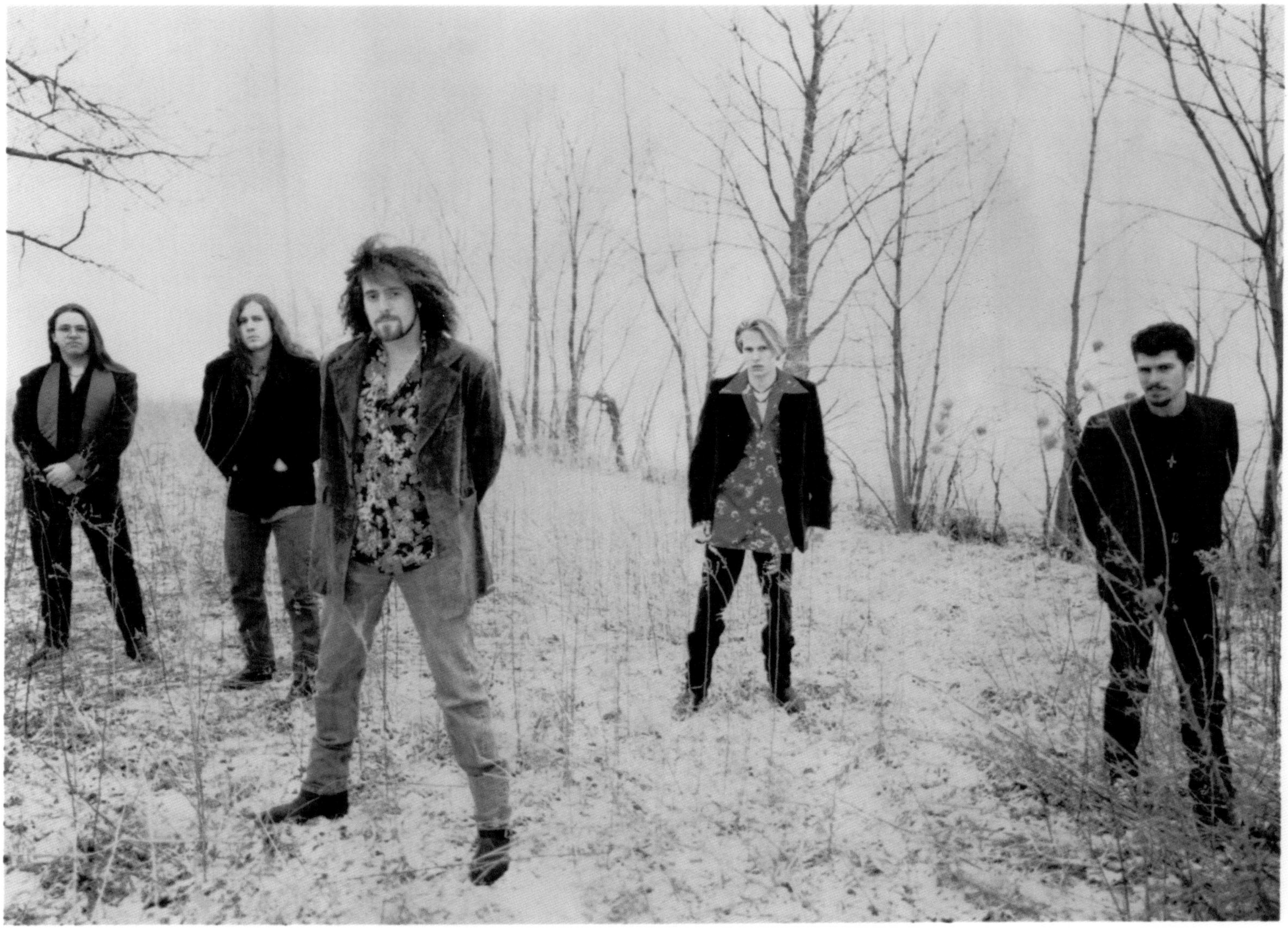

Photo Credit: Ralf Strathman

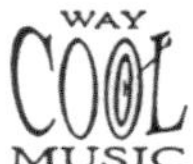


# the why store

MCA. 3/96

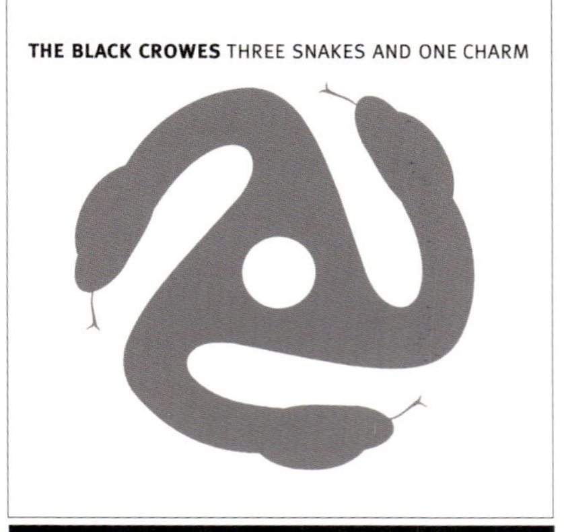


*Billboard* 200: *Three Snakes and One Charm* (#15)

# The Black Crowes were shown appreciation with a grooved-on gig in support of *Three Snakes and One Charm*.

**WHEN JERRY** Garcia died in August 1995, the lives of faithful fans ceased to be dictated by the touring schedule of the Grateful Dead. But the journey had resumed with the Furthur Festival, an antidote for those suffering from Dead withdrawal. The concerts were the brainchild of two former band members, guitarist Bob Weir and drummer Mickey Hart, who wanted to add a new band that could appreciate the Dead's blues roots, eloquence and decadence. So they invited the Black Crowes to headline the tour.

Despite the generational difference, the bands shared a sensibility that transcended musical style and connected them on a higher level of dedication. "I was ten feet tall when I walked out of my first Dead show—'Wow, okay, we're on the right track,'" drummer Steve Gorman recalled. "It's not that we sound like the Dead. It's a mindset, an attitude. When some people in bands say, 'Music is my life,' that just means you're drunk all the time and you're always looking good for photos. But if music is your life, then you can't go very long without playing it.

"We had the good fortune to open for the Dead back in April 1995 at Tampa Stadium, and that's how we saw it. There is something that goes beyond those surface levels that's a little more consistent and meaningful. The Dead were simply carrying on an old tradition—troubadours getting out and traveling, singing and writing songs. It's just what a musician does. You do good work, the rest falls in line."

On the tour, as usual, the Crowes reordered set lists for each date and invited fans to bring their tape recorders. "We go out and try to play a good show every night," Gorman said. "Just because we have a new record out doesn't mean you're going to hear it and our previous singles. Half of the master song list is covers, if not more. You can't cut off your roots. There's so much out there—to just worry about your own music, you're selling yourself short. We do as many covers as we can learn on tour."

The Black Crowes did have a new record out, and concurrently carried a torch for Southern soul and Seventies rock on *Three Snakes and One Charm*, the band's best album since its debut. The funky "Blackberry" kicked serious booty as singer Chris Robinson prattled the raunchy lyrics—"Hey blueberry, look at my bumblebee." "It's about wanting to get with a Black girl," he admitted. ■

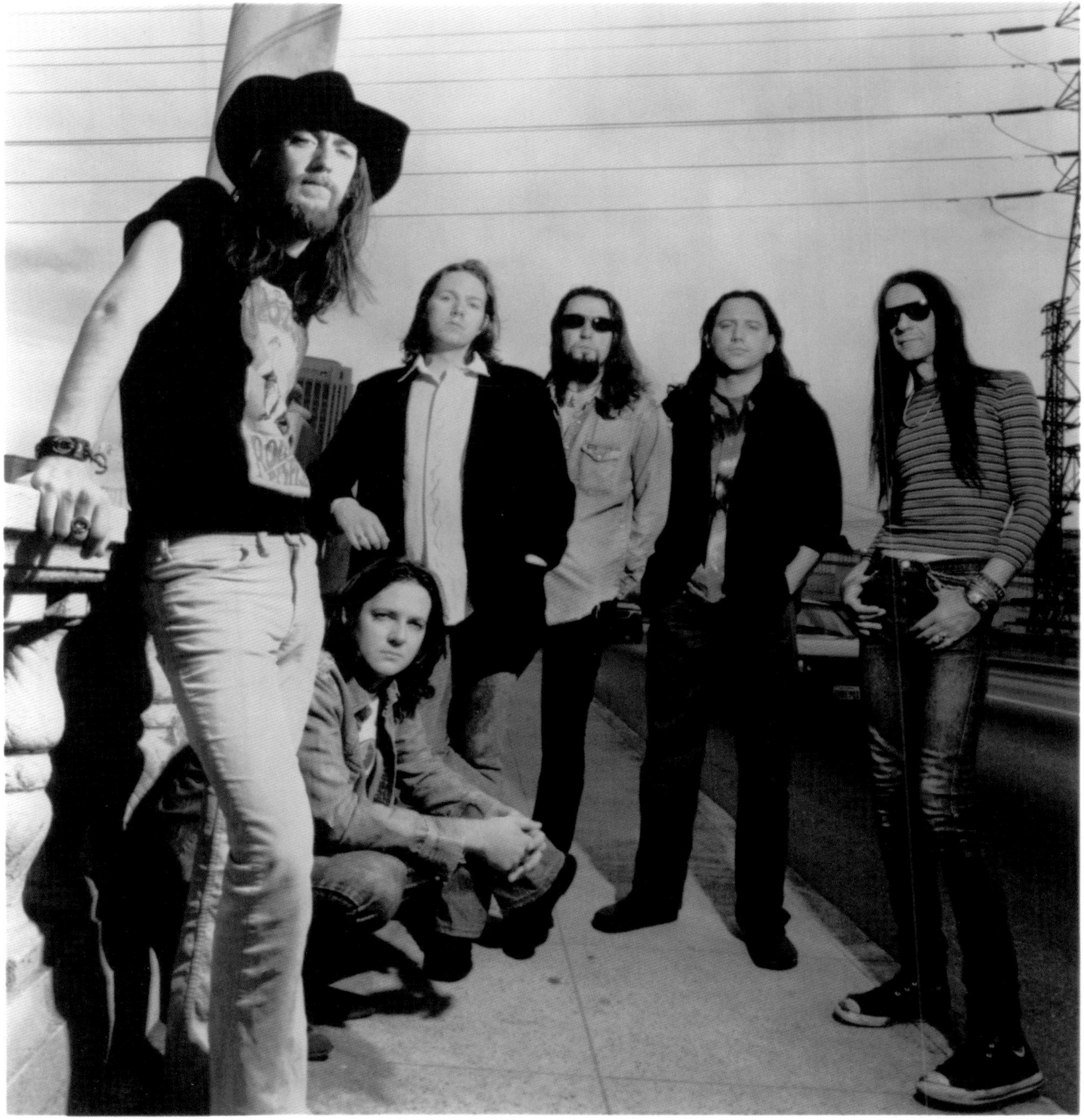

Photo Credit: American Recordings

Chris Robinson Marc Ford Rich Robinson Johnny Colt Steve Gorman Eddie Harsch

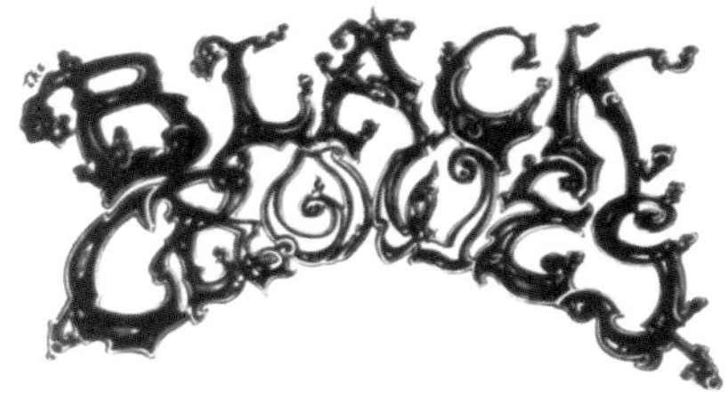


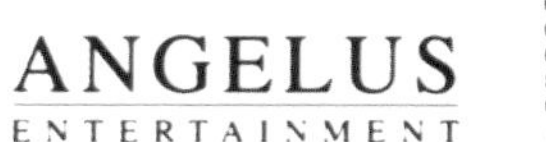


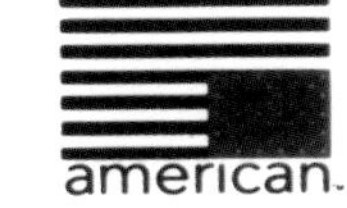

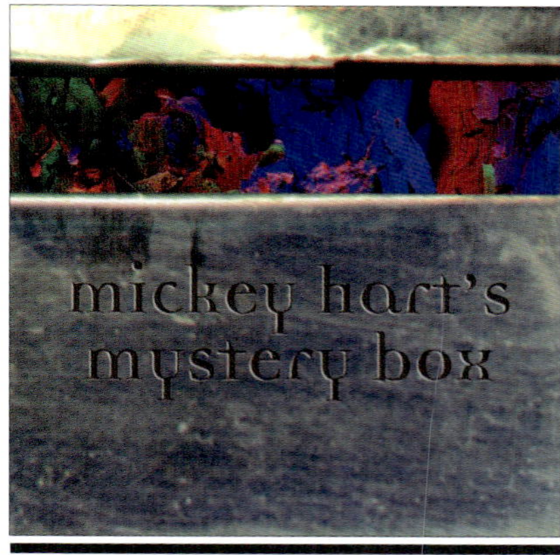


## Former Grateful Dead drummer Mickey Hart released a pop-oriented collection as Mickey Hart's Mystery Box.

**WITH THE** death of leader Jerry Garcia in August 1995, the Grateful Dead saw thirty years of nonstop touring come to a close. Everyone speculated about the future of the legendary band's surviving members and millions of Deadheads. Was there life after the Dead?

The legacy lived on with the Furthur Festival, a traveling road show in the tradition of the Dead's caravans. Highlighting the event were co-headliners Ratdog (guitarist Bob Weir's new band) and Mickey Hart's Mystery Box (the Dead drummer's new band). Hart said he didn't grieve for Garcia as much as he communed with his spirit. "It's not an exercise in nostalgia," he said. "Yeah, everyone thinks of Jerry every day, but it's new music."

Hart, who had championed world music for nearly a quarter-century, arranged and produced an acclaimed fusion of genres for the pop mainstream. *Mickey Hart's Mystery Box* weaved together lyrics by Robert Hunter, vocals by the Mint Juleps (a six-member, predominantly Black, all-female, a cappella group from London), guests Bruce Hornsby and Weir, and Hart's Grammy-winning Planet Drum ensemble.

"The thought came to marry percussion to chant," he explained. "But I wanted to deliver more emotional content in the music, and that meant adding English lyrics. I wasn't trying to make a strict pop record, or I would have used guitars. It has the form. There are things that make it ear-friendly, but I mixed it up pretty good."

Hart contributed vocals to several tracks, including the album's emotional high point, "Down on the Road." "I heard a sweet guitar lick, an old familiar sound/I heard a laugh I recognized come rolling from the earth," he talked-sang in the homage to deceased heroes. "It sounded like Garcia but I couldn't see the face/Just the beard and the glasses and a smile on empty space." "It crystalizes Garcia's most endearing characteristics," Hart said. "How to do it without being maudlin or corny was the trick, and Hunter pulled it off."

At "Deadapalooza," as fans called the Further Festival, Hart unveiled a "soundroid" that was known as RAMU—Random Access Music Universe. "It's part drums, part digital. I stand in the middle and manipulate it. All the sound library I've collected over 25 years is in RAMU's brain, and it allows me to go from sound palette to sound palette on the touch of a switch. It's a percussionist's fantasy." ■

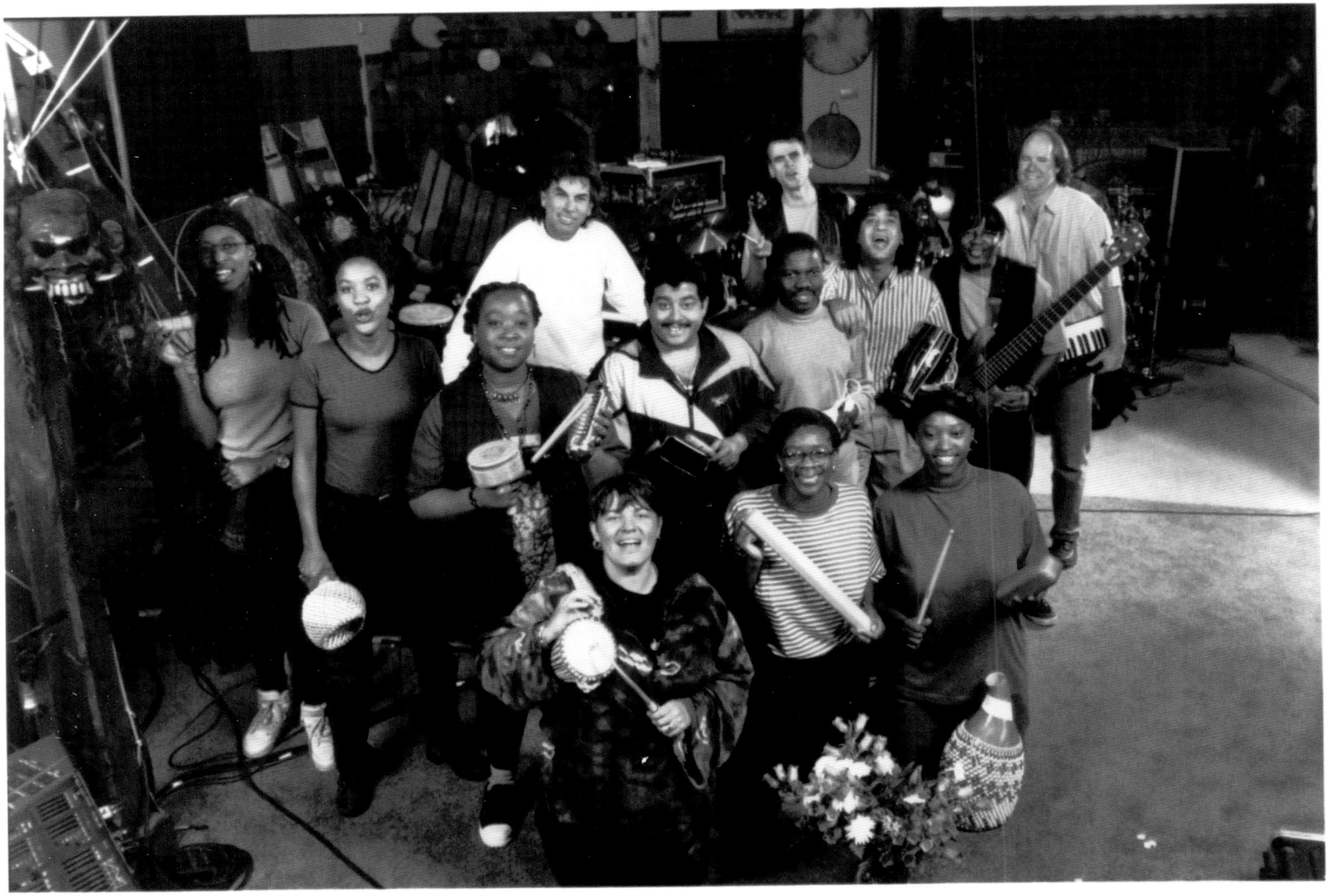

Credit: John Werner

# MICKEY HART'S MYSTERY BOX

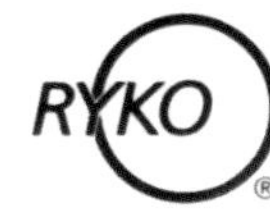

*Billboard* 200: *The Great Southern Trendkill* (#4)

## Pantera released *The Great Southern Trendkill*, an album alluding to drug use and self-destructive behavior.

**FEW BANDS** could match the fury of Pantera's harsh, grinding thrash-metal. Hailing from the Lone Star state, the "cowboys from hell" developed a buzz thanks to punishing live performances, and their fan base grew with each release—the platinum smash *Far from Driven* debuted at No. 1 on Billboard's album chart in 1994.

"It completely flips me out sometimes," drummer Vinnie Paul said. "You can go to a Pantera show and see everything from long-haired dudes to no-haired dudes, from girls to doctors and lawyers. One night I had a 60-year-old guy come up to me backstage and hand me a bunch of CDs to sign. I said, 'What's your kid's name?' and he said, 'No, these are for me—I'm your biggest fan in the world!'"

*The Great Southern Trendkill* offered more angry and terrifying lyrics, Dimebag Darrell's sinuous, aggressive guitars and Philip Anselmo's gargling-with-battery-acid vocals. "The title refers to current music," Paul explained. "A lot of people outside the US think all the good bands come from New York City, Los Angeles or Seattle. We wanted to put the Southern cities on the map, because there's a lot of great music from here. And there are a lot of trendy bands changing their style just to go with the flow, to try and be accessible. We don't feel like we have to do that. We want to remain true to our roots."

A song like "Drag the Waters" was exactly what fans expected from Pantera, a grim but wickedly pleasing going-over. But "Suicide Note Pt. 1" and "Floods" were jarring in their gentleness—there was haunting acoustic guitar accompaniment, and Anselmo actually sang. It wasn't what some longtime loyalists wanted to hear.

"It was a natural progression," Paul claimed. "'Suicide Note Pt. 1' started out with the fast, heavy version, which is 'Suicide Note Pt. 2.' Then we played a New Year's Eve show in Dallas—we woke up the next day all hung over and wrote that. We never re-recorded it—that's the actual four-track recording out of Dime's bedroom." ■

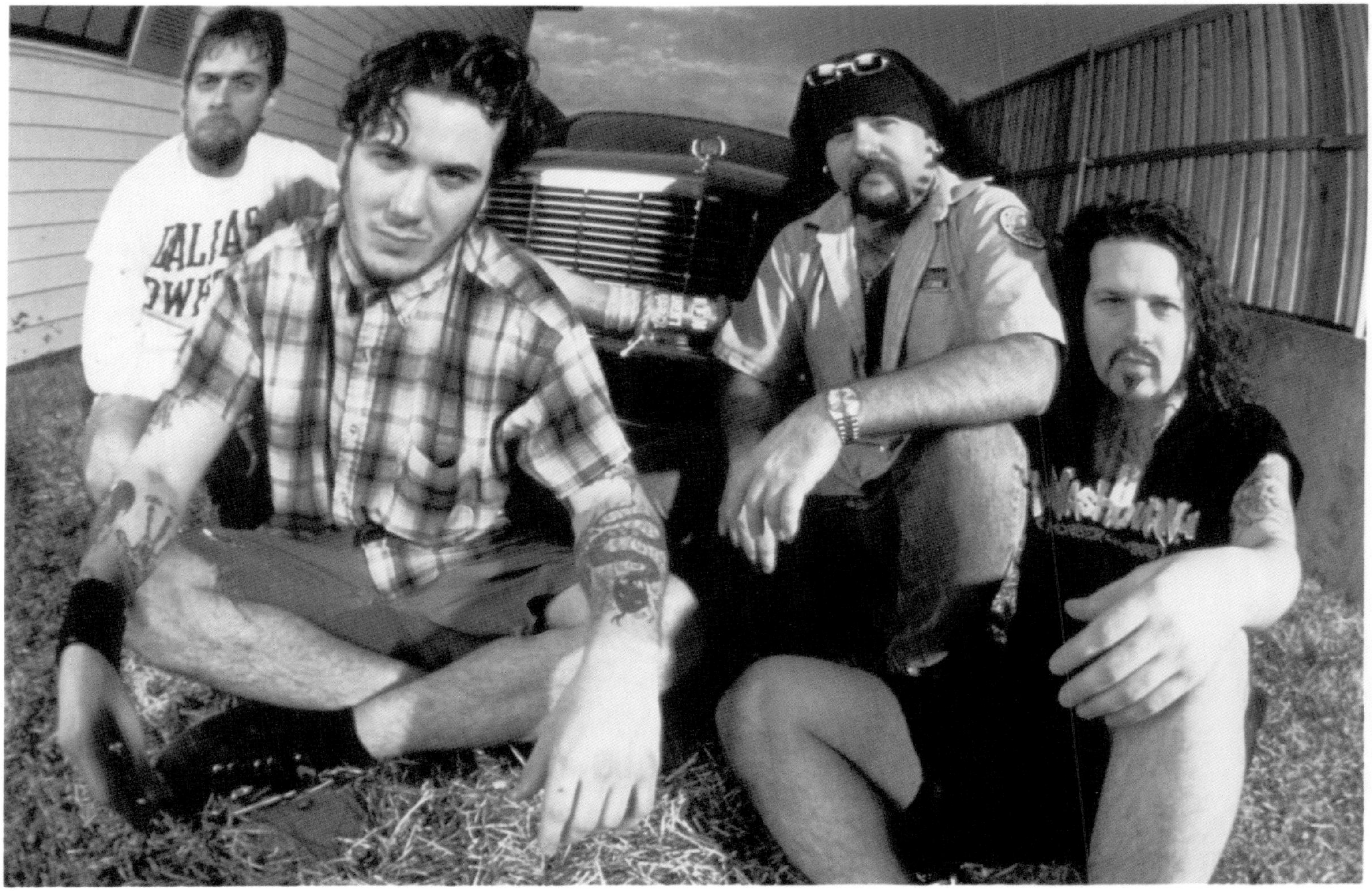

PHOTO CREDIT JOE GIRON 1996

L R : REX, PHILIP ANSELMO, VINNIE PAUL, DIMEBAG DARRELL

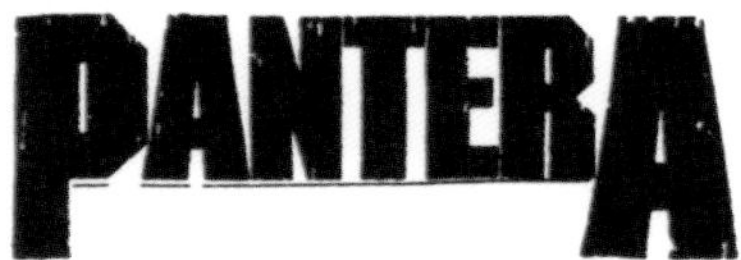


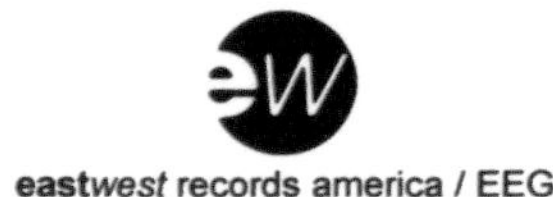


east*west* records america / EEG

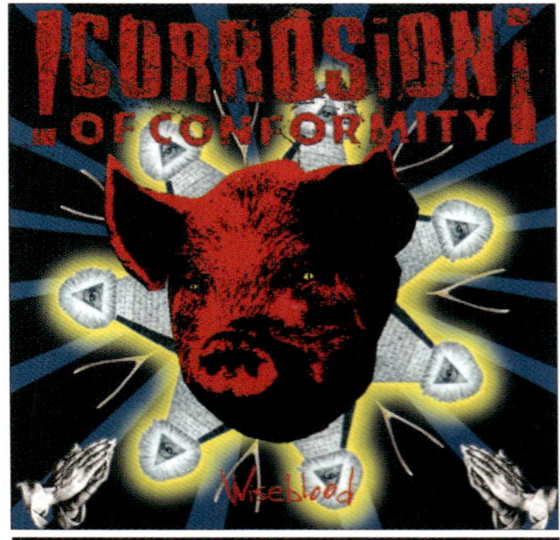


*Billboard* 200: *Wiseblood* (#104)

## The taut, ferocious *Wiseblood* further sharpened the alt-metal niche Corrosion of Conformity had established.

**STARTING OUT** as a pure hardcore punk outfit, Corrosion of Conformity had gone through many stylistic changes through the years. With 1994's *Deliverance*, guitarist and vocalist Pepper Keenan, guitarist Woody Weatherman, bassist Mike Dean and drummer Reed Mullin twisted traditional British-style metal and gritty Southern rock stomp, yielding a pair of radio hits, "Albatross" and "Clean My Wounds."

*Wiseblood*, the veteran quartet's sixth album (named after Keenan's oddball experience at a Raleigh, North Carolina, boarding house), marked the first time the lineup had remained intact from a previous album, mining the musical territory established with *Deliverance*.

"You spend years and years getting your shit together, and you finally get a sound and style that's your own, and you just perfect it from there," Keenan said. "We try to explore many different possibilities without being self-righteous artists. The main thing is you're still writing songs for other people."

The strongest tracks were "Drowning in a Daydream" and "King of the Rotten." "We didn't use a lot of fancy equipment—engineering-wise, we did everything extremely wrong," Keenan said. "We hit tape levels so hard, everything was in the red—ridiculous stuff that most people would freak out if they heard the rough mixes. But that's the way we like to do it. I don't care if it's right or wrong, it just feels right when you play it back."

*Wiseblood* turned up on a profusion of "best of" lists, but touring the world with Metallica in support of the album didn't rev up C.O.C. "We try to just be a touring band that makes good records and is honest with our fans—we're not going to put on silver space suits and go jumping around next month," Keenan said. "It sounds weird, but I think we have more in common with timeless bands like the Allman Brothers that keep doing their own thing, honing their craft and not somebody else's ideas.

"Until we're onstage, we really don't realize much going on around us. We get back to Raleigh, and we're just jamming in a little cubicle practice room underneath a wig shop, and I'm roaming around town in my pickup truck trying to fix the damn thing. It's a weird dichotomy." ■

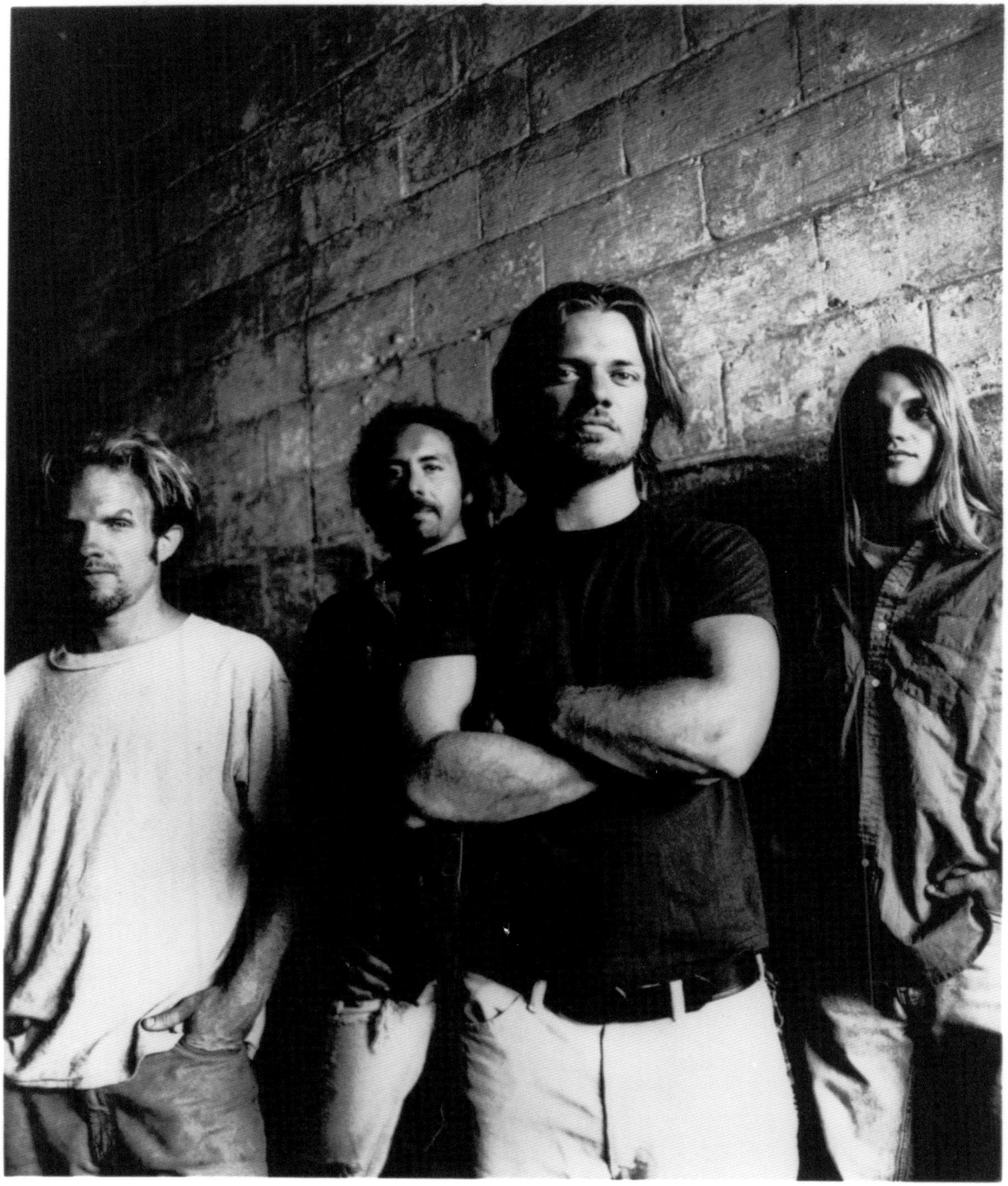

PHOTOGRAPH: DANNY CLINCH

Mike Dean | Woody Weatherman | Pepper Keenan | Reed Mullin

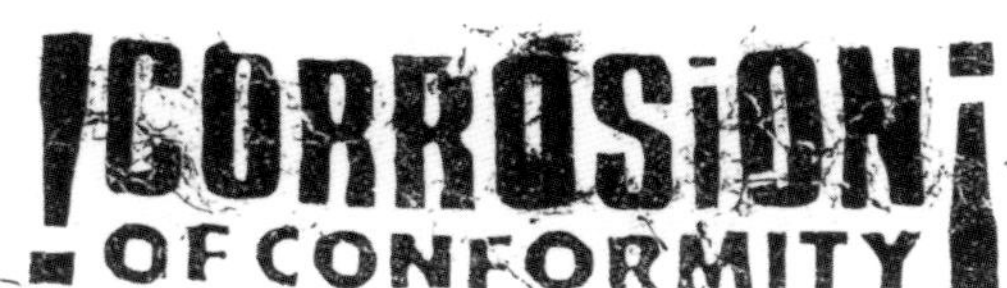


COLUMBIA
9608

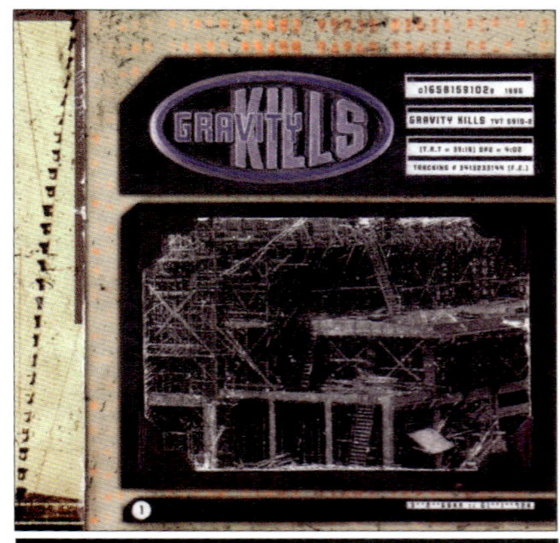

*Billboard* 200: *Gravity Kills* (#89)
*Billboard* Hot 100: "Guilty" (#86)

## Airplay for the abrasive industrial-rock direction of "Guilty" brought mainstream popularity to Gravity Kills.

**UBIQUITOUS ON** alternative-rock airwaves, the pulsating "Guilty" by Gravity Kills bristled with industrial flavor—factory clangs, a corrosive riff and dance beat—that owed a debt to Nine Inch Nails.

"I've had to answer to those comparisons all year," singer Jeff Scheel said. "What we do is more of a fusion of straight-ahead rock with a lot of industrial influences. Music is a culmination, your own interpretation of all the bits and pieces you carry along with you. Industrial music isn't what it was 10 years ago, what Skinny Puppy or Ministry was doing."

Those industrial bands took years to build underground followings, but Gravity Kills had a fast rise to a commercial breakthrough. "Guilty," the first song the foursome ever wrote together, was rush-recorded to appear on a compilation put out by a radio station in St. Louis. After winding up as that station's most requested song, "Guilty" graced the soundtrack to the film *Seven* (used in the scene where Brad Pitt and Morgan Freeman enter an S&M shop). The band was signed to a record deal without ever playing live. The single and video for "Guilty" soared to renown at modern-rock radio and MTV.

"But people don't quite get a sense of what the band is," Scheel said. "As soon as they see the live show, the light goes on—'Wow, these guys aren't trying to be Nine Inch Nails, they're trying to do their own thing.' In the Eighties, industrial bands were dark and gloomy—the shows didn't really involve the audience. Our show is very aggressive, but there's a little bit of arena-rock that seeps out, even when we do a small club—I tell people to make noise and we jump around. We have a sense of entertainment." ■

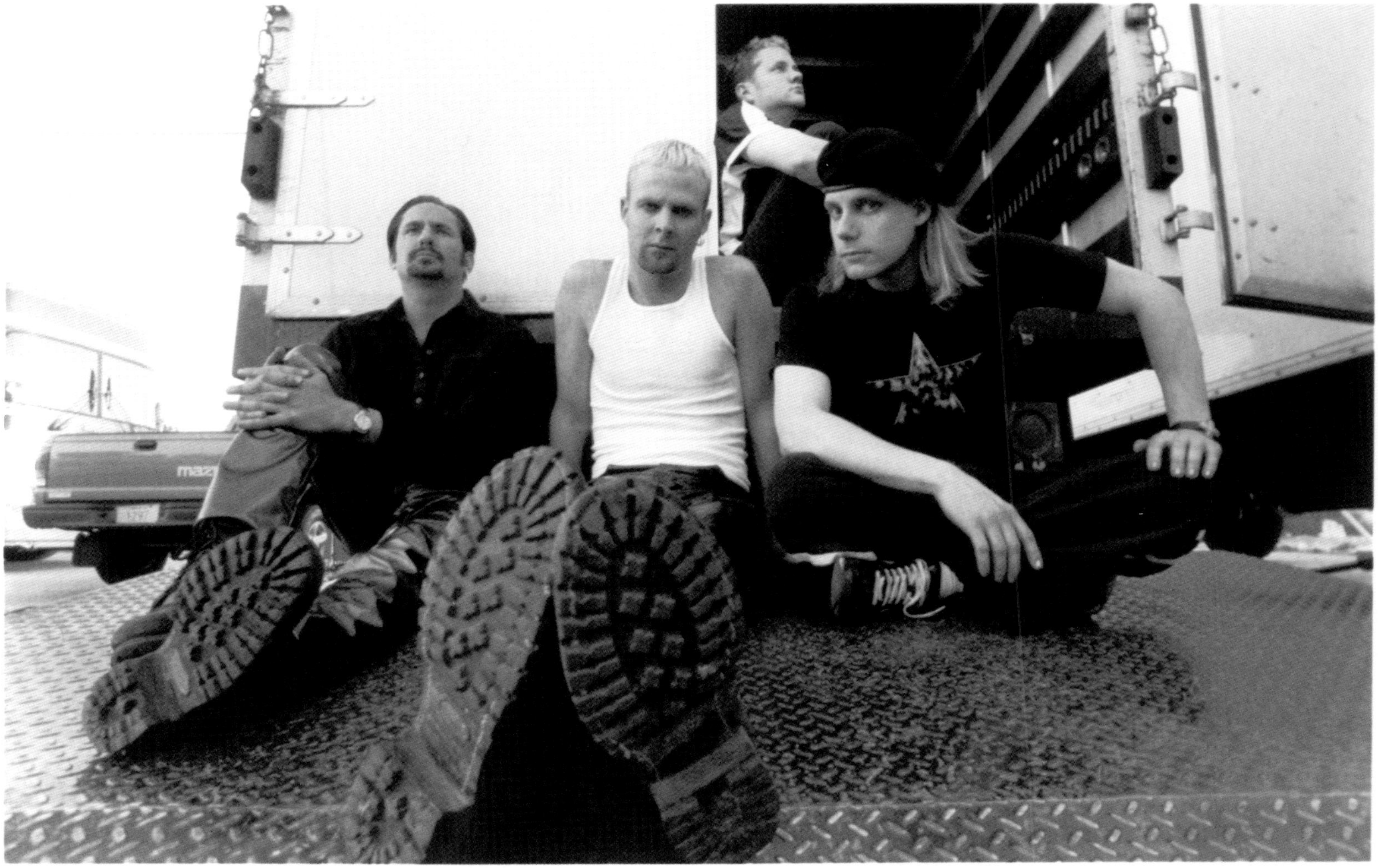

# GRAVITY KILLS

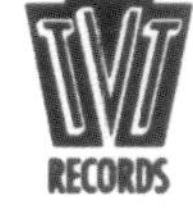


**FOR PRESS INFORMATION PLEASE CONTACT:**
LOIS NAJARIAN AT SUSAN BLOND 212.333.7728 OR
CARLEEN DONOVAN & CHARLIE AMTER AT TVT RECORDS 212.979.6410

**MANAGER INFO:**
GLORIA BUTLER AT GLORIA BUTLER MANAGEMENT
314.532.4541 OR 011.44.156.478.2341

**BOOKING INFO:**
ALEX KOCHAN OR DEBBIE MORRISON
AT ARTISTS & AUDIENCE 212.721.2400

**A & R CONTACT:**
TOM SARIG AT TVT RECORDS
212.979.6410 EXT. 269

TVT RECORDS, 23 EAST 4TH STREET, NY, NY 10003 TEL 212.979.6410 FAX 212.979.6489

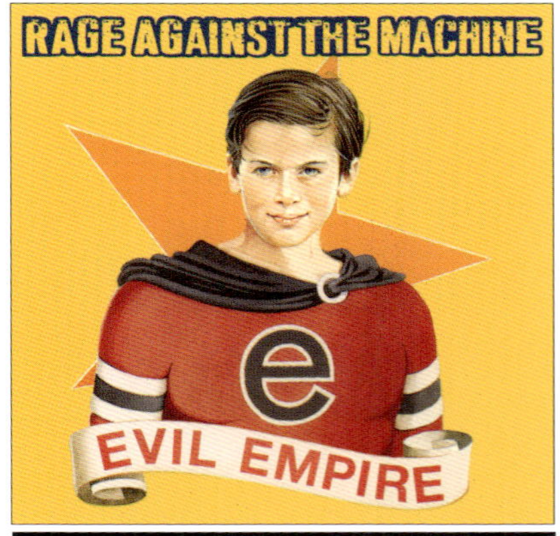


*Billboard* 200: *Evil Empire* (No. 1)

## Acclaimed and commanding, Rage Against the Machine dispatched more rants of dissention on *Evil Empire*.

**ON A** *Saturday Night Live* appearance, Rage Against the Machine wanted to protest the guest host, wealthy former Republican presidential candidate Steve Forbes, but the network vetoed the idea of hanging American flags upside down during the band's set. Nevertheless, the firebrand members continued to push their antiauthoritarian and revolutionary message.

"Politics bubbles a little closer to the surface in election years," guitarist Tom Morello noted. "The conventions are such grim affairs, such criminal political theater. The attempt is obviously to keep people stupefied—the emotionally potent oversimplifications, the consumption of fantasy. There's a growing realization that there's no room for ordinary people in the current structure. While people have their choice between different puppets, the puppet masters are beyond any electoral control.

"That's the crucial thing we're trying to get across—people should rebel. All substantive social change has come through struggle, not through the calm deliberations of Congress or the wisdom of the Supreme Court. It's people standing up against injustice and being unwilling to budge."

While the commentary rubbed some folks the wrong way, the band offered fans what they wanted. After a long layoff, the message rockers returned with a second album—*Evil Empire*, an eruption of buzzsaw grooves, grinding guitars and lyrical swipes at social intolerance and political injustice that debuted at No. 1 on the album charts.

"We've always been a prolific band," Morello said. "We stepped off the road and wrote about 30 songs—and we couldn't agree on one of them. That's the irony. Rage is more in tune with each other's political outlook than our musical outlook. It was a matter of finding the right combination of songs that we could be proud of."

"Bulls on Parade" was fueled by the opening salvo, a bastardized heavy jazz riff that was rounded out with frontman Zach De La Rocha's venomous ravings against the system. "People of the Sun" was a funky version of the ferocious Rage sound. The written legacies of Bob Marley, Malcolm X, Che Guevara and others were pictured on the inner sleeve.

"At shows we meet young people who say, 'I can't do anything, I'm just one person,' but don't let anybody tell you anything about the odds against you," Morello said. "Serfdom, slavery, child labor and the subjugation of women were all taken for granted at one time, but were overcome through struggle, not passivity. People get tricked all the time into fighting and dying and killing for Uncle Sam's business wars, but if you're going to fight for justice here at home, at least you know what you're fighting for." ■

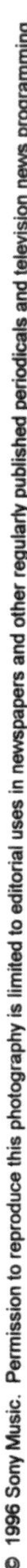

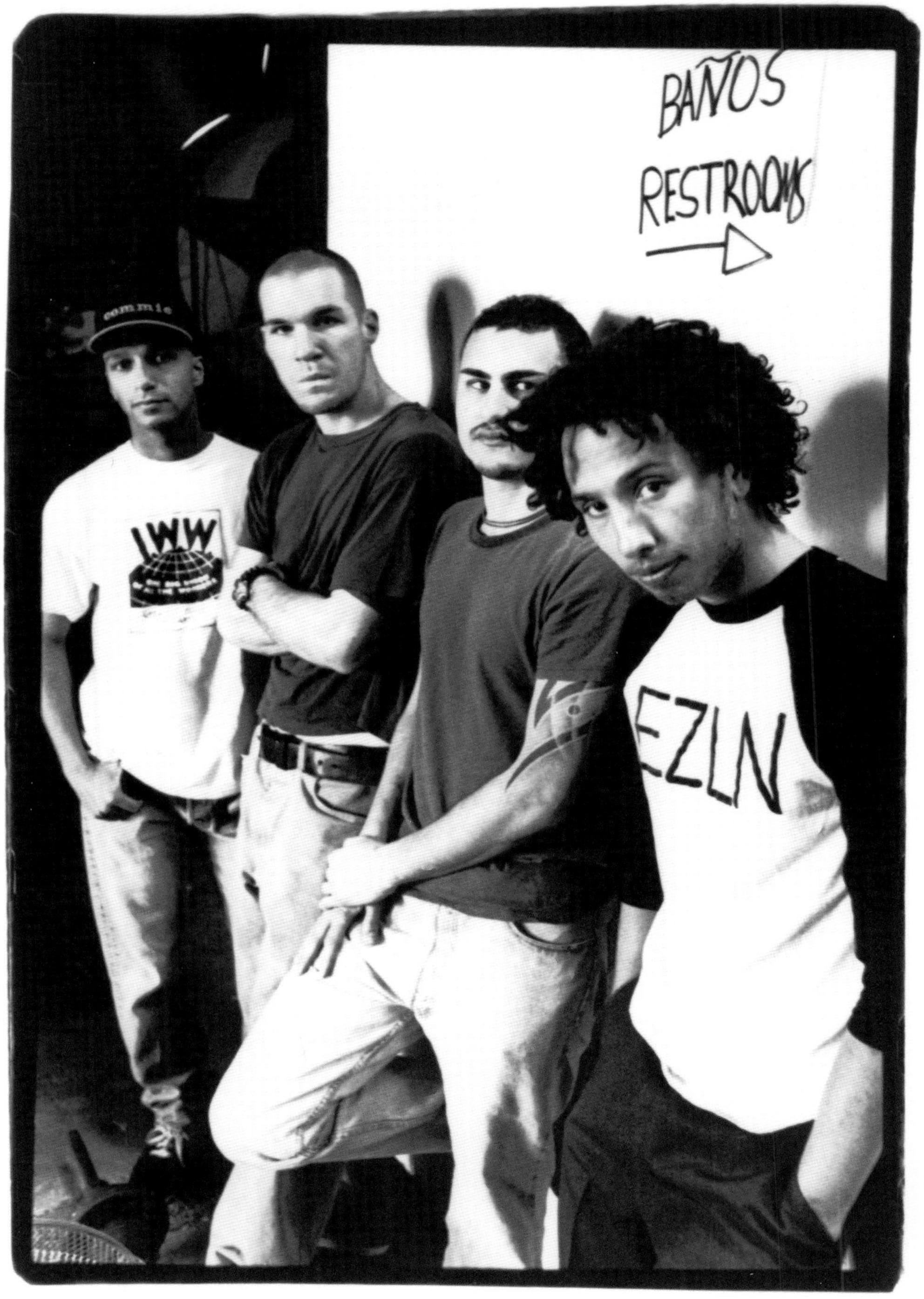

PHOTO CREDIT LISA JOHNSON

| TOM MORELLO<br>GUITAR | TIM BOB<br>BASS | BRAD WILK<br>DRUMS | ZACK DE LA ROCHA<br>VOCALS |
|---|---|---|---|

# RAGE AGAINST THE MACHINE

9602

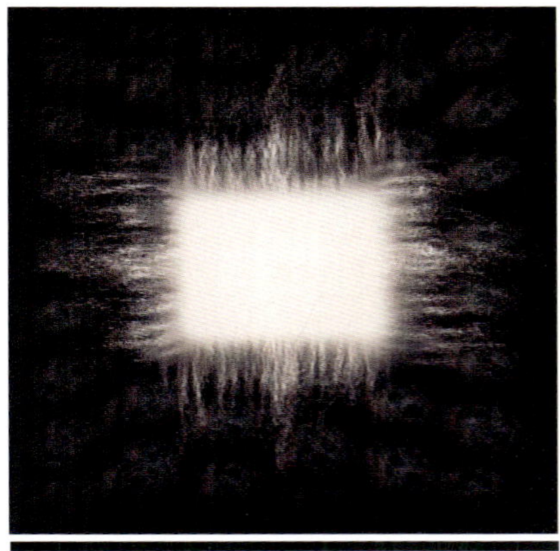

*Billboard* 200: *Ænima* (#2)

# With *Ænima*, the band's second release, Tool emerged as the leading force in the progressive-metal movement.

**THE FOUR** members of Tool consciously eschewed the modern rock band archetype. They rarely appeared in their videos or album art, seldom granted interviews and refused to discuss their private matters. Onstage, they played in near darkness, flanked by striking visuals.

But in an era of alternative music, the popular Los Angeles band—singer Maynard James Keenan, guitarist Adam Jones, drummer Danny Carey and bassist Justin Chancellor—proved heavy rock didn't have to be dumb, and that intelligent art-metal didn't have to be boring.

Tool crunched and lumbered about with Alice in Chains, Stone Temple Pilots, Helmet and the rest of the hard-rock class of 1993 on the debut album *Undertow*, a malicious rush that was best appreciated on the singles "Prison Sex" and "Sober." Tool turned out to be the surprise attraction of the Lollapalooza tour—Keenan, a riveting frontman, became known to take the stage gaudily dressed in drag, or decked out in a business suit and gray wig, or beautified in nothing more than underwear and face paint.

Tool delivered *Ænima*, a jagged, sullen nightmare filled with roaring guitars, abrupt rhythm shifts and jarring, evocative sound effects. The band's songwriting had become darker and more adventurous—the angry intensity and penchant for difficult lyrical subjects left fans either scratching their heads or cheering. Some of Tool's following was inclined to good ol' moshing and hooting. Most, however, picked up on the band's ambitious reference to Jungian philosophy.

"It's a collective thing," Jones said. "There are no rules, no politics. Tool is a very selfish relationship between the four band members—we do it for us. It's self-fulfillment. So whatever people decide they want to get out of it is fine."

The singles "Stinkfist," "H," the title track and "46 and 2" all were hits on the rock charts, Jones, who worked as a Hollywood movie special-effects designer before joining Tool, was interested in presenting the band's music visually. He directed and oversaw the production of the quartet's creepy award-winning videos, collecting images from his twisted imagination.

"We just write music until we like it, and then we put it out and see what it does," Jones said. "Any four people who get together, there's going to be four different perspectives—things are really good and things really suck at the same time, and you've got to work through that." ■

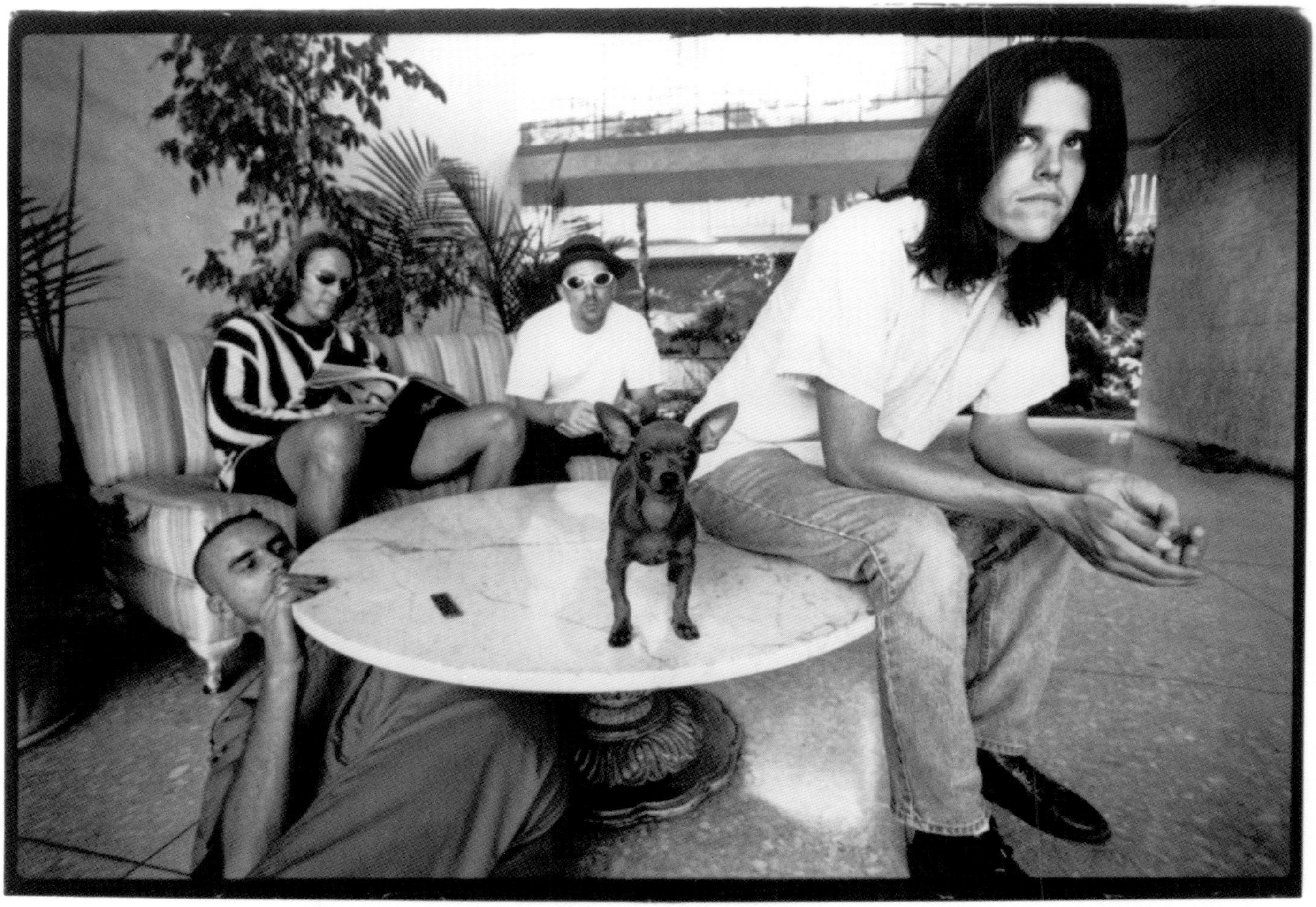

Photo Credit: Syd Kato

(L-R) Justin Chancellor (Bass), Danny Carey (Drums), Maynard James Keenan (Vocals), Hugo (Blue Chihuahua), Adam Jones (Guitar)

http://www.zoology.com

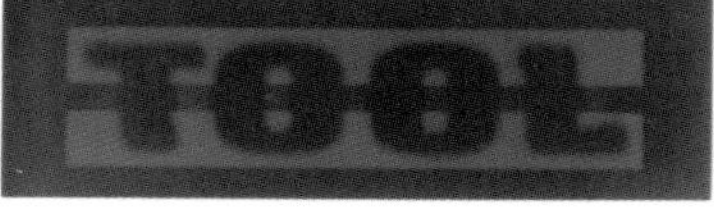


Larrikin Management
(213) 930-9130

ENTERTAINMENT 8750 Wilshire Blvd., Beverly Hills, California 90211 TEL 310 358 4218 FAX 310 358 4299

9609

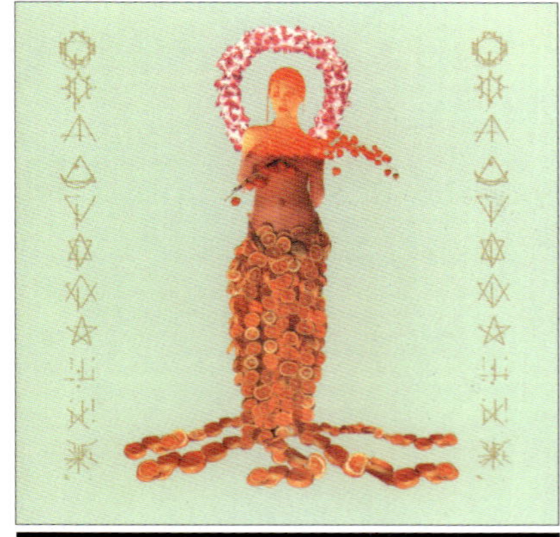

*Billboard* 200: *Good God's Urge* (#20)

# Commanded by Perry Farrell, Porno for Pyros concocted a laid-back follow-up to their gold-certified debut.

**AN ALTERNATIVE** impresario, Perry Farrell was famous for three things—masterminding the annual Lollapalooza festival, fronting his groundbreaking former band Jane's Addiction and experimenting with drugs ("Heroin's not for everyone—but it's for me.").

Farrell was focusing his efforts on Porno for Pyros. He could write his own ticket with devotees who thought the band was art, but others scratched their heads. Jane's Addiction and Porno's debut ("Pets" was the big hit) had a hard-rock feel, but the songs from the second album, *Good God's Urge*, took a tender turn. They were inspired by the band's frequent surfing vacations to the South Pacific.

"The first Porno record was written during the riots in Hollywood, and you could hear it in the lyrics and music," drummer Stephen Perkins, a Jane's Addiction holdover, said. "We played for the natives on bongos and acoustic guitar. That's where we learned to communicate without electricity or amplification. But the best thing is that we became friends. Jane's Addiction would have never gone to an island for 10 days alone—we'd have hated each other."

Farrell thought his peace-and-love lyrics were important, and he'd set them to spacey hippie-rock soundscapes. "Tahitian Moon"—a melodic chorus and a punk-rock Motown rhythm with a flamenco-style guitar part put through an electric crunch—was noteworthy. But other songs were dissonant, annoying or inert.

Farrell might've been distracted. He had conceived and organized the first Lollapalooza festival in 1990 as a sort of cutting-edge rock-culture traveling circus with an ideological bent. Since then, it had become a cash cow, but Farrell became gradually less involved, and Metallica headlining the 1996 event pushed him over the edge. So he walked away from Lollapalooza with a movable fest of his own. Christened Enit, it embarked with Porno for Pyros headlining.

"We're gonna plant trees, 5,000 for each show," Farrell said. "We're gonna have yoga sessions in the morning and serve tea for everybody. We're gonna put the food in leaves that won't cause as much trash, and everybody's going to eat at the same time as opposed to a bunch of little stands. We're gonna get back to nature."

But Farrell had problems booking sites, and the Enit festival was discontinued, owing to high production costs and a lack of fan interest. ■

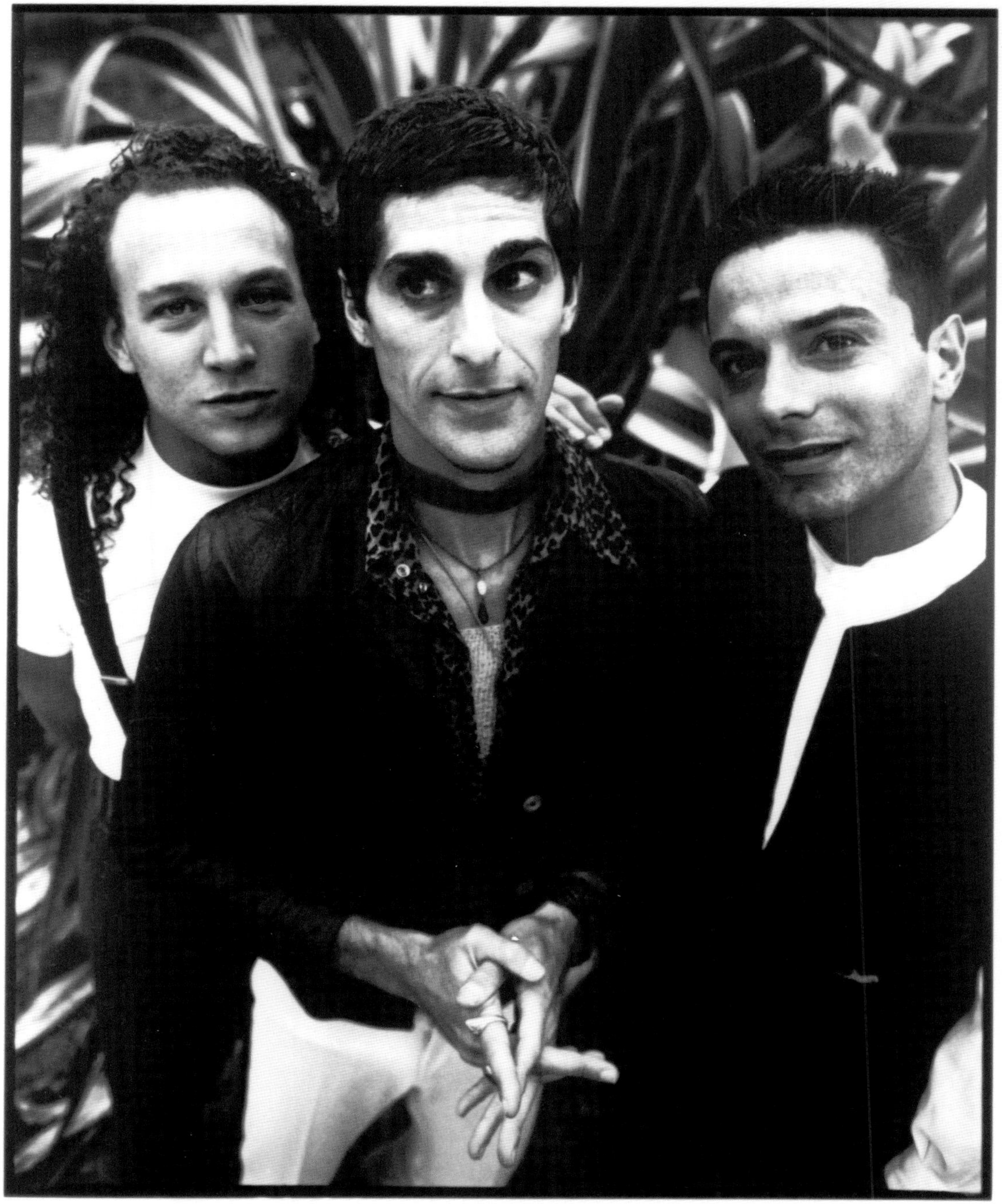

Photo Credit: John Eder

Stephen Perkins Perry Farrell Peter DiStefano

# Porno For Pyros

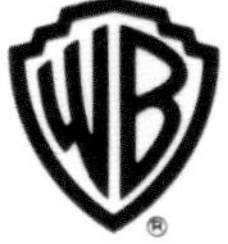

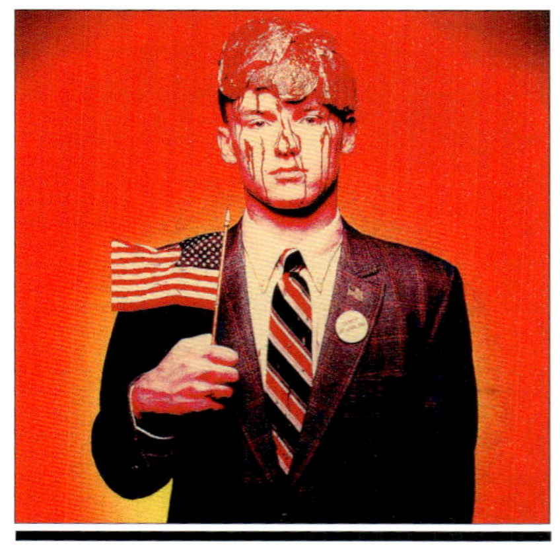

*Billboard* 200: *Filth Pig* (#19)

# With the *Filth Pig* album, recording wasn't a barrel of laughs for the first time in Ministry's uncommon career.

**THE GODFATHERS** of industrial noise, Ministry partners Al Jourgensen and Paul Barker evolved their over-the-top sonic assault with the 1992 album *Psalm 69*, a new height in harsh electronic histrionics. Ministry appeared on the bill at Lollapalooza and all over MTV with "Jesus Built My Hotrod."

When Ministry returned with *Filth Pig*, fans were anticipating an album that was as abrasive and punishing as *Psalm 69*. But there was a more restrained edge, grinding and foreboding. "*Psalm 69* left a bad taste in our mouths—we realized we'd painted ourselves into a corner stylistically," bassist/programmer Barker said. "We're fairly mischievous. We don't want to spoon-feed people. We knew we weren't going to make the same record over again."

Ministry's ethos was still antagonistic, but the duo's adrenalized beats, layered samples and electronically altered exhortations gave way to disjointed time signatures, crunching riffs and odd instrumental entries like steel guitar and piano (the descending figure on "The Fall"). "We were bored with industrial music," Barker said. "We wanted to throw out all of our studio techniques and tricks, everything we could always fall back on, and still do something competent. We got ideas by jamming in a band context. Now we've got six guys onstage."

*Filth Pig* was recorded in disarray. Jourgensen and Barker left Chicago (where Ministry began in 1981), moved to Texas and built a studio in an abandoned bordello. Then equipment broke down, and they were on each other's nerves. Barker left and came back. Guitarist and vocalist Jourgensen, a guy with a propensity for various pharmaceuticals and sexual fetishes, was harassed by the local police. "We had a lot of shit happen, there were frustrations," Barker admitted. "But it had to do with the process, not the music."

"Brick Windows" was highlighted by Jourgensen's sonically stressed vocal. A droning, distorted cover of "Lay Lady Lay" didn't sound remotely like Bob Dylan's original version. "One of our favorite songs is Jimmy Webb's 'Wichita Lineman' (a Glen Campbell hit)—we totally dig it, but Urge Overkill covered it first," Barker explained. "Al was bummed, but 'Lay Lady Lay' has the same chord progression." ■

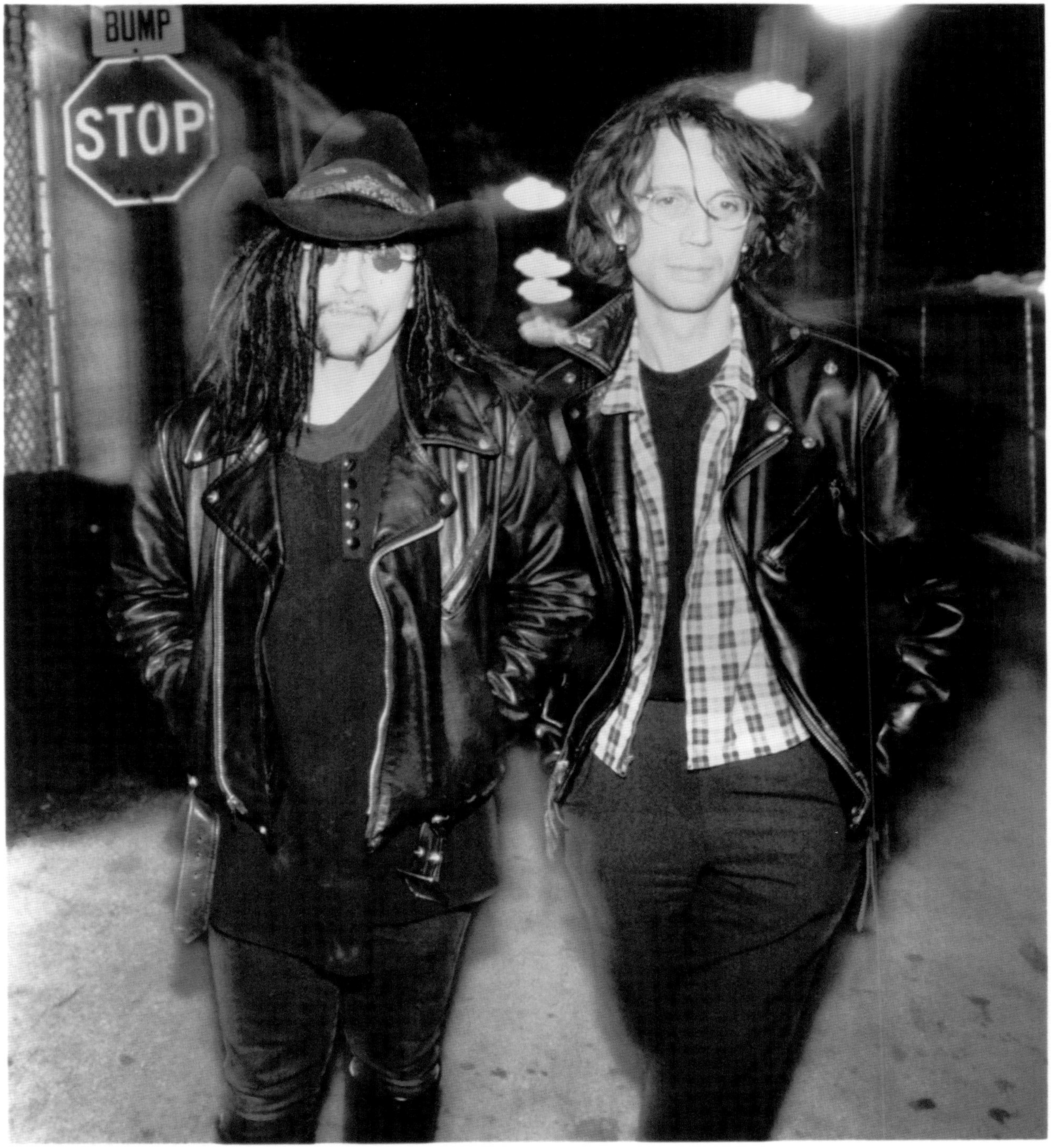

Photo Credit: Paul Elledge

# MINISTRY

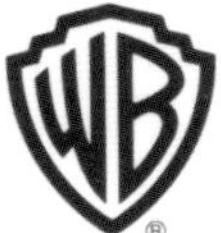

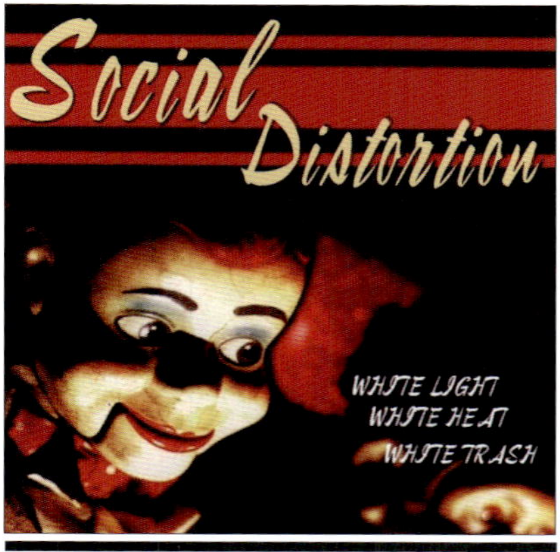


*Billboard* 200: *White Light, White Heat, White Trash* (#27)

## Social Distortion's *White Light, White Heat, White Trash* held fast to Mike Ness' simple punk underpinnings.

**PLAYING AND** living hard since the early Eighties, Social Distortion had its sound described by singer and guitarist Mike Ness as "kind of like if Hank Williams got in a car wreck with the Ramones." In the Nineties, Ness was galled at the poseurs whose prefabricated wrath passed for punk rock.

"All I have to do is turn on MTV and watch it for five minutes and I'm exasperated—I feel like some of the hardcore rappers felt when Vanilla Ice hit," Ness said. "There's a lot of punk rock out there that is capitalizing on the media and fashion. When a cool thing becomes popular, it starts getting uncool—a lot can get lost in the translation."

It had been four years since fans had heard from Social Distortion. On the way to making *White Light, White Heat, White Trash*, the Southern California quartet changed drummers twice, with Chuck Biscuits (ex-DOA, Black Flag) taking over. And a dozen songs were recorded and scrapped—at one point, producer Michael Beinhorn (of Soundgarden and Red Hot Chili Peppers fame) told Ness to go off and write more.

"My songwriter ego was bruised," Ness admitted. "My first reaction was, 'Who is this guy?' But I've learned to keep an open mind. Just because something is hard doesn't mean it shouldn't be done. It's easy to become complacent. You can write catchy songs all day long, but are you going to like them in a year? I was forced to dig deeper and get in touch with stuff that isn't necessarily at the surface when you pick up a guitar. "And I had to get out of California. It was like having a gym in your home—to get to it, maybe you pass the TV and the refrigerator, and chances are you may not work out that day because *The Honeymooners* is on. I wrote a lot of this record in New York City. Getting that different environment was essential for me."

*White Light, White Heat, White Trash* was a badass recording—irresistible guitar riffs, thundering backbeats and gritty vocals by Ness, a working-class tough guy whose past included heroin addiction, alcoholism and jail time. His confessional tunes were still motivated by rage and resentment, but he was now thoughtful and sometimes penitent.

The smoking single "I Was Wrong," which held a Top 5 slot on the modern-rock charts, burned with pain and raw feeling. "I used to go through people's lives like a tornado," Ness mused. "'I Was Wrong' could go to anyone who was in the way—if they were there, they know. It's kind of a smug apology, but it's more of a self-acceptance song."

Ness drew his inspiration for the album from the first wave of American punk rock. "The late Seventies is when the attitude and angst and style was pure and undiluted. Musically speaking, that period was all blues-based rock. Those bands had grown up influenced by Chuck Berry and the pop of the Sixties."

Social Distortion aspired to achieve the big time with *White Light, White Heat, White Trash*. "It's exciting, frankly. We've tried hard to hold on to our dignity and ideals without compromising, and it's paid off. Wow, we're getting across without having to change." ■

PHOTO: FRANK OCKENFELS


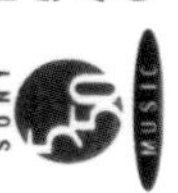


RECORD COMPANY:
550 MUSIC
ATTN: DAVE GOTTLIEB
(212) 833-8491 FAX (212) 833-4060

PRESS:
MSO
ATTN: TRESA REDBURN
(818) 380-0400 FAX (818) 380-0430

US BOOKING:
ICM
ATTN: ANDY SOMERS
(310) 550-4341 FAX (310) 550-4108

INTERNATIONAL BOOKING:
ITB
ATTN: MARTIN HORNE
(0171) 379-1313 FAX (0171) 379-1744

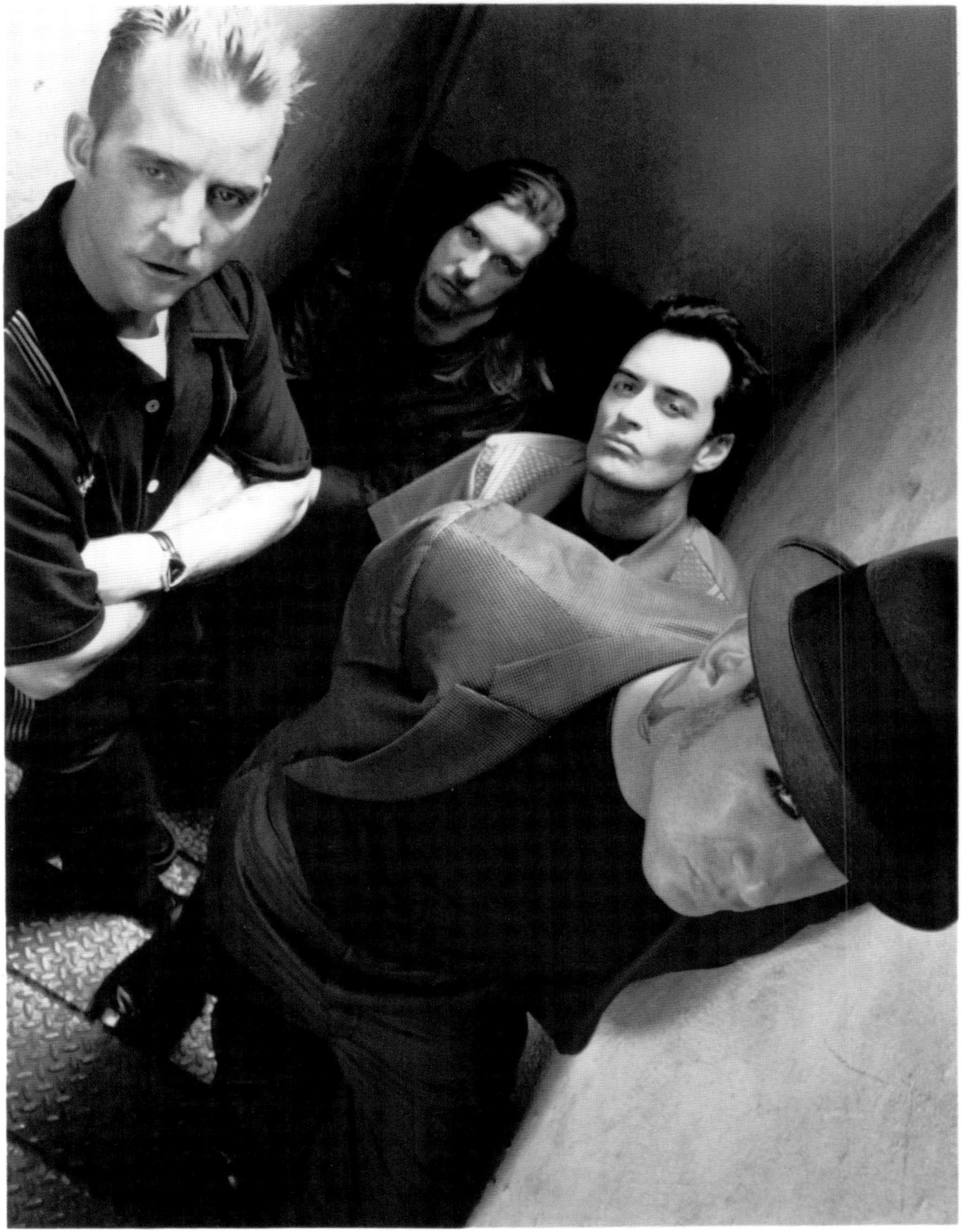

# SOCIAL DISTORTION

REBEL
WALTZ, INC.

*Billboard* 200: *Goldfinger* (#110)

# Captivating a loyal fan base with "Here in Your Bedroom," Goldfinger considered its ska-punk dues paid in full.

**IT WAS** quite a year for Goldfinger, a light-hearted Southern California outfit fusing punk and ska. The four members went from clubbing around the Orange County scene in virtual obscurity to the catchy "Here in Your Bedroom" becoming a Top 10 track on alternative radio. And it all began with lead singer and guitarist John Feldmann working in a Santa Monica punk-rock shoe store.

"I wrote 'Here in Your Bedroom' on New Year's Eve of '95," Feldmann explained. "I had a crush on a girl who worked in the dress department for eight months. Finally, we went on a date and she slept with me. And I was so nervous about how the morning after was going to be. So that song is about those wacky feelings that a sensitive guy like me gets at those times. She dissed me not long after that, but out of the dumpage I got three of my best songs. A lot of our songs are about my failed experiences with girls!"

Selling shoes had other benefits. Feldman stuck an employee of Mojo Records with a pair of green suede creepers. "He recognized me from an old band I was in. I told him about Goldfinger and to check it out—I slipped a demo in his box. I guess he liked it."

The transaction ended in a record deal. In support of a self-titled debut album, Goldfinger played as an opening act on 217 shows in 264 days. *Goldfinger* turned gold, and the energized songs "Mable" and "Pictures" also received airplay.

"We definitely had to prove ourselves," drummer Dangerous Darrin Pfeiffer said. "People say, 'Ah, you just came out of nowhere and exploited punk and took over.' That's not true—we've been into punk for a long time. Or people bag on us, 'Oh, you guys aren't ska.' John was listening to the Specials and Madness in high school—the first concert he ever saw was the English Beat. I go through all of the e-mail, about 60 letters a day. The majority are good, but two percent want to rip on you, call you losers and poseurs. I love it—I can kill them with kindness. I explain to them how the music's in my heart, and they're like, 'Whoa, I never thought a guy in the band would read that!'" ■

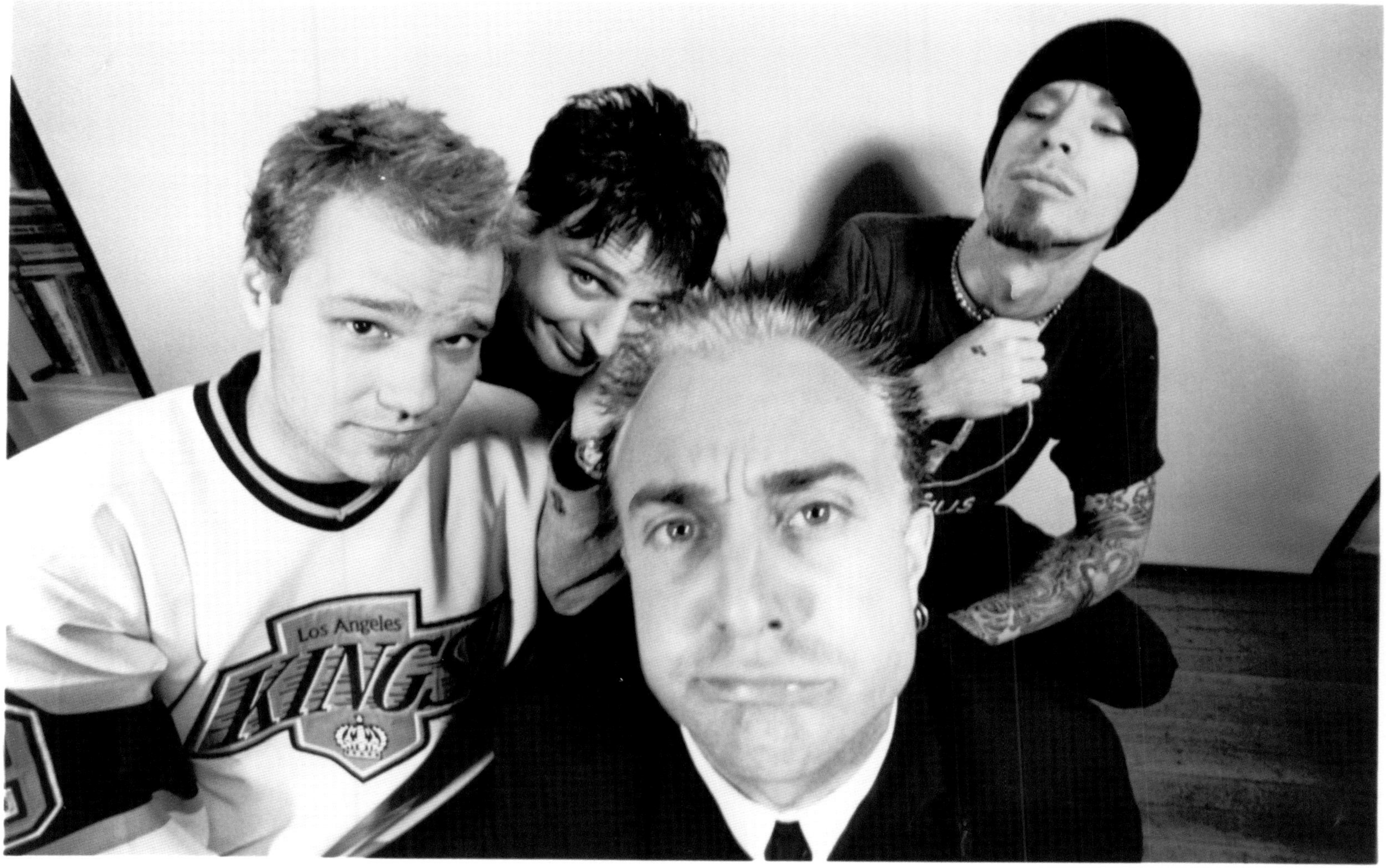

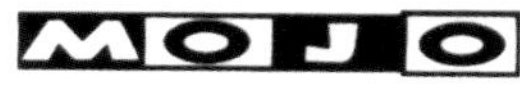


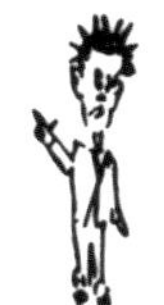

Photo Credit: Carla Cummings

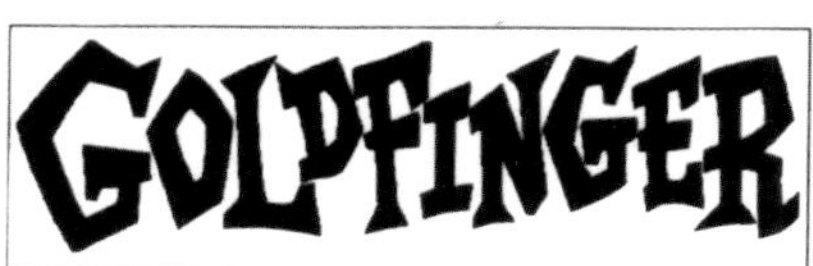


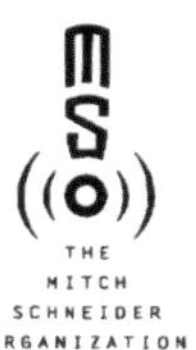

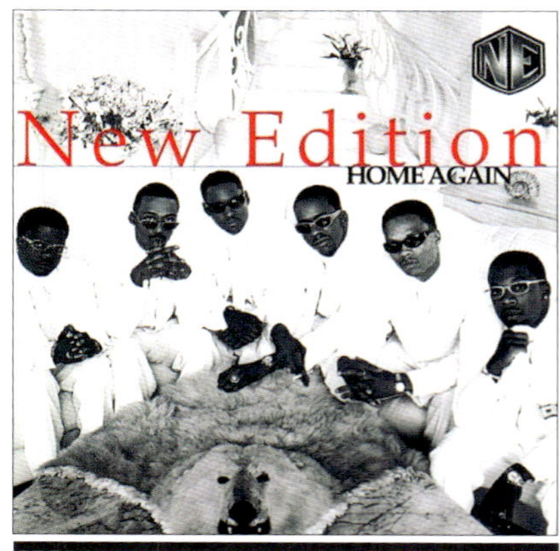


*Billboard* 200: *Home Again* (No. 1)
*Billboard* Hot 100: "Hit Me Off" (#3); "I'm Still in Love with You" (#7); "One More Day" (#61)

## All six former members of New Edition depended on the celebratory *Home Again* to resuscitate their fortunes.

**THE PUBLIC** loved the idea—past New Edition members Bobby Brown, Ralph Tresvant, Michael Bivins, Ricky Bell, Ronnie DeVoe and Johnny Gill (who replaced Brown) reunited to record a comeback album. "We've had to check our egos at the door, and there have been ups and downs," DeVoe allowed. "But we've done it."

In the early Eighties, New Edition busted out of the projects of Boston's Roxbury district with the Jackson 5-inspired hits "Candy Girl," "Cool It Now" and "Mr. Telephone Man." The teen group's performances featured a bubblegum soul sound, a hip-hop attitude and precision choreography. But the guys were seen as puppets of pop entrepreneur Maurice Starr (who, after an acrimonious split, was keen to find a "white New Edition" and organized New Kids on the Block).

After New Edition was finished, the members became some of the biggest R&B stars of the decade. Brown emerged with the influential album *Don't Be Cruel*. The rest scored No. 1 R&B hits—Tresvant with "Sensitivity," Bell Biv DeVoe twice and Gill four times.

New Edition's appeal hadn't diminished much. *Home Again* debuted at No. 1 on *Billboard*'s album chart and sold millions. But skeptics pointed to the last releases by Brown, Gill, Tresvant and Bell Biv DeVoe, which were commercial disappointments. Was the reunion needed to jump-start their careers? DeVoe didn't argue. "You never know how things in life are going to go—it's a roller-coaster ride," he said. "It's just a matter of timing. It's not like we lost contact with each other—we'd been planning to regroup all along."

On *Home Again*, the gangsta-derived "Hit Me Off" had street credibility and mass appeal. Tresvant recalled the group's first night in a New York City studio recording the single. "We toasted the session with Champagne and everything sounded great," he said with a laugh. "We had fun laying the recording and the vocals, but the next day it sounded horrible. It was the Champagne. We had to cut it all over again."

The chugging "Something About You" was knockout new jack swing. "We have more fans as individuals than we had when we were a group," DeVoe explained. "You can hear bits of those elements on the new record, but we had to keep the collective concerns of the New Edition sound."

The entire crew took the music on the road, mixing songs from *Home Again* and solo hits. But it was hard for the matured New Edition to do the old kiddie pop hits, especially a paean to puppy love like "Mr. Telephone Man." "Oh, man," DeVoe said with a moan. "But we have to respect the people who buy our records and come to our concerts." The tour proved ill-fated, as egos flared and both Brown and Bivins quit the group. ■

Ronnie
Bobby
Ricky
Mike
Ralph
Johnny

Photo Credit: Albert Watson

NE
NEW EDITION

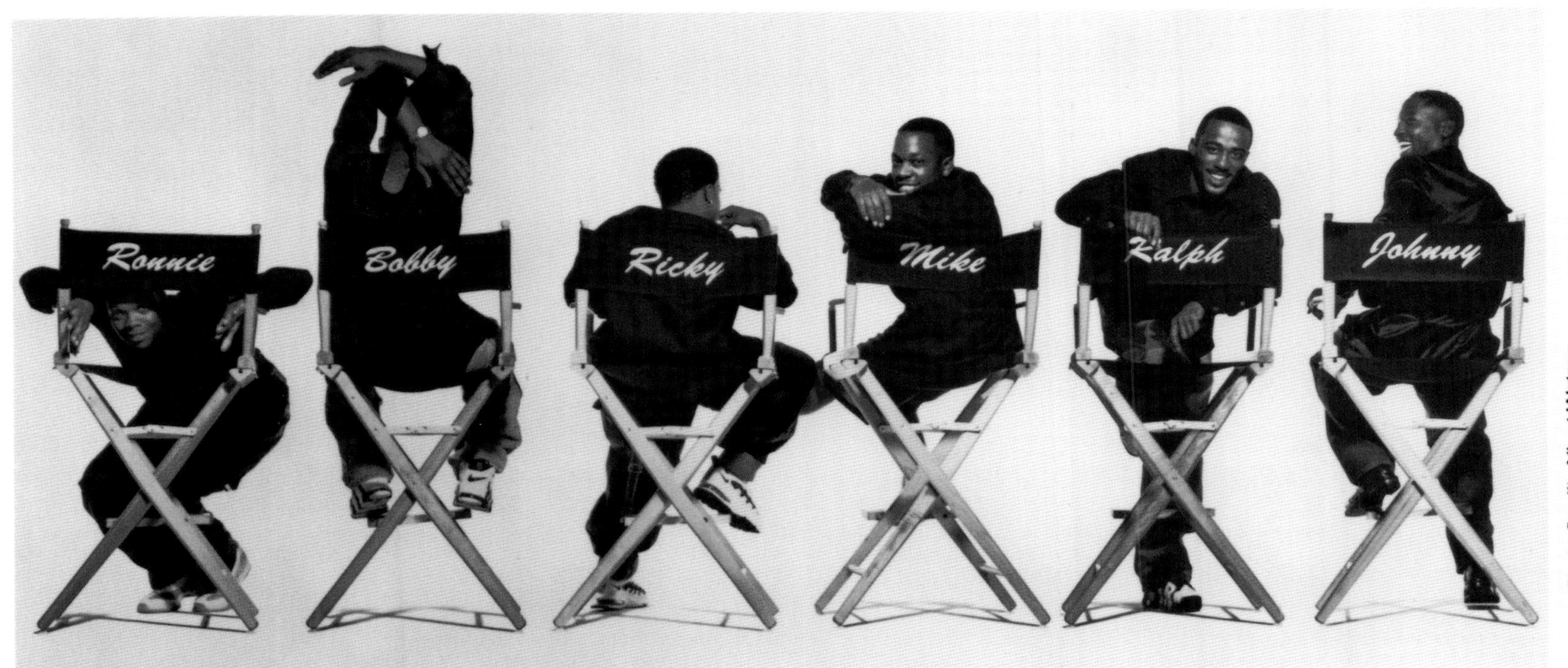

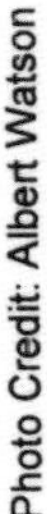

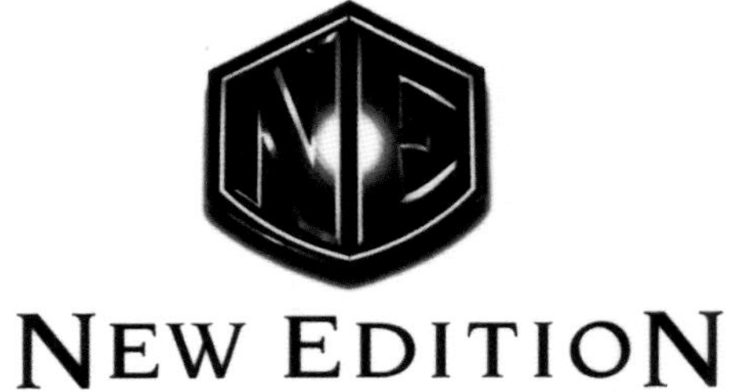

7/96

MCA.

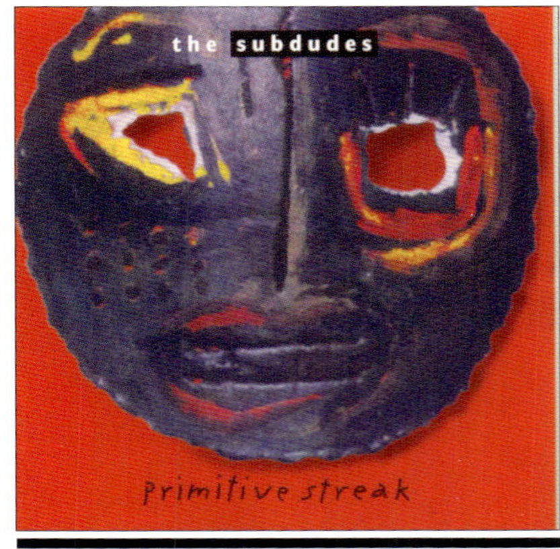


# The Subdudes opened the way for a new breed of Americana artists, but the mainstream was slow to catch on.

**ANYONE WHO** ever saw the Subdudes live surely never forgot them. Since the band's inception in the late Eighties, the four members had always delivered both charm and top-notch musicianship, masterfully blending elements of New Orleans R&B, roots rock, gospel and country. They had good word-of-mouth from peers in the music industry—Bruce Hornsby, Shawn Colvin, Huey Lewis, Eric Clapton, Joni Mitchell, Roseanne Cash and Bonnie Raitt were big fans.

*Primitive Streak*, touted as "the best 'Dudes record yet," stretched the soulful essence of their signature sound. On "All the Time in the World," Tommy Malone's reckless slide guitar work would have done Lowell George proud. The band indulged in five-part harmony with the help of Willie Williams of the Zion Harmonizers on "Faraway Girl." They recorded "Too Soon to Tell" with Raitt, and the buoyant "Sarita" and the stomping "Love Somebody" should have gained significant radio play.

But the album didn't elevate the Subdudes beyond the cult status they enjoyed for years in their native Louisiana and their adopted home of Colorado. The guys resided in different parts of the country, losing some of the chemistry they had developed in the early years. So they called it a day.

"We got a little bit discouraged with the day-to-day business—we were expecting more to happen with our fourth album," accordionist/keyboardist/vocalist John Magnie said. "And there are some musical reasons, some diverging paths between us—we haven't been writing songs together as much. It's a feeling that we've been doing it for a while, run the course with this style that we came up with. We needed to take a vacation, and that progressed into breaking up, letting it rest for the time being."

Percussionist Steve Amedee planned to make an instructional video—his distinctive tambourine work had become the Subdudes' trademark. On a fateful night in March 1987, Malone, Magnie, Amedee and bassist Johnny Ray Allen did a club gig in reaction to comments that their music was too loud and complicated. So they performed with two acoustic guitars and an accordion—and, in keeping with the unplugged ethos of the evening, Amedee lifted a tambourine from Malone's landlady. He quickly got serious and developed a unique percussion setup that had the drive of a full drum kit, using a thumb and forefinger to alternate between bass and snare sounds. ■

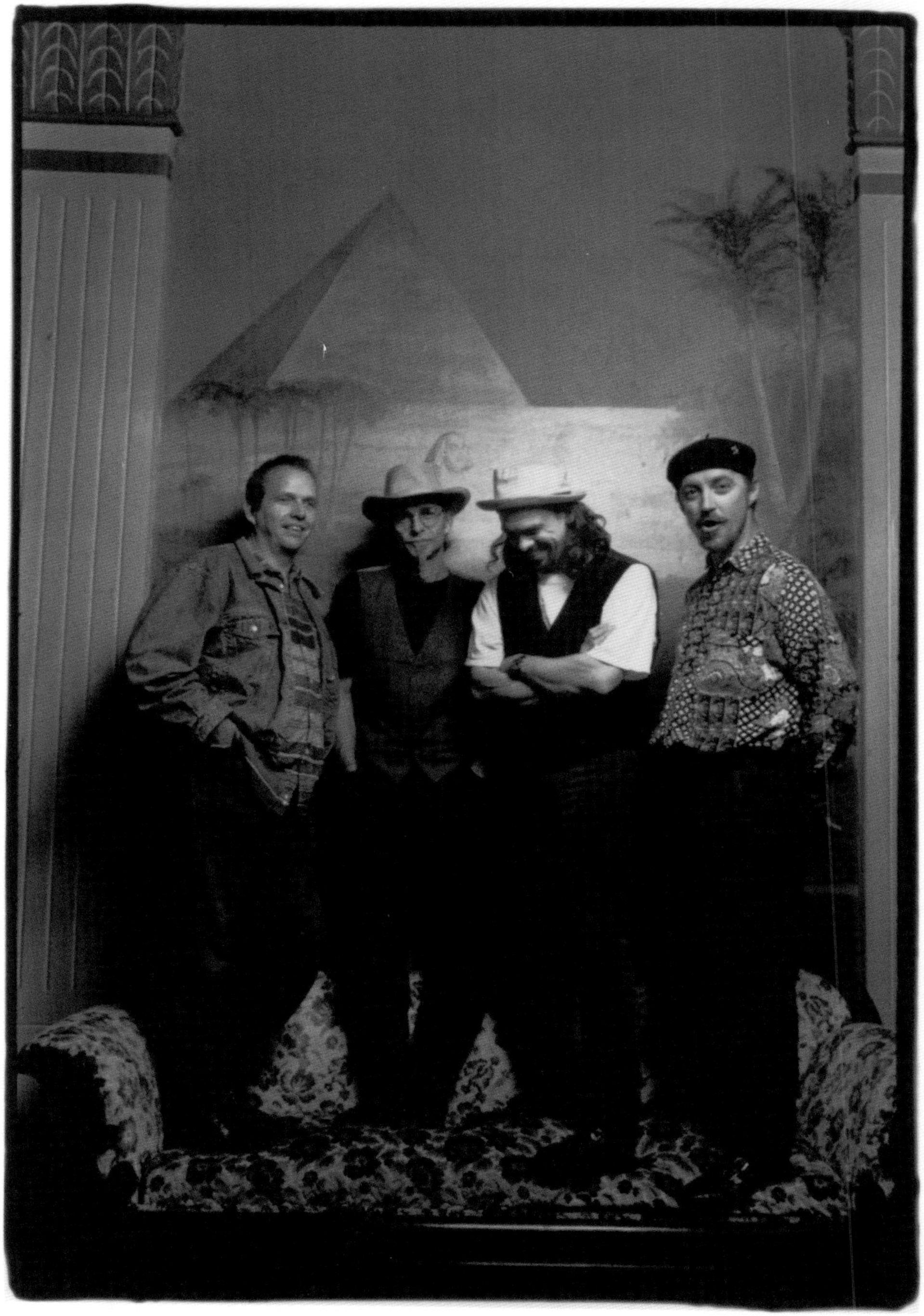

Photo: Michael Wilson

High Street Records™ Recording Artists

# the subdudes

High Street Records Publicity Office, PO Box 9388, Stanford, CA 94309 (415) 329-0647
Booking Agent: Monterey International, 200 W. Superior, Suite 202, Chicago, IL 60610 (312) 640-7500

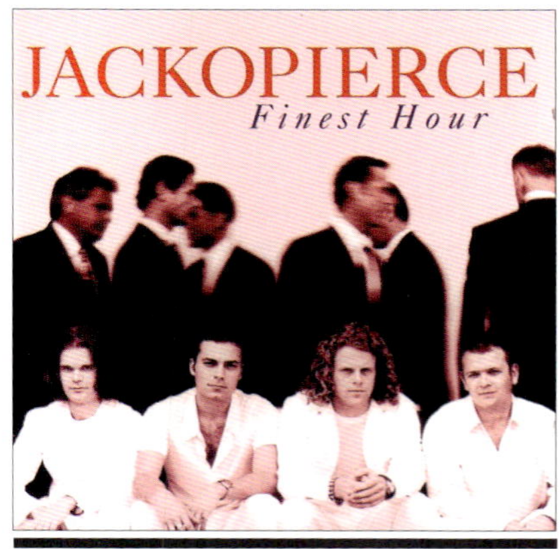


**Jackopierce** was at its best touring, yet the band fashioned a choice collection of pop songcraft, *Finest Hour*.

**THE FOUNDERS** of Jackopierce, Jack O'Neill and Cary Pierce, met as freshmen at Southern Methodist University in Dallas. The duo packed up an unregistered Volkswagen van and took their act on the road. Playing a wealth of small concerts in college towns, Jackopierce built up a devoted fan base and released three albums independently before A&M Records snatched them up in 1993.

Since then, Jackopierce had evolved into an exceptional acoustic-flavored pop-rock band, relying on crafted melodies and splendid harmonies. *Finest Hour* reflected the different writing styles of O'Neill and Pierce—the former's dark, brooding lyrics, and the latter's upbeat, energetic melodies. "Trials" and "Vineyard" were celebrated in the radio market for adult album alternative (Triple A), a nascent format with a broader playlist.

"I learned a lot about the music business—stuff that's not shocking but pretty interesting for a young, naïve kid," O'Neill noted. "A lot of it was feeling my way around, and, unfortunately, I was doing it in a very public medium."

But Jackopierce never experienced major radio play, nor videos on MTV and VH1. After nearly a decade on the road, O'Neill and Pierce were still best buddies, but they were ready to, in typically ambiguous public-relations prose, "pursue other interests." They announced their farewell tour. "To suddenly not be doing it anymore would leave a lot of question marks in people's heads when we move on with our careers—'So what the hell happened?,'" O'Neil said. "It's cool to know that we're working for a really specific goal, to make a definitive end to a really good run. I've never done anything in my life for nine years."

What if "Trials" had brought about the notice that Jackopierce deserved? "It happens a lot, where one song takes a band from a near-hit to a hit—there were a few songs in our catalog that could have done that," O'Neill said. "But there's the politics of radio and record labels, the way they interact and dictate what people listen to. That's when luck plays a part. There's no reason to be bitter, but some things could have been done differently. If we'd just played on *The Rosie O'Donnell Show* on Thursday instead of Wednesday—who knows? There's a reason for everything.

"But what an amazing ride—two guys who started playing for free beer around town, finding themselves working with T-Bone Burnett and touring the world. That's the stuff of dreams." ■

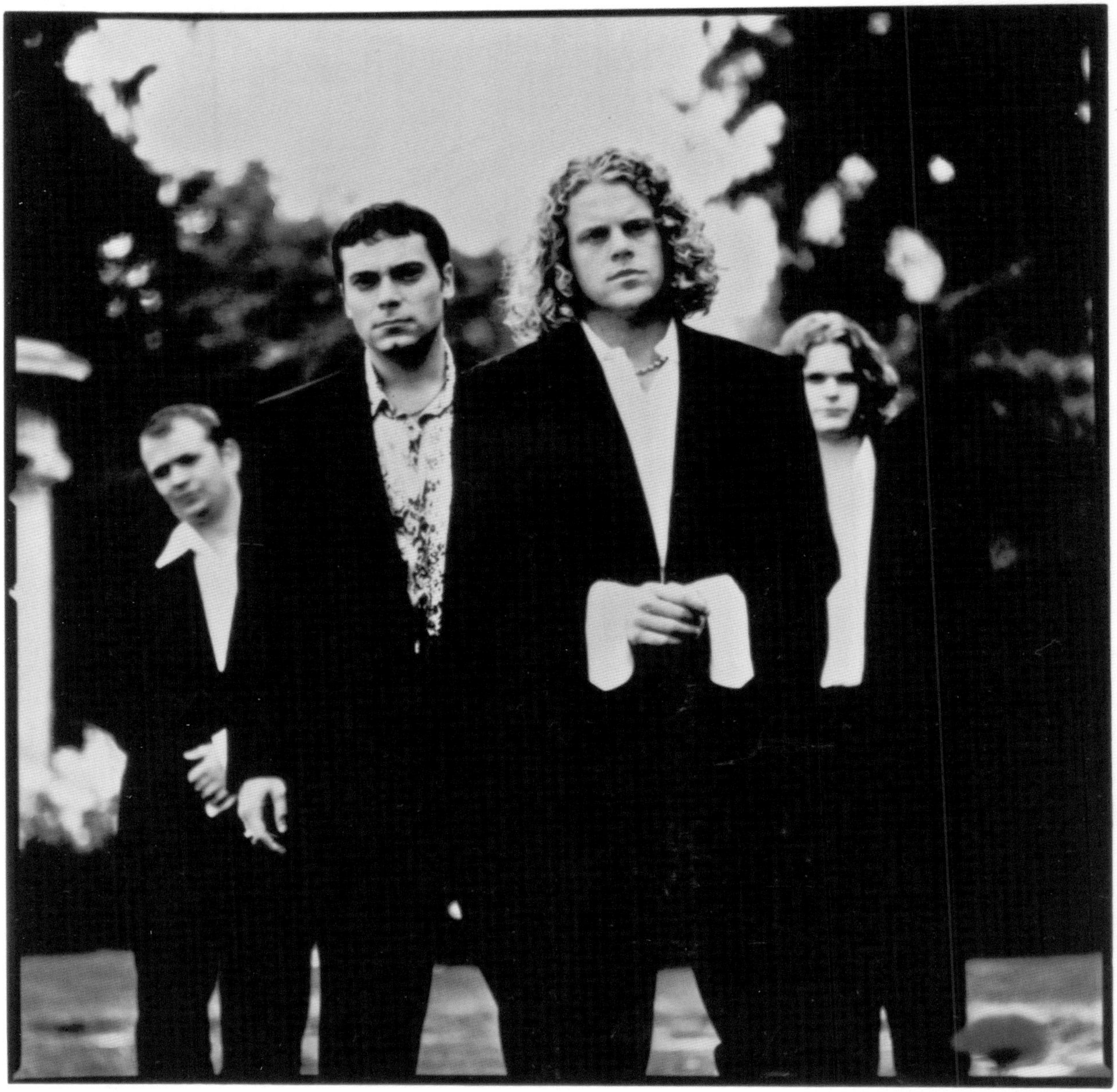

Photo: F. Scott Schafer 6/96

Earl Darling Jack O'Neill Cary Pierce Clay Pendergrass

# JACKOPIERCE

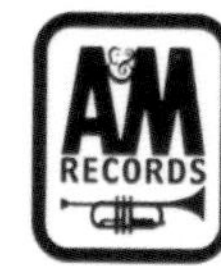

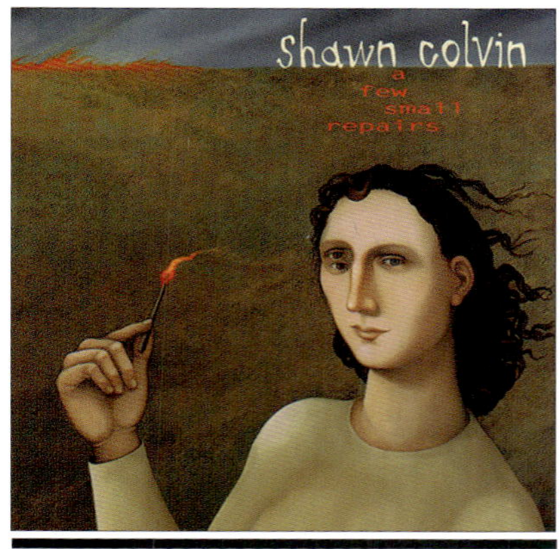


*Billboard* 200: *A Few Small Repairs* (#39)
*Billboard* Hot 100: "Sunny Came Home" (#7)

## Shawn Colvin's "Sunny Came Home" earned her Grammy Awards for Record of the Year and Song of the Year.

**IT WAS** written after a divorce, so some listeners considered Shawn Colvin's *A Few Small Repairs* album an emotional payback. But not every song was angry. "They're all breakup records—it's what I do," the singer-songwriter said with a laugh.

Colvin was the darling of the "new folk" scene when her debut album, 1990's *Steady On*, won a Grammy for Best Contemporary Folk Recording. Two nominations followed for 1992's *Fat City*. In 1994 she recorded *Cover Girl*, an interpretive collection of other people's songs. Cynics said it stalled the momentum she had going. "I never felt that way—from my point of view, it was really fun to make that record, and I needed to have a little fun," she said. "In the long run, I broke through some sort of demon that was sitting on my shoulder. I don't feel frightened of the studio now."

The songs had their roots in catharsis, but Colvin asserted that *A Few Small Repairs* was "the easiest record I've ever done." It rejoined her with John Leventhal, the producer who guided *Steady On* and was her lover through much of the Eighties (he then married Rosanne Cash). Leventhal weaved textures into the lovely melodies. It was piquant electro-acoustic folk rock with some aggressive fuzz guitar and strings here, a trace of recorder and flute there.

"I just missed writing with him—I didn't care what came of it aside from that," Colvin said. "He'd done work with Marc Cohn, with Patty Larkin. I never had a feeling that it would be any different. We were a little anxious when we got together, hoping that we'd have a good time. But after the first day, it was clear that it was going to go okay."

The poignant record was a testament to Colvin's maturing sense of message and skill at lyrical imagery. In the opening track, "Sunny Came Home," a troubled woman sets her house on fire. The Tom Petty-flavored "Get Out of This House," with a wailing harmonica, included a time-observed kiss-off: "Go jump in the lake."

"In general, the record has to do with the dreams people have that change as they grow into middle age," she said. "That's what I felt happening to me in all areas of my life—seeing things more clearly and being disillusioned. Nonetheless, I think it's kind of hopeful and funny. It has that attitude that you begin to acquire as you get older—life is obviously not going to be what you thought it was, yet there are a lot of payoffs in sticking around long enough to appreciate things and understand yourself better." ■

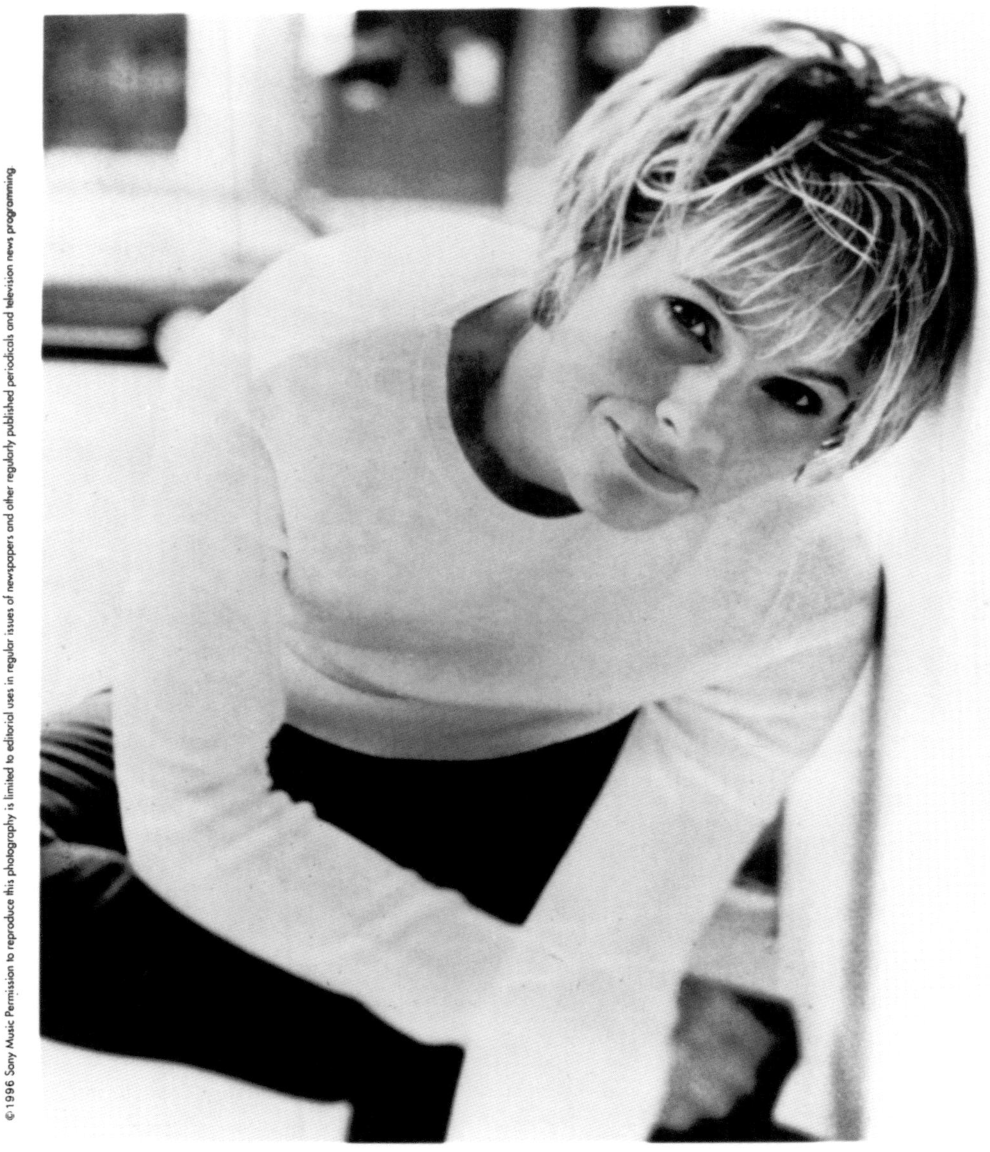

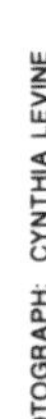


**SHAWN COLVIN**

COLUMBIA
9610

Billboard 200: *You? Me? Us?* (#97)

## British folk-rock master Richard Thompson separated his double album *You? Me? Us?* into two distinct formats.

**THROUGHOUT HIS** long career, Richard Thompson had long been praised by musicians, fans and the music industry for his expressive guitar work, moody songwriting and grimly witty performances. His electric and acoustic work had coexisted almost independently, and he embraced the dichotomy on *You? Me? Us?*, a double CD divided into halves—*Voltage Enhanced*, a blistering collection of songs, and *Nude*, a more contemplative recording.

"I suppose I'm happy to try to appeal to all factions," the affable and unassuming Brit said. "There are definitely people who only want to hear acoustic music, which is fair enough. There are people who only want to hear electric guitar playing, and the song is something that's a bit in the way—that they have to wade through to get to the guitar solos—and that's fair enough as well. So doing two discs was the best way to sequence this material."

A founding member of the pioneering English folk-rock group Fairport Convention, Thompson went solo in 1972 and had since written hundreds of witheringly sad and mirthfully vicious tunes. "It's an easy job, to tell you the truth. It's not like writing novels or something. Hell, what am I expected to do, 12 songs a year? Gosh that's only one a month.

"I shouldn't be belittling myself. I suppose I should be saying how hard life is, how drugs and pain keep one creative. But I've probably figured out how to sit down and have a full day's work better than I used to. In the old days, I started to write around midnight and by four o'clock I'd be in the mood—and then by 4:30 I'd be too tired to carry on. Now I start really early in the morning. If it gets going well, I can get an eight-hour working day. There's always a lot to write about, no shortage of subject matter."

The *Voltage Enhanced* side was Thompson's most basic guitar/bass/drums record since *Shoot Out the Lights*, his 1982 masterpiece made with his ex-wife Linda. The *Nude* disc had a timeless sound. "The whole 'new age' thing killed acoustic guitar for me," Thompson said. "I'm fairly sick of those pristine records, so we ran the acoustic guitars through amps to tweak them a bit, give them an indefinable sound."

Lyrically, songs took a hard look into spiritual and romantic longings. Thompson sang "Dark Hand Over My Heart" in a bleak baritone: "Becky loved me and I let her/Wish I could have loved her better/On the day we pulled apart/She primed a time-bomb in my heart."

*You? Me? Us?* was heralded as an intense, intelligent album, but Thompson still sought the commercial heights that peers like Eric Clapton had reached. "In terms of career, the biggest change I could have would be to get on the radio more," he expressed. "But I've never really manufactured hits, or compromised albums in a way that made me unhappy with them." ■

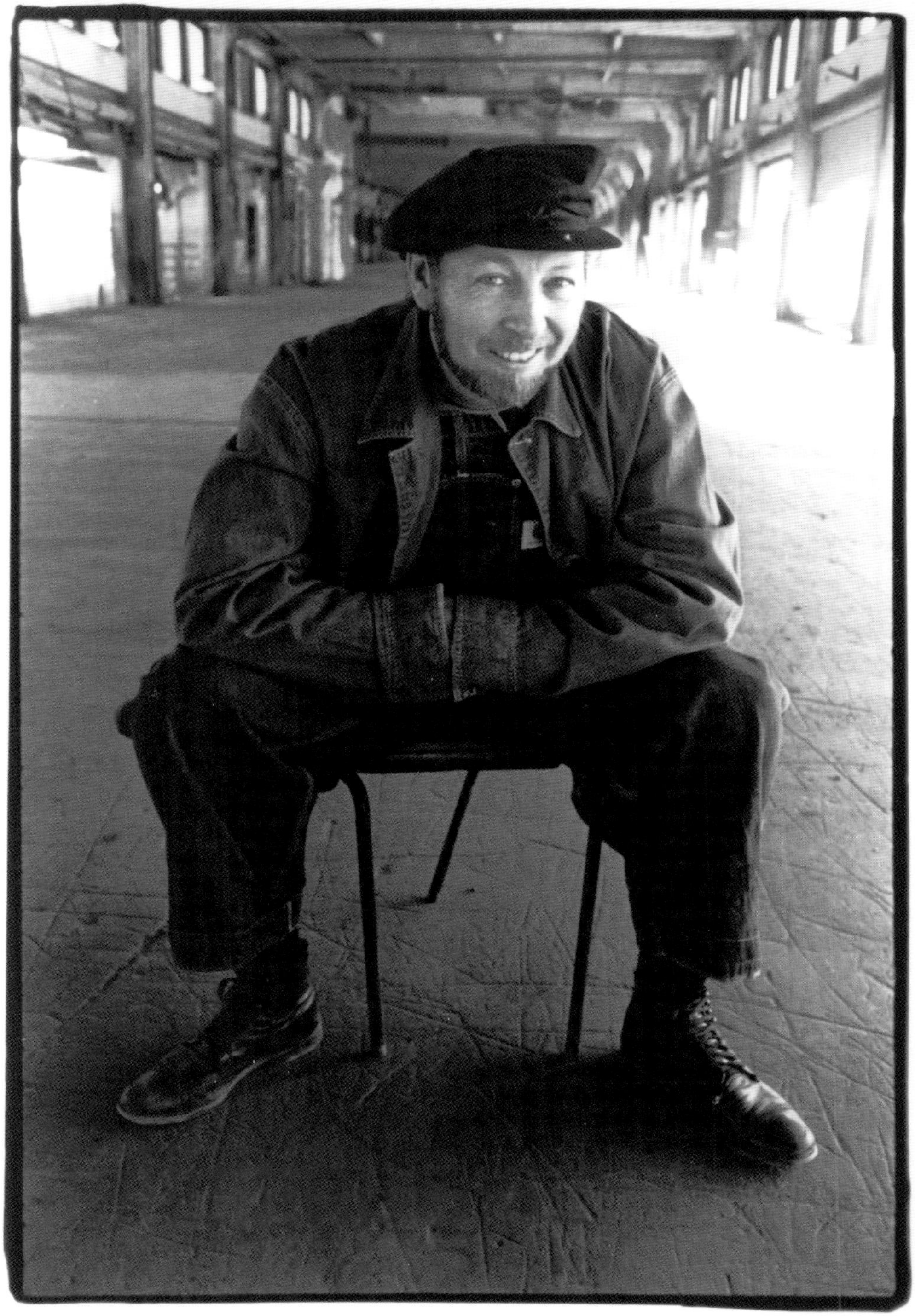

Photo Credit Michael Wilson © 1995

**RICHARD THOMPSON**

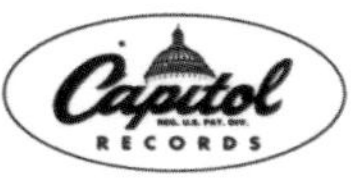

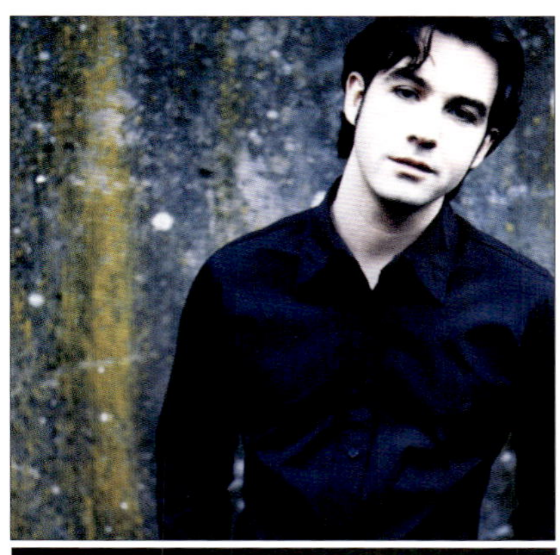

*Billboard* 200: *Duncan Sheik* (#83)
*Billboard* Hot 100: "Barely Breathing" (#16)

# "Barely Breathing," Duncan Sheik's thoughtful, snappy debut single, ruled the airwaves for months on end.

**IT WAS** an unusual singer-songwriter whose obvious influences were artists whose brooding impressionism evoked a great number of images and sentiments. But Duncan Sheik's self-titled debut album conjured up that pre-MTV era. It was a rainy day/late night record—sensitive, subtle, progressive and intimate.

"There's a certain group of beautiful records—Nick Drake's *Five Leaves Left* and *Pink Moon*, the first two Blue Nile records, but also David Sylvian's solo albums and Talk Talk's *Colour of Spring*—that are all genius works of insane sonic beauty," Sheik enthused. "I listened to them a great deal when I wrote my songs. If you looked at the production notes, all those names were bandied about quite a bit. It's something I'm profoundly affected by."

Sheik was born in South Carolina and started making music when he was "little." At 12, he had a heavy-metal cover band, and he spent his teens worshipping Seventies art-rock. "Being a musician in some capacity has always been the case—I never questioned it. But it took me a long time to become a good performer. I was very self-conscious about my voice growing up. It wasn't until I had a few years of voice lessons that I was able to get rid of my psychological and technical problems in that department. That helped me to come around, to be confident to get up and sing in front of people, but it was like pulling teeth for a while."

Sheik refined his music at Brown University, where he majored in semiotics. "I'd like to call it 'contemporary philosophy of cultural production,'" he said. "You're talking about how all these mediums, whether it's music or film or visual arts or literature, affect society and in turn how society affects these forms of culture. It's in the theoretical realm—you're looking at them from different points of view, under the psychoanalyst microscope or the feminist microscope. It's interesting if not the most practically useful discipline in the world. But a lot of people who study semiotics go on to do criticism of some kind or make films. Not so many musicians, maybe."

*Duncan Sheik* was recorded at a 150-year-old French château owned by producer Rupert Hine, best known for his work with the Waterboys, Kate Bush, Tina Turner and Howard Jones. Sheik handled vocals, guitar, keyboards and accordion. The album opened with the striking "She Runs Away," but it was "Barely Breathing" that moved breathlessly up the singles charts.

"It was the last song written for that collection," Sheik said. "It's almost a typical story that the throwaway track becomes the big hit. For me, it's the most conventional pop song on the album in some ways. I don't want to take anything away from it—I'm proud of it as a track. There is much more adventurous music on the rest of the record—but that depends on whether you think adventurous is a good thing." ■

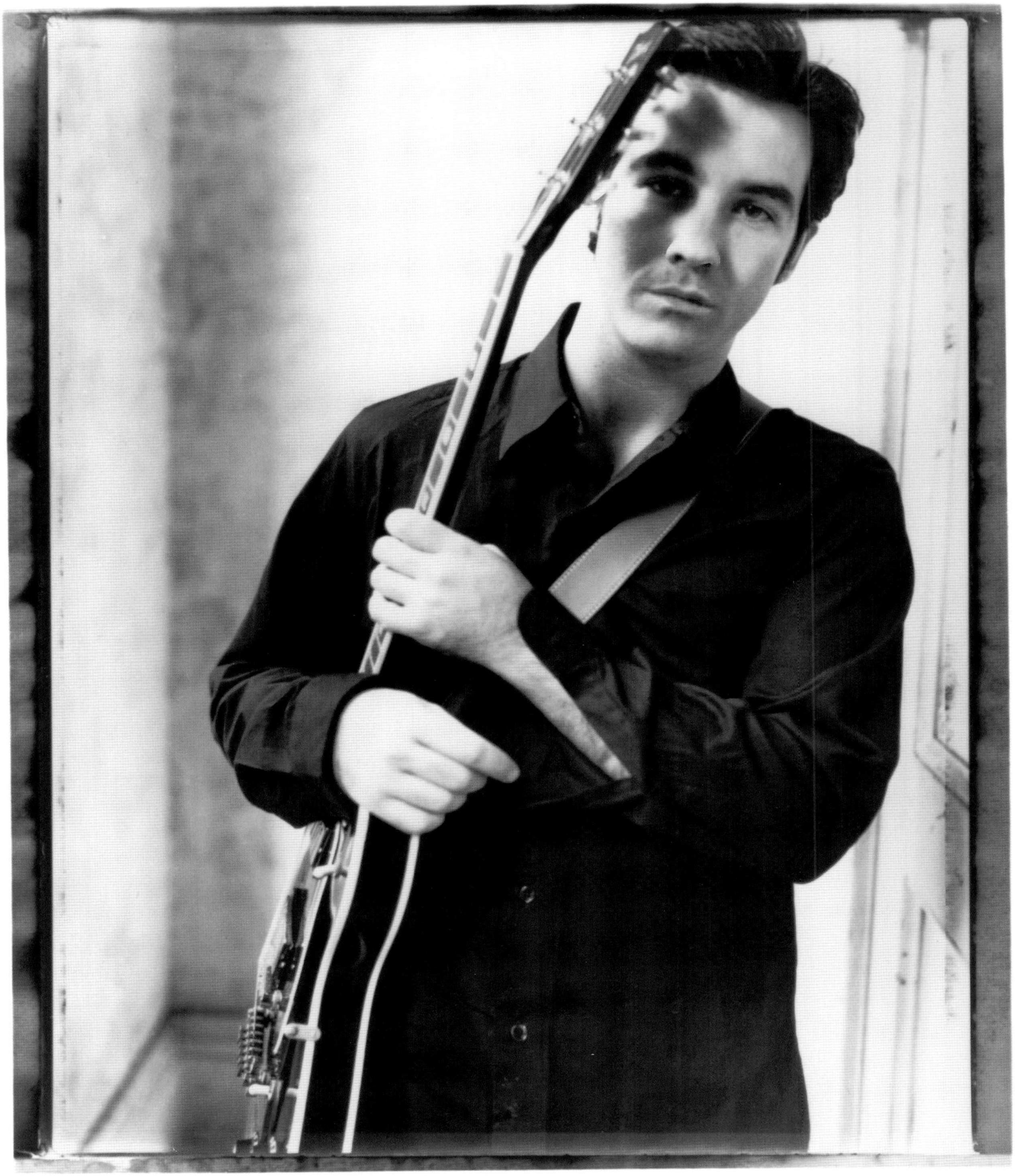

Photo: Danny Clinch

duncan sheik

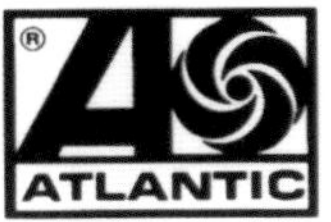

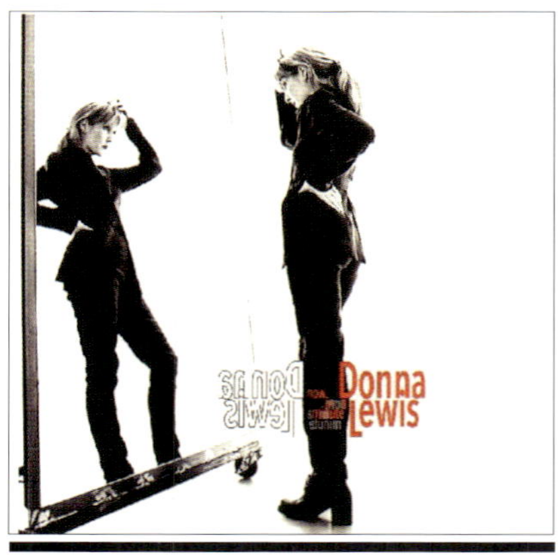


*Billboard* 200: *Now in a Minute* (#31)
*Billboard* Hot 100: "I Love You Always Forever" (#2); "Without Love" (#41)

## The catchy refrain of "I Love You Always Forever" drew global notice for Welsh singer-songwriter Donna Lewis.

**AS HER** smash "I Love You Always Forever" became a huge hit on its own merit—sans exposure via a movie soundtrack, the Olympics, a soap opera, etc.—Donna Lewis quickly made a name for herself. In *Billboard*, the track broke every record in the magazine's radio airplay detections, and it made a major impact on the international pop charts.

The single was inspired by the H.E. Bates romantic novel *Love for Lydia*—the chorus/bridge lyric ("I love you always forever/Near and far, closer together/Everywhere I will be with you/Everything I will do for you") was taken from the book. "I Love You Always Forever" was originally titled "Lydia," but it was changed for promotional reasons by the record company.

"I was writing this piece, about what it's like when you first fall in love—you're pretty naïve at the time and you think that love is going to last forever and ever. And at the same time, I was reading *Love for Lydia*. What's great is that H.E. Bates wrote in a very beautiful and descriptive way—it had this wonderful, dreamy atmosphere set in the Twenties in the English countryside, so that's what I wanted to try and use in my song."

The classically trained Lewis taught flute and performed with cover bands before her label tracked her down. "Somebody passed on my demo tape to a musician in Woodstock, who sent it to the record company. Because he wanted to produce the record with me, and the company didn't feel he was the right guy, he wouldn't give them my phone number. They were desperately trying to find me—one of the A&R reps was on the verge of hiring a private investigator."

Lewis' debut album *Now in a Minute* was co-produced by Kevin Killen (U2, Elvis Costello, Kate Bush). Lewis called her soothing synth-based sound "atmospheric pop." Her breathy, dulcet voice was girlish—she often sounded like a less unusual Cyndi Lauper. "And I'm nothing like Enya, but I can see the comparison in a way—she's ethereal and so are some of my sounds, my layering of my vocals," Lewis said.

"When I wrote 'I Love You Always Forever,' I was really pleased—people I played it for used to say, 'That's a great little song.' But never in my wildest dreams did I think it was going to be this big all over. I'm itching to do some more recording, but the record is starting to happen around the world. When we speak to friends at home and they say, 'What's going on?' and we say, 'Well, we're in Paris today and then we're in Rome tomorrow and then the States the next day,' they think, 'Oh, God, it sounds so fantastic.' But at the moment, it's just tiring." ■

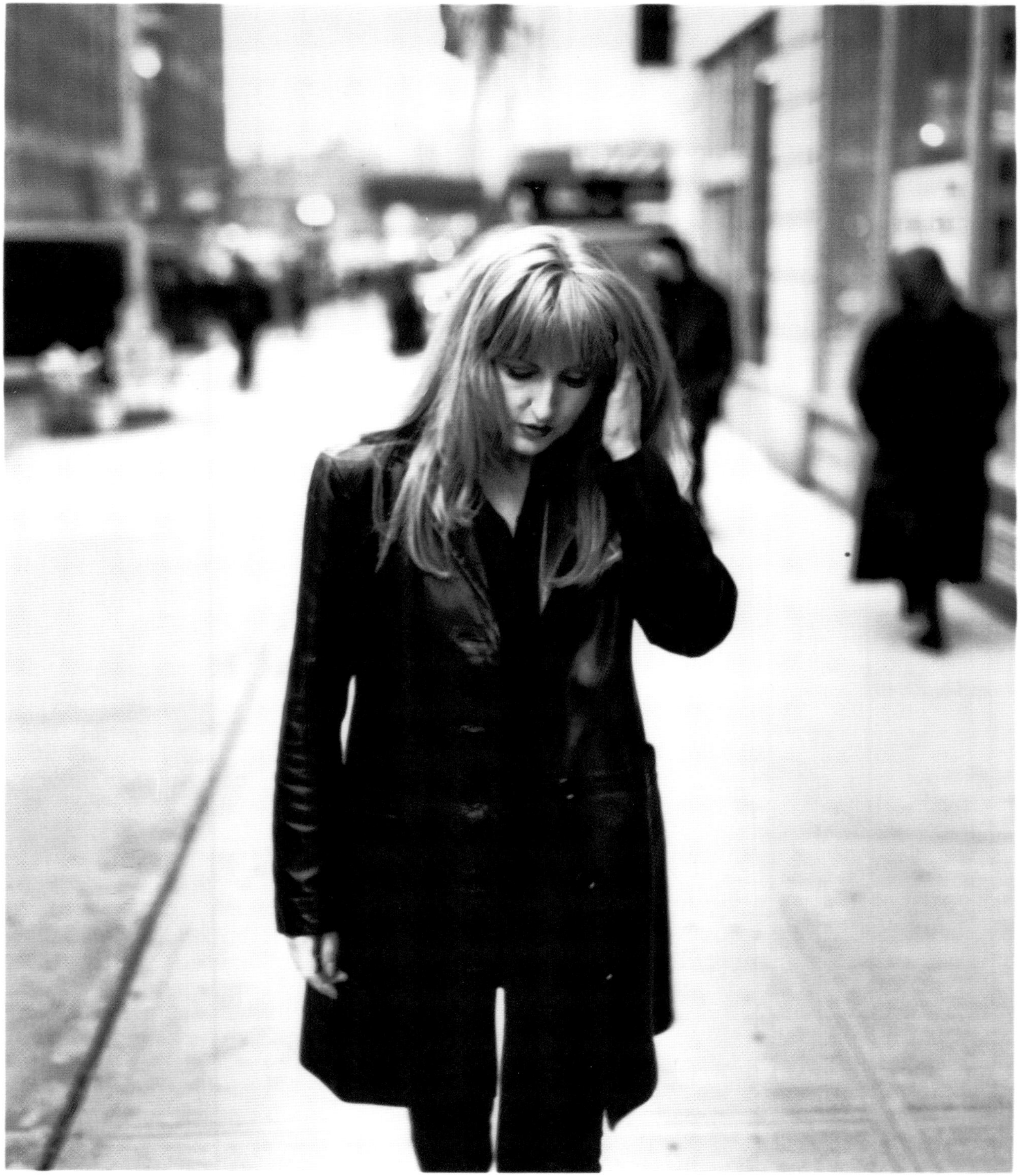

**DONNA LEWIS**

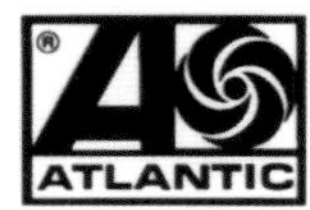


Photo Credit: NORMAN JEAN ROY

*Billboard* 200: *The Burdens of Being Upright* (#54)

## In the US and other countries, Tracy Bonham topped the modern-rock charts with the angsty "Mother Mother."

**WITH HER** hit "Mother Mother," a No. 1 track on alternative radio, Tracy Bonham joined the club of irascible female artists. And she was uncomfortable with it. "I don't see the big deal," she said. "There have been a million strong female musicians for a long time. I never felt anything different being a woman in rock—until it became such a big media thing. But it's the ongoing fad right now. It's so hyped that the pendulum is going to swing back, I know it. The public is already closing the door. Once Alanis Morissette comes out and she sells 18 billion records, it seems like everyone else pales—'Oh, yeah, we've heard that before.'"

Bonham grew up in Oregon with eight older siblings. At age 9, she received classical training on violin, but she was also drawn to rock music. "I went through a year of wearing safety pins on an army jacket—my mom hated it—and I thought I was really punk, but I wasn't at all. I had friends who listened to the Sex Pistols, that's as close as I got. I listened to bands like the Police and the Specials, the Who and the Beatles. Then I got into vocal jazz, just dabbled in everything."

Bonham made her home in Boston and learned to play guitar. A one-time student at the Berklee College of Music, she got her start in the city's vibrant club scene and was voted the best local artist. Her major label debut, *The Burdens of Being Upright*, garnered rave reviews and airplay. "To get a record deal, it's really luck—that means opportunity meets preparation," she said. "I'd been a musician over a long period of time, not knowing what path I was going to take. And then when I was 27, thank God I was ready for it. If this came to me when I was 21, no way. I didn't know what the hell I was doing."

Bonham had a knack for embellishing her rage with bouncy melodies, and "Mother Mother" juxtaposed the desire to establish a sense of independence with the terror of leaving the nest. It was singer-songwriter fare, then *wham!* a near-maniacal rant: "I'm freezing, I'm starving/I'm bleeding to death, everything's fine!"

"There are unwritten rules if you want to have a pop song, but I try not to follow any of them," she said. "I do know that I have some catchy choruses, but it wasn't intentional—'Okay, I'm going to write one that everybody's going to sing like a jingle.' Now it's very disappointing, because somebody will come up to me and go, 'So, you write any hits lately?' That's not what it's all about, like you're selling cars. I've met a lot of car salesmen lately."

With her electric guitar strapped to her 5-foot frame, Bonham looked like a kid sister. "The rug has been swept out from under my feet. I had no idea my life would change like this. All my life I practiced my craft every day, either piano, voice or violin. Now there's no free time. 'Yeah, I used to write songs—and then I got a record deal.'" ■

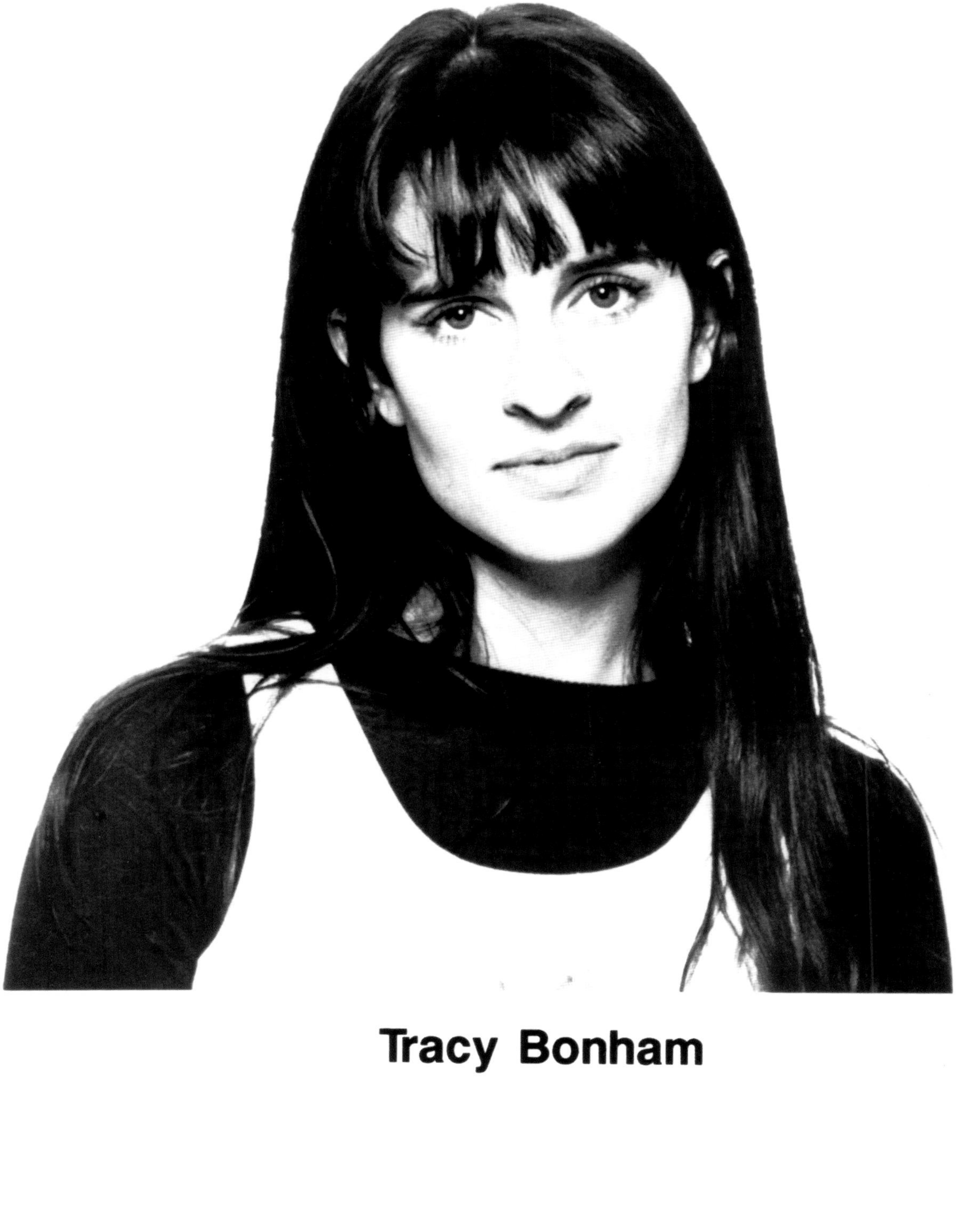

**Tracy Bonham**

Photo Credit: Frank W. Ockenfels 3

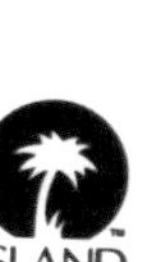

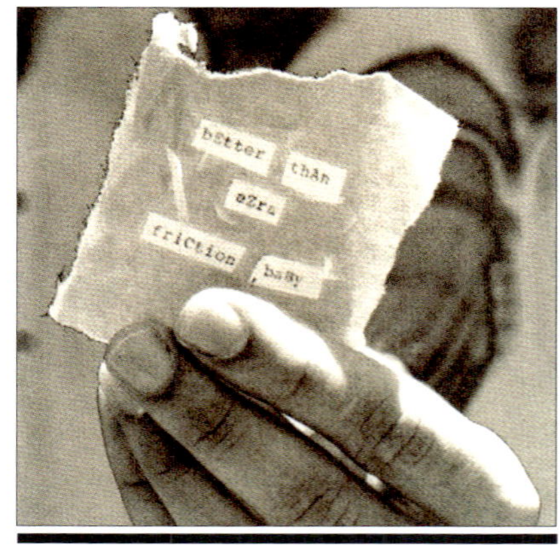


*Billboard* 200: *Friction, Baby* (#64)
*Billboard* Hot 100: "King of New Orleans" (#62); "Desperately Wanting" (#48)

## The alt-pop singles "Desperately Wanting" and "King of New Orleans" maintained attention for Better Than Ezra.

**WITH THE** debut release *Deluxe*, Better Than Ezra gained a lot of national attention in 1995. The album was certified platinum and spawned the hit "Good," which was a No. 1 record on alternative radio for more than six weeks. But success had a downside.

"We were a band that didn't have any kind of flamboyant character like a Courtney Love that was going to generate a lot of press," singer and guitarist Kevin Griffin said. "So 'Good' was perceived as one of those songs that radio made from a band that had no history. And nothing could be further from the truth—we'd been together for seven years and had toured and toured all over the place, and we had developed a great fan base before that."

In fact, before *Deluxe* was picked up by a major label, Better Than Ezra had already sold 30,000 units independently. The Louisiana threesome was back with a sophomore effort, *Friction, Baby*, to try and get set apart in a world of one-hit wonders. "Desperately Wanting" snagged radio airplay, with Griffin's crashing guitar riff and yearning vocal beefing up the hook. "King of New Orleans" was about "gutter punks," the controversial homeless kids who lived in the French Quarter. The video was shot in an abandoned building on Annunciation Street.

"I saw their plight as an analogy for what happens in everyday life," Griffin explained. "The wealthy landowners don't like seeing them in the French Quarter, so they complain to the city council, and the councilmen complain to the police department, and the police come down on these kids who are really just the scapegoats for the frustration that tends to be passed down to subordinates.

"You can look at it as a law of physics—matter is neither created nor destroyed, it just changes form. People transfer negative energy, and it comes to rest on the most defenseless people—in this case, these gutter punks who've never had any love in their lives and whose only family is this loose network of kids. If there's a message to the song, it's being tolerant of people who aren't like you and seeing their weaknesses."

Better Than Ezra had a slightly different lineup—drummer Travis McNabb had replaced Cary Bonnecaze—as the market got more competitive. "Ten years ago, if you had a platinum-selling album, you were suddenly an established artist or you could rest on whatever laurels you perceived you had," Griffin said. "But these days there are so many bands, you can't afford to slack off. Not that we want to, but that's the nature of the biz." ■

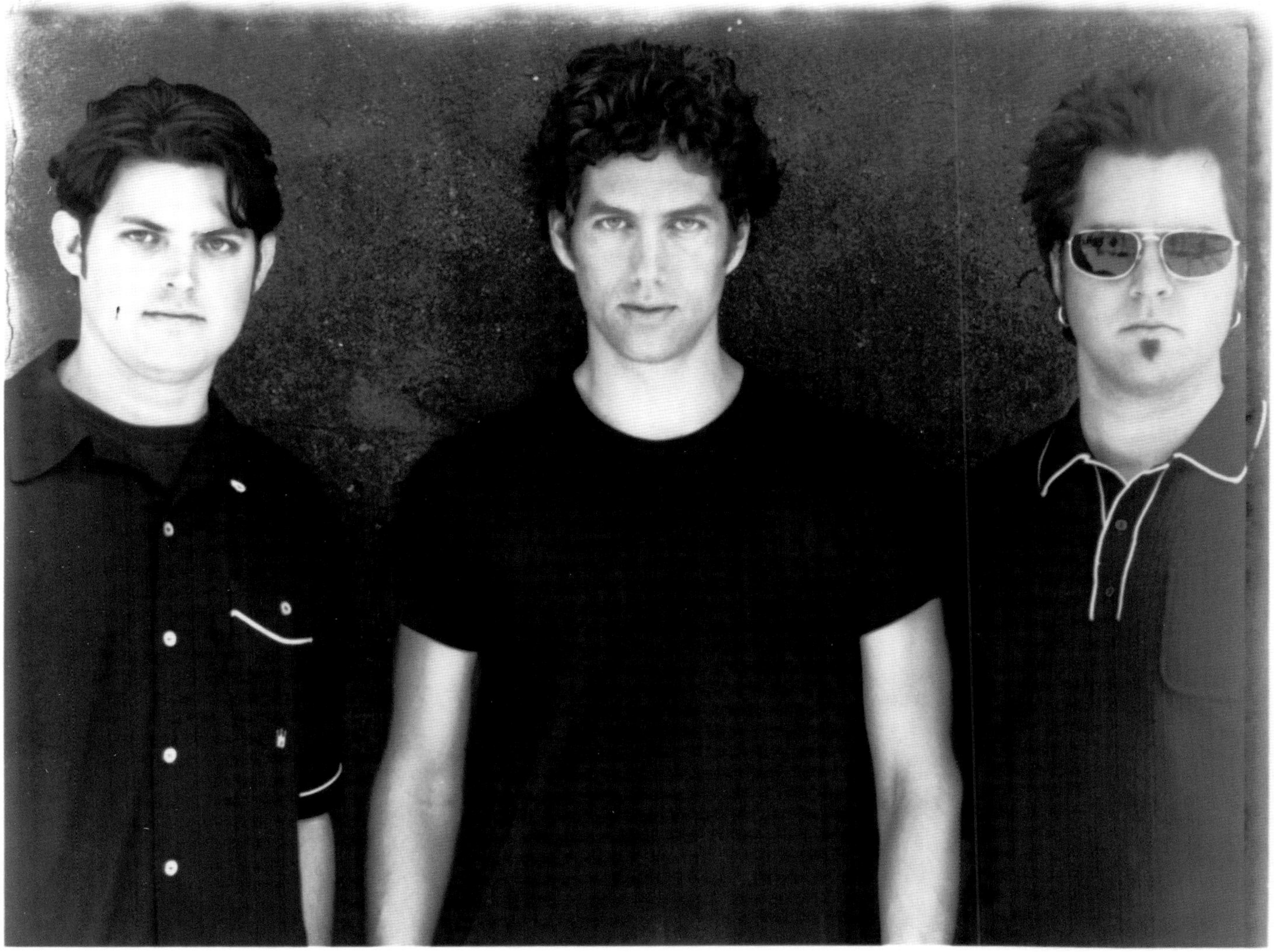

PHOTO CREDIT FRANK OCKENFELS

L R : TOM DRUMMOND, KEVIN GRIFFIN, TRAVIS McNABB

# bEtter thAn eZra

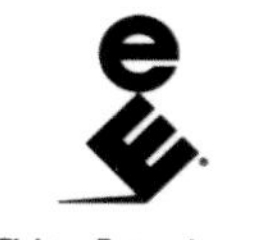


EEG

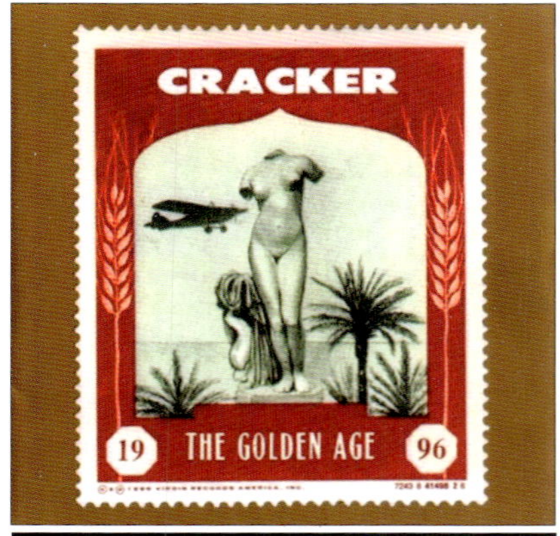


*Billboard* 200: *The Golden Age* (#63)

## Cracker's *The Golden Age* brought to pass another irreverent hit with the rampaging "I Hate My Generation."

**THE ALBUM** *The Golden Age* heralded the return of Cracker. The first single was the unapologetic rocker "I Hate My Generation," in which David Lowery bemoaned the sorry state of his peers—and had a great time doing it. "The song is about being pissed-off at hearing pissed-off songs—that's a pretty complicated thing to explain to people," Lowery said. "It just came out in five minutes. My first question after we wrote it was, 'Is that too stupid?' And everybody said, 'No, it's great.'"

It was reminiscent of the capers of Lowery's previous band, Camper Van Beethoven, or the early Cracker single "Teen Angst (What the World Needs Now)" with its memorable lyric: "What the world needs now is another folksinger/Like I need a hole in my head." "I get pinned with that 'misanthropic bastard' tag, and that's always bugged me," Lowery said. "It's people who just hear one song on the radio or read about it, or other musicians. That's how they've perceived me for a decade. I've always felt like a good author or filmmaker will use irony or sarcasm or humor or absurdity or just completely go off on a tangent that doesn't make any sense, to tell a story."

Joan Osborne sang backing vocals on the rousing, gospel-smacked "Nothing to Believe In." "A lot of radio stations switched to that song—they found 'I Hate My Generation' too punk rock," Lowery said. "Which is great. I just love that idea, because I'm 35. Everybody's been playing punk rock on these alternative stations, so we do something I think is real punk rock, and a lot of people are going, 'Well, that's a little hard for us, we're gonna play the softer track.'"

*The Golden Age* established a balance between the cynical moments and heartfelt songs—some even featuring a string section. Lowery felt encouraged. "Our actual fans, people who've bought the records, understand what I'm doing. But you go to a Cracker show and a quarter of the audience wants to hear the singles. This goes back to Camper Van Beethoven days. Our fans wanted to hear 'O Death,' and the oblivious frat boys would show up and scream for 'Take the Skinheads Bowling.' Now I bet people will figure out that we're more complex than they've assumed. We don't always have to have wacky punk-rock songs to get on the radio anymore." ■

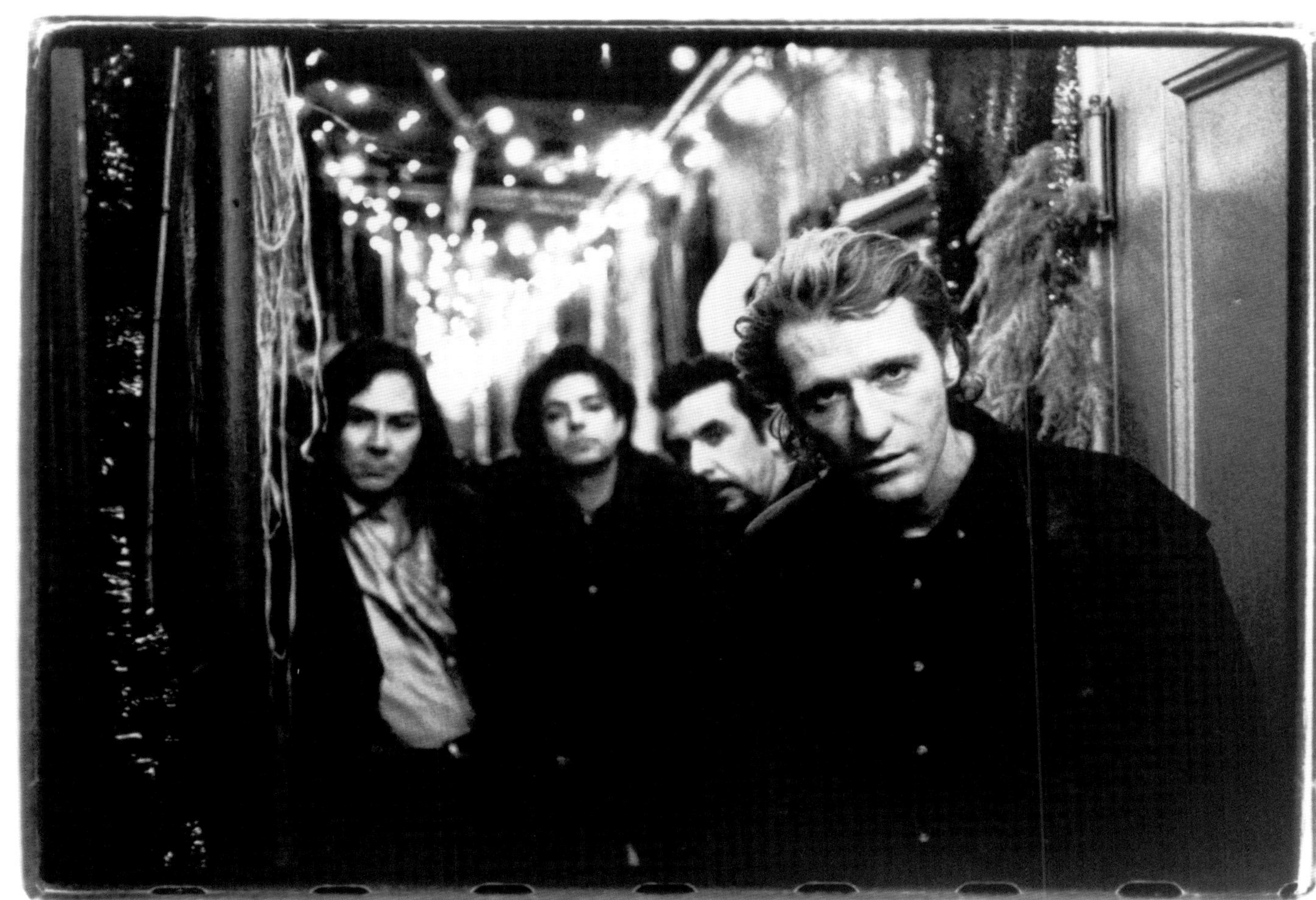

Photo Credit: Danny Clinch 2/96

**CRACKER**

Virgin

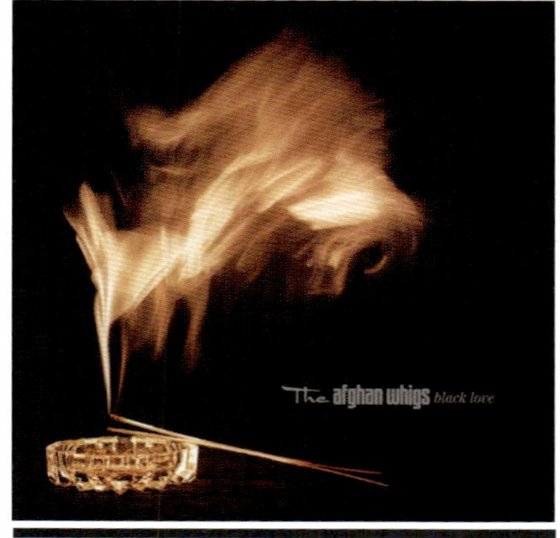


*Billboard* 200: *Black Love* (#79)

## The Afghan Whigs acknowledged R&B while dispatching Greg Dulli's apprehensive accounts of erotic torment.

**ON RECORD**, Greg Dulli had cast himself as a swaggering stud, a misogynistic heel and a bitter soul with a suave allure searching for meaning in a lying, deceitful world. The press anointed him "alternative rock's most complex frontman," but the leader of the Afghan Whigs questioned that point.

"I'm not writing anything that anybody couldn't understand if they thought about it long enough," Dulli said. "Most of the songs are inspired by ordinary people in extraordinary circumstances. You're not given any credit for your imagination or your social observation. People tend to dwell on the more sensational aspects—'Wow, this bastard is you!'—when the moments of transcendence or levity are ignored in the process."

The Afghan Whigs had verged on big-time status for a few years. The Ohio band was signed to Sub Pop and released four albums, playing its own hotshot brand of haunting guitar rock. The band survived the leap to a major label with 1993's acclaimed *Gentlemen*, a distillation of the emotional and physical cruelties in a failed relationship.

The quartet returned with the darker, more free-wheeling *Black Love*. The album stunned with sludgy, spiraling guitars and frayed vocals at one moment, only to seethe with melancholic strings, keyboards, ambient sounds and soft crooning the next. The grandeur was gripping at times, and *Black Love* came off like a cinematic song suite.

"When I was a kid, I wanted to figure out two things in my life—how do you make movies and how do you make records?" Dulli said. "Making movies was my first obsession. Once I figured out how to tell a story, it carried over into how I write music. That influenced me as much as other records. It's hard to say without sounding pretentious, but that's something to aspire to."

*Black Love* was a treatise on the conflict between morality and desire. Dulli described the adversarial "Honky's Ladder" as "the ultimate revenge fantasy"—the line driven by his howling was "Got u where I want u motherfucker!" "It was based on brattiness, not commercial motivation," the singer laughed. "In a perverse way, I wanted to see if they would play it on the radio. They bleeped the regular version in some places. The cleaned-up edit is probably naughtier—it's a moan lifted from a porno movie!"

"Going to Town," about lovers who set their city on fire, had trappings of mid-Seventies funk, a Stevie Wonder-esque hook. Dulli always combined his tunes with a groove, and few of the Whigs' alternative colleagues shared that penchant for Sixties R&B and classic Motown. There were risks for a Midwestern white rocker drawing from sweet soul music's dark, sensual passion.

"You end up answering to semi- or over-educated white men who consider themselves liberals," Dulli mused. "The irony isn't lost on me. Just go back to the Rolling Stones—they were so avid in their pursuit of sounding like a Black group, and they got called minstrels. We're not doing anything that hasn't been done before. We might not be able to do it like Bootsy (Collins), but it's better than being Pat Boone." ■

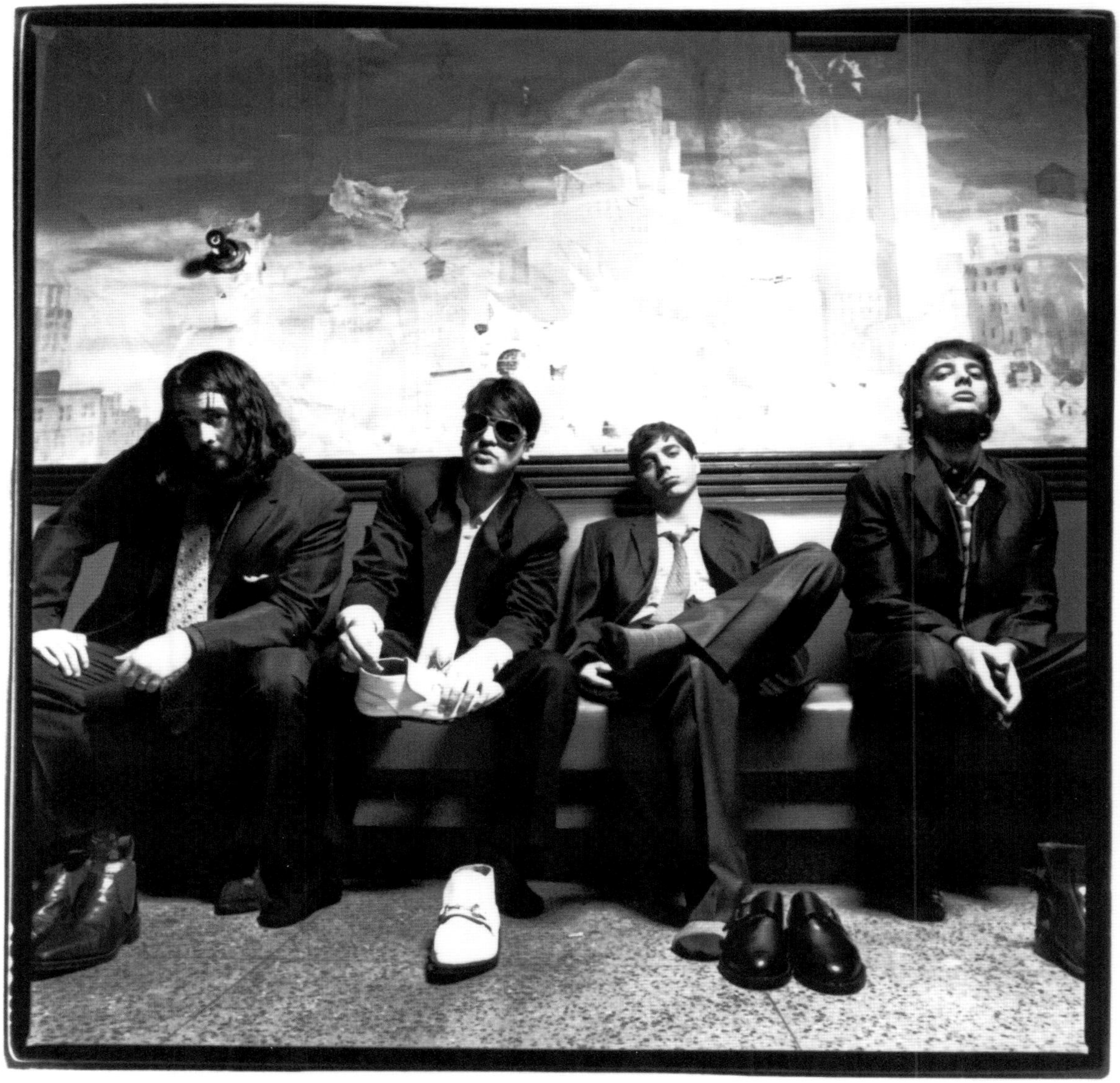

PHOTO CREDIT DANNY CLINCH 1996

L R : JOHN CURLEY GREG DULLI, PAUL BUCHIGNANI, RICK McCOLLUM

# The afghan whigs

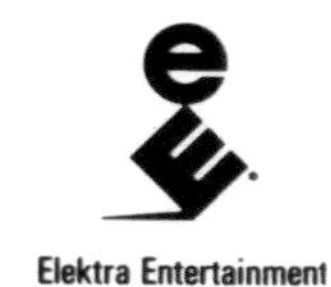

Elektra Entertainment

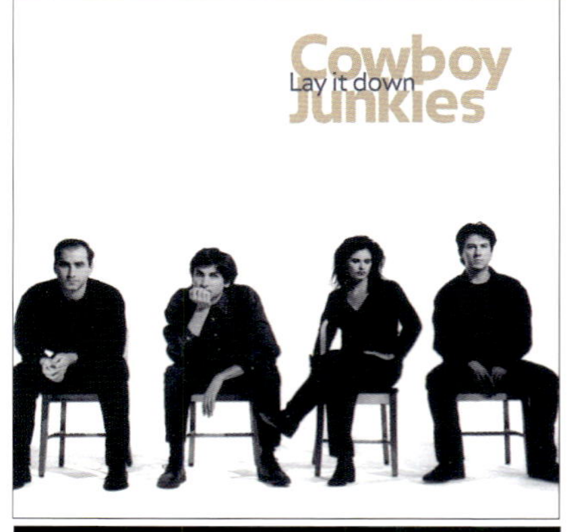


*Billboard* 200: *Lay It Down* (#55)

## The guitar-drenched *Lay It Down* heralded a return to Cowboy Junkies' sonic origins and incipient influences.

**WITH ITS** stark beauty and simplicity, Cowboy Junkies' *The Trinity Sessions*, featuring a distinctively narcotic reading of the Lou Reed/ Velvet Underground classic "Sweet Jane," sparked a sensation in 1988. The hallmarks were Margo Timmins' haunting, detached vocals and her brother Michael Timmins' languorous yet tasteful guitar playing. But that signature sound had been virtually unheard since.

"Over the last few records, we began to bring in a lot of different outside musicians—I wanted to have a bit of space for them so I was concentrating on rhythm playing," Michael Timmins said. "Also, I got into writing songs more heavily."

*Lay It Down* heralded a return to the Junkies' country-blues-on-Valium roots. The Canadian band went to Athens, Georgia, to work with John Keane (R.E.M., Indigo Girls). "His studio is in a big-porched house," Timmins said. "We wanted an environment that would add something to the recording process. We'd always liked Georgia. There's a laziness to the lifestyle—you can't move too fast because it's too hot. It seemed perfect for us.

"We wanted to get back down to the four of us playing again, start a new cycle. By stripping the band down, more space appeared to play a lot of guitar. And I've been able to hone my composing style so that it's a bit simpler in a structural way. I feel like I've become a songwriter. I can say that now without blushing."

The song "A Common Disaster" was revered by the group's diverse, dedicated following. "It's an attitude song, sort of tongue-in-cheek," Timmins said. "'Common' can mean everyday or shared." Though it was spiced with subtle organ, strings and Keane's pedal steel, *Lay It Down* was the most bare-bones record the Junkies had made since they recorded their first album in the family garage.

"You almost have to survive your success," Timmins said. "*The Trinity Sessions* was a great surprise for us, and then it became a matter of living up to that. We feel we've always done that on an artistic level, but the commercial side of things works on sales. It's been a constant battle to keep both sides happy. I think we've done a pretty good job of that. Now we're beginning to attract a younger audience that would have been 10 years old when *The Trinity Sessions* came out. That's a neat feeling." ■

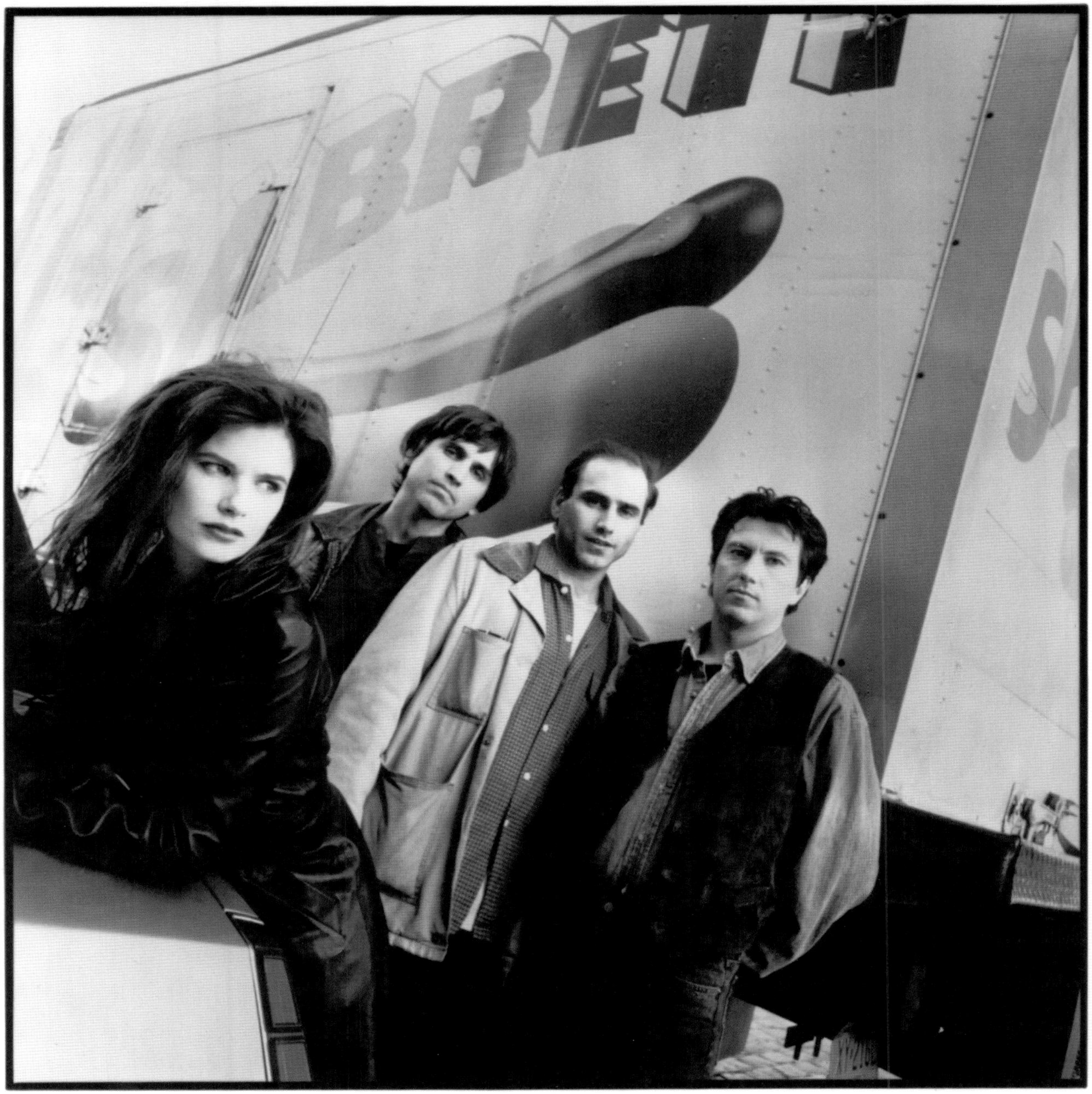

Photo Credit: Guzman

Margo Timmins Michael Timmins Peter Timmins Alan Anton

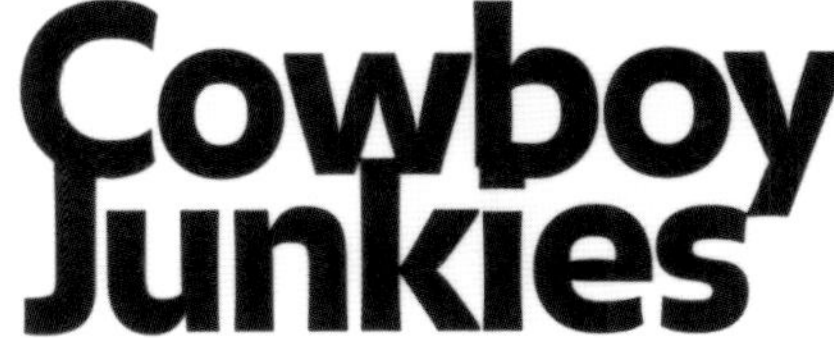


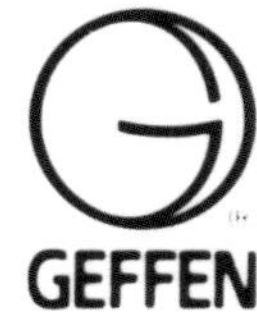

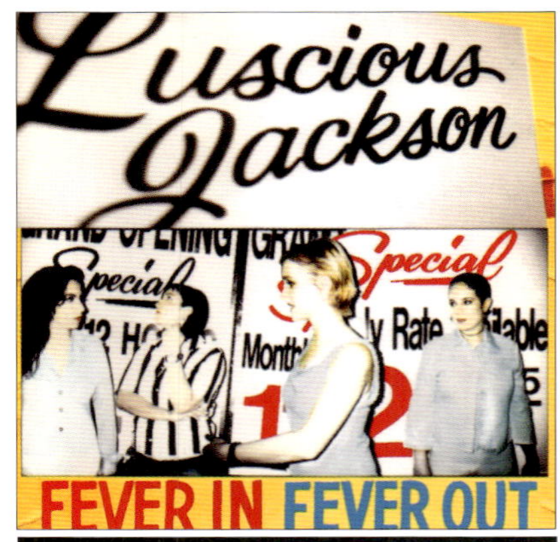


*Billboard* 200: *Fever In Fever Out* (#72)
*Billboard* Hot 100: "Naked Eye" (#36)

## The casual charm of "Naked Eye" extended Luscious Jackson's body of friends and supporters substantially.

**WITH SAMPLE-HEAVY** collages of hip-hop informed experimentation, Luscious Jackson's first album, 1994's *Natural Ingredients*, re-created the feel of New York from a uniquely female perspective. After two years of playing Lollapalooza, touring with R.E.M. and selling some 200,000 albums, the band took a sophisticated step on *Fever In Fever Out*.

"We thought it would be a good idea to emphasize live instrumentation in the studio," vocalist, bassist and guitarist Jill Cunniff said. "We'd played as a band for three or four years and never spent time exploring sounds and using good equipment. That's the reason we worked with Daniel—he's good at that stuff."

In shaping the soundscapes of *Fever In Fever Out*, the band had enlisted Daniel Lanois, producer of such monster artists as U2, Peter Gabriel and Bob Dylan. They recorded the album in New Orleans at his studio and in New York City at drummer Kate Schellenbach's West Village studio loft. Radio and MTV came around to the single "Naked Eye," which featured enchanting harmonies and a swanky groove. "We've always had a lot of press," Cunniff said. "But 'Naked Eye' has given us our big boost, a whole other level of exposure. It's pretty amazing, how far radio goes."

*Fever In Fever Out* featured a guest appearance by Brand New Heavies diva N'Dea Davenport and, unexpectedly, the bittersweet soprano of country maverick Emmylou Harris. "That made total sense," Cunniff said. "She's such a great woman, it was so comfortable in the beginning. She came in and liked the music. She loves to sing, anywhere, anytime."

Like her bandmates, Cunniff led a punk-rock lifestyle of the early Eighties. Born and raised in New York City, she, Schellenbach and vocalist/guitarist Gabby Glaser came of age in the Lower East Side punk scene. "We're nutty New Yorkers, but we definitely pursue modes of relaxation," Cunniff said. "We're very mellow. I practice yoga and I hope to move to the country sometime soon. I'm really into health and fitness."

According to Cunniff, the band's primary lyricist, the album's themes were more introspective, yet the members of Luscious Jackson found themselves forced into women-in-rock discourses. "The stupidest questions are 'Why aren't you more angry?' or 'Why aren't you more like the type of woman that we've seen?' That tees me right off," Cunniff said. "I look forward to the day when women don't have to fit into a mode like 'angry woman' or 'sexy woman' or 'tough woman.' On this record, I find we've been accepted as we are a lot more. Our fans are pretty great—a lot of girls and a lot of cool guys. No macho problem or anything that bugs me. They get it—they accept us as normal girls." ■

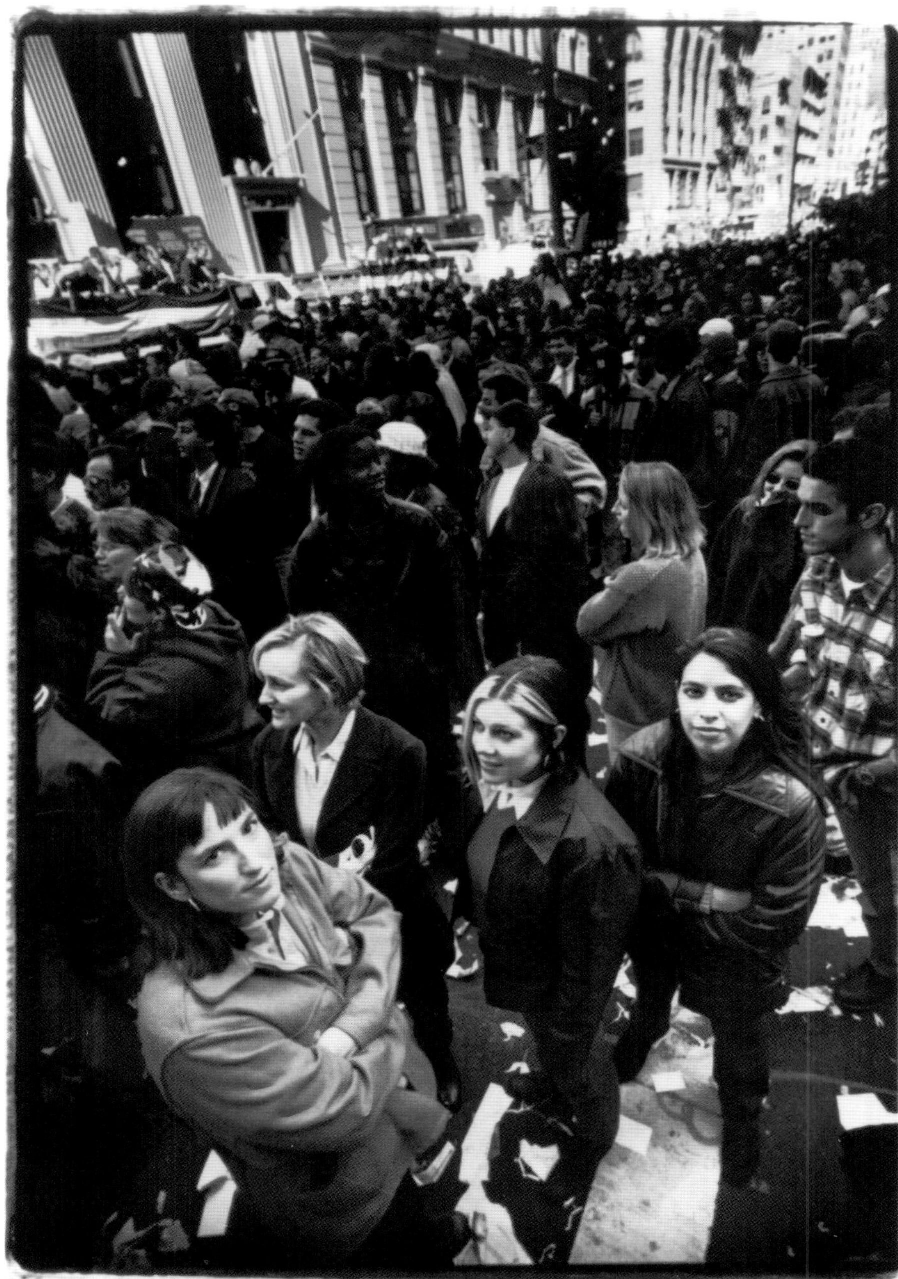

Photo Credit: Danny Clinch/1996

L-R: Kate Schellenbach Vivian Trimble Jill Cunniff Gabby Glaser

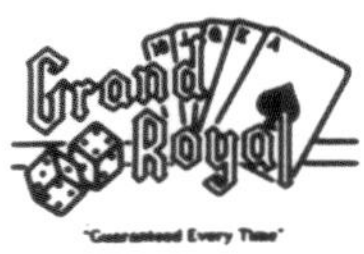


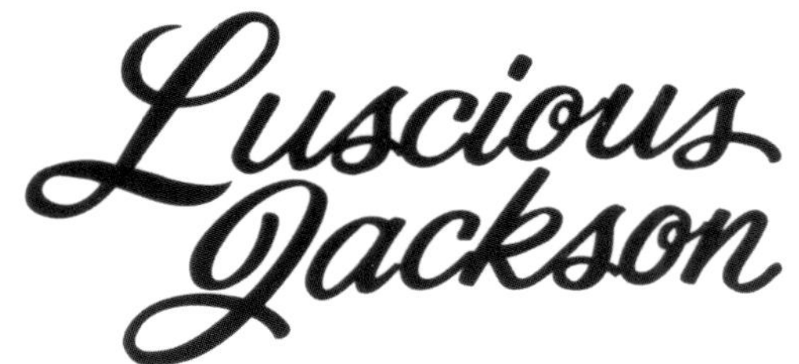


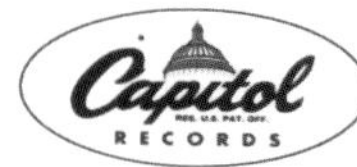

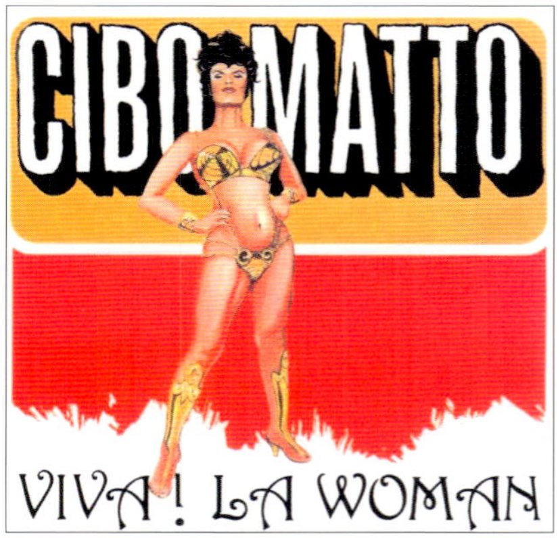

# Cibo Matto's food-focused music, reflecting the melting-pot ways of New York City, was just a matter of taste.

**THE DEBUT** album *Viva! La Woman* by Cibo Matto made an appetizing impression—keyboardist/sampler Yuka Honda and singer Miho Hatori were giddily preoccupied with food, devoting songs to the fascinating powers of "White Pepper Ice Cream" and "Beef Jerky" in choppy Japanese-accented English. The duo's cheeky charm established Cibo Matto (Italian for "crazy food") with New York art-scene tastemakers like John Zorn and Beastie Boys. "I probably wouldn't have become a musician if I didn't live in New York," Honda explained. "It was destiny to move there. I was thrown into the pond of musicians and started to play music."

An album of off-kilter sampling, funk and hardcore, *Viva! La Woman* ranged from the quixotic pop of "Sugar Water" to the rowdy riot-grrrl rap of "Birthday Cake." "Know Your Chicken" was crammed with strange beats, dub grooves, loops, riffs and found sounds. Composing with samplers was an art form requiring heavy musical skills, Honda maintained—instead of refining songs through jams and rehearsals, she labored over them for weeks in her living room, then performed the samples live. "Our songs were written to be played live in tiny places like CBGB's Gallery," she said. "People are mistaken if they think sampling is just patching together some cool old music."

*Viva! La Woman* spent six weeks at No. 1 on the *CMJ* charts, compiled by the music trade magazine aimed at college radio stations, but cute and quirky Honda and Hatori were disillusioned when they were tagged as a novelty act. "Definitely the fact that there are not many Japanese female musicians in America make people put us into one little box," Honda said. "We're getting sick of people not understanding food as an art form." "People always expect you to choose sides between digital or analog, old-school or new-school, even between Chinese and Italian food," Hatori joked. "Well, we eat everything." ■

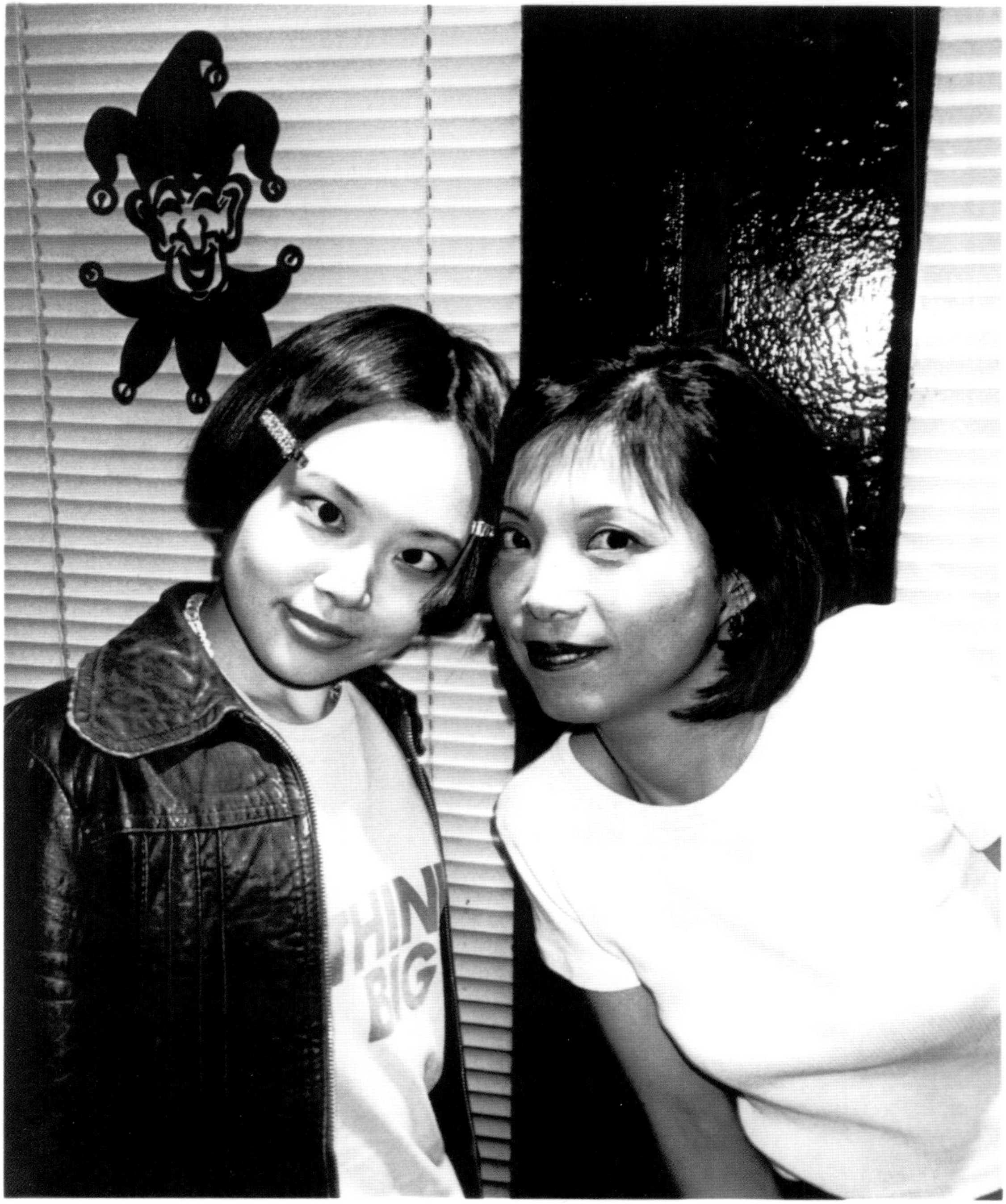

Photo Credit: Dave Aron

Miho

Yuka

# CIBO MATTO

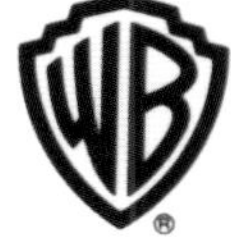

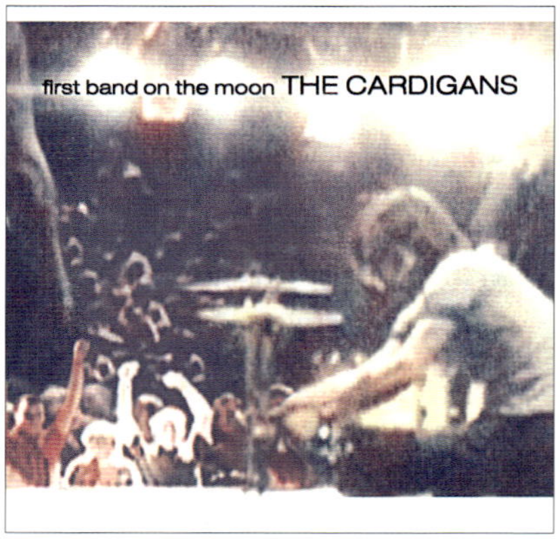

*Billboard* 200: *First Band on the Moon* (#35)

## The Cardigans, a Swedish quintet, found immense US airplay as well as international success with "Lovefool."

**THE BREEZY** single "Lovefool" endeared the Cardigans to America—the "Love me love me/Say that you love me" chorus was all over radio and MTV. The song was a highlight of *First Band on the Moon*, a blithe collection of cool Sixties lounge-pop grooves that revolved around Nina Persson's winsome vocals. How did the Cardigans become Sweden's newest musical export? "I never listened very much to Swedish music sung in Swedish—it's very difficult to write good lyrics in Swedish," bassist and co-lyricist Magnus Sveningsson said. "Most of the acts who sing in Swedish are mainstream—the Swedish Mariah Carey, the Swedish Bob Dylan, whatever. It's not very interesting."

The Cardigans' candy-coated sound was shaped when the members hooked up with producer Tore Johannson, who introduced them to his retro tastes and vintage instruments. "We existed as a band for one year when we were asked to come down to his studio in 1993," Sveningsson said. "We were in our 20s, very green—we didn't know anything about the music business. He's older than us, one of those people you respect a lot—he's not very social or talkative, but he has an aura of power. We didn't have a strong identity at that time, but he pointed out what we were good at. Ever since, he's been our biggest influence, much more than any other group or record."

"Lovefool" was cute fun—it was used in the film *Romeo + Juliet*—but on "Been It," the words were as dreary as the music was cheery. "That's one of the things I like the most about our little band," Sveningsson said. "This happy love song has a bit of a monster hidden beneath the surface. Maybe that's the Scandinavian temperament. People thought ABBA wrote silly love songs, but if you really listen, knowing that it was actually two couples in the band, those lyrics have self-denial going on—sad lyrics were matched to perfect pop songs. In that sense, I hope we have something in common—ABBA was one of the best bands in the world, ever."

In addition to ABBA, the Cardigans had diverse influences, ranging from Eighties British pop bands to the heavy metal sounds that Sveningsson and guitarist Peter Svensson preferred as youths. *First Band on the Moon* included a tasteful rendition of "Iron Man," Black Sabbath's anthem. "Black Sabbath is the perfect group for us to cover. Those hard-rock riffs might seem the most significant thing about the songs, but beneath them they had a deep influence from British folk music. We've added some influence from Swedish folk music, which is also quite sad and melancholic. I don't think we could do an AC/DC cover, for instance. I love AC/DC, but their music is much more blues-oriented—I don't think it would fit. We are not a blues band, I can tell you." ■

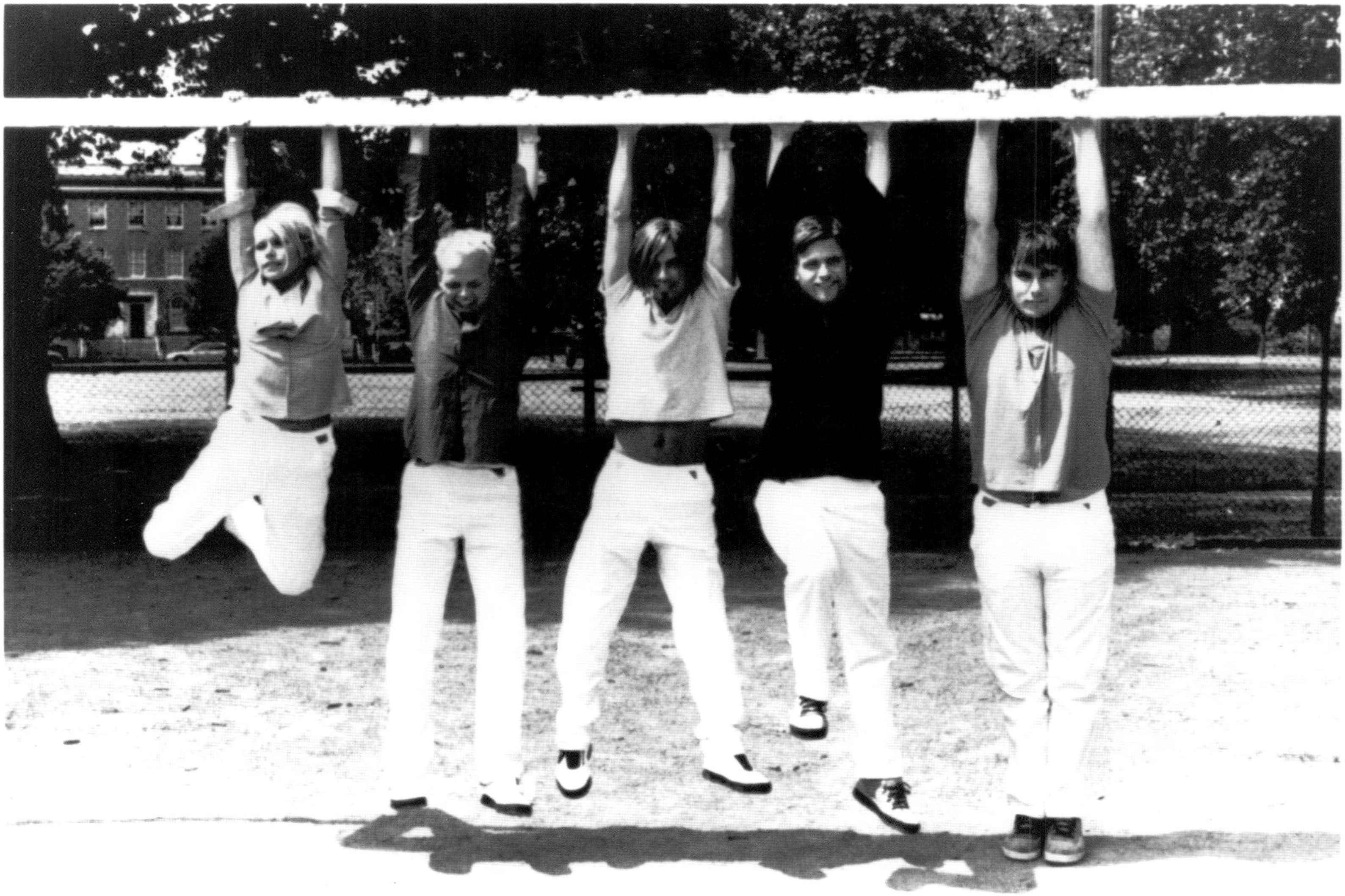

THE CARDIGANS

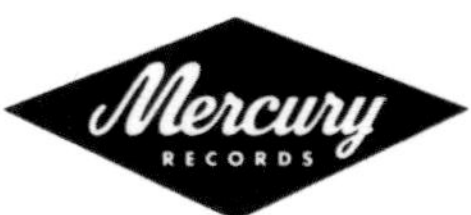

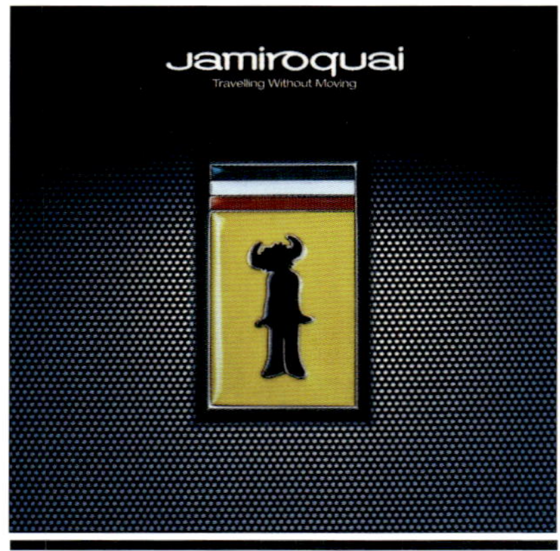


*Billboard* 200: *Travelling without Moving* (#24)

# An award-winning music video for "Virtual Insanity" secured a place for Jamiroquai in the pop music pantheon.

**THE MOST** successful soul act in Britain, Jamiroquai came out of the same UK funk scene as Soul II Soul and the Brand New Heavies. A 1993 debut album made lead singer Jason Kay a loud, opinionated and controversial star in Europe. The band sought stateside success, sounding more playful on *Travelling without Moving*. There was a sharper pop sense, and a reverence for Stevie Wonder—the charismatic Kay sounded just like him.

"Mentioning my name and Stevie Wonder's in the same sentence is really flattering," Kay said. "But I can't understand why anyone would make the comparison." "Our new songs are more like a light beer than a heavy ale, good for the summer," keyboardist Toby Smith added with a laugh. "We were at risk of being branded as eco-conscious troubadours, so we concentrated on the more funky, dancy, party aspects of our music."

The multiracial quintet cranked out a dense "all-natural" mixture of soul, jazz, funk and even disco. But the focus was on Kay, a free-wheeling funky white boy. With an oversize hat concealing everything but a scruffy goatee and ponytail, he established an ethos of "get down, get stoned," fronting trippy booty-shaking tunes like the sunny "Cosmic Girl" and "Alright."

The spirit of Wonder, Kool & the Gang and Earth, Wind & Fire soared through the jams, and young fans who had no memories of late-Seventies funk found Jamiroquai's silky grooves to be infections. A vertigo-inducing promotional video for "Virtual Insanity" was named Video of the Year at the MTV Video Music Awards, and the song won a Grammy for Best Pop Performance by a Duo or Group with Vocal. ■

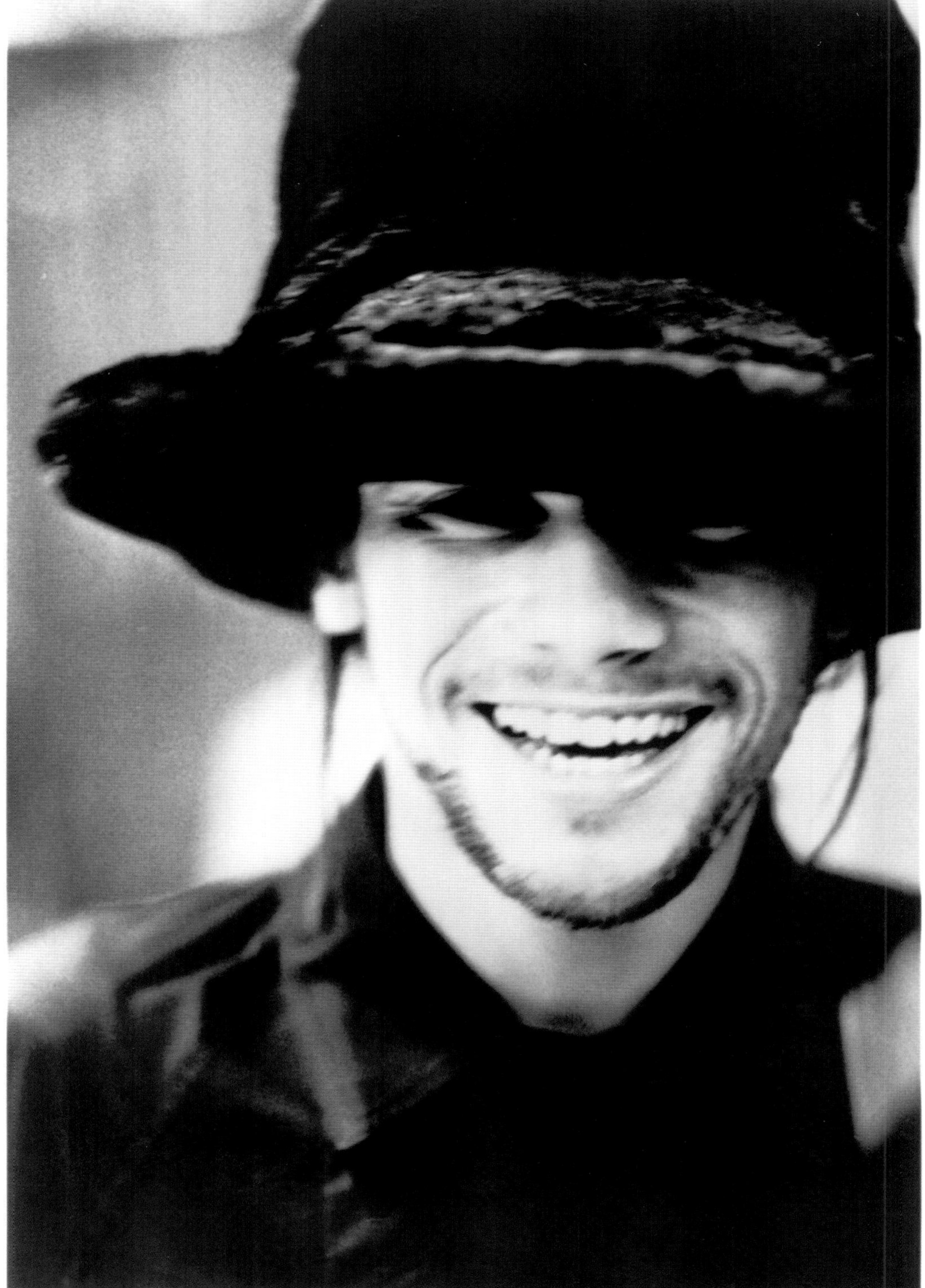

Photo Credit: Ellen Von Unwerth



WORK

JAMIROQUAI

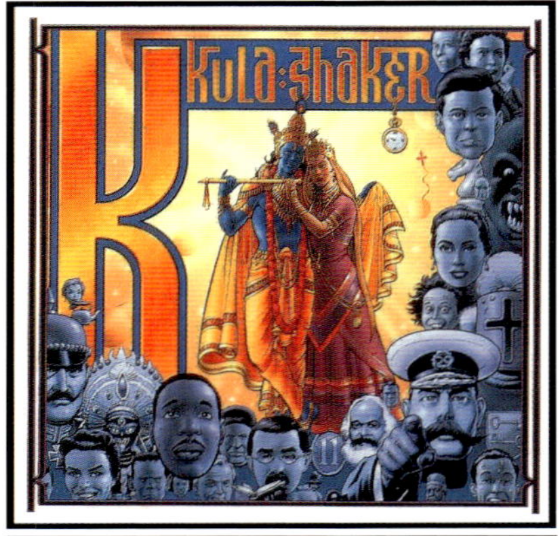

*Billboard* 200: *K* (#200)

# Infused with Indian mysticism, the neo-psychedelic rock of "Tattva" drew accolades for Britain's Kula Shaker.

**FANS DIDN'T** need to get their ears checked if they'd misheard the lyrics to Kula Shaker's alt-rock hit "Tattva." The refrain was sung partly in Sanskrit: "*Tattva, acintya bheda abheda Tattva.*" Misunderstood versions of the words had reached the ears of guitarist and singer Crispian Mills. "The first one I heard was from (Oasis guitarist) Noel Gallagher—he insisted it was really 'Ginger Baker bagel snack bar.' That did it for me—from then on, I found myself singing it!"

Gallagher also anointed Kula Shaker as "the best band in Britain"—Mills and his bandmates were huge in the UK with a blend of retro psychedelic rock, ancient Indian mantras and pop melodies. The quartet emerged on the US music scene with the release of the debut recording *K*. Mills was the son of Hayley Mills, the Sixties Disney teen ingenue who starred in the movies *Pollyanna* and *The Parent Trap*. With the humble meditativeness of a seeker, he credited Kula Shaker's success to his immersion in eastern spirituality.

"I headed to India for enlightenment in 1993 and became fascinated with Hindu culture. I didn't have one moment of great inspiration where it all suddenly made sense—you're always learning. It's an important side to the band's character, but people have made a big thing out of it—for young pop stars to go to India reminds them of something that happened in the Sixties. But if you feel the need to present your views and express your feelings lyrically, you can't stop yourself. You have to do what's natural."

*K* was derivative but undeniably enjoyable. Warm electric guitar and swirling Hammond organ merged with tamboura, table and sarod. "Hey Dude" was catchy psychedelia, and "Govinda" was a rocking version of a Sanskrit mantra. And "Tattva" rated as one of the year's best singles. Mills described Kula Shaker's sound as the best elements from the past few decades of British pop.

"You can hear that whole Sixties thing, obviously—the setup we're using with the Hammond and harmonies, getting right into the melodic trip. But we certainly took a lot rhythmically from the Seventies, those grooves we laid down. From the Eighties, we learned a lot about mistakes! We did like that whole Manchester thing—the Stone Roses crossed over between dance and guitar bands, and you couldn't do that before."

Mills swore by numerology, planetary movements and the might of the letter K—drawings of King Kong, Martin Luther King Jr., Krishna, JFK, Katharine Hepburn and others appeared on the cover of the CD. How was he dealing with rock stardom? "I'm getting to the point where I could have a full-on egomaniacal fantasy—if I wanted to. It's a temptation if you want to submit yourself to it and do a lot of cocaine. But you can work around whatever reality you want. I'm playing music, I'm communicating. I'm fortunate we're doing this kind of work, if you can call it that." ■

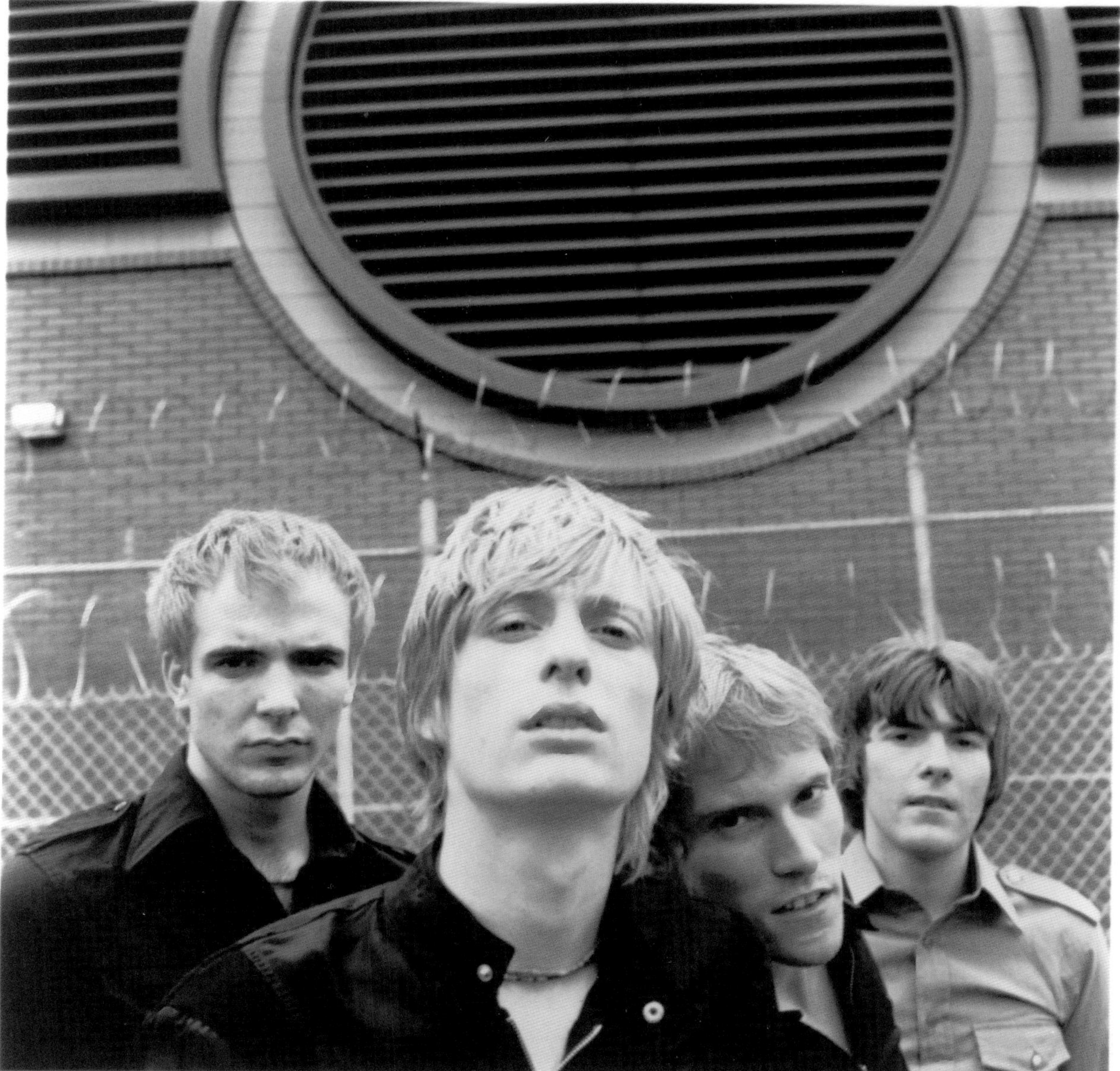



Photo Credit: Joshua Kessler

Left to Right: Alonza Bevan, Crispian Mills, Paul Winter-Hart, Jay Darlington

Kula Shaker

COLUMBIA

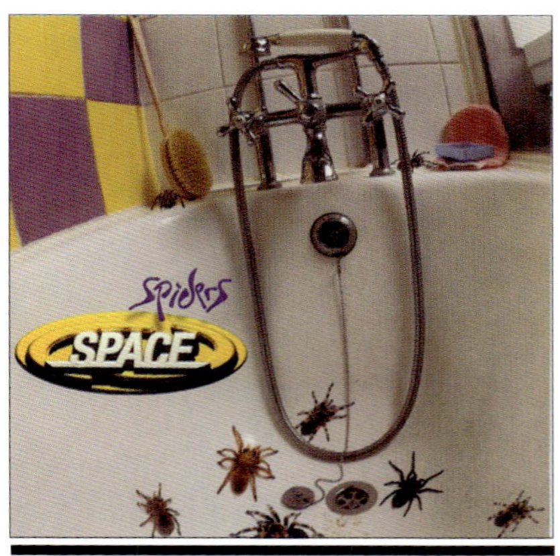

*Billboard* 200: *Spiders* (#189)

# The uncommon sound and lyrics of "Female of the Species" helped to establish Liverpool's Space in the US.

**ON MODERN-ROCK** radio, the most insidious hit to gain traction was "Female of the Species" by the English band Space. Over a mingling of cocktail lounge-type jazz, timpani and vibraphone, lead singer and bassist Tommy Scott reordered secondary lines from B-movies into a creepy tribute to the fairer sex: "The female of the species is more deadly than the male." For Scott, the song bore a particular importance. He wrote it for his father, a piano player who had died of cancer.

"'Female of the Species' is a mishmash of Frank Sinatra songs," Scott explained. "My dad used to come home drunk, put Sinatra on and listen to it full blast. I grew up listening to that and Nat King Cole and Ella Fitzgerald, even Frankie Laine and Dionne Warwick. I used to hate it! When I got my first guitar, my dad said, 'That's rubbish! Why don't you write a decent song?' I tried, but it was all these difficult jazz chords. I learned 'Everybody's Talkin'' and 'The Girl from Ipanema' to please him. He died before our success, so I wrote 'Female of the Species,' and it sounds corny, but I do believe he helped. I'd give this band up any day to have him back, but it does drive me."

Space's second single, "Neighbourhood"—"In 666 there lives a Mr. Miller/He's our local vicar and a serial killer"—reached the Top 10 on the UK charts (after being temporarily banned during the week a shooting massacre occurred at a Scottish school). Scott said he intended the other songs on Space's debut album *Spiders* to be "the sort of thing you'd hear in film soundtracks or Broadway musicals," combined with Happy Mondays guitar rave-ups and updated techno/hip-hop stylings by keyboardist Franny Griffiths.

"In my teenage years, I was always more interested in movies that music," Scott said. "Songs are like mini-movies to me, a soundtrack to a plot and a story. When Franny joined, it allowed my imagination to be put to songs. I couldn't do it with just guitar, drums and bass. Everyone says my songs are quirky, but they're sad. It's just like the Dustin Hoffman character in *Midnight Cowboy*—he was sad, but you could laugh at him. *Midnight Cowboy* sums up every song I write. I just want a few people to like our songs, not think that we're the greatest thing in the world like some British bands want. None of us has a big ego. We've been successful in Britain, but I don't feel any different from when I was unemployed." ■

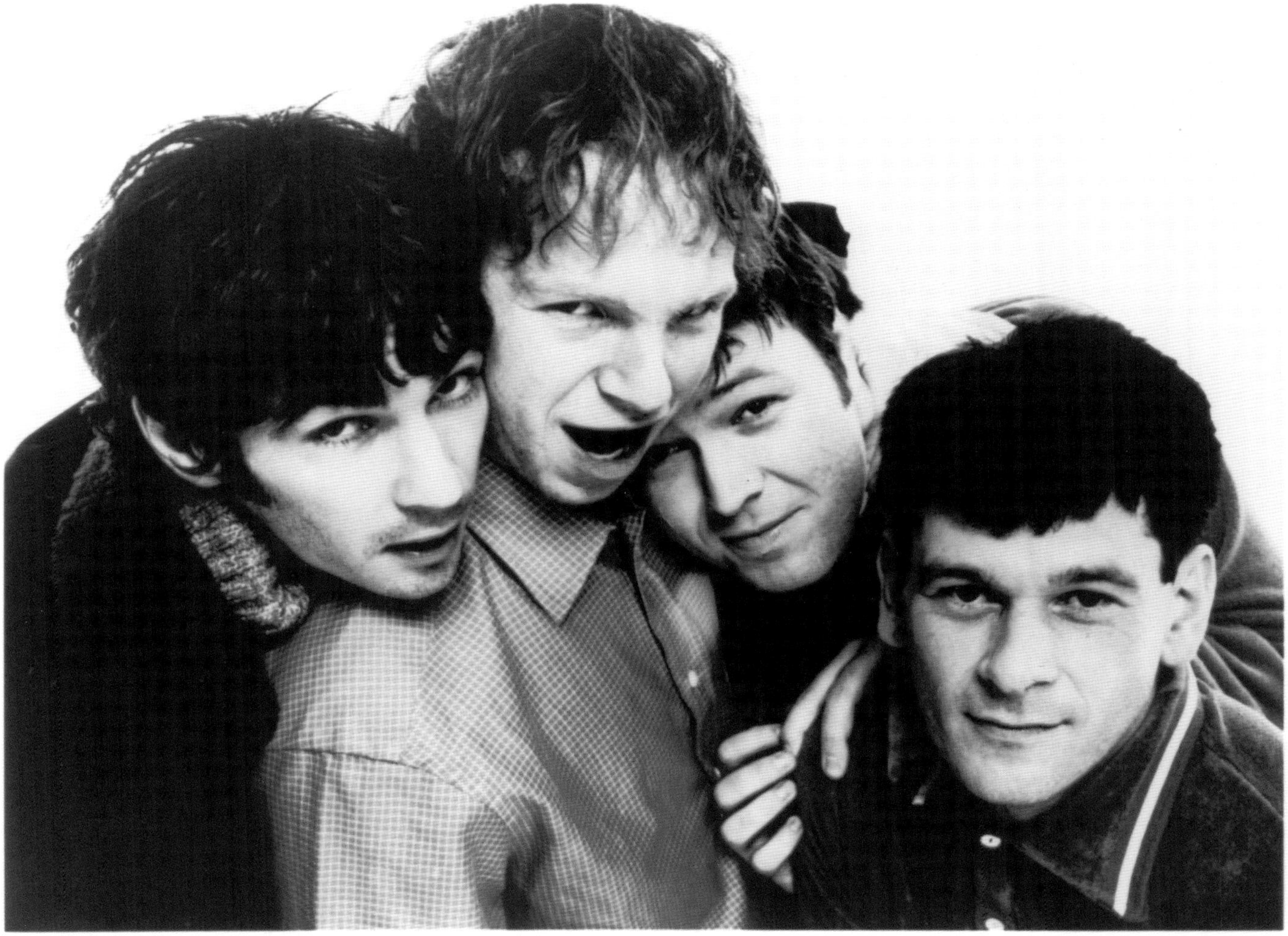

Photo credit: Peter Ashworth

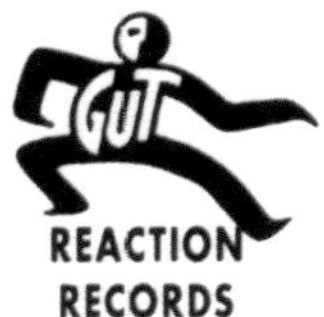


# SPACE

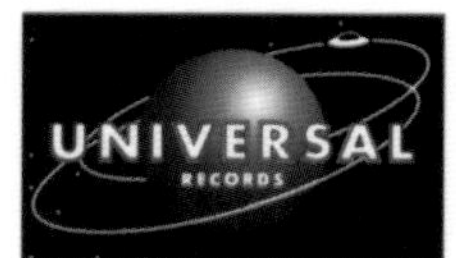

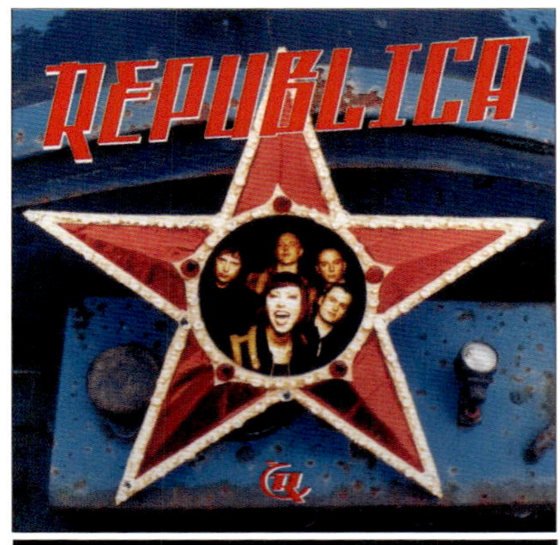


*Billboard* 200: *Republica* (#153)
*Billboard* Hot 100: "Ready to Go" (#56); "Drop Dead Gorgeous" (#93)

## Appearing amid a profusion of female-fronted rock bands, Republica broke in America with a self-titled album.

**ACCORDING TO** Republica, it wasn't so tough for a new UK group to go to the US. Two lively, catchy hits, "Ready to Go" and "Drop Dead Gorgeous," stood out on the radio and were perfect for club nights. *Republica*, the band's debut release, unified the slick hook-laden pop of early Eighties new wave and energetic Nineties techno beats.

"We're actually getting better known over here than in England," lead singer Saffron said. "There, our album hasn't been released, no one's written about us. Basically, we don't fit into any fashion—we're not Brit-pop, we're not another dance act. Here, when the 'Ready to Go' single was starting to get played, we got phone calls, so we came straight out. The last few months have been so brilliant, just go-go-go for us,"

Saffron, who had sung with Prodigy and sharpened her chops with the Shamen and N-Joi, met keyboardists Tim Dorney (of Flowered Up) and Andy Todd (who had mixed dance tracks for divas from Björk to Barbra Streisand) in London three years prior. They added guitarist Johnny Male. "We all work together, and everyone has the power of veto—usually, Tim and 'Toddy' do a backing track and I come up with a lyric," Saffron said. "We'd written the album and then we got a drummer (Dave Barbarossa, formerly of Bow Wow Wow and Adam & the Ants), and so our live sound suddenly became a lot harder and guitar-led. We concentrated a few months on getting the touring thing fully up and running, to put the album's electronics across live as best we possibly could."

"Ready to Go" featured Saffron's brattish charm. Two versions of the song, a rousing US mix and an original mix, started and finished *Republica*. "The American record company came along and said, 'Oh, we could do a mix.' We knew it was our best song, but I don't think we knew it would do half as well as this." The video was nothing but extreme zoom shots. "The original cut was four times faster, but we weren't allowed to use it. The record company said, 'Oh, no, you'll get sued for giving people epileptic fits.'"

The fun, upbeat "Drop Dead Gorgeous" was Saffron's ode to bad boys, with frenzied percussion and bass and her exultant vocals. "It's everything we've worked for, the realization of all those years trying to get somewhere. Is this really it? The main thing is to keep our feet on the ground, just carry on and hopefully make a living out of it if we can. People ask me, 'What would you buy?' and I have enough trouble paying my rent as it is. I haven't had time to think about anything that far ahead." ■

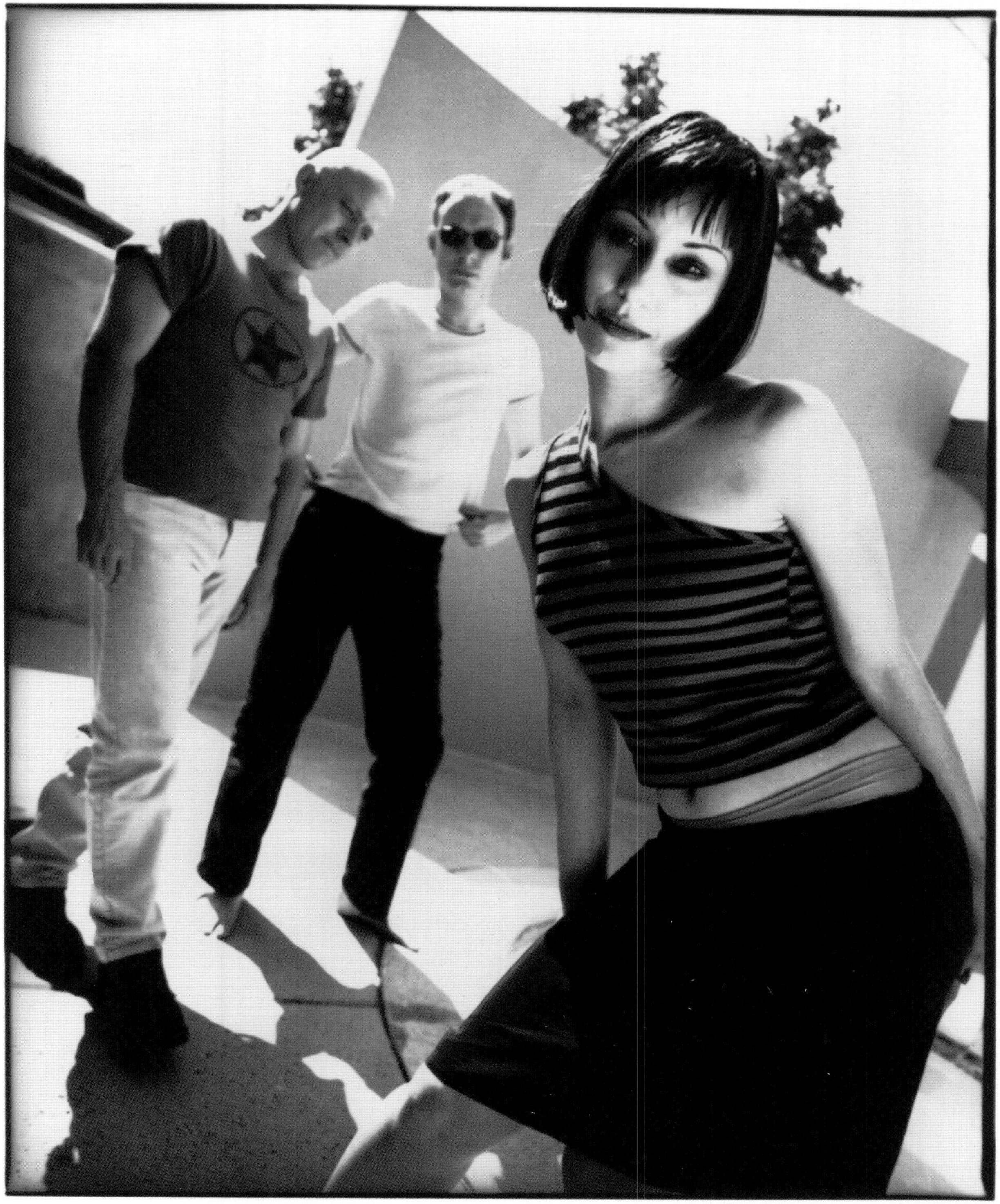

Andy Todd Tim Dorney Saffron

Photo Credit: Kate Gardner

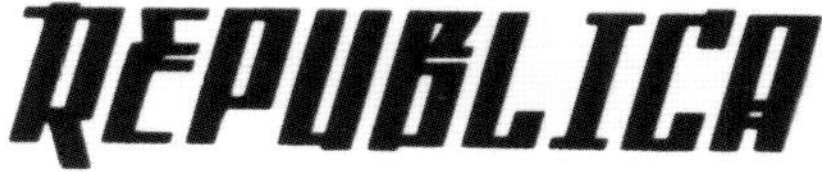


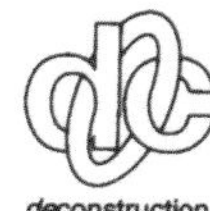


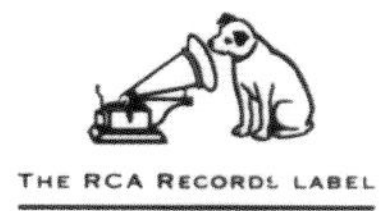

*Billboard* 200: *Walking Wounded* (#37)
*Billboard* Hot 100: "Wrong" (#68)

## On *Walking Wounded*, Everything but the Girl smoothly assimilated new electronic sounds into the music.

**COMMENCING IN** 1982, Tracey Thorn and Ben Watt formed Everything but the Girl and began making works categorized as "sophisti-pop," a blend of jazz, soul and pop elements with sumptuous production. Six albums later, Watt endured a lengthy recovery from an unexpected and potentially fatal auto-immune disease. EBTG returned to work with renewed dedication and, a year after the 1994 release of their seventh album, *Amplified Heart*, garnered a massive worldwide hit with Todd Terry's thumping, melancholy house remix of "Missing."

Buoyed by the success, Watt and Thorn seized the occasion and dove headfirst into an electronic music turn. They fashioned the self-produced *Walking Wounded*, a dance-friendly album inspired by a collaboration with Massive Attack.

"There's a sense of rebirth in the air," Watt said. "People know the trials we've been through in our personal lives, and generally they're pleased that we've managed to draw some kind of strength and energy out of ourselves to create music. Before that point, I was frightened that if I took textures and arrangements and production in a more extreme direction, people would just walk away. But I could see how my genuine interest in 'drum and bass' would really complement and contrast our natural sound. Drum and bass is like hardcore club music—its genesis lies in techno and jungle, a combination of frenetic programmed breakbeats taken from hip-hop records and then sped up, set against dark, deep, slow-moving bass lines."

*Walking Wounded* brimmed with subtle, sultry songs like the title track and "Wrong," which topped the dance-club charts. "On paper, it looks like a very unlikely combination with what we've done in the past," Watt admitted. "But you have this balance, something you get in reggae and even be-bop, when you can feel the slow hard-time pulse in the song while tapping your foot to the double-time feel. We could write laid-back, mellow songs and Tracey could sing in her natural style, but I could find the kind of tension that I was yearning to put into music by programming these hard, fast beats. It all fell into place." ■

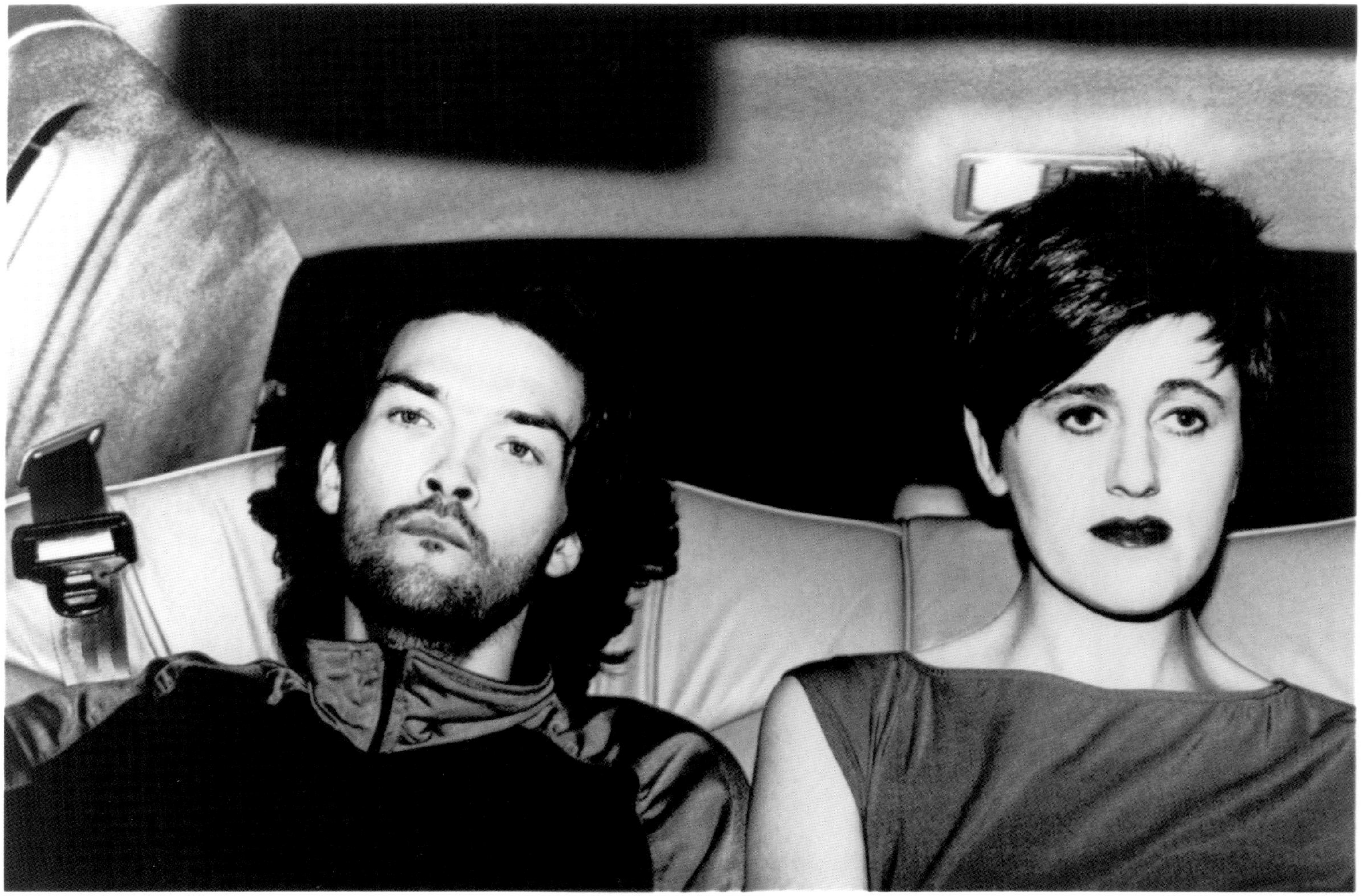

Photo Credit: MARCELO KRASILCIC

Ben Watt

Tracey Thorn

EVERYTHING BUT THE GIRL

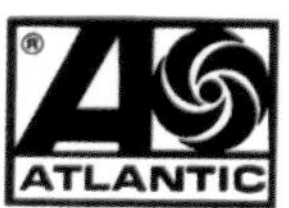

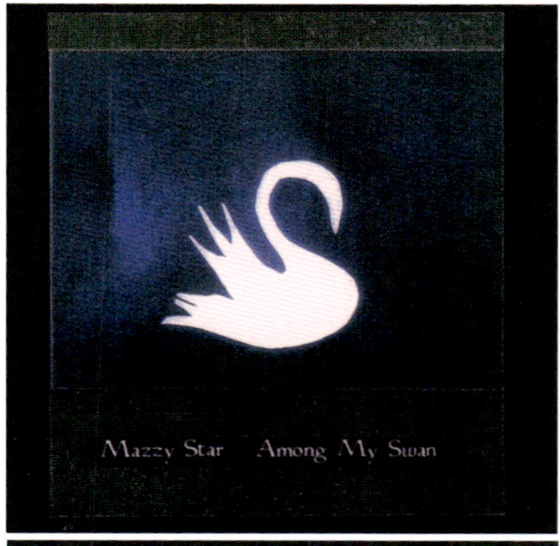


*Billboard* 200: *Along My Swan* (#68)

# Hope Sandoval's torpid performances arrived at a haunting, serene beauty on Mazzy Star's *Among My Swan*.

**THE ELEMENTS** in Mazzy Star's music were Hope Sandoval's soft, ethereal voice and David Roback's hazy, wistful touches of guitar and organ. And a mystique cloaked the pair's slow, dreamy "nod-pop." Roback and Sandoval were reticent interviewees—some rock scribes had published actual counts of the seconds between questions and "Maybe...I don't know" answers.

Mazzy Star's roots lay in Los Angeles' "paisley underground" scene of the early Eighties. Roback split the Rain Parade after that group's only album and formed Opal. Around the same time, Sandoval was singing in Going Home (Roback produced the folk duo's unreleased first album). When things soured for their respective bands, they got together. Roback's simple, atmospheric arrangements, the fuzzy strum of his guitar work and touches of neo-psychedelia highlighted Sandoval's languid, morose vocals. *She Hangs Brightly*, Mazzy Star's debut album, established a cult following, and *So Tonight That I Might See*, from 1993, spawned the beautiful MTV video hit "Fade into You" and went platinum.

There were jumps in style on *Among My Swan*. "I've Been Let Down" moved along like an acoustic country tune, and "Flowers in December" used an unassuming Neil Young-ish harmonica to accompany a message of longing, with Sandoval sounding more little-girl-lost than ever. "We wrote that song pretty quickly, right after we released *So Tonight That I Might See*—we played it live a lot and it basically stayed the same," she said. "But I still have a lot of problems playing live. When a small band is in the middle of getting to be a popular big band, the audience doesn't know what's going on. It's harder to control everybody when there's so many more people in one room.

"If you've never been to a Mazzy Star show, you don't know that it's really awkward to show up and socialize and have some kind of party while the band is playing. It's not background music. It's frustrating to go onstage. I just think it's rude when somebody's talking and chatting over a very quiet song and not paying attention. I don't see the point in showing up. I know I can't do the songs. I know people don't care." ■

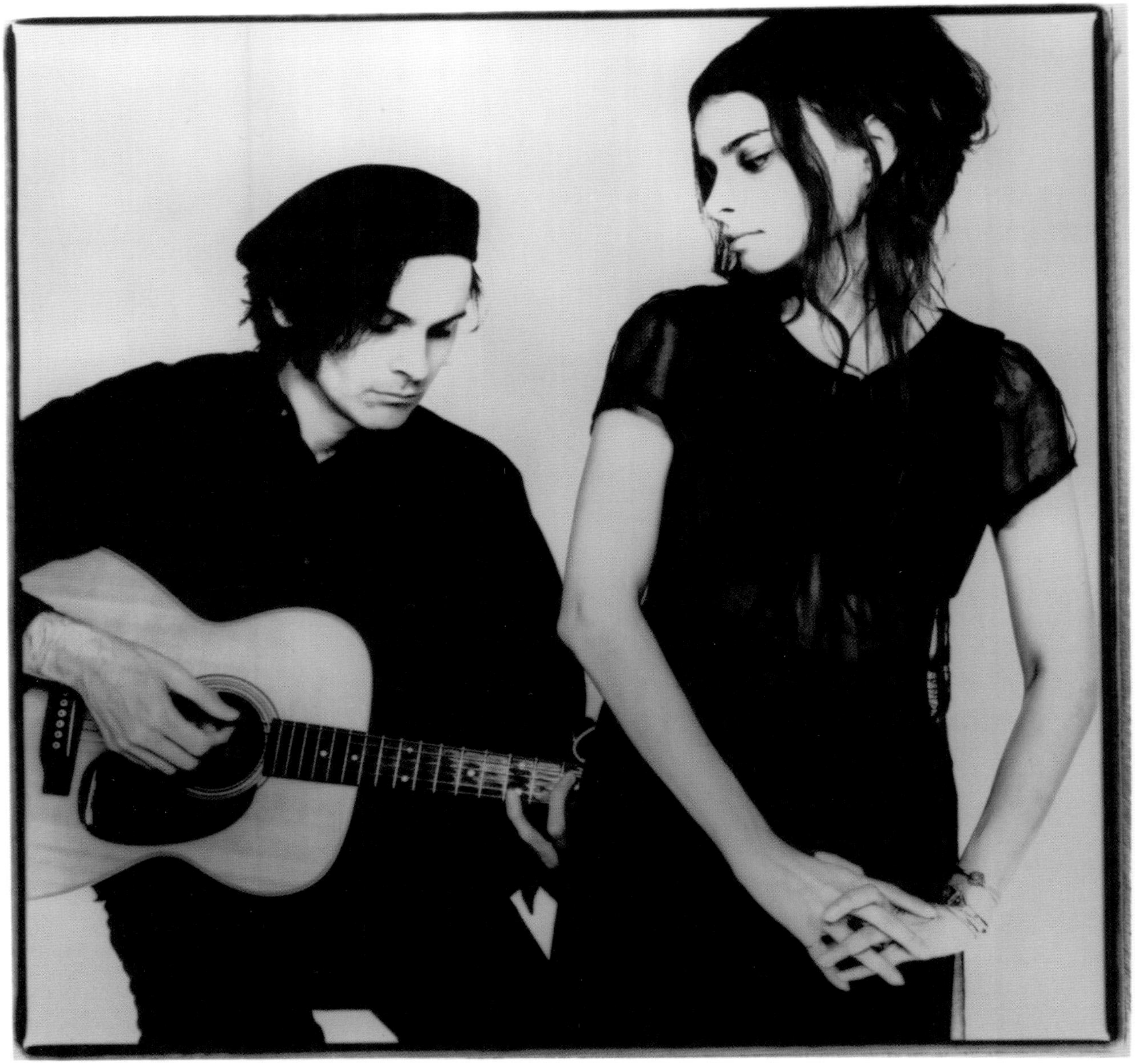

PHOTO CREDIT: ANDY CATLIN/1996

Mazzy Star

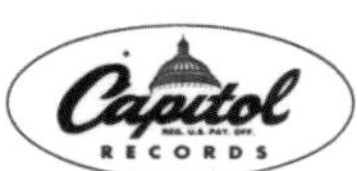

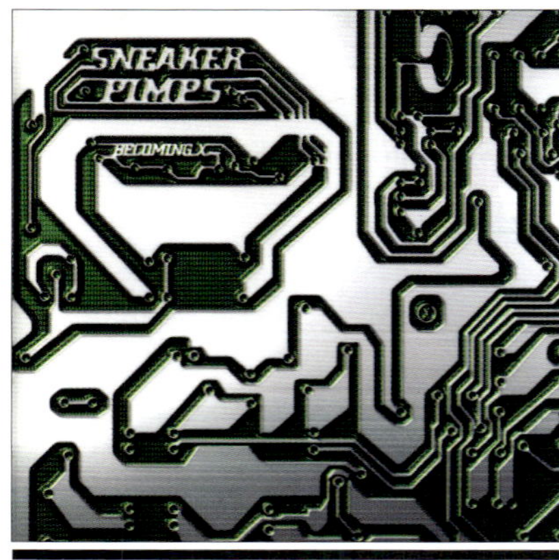


*Billboard* 200: *Becoming X* (#111)

England's **Sneaker Pimps** experienced a wave of acclaim in the States with the casually aloof "6 Underground."

**THERE WAS** an apparently inexhaustible supply of alternative dance acts that had become sensations in the UK. Following the success of Massive Attack, Portishead and others, Sneaker Pimps became the latest band promoting the electronica movement. Citing influences that ranged from Shirley Bassey to Kraftwerk, the core members—guitarist Chris Corner, keyboardist Liam Howe and vocalist Kelli Dayton—took on mesmerizing trip-hop rhythms and guided them into innovative tones.

Corner and Howe had been producing dance music since the early Nineties. Dayton left a punk band to join the remix duo—they recorded the debut album *Becoming X* in a few weeks in Howe's bedroom studio at his parents' home. "Chris and Liam didn't expect to work with somebody like me, and I didn't expect to work with somebody like them," Dayton said. "We never constructed a master plan—'I'm a bit punky, you're a bit dance-y, we'll get together and do this thing.' We were of such different pasts, doing such different things musically. But we developed a friendship, and before we knew it, we had 10 songs—most of the music was written before I ever met them. It was that easy, that quick."

On record, Sneaker Pimps' sound was suave, subtle and suggestive. Something about "6 Underground" made it stand out from the rest of the hits on modern-rock radio, and "Spin Spin Sugar" edged its way onto the dance charts. Sneaker Pimps were one of the few groups who saw the value in crafting songs instead of just loops and beats.

In concert, Sneaker Pimps (a Beastie Boys name to describe someone who was paid to look for prime footwear) were less exotic. After an intense international touring schedule that left the band away from their friends and family for months, the group parted with Dayton. "We originally did the demos with Chris singing on the songs," Howe recalled. "We recorded them with Kelli and it sounded right with her. We never wanted to push the idea of a 'lead singer' because the focus was always the music, but the album did well—it suddenly just ran away with itself." ■

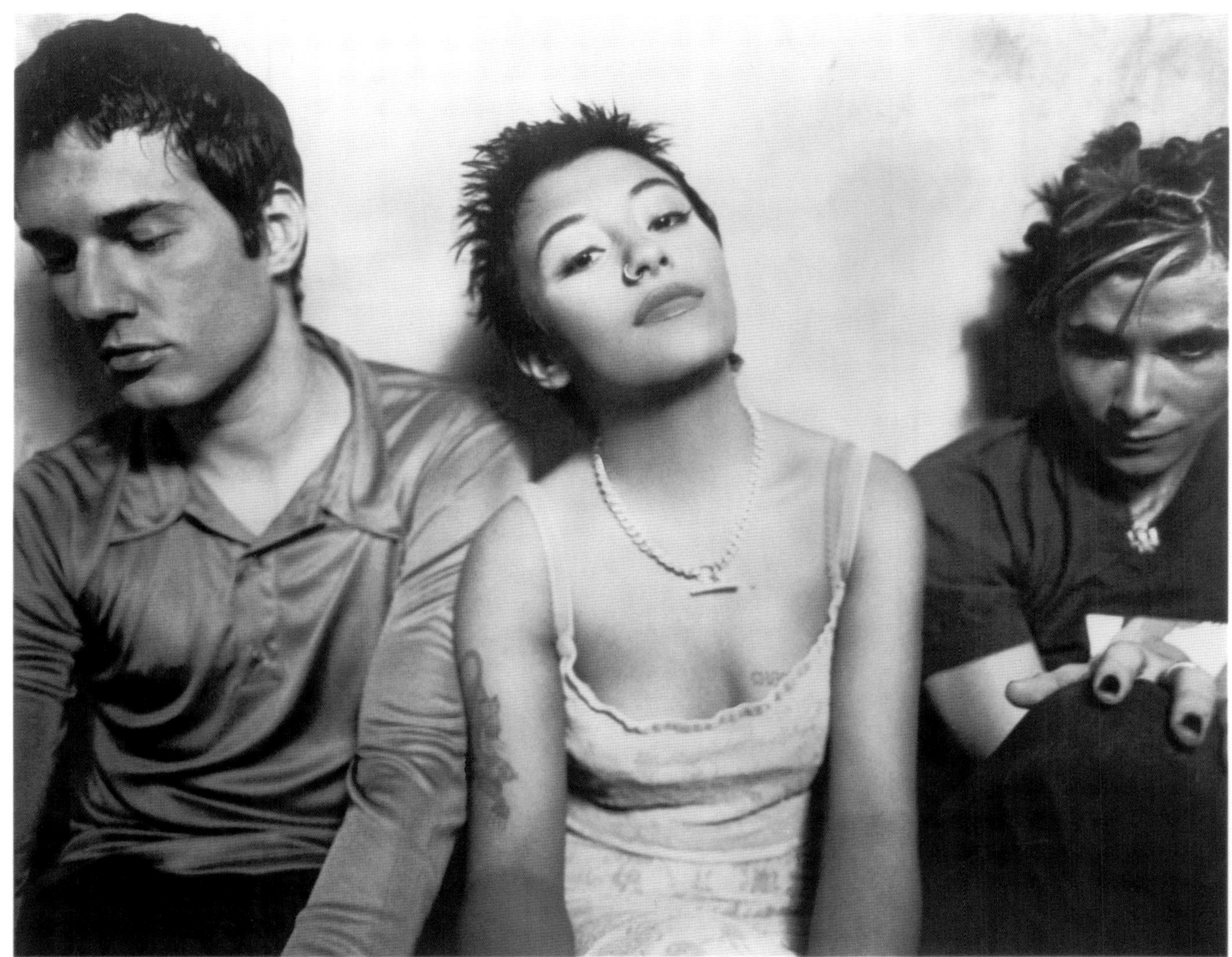

Photo Credit: Jeff Reidel 1/97

**Liam Howe** **Kelli Dayton** **Chris Corner**

# Sneaker Pimps

Virgin

*Billboard* 200: *Signs of Life* (#20)

## On *Signs of Life*, his ninth album, Steven Curtis Chapman moved his Christian songwriting in a new direction.

**ONE OF** the biggest names in the contemporary Christian music industry, Steven Curtis Chapman had scored 16 No. 1 CCM singles, won three Grammys and garnered three gold records. But his catchy brand of sanctified pop, rock 'n' roll, blues and country had yet to cross over to a mainstream audience.

"I guess I still have an identity problem," Chapman said. "My wife and I joke about it. We get dressed up and go to the Grammys and pretend that we belong there—we feel like we're sneaking around hoping we don't get caught. It's a different community of people. A lot of them cross paths on television shows or tours. But they hear my name and think I'm married to Amy Grant—'No, that's Gary Chapman.' Or I'm the guy who shot John Lennon—'No, that was Mark David Chapman.'"

Chapman's fans related to his songs because he didn't jam religion down their throats—he was a peer. There was a more aggressive edge to Chapman's music on *Signs of Life*, a deliberate shift toward a sparer, rootsier sound. "I felt like I was on the verge of becoming a victim of my own success," he explained. "When that machine starts running and churning, it's hard to break out of that. Fortunately, I had my record company's blessing. They said, 'Go make the record you always wanted to make.' My real goal was to recover some sense of passion for music, and not just allow myself to go through the motions."

Chapman retreated to the music of his Paducah, Kentucky, boyhood. "I went back and got CDs of all the first records I remembered owning—Andrae Crouch & the Disciples' *The Best of Andrae*, Billy Preston's *That's the Way God Planned It*, the Doobie Brothers' *Best of the Doobies*. That was real music, when a bunch of guys got together and jammed, and it felt good."

Chapman was inspired to record with fewer overdubs and synths, mainly with pop players he'd never worked with before. And he did all his own guitar parts—bluesy songs like "Lord of the Dance" and "The Walk" confirmed he knew his way around his instrument. Chapman agonized over the record for months. "My wife accused me of having a midlife crisis. I laid in bed the night before it was released thinking, 'What if they don't like me?'"

But *Signs of Life* entered the charts in the Top 20, right up there with secular albums by Dave Matthews Band, Shania Twain and Garbage. Chapman said some of his fans weren't so sure of one change—they saw that his trademark wavy blond hair was gone. "My America Online account is in the trash," he said with a laugh. "I logged on and came across the debates on my short haircut. It was amazing to me how all of a sudden people are affected—they get used to the way you look. I've seen everything from 'Can you believe his hair? It's awful! What was he thinking?' to 'I like it, personally—get off his case!' Unless we have very thick skin—and I don't, I have tissue-paper skin—we artists should be banned from the internet." ■

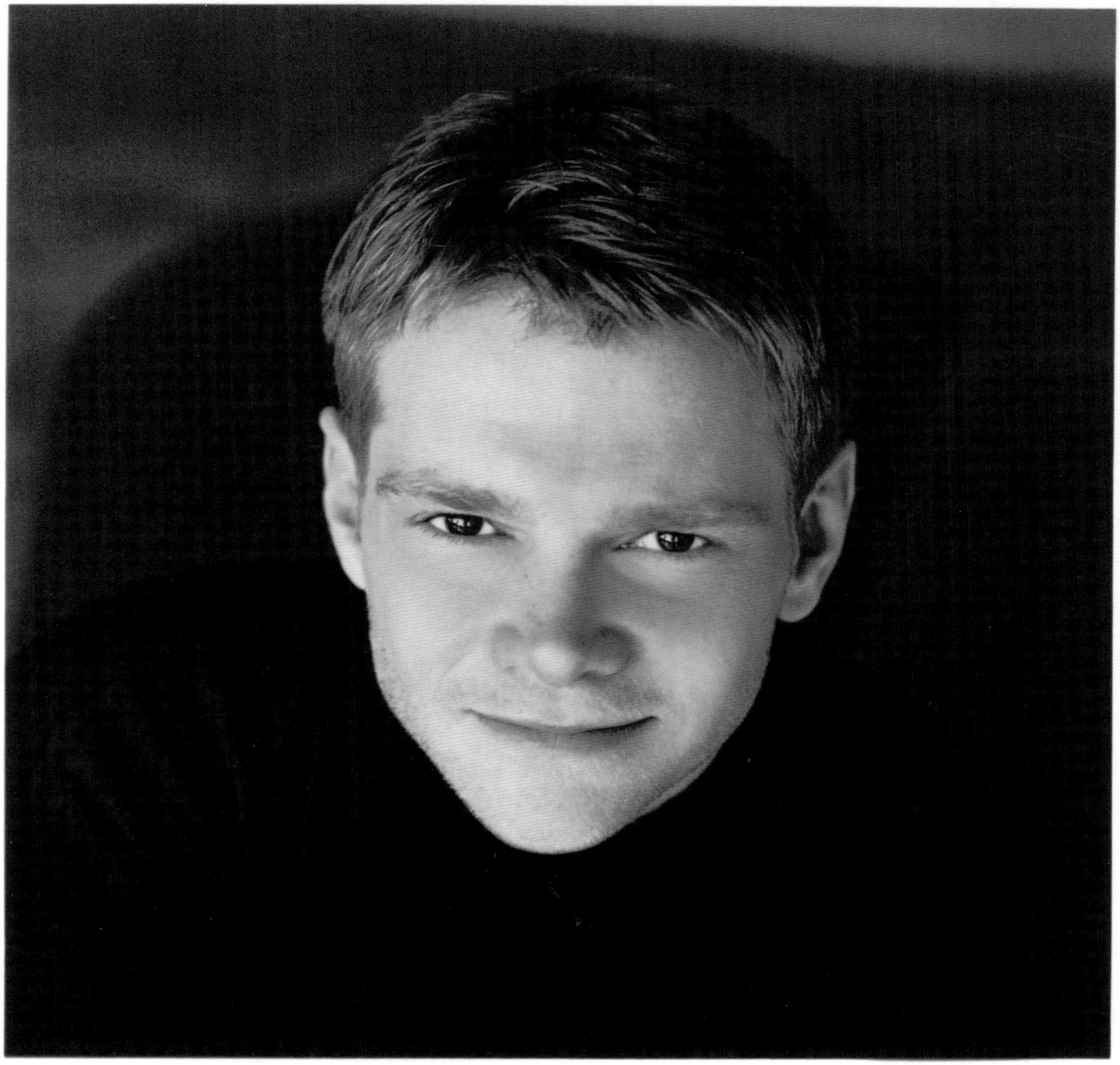

# STEVEN CURTIS CHAPMAN

Management: Creative Trust
(615) 297-5010
Booking: Creative Artists Agency
(615) 383-8787
Publicity: Sparrow Media Relations
(615) 371-6800

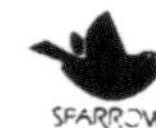

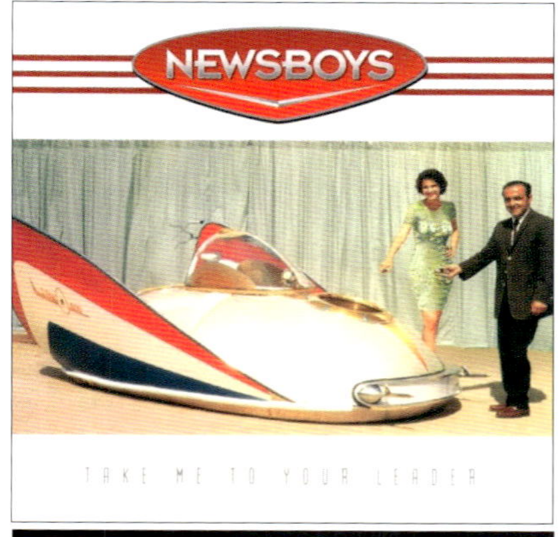


*Billboard* 200: *Take Me to Your Leader* (#35)

## Newsboys' *Take Me to Your Leader* album evinced a new chapter in the ongoing growth of non-secular rock.

**SINCE COMING** to the US from tiny Mooloolaba, Queensland, Australia, Newsboys had achieved enough popularity in the contemporary Christian marketplace to edge into the modern-rock scene. Based in Nashville, the home of the Christian music industry, the band had earned Grammy nominations and won Dove Awards. At the root of the religious band's success was vocalist John James, who co-founded the outfit with drummer Peter Furler. Steve Taylor, a legendary singer-songwriter in the Christian music scene, had formed a partnership with the group, producing the last few releases.

Newsboys signed with Virgin Records, the label that also had Spice Girls, Janet Jackson and the Rolling Stones. *Take Me to Your Leader* was the band's gold-certified major-label debut. Tom Lord-Alge, a renowned mixing engineer (Goo Goo Dolls, Live, Dave Matthews Band, Steve Winwood), worked on the album. "The word we keep hearing about this one is 'organic'—like we have an herb garden on the album or something," Furler said with a laugh. "But the word keeps coming up because the album is mainly performed live—we didn't use any sequencers."

All but one track became a hit on the contemporary Christian charts, and a zany video accompanied the title track. "If you're a Christian band, making a video isn't a high priority because there's really no outlets except regional, low-budget TV shows here and there," keyboardist Jeff Frankenstein explained. "Actually, video is the least stressful thing for a band to make because everything else is taken care of. You turn up, and the director's in charge of the crew and cameras—you just have to slip behind your instrument and lip-synch." ■

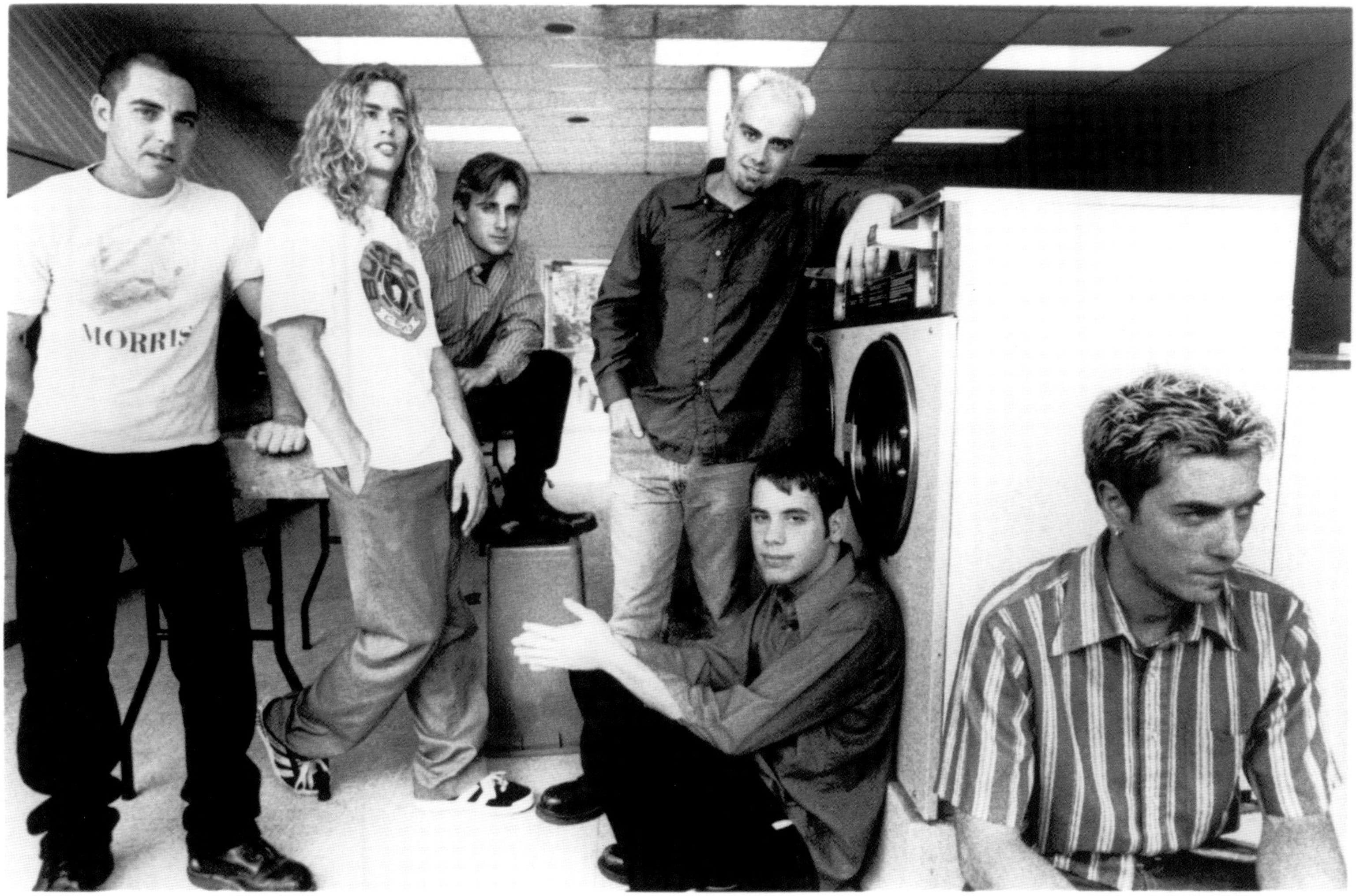

Photo Credit: Jeff Frazier 7/96

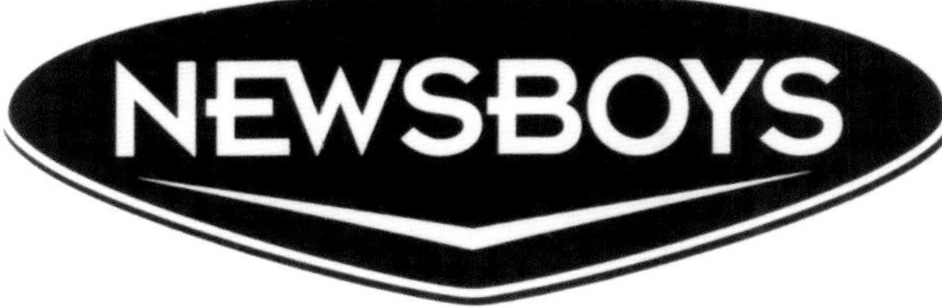


Virgin

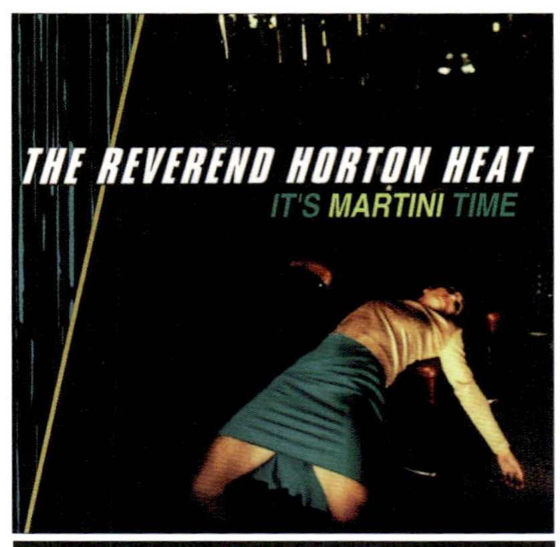


*Billboard* 200: *It's Martini Time* (#156)

**The Reverend Horton Heat undertook rowdy, razor-sharp live shows in support of the *It's Martini Time* album.**

**WITH A** brand of revved-up rockabilly, the Reverend Horton Heat had crisscrossed the country hundreds of times to bring the music home to the "Heatheads" who believed. Dubbing its sound "psychobilly," the Texas trio added a big dose of punk adrenaline and a dash of surf, Tex-Mex and country music, paying homage to the ladies, cars and getting wasted. The cats were led by vocalist and guitar virtuoso Jim "the Rev" Heath, a professed former pool shark and teen truant.

"There are a lot of good traditional rockabilly bands out there that won't be heard by anyone," Heath explained. "A lot of people don't even know they like rockabilly until they hear it. It's the kiss-of-death word for bands if they want to pursue a career, because it's a limited market. Somehow, we broke through that, and we'll keep on doing our twisted Texas version of it. We borrow from a lot of roots, not just rockabilly. We like AC/DC and Pantera and the Ramones. It's harder-edged, but we still keep the 'billy in there."

Raw, energetic performances were the Reverend Horton Heat's life work. With the stage as his pulpit, the irreverent Rev, in snappy suits and hair shined up with grease, preached—his fast-reverb-drenched guitar holding things together as bassist Jimbo Wallace slapped his stand-up silly and drummer Scott Churilla beat his kit within an inch of its existence. The band had steadily built an enthusiastic cult fan base.

"That's our whole plan—a lot of bands that have big hits on the radio don't have as big a following as we do," Heath said. "It comes from a lot of hard work. We started out in a little van with no record and said, 'We've got some good songs, and we're going to take this on the road.'"

In 1990, the Reverend Horton Heat signed with Seattle's seminal grunge label, Sub Pop. After releasing two albums, the band caught the ear of a major label and inked a deal with Interscope for 1994's *Liquor in the Front* (with Ministry's Al Jourgensen behind the board). *It's Martini Time* continued in the grand scheme of, say, Tennessee Ernie Ford fronting the Cramps. But neither the swingy title track nor "Slow" would become breakout songs for the Reverend Horton Heat.

"I'll never understand radio," Heath said. "Who would have expected the big ska craze that was taking over for a while? The female folksinger thing is still popular—they're getting the multimillion-dollar contracts, and that's all you hear. There's a wide variety of music out there that I'd like to hear on the radio, but I'm not going to hold my breath." ■

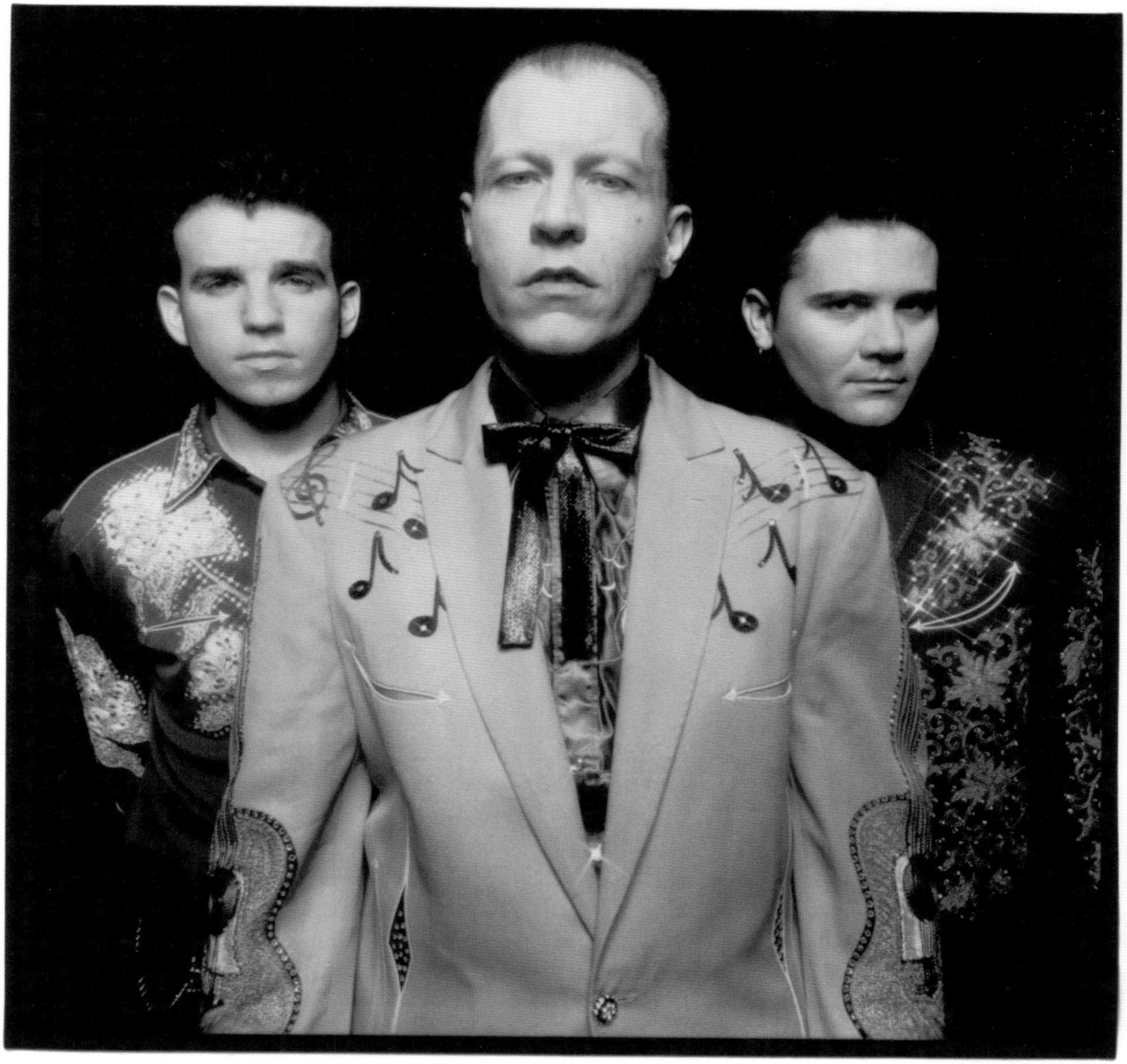

Photo credit: Marina Chavez

Scott The Rev Jimbo

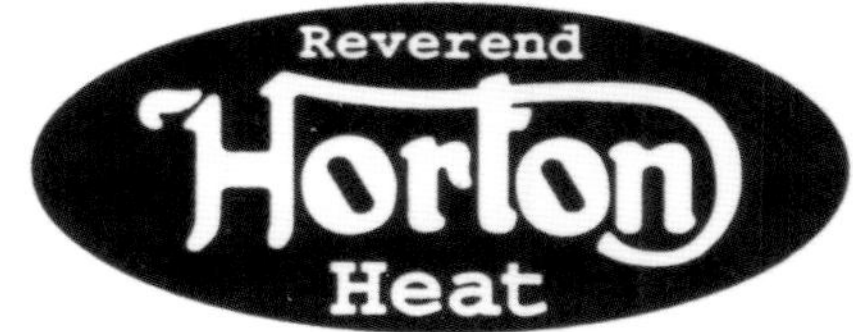

*Billboard* 200: *Hot* (#27)

## Squirrel Nut Zippers succeeded in transforming infectious retro swing into major commercial success with *Hot*.

**LOOKING FOR** an alternative to alternative rock and a diversion from the era's disaffected stars, some of the post-grunge crowd were ready to jitterbug. They packed away the T-shirts and long shorts and decked out in gowns, fedoras and the closest thing to zoot suits they could find at thrift shops. And they bought *Hot*, Squirrel Nut Zippers' second album, a take on the big-band swing and Harlem hot jazz of the Twenties and Thirties.

"Something's in the air—other bands are starting to do some wacky stuff, familiarize themselves with the connotations of music that don't use traditional guitar/bass/drums instrumentation," guitarist Tom Maxwell said. "People can't believe that we found seven musicians who would play this stuff. Not everyone was familiar with the genre, but they jumped on it immediately, understood it intuitively."

The mission to keep the jive alive wasn't a cynical pose. The original tunes on *Hot* referred to the jazz musicians admired by the snazzy North Carolina septet—Fats Waller, Louis Armstrong, Cab Calloway—but they sparkled with up-to-date zeal. "Hell," an old-time calypso number, smoked up America's modern rock airwaves—and it was a little jarring to hear the extremely retro banjo-and-horns tune next to the Smashing Pumpkins and Nine Inch Nails.

"I can guarantee you 'Hell' is the only Top 30 song that has a reference to Lord Executor in it," Maxwell enthused. "I'm very much into calypso from Trinidad, the music from the Twenties to the early Forties. The strength of it was in the individuality and personality of the calypsonian. Most of the song structures were totally insane, and no one wasted too much time on that—they just got down to writing these incredibly brutal, frank lyrics where they would kick each other's asses all over the island.

"English was their second language, and the way they put words together was beautiful. Lord Executor's songs were really scary—they sound like he's reading the news. I completely immersed myself in that style. I read a book called *The History of Hell*. It was full of fun facts about hell's inception and its place in western culture and art, right up to *Portrait of the Artist as a Young Man*. Talk about fertile ground."

The pre-rock sound reeled in fans, and *Hot*, the highest charting indie record in the country, was certified gold. Maxwell and his bandmates had to deal with sudden celebrity. "Once you reach a certain degree of success, you're guaranteeing a backlash—no one will be able to listen to your song again, ever," he mused. "I don't want 'Hell' played into the ground—it's good, but it's no better than any other song on the record.

"But it's too late. I'd rather this whole thing be over with, to be honest. I've already sold more records than I thought I'd ever sell. I love *Hot*—I'm proud of it. But I'm more interested in people understanding the diversity of what we have to offer. I don't want to get burned out." ■

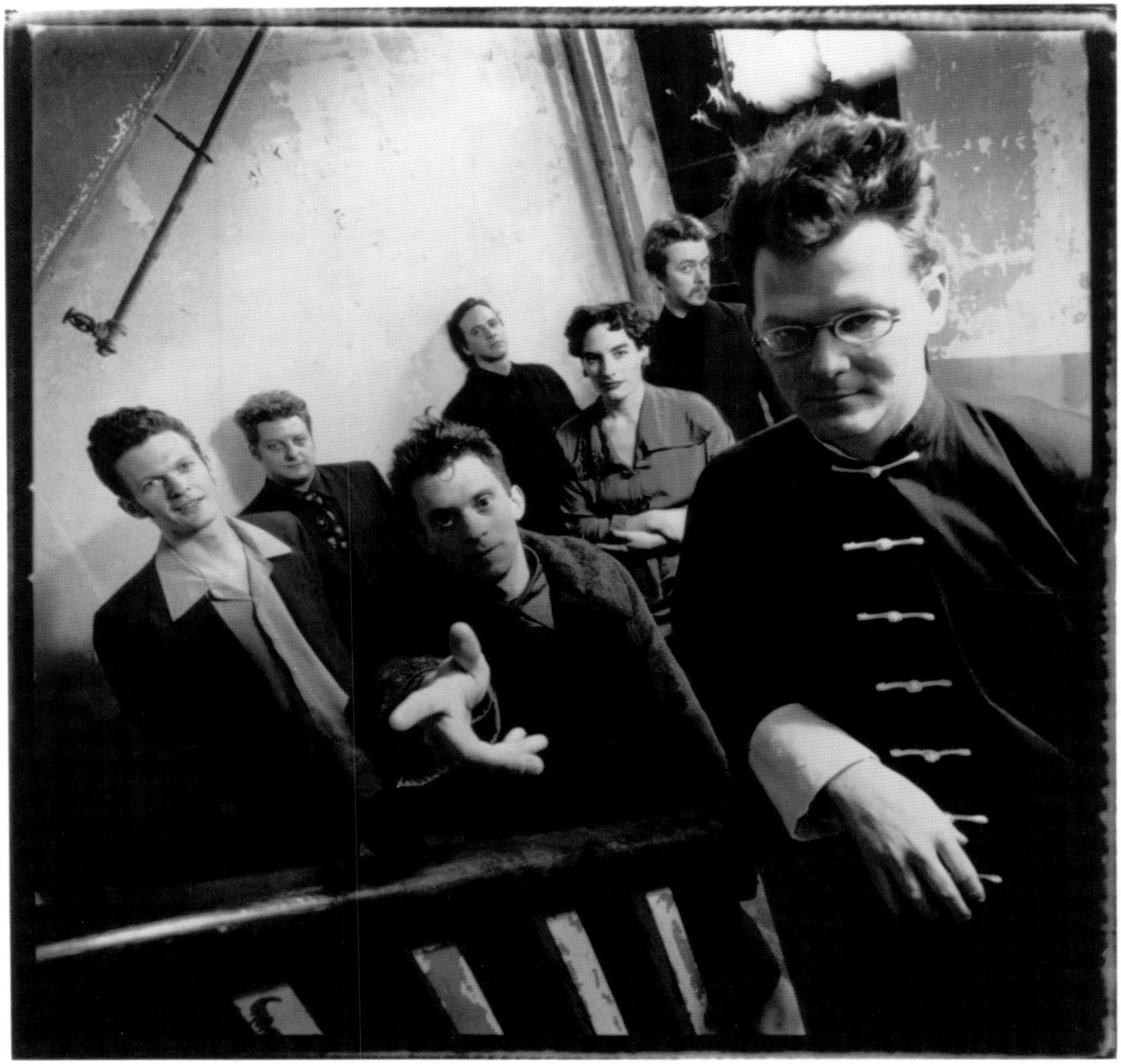

Photo: Mark Van-S

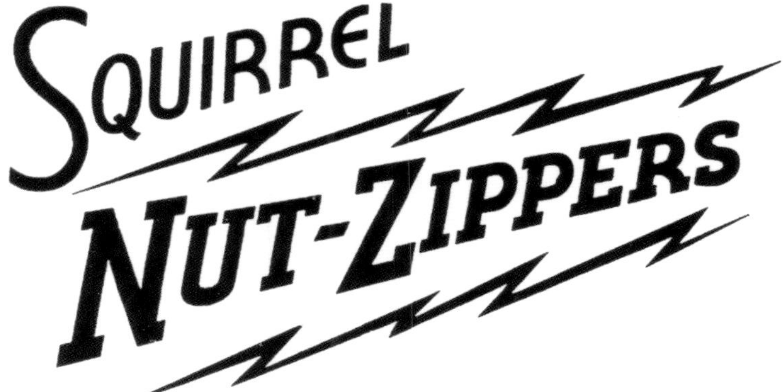


mammoth

Mammoth Records
101 B Street, Carrboro, NC 27510
Mammoth NC: 919.932.1882
Mammoth NY: 212.707.2830
Mammoth LA: 310.205.5732
E-mail: info@mammoth.com

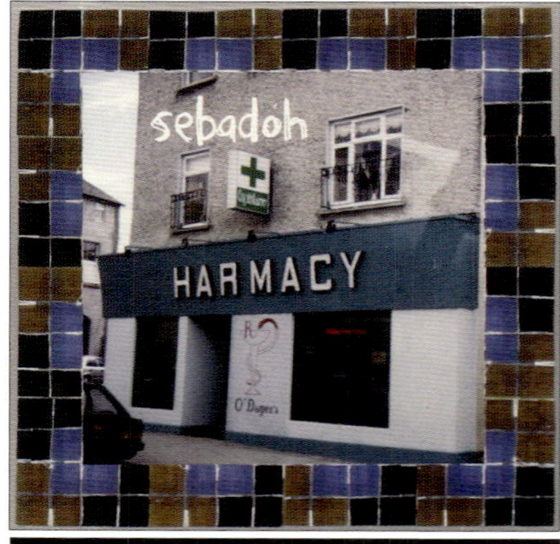


*Billboard* 200: *Harmacy* (#126)

# Deriving benefit from a cohesive production ethos, *Harmacy* became Sebadoh's first album to enter the charts.

**CO-CREATED AS** an outlet for Lou Barlow when he felt limited in Dinosaur Jr, Sebadoh helped pioneer indie-rock's "lo-fi" movement. Early albums were mostly home recordings in his intimate and confessional songwriting style.

"When I was 19, I couldn't walk into a studio and expect to blow out microphones and overload gear and layer sounds on top of each other to see what would happen while someone was looking over my shoulder and charging me $20 an hour," Barlow explained. "Now that I'm branching out a bit, I have the money to go into a studio. I want to figure out a way to make it my own personal instrument like I made the four-track. I haven't gotten there yet, but it's all part of the process."

Barlow had experienced an unlikely kind of fame—his song "Natural One" (credited to Folk Implosion, an ongoing side project with his friend John Davis) was featured on the soundtrack to Larry Clark's notorious film *Kids* and became an improbable Top 40 smash. For the first time, Barlow felt under real pressure to expand on the success.

Sebadoh had become a traditionally functioning band with bassist Jason Loewenstein and drummer Bob Fay, but the controlled recording process of *Harmacy* was protracted and difficult. With the commercially viable album, the sensitive Barlow's indie-rock credibility was questioned, but he strived for a sense of calm.

"You know, 'How can you write about all this confusion when you have everything together?' I had a pretty nice childhood. My parents gave me a lot of space and support, they let me become who I was bound to become. And the woman I married, I met nine years ago. But there's a limitless supply of insecurities. People are so very insecure of themselves, second-guessing things. I'm always trying to understand that, and that's where all of my songs come from.

"I don't ever put it to myself, 'God, I should be happy.' I don't think writing a sad song is about being sad—it's about catharsis, about moving beyond something and understanding it. The only way I can be happy is to write about what makes me feel bad. Hopefully, as I get older, I'll be able to celebrate more of what I have."

On *Harmacy*, Barlow's short tunes were sharp (the deceptively upbeat kiss-off "Ocean") and sweet (the beautiful ballad "Willing to Wait" was his finest hour as a writer). "I feel like I've gone through musical puberty in the last year," he said. "Rather than being this center of confusion, maybe I'd rather be a center of inspiration.

"I feel like I've just begun. I'm not even gonna bother getting defensive about it. Sure, I've written plenty of adolescent angst songs. Maybe I'll continue to do that, maybe that's how they'll continue to come off. But it's not what I'm thinking. Personally, when I hear stuff like Smashing Pumpkins and Bush, all of that shit is so whiny—it doesn't even have any particular poetic flow to it. Then when people start giving me shit, I'm like, 'What are you talking about? I'm trying! Work it out!'" ■

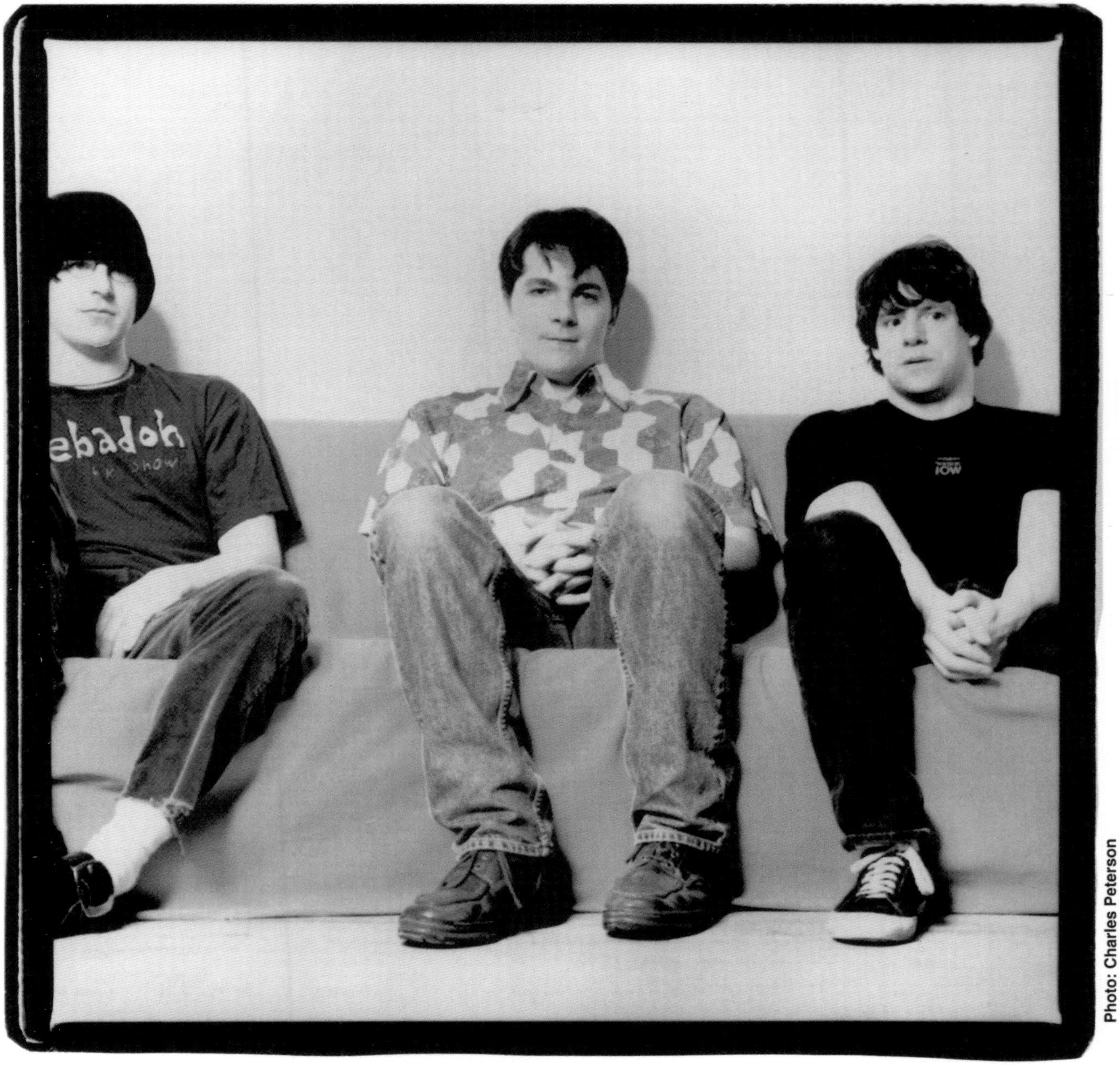

Photo: Charles Peterson

**LOU BARLOW** | **JASON LOEWENSTEIN** | **BOB FAY**

# SEBADOH

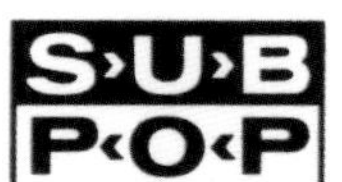


SUB POP RECORDS
1932 First Avenue
Suite 1103
Seattle, WA 98101
TEL. (206) 441-8441

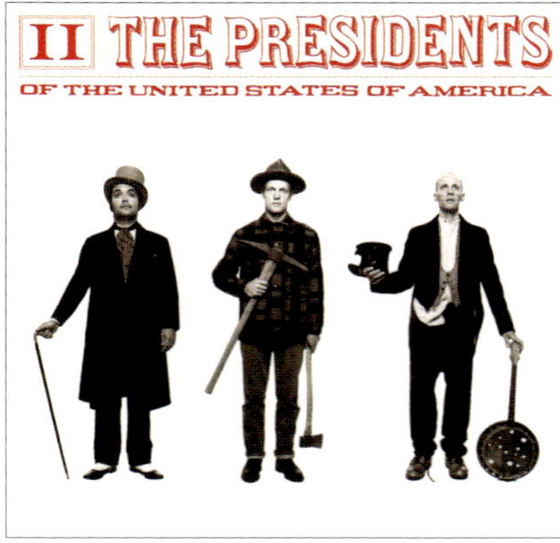


*Billboard* 200: *II* (#31)

## The Presidents of the United States of America's November release of *II* jibed with the US presidential election.

**HAVING MORE** fun than most bands, the Presidents of the United States of America performed with unrestrained joy and enthusiasm, partying with loony tunes and meager instrumentation—two strings on Chris Ballew's basitar and three on Dave Dederer's guitbass. They were talented players, but the Presidents' canniness revealed itself most conspicuously in their playfully saucy songwriting. Some listeners pogoed along oblivious to the hilarity, but others caught the ironic tenor. *II* was a silly satire of arena-rock—the first track, "Ladies and Gentlemen Part I," asked the musical question "Are you ready to rock?" with as much pretension as the members could evoke.

"Both records are excellent documentations of what we've sounded like at the time," Dederer said. "The first record sounds intimate—we were playing these small clubs. The second record, we were playing huge festivals in Europe and hockey rinks in Australia for months. We were in this super-tight mode of rocking out to bigger and bigger audiences—which means very broad strokes, very aggressive and fast, basically just spraying energy off the stage."

The Seattle trio's quick, quirky offerings from II included "Mach 5," which could have been a tribute to the animated hero of *Speed Racer*, and "Volcano," a catchy rocker with hysterical singalong lyrics that mixed a metaphor for stereo equipment. The Presidents were trying to prove that they weren't a flash in the pan. Their debut album had been certified multiplatinum, helped by the hits "Lump" and "Peaches," but *II* only sold enough copies to go gold.

"We never formed the band with the ambition of having a major record deal—it all fell into our laps," Dederer explained. "We were explicit—we didn't want to be gone all the time touring. Once we saw our first record start to take off, we realized, 'Okay, this is a chance to grab for the brass ring—we need to suck it up this one time and go for it and tour nonstop for more than a year.'

"And we did it. Now we know what the spoils are and what it will take out of us. The entertainment business is crazy—we don't want to live immersed in it. Chris and I are both married—we don't want to be away from our wives all the time. We're rethinking how we're going to run the band in a way that will allow us to make records and play to people who want to see us without going completely out of our minds." ■

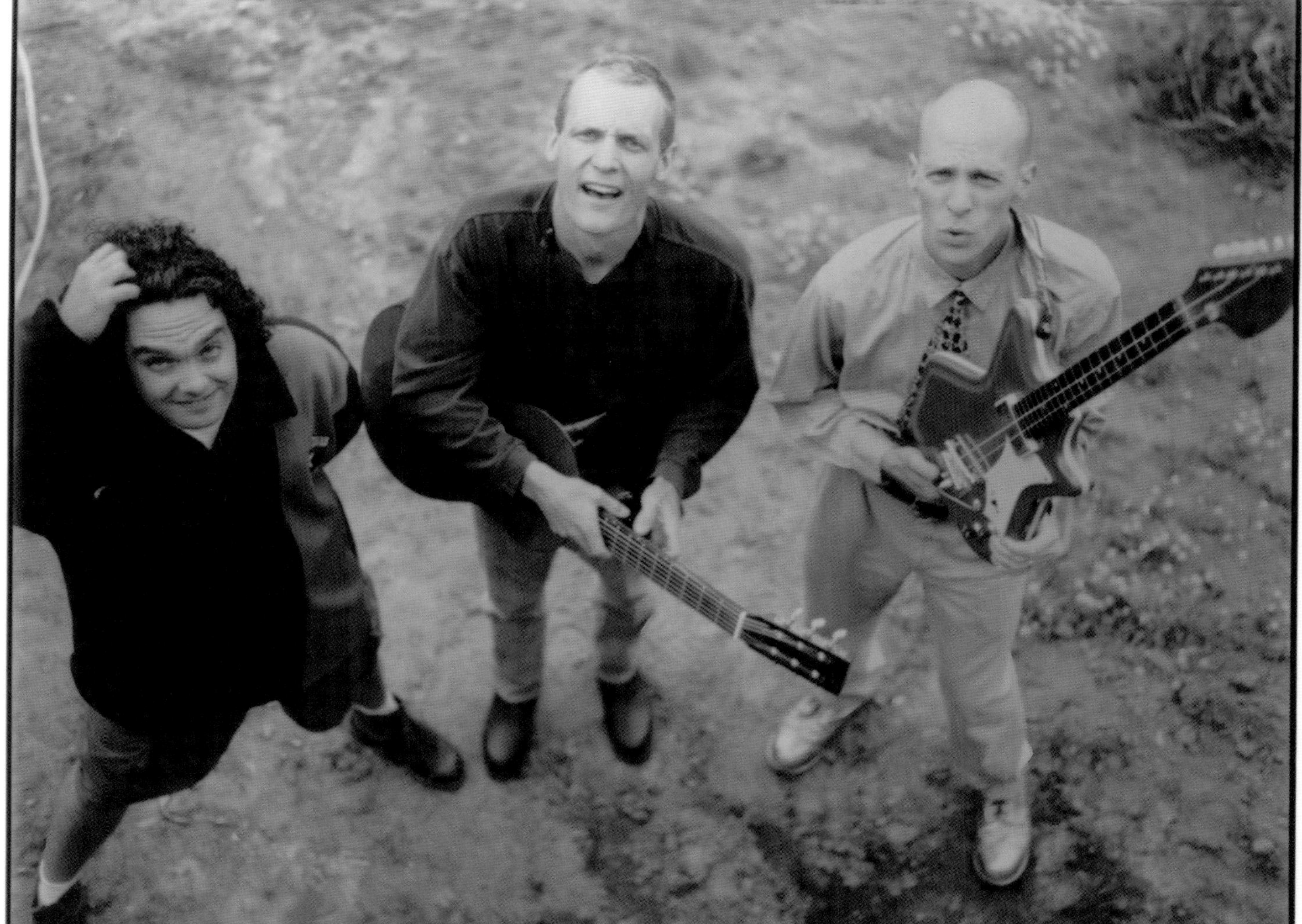



Photo Credit: Lance Mercer

JASON FINN DAVE DEDERER CHRIS BALLEW

# THE PRESIDENTS OF THE UNITED STATES OF AMERICA

COLUMBIA
9610

*Billboard* 200: *Rocket* (#36)

# "Standing Outside a Broken Phone Booth with Money in My Hand" sparked interest in Primitive Radio Gods.

**A MESMERIZING** blend of a scratchy hip-hop beat, half-spoken lyrics, subdued instrumentation and a haunting sample from B.B. King's "How Blue Can You Get"—"I've been downhearted baby/Ever since the day we met"—"Standing Outside a Broken Phone Booth with Money in My Hand" ruled alternative-rock radio and MTV. Even late-night television talk show host David Letterman made an on-air habit of muttering, "I've been downhearted baby."

But there was a surprising story behind the hit single. Like the rest of *Rocket*, the first album from Primitive Radio Gods, it had originally been recorded five years prior. Chris O'Connor began his musical career with the I-Rails, a Santa Barbara band that released four indie albums between 1988 and 1990. When they failed to land a major-label recording contract, the other I-Rails abandoned music to take regular day jobs. On a $1,000 shoestring, O'Connor recorded the rest of an album in a friend's garage on a broken-down '96 Ampex 16-track tape deck.

"I started out 'Phone Booth' looping an old Fifties R&B drum sound I had," O'Connor said. "I played with that and put an acoustic bass line in there, and the lyrics and melody came together. But I built in a lot of space—I wanted something different. That's when the B.B. King element fell in. "But it wasn't like I listened to a bunch of old blues records and decided to put one in a song. I'm not a blues fan in a traditional sense. It was an accident. I went to a music store and copied a bunch of random sounds for my computer, everything from rocks falling down a cliff to the B.B. King sample. I put it in, hit the key, broke up the melody to fit the timing of the song, and it sounded cool."

Then O'Connor bailed on music. Three years later, he decided to release the album himself, ascribing it to an assumed band name, Primitive Radio Gods. But, frustrated by an indifferent response, he returned to his job. A year after that, O'Connor discovered a cache of the CDs while cleaning his closet and decided to mail out a few more copies. *Rocket* passed into the hands of a music biz exec, and "Standing Outside a Broken Phone Booth with Money in My Hand" began to take off.

The hit song was also featured on *The Cable Guy* soundtrack, and O'Connor, who reassembled the band to tour, was trying to build on that success. "It's weird, I'm having problems. I can't connect a lot of it to the reality of who I am. I'm sitting in a hotel room, and the perception is that I'm riding around in a limo with babes on each arm. Someone wins the lottery every once in a while, and that's what happened to me. There's no formula. I'm trying to have fun and not take it too seriously. I've been enjoying my 15 minutes of fame, if that's all it is." ■

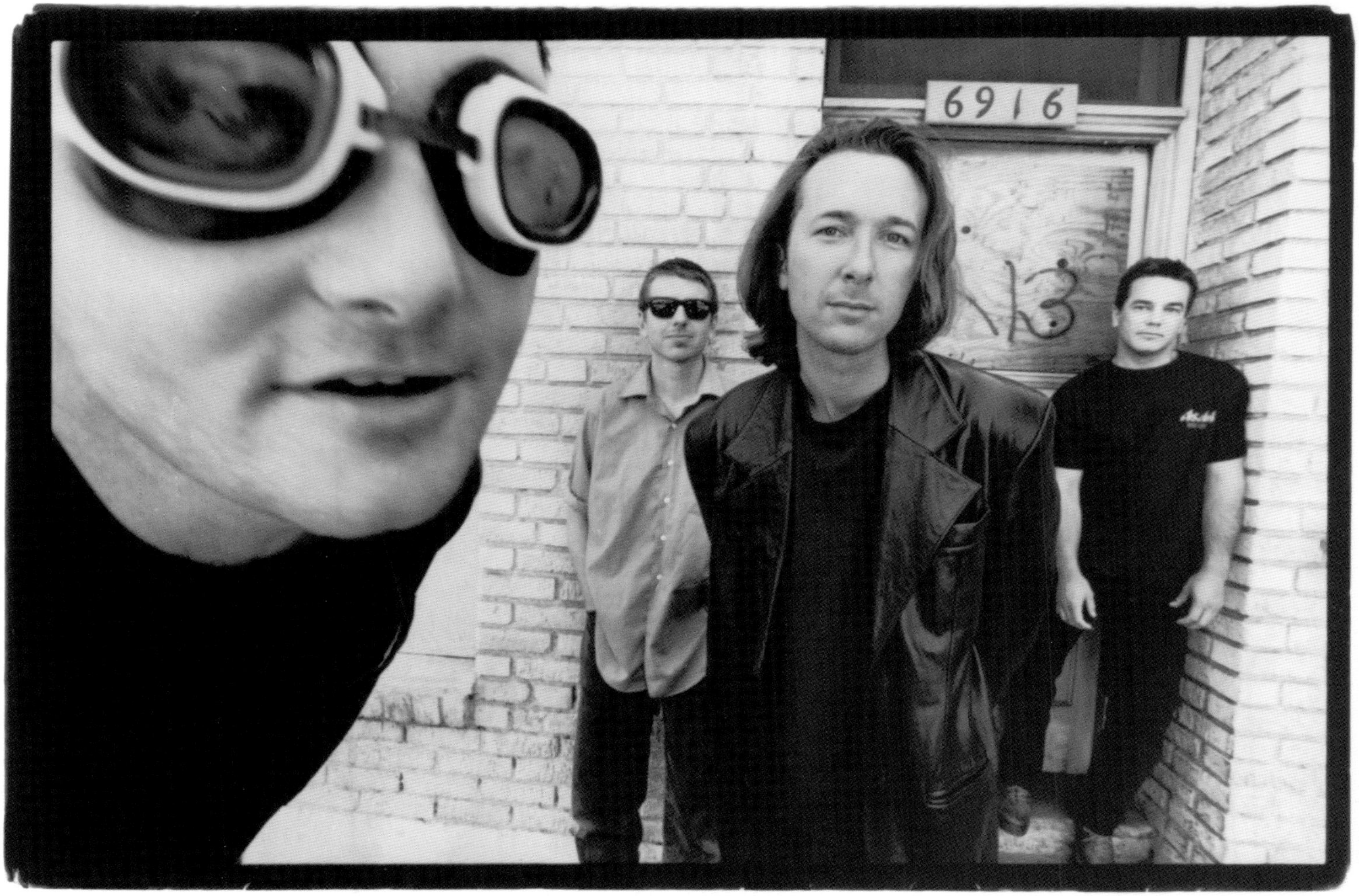

PHOTOGRAPH: LISA JOHNSON

Luke McAuliffe    Jeff Sparks    Chris O'Connor    Tim Lauterio

**primitive radio gods**

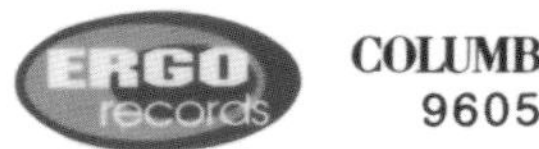


COLUMBIA
9605

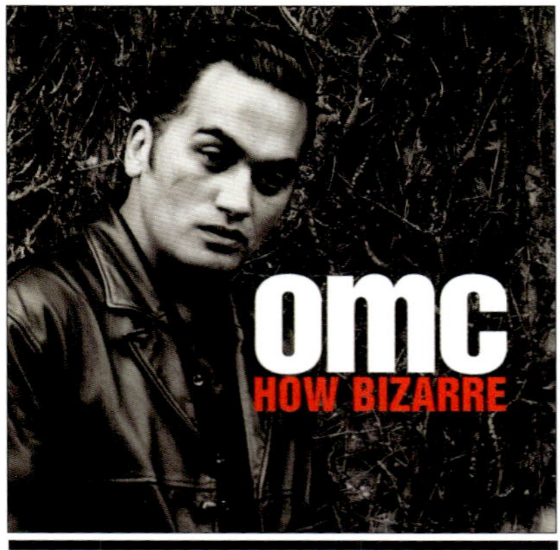


*Billboard* 200: *How Bizarre* (#40)

## A summer anthem by a pioneering South Auckland musician, OMC's "How Bizarre" took the world by storm.

**WITH THE** insidiously catchy "How Bizarre," OMC attracted global attention. The breezy single streaked to No. 1 in 10 countries, with the song's title becoming a catch phrase—listeners mimicked singer Pauly Fuemana's lilting, accented delivery, exclaiming "How bizarre!"

Fuemana, who basically was OMC, learned the effects of having surprise international success. "At home in New Zealand, everyone said, 'That's the worst song, no one's going to like it,'" he said. "It's been a year and a half, and I've been around the world three times. People are now saying, 'I knew it was going to be successful.'"

Before his career took off, Fuemana had it tough. A street kid born to a Nuiean father and a Maori mother, he was raised in Otara, a rough section of South Auckland. But the charismatic Antipodean found salvation in music. He fronted the Otara Millionaires Club until the local band split up in 1995, leaving him to hook up with producer and co-writer Alan Jansson and pursue a solo career under the band's acronym.

"Poverty is the same everywhere—you end up doing some really stupid things to survive," Fuemana explained. "You don't regret it, but you grow up cautious about who you talk to, what area you venture into. I'm so glad I had the opportunity to leave that lifestyle behind me and do music. I'm not focusing on my problems from the past. We're not trying to push anything, no hidden messages. We just want people to have a good time.

"How Bizarre" made accordion and a bullfight trumpet as fundamental as guitar, bass and drums. "The Tijuana trumpet was the main part I really pushed for, or it would be like Neil Diamond doing 'Solitary Man' without the French horns," Fuemana said. "I grew up with some beautiful songs created by great people. I wanted to be involved with a song that had those elements."

On the rest of the *How Bizarre* album, Fuemana made a diverse sound that could have been called "urban Pacific Rim"—a blend of Western pop, rap, country and lounge with Auckland rhythms and harmonies. "Right On" was as irresistible as the title track.

"Alan and I wanted to use everything we could, from Roxy Music to David Bowie to Sergio Mendes to Bob Marley, without stepping on anyone's toes. It's like an homage. New Zealand is such a small country, and Europe and America have been bombarding it with music for the last century. We're taking ingredients from the two influences."

The media compared Fuemana with everyone from Marvin Gaye (his "sharp easy grace") to Beck (his playful rap 'n' roll) to Elvis (his heavy-lidded eyes, full lips and jet-black pompadour). He embraced the assertion that "How Bizarre" was a quasi-novelty smash. "New Zealand bands have always had to move to Australia or London or America to try and make their mark. It's been a great privilege to be part of something in New Zealand and succeed all the way here—and I can still jump on a plane and go home." ■

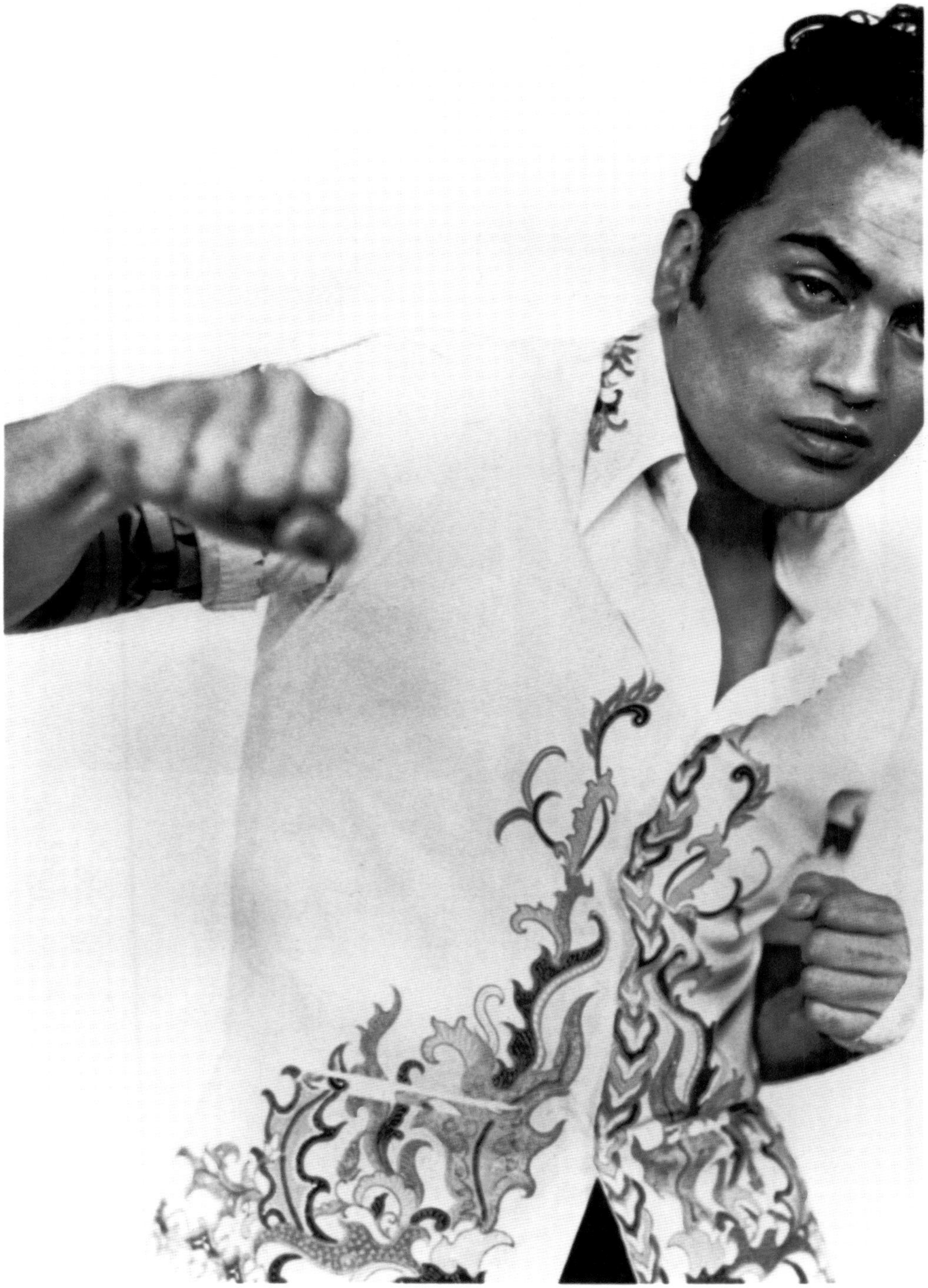

PAULY FUEMANA

huh!

omc

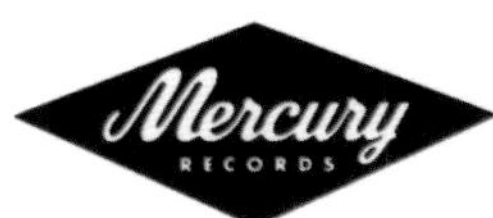

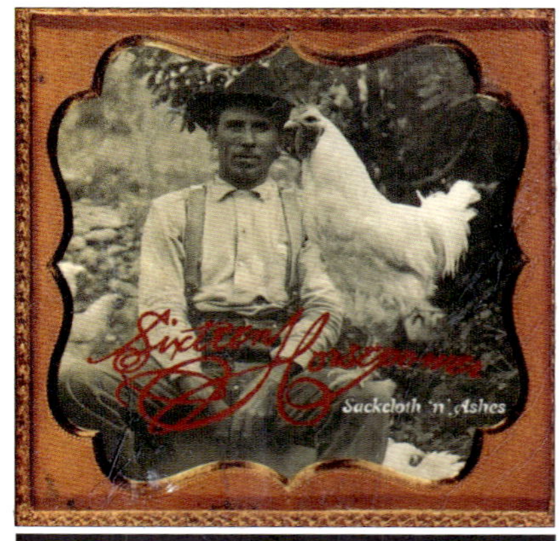


## *Sackcloth 'n' Ashes* established the mesmerizing alternative-country interpretations of Sixteen Horsepower.

**THE GRIPPING**, atmospheric style of Sixteen Horsepower sounded nothing like a take on post-grunge music. The sound, described as "roots-gloom," "American gothic" and "spooky campfire," was a mix of rustic blues wailings, old-time country tunes and modern-rock dramaticism. But it helped the Denver-based trio attain big-league status—the debut album *Sackcloth 'n' Ashes* was released by A&M Records.

Wan and lanky David Eugene Edwards fronted bassist Keven Soll and drummer Jean-Yves Tola, creating an edgy, earthy mood on vintage instruments—Edwards switched between slide guitar, banjo and the distinctive cry of a bandoneon (a turn-of-the-century small button accordion), his songs propelled by Tola's stripped-down kit. Edwards' voice was creaky and eerie. The vibe reflected a love of traditional music.

"I played electric guitar in punk rock bands in high school, but I've always played the acoustic guitar," Edwards said. "I started getting into other types of music, not necessarily quiet, folky music, just 'rootsy' music from all over—Russia, Hungary, Czechoslovakia. That's my family's heritage. My grandfather and father are Nazarene preachers, which is an old, Southern-style sect. I always liked the music around church—that's my main influence. Somebody found a banjo in the trash and gave it to me, and I started playing it. I went looking for an accordion and saw the used bandoneon in the window of a music store."

Edwards, who'd grown up in Colorado, was in Los Angeles working as a carpenter on Roger Corman's film set in 1992. He met the jazz-trained Tola, who had emigrated from Paris. They relocated back in Denver to team with Soll, a luthier by trade who performed on his own handmade flat-top acoustic basses. Within six weeks, Sixteen Horsepower was playing clubs.

"L.A. isn't a fun place to live, and I missed Colorado," Edwards said. "In L.A., there are so many money people into the alternative scene. In Colorado, nobody cares except the people who go see the music—they're more supportive. And we had friends there, so I knew at least five people would be at our first show."

Warren Burleigh, a producer who'd been behind the board for the Violent Femmes, saw a gig and offered his services. He was at Ardent Studios in Memphis when the band cut *Sackcloth 'n' Ashes*. Listening to Edwards' apocalyptic wailing on songs like "Heel on the Shovel" brought the names of Leonard Cohen and Nick Cave to mind. "Black Soul Choir" entered the playlists at most college radio stations—Edwards chose the banjo as his lead instrument and combined it with Soll and Tola's bent rhythm.

"We're just trying to have a positive attitude," Tola said. "This music came out of what we like—we didn't think other people would like it as much as they have. The record company doesn't want to force the album down people's throats, but they've seen the reaction to the live show. It's going to take a couple of years of touring the world for people to understand what we're about." ■

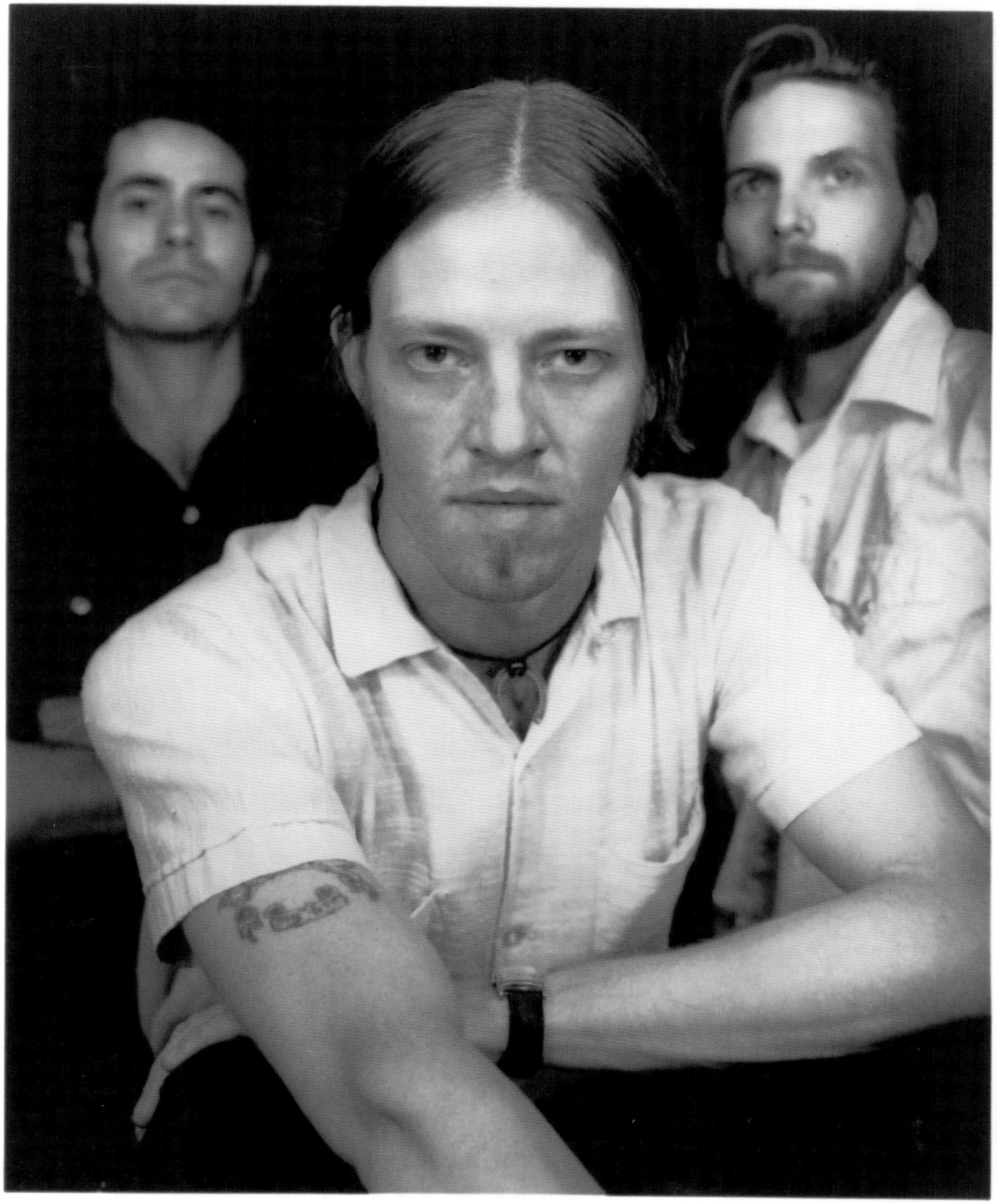

Photo: Tony Nelson 7/96

Jean-Yves Tola David Eugene Edwards Rob Redick

Amy Berg/Steve Stewart Management
(213)468-0250

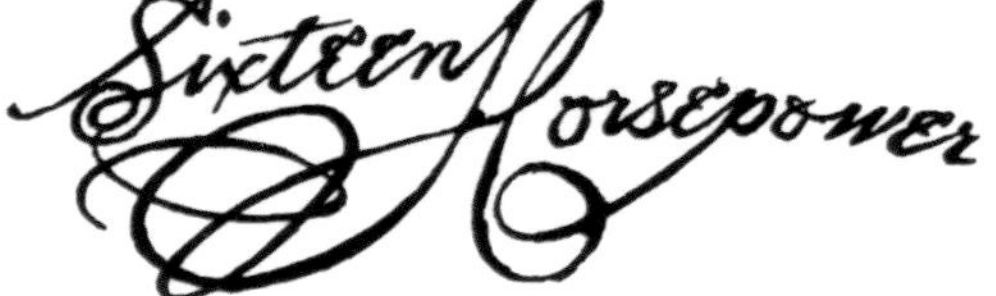


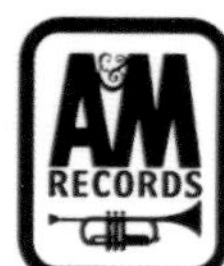

*Billboard* 200: *Wild Mood Swings* (#12)
*Billboard* Hot 100: "The 13th" (#44); "Mint Car" (#58)

# The Cure followed its commercial and critical pinnacle with personnel congruousness and *Wild Mood Swings*.

**IN THE** early Seventies, Cure auteur Robert Smith started specializing in brooding, frightening melodramatics. Since then, the British group had continually evolved from his original mope-rock presentation, switching from synth-pop to pop-jazz to the jaunty, spirited "Friday I'm In Love"—the band's last worldwide hit. "There have been five different Cures—the band has changed with my outlook," Smith noted. "Unfortunately, we seem to be the only band in the world that's not allowed to be whatever we want. This 'doom-and-gloom' label is still put on us."

But the singer/guitarist knew that his dark, obsessive image led the Cure down that career path. "There's a lot of baggage," he admitted. "But I'm proud of what we've done. I don't do it for the same reasons as other people. I'm not driven to be successful, just to play music and write songs. I'm being slightly disingenuous because they've gone hand in hand, but all I ever wanted was a means of self-expression. The last year has been the best of my life. This might be it for the Cure, and I want to get the most out of it."

Smith considered *Wild Mood Swings*, the Cure's first studio album since 1992, a band effort. "I'm four years older—there's a difference in me," he said. "I determined that I would rid myself of the things that I disliked about being in the Cure, whether it be the methodology or the interaction between band members. In the past, I tried to get them involved, and it worked on various levels. But ultimately, they always looked to me to sort things out and get the best out of people. It was a strain, looking out for telltale signs—who was going to crack up next, who was going to jeopardize the entire thing. I figured this time around the onus shouldn't be on me."

*Wild Mood Swings* found the veteran alternative band with another new lineup. Jason Cooper made his debut replacing long-time Cure drummer Boris Williams, and keyboardist Roger O'Donnell (a member of the group between 1987 and 1990) had returned, with bassist Simon Gallup and guitarist Perry Balmonte. "We started the demos when Boris was in the group. After he left, I was down, and I had a rethink—the album was going to be entirely acoustic, with a string quartet and a pianist, no drums. Then I had another change of heart—I decided I wanted to put a group together. So it was a long process, but it was good. I needed a break."

A recording sojourn at two different country houses in western England had rejuvenated the band. "In that environment, we cooked for each other, took turns cleaning up. We quickly developed an emotional bond that can only grow out of living together. We're all a little bit calmer—we're less likely to hit each other than the last time we were together on a tour bus." *Wild Mood Swings* featured an eclectic mix of styles and tempos. The unusual "The 13th" was spiced with salsa music, and "Mint Car" was sunny. "I like that kind of dumb pop," Smith explained. "It adds a bit of humor." ■

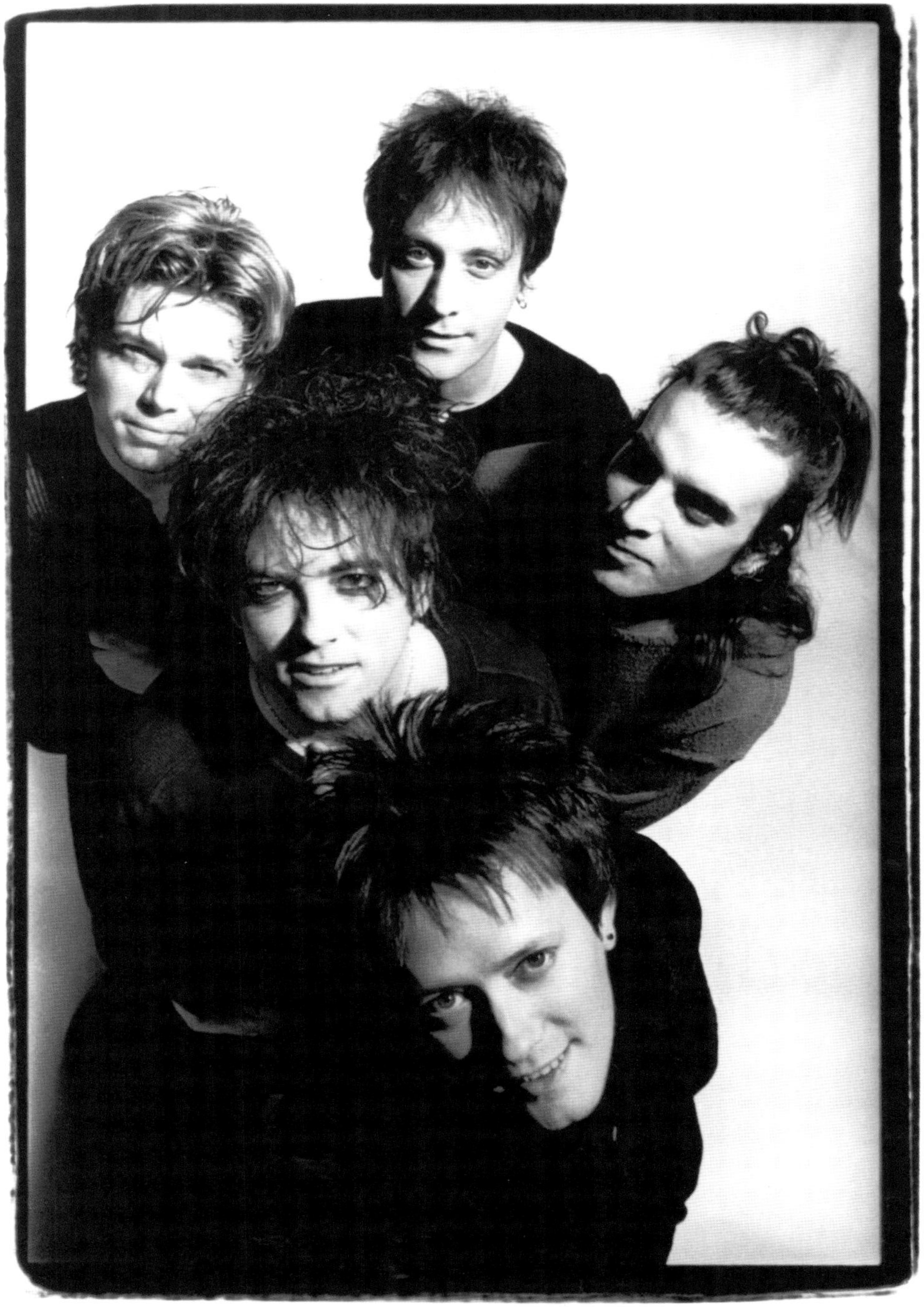

PHOTO CREDIT PAUL COX / 1996

CLOCKWISE FROM TOP CENTER : PERRY BAMONTE, SIMON GALLUP, ROGER O'DONNELL, ROBERT SMITH, JASON COOPER

# THE CURE

FICTION

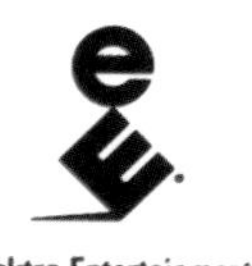

Elektra Entertainment

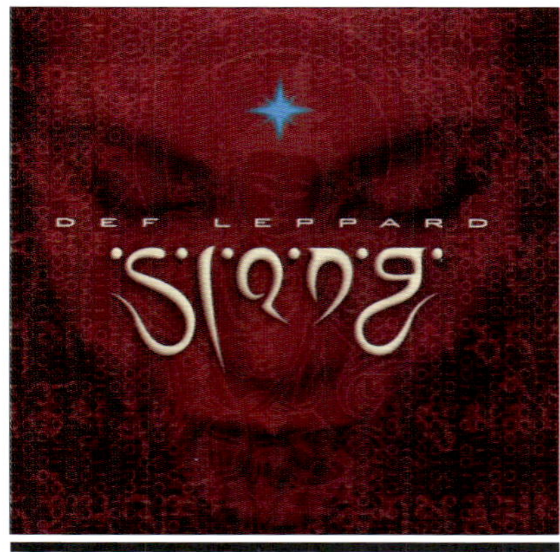


*Billboard* 200: *Slang* (#14)

## Def Leppard's *Slang* album signified an acute musical departure from the pop-metal band's trademark sound.

**FINDNG ENORMOUS** success in the Eighties, Def Leppard became the first band ever to sell more than 9 million albums consecutively in America—*Pyromania* and *Hysteria* spawned such extravagantly produced pleasures as "Pour Some Sugar on Me," "Animal" and "Photograph."

Tastes had changed, however, in the four years since *Adrenalize*, the British quintet's last studio album. Their carefree power-rock had taken a hit at the hands of the alternative outbreak. But who said a Leppard couldn't change is spots? The album *Slang* opened with an aggressive sound—mechanical tempo, abrasive guitars and distorted vocal. "We'd done so many albums in a certain way, it was time to move on," guitarist Phil Collen said. "I think it's the most creative thing we've done, exactly like we wanted it to be. The emphasis was on the songs and performance, not the production and gloss."

"Work It Out," which reached the Top 10 on the mainstream rock charts, had industrial-funk overtones. There were no choral-backing vocals—Joe Elliott's singing was stripped-down. And drummer Rick Allen, who'd lost his arm in a 1984 auto accident, traded in his electronic kit. "'Work It Out' was a pop song initially, but we wanted to give it a harder edge influenced by different stuff like Nine Inch Nails," Collen said. "The guitar playing on this album was the easiest we've ever done, a lot of first-take stuff. The sound was very black and white—either it worked or it didn't. We didn't go looking for it months on end.

"The crooning quality that Joe managed helped as well. The demo had a very high, pure voice, and normally that would have been Joe's range, but it was out of context. I said, 'Sing it like Iggy Pop,' and bang, it was there. Obviously, Rick had to get over a lot of personal demons—electronic drums allowed him to be able to play at all. So it was a big step for him to say, 'Okay, I'm going to play real drums now.' Once he did, we sounded like a different band. There were dynamics that we hadn't had in 12 years."

*Slang* got a boost from market-savvy craftsmanship—Def Leppard applied the expected melodic hooks and pop sensibilities to "All I Want Is Everything," a sparkling ballad. "Anyone who's heard the album loves it, but getting people to actually listen is a difficult thing—it's not a given like it used to be," Collen said. "It's a very weird time for rock bands to get national radio exposure unless you fit into an alternative format. Plus people have so many distractions. I don't think rock music is as important in their lives as it used to be."

The members' actions outside the studio had created a speed bump on their return road to success. Elliott and his wife were arrested for assaulting each other, then Allen was charged with spousal battery and convicted. "But everyone's getting along great," Collen assured. "It's grown-up to be able to correct the problems in their personal lives." ■

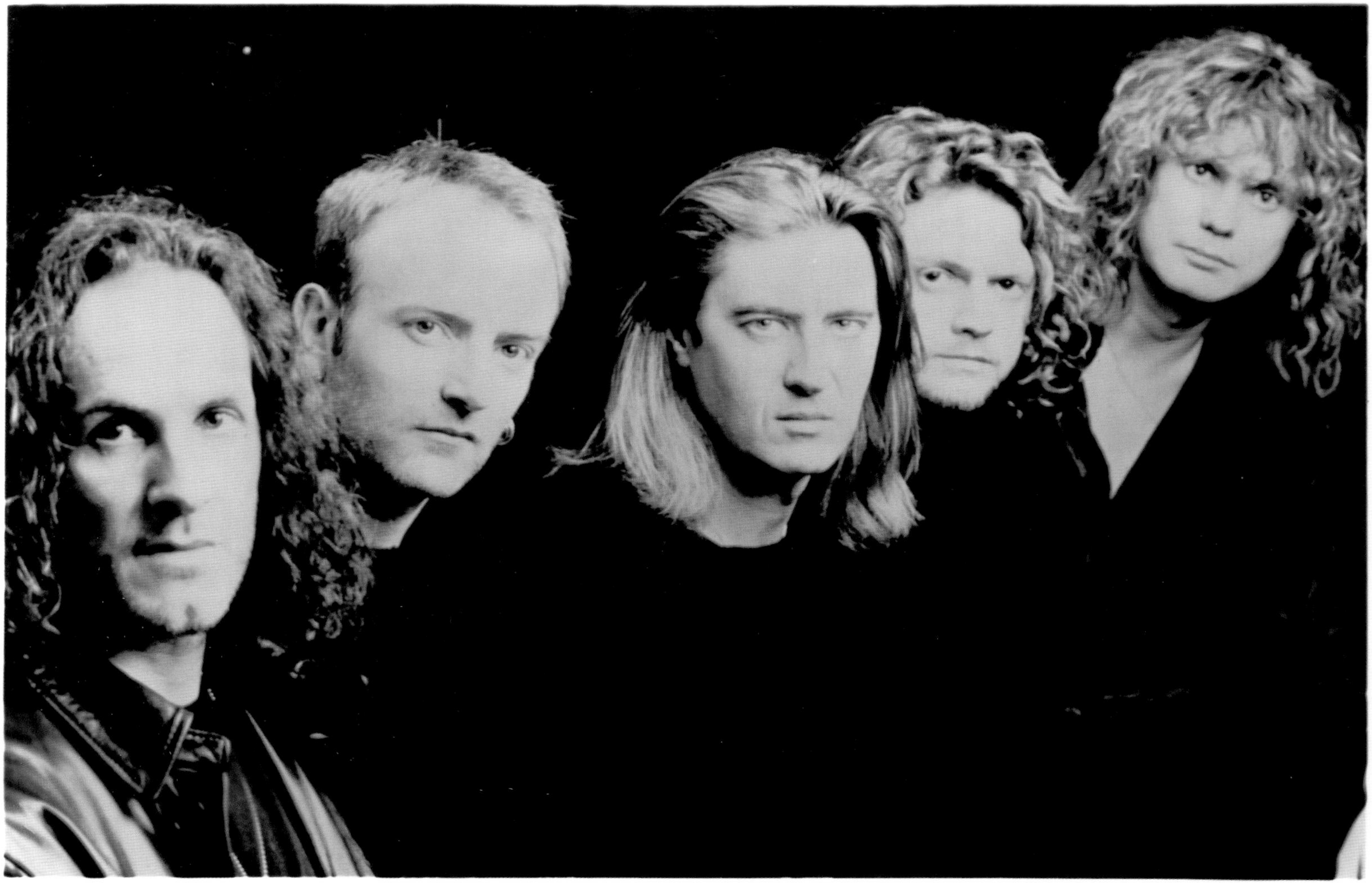

PHOTO CREDIT: CYNTHIA LEVINE

L to R: Vivian Campbell, Phil Collen, Joe Elliott, Rick Allen, Rick Savage

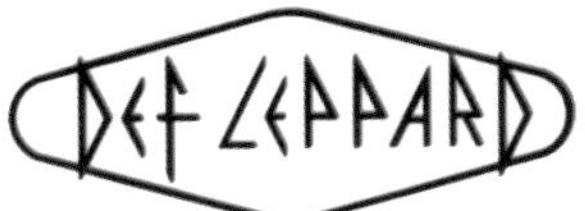


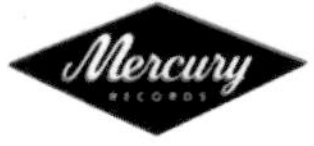

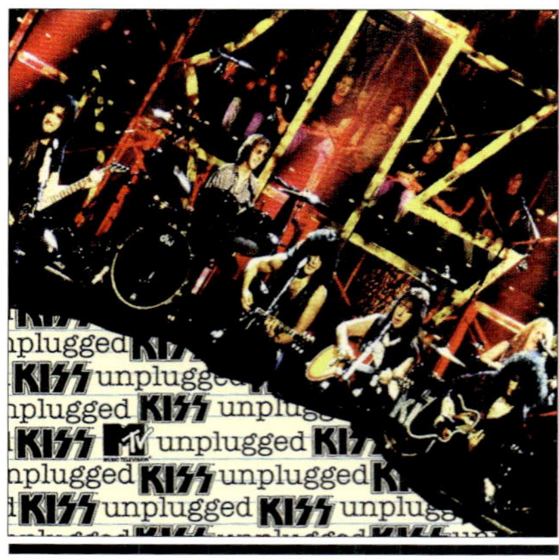


*Billboard* 200: *Kiss Unplugged* (#15)

## An *MTV Unplugged* appearance culminated in a reunion tour with the four estranged founding members of Kiss.

**COUNTLESS YOUNG** musicians had been inspired by Kiss, from Nine Inch Nails' Trent Reznor (who dressed up as bassist Gene Simmons in a Halloween parade when he was 13 years old) to Garth Brooks (who had all of Kiss' 8-track tapes in high school). So the rock world could do worse than a full-scale Kiss renaissance.

It began when the band joined the long line of musicians to perform on a historic episode of *MTV Unplugged*. Simmons, guitarist Paul Stanley and current members drummer Eric Singer (drums) and Bruce Kulick (guitar)—were joined by original Kiss members Ace Frehley and Peter Criss. The set, released as the album *Kiss Unplugged*, spanned the band's career, showing young whippersnappers the importance of hooks and harmonies and a sense of trashy fun.

And then Simmons, Stanley, Criss and Frehley—Kiss' first lineup—bludgeoned their way back onto the stage, reuniting for the first time since 1979 with their renowned makeup and special effects. Simmons, everybody's favorite flame-spitting, blood-spewing, tongue-wagging rock star, was feeling shrewd and practical. He was the group's businessman—he owned the rights to Kiss' likeness in makeup. Clearly, money—the gross from ticket sales, merchandising and cross-promotions—was an incentive for Kiss to reform. Simmons' exuberance sealed the deal.

"Ace and Peter decided to get their lives in order," he said, referring to Frehley and Criss' immoderation of the last decade. "When you look into somebody's eyes and you start to see the chemistry that attracted you to them in the first place, you're reminded of why the band was put together with these four members as opposed to others. Everybody brought a piece of the puzzle that was missing.

"I wouldn't have done this a year earlier or 14 years earlier, because a team is only as good as every one of its members. The original Kiss was a dysfunctional family—that's why it broke up in the first place. (Frehley and Criss) have realized that it's a blessing, and Axl Rose-like behavior is just not tolerated. The same rules apply to everybody, and we believe in the working man's ethos—you do the best you can, every time, no excuses, no whining."

Kiss' fan base was second in loyalty only to that of the Beatles, and devotees got what they came for—the Seventies revisited, a live display that was the ultimate in extended adolescence. Simmons made no apologies for the band's excesses.

"Yes, we're going to make an awful lot of money. Fine. We get paid for our living, so does everybody else. Everybody gets paid different amounts, but so what? Welcome to life. But we've never shied away from putting our money where our mouth is. Our competition was never whether John Denver was changing a tie-dyed T-shirt. We've always competed with only one very big band—Kiss." ■

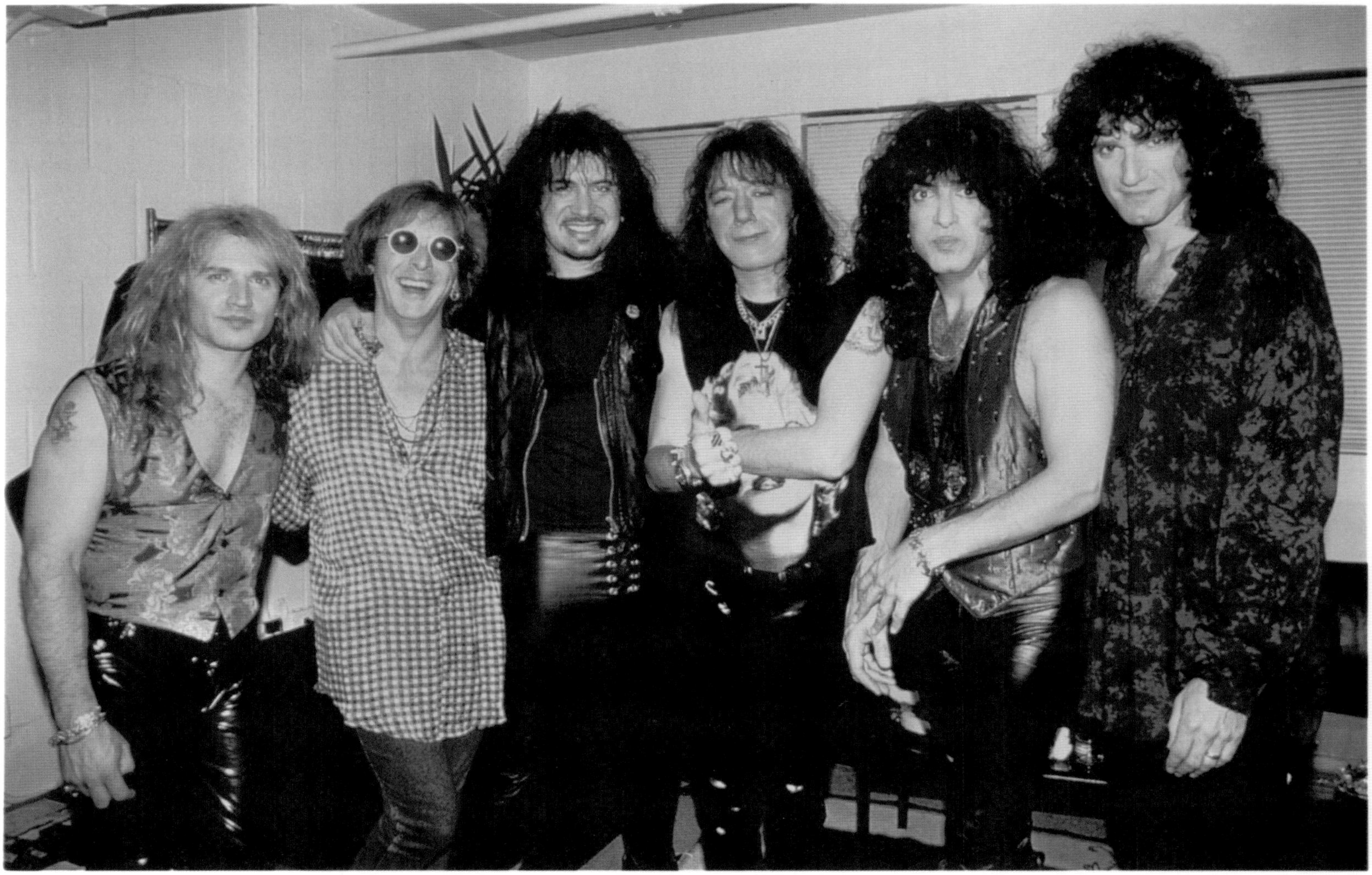

L R : ERIC SINGER, PETER CRISS, GENE SIMMONS, ACE FREHLEY PAUL STANLEY BRUCE KULICK

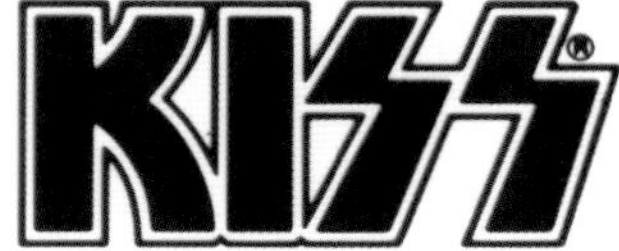


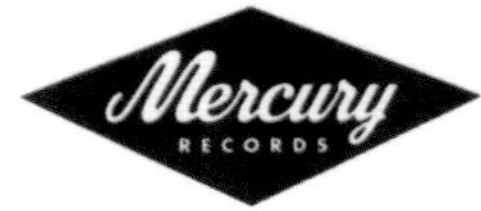

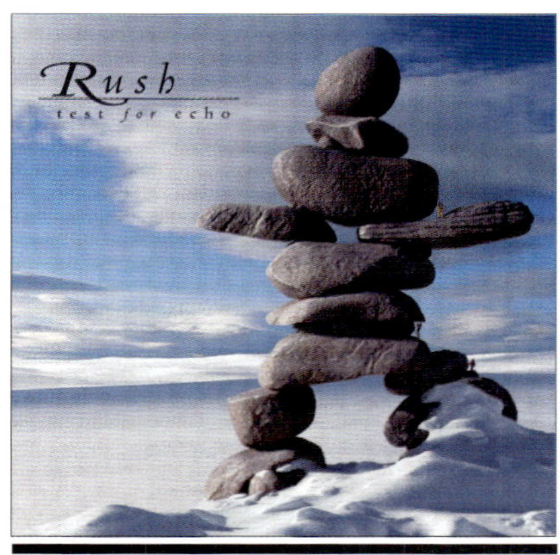


*Billboard* 200: *Test for Echo* (#5)

## The members of Rush concentrated on their individual performances for the guitar-driven *Test for Echo* album.

**IN 1993**, after making music for more than 20 years with hardly a break, Rush decided to take a vacation—and risk losing touch with fans. Guitarist Alex Lifeson released his first solo album under the name Victor, and drummer Neil Peart worked on a Buddy Rich tribute. Bassist and vocalist Geddy Lee spent time with his family. "In the world of making rock records, three years really is a long time—enough to totally fade from memory," Lee said.

Yet Rush returned more inspired than ever. *Test for Echo*, the Canadian power trio's 20th album, was the hardest-edged record since 1981's *Moving Pictures*, which yielded the hits "Tom Sawyer" and "Limelight." The sound focused on Peart's tricky time signatures and Lifeson's busy solos, with fewer of the keyboards and production flourishes that bound the band's recent progressive hard-rock work.

"With this one, what the music was saying and how it was being put together was the result of numerous experiments," Lee explained. "There's no guitar player alive who likes to play with a keyboard, so usually Alex brings up his feelings about that. Over the previous three albums, I had found myself getting a little bored with that over-arranged approach that naturally occurs when you use keyboards at an early stage of writing. These days I prefer to use it only to provide something extra that a song lacks."

Three songs from *Test for Echo*, produced by Peter Collins (Jewel, Queensryche), ascended the mainstream rock charts. The crisp title track explored the puzzle of global communication, acoustic guitars passed through the enchanting "Half the World," and dizzying licks darted around "Driven."

"Fortunately, technology keeps changing—the methods of working on your music get more confusing and complicated, so that brings a different challenge every time around," Lee said. "Those are good things, although sometimes frustrating, because they stimulate you and take you away from your normal mode of expression. That new look at the same thing is very important to keep us from falling asleep at the wheel."

All three members of Rush had developed awe-inspiring chops on their instruments. "When you're a young band first starting, all you want to do is practice, because gigs are few and far between," Lee said. "Then you're touring, and you're practicing every day. Then when you achieve a measure of success and you're able to slow down, your practice subsides a bit. And you suddenly find yourself in the unfortunate position of feeling a little detached from your muse. You feel the urge to start woodshedding again.

"What we learned from this album was, all the extra practice we did was actually able to take us to a higher level. Every time you think you've flattened out in your learning curve, you find out that that's not true—there's so much farther to go. Like any craft, you have to work on it your entire life to keep on getting better and better." ■

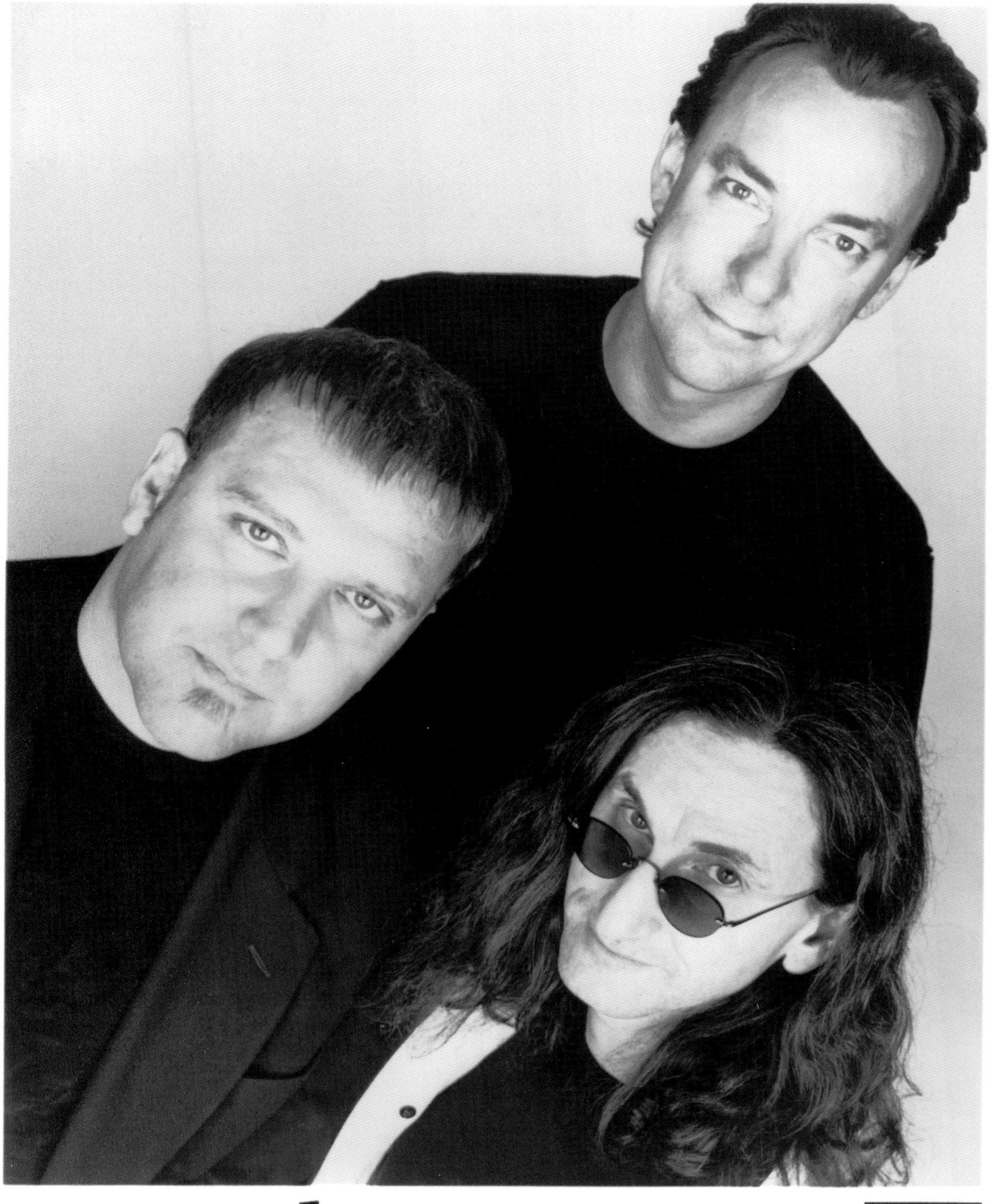

Rush

Photo Credit: George Whiteside

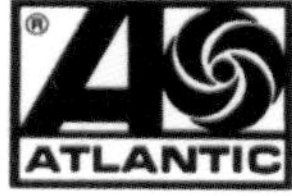

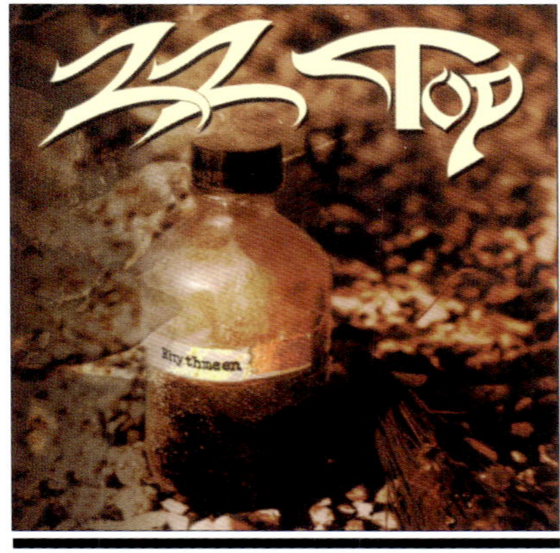


*Billboard* 200: *Rhythmeen* (#29)

## Blues-based rock 'n' roll guitar workouts made *Rhythmeen* the most impressive ZZ Top effort in many moons.

**LESS ABOUT** production and more about what ZZ Top did best, *Rhythmeen* harkened back to stripped-down blues rather than the synth-based rock that characterized the venerable Texas trio's Eighties hits. "It's low-down, brother," guitarist Billy Gibbons said. "The old fans say it reminds them of early ZZ, and then the newer fans that came aboard around the *Eliminator* period say, 'Gee, this is something new for you guys.' It's a whirlwind."

The return to roots was stimulated by a session of the Robert Rodriguez/Quentin Tarantino film *From Dusk till Dawn*. "They were nearing completion of their vampire picture, and their incoming call stated that they were interested in having a ZZ Top offering included, perhaps as a theme song," Gibbons explained. "We said, 'Well, gee, we'd be most interested—when do you need it?' And they said, 'Tonight.' So, with that in mind, we composed and recorded 'She's Just Killing Me' and a second track within the space of an hour. When it was delivered that night, they said, 'Hey, this is ZZ as we like it, no change is required.'

"I credit the unsuspecting moment of the mad scramble to make a deadline. The pressure was on, and in this case it seemed to be positive—it set a focus and we kept it. You might see some interesting collaborations with the engineering staff on the songs, and a lot of observers have patted ZZ on the back for expanding their horizons. The reality is we had very little prepared, and many of the late-night sessions were a result of picking through the afternoon song ideas and rewriting in the studio."

In the title track from *Rhythmeen*, Gibbons said it all when he sang "the backbeat's the big boss." Songs like "What's Up with That" blended his salacious rasp and gritty, unpredictable solos with tough, funky rhythms. The band's sound was live, but there were some revealing drum-machine blips on a few tracks.

"For us, *Rhythmeen* is probably on the shier side of techno and leaning heavy on the grease," Gibbons said. "Frank (Beard, drummer) brought along some of his favorite drum loops, and as a shadow they support the title of this record—'mean rhythm.' But it didn't get in the way, and it didn't stamp the songs out of the ZZ three-guys-three-chords-three-beat format. We're managing to retain our interpretation of the blues and integrate sensible conveniences, shall we say.

"In the midst of the garage-sounds-are-cool trend, we've arrived quite fashionably. If it holds, maybe we could do the whole next album in an hour." ■

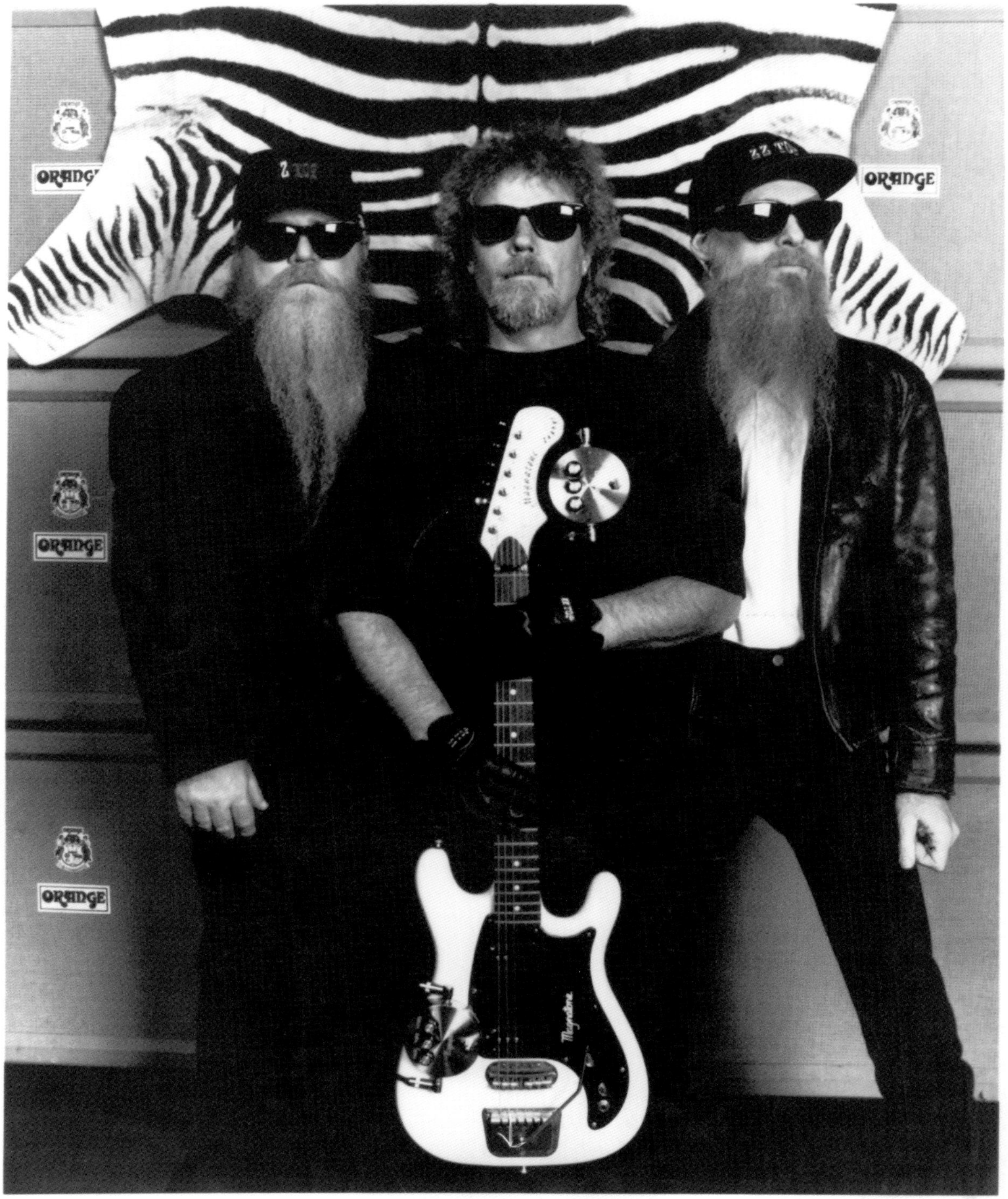

Photo Credit: James Bland

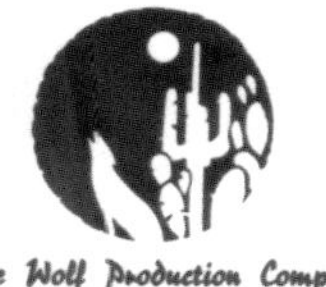


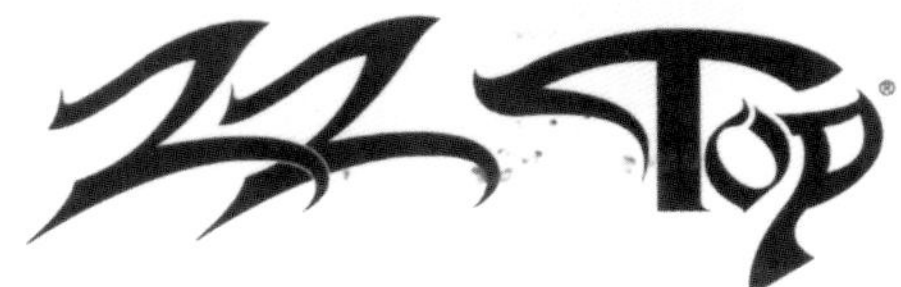


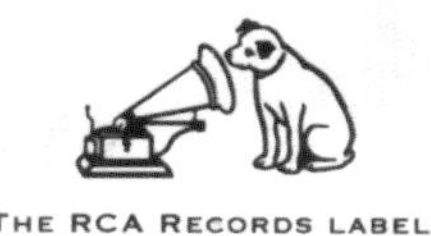

donovan sutras

## Sixties icon Donovan sallied forth on a new crusade, recording *Sutras* with sought-after producer Rick Rubin.

**ONE OF** the most distinctive talents in the heady days of the Sixties, Donovan blossomed from scruffy folk singer ("Catch the Wind") to a member of the British pop aristocracy. The young Scotsman rode a giant wave of success with "Sunshine Superman," "Mellow Yellow," "Atlantis," the great "Hurdy Gurdy Man" and other Top 40 hits.

But Donovan's commercial prominence had been clouded by his lasting flower-power image as a transcendental troubadour associated with peace-and-love idealism. With millions of people now involved in various forms of alternative consciousness, the icon believed that the world was once again ready for what he described as his "mystic pop" and his message of universal oneness. He recorded *Sutras*, his first album in more than a dozen years, "with one foot in Buddhism and the other in Tower Records."

"I purposely walked away, now I'm purposely coming back into it," Donovan said. "The Sixties were a mix—in the worlds of fashion and film and literature and dance and theater, anything went then. I was absorbing so much music—that was an exciting time for me, it broke open all the doors. But post-fame was difficult, because it wasn't just fame—it was a super-fame of a kind that few have."

After a string of indistinctive Seventies albums, Donovan withdrew, pursuing painting and photography and focusing on his family. "By 1983, I'd made 26 albums, and I said, 'That's enough.' I was never an entertainer in the sense that I had to keep going. There wasn't much happening for me musically. It was a private time, a lessons-to-be-learned time. I was in retreat at the Joshua Tree National Monument until U2 made the place famous. Then I moved back to Ireland.

"My wife Linda turned on the television and said, 'The Nineties look like the Sixties turned inside out.' So many subjects that were taboo were now establishing themselves. The 'new age' was in the shopping mall—the self-awareness and unconventional healing, the airing of minority views, the collections of ethnic music available. This was very different, a world I could respond to. I felt drawn back into it."

Donovan's return was guided by Rick Rubin, the rap/metal impresario who had just completed the highly acclaimed comeback album by Johnny Cash. Rubin sought out the reclusive singer and signed him to his American Recordings label. They spent more than two years writing and recording *Sutras*. "Linda said, 'You'll need a producer and a record company.' Ah, the hot-and-cold relationship with the music business. But she said, 'There will be a guy who's in control of his own destiny.' We waited, and Rick called. My young friends said, 'What are you going to do, Donovan hip-hop?' I laughed. Rick said, 'Let's just start recording you solo and see what happens.' We have a shared interest in Eastern mysticism."

The simple arrangements on *Sutras* were centered on Donovan's vocals and acoustic guitar. The stunning ballad "Please Don't Bend" was a love song with a haunting hook. "Rick wanted to go back to the beginning," Donovan said. "And I went with him." ■

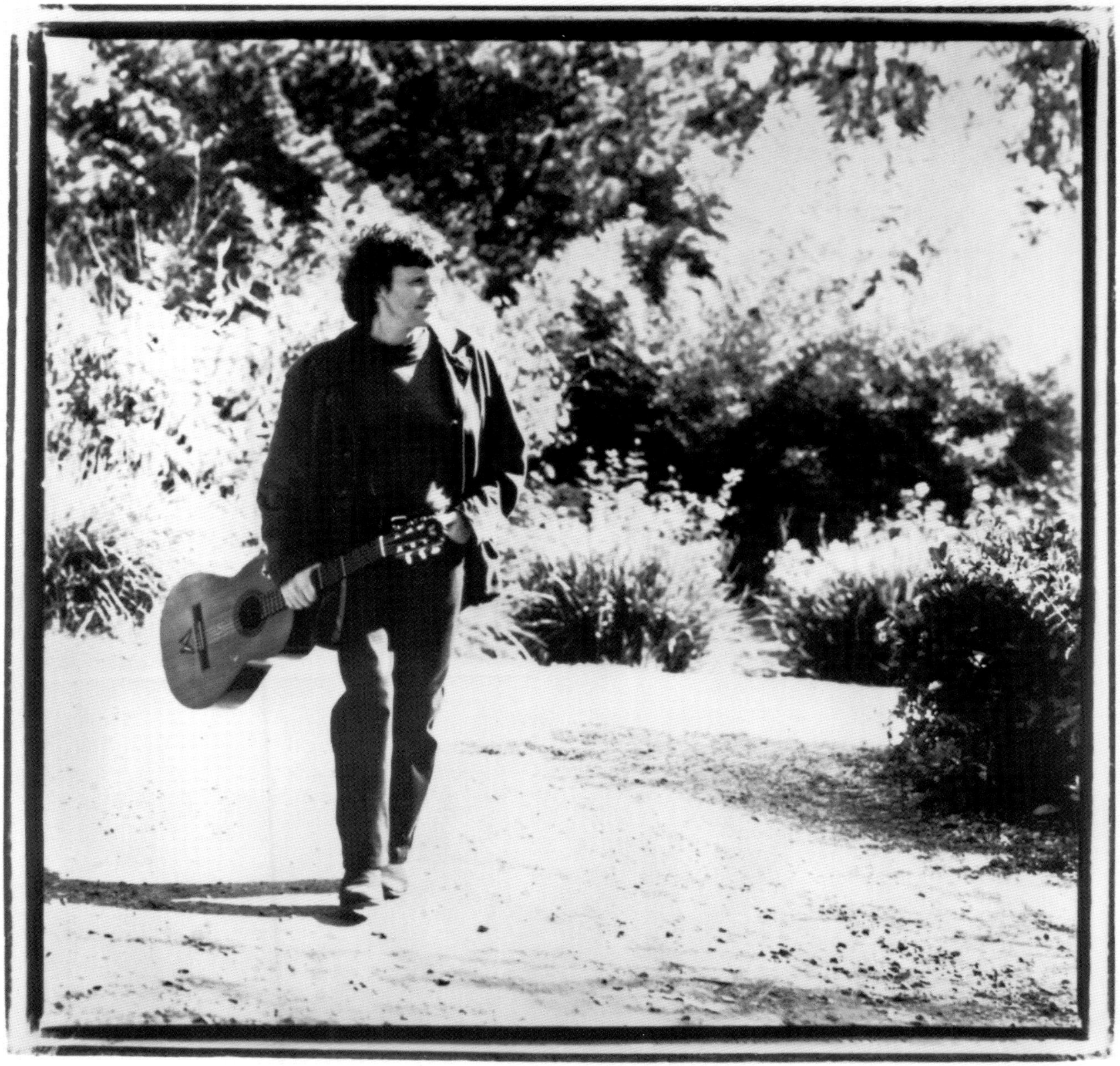

Photo Credit: American Recordings

# donovan

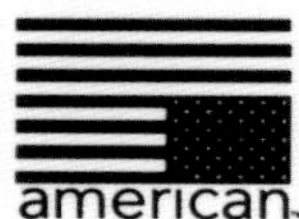

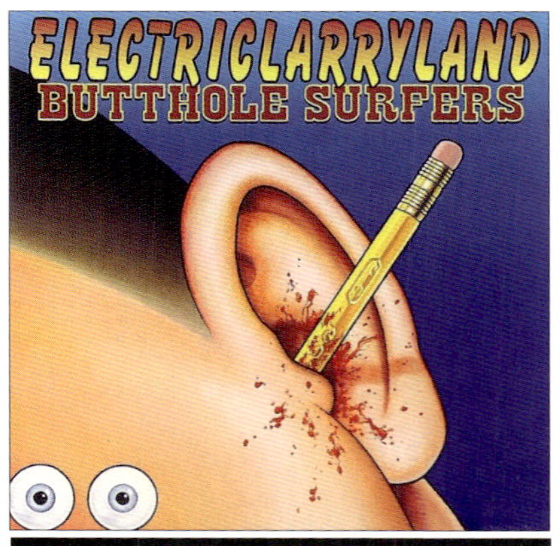


*Billboard* 200: *Electriclarryland* (#31)

## Many years of cultdom came to an end when Texas' Butthole Surfers experienced a surprise hit with "Pepper."

**MAINSTREAM FAILURE** was almost guaranteed when Butthole Surfers first got together on the campus of San Antonio's Trinity University in 1981. Many newspapers wouldn't print their scatological name in ads, and only underground radio stations would have anything to do with them.

But the world was finally ready for the shock-rockers—the Surfers had a hit when "Pepper" climbed to No. 1 on the modern-rock charts. "We've never had obscenity-ridden records, nor are we particularly political," ranting frontman Gibby Haynes said, acknowledging the band's "really stupid name."

Butthole Surfers had spent their career reveling in noisy, cheerfully demented work. *Locust Abortion Technician* (1987) and *Hairway to Steven* (1988) featured savage psychedelic mayhem, with Haynes' tortured screams and Paul Leary's overwrought guitar splotches. The band gained increased notoriety through frenzied, decadent live shows. Haynes was prone to antics such as pyromania and blasting a shotgun above his audience.

The Surfers didn't set out to align with a major label, but Capitol Records released *Electriclarryland*, creating a marketing strategy and major airplay for the trip-hop pop of "Pepper." "I don't know what to think of that song—I like it, but I don't expect anyone else to," Haynes mused. "King (Coffey, drummer) and I were talking about doing a record called *Trying Hard* where we totally cop the hits of the day, cover all the different genres. If we could really fool the people into thinking that we were really going for a pop record that would sell a lot, it would be a great deal of satisfaction to us."

The "Pepper" video contained a kidnap scene with Erik Estrada (famous for his role on the television police drama *CHiPs*) as the victim and the band members being pursued by federal agents. "People are like, 'Well, now you guys are trying to sell out.' I say, who'd you rather be right now, Kenny G or Kurt Cobain? My heart says Kurt Cobain, man, but my mom says Kenny G," Haynes laughed. "We've made so many records, it's hard for people to think of us as this semi-successful band that's part of rock history at this point. But it's gotta be true." ■

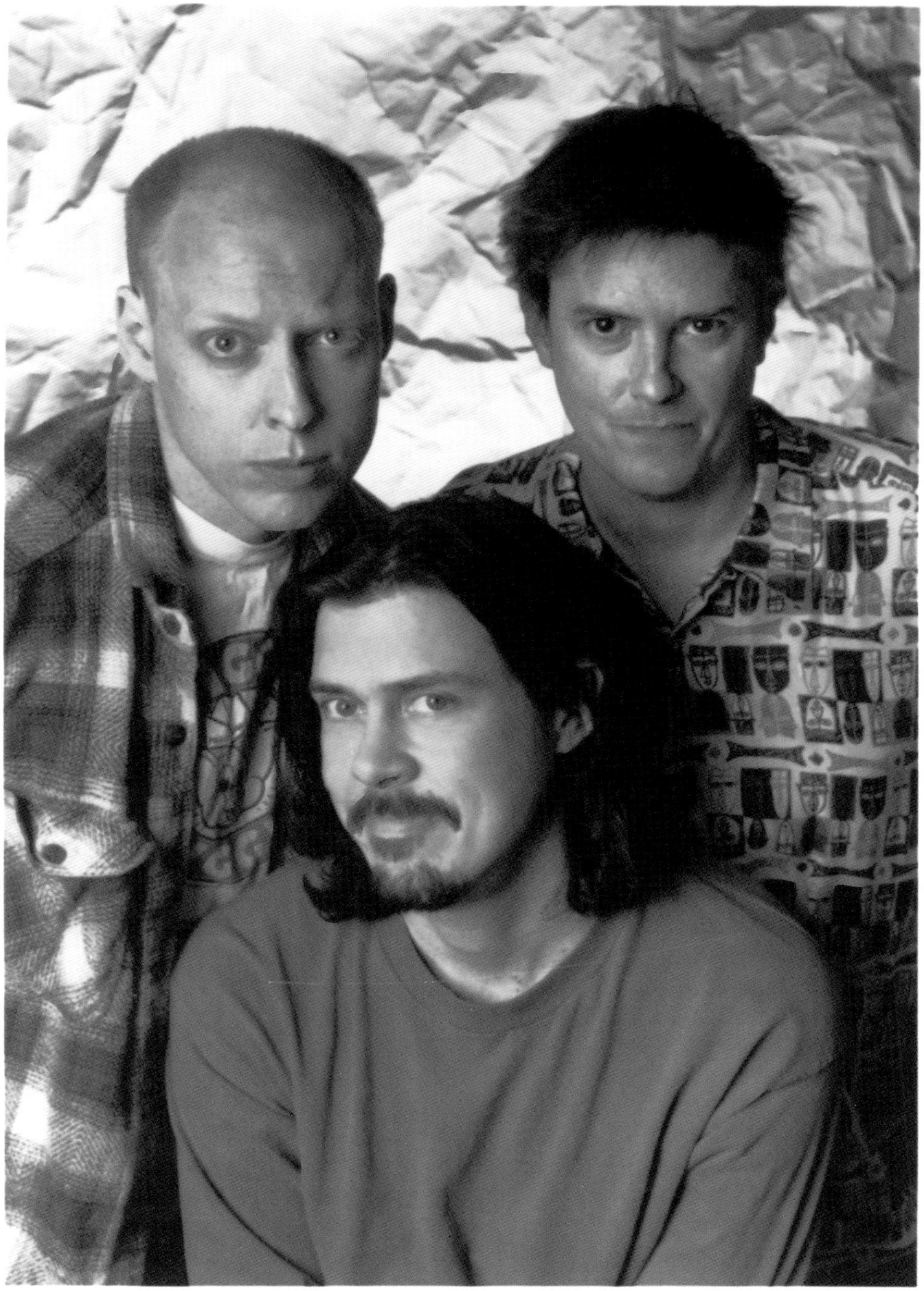

Photo Credit : Will van Overbeek © 1996

(L - R) : King Coffey, Gibby Haynes, Paul Leary

# BUTTHOLE SURFERS

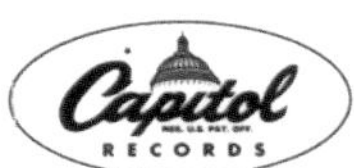

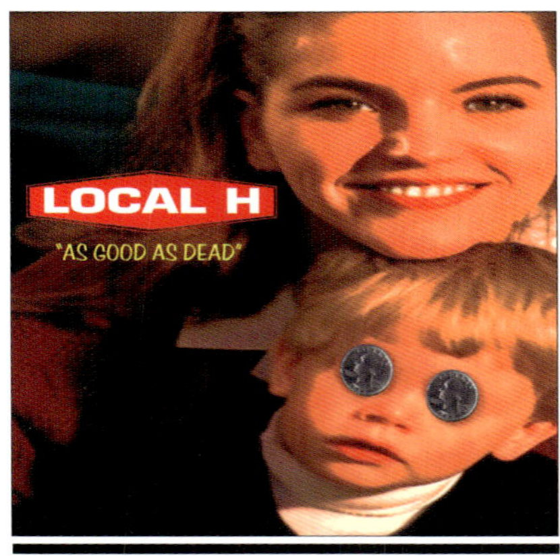


*Billboard* 200: *As Good as Dead* (#147)

## Alt-rock fans improved their word power through "Bound to the Floor" by Local H, the pride of Zion, Illinois.

**FOR TWO** guys, Local H made an enormous racket. The smart, funny duo—singer and guitarist Scott Lucas and drummer Joe Daniels—put energy, humor and presence into their music. They got compared with Nirvana, Lucas said, "because we play catchy songs, really fucking loud."

The album *As Good as Dead* was about the frustrations of growing up in a slow, dreary, small town like Zion (45 minutes north of Chicago). "What's interesting is that I wrote it from the point of view of someone who's in their 20s and goes to bars and is a loser—and it seems like a lot of kids are looking at it like a high-school record," Lucas said. "It weirds me out a little when people want to talk about these personal lyrics, because they're taking it on their own level."

*As Good as Dead* featured a hit radio single, "Bound to the Floor" (or "that copacetic song," as it was known on request lines): "You just don't get it/You keep it copacetic/You learn to accept it/You know you're so pathetic." "That was probably the hardest song on the record to write," Lucas said. "It used to have this big, majestic bridge in the middle, and it just took the song some other place. We fucked with it for quite a while, and it just wasn't working—it was too long, it got really boring. Then once we stepped back from it and realized that we should just simplify it and play that riff over and over, the song came together."

Other cool songs were "Fritz's Corner," about a bar in Zion, and "Eddie Vedder," a tale of rejection ("If I was Eddie Vedder/Would you like me any better?"). "I just always thought it was funny—I guess it's not *that* funny," Lucas said. "But 'Vedder' screamed to be rhymed with something. That's one of the lyric-writing techniques we do a lot—you just keep an ear open for slang and you pick it and put it in your songs."

"High-Fiving MF" was an excoriation of the macho jocks in the mosh pit. "What's interesting is that the hard-rock stations play it. You wouldn't think that they would be apt to play somebody new, because they've got one foot in classic rock and old metal. Which I think is great. I'd rather hear Ozzy Osbourne next to us than No Doubt."

Lucas and Daniel formed Local H during their high school years. The band was originally a quartet, but the guitarist and bass player left and were never replaced. "For a year we were basically writing and recording, and then we were starting to get interest based on that. These people thought we had a band together, and we weren't going to pass up any opportunity for a show coming up to say that we didn't."

So Lucas added a bass pickup to his guitar to accommodate the two low strings. "You've got to realize that you're backing yourself up," he explained. "If you're going to play anything melodic, you're going to have to hold down your bass notes. You start to look at each guitar string as a different possibility. It's like what Jimi Hendrix did—he would divide his guitar in two, and he'd have the bass doing one thing and the treble strings would do something. At first it's hard, and you get used to it." ■

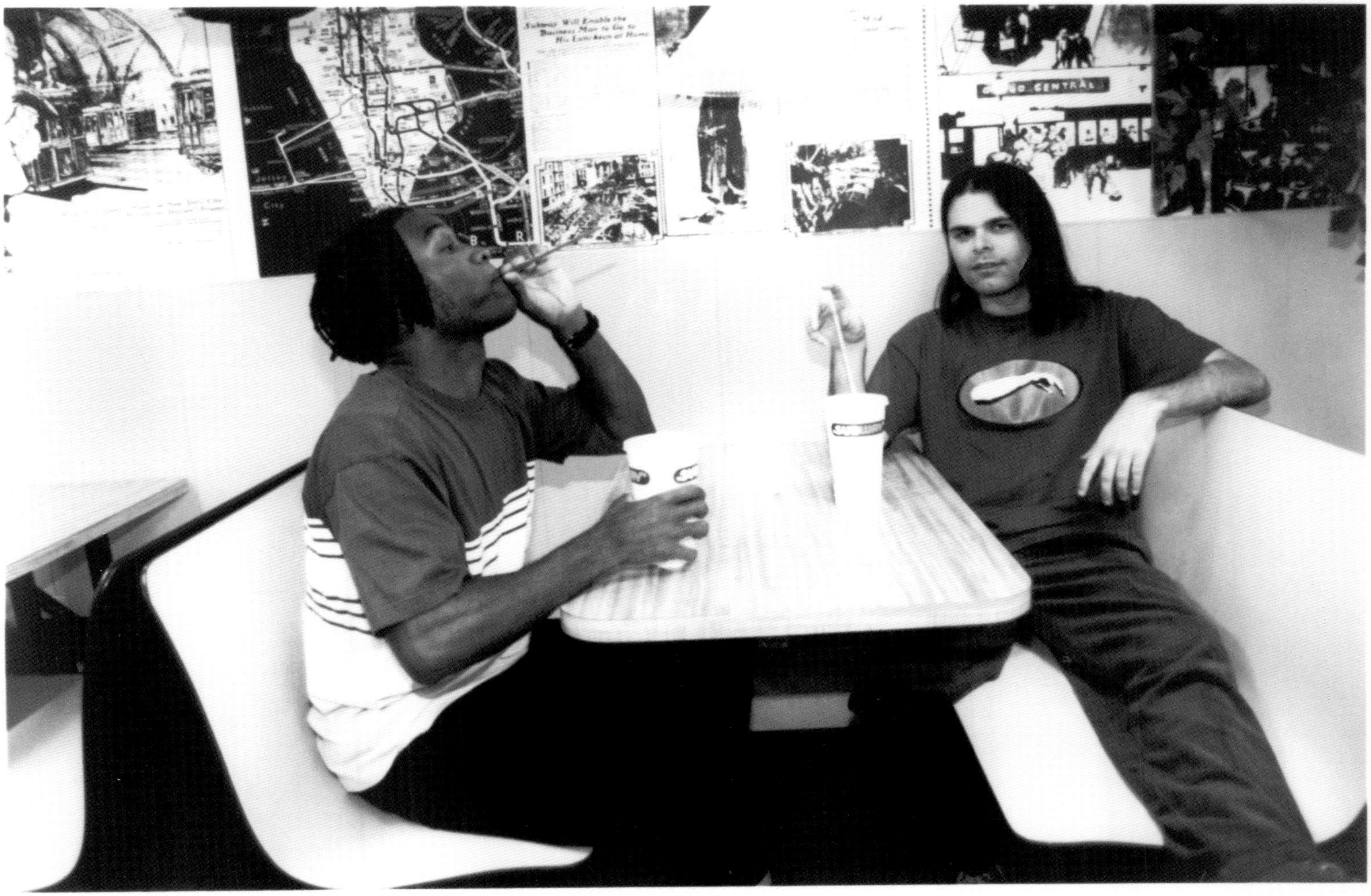

Joe Daniels

Scott Lucas

Photo Credit: John Nguyen

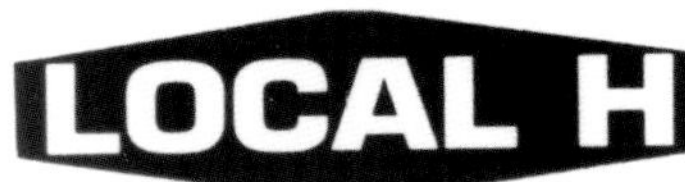


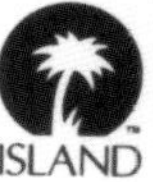

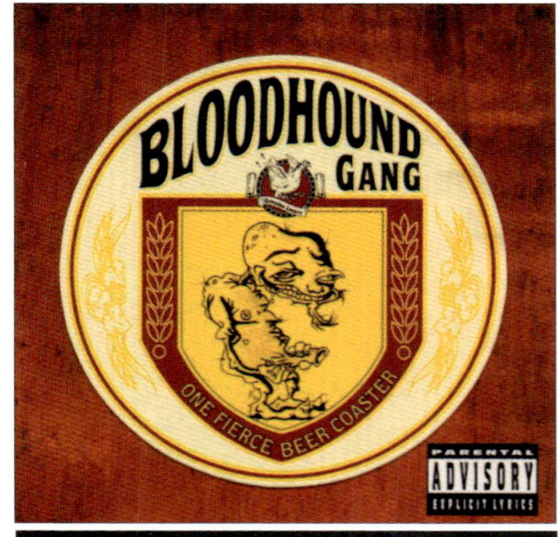


*Billboard* 200: *One Fierce Beer Coaster* (#57)

## Bloodhound Gang sniffed the boundaries of good taste with a bratty second album, *One Fierce Beer Coaster*.

**ENOUGH FOLKS** found the humor in Bloodhound Gang's offensive song titles and lyrics to make *One Fierce Beer Coaster* a surprise hit album. Jimmy Pop Ali, the Pennsylvania band's charismatic front man, knew why his lowbrow approach sufficed.

"Our manager said, 'You've got to be the first, you've got to be the best, or you've got to be completely fucked up," Ali said. "And that's what basically comes to the top. With us, we're something stupid and different. Lyrically, it's something people can relate to a lot more. It's not these universals about love and hate. It's about the robot Vicky on the TV show *Small Wonder*, and how Screech always gets Zach from *Saved by the Bell* in trouble. It's a very American record."

"Fire Water Burn" was a top request on modern-rock radio stations. Sinking the hook with a deadpan vocal delivery, Ali ranked on white-guy rappers (which he was) with lines like: "This hard-core ghetto gangster image takes a lot of practice/I'm not black like Barry White, no I am white like Frank Black is" while giving shout-outs to everyone from Lawrence Welk to Emmanuel Lewis (from TV's *Webster*).

He used a favored 12-letter expletive, so a "donkey-version edit" of "Fire Water Burn" was made for radio. "I have a list of ways to censor myself," Ali said. "One idea that was too topical was having O.J. Simpson saying his own name, so the chorus would be 'Burn (O.J. Simpson) burn.' But the donkey sound effect was pretty annoying so that was the choice."

Some of Ali's jokes were smart. "Why's Everybody Always Pickin' on Me?" was a song Beck might have killed for—a sample from the Classics IV's "Spooky," self-conscious rapping ("The drummer from Def Leppard's only got one arm!"). But Bloodhound Gang sparked concerns with other attention-grabbing songs on the album, including "I Wish I Was Queer So I Could Get Chicks" and "Yellow Fever." "All the jokes in the middle are out of *Truly Tasteless Jokes* books," Ali said.

It came as no surprise that Ali was an idolater of Howard Stern, radio's hugely popular "shock jock." He held the distinction of being rejected for a free internship with Stern's show on three separate occasions. "The fourth time, I wrote so many lies on my résumé that they couldn't refuse. I got the internship the same day we got a record deal. So I couldn't do it, even though I had been begging them for who knows how long." Stern heard *One Fierce Beer Coaster* and had Ali on his show. "We came in and talked about what a loser I am and he gave me his title of Most Successful Intern. I'm pretty happy. I might as well die now that 'Yahweh' has recognized me." ■

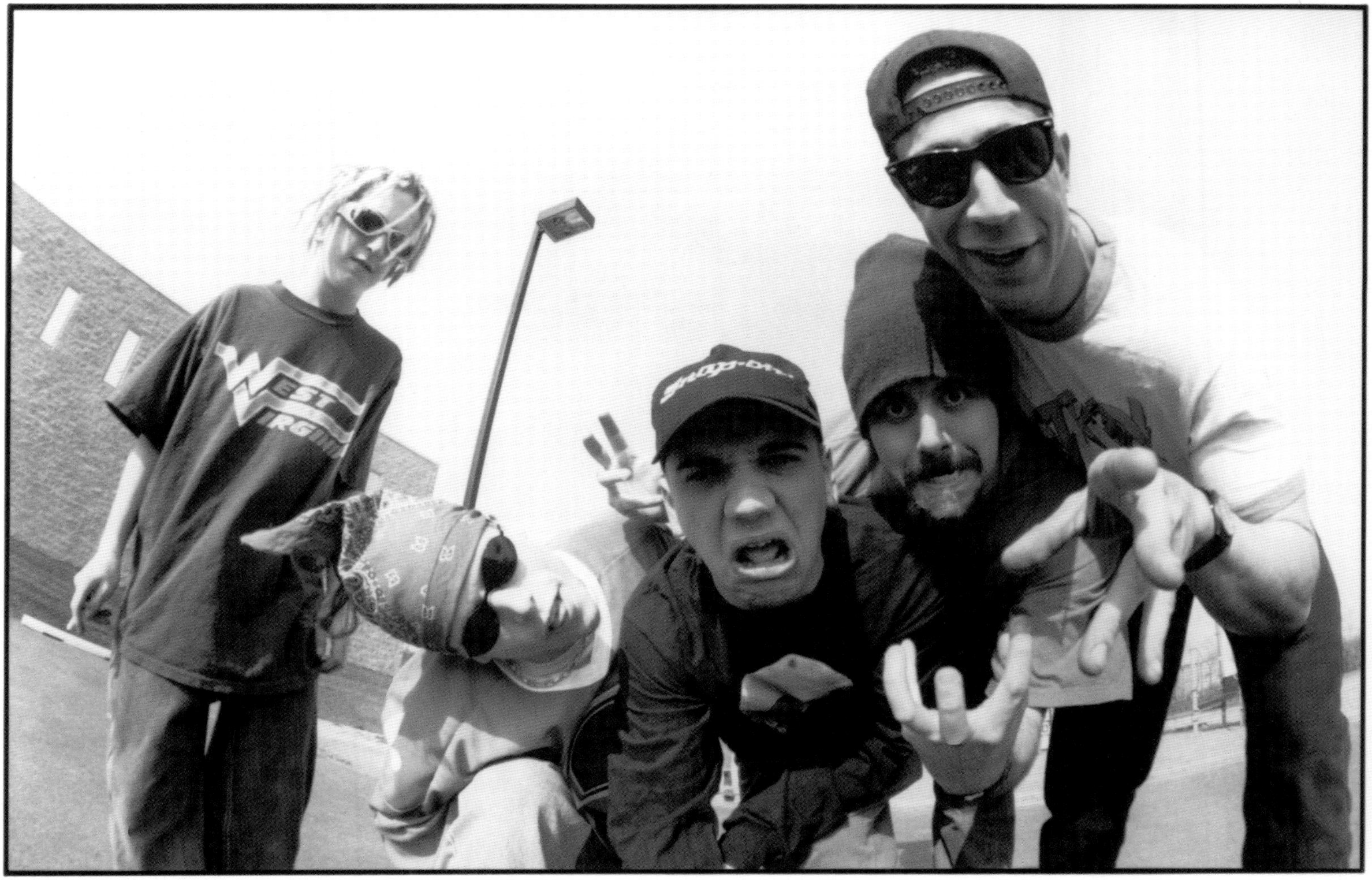

Photo Credit:: Celeste Angello

Spanky G Q-Ball Jimmy Pop Ali Lupus Evil Jared

**BLOODHOUND GANG**

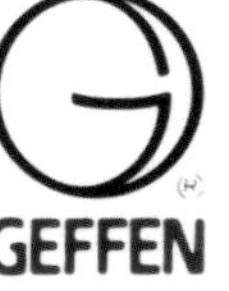

GEFFEN

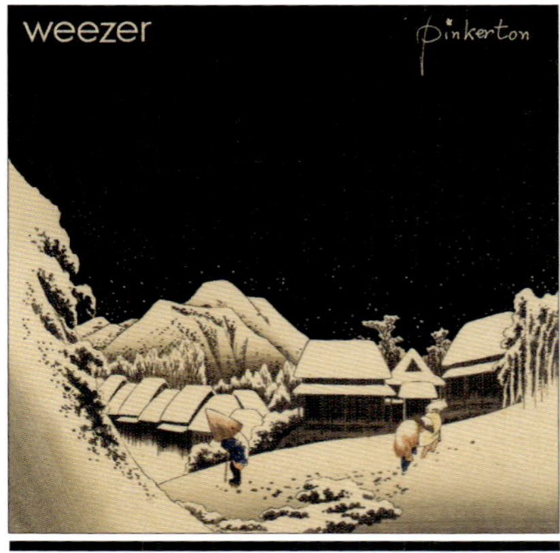


*Billboard* 200: *Pinkerton* (#19)

# While it initially foundered commercially, Weezer's gloomy, abrasive *Pinkerton* soon amassed a cult following.

**WHEN A** 1994 debut album spawned three modern-rock hits—"Undone - The Sweater Song," "Buddy Holly" and "Say It Ain't So"—Weezer traveled thousands of miles touring the world. And Rivers Cuomo was an unhappy guy.

"I was miserable at that point," the notoriously press-shy singer/songwriter/guitarist said. "We had 10 songs. We were terrible—I was an awful singer. But we had an incredible amount of exposure. I'm such a huge fan of pop music, and it was really exciting to be a part of the whole tradition of shallowness and fickleness. I always said I wanted to be a one-hit wonder, and then we ended up having three hits. I just felt like running and hiding. And I wasn't drinking, I wasn't having fun, I wasn't meeting girls."

After two years in hibernation, the band re-emerged with *Pinkerton*, the follow-up to the double-platinum *Weezer*. Weezer bypassed Ric Ocasek—who'd given the debut its sunny, geeky spark and vigor—and produced the album alone. The sound was rawer, and Cuomo took fans through his dark, juvenile take on personal relationships. Sales for *Pinkerton* struggled, and there were rumors of inner-band turmoil. After a tour, Cuomo started another semester at Harvard. The rest of Weezer—bassist Matt Sharp, drummer Pat Wilson and guitarist Brian Bell—returned to work on their own projects.

Then Weezer went back out on the road. "This time, the whole experience is a party," Cuomo reflected. "On the first tour, we were painted as 'the nerd group'—it was the next big thing. There are definitely times when I want to be alone and I don't want to party. I just want to be by myself and write songs or read books, which is kind of nerdy. But then the other half of the year, I'm out on the road just totally drunk, picking up girls, getting in fights, whatever. And those things are not considered traditionally nerdy."

The guys were still dorky, but Weezer rocked with playful, catchy pop-punk tunes. "You name it, we've done it on this tour," Cuomo admitted. "It's been crazy. I've gotten in a couple of brawls, mostly with girls. This psychotic girl came backstage the other night and beat the crap out of me. I couldn't believe it—I'd just gotten really high in the parking lot, too, so I was not in the right space to think logically and defend myself. And she was very large. It pretty much happens every night."

Weezer was in such high spirits that another song from *Pinkerton* was released to radio, the heartbreak of "Pink Triangle." Cuomo discovers that the woman of his dreams is a lesbian: "Everyone's a little queer/ Why can't she be a little straight?"

"It's about a girl I met at school," Cuomo explained. "Whenever I write about a character or a story, something fictitious, it comes out sounding really cheesy. I don't have that skill yet. I've only been able to write about the events of my life using all the little details. I've got to try to do something else. Next year, I'll be done with school, which will be very strange. I've been going back on and off since I was four. I'll probably move to New York and just rock for the rest of my life—which may be very short at the rate I'm going." ■

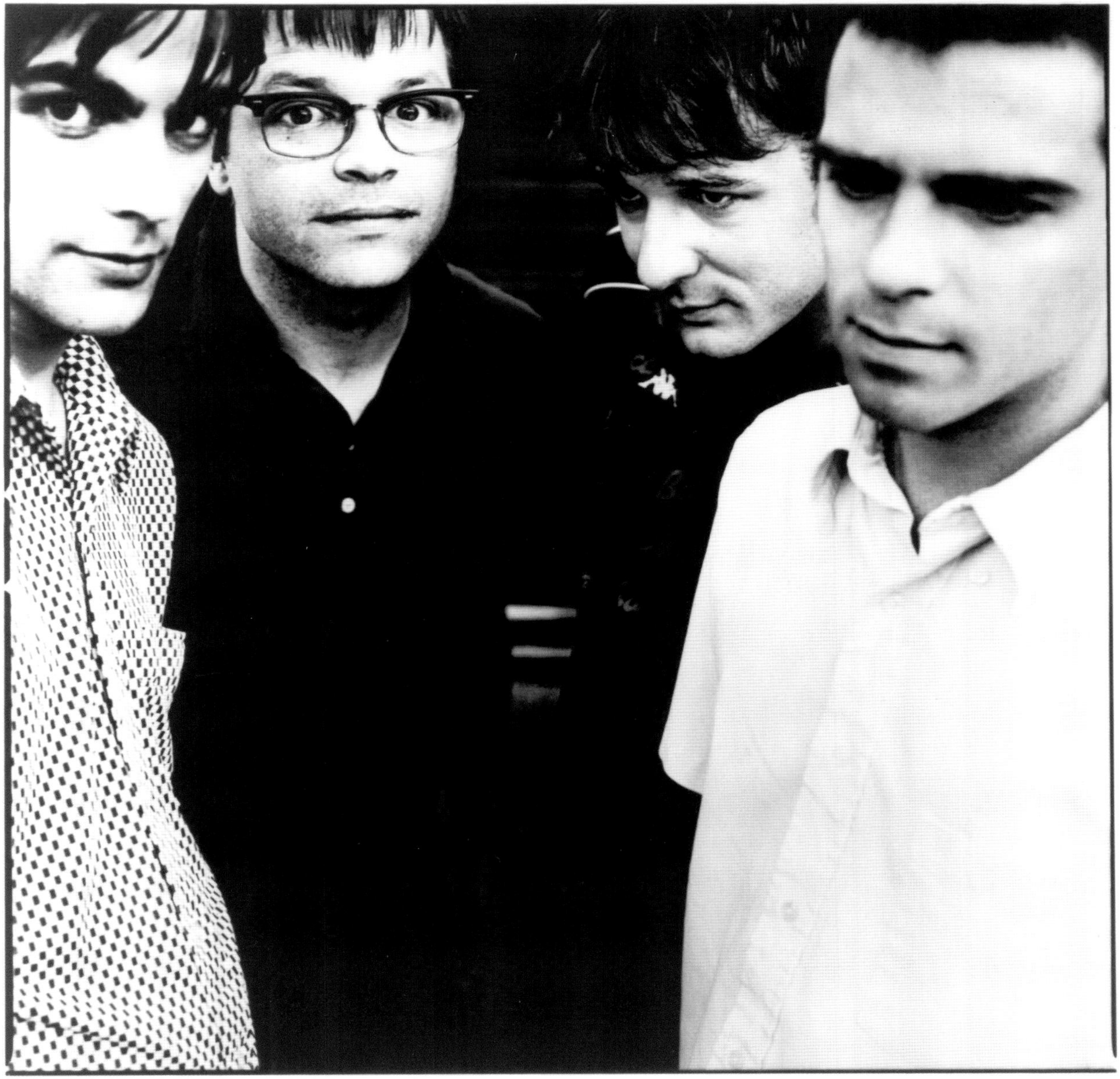

Photo Credit: Anton Corbijn

Brian Bell Patrick Wilson Matt Sharp Rivers Cuomo

# weezer

GEFFEN RECORDS, INC.

## Winding up with a tribute of sorts, Nerf Herder recorded "Van Halen" and the plight of that band's loyal fans.

**A GOOFY** guitar-driven ditty, Nerf Herder's ode to "Van Halen" oozed with album and song titles, a hilarious attempt at Eddie Van Halen's memorable finger-tapping technique and an ultimatum that played off that band's controversial lineup change: "Sammy Hagar, is this what you wanted, man?/Dave lost his hairline but you lost your cool buddy/ Can't drive 55/I'll never buy your lousy records again…"

"We haven't really played that much," lead singer and guitarist Parry Gripp admitted. "We started about two years ago in Santa Barbara and practiced twice a week for two hours—that's been our regular schedule. Suddenly, this stuff started happening. We were so happy when an indie label offered to make a CD of our music—I never thought I'd be on a CD."

When "Van Halen" began to get alternative airplay around the country, Nerf Herder signed with a major label, re-releasing a self-titled album of hilarious punk-pop songs referenced as "nerdcore." In "Sorry," the protagonist apologizes to a girl for a million transgressions ("Sorry I showed up at your party/Sorry I drank up all the Bacardi").

"'Van Halen' was a novelty, a fluke—it got us signed to a larger record deal, but I don't know if we'll ever have another song that gets played that much or gets that much attention," Gripp said. "I guess those guys liked it—we've never heard from them one on one. It was nice that Eddie let us use all the Van Halen posters in our video—that was something that we had to get permission for. But we haven't talked to Sammy. I really don't want to."

The trio's name was derived from a scene in *The Empire Strikes Back*, the second film in the *Star Wars* series, in which Princess Leia spews an insult at Han Solo—she calls him a "stuck-up, half-witted, scruffy-looking nerf herder"—so the boys were thrilled that the video for "Sorry" had a special guest appearance—Mark Hamill, who portrayed Luke Skywalker in the *Star Wars* franchise, played the role of a detective who interrogates the band. "He was very nice, like he was hanging out and joking around at a barbecue," Parry enthused. "He was happy to talk about (the theatrical re-release of) *Star Wars*."

Nerf Herder had a reputation as a fun live band. "Our music is really simple," Parry noted. "Anyone could take our songs and play them reasonably well—it's not difficult. We're kind of corny. It comes from the terror of being onstage and seeing the crowd stand there looking bored and wanting to do something that will get a reaction." ■

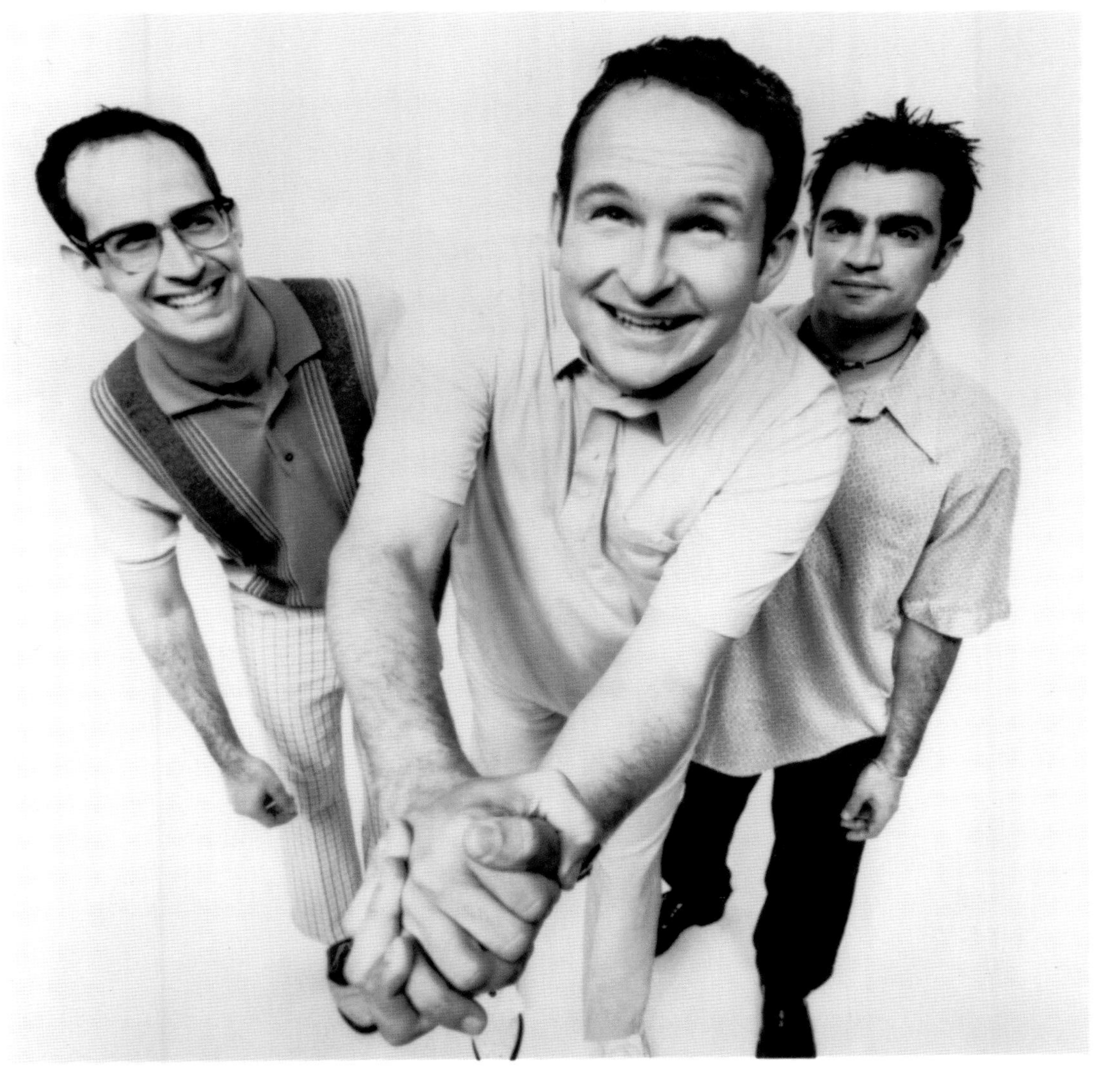

PHOTOGRAPHER: MARINA CHAVEZ

# NERF HERDER

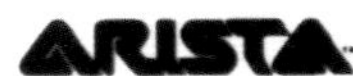


MANAGEMENT: CAHN-MAN

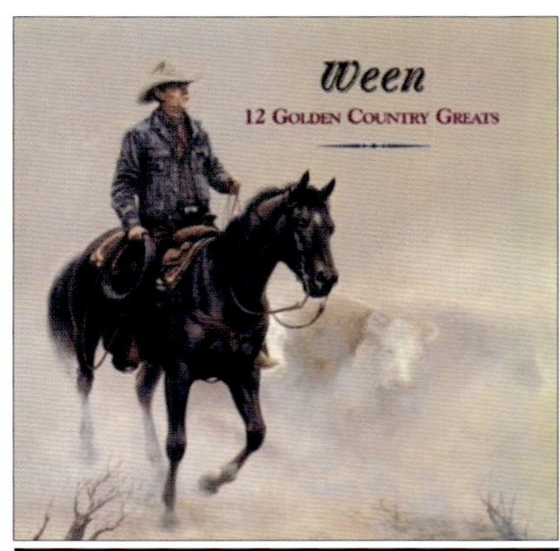


## The goofy duo Ween enlisted Nashville studio musicians and went for the gusto on *12 Golden Country Greats*.

**IN THE** mid-Eighties, Ween—the duo of Gene and Dean Ween (Aaron Freeman and Mickey Melchiondo)—sauntered out of New Hope, Pennsylvania, with a do-it-yourself work ethic and four-track tape recorder. Since then, the self-described "spoiled, overeducated, suburban" fake brothers had built a cult following with an outflow of homemade, lo-fi songs. And they hadn't matured a bit.

"We reach stages of pitiful intoxication," Dean said. "And I'm a really, really, really bad sports fan. My wife is going to leave me on account of it, actually. I watch two or three baseball games a day. I'm a huge basketball fan all year long. There's hockey—I'm a Flyers season-ticket holder. And I play four or five rounds of golf a week."

So what was the fascination with the crazy world of Ween? Part of it was the two-man band's ability to copy a dizzying range of styles and genres, from Seventies heavy metal to the Motown sound. There was also Ween's dysfunctional sense of humor—it could be hilarious if the mood was right, puerile and depraved if it wasn't. "All of our records are like greatest hits of that year," Dean explained. "We write and record, we throw away the bad stuff and pick out the best stuff. The people who know, know."

"Push th' Little Daisies" (Ween's version of a hit single) was professionally recorded, and 1994's *Chocolate and Cheese* was tops among fans. Ween then trampled on cowboy crooning with the repellent *12 Golden Country Greats*—Dean and Gene went to Nashville for nine days and rented some of the great session players from country music's golden age, who couldn't have been too gratified about songs like "Piss Up a Rope."

"That's the biggest beating we've ever taken," Dean admitted. "We weren't stupid—we fully knew that people were going to be pissed. But we spent too much time worrying about what those guys were going to think before we went down there. The reality of it is that they're so professional and relaxed, literally a bunch of old cats sitting around laughing and talking. They're not wearing cowboy boots and hats and string ties—they're regular-looking men who are so badass working with songs and singers.

"We've never had that kind of talent at our fingertips, but we didn't put enough work into it. We treated it like it was a session—it wasn't supposed to be a record. But we had songs laying around and called it a record. If I could rewind time, I'd love to have another crack at that. If I lived in Nashville, I could collect a billion dollars making the best country record of all time." ■

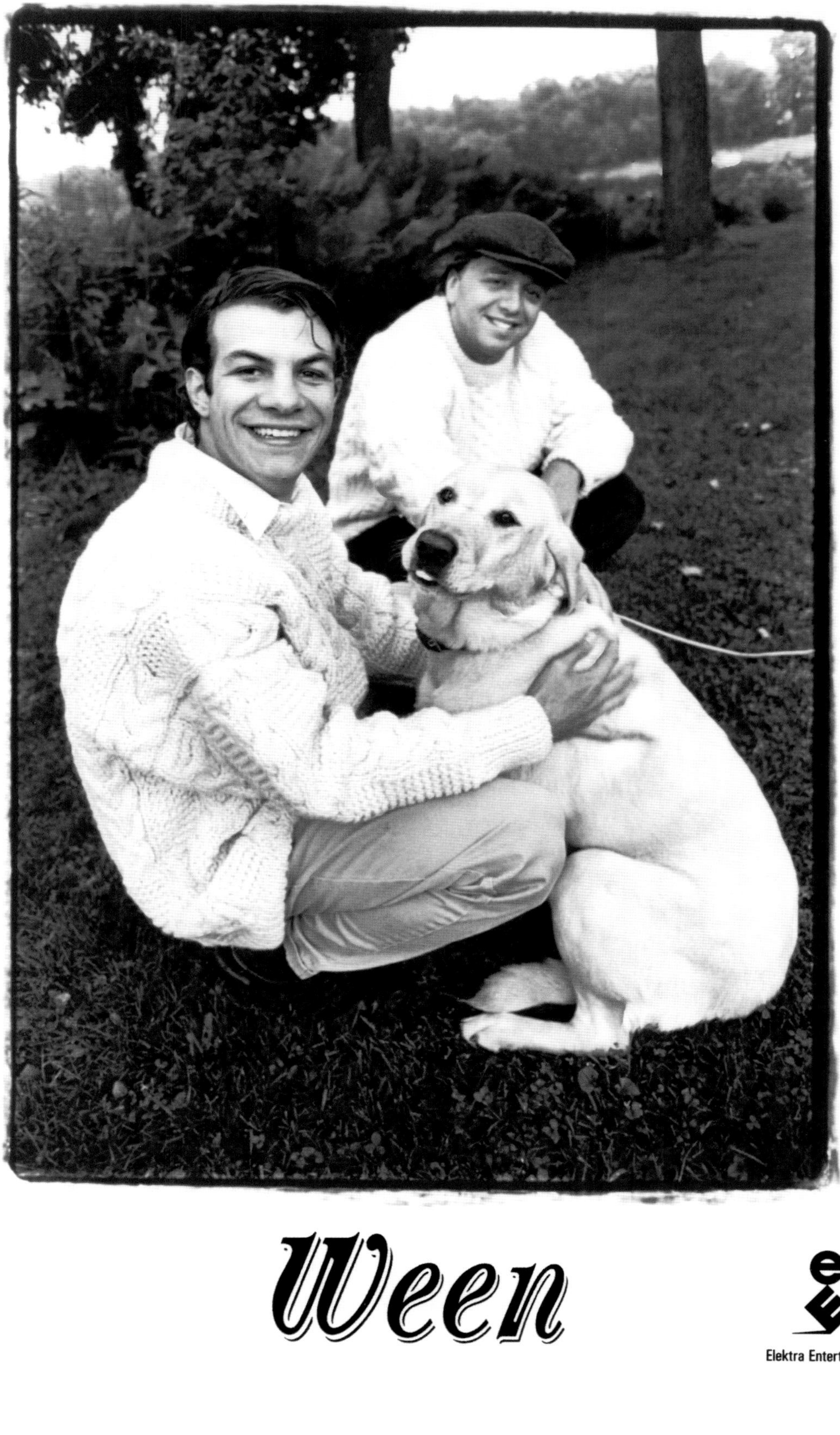

PHOTO CREDIT DANNY CLINCH

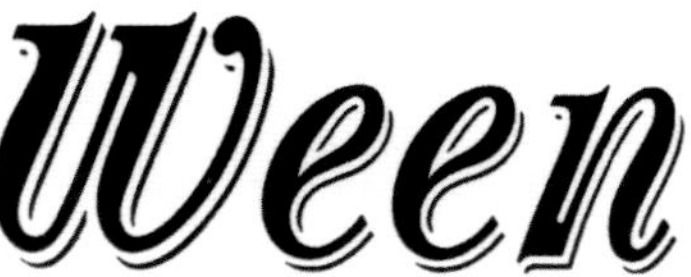


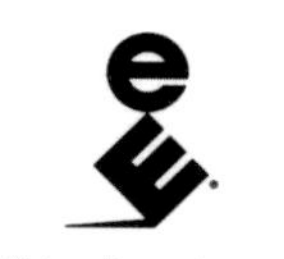

EEG

Elektra Entertainment

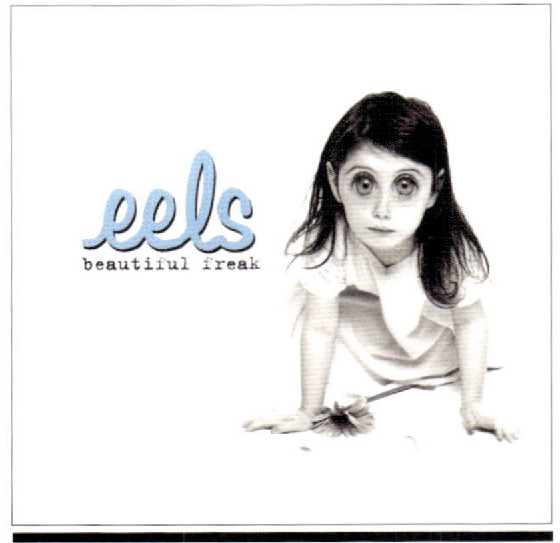


*Billboard* 200: *Beautiful Freak* (#114)

## The quirky *Beautiful Freak*, eels' debut album, brought forth a joyless alternative hit, "Novocaine for the Soul."

**A SINGLE** getting massive radio play, "Novocaine for the Soul" by eels expressed isolation and loneliness, pairing the despairing lyrics with pop hooks and moody strings. "I was obviously going through a pretty dark period—it's not a happy sentiment," singer and guitarist E said. "I was really thinking about this one before I wrote it, and I wanted to write a nonjudgmental view of our need for numbness. I was just noticing how everybody's desperately trying to cut themselves off from their feelings at any possible chance, by drugs or alcohol or even watching TV—there's always something to keep you occupied.

"And it's certainly not meant to be an anthem. It's the No. 1 alternative song right now, and at our concerts we play it and everybody starts cheering and singing along, which is a great feeling, but it's also really weird—I start to feel like I want to smile, but it's not really a smiling kind of situation."

Much of the material on eels' *Beautiful Freak* was intended for E's third solo album, but things changed when he met Tommy (bass) and Butch (drums) in a club (the Los Angeles trio liked to be on a first-name basis with everyone). E co-produced *Beautiful Freak* with Michael Simpson of the Dust Brothers (Beck, Beastie Boys). The music had a variety of unconventional sounds and strange instruments in the mix, careening from glockenspiel to guitar rock to jazzy samples within the space of a song.

"Pop has become a dirty word to me because of all these bands that are playing in L.A.—they sound like bands full of record collectors instead of bands full of artists. I never intended to be part of that. I wanted to experiment a little. Rather than try to sound like the Beatles, I wanted to do as the Beatles did. They soaked up everything around them at the time, and then put their own stink on it. We have enough of our own stink to make something unique."

The evocative video for "Novocaine for the Soul" featured members of eels attached to wires to simulate the action of flying. "Like a lot of artists, I subscribe to the cliché that videos are evil, but I knew that we weren't Pearl Jam and we needed to make a video, so I just wanted one that was going to be different and stick out—and that MTV was going to play, which is a tough combination. I've been in the situation where you make an $80,000 home movie that no one sees because they don't air it."

The milieu of urban tension and bohemia had an impact on eels' sound. "I thought the West Side was all there was in L.A.—all the 'plastic people' clichés came true before my eyes," E allowed. "I didn't know about Echo Park and Silverlake and the great underground art scene. I don't think of Los Angeles the same way I used to. I really like it now." ■

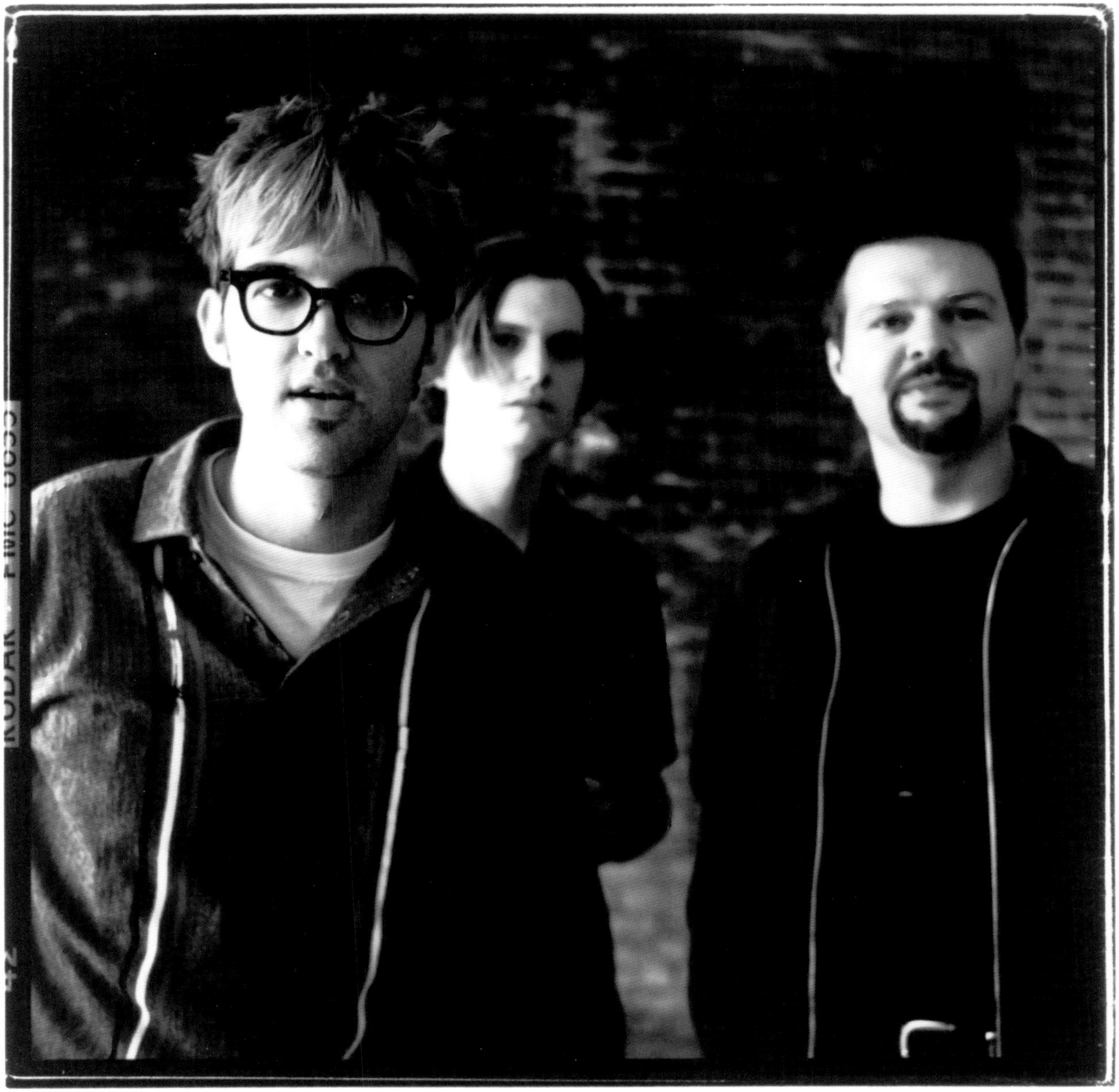

Photo Credit: Ann Giordano

E Tommy Butch

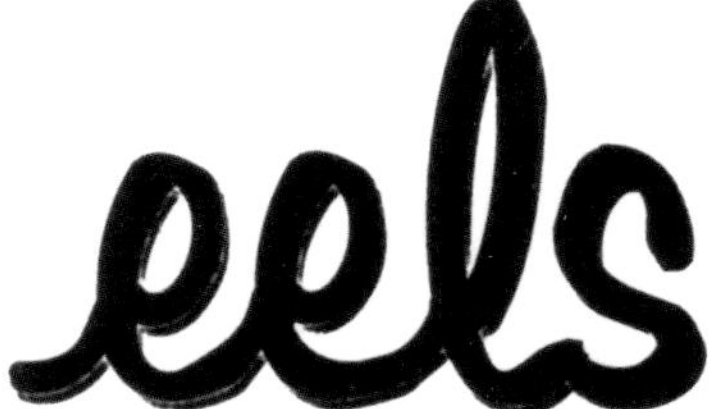


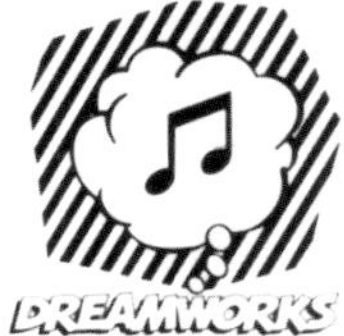

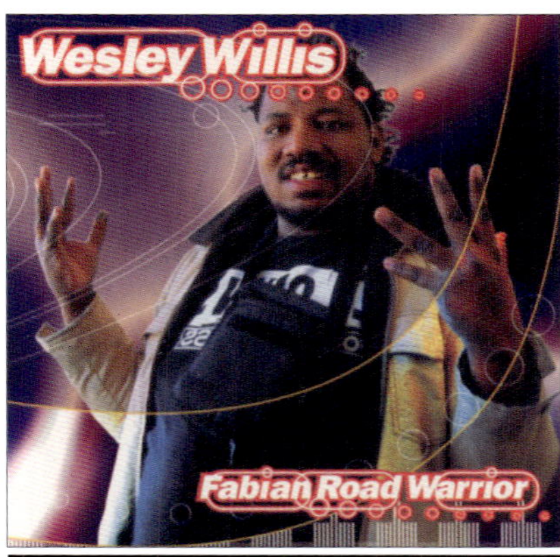


## Adhering to his minimalist approach, garrulous Wesley Willis occupied a completely unorthodox musical niche.

**THE MOST** talked-about cause célèbre in the music business wasn't another hotshot alternative rocker with a sarcastically distant persona. It was Wesley Willis, a former Chicago street person who had been diagnosed as a chronic schizophrenic in 1989. Reportedly the victim of lifelong episodes of random violence and domestic abuse, the affable Willis heard voices that told him to doubt his creative side.

But music had become both his most effective therapy and a career. He was a one-man record label who'd released 20 CDs on his own. Most of the sales had been made at random encounters—he carried copies with him just in case he met someone with $10. Major labels had hesitated to deal with Willis—they didn't want to appear to exploit someone whose eccentricity was the result of mental illness. But Willis signed with American Recordings, and the attention in support of *Fabian Road Warrior* thrust him before nightclub audiences, photo sessions and film crews.

There was a sincere affection for Willis' crude, repetitive songs. Most of them were odes to musicians, and they followed the same format. Using the same pre-programmed Casio keyboard music, he rapped about the artist's show career, then howled a chorus of the honoree's name, and ended with a slogan or catch phrase from a TV commercial ("Taco Bell, make a run for the border!" or "Rice-A-Roni, the San Francisco treat!").

Willis was already famous in his hometown. He was an intimidating presence—a hulking 6-foot-4, 320-pound frame, facially scarred. Small unkempt dreadlocks sprang from his head, and he dressed in thrift-store duds. But most of the time, Willis was reaching out for friendly contact. He had a chronic bruise on his forehead from his trademark headbutt greeting. He was skilled at self-promotion. "I like to sing, I like to have fun, I like to keep out of trouble like a man should," he said in Ali-style braggadocio.

The guys in the band said Willis wasn't on his medication consistently on tour. Sometimes the demons prevented him from traveling on airplanes. But he was usually determined to put on a rock show. He stood pigeon-toed at the microphone, his long-sleeve T-shirt barely containing his girth. He thumbed through one of his many dog-eared spiral notebooks, bellowing his spoken-word verses and fervently chanted choruses.

Cursed with an inner conflict, it was difficult for Willis to avoid a freak-show relationship with an audience, but the laughter he drew wasn't at his expense. He enjoyed conveying the different reality he lived in, and he wanted his songs to be heard. And unlike a lot of musicians, he didn't just talk about gigs, he got them. Selling CDs beside the stage after his shows, he got the last word. "I'm a big man, I'm a rock 'n' roller," he shrugged. "I just make music." ■

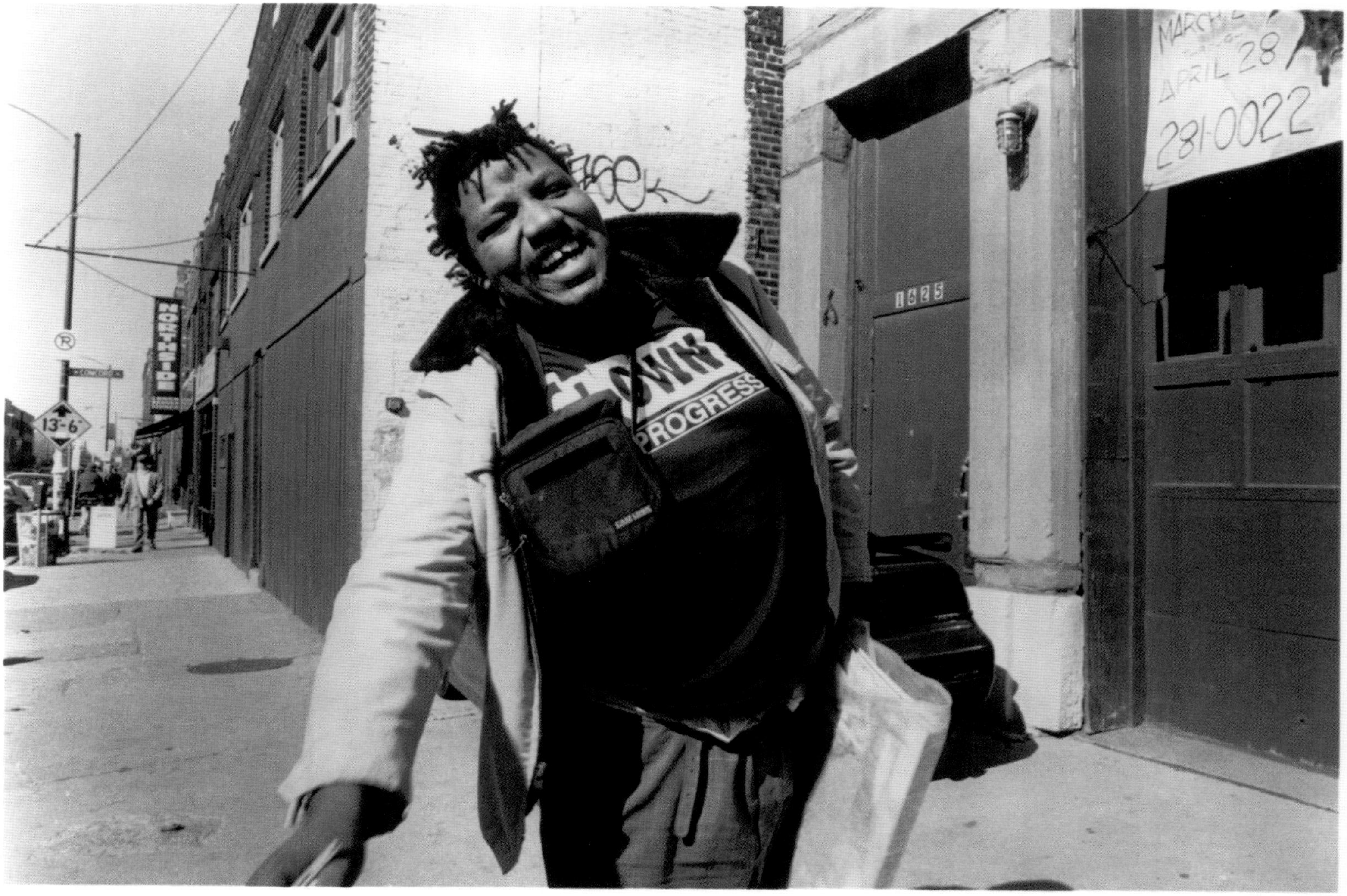

# Wesley Willis

Photo Credit: American Recordings

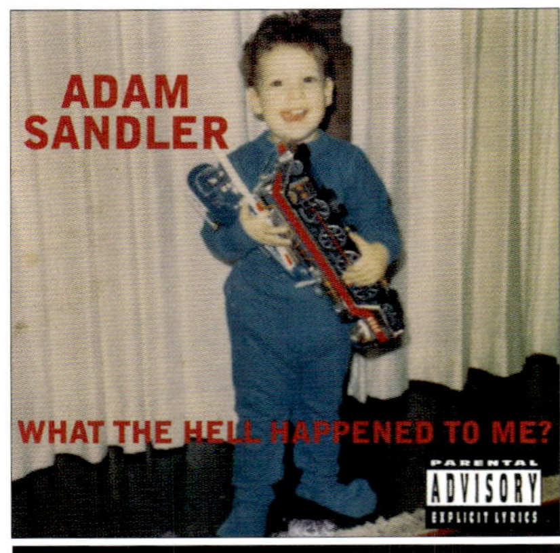


*Billboard* 200: *What the Hell Happened to Me?* (#18)
*Billboard* Hot 100: "The Chanukah Song" (#80)

## First performed on *Saturday Night Live*, "The Chanukah Song" panned out as a holiday staple for Adam Sandler.

**ON THE** iconic television property *Saturday Night Live*, comedy star Adam Sandler made a name for himself by impersonating Pearl Jam's Eddie Vedder and Axl Rose of Guns N' Roses—and performing his amusing original songs.

"When I first did standup comedy, I would do jokes about music—going to concerts, what music means to you growing up," Sandler explained. "And I played a few songs. When you have a guitar in your hand, you don't have to be thinking as much. You're prepared, you have your three-minute song ready to go. I wasn't so nervous, and that definitely helped me in the beginning."

Not everyone found Sandler's emotionally stunted man-child comedic persona funny—sometimes he was just annoying. But he had spent five years with *Saturday Night Live* as both a writer and performer, and his film career had kicked into high gear—he was the star of *Billy Madison* and *Happy Gilmore*. And he had also gained national recognition with his comedy albums. 1993's *They're All Gonna Laugh at You* reached platinum status and spawned the hit "Lunchlady Land."

His second release, *What the Hell Happened to Me?*, maintained explicit—and hilarious—scatological skits and introduced new song selections ("Ode to My Car," a laid-back reggae tune). "The Chanukah Song" instantly received radio airplay and deservedly became an unofficial anthem for those "eight crazy nights." Sandler stood up for his people, listing Jews from Rod Carew ("He converted") to Harrison Ford ("a quarter Jewish, not too shabby").

To support *What the Hell Happened to Me?*, Sandler took to the road in what he called a "backyard rock 'n' roll party for you and 5,000 of your friends," incorporating a mixture of comedy and musical curiosities from his two albums. "I remember when I was 16, playing in garage bands, I thought I was a badass on guitar—until I saw everybody else play," he said with a laugh. "It was a smack in the head. This is the most fun ever. I run and dance around the stage like a fool, goofing around and getting everyone in the crowd to do silly stuff. It's a cool feeling, something I don't know if I'll get to do again."

Sandler traveled with some prestigious players. Musical director and guitarist Waddy Wachtel had produced records by Keith Richards and Warren Zevon and performed or recorded with Stevie Nicks, James Taylor and Linda Ronstadt. Live, there were silly videos and covers, notably of Foghat's version of "I Just Wanna Make Love to You."

"Alternative music is so huge, you don't hear so much classic rock going on. *Foghat Live* is the greatest! On the bus yesterday, Waddy and my buddies were rocking out to the Who with me. Five of us started a spontaneous mosh pit, everybody flying and jumping around the moving bus—all because of 'Substitute.' I was gonna call Townshend up and tell him he started trouble." ■

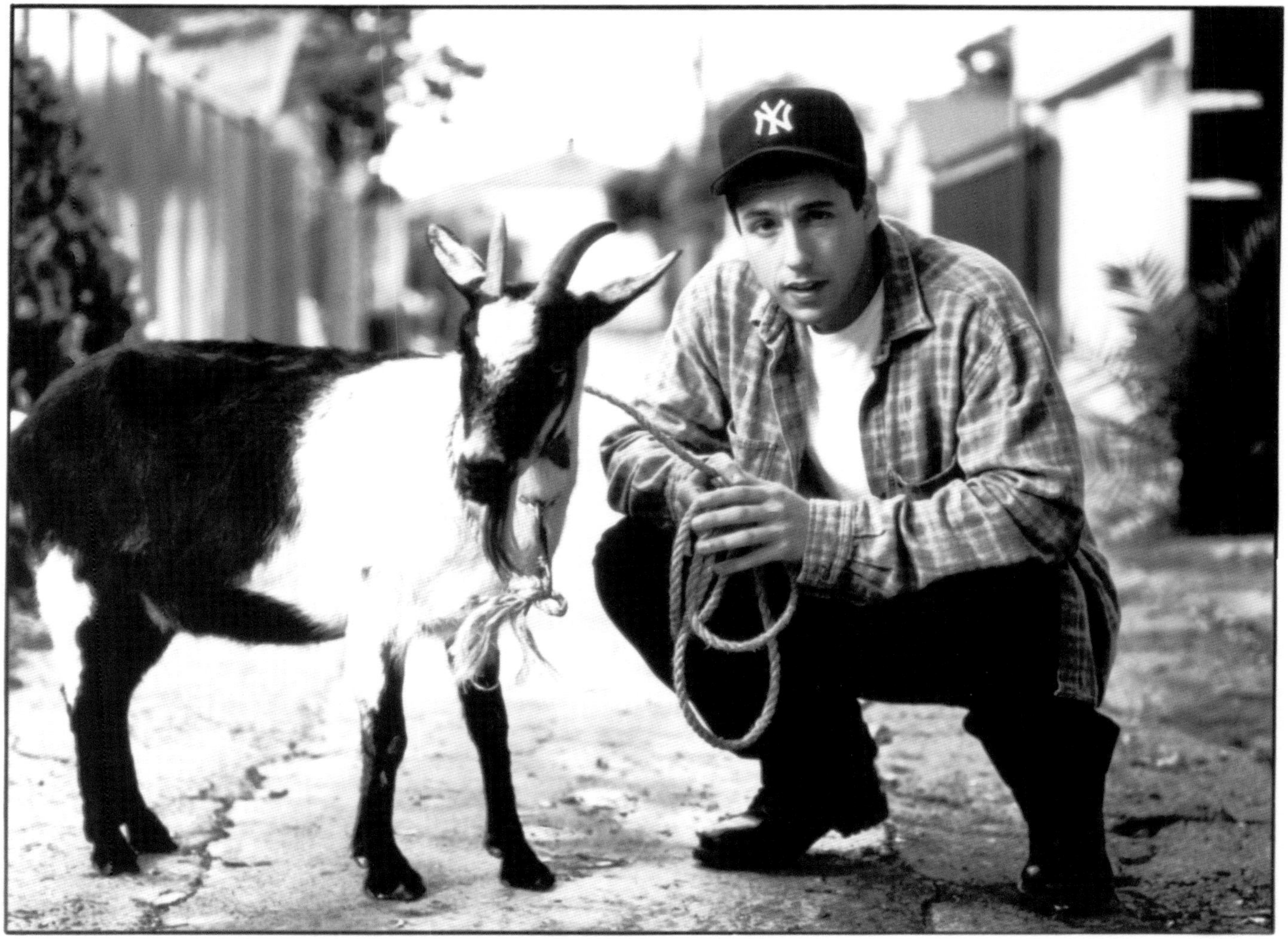

PHOTO CREDIT: Bonnie Schiffman

# ADAM SANDLER

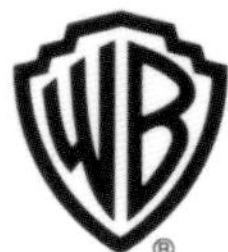

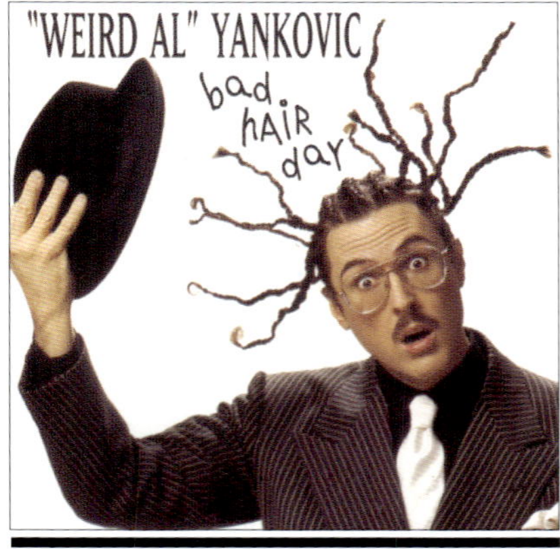


*Billboard* 200: *Bad Hair Day* (#14)
*Billboard* Hot 100: "Amish Paradise" (#53)

## A lampoon of a hit by Coolio, "Weird Al" Yankovic's "Amish Paradise" touched off an insignificant controversy.

**SUCH HUMOROUS** classics as "Eat It," "Smells Like Nirvana," "Like a Surgeon" and "Another One Rides the Bus" had earned "Weird Al" Yankovic his title as the master of musical parody. And the novelty hadn't worn off—with *Bad Hair Day*, Yankovic delighted in the most successful release of his career. The album featured "Amish Paradise," a send-up of Coolio's "Gangsta's Paradise" that relocated from the mean streets of the ghetto to the fields of Lancaster County: "But if I finish all of my chores and you finish thine/Then tonight we're gonna party like it's 1699."

"I had a note in my idea notebook to do a song about the Amish for a couple of years," Yankovic explained. "I was going through the *Billboard* charts looking more toward alternative songs because *Bad Hair Day* was going to be my alternative album. But the Coolio song had been No. 1 for eight weeks, the biggest song of the year. I thought, 'Oh, gee, that would be so perfect, Amish instead of gangstas—I gotta do this!"

It was safe enough for Yankovic to send up the Amish, since they were forbidden to listen to rock music. The artists who were victims of his satire usually got the joke. "At this point, I could probably get away with doing parodies without asking permission from the original songwriters," he explained. "But ethically, I think it's better to get it. You can still sue anybody for anything in this country without legal grounds, so you don't want to get someone upset. And I've developed a track record with a lot of songwriters—I don't want to tick them off."

But Coolio wasn't thrilled when Yankovic served as a presenter on the American Music Awards sporting the rapper's Medusa-like hair. "He seemed to get a kick out of it—he laughed and shook my hand," Yankovic said. "But at a press conference after the Grammys, somebody asked him about 'Amish Paradise' and he went off—'I never gave him permission for it, I don't appreciate him desecrating my song like that.' I don't know if he changed his mind or if my record company lied to me about talking with him or if it was a big-time miscommunication between my posse and his posse. It's heartbreaking for me, because it ruins my perfect record of satisfied customers."

Although Yankovic was best known for his parodies, half of *Bad Hair Day* consisted of original songs. "The Night Santa Went Crazy" was released as a single during the Christmas season. "The fact that my originals are ignored has always been a pet peeve of mine," he said. "People still know me as the parody guy—and people even more out of touch just know me as the 'Eat It' guy, sadly enough. I'm not going to hold my breath." ■

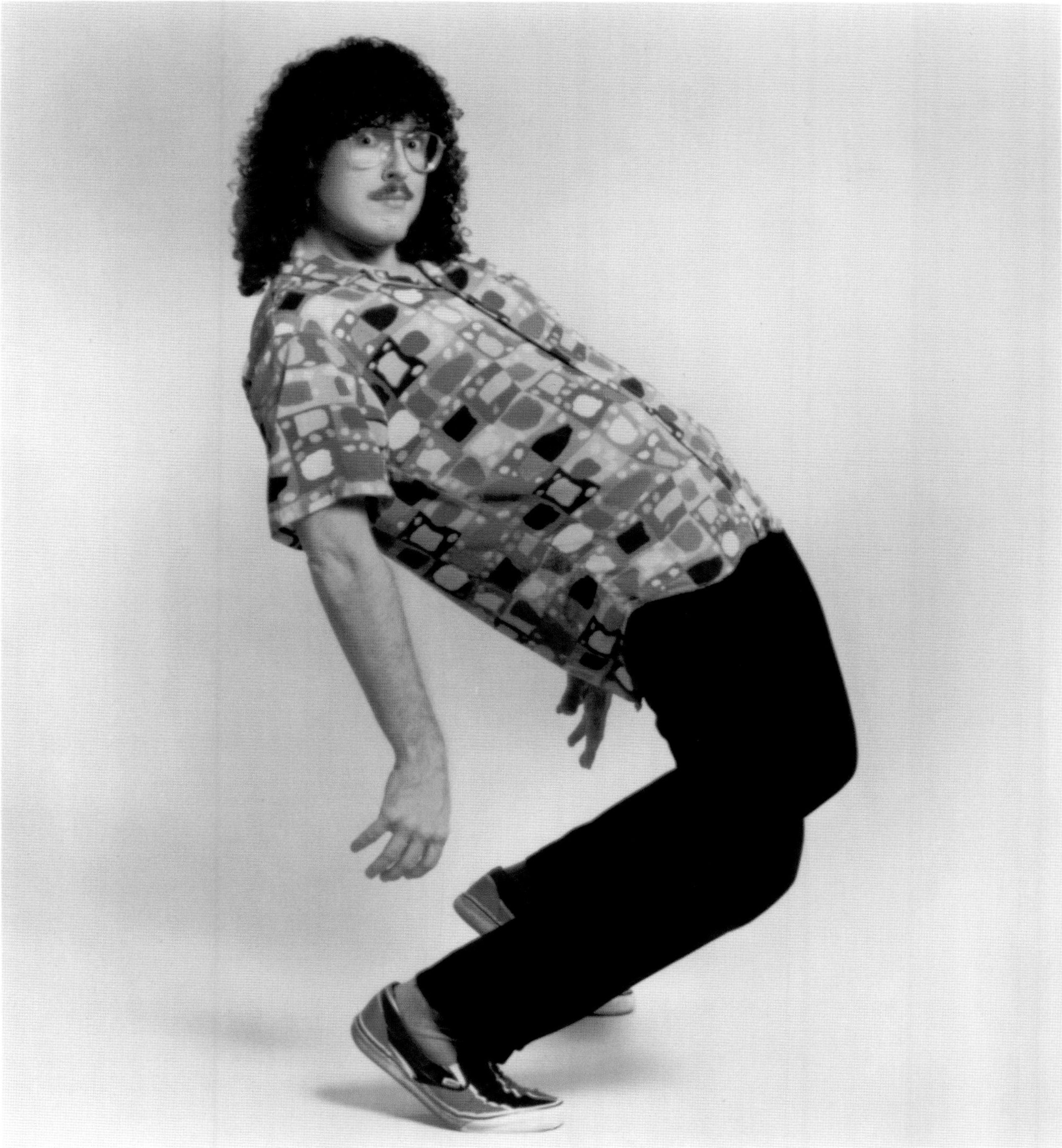

PHOTO CREDIT: Carl Studna

IMAGINARY ENTERTAINMENT

JAY LEVEY

925 WESTMOUNT DRIVE • LOS ANGELES, CALIFORNIA [illegible]

# "WEIRD AL" YANKOVIC

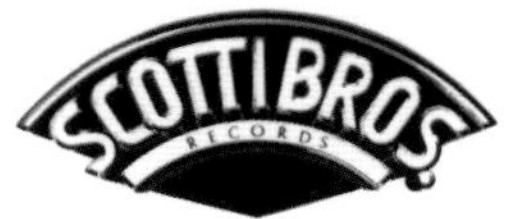

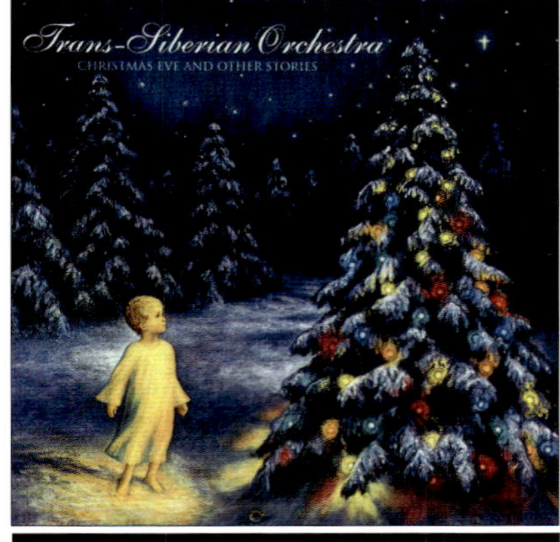


*Billboard* 200: *Christmas Eve and Other Stories* (#48)

## Trans-Siberian Orchestra's conceptual symphonic rock came to light as the next engendering of rock opera.

**MERGING HOLIDAY** and classical music with the heavy-metal strains of screaming guitars, crashing drums and bombastic keyboards, Trans-Siberian Orchestra grew out of Paul O'Neill's songwriting and producing work with hard-rock bands. Savatage was on its last legs when O'Neill put "Christmas Eve/Sarajevo 12/24" on the progressive metal outfit's *Dead Winter Dead* album in 1995. The epic was inspired by the real-life tale of a cellist who went to the town square in his native city of Sarajevo and performed as the Bosnian war raged around him.

"I had the song in my head for years, since the late Seventies—just the counterpoint of 'God Rest Ye Merry Gentlemen' over the choir and bells and then new music to tie the whole thing together," O'Neill said. "Then I heard the story of the cello player. In the original version, I had the melody being played by a guitarist. We put in the single cello to represent the old man in between the orchestra representing the Muslims and the rock band representing the Serbs."

O'Neill invented Trans-Siberian Orchestra to follow in the manner of *Tommy* and *Jesus Christ Superstar*. In the studio, the TSO lineup was built around him and his longtime creative partners Jon Olivia and Robert Kinkel, who added singers and musicians as needed. The first holiday release, *Christmas Eve and Other Stories*, struck a nerve when it debuted, and "Christmas Eve Sarajevo 12/24" became an unlikely seasonal classic.

The New York City-based collective combined the elegance of an orchestra with the riffs of a hard-rock band. "Every generation has roots in some kind of rock—it goes back that far now," O'Neill said. "And the marriage of classical and rock is incredibly natural. I always thought that Beethoven was the first heavy-metal star. '*Dun dun dun duh, dun dun dun duuhh*' (the opening to Beethoven's Fifth Symphony)—Black Sabbath could have written that riff.

"Fifty percent is writing a great song. The other fifty percent is getting the right people to play it. I tended to give rock operas to Savatage, but there were artificial limits. By their very nature, rock operas want multiple lead singers—as the characters change, the voices want to change. With Trans-Siberian Orchestra, we didn't want to stay in any certain style—we got classical, rock, blues, gospel.

"It always goes back to timeless Christmas melodies. We all grew up on them—it's a touchstone that crosses generations, nationalities and cultures, that instant familiarity. Plus, there's something genetic in all human beings that we love to hear a good story. Every single one of us has been late for work once—you're watching something on TV, and you stay even though you know you're going to be in trouble, because you've got to see what happens next. TSO has that advantage as well." ■

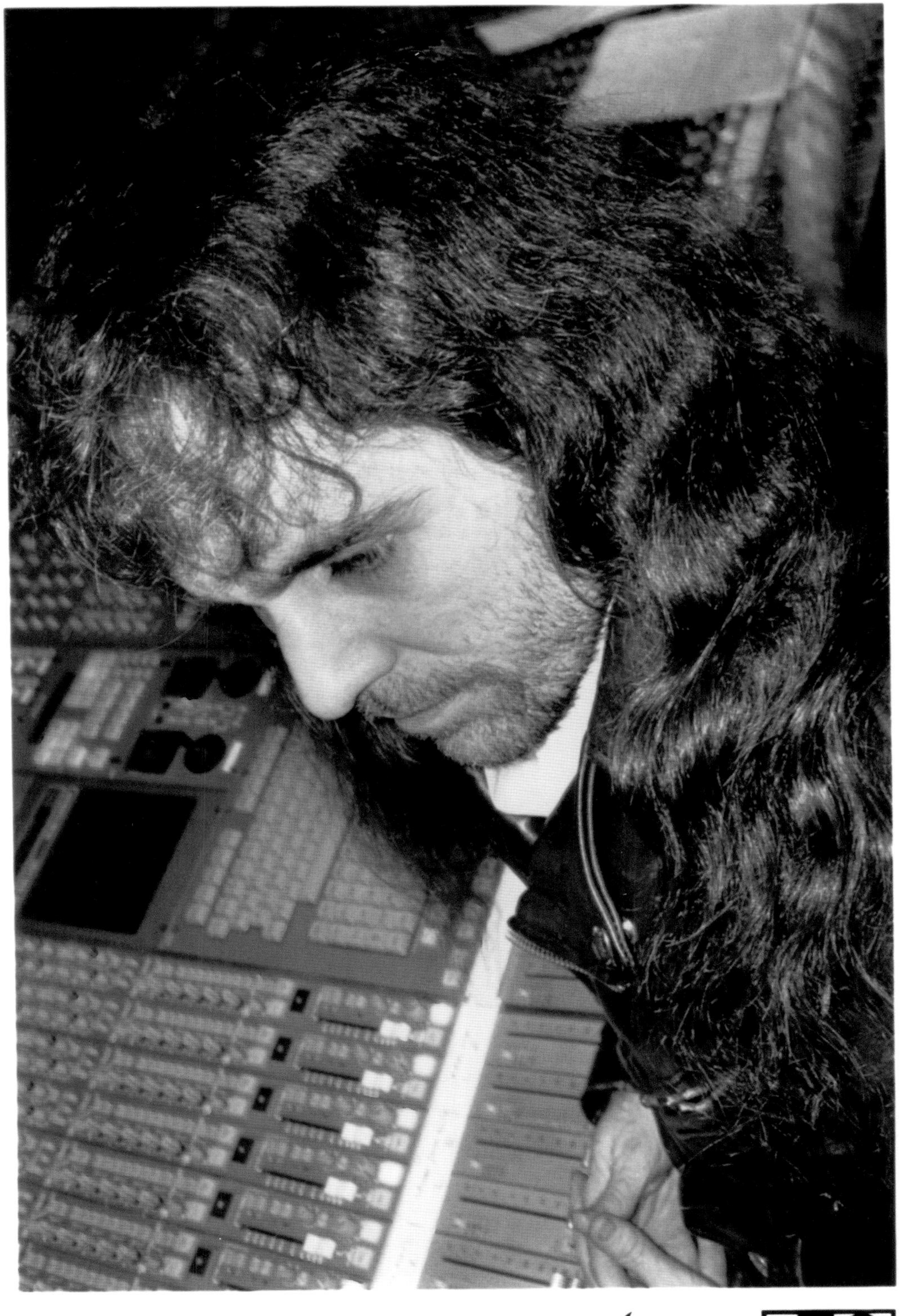

Photo Credit: Mick Rock

*Trans-Siberian Orchestra*

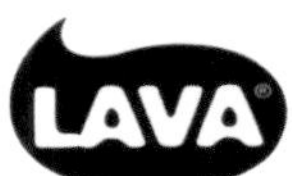


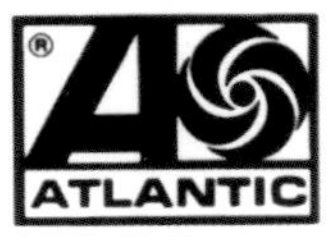

## Carl Perkins' last album, *Go Cat Go!* found "the father of rockabilly" singing duets with some big-name guests.

**THE STORY** of Carl Perkins was an essential account of the birth of rock 'n' roll. The sharecropper's son grew up dirt-poor in Tennessee. With his brothers, he started playing honky-tonks and country dances, fusing elements of traditional country and bluegrass with Black blues. Along with Jerry Lee Lewis, Elvis Presley and Johnny Cash, he started recording for tiny, Memphis-based Sun Records.

When Sun owner Sam Phillips sold Presley's contract to RCA, he assumed that he had another guy as good in Perkins. Perkins wrote his own songs and was a great rock 'n' roll lead guitarist, combining fingerpicking chording and rapid-fire licks. Turned loose to rock out at his third session, he produced the redoubtable "Blue Suede Shoes." The rockabilly anthem of teenaged identity was inspired at a dance where Perkins was playing, when a boy upbraided his date for stepping too near his fancy footwear

"In 1956, the teenagers in this country were ready for their kind of music," Perkins explained. "Some of the preachers around the South and the disc jockeys who busted up our records were saying, 'This music's got to go,' or 'It was sent by the devil.' I say it makes people happy, brings back memories, plants a thought. I knew in my soul there was nothing wrong with kids dancing and getting their frustrations out through the beat. I loved it—there ain't nothing prettier than two clean teenagers out there jitterbugging."

"Blue Suede Shoes" topped the pop, R&B and country charts simultaneously, and it seemed to herald the start of an important career. But the rug was pulled out from under Perkins. While he was on his way to New York to appear on television, he was almost killed in a serious car accident. He was hospitalized for the better part of a year recuperating. Meanwhile, Presley had cut his own cover of "Blue Suede Shoes" and was becoming a worldwide phenomenon.

Perkins churned out some classic rockabilly s des that made a profound impression on the next generation of guitarists, pickers like George Harrison and Eric Clapton. But the pop world left rockabilly behind, and Perkins never followed "Blue Suede Shoes" with anything approaching that success. By 1958, he was deep in the throes of alcoholism. A 10-year stint with Johnny Cash saw Perkins regain his confidence, and Cash had the top country record in 1968 with his interpretation of "Daddy Sang Bass."

In the early Seventies, England went rockabilly crazy, and Perkins experienced a comeback. Backed by a band that included his sons, he worked steadily through the Eighties. Perkins was elected to the Rock and Roll Hall of Fame on the second ballot. He had a bout with throat cancer, but the rockabilly king kept on pickin'.

*Go Cat Go!*, a tribute album, featured Perkins performing with all-stars Tom Petty, Johnny Cash, Bono, Willie Nelson, John Fogerty, Paul Simon and ex-Beatles Paul McCartney, George Harrison and Ringo Starr. Both John Lennon and Jimi Hendrix appeared via their previous recordings of "Blue Suede Shoes." It was a testament to an upright, self-effacing, devout man. "Family is what Carl Perkins is all about. My music will always be a part of my soul, but my love for family is the foundation of my soul." ■

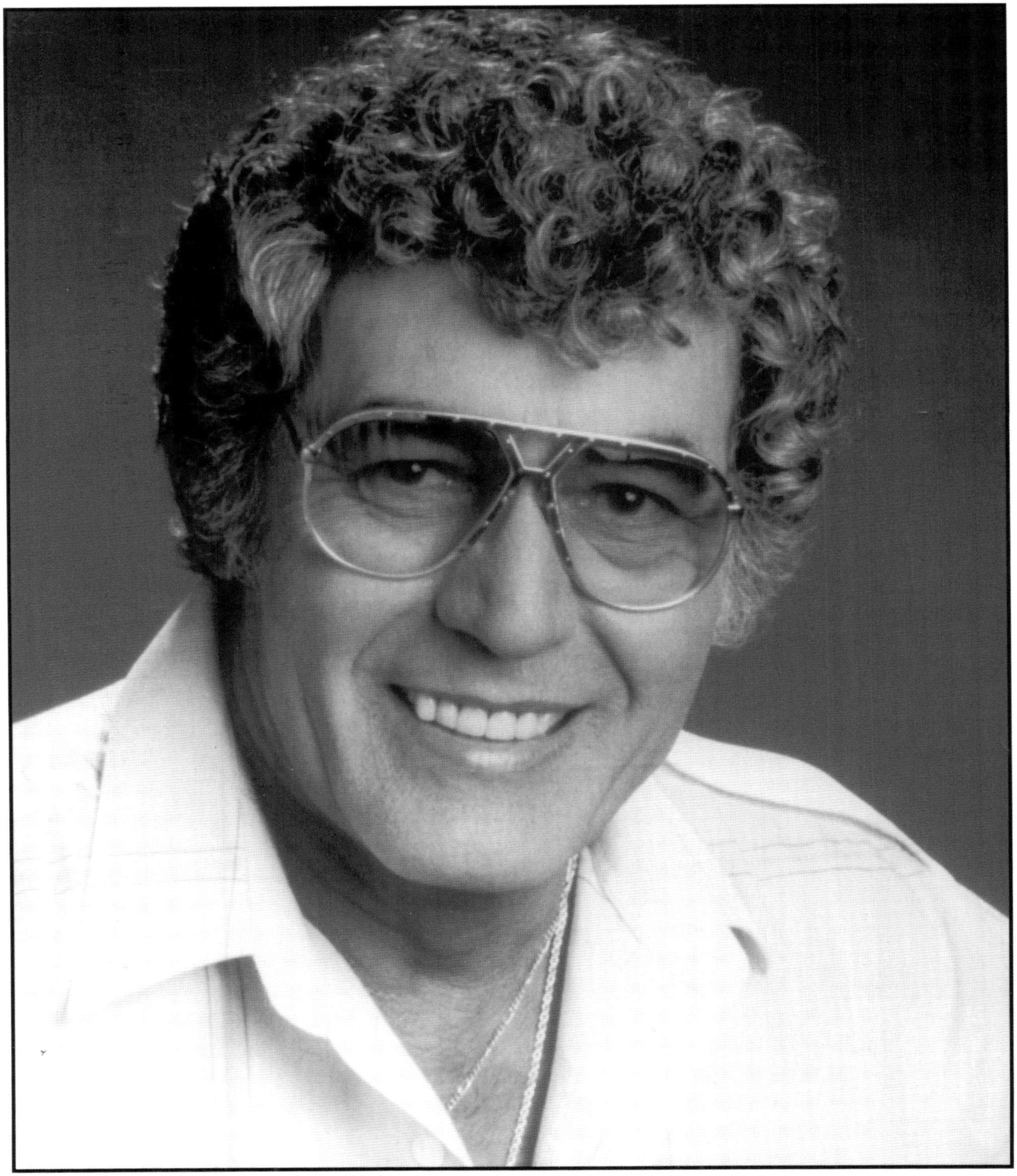

Carl Perkins

**Dinosaur Entertainment Corporation**
2115 Magazine Street, New Orleans, LA 70130
(504) 529-3033 Fax (504) 529-1387

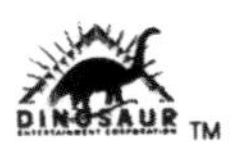

TM

*Billboard* 200: *Anthology 2* (No. 1)
*Billboard* Hot 100: "Real Love" (#11)

## The Beatles' *Anthology 2*, another clutch of unissued tracks, included "Real Love," a honed John Lennon demo.

**A MULTIMEDIA** project charting the band's career, *The Beatles Anthology* had captivated the interest of music fans. They loved seeing the archival footage that elevated a film documentary broadcast on national television, and *Anthology 1*, the first double-CD of a trilogy, went straight to No. 1 and sold 3 million copies.

Yet the initial archeological appeal of Beatlemania redux wore thin. While some music caught on among bootleg fiends who had never heard many of the tracks, most devotees quickly grew bored with *Anthology 1*—outtakes of "Kansas City" didn't seem all that interesting after one listening. It just wasn't quite as good as the ubiquitous marketing blitz had built it up to be.

The good news was that the Beatles' *Anthology 2* delivered more pleasure. The 45 unreleased tracks covered the experimental "studio years" from 1965 to 1968, after the Fab Four tired of playing to screaming fans in stadiums and developed their genius under the aegis of producer George Martin. It's the way they created the seminal albums *Rubber Soul*, *Revolver* and *Sgt. Pepper's Lonely Hearts Club Band.*

The songs started out differently from the classics that everybody knew. On "And Your Bird Can Sing," John Lennon and Paul McCartney collapsed into giggles while recording a vocal overdub, and a folksy first take of "Yesterday" resonated, eavesdropping on the making of McCartney's most successful song.

*Anthology 2* also included "Real Love," the second song from 1995's "reunion sessions." Like "Free as a Bird" from the first anthology, McCartney, George Harrison and Ringo Starr recorded a song written but never released by Lennon. It was pure pop produced by Jeff Lynne, sounding like Lennon backed by the Traveling Wilburys.

"'Real Love' had all the words and music—this was more like we were sidemen to John," McCartney said. "Which was joyful and good fun, and I think we did a good job. There was a crazy moment, because not having done it for so long, you become an ex-Beatle. But working on this anthology, you're in the band again, there's no two ways about it. And it was good being them again for a little while.

"We just work well together, that's the truth of it. When you find someone you can talk to, it's a very special thing. But if you find someone you can play music with, it's really something." ■

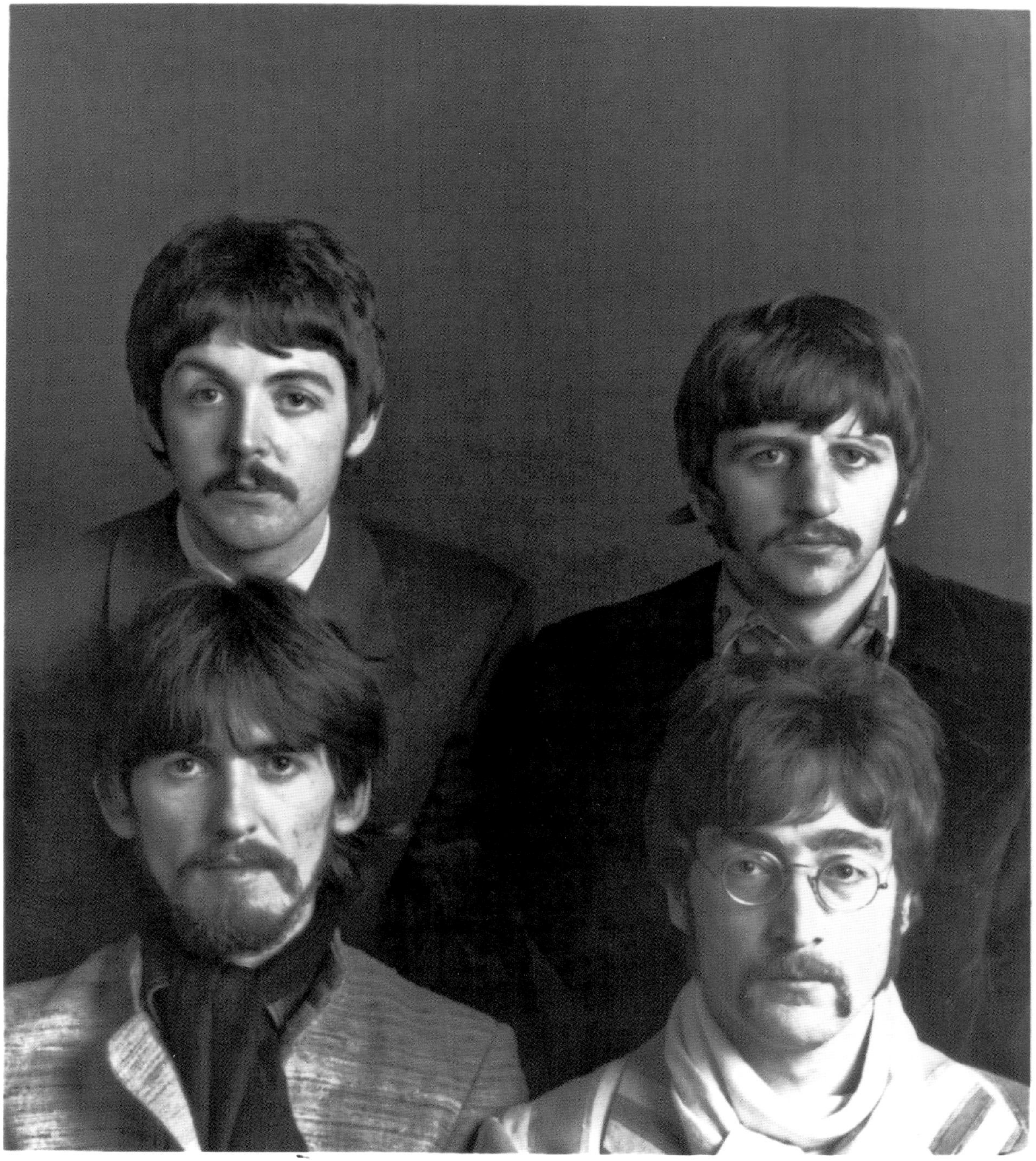

1996 / 37361



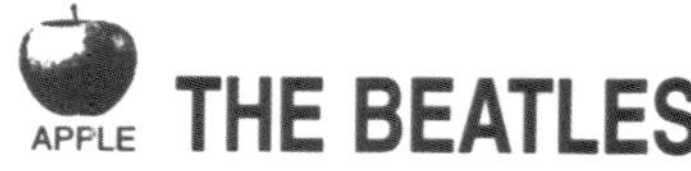


**JANUARY 1967**

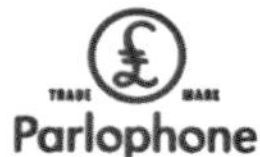

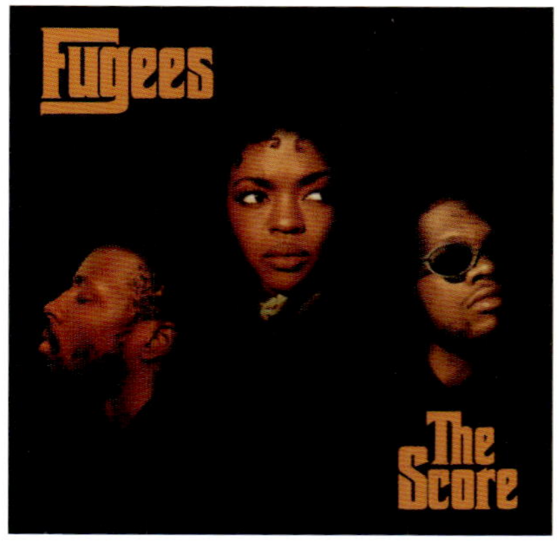


Rejecting the commonplace crotch-grabbing approach to making hip-hop, **Fugees** topped charts worldwide with *The Score,* the trio's sophomore album.

*Billboard* 200: *The Score* (No. 1)
*Billboard* Hot 100: "Fu-Gee-La" (#29)

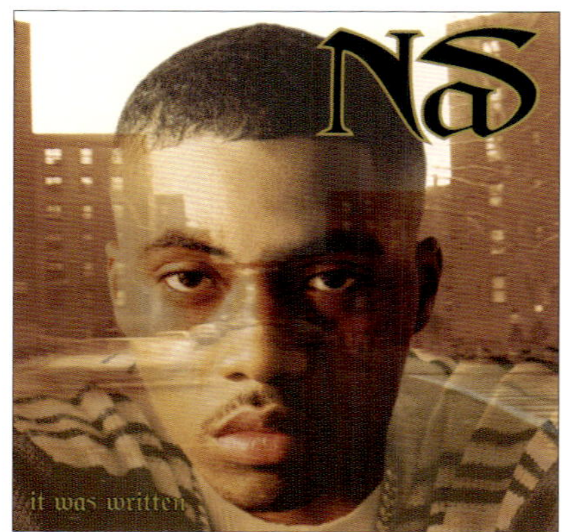


**Nas**' *It Was Written* album reached No. 1, and "If I Ruled the World (Imagine That)" featuring Lauryn Hill vaulted the New York rapper to mainstream fame.

*Billboard* 200: *It Was Written* (No. 1)
*Billboard* Hot 100: "If I Ruled the World (Imagine That)" (#53); "Street Dreams" (#22)

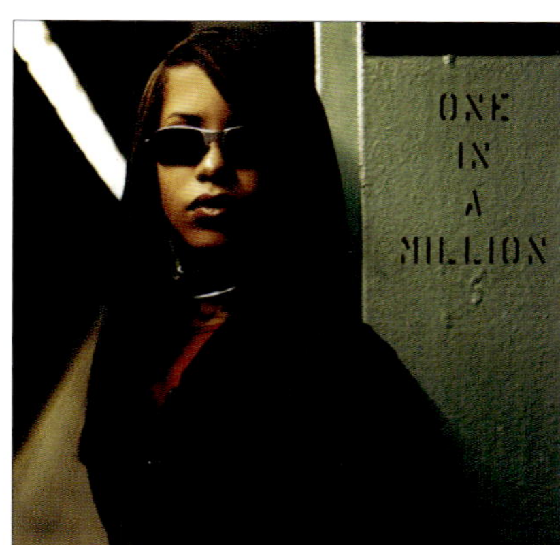


For *One in a Million,* her second album, the 17-year-old singer **Aaliyah** teamed up with young producer Timbaland and his writing partner Missy Elliott.

*Billboard* 200: *One in a Million* (#18)
*Billboard* Hot 100: "If Your Girl Only Knew" (#11); "The One I Gave My Heart To" (#9)

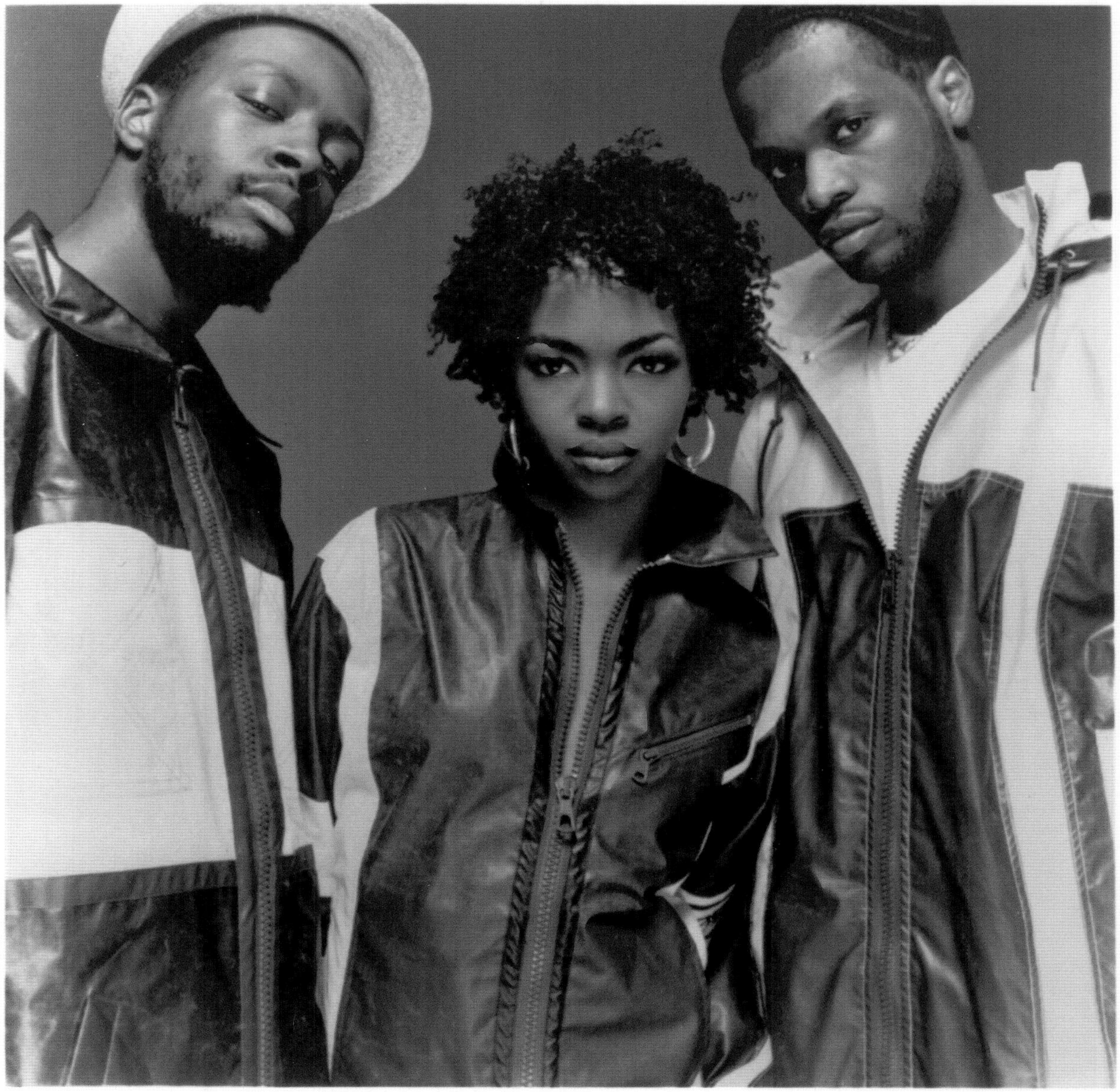

PHOTOGRAPH: MARC BAPTISTE

Wycleff Lauryn Pras

DAS Communications
83 Riverside Drive
New York, NY 10024
Phone: 212 . 877 . 0400

# FUGEES

COLUMBIA
9602

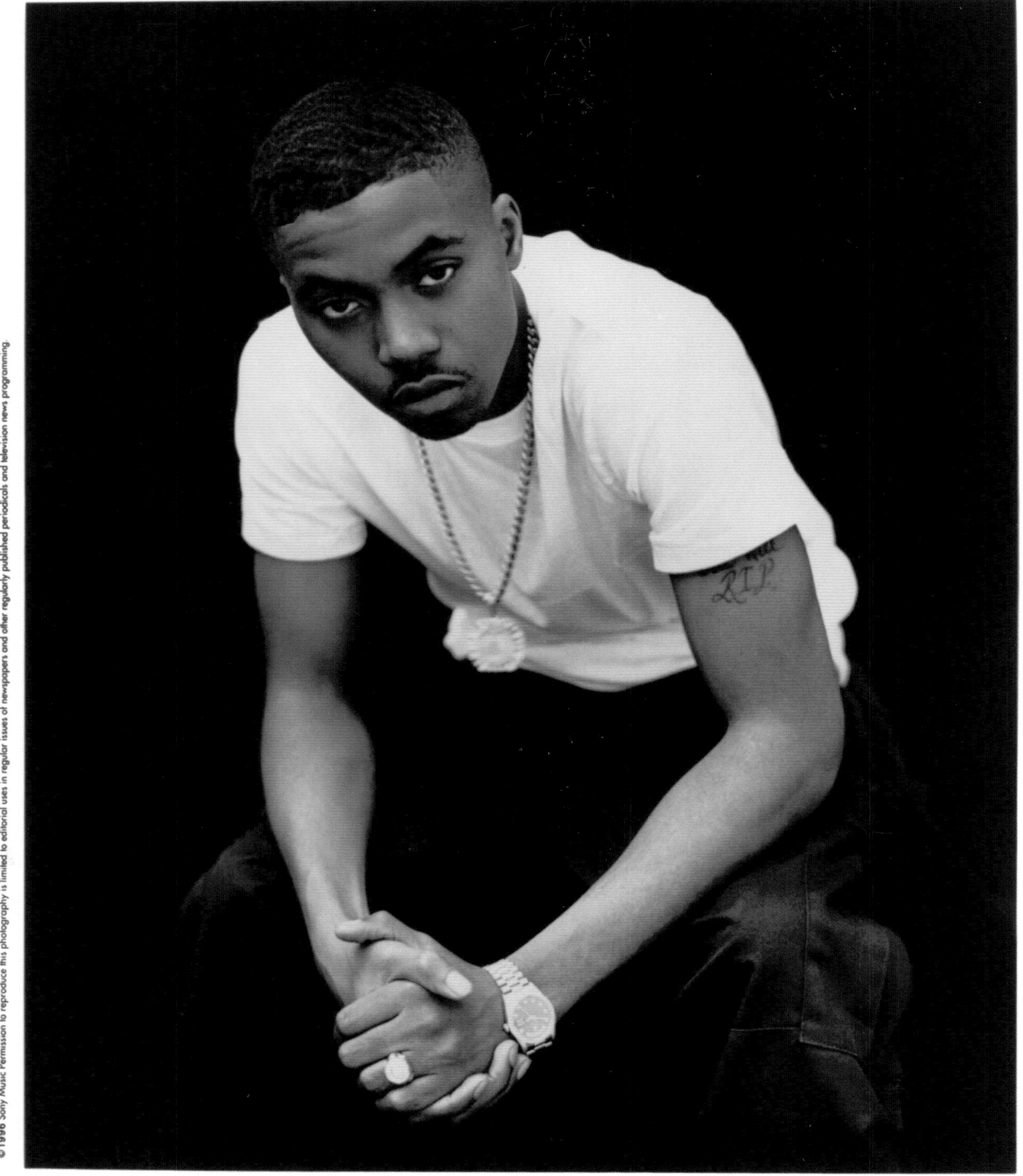


PHOTOGRAPH: DANNY CLINCH

Management:
Steve Stoute
212-889-6888

# NAS

COLUMBIA
9607

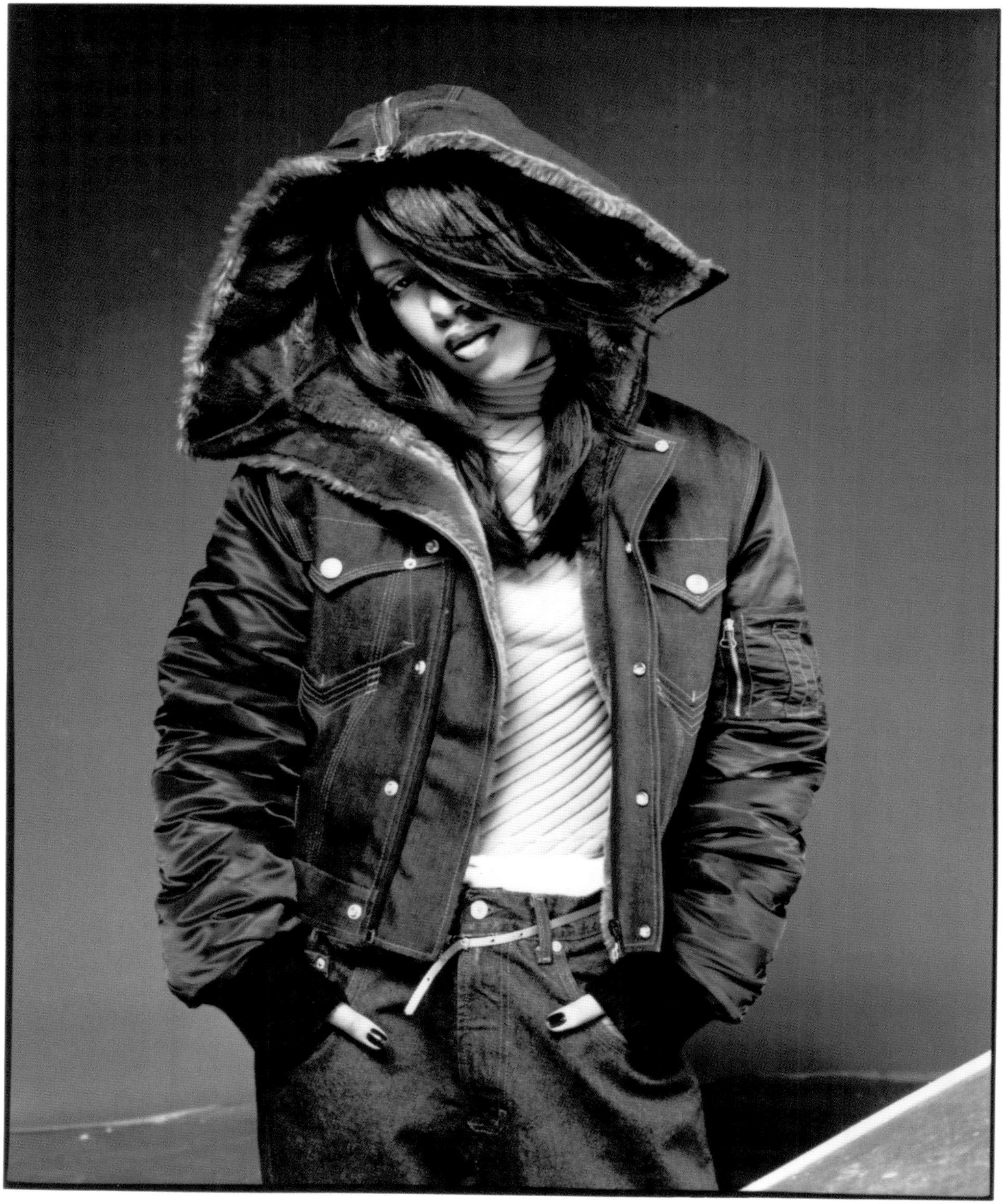

Photo Credit: Marc Baptiste

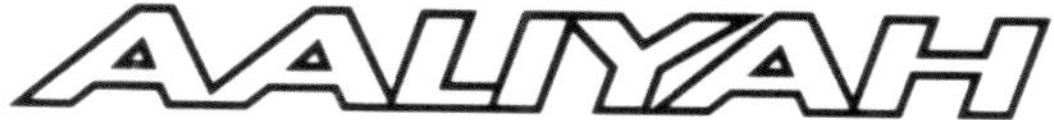


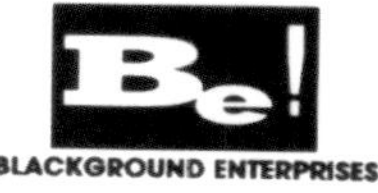


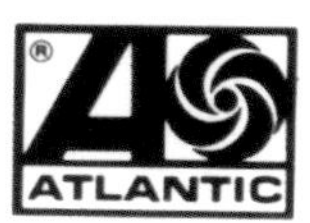

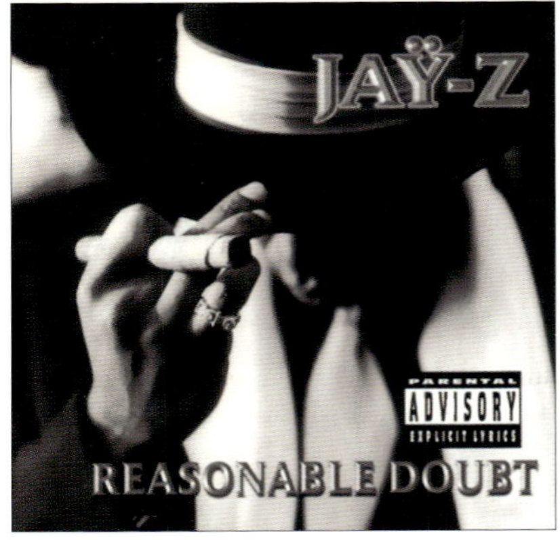


With no major label willing to sign him, rapper **Jay-Z** formed Roc-A-Fella Records and released *Reasonable Doubt*, his debut album of street exploits.

*Billboard* 200: *Reasonable Doubt* (#23)
*Billboard* Hot 100: "Dead Presidents"/"Ain't No Nigga" (#50); "Can't Knock the Hustle" (#73); "Feelin' It" (#79)

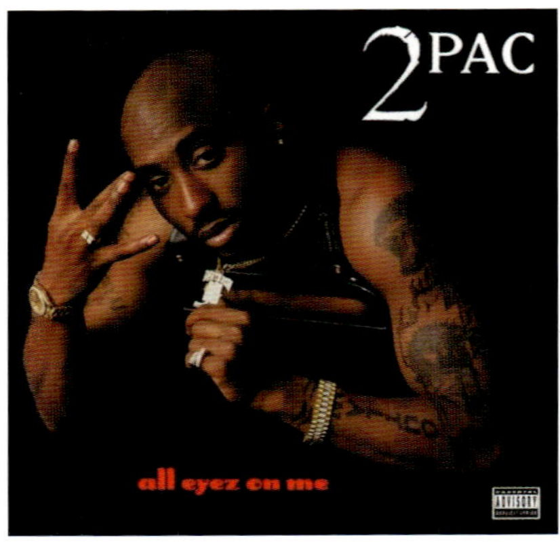


*All Eyez on Me*, the first double album in hip-hop history, emphasized **2Pac**'s volatile gangsta lifestyle and attained critical and commercial success.

*Billboard* 200: *All Eyez on Me* (No. 1)
*Billboard* Hot 100: "How Do U Want It"/"California Love" (No. 1)

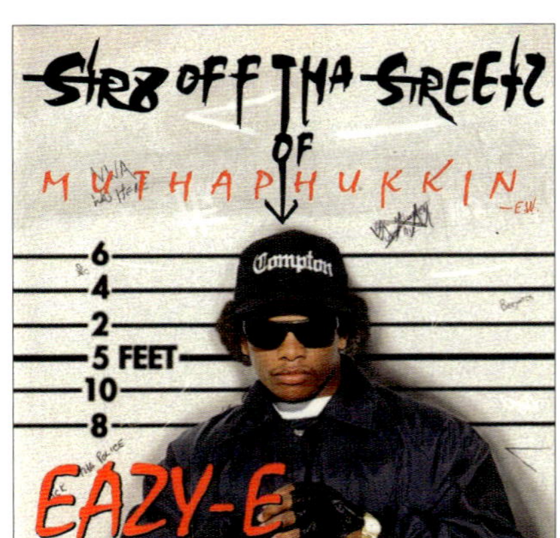


Ten months after his death by complications from AIDS, gangsta rapper **Eazy-E**'s last album, *Str8 off tha Streetz of Muthaphukkin Compton*, was issued.

*Billboard* 200: *Str8 off tha Streetz of Muthaphukkin Compton* (#3)
*Billboard* Hot 100: "Just tah Let U Know" (#45)

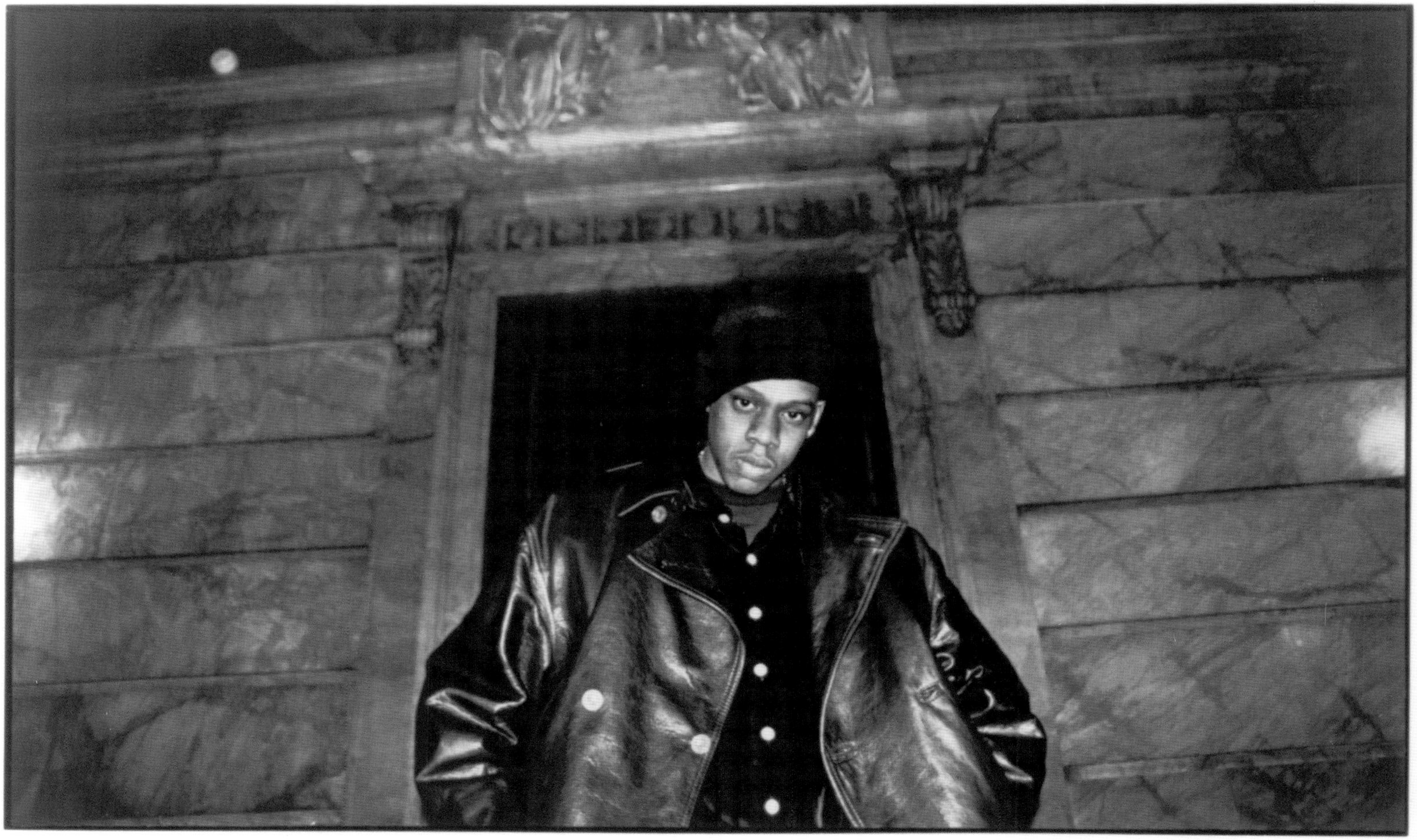

PHOTO: ABDUL ABBOTT

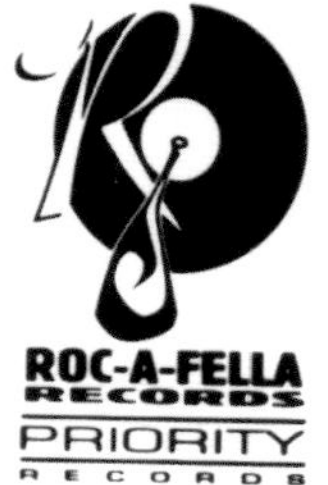


# JAŸ-Z

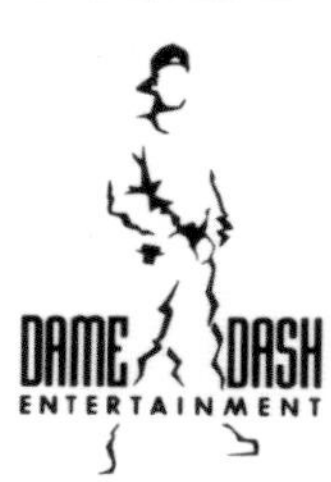

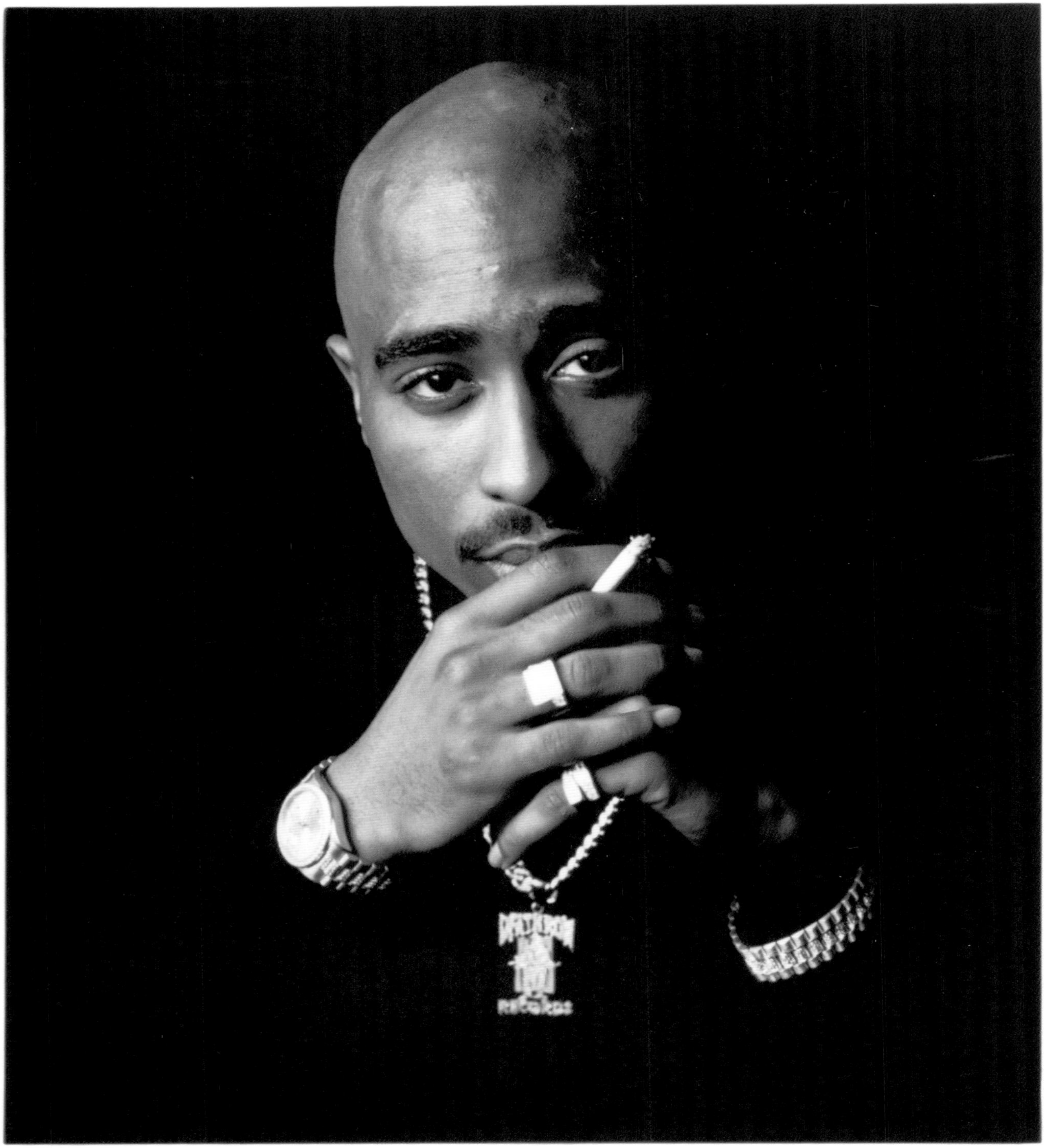

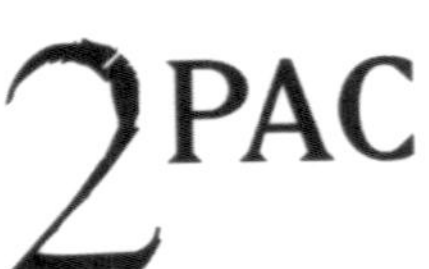
2PAC

DEATH ROW
RECORDS

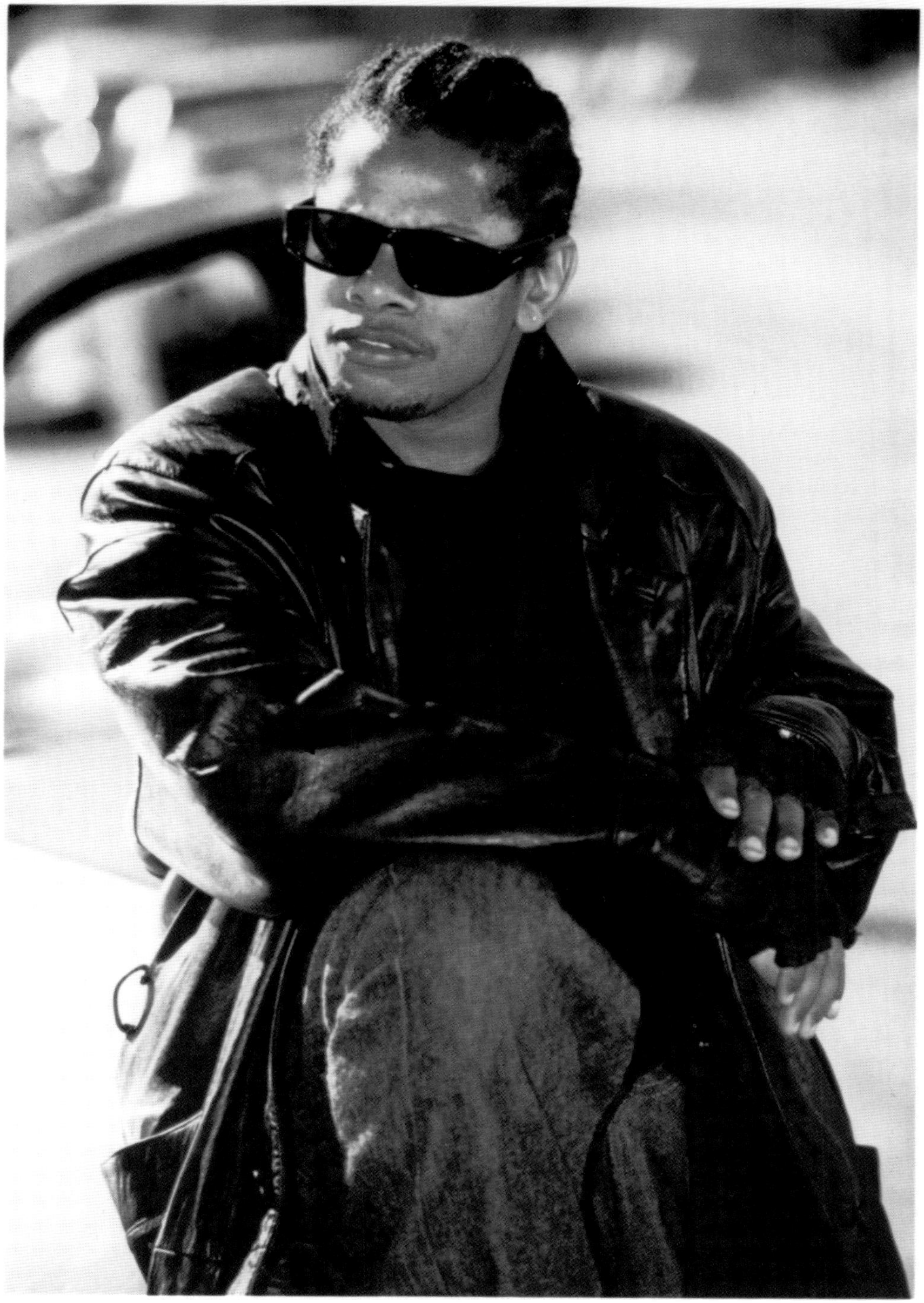

Photo: Kenneth Samuels

# EAZY-E

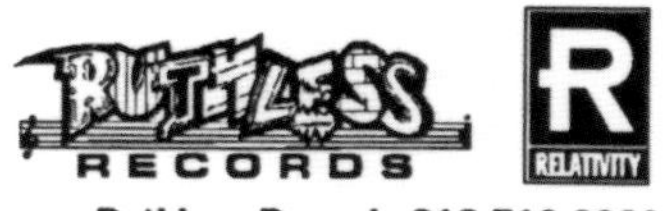


Ruthless Records 818.710.0060

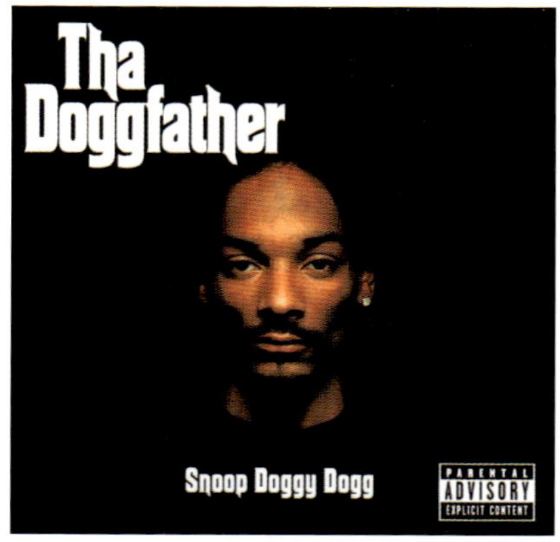


Acquitted in a much-publicized murder trial, rapper **Snoop Doggy Dogg** watched his second album, *Tha Doggfather*, debut on top of the pop and R&B charts.

*Billboard* 200: *Tha Doggfather* (No. 1)

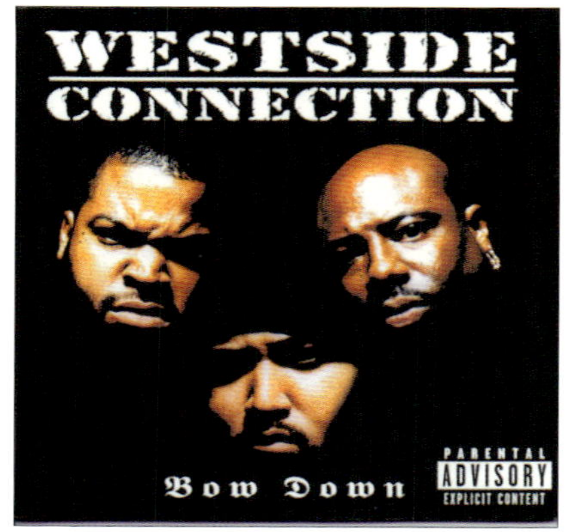


Hip-hop supergroup **Westside Connection** scored a No. 1 rap hit with "Bow Down," a directive to any detractors dissing the West Coast gangsta kingpins.

*Billboard* 200: *Bow Down* (#2)
*Billboard* Hot 100: "Bow Down" (#21);
"Gangstas Make the World Go Round" (#40)

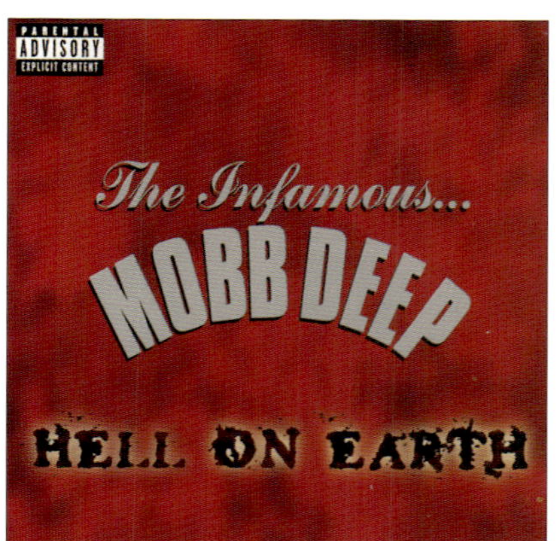


**Mobb Deep**'s third album resumed the East Coast hardcore rappers' portrayal of harsh street life, reflected in the hypnotic "Hell on Earth (Front Lines)."

*Billboard* 200: *Hell on Earth* (#6)

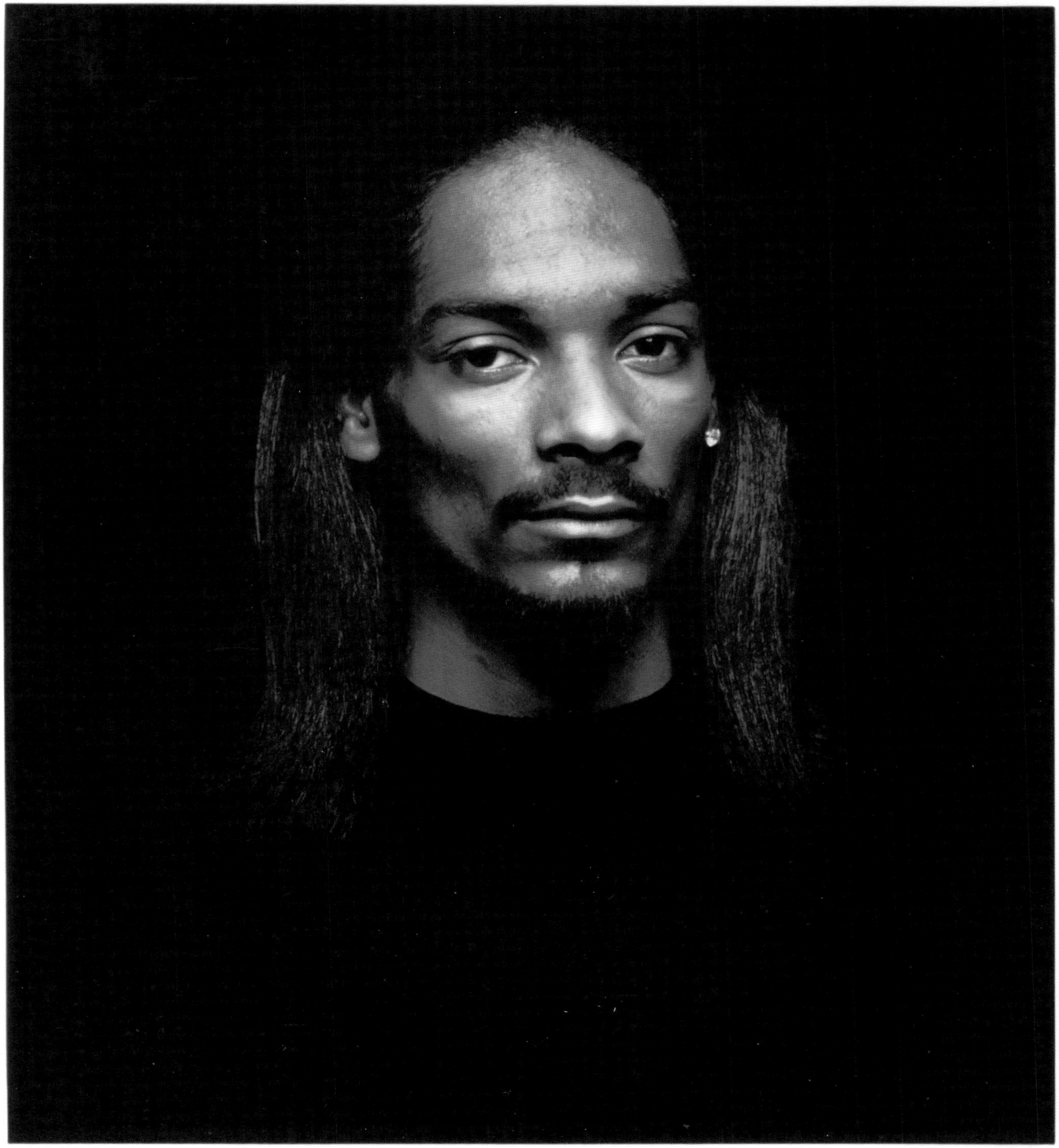

**SNOOP**
**doggy dogg**

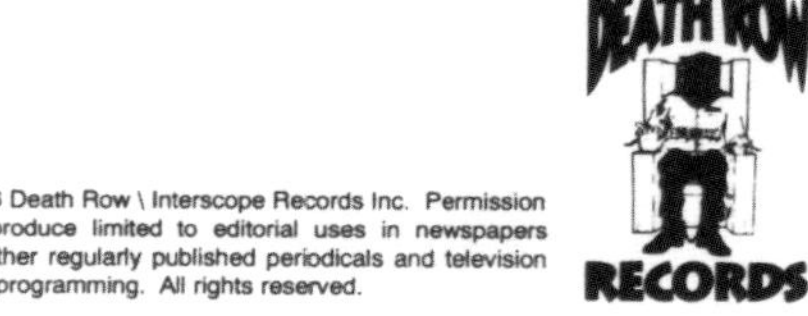

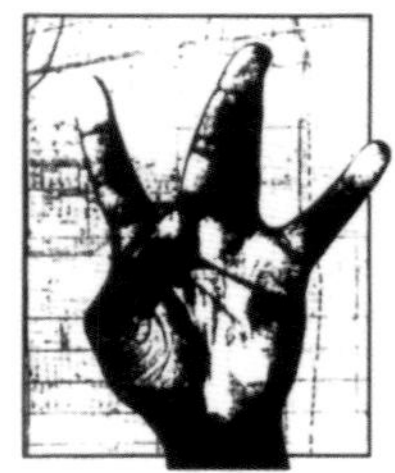

# WESTSIDE CONNECTION

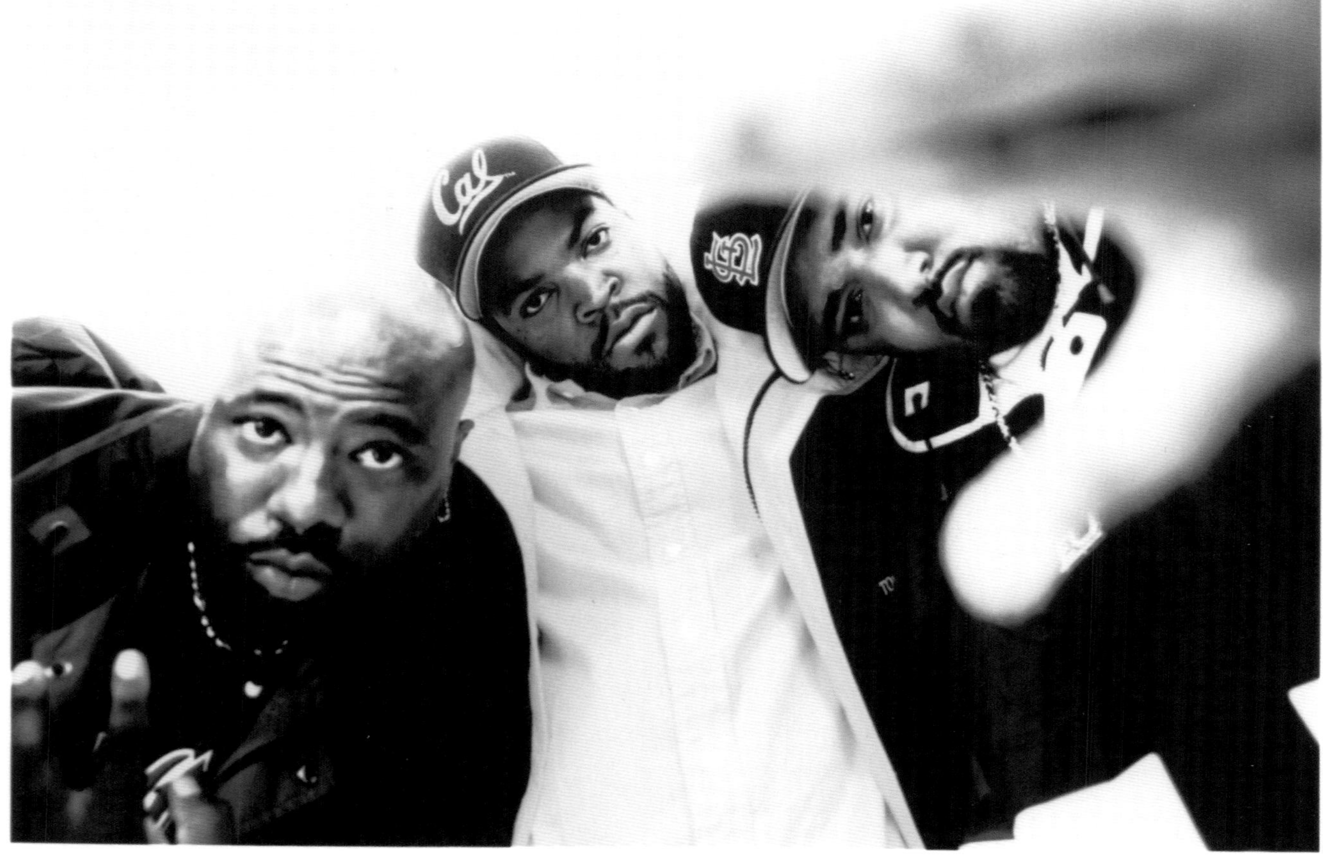


Photo: Michael Miller

**WC** **ICE CUBE** **MACK 10**

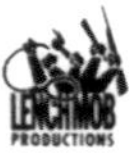


PRIORITY RECORDS

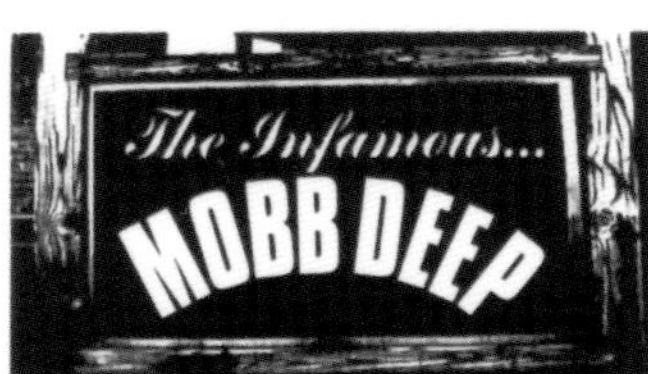

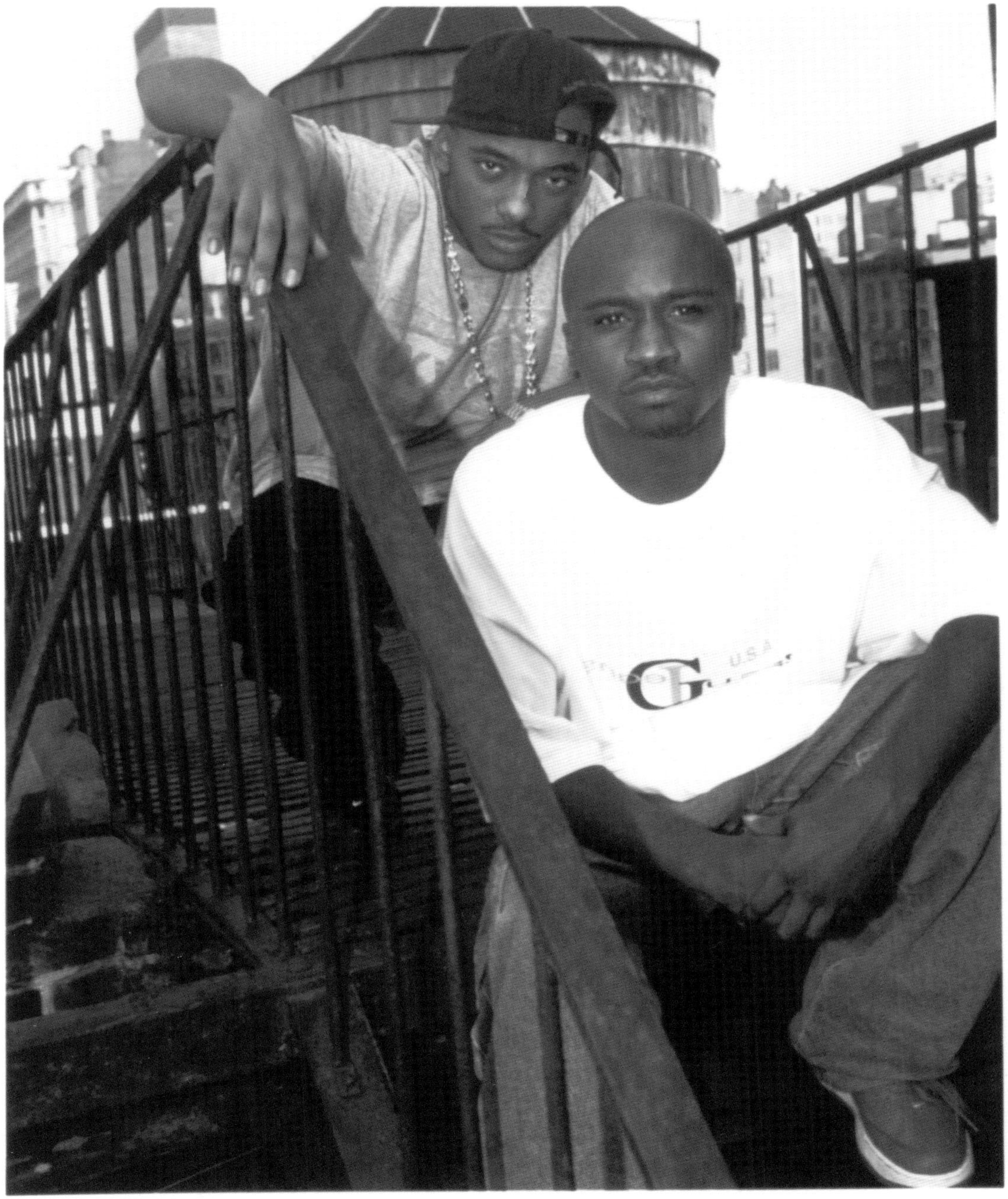

Prodigy Havoc

Violator Management (212) 229-5267

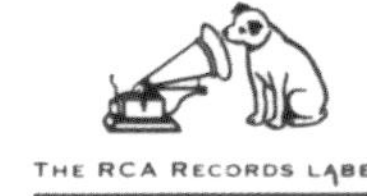

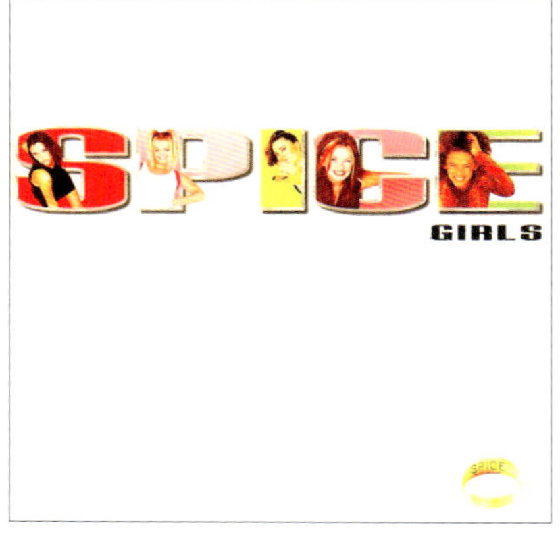


**Spice Girls** became pop culture icons with *Spice*, the British girl group's first album, and the smash "Wannabe," a No. 1 hit in more than 30 countries.

*Billboard* 200: *Spice* (No. 1)
*Billboard* Hot 100: "Wannabe" (No. 1);
"Say You'll Be There" (#3); "2 Become 1" (#4):

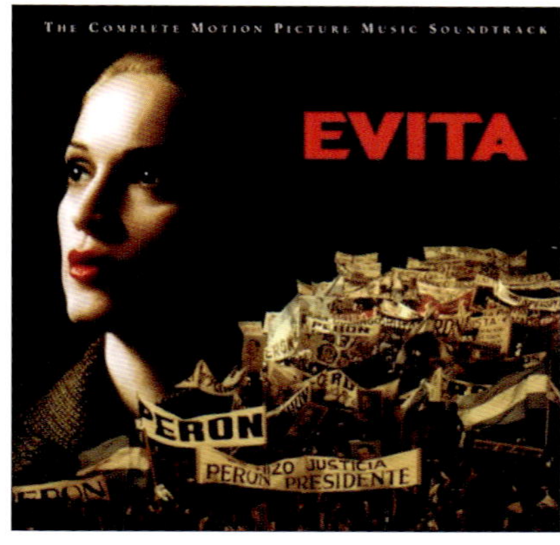


Reinforcing her celebrity by playing the title role in the screen version of *Evita*, **Madonna** performed most of the songs for the movie's soundtrack.

*Billboard* 200: *Evita* (#2)
*Billboard* Hot 100: "You Must Love Me" (#18);
"Don't Cry for Me Argentina" (#8)

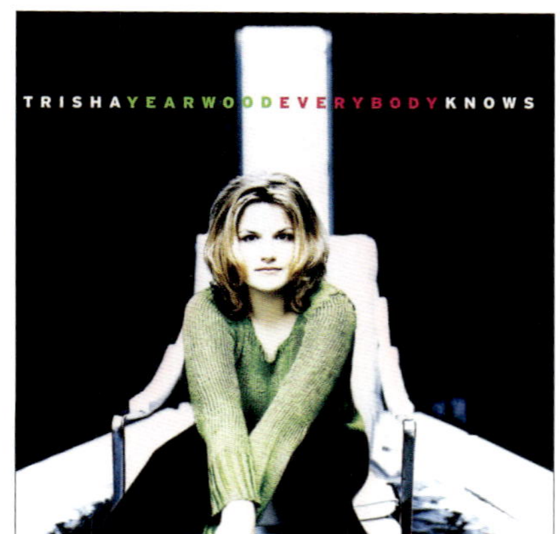


Singer **Trisha Yearwood**'s spate of country-pop hits extended to *Everybody Knows* and the massive singles "Believe Me Baby (I Lied)" and the title track.

*Billboard* 200: *Everybody Knows* (#52)

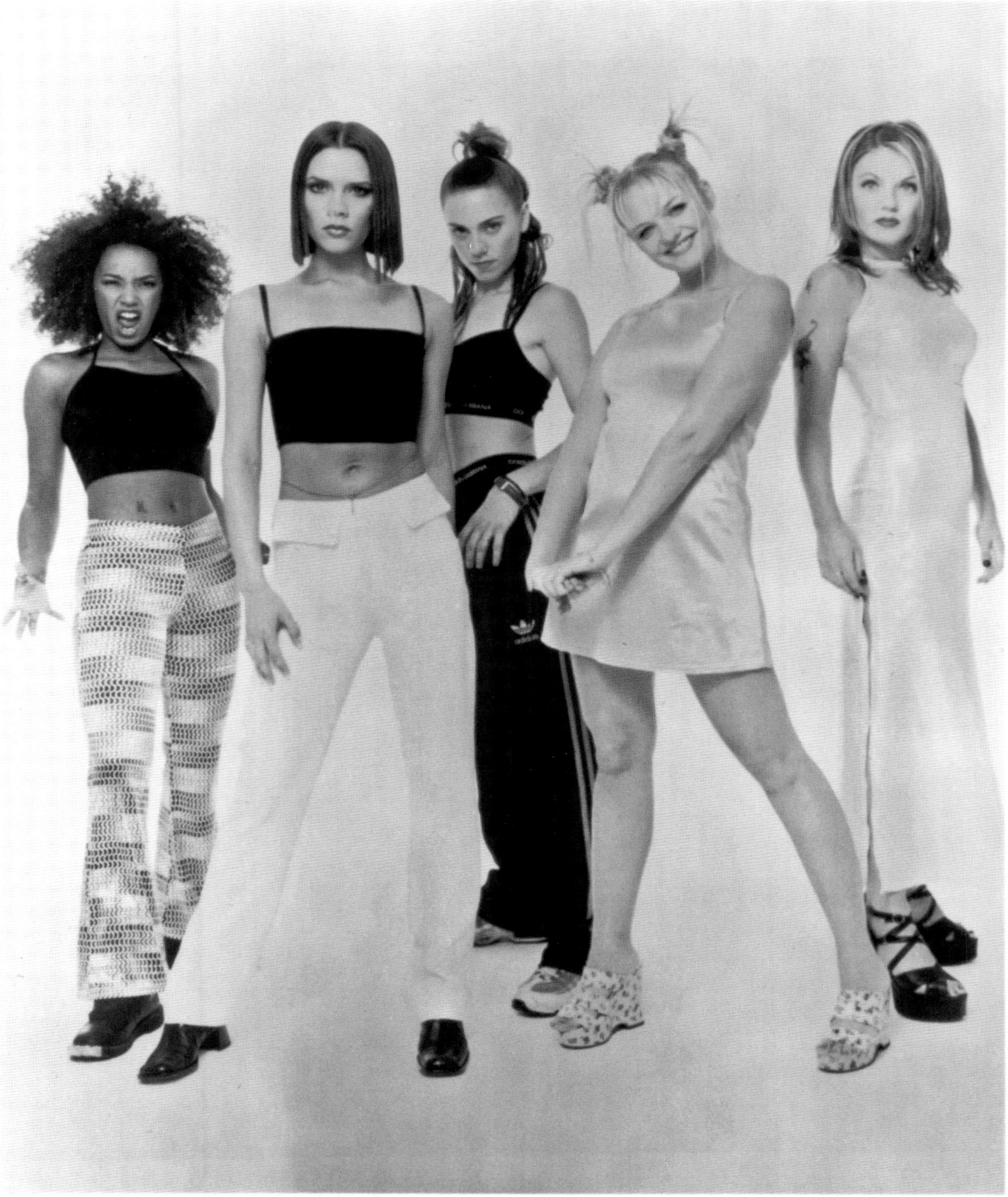

Photo Credit: Francessca Sorrenti 9/96

Melanie B. Victoria Melanie C. Emma Geri

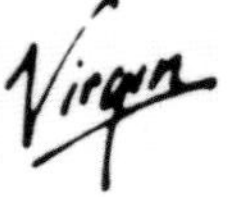


# SPICE GIRLS

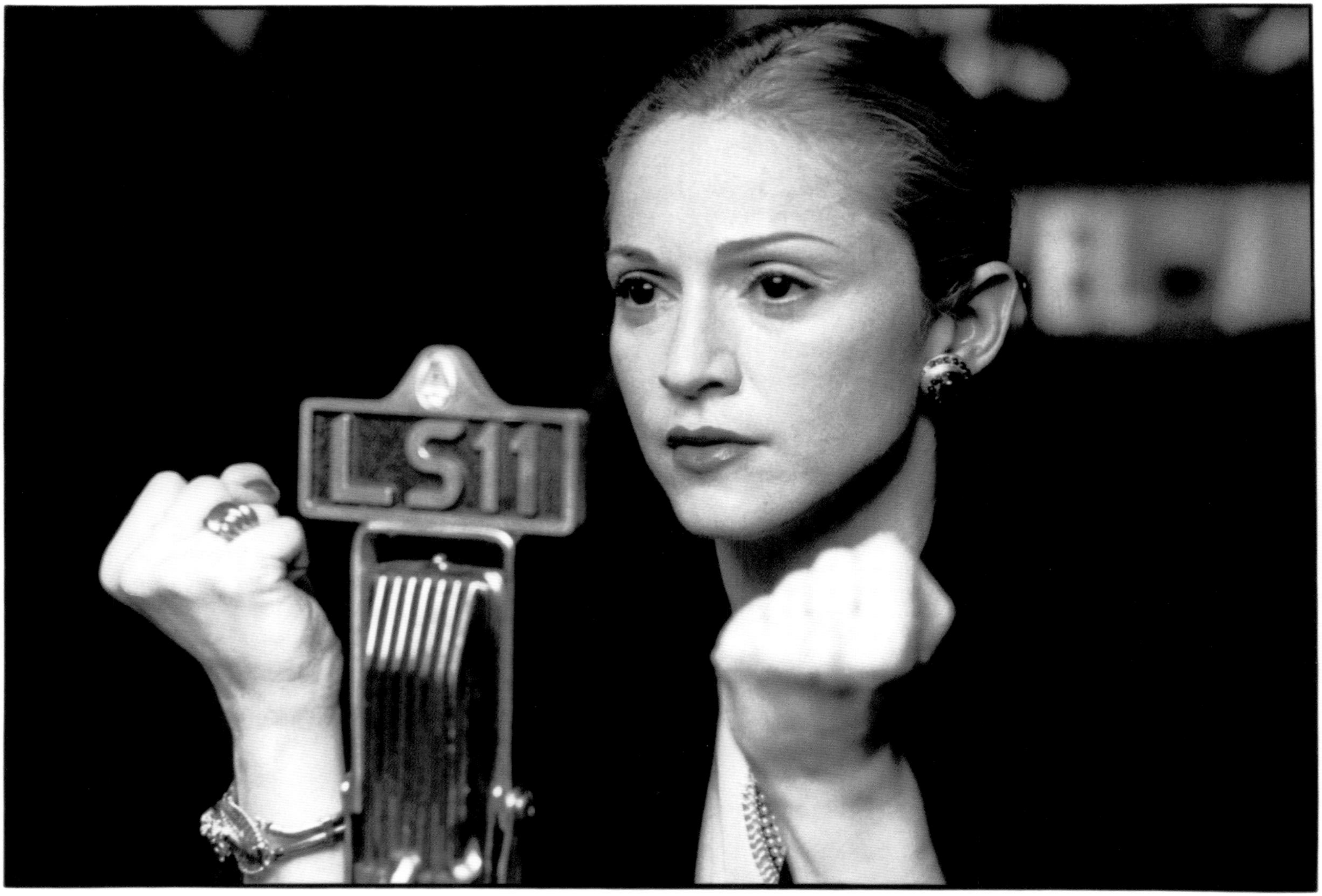

Photo Credit: David Appleby

# EVITA

**The Complete Motion Picture Music Soundtrack**

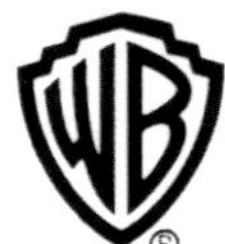

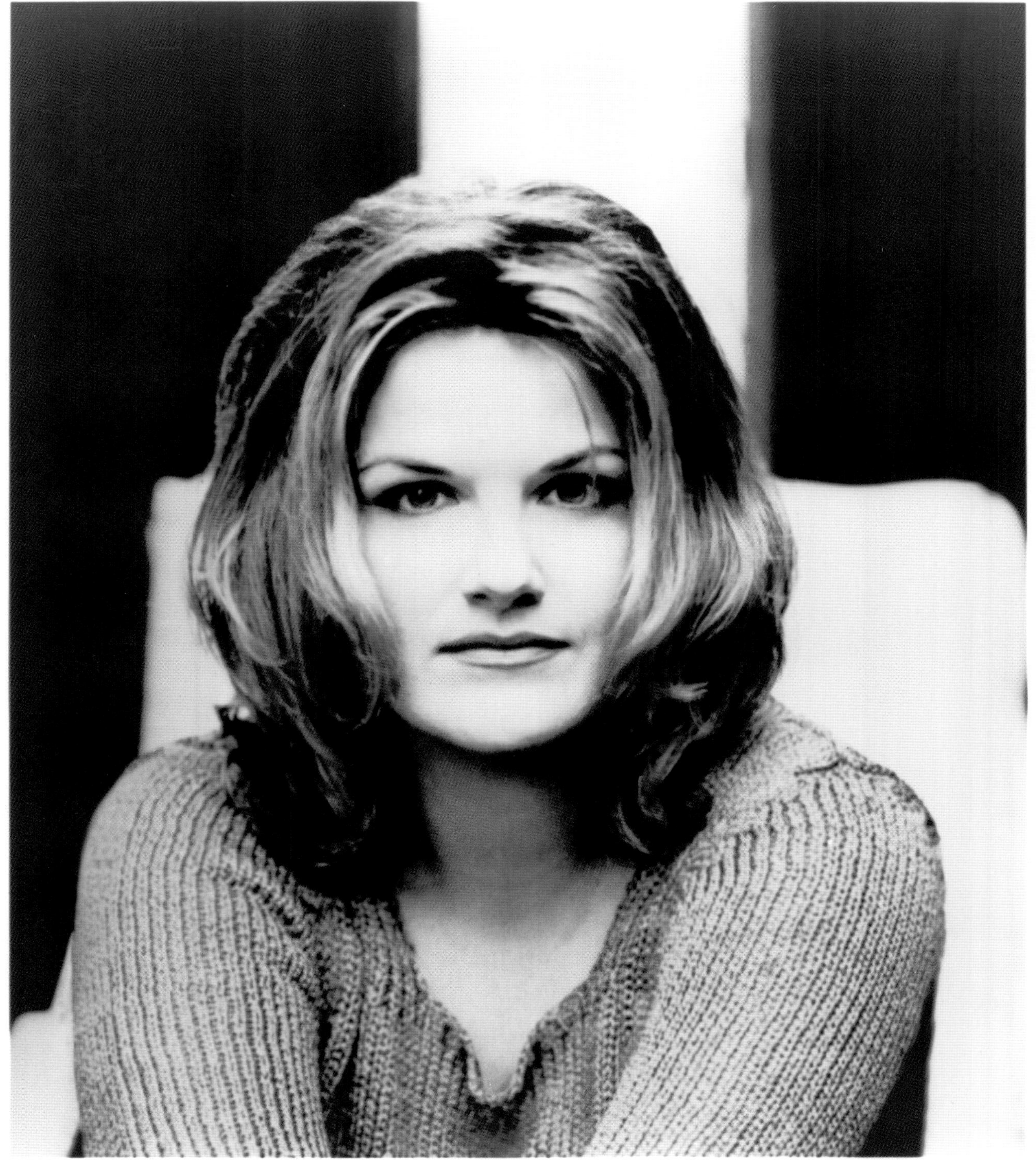

photo: Russ Harrington 0796A

TRISHA YEARWOOD

MCA NASHVILLE

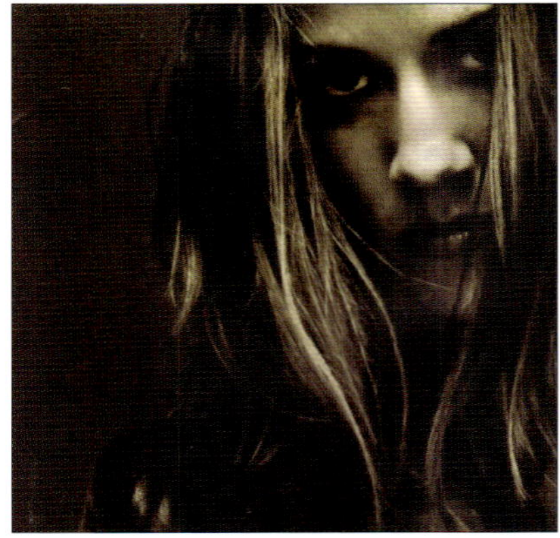

Producing her self-titled second album herself and playing most of the instruments, **Sheryl Crow** netted a worldwide hit with "If It Makes You Happy."

*Billboard* 200: *Sheryl Crow* (#6)
*Billboard* Hot 100: "If It Makes You Happy" (#10);
"Everyday Is a Winding Road" (#11)

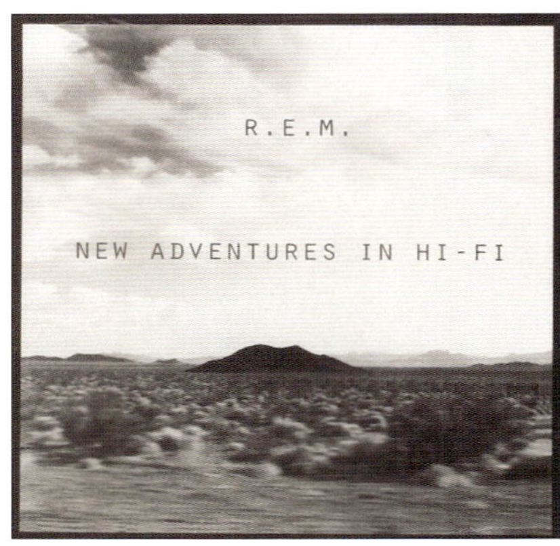


After inking a new record deal for a reportedly unprecedented sum, **R.E.M.** crafted *New Adventures in Hi-Fi* in various locales on and around a world tour.

*Billboard* 200: *New Adventures in Hi-Fi* (#2)
*Billboard* Hot 100: "E-Bow the Letter" (#49);
"Bittersweet Me" (#46); "Electrolite" (#96)

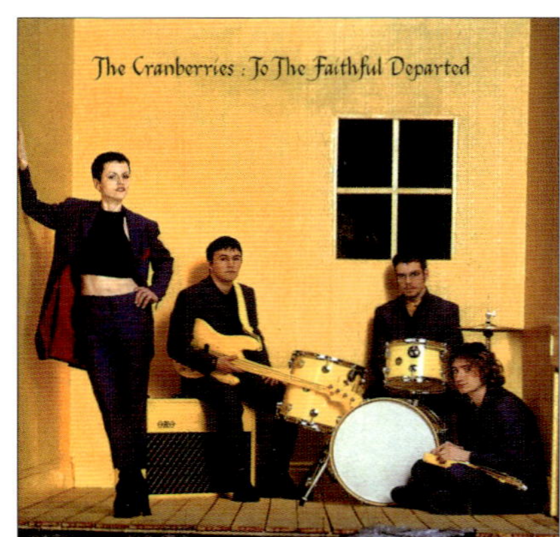


**The Cranberries**, an Irish band fronted by singer Dolores O'Riordan, looked for ironic meaning in drug culture with the No. 1 alternative-rock hit "Salvation."

*Billboard* 200: *To the Faithful Departed* (#4)
*Billboard* Hot 100: "Free To Decide"/"When You're Gone" (#22)

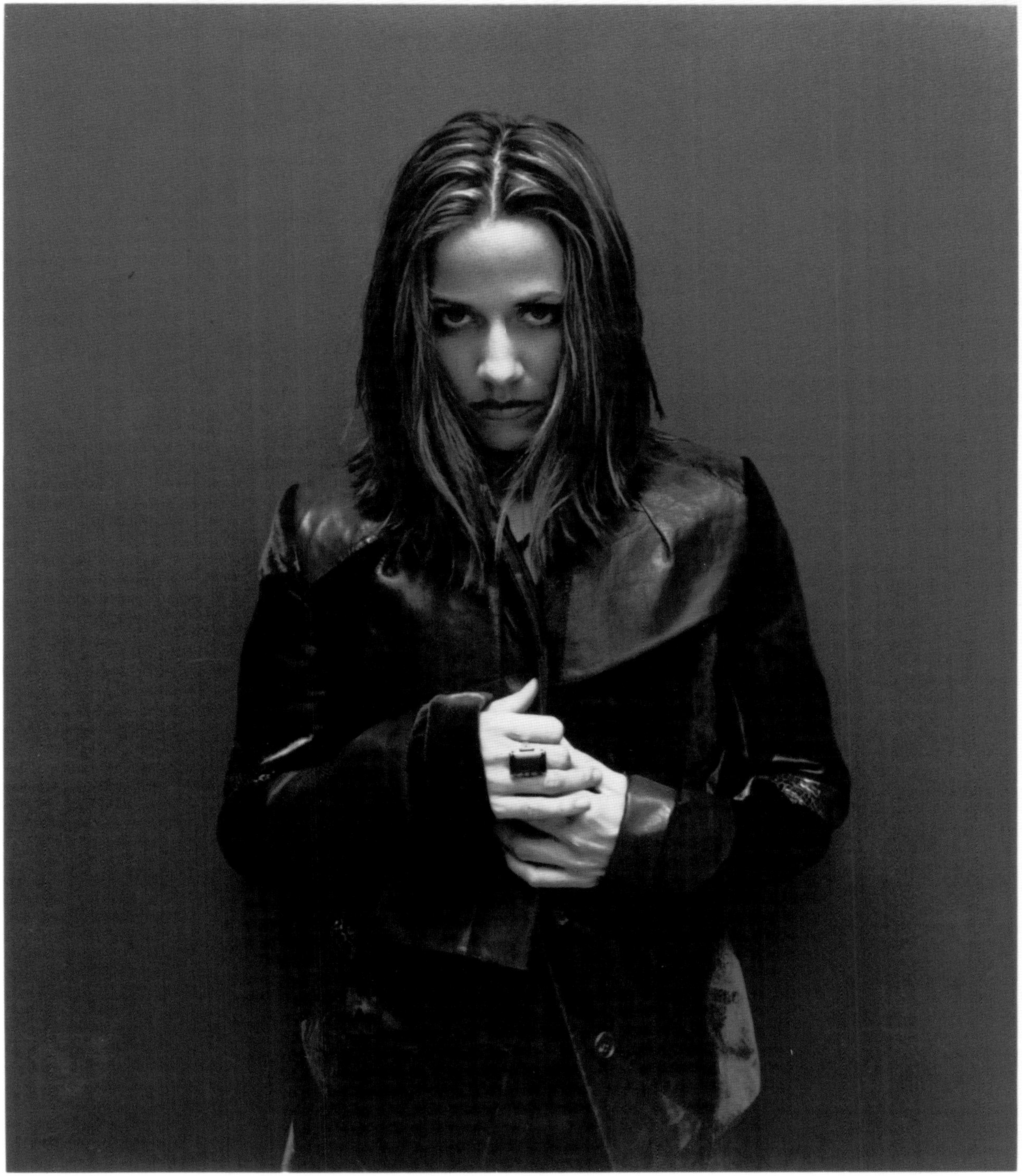

Photo: Steen Sundland 9/96

SHERYL CROW

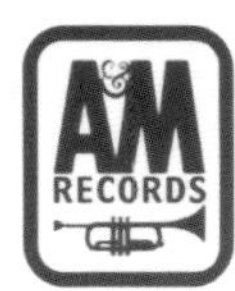

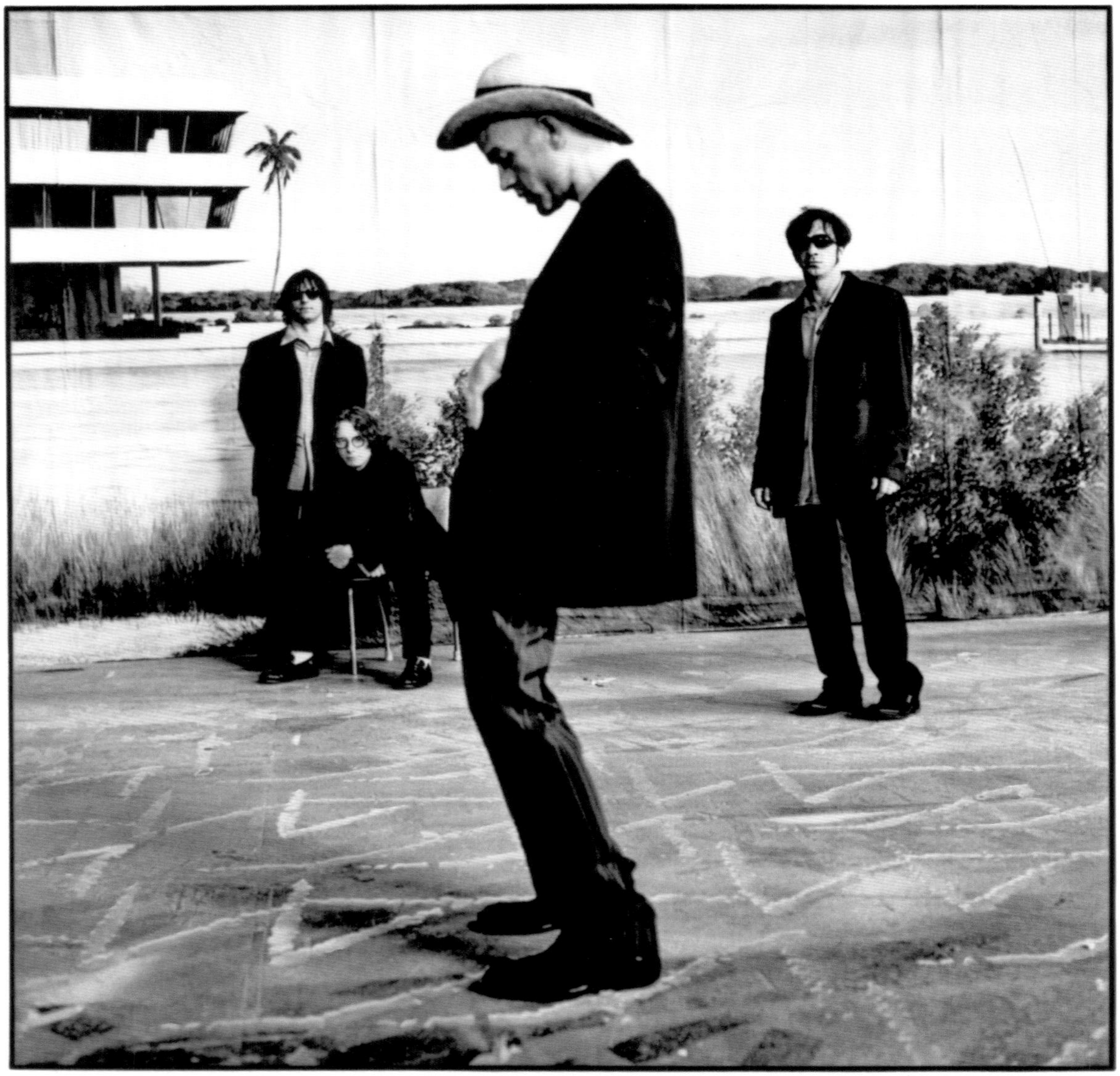

Photo Credit: Anton Corbijn

# R.E.M.

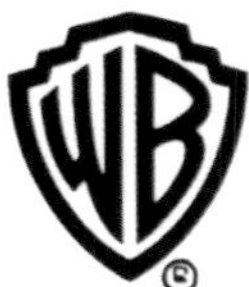

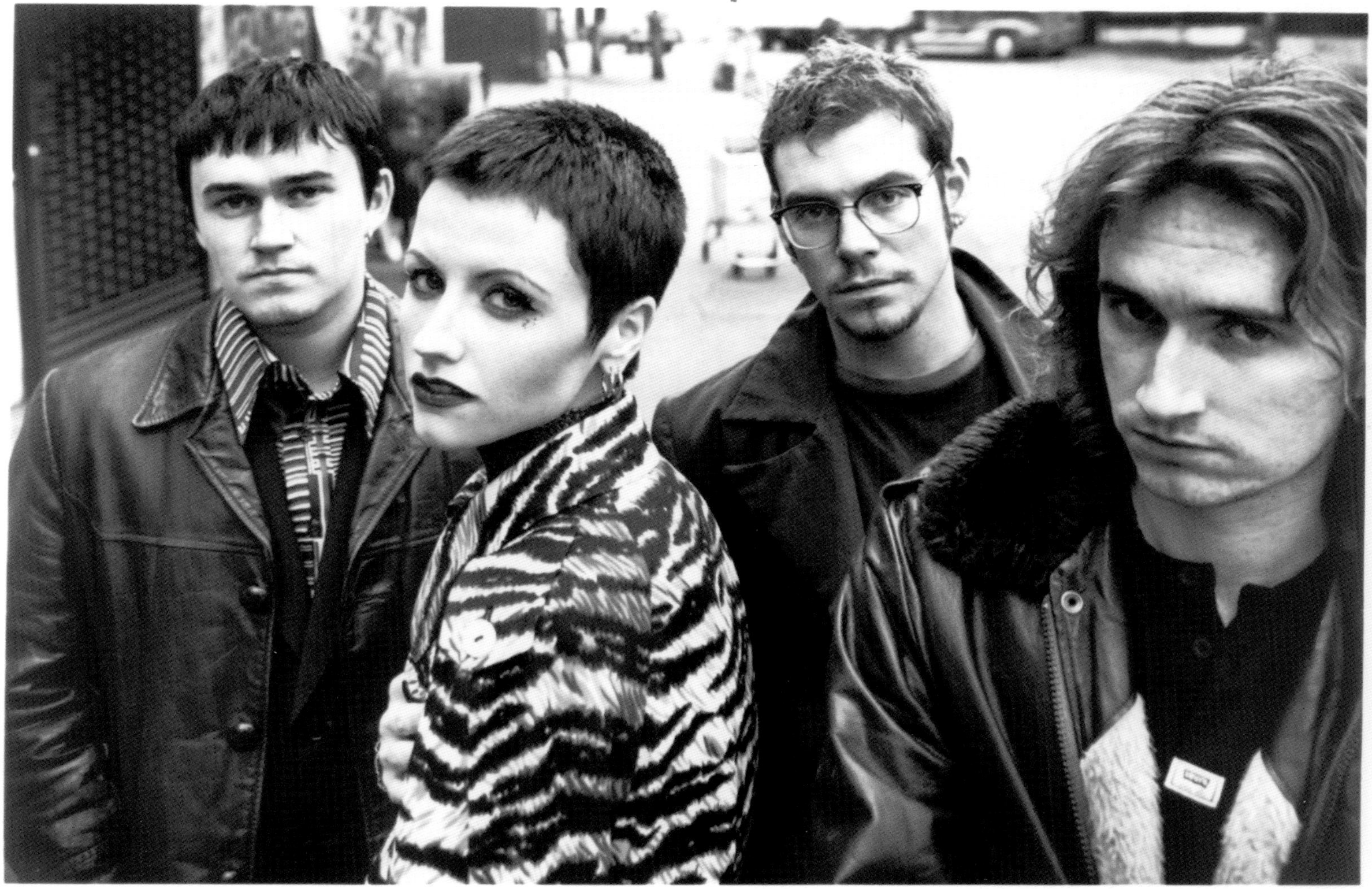

Photo Credit: Mark Seliger

Mike Hogan Dolores O'Riordan Fergal Lawler Noel Hogan

# The Cranberries

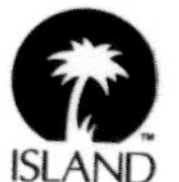

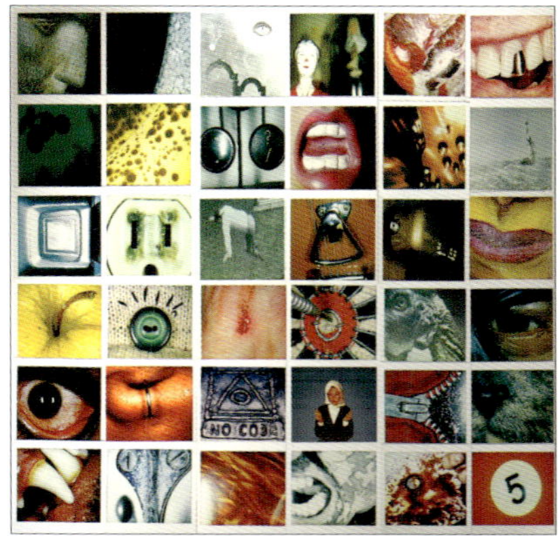


**Pearl Jam**'s diverse *No Code* debuted at No. 1 on the charts, but touring to boost album sales was curtailed due to the band's battle with Ticketmaster.

*Billboard* 200: *No Code* (No. 1)
*Billboard* Hot 100: "Who You Are" (#31)

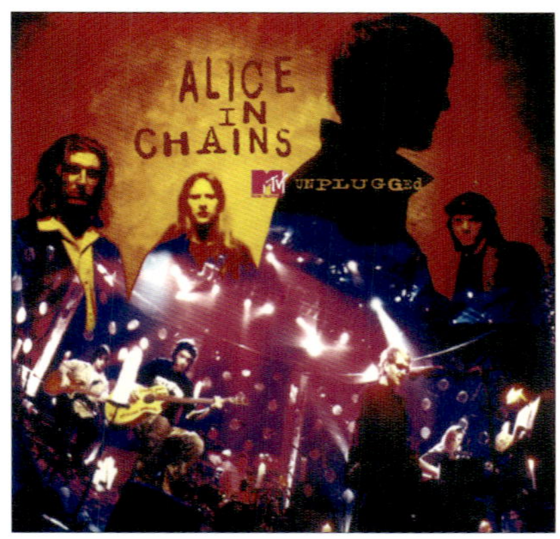


*MTV Unplugged*, a recording of **Alice in Chains**' first live performance in nearly three years, highlighted an all-acoustic set list.

*Billboard* 200: *MTV Unplugged* (#3)

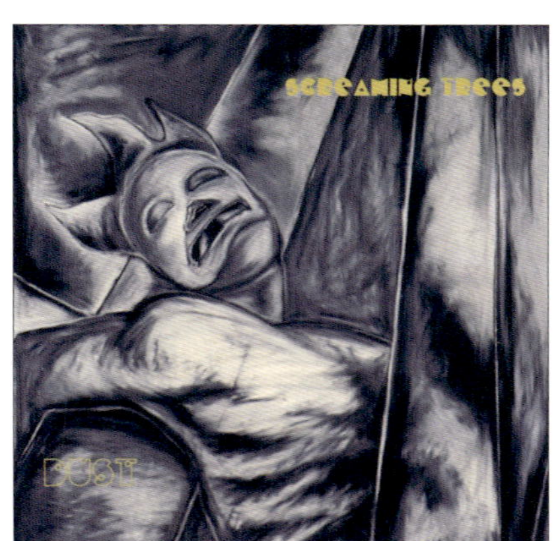


An entire album was recorded but then rejected by **Screaming Trees** themselves, yet *Dust* finally settled and "All I Know" became a favorite on rock radio.

*Billboard* 200: *Dust* (#134)

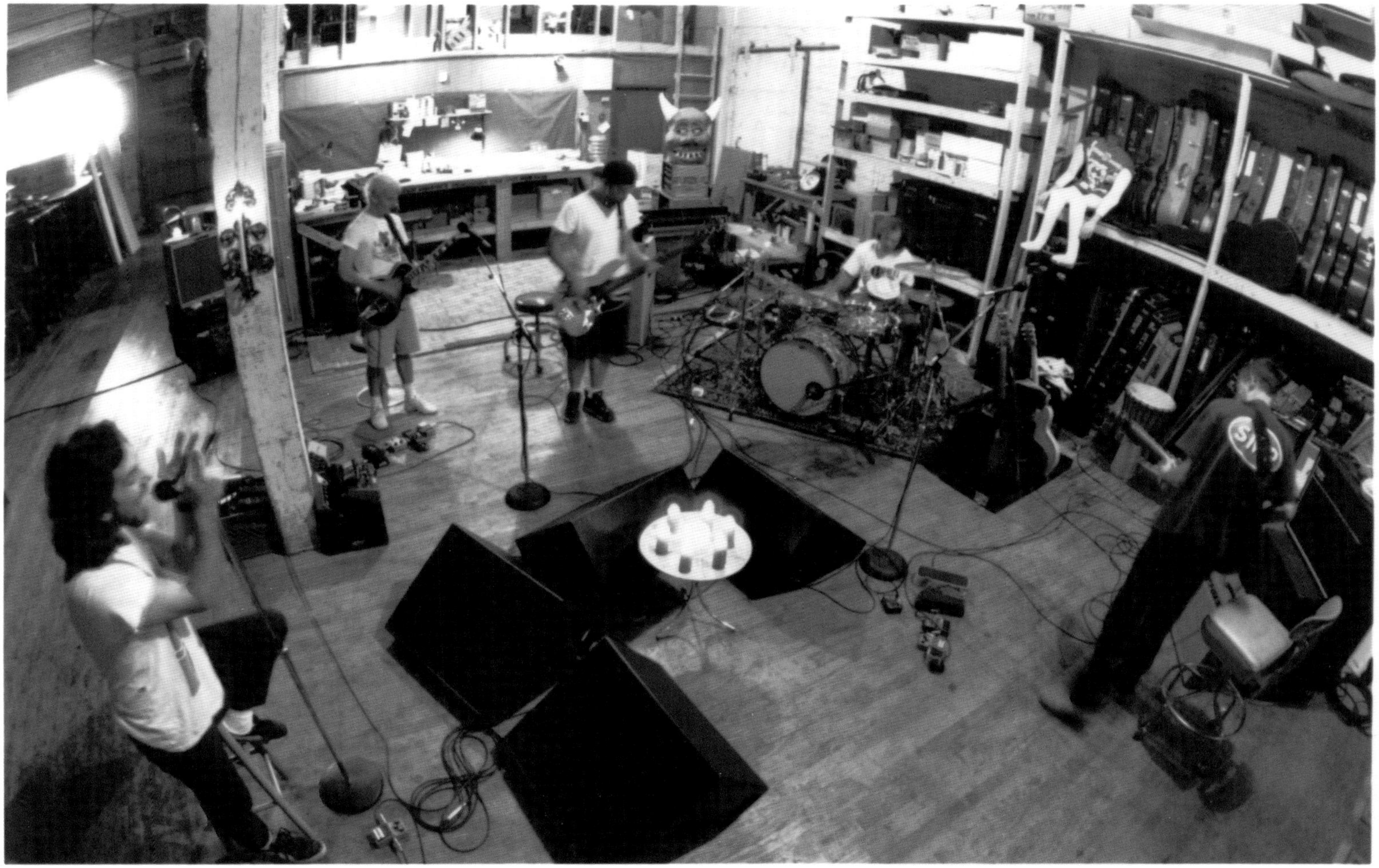

PHOTO CREDIT JEFF AMENT

L R : EDDIE VEDDER, MIKE McCREADY JEFF AMENT JACK IRONS, STONE GOSSARD

# PEARL JAM NO CODE

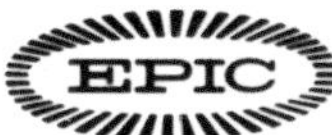

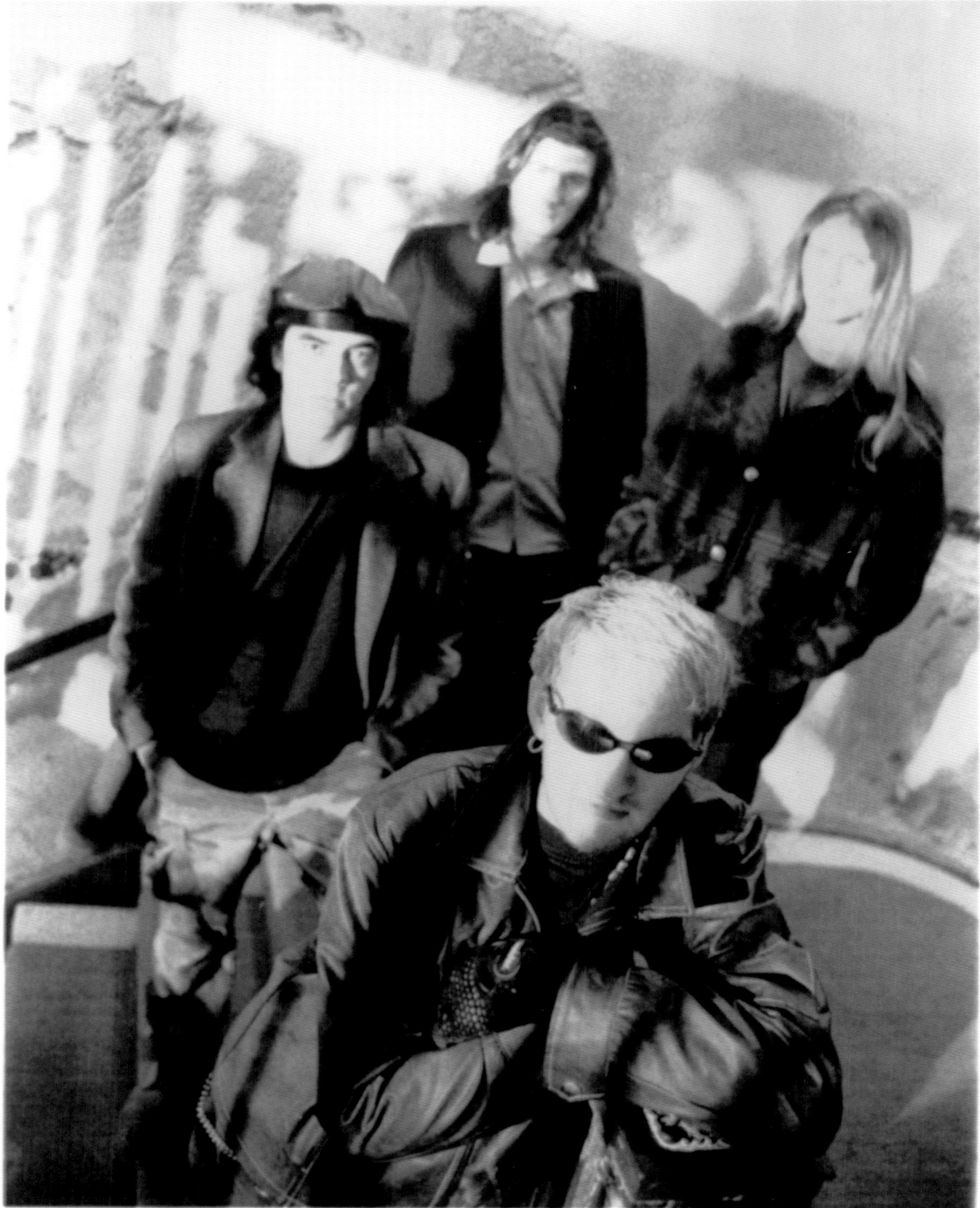



Photo Credit: Danny Clinch

Clockwise from top: Sean Kinney Jerry Cantrell Layne Staley Mike Inez

ALICE IN CHAINS

COLUMBIA
96/06

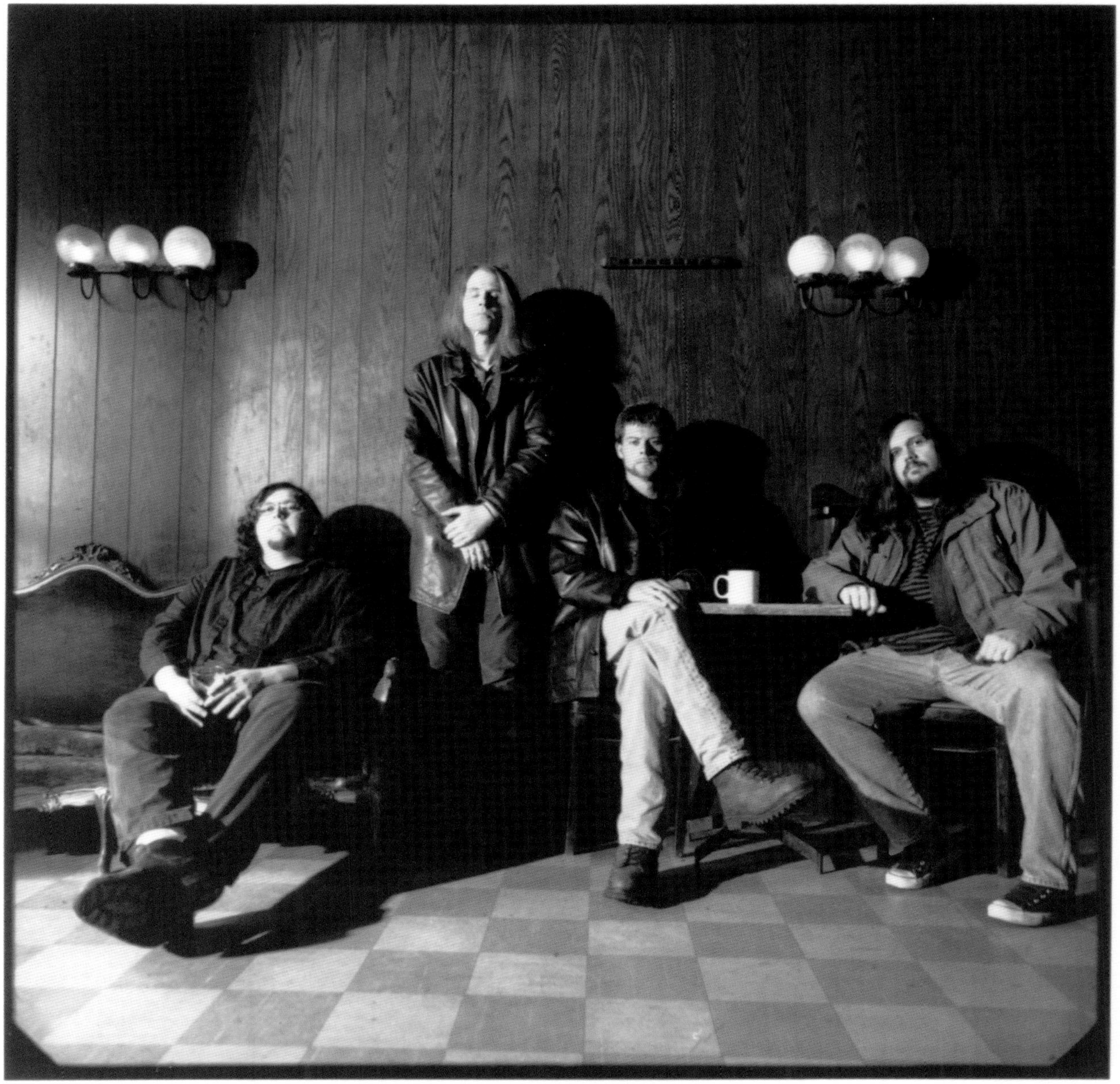

PHOTO CREDIT DANNY CLINCH

L R VAN CONNER, MARK LANEGAN, BARRETT MARTIN, GARY LEE CONNER

# SCREAMING TREES

9605

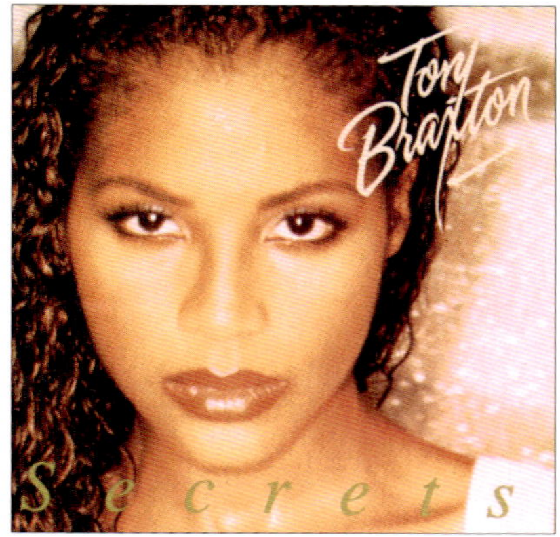


Singer **Toni Braxton** realized overwhelming success with her *Secrets* album and the No. 1s "You're Makin' Me High" and the iconic "Un-Break My Heart."

*Billboard* 200: *Secrets* (#2)
*Billboard* Hot 100: "You're Makin' Me High"/"Let It Flow" (No. 1);
"Un-Break My Heart" (No. 1);
"I Love Me Some Him"/"I Don't Want To" (#19)

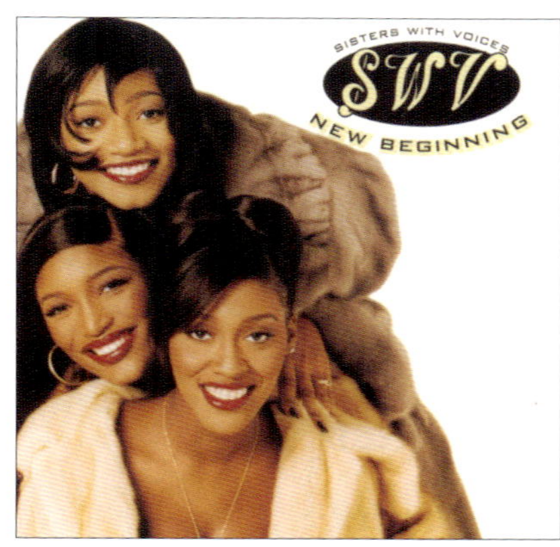


"You're the One," a flirtatious flow from **SWV**'s sophomore release, *New Beginning*, became the female trio's third song to reach the top of the R&B charts.

*Billboard* 200: *New Beginning* (#9)
*Billboard* Hot 100: "You're the One" (#5); "Use Your Heart" (#22);
"It's All About U" (#61)

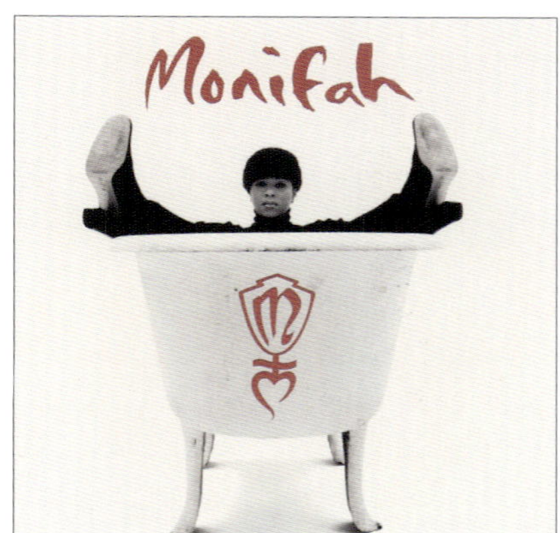


Heavy D guided a good deal of **Monifah**'s *Moods...Moments* album, and the sensual "You" earned the R&B songstress a gold single and critical accolades.

*Billboard* 200: *Moods...Moments* (#42)
*Billboard* Hot 100: "I Miss You (Come Back Home)" (#56);
"You" (#32); "You Don't Have to Love Me" (#82)

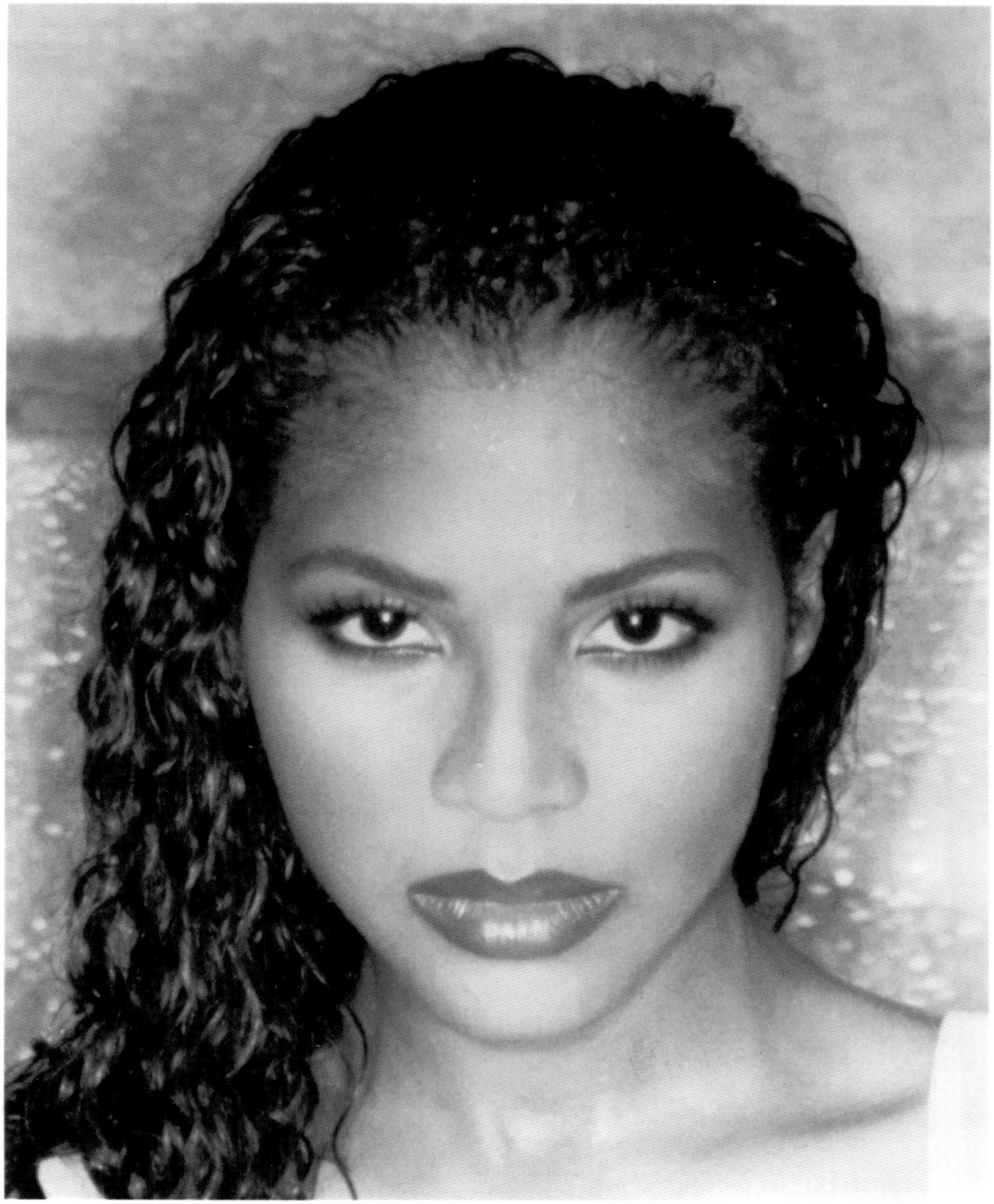

Toni Braxton

Management by Arnold Stiefel and Randy Phillips

STIEFEL•PHILLIPS
ENTERTAINMENT

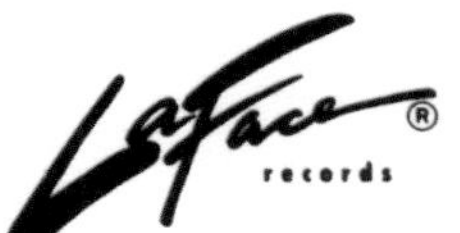

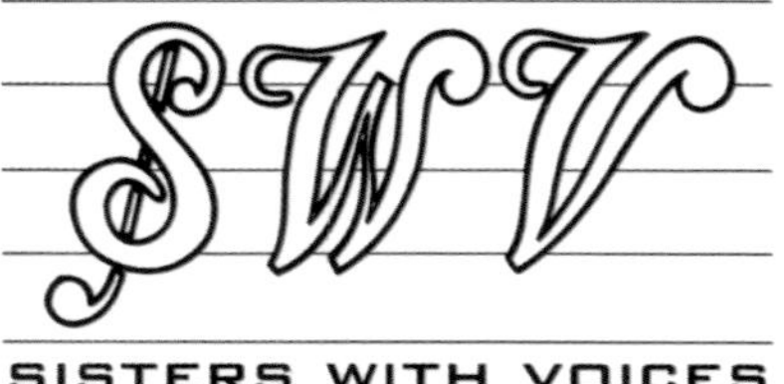
SWV
SISTERS WITH VOICES

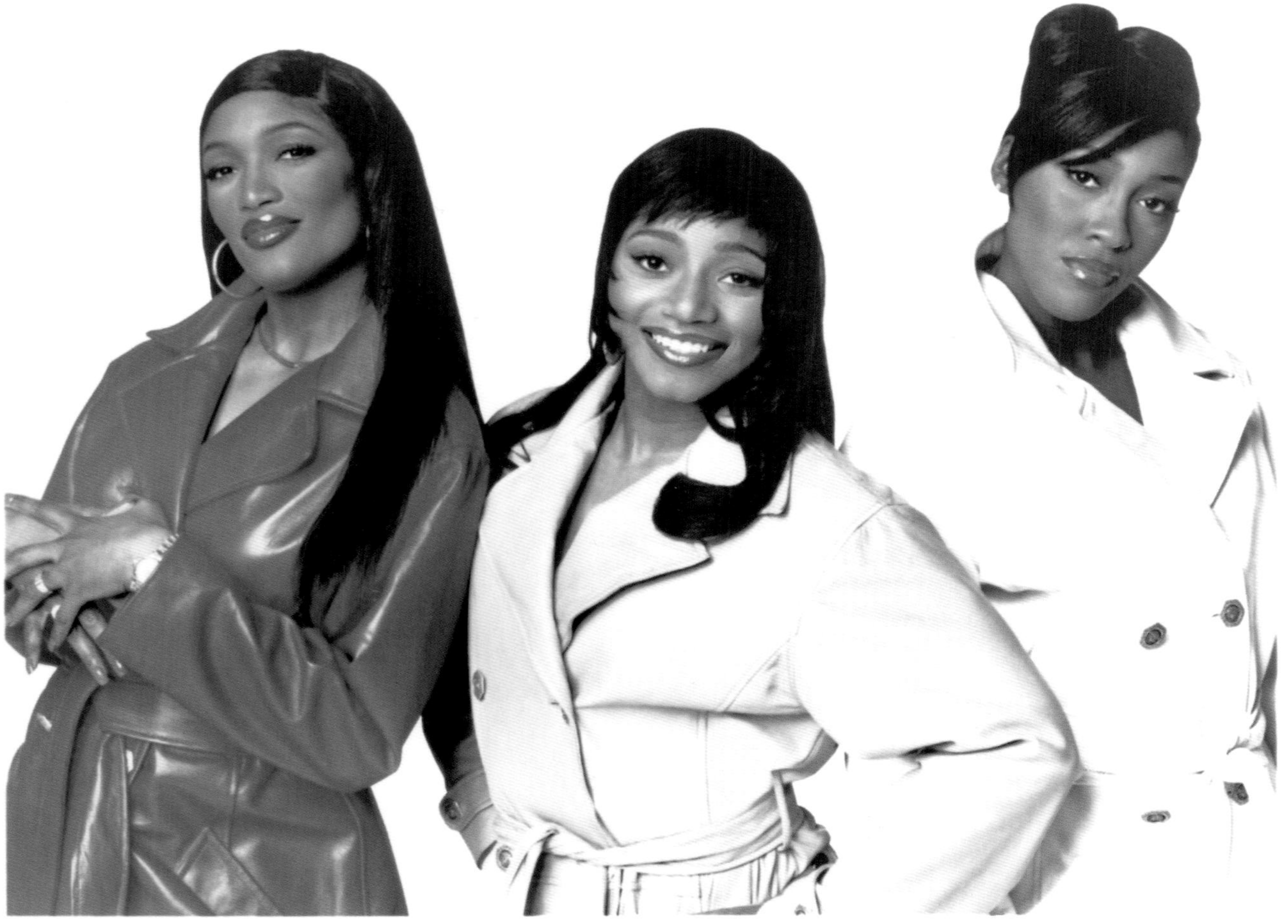

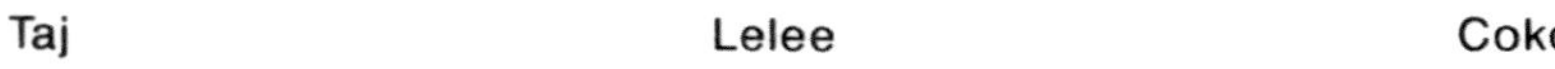
Taj
Lelee
Coko

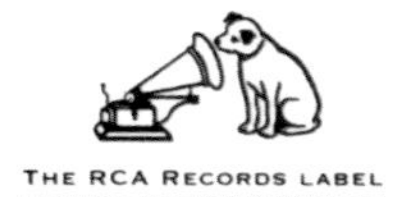
THE RCA RECORDS LABEL

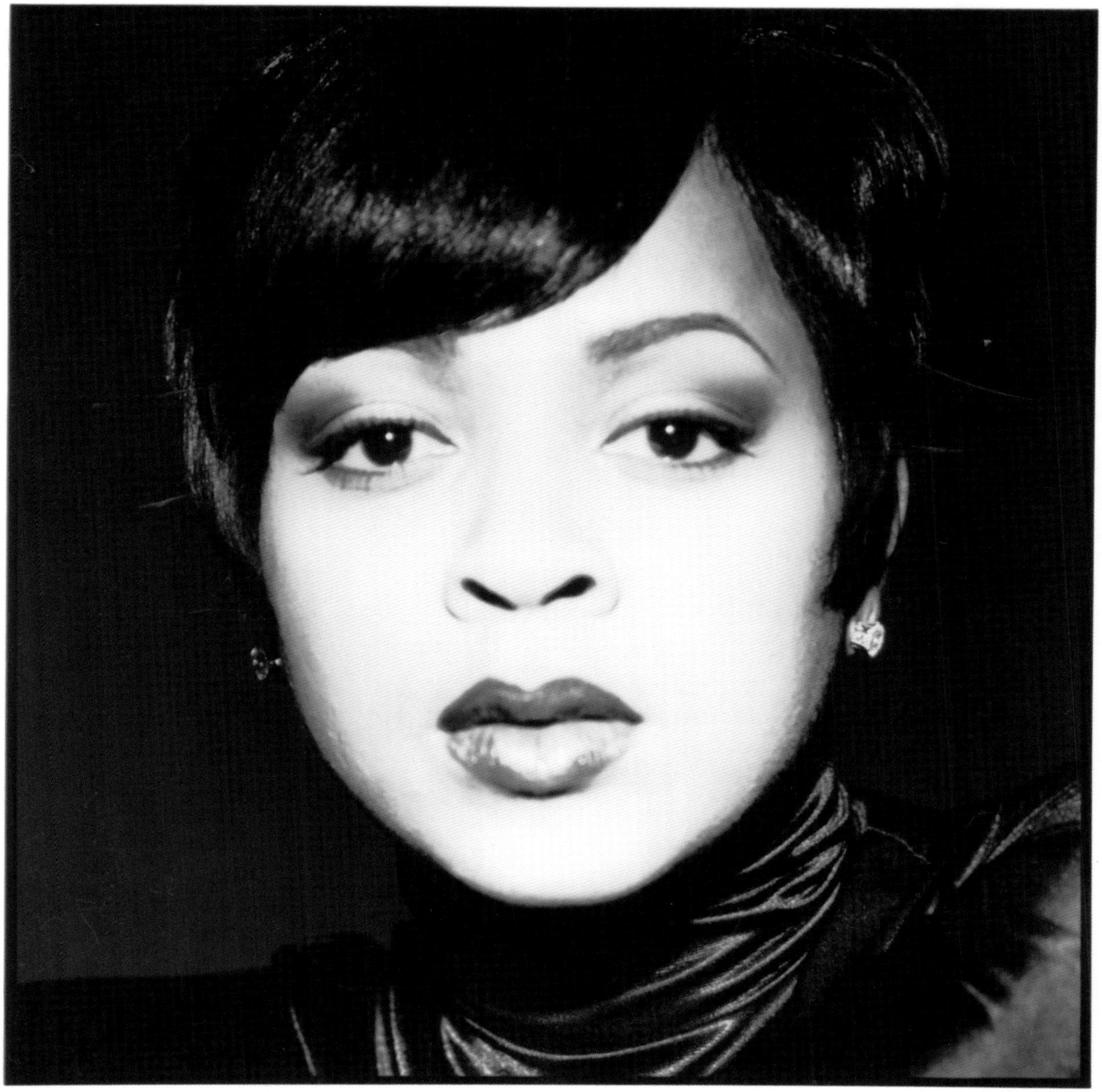

Photo credit: Daniella Federici

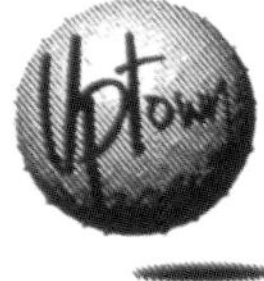


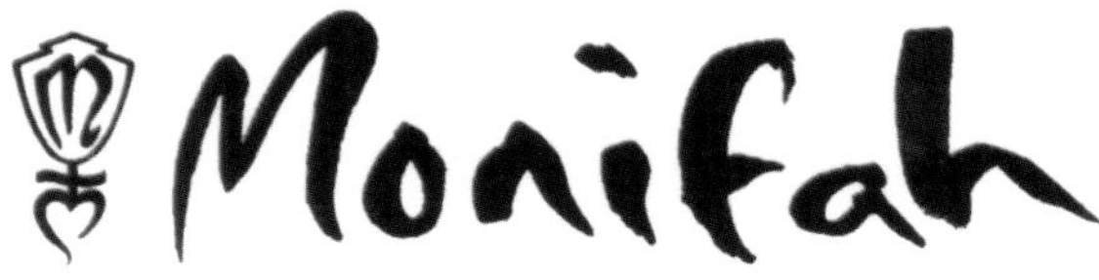


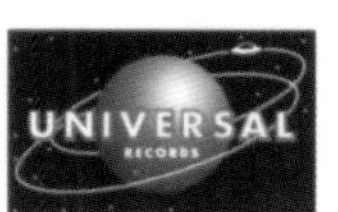

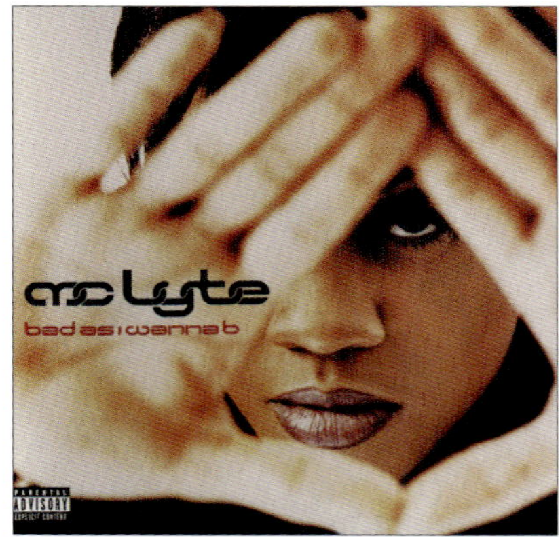


Lady rapper **MC Lyte** bagged her two highest-charting singles, "Keep On, Keepin' On," featuring Xscape, and "Cold Rock a Party," a duet with Missy Elliott.

*Billboard* 200: *Bad as I Wanna B* (#59)
*Billboard* Hot 100: "Keep On, Keepin' On" (#10); "Cold Rock a Party" (#11)

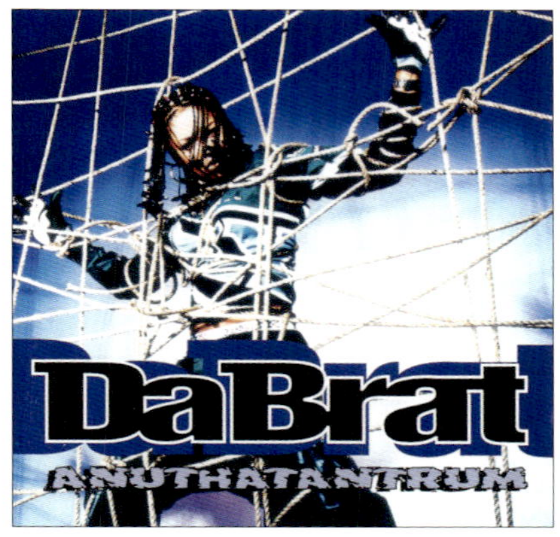


Turning out a second album, *Anuthatantrum*, female emcee **Da Brat** scored the hits "Sittin' on Top of the World" and "Ghetto Love" featuring TLC's T-Boz.

*Billboard* 200: *Anuthatantrum* (#20)
*Billboard* Hot 100: "Sittin' on Top of the World" (#30); "Ghetto Love" (#16)

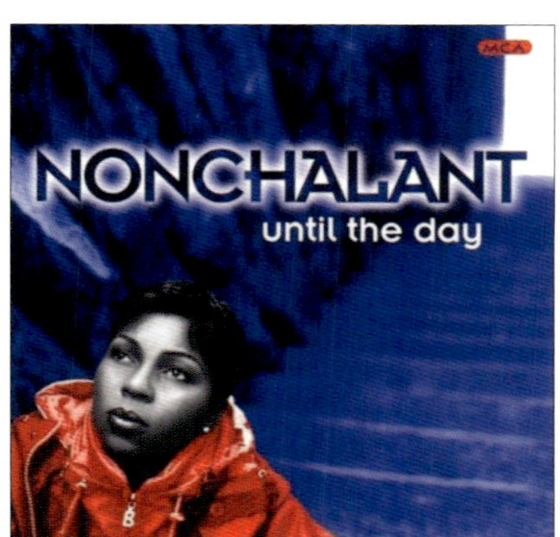


Washington, D.C. rapper **Nonchalant** delivered a message with "5 O'Clock," a song confronting an addled dope dealer who poisoned his neighborhood.

*Billboard* 200: *Until the Day* (#94)
*Billboard* Hot 100: "5 O'Clock" (#24)

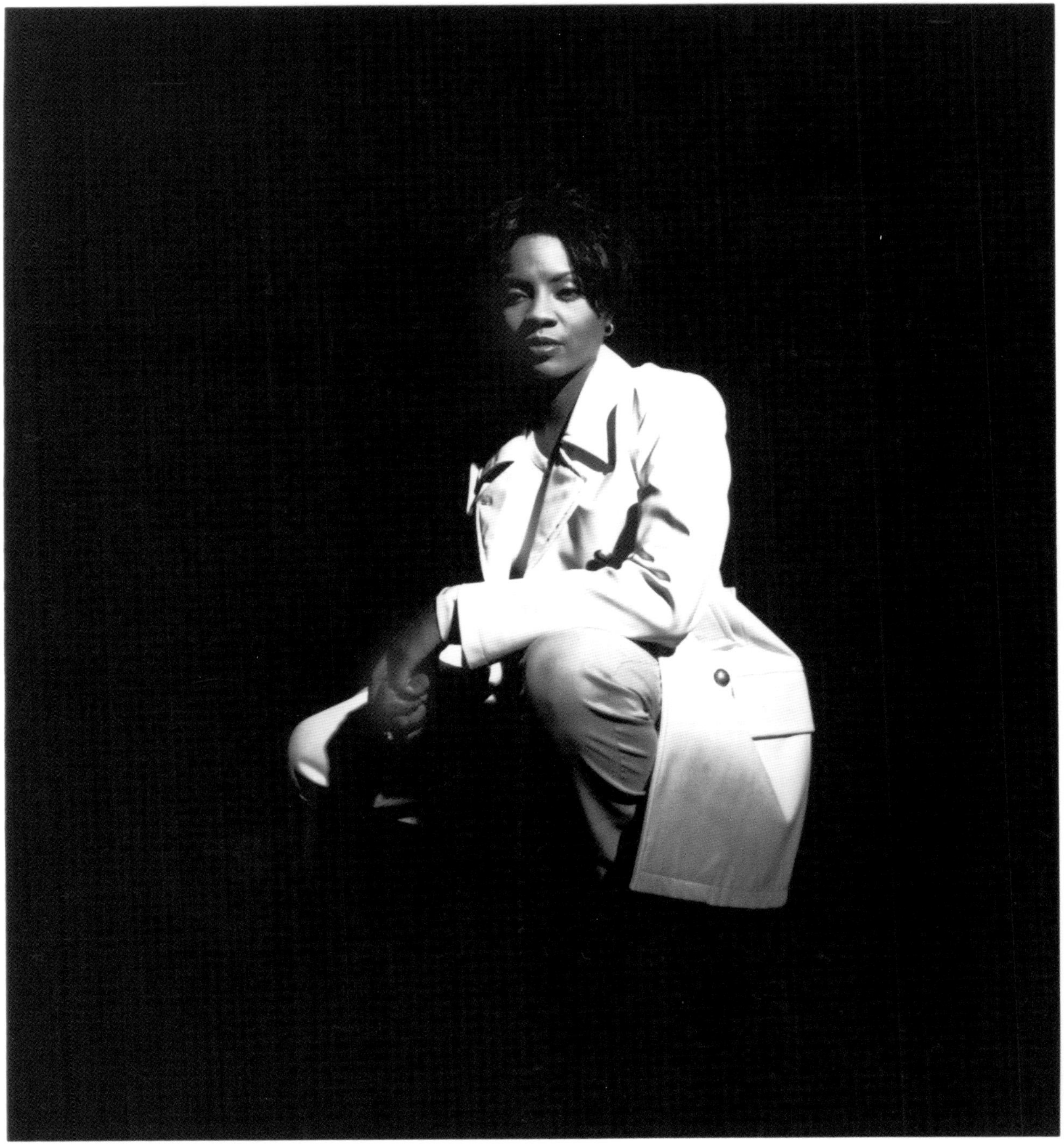

PHOTO CREDIT MICHAEL S. MILLER

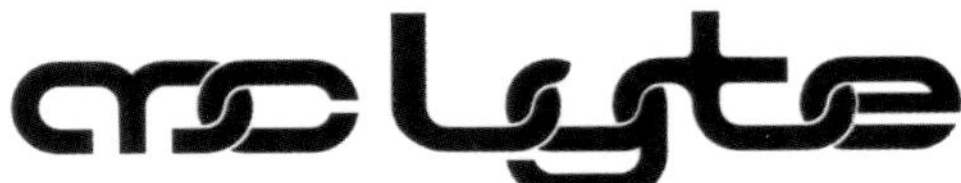


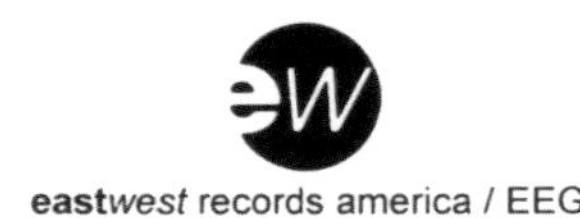

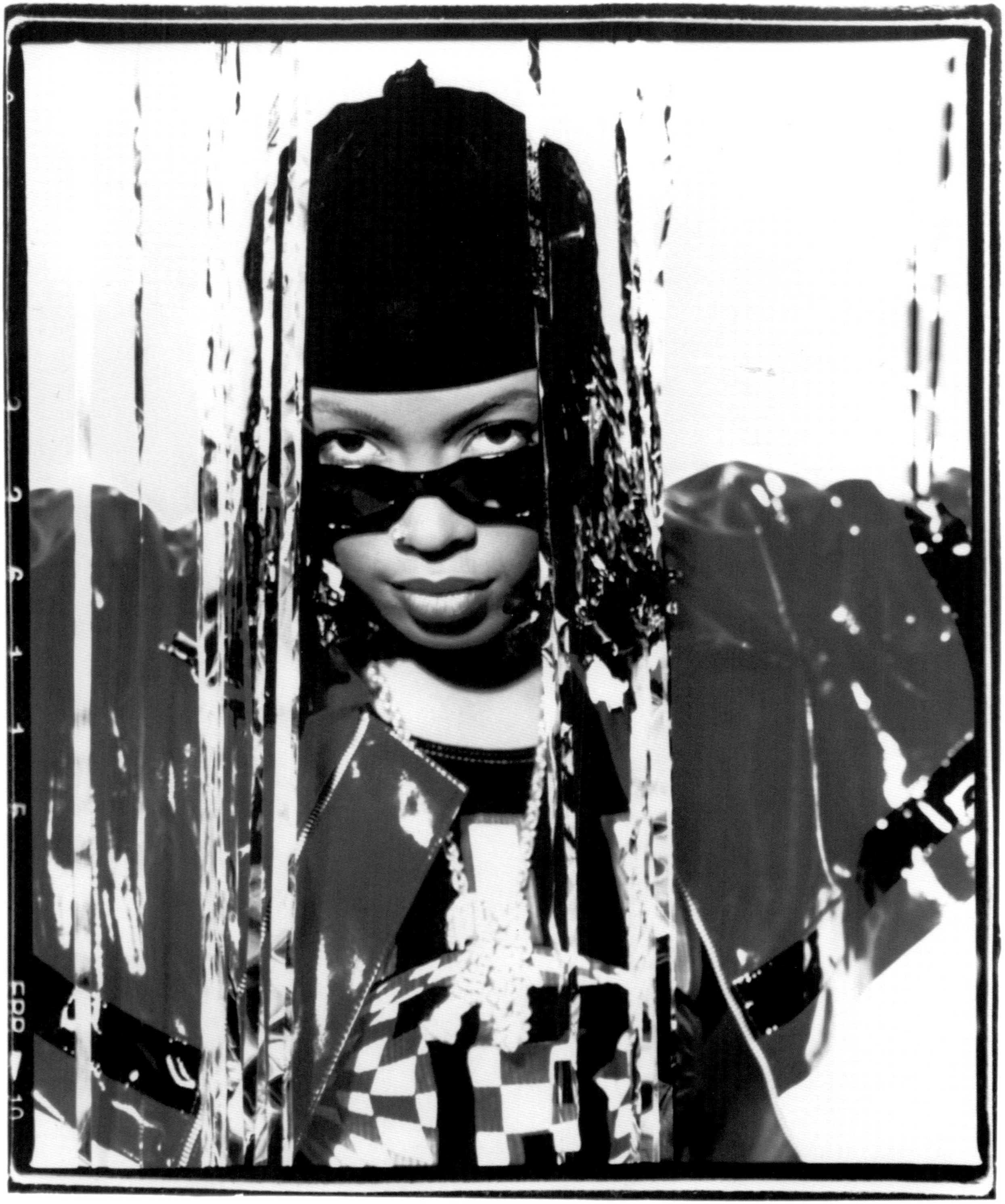

Photo Credit: Silvia Otte

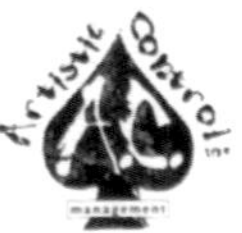


# DaBrat

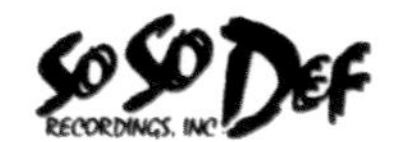


COLUMBIA
9610

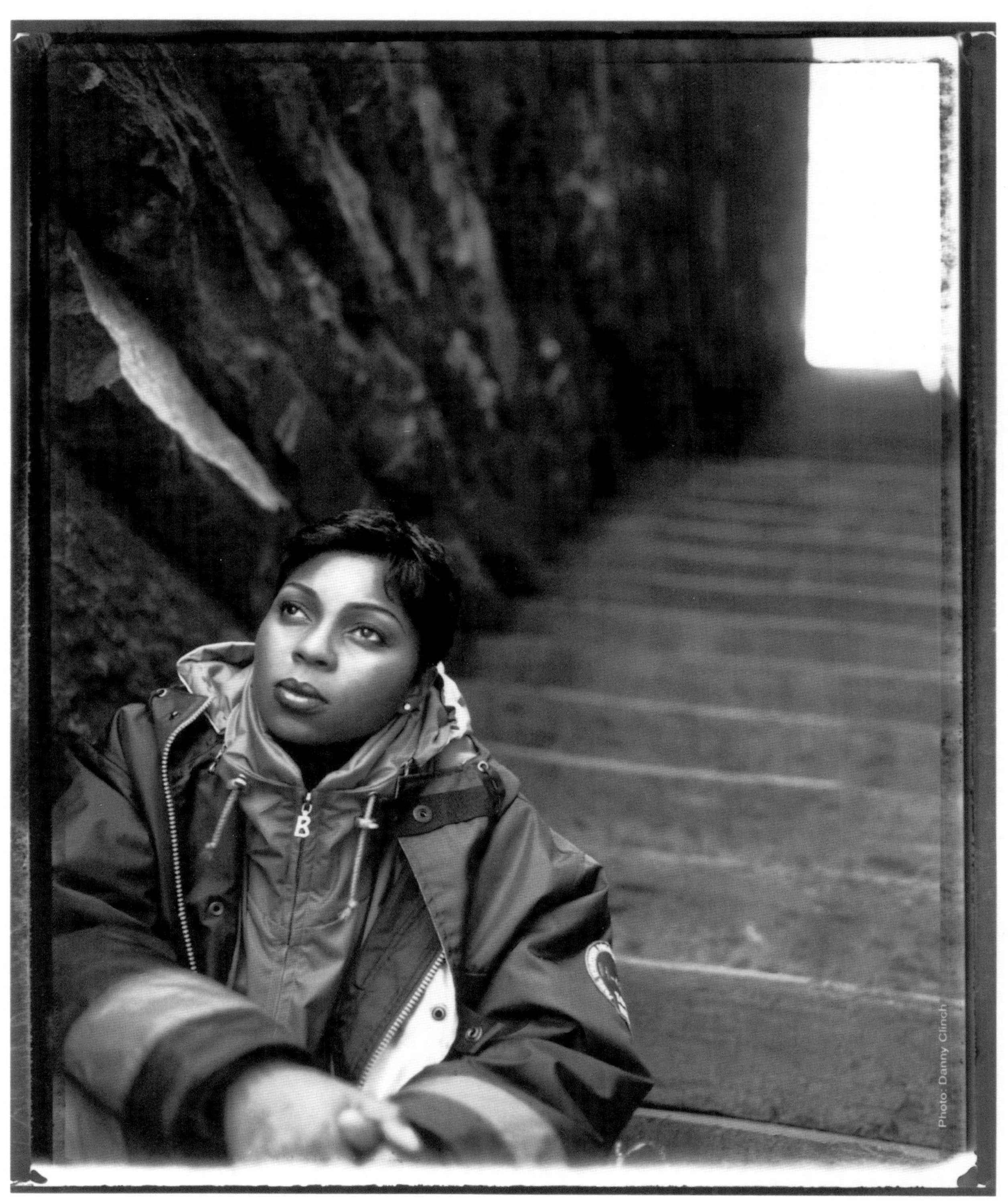


NONCHALANT

MCA '96

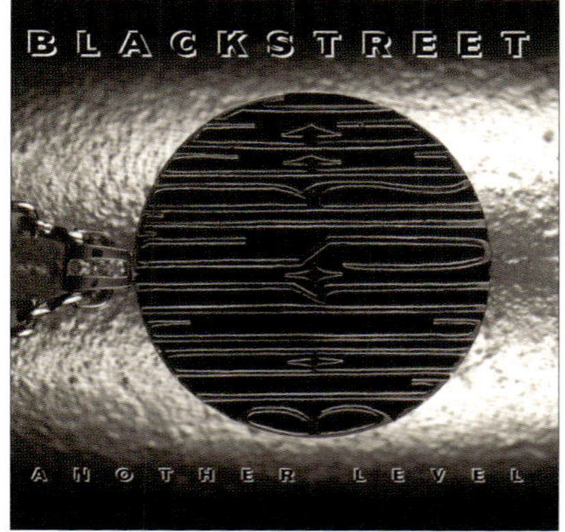


Created by new jack swing producer Teddy Riley, R&B group **Blackstreet** hit No. 1 and took home a Grammy Award for "No Diggity" featuring Dr. Dre.

*Billboard* 200: *Another Level* (#3)
*Billboard* Hot 100: "No Diggity" (No. 1); "Fix" (#58)

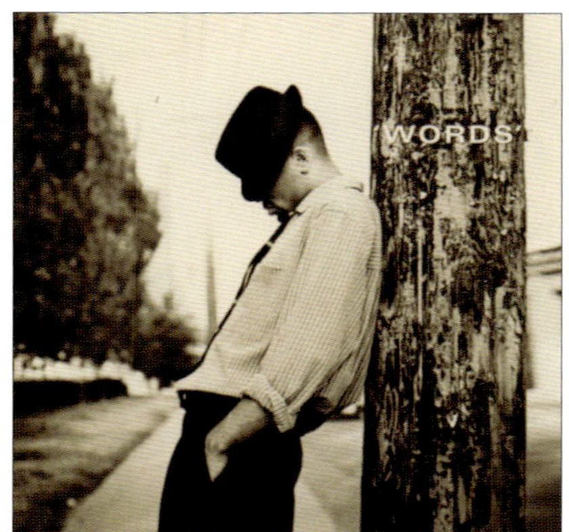


**The Tony Rich Project**, a handle for the versatile musician, offered a wistful single, "Nobody Knows," and *Words* won a Grammy for Best R&B Album.

*Billboard* 200: *Words* (#31)
*Billboard* Hot 100: "Nobody Knows" (#2);
"Like a Woman" (#41); "Leavin'" (#88)

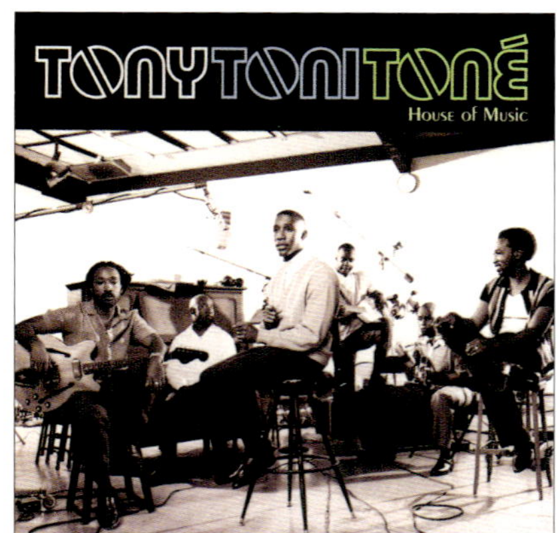


Stylishly merging traditional and contemporary R&B styles, **Tony Toni Toné** reformed for an accomplished fourth album, *House of Music*, before disbanding.

*Billboard* 200: *House of Music* (#32)
*Billboard* Hot 100: "Thinking of You" (#22)

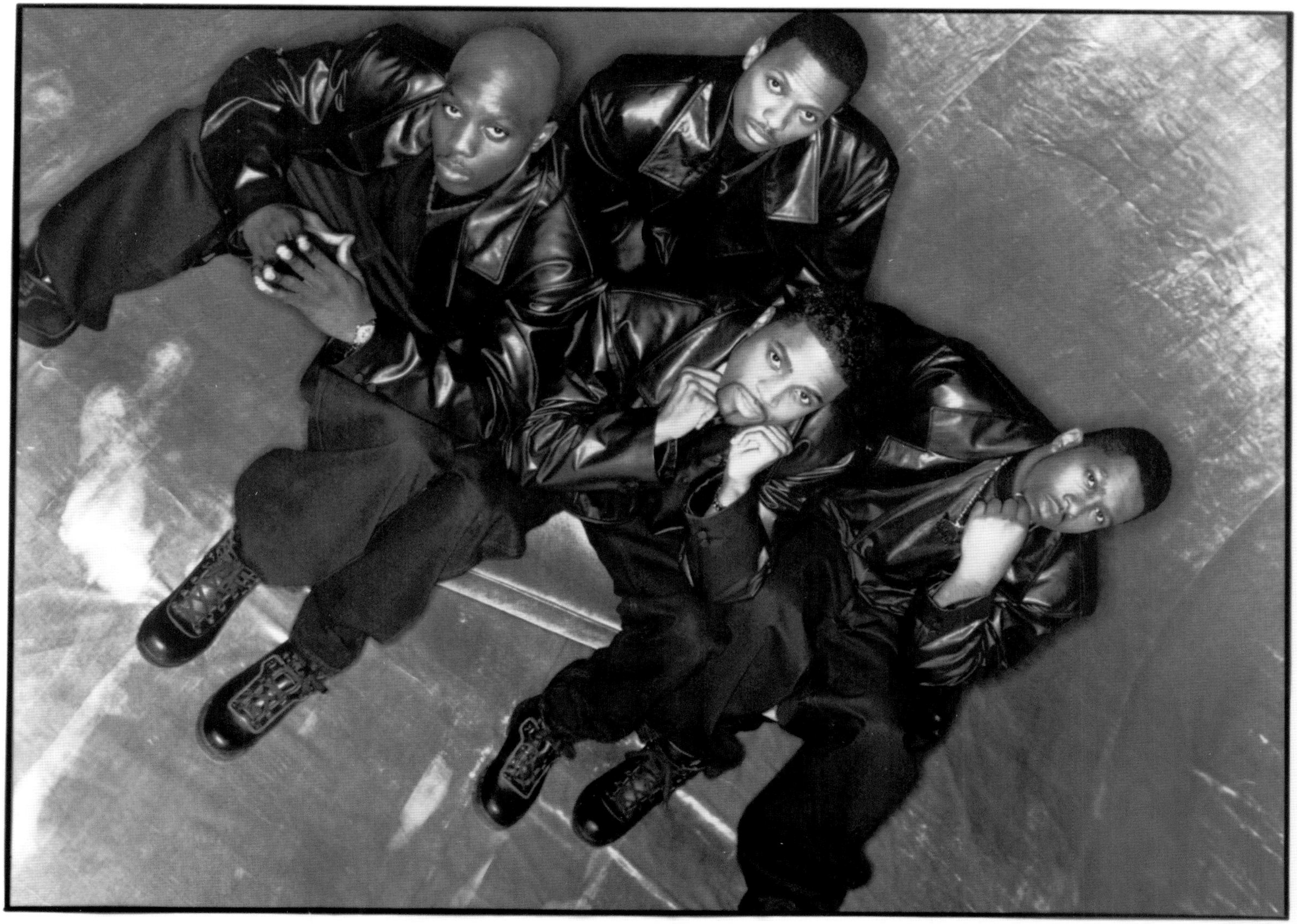

CHAUNCEY "Black" HANNIBAL    MARK MIDDLETON    TEDDY RILEY    ERIC WILLIAMS

Photo Credit: D.Low

# BLACKSTREET

ANOTHER LEVEL



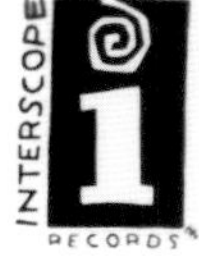

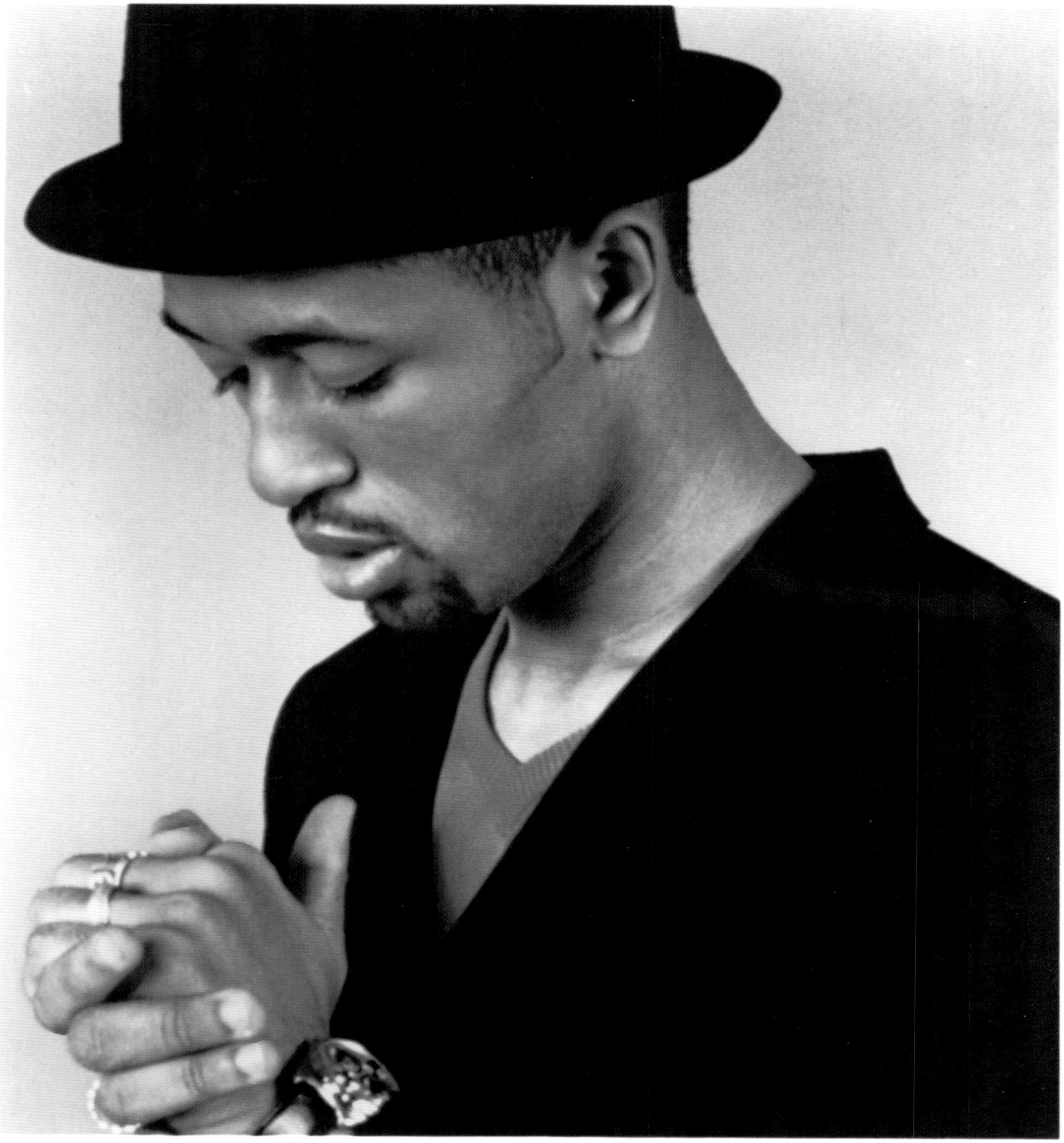

Photo: Daniel Soder

# THE TONY RICH PROJECT

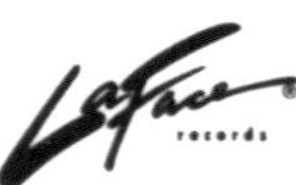

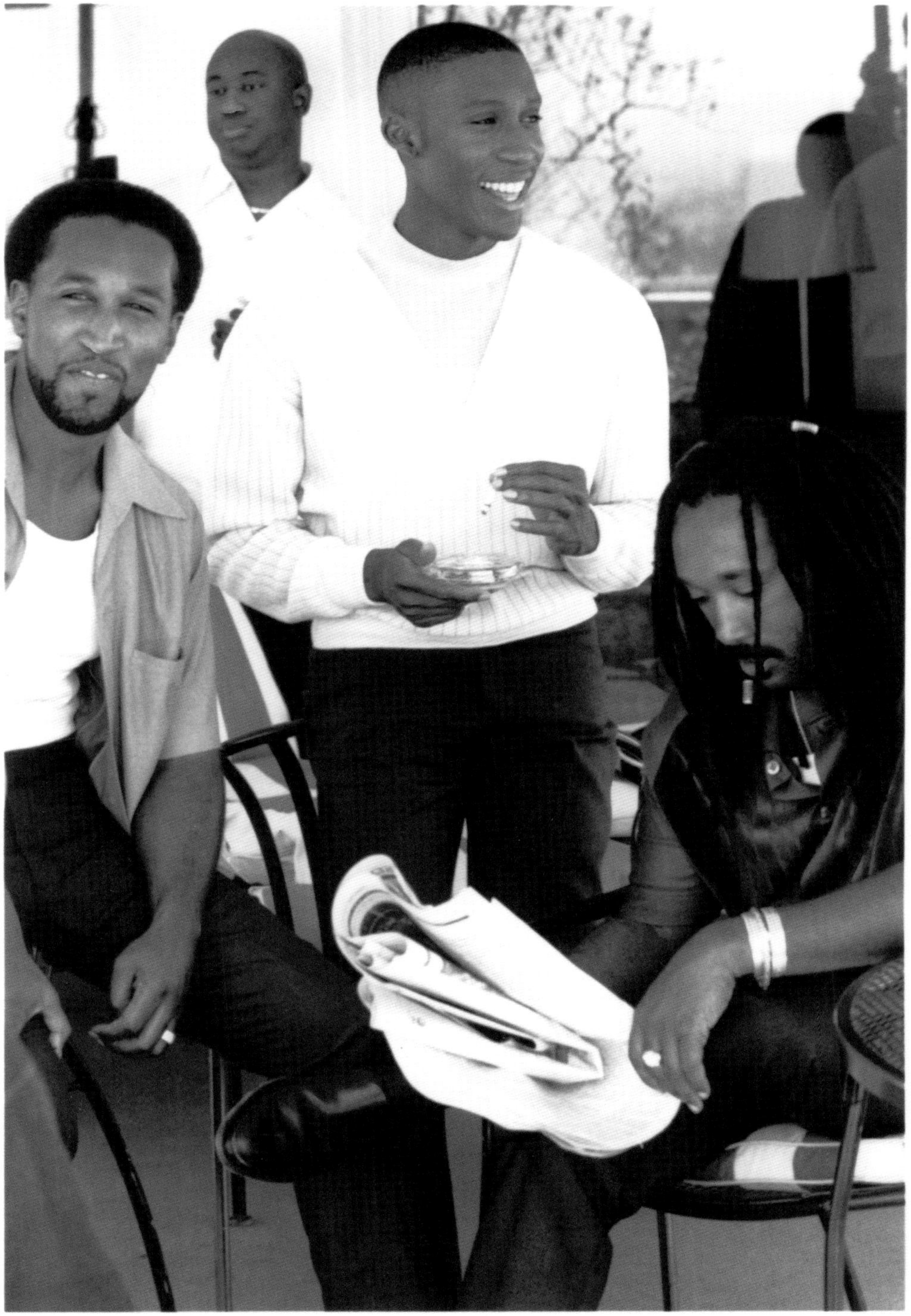

PHOTO CREDIT WILLIAM CLAXTON

L R : TIMOTHY CHRISTIAN RILEY RAPHAEL SAADIQ, D'WAYNE WIGGINS

TONY TONI TONÉ

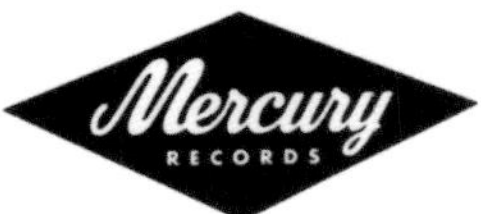

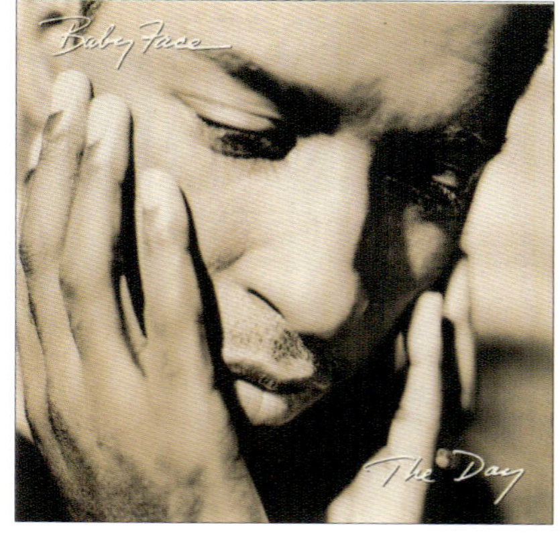


A Grammy Award-winning composer and producer of landmark hits for other acts, **Babyface** rose with *The Day*, his fourth album as a solo recording artist.

*Billboard* 200: *The Day* (#6)
*Billboard* Hot 100: "This Is for the Lover in You" (#6); "Every Time I Close My Eyes" (#6)

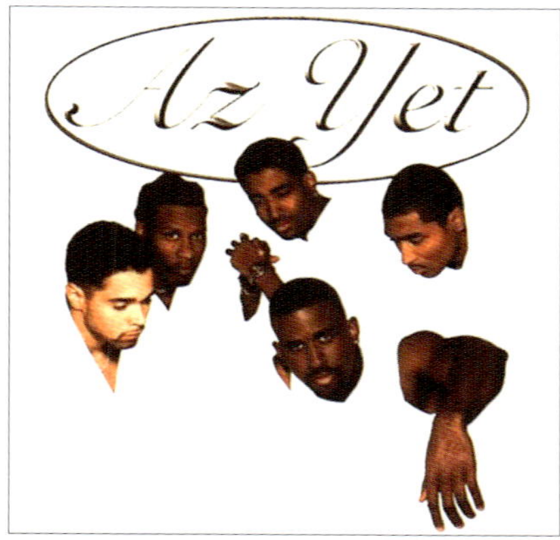


**Az Yet**, a soul quintet from Philadelphia, generated attention with the gold single "Last Night" and a cover of Chicago's classic "Hard to Say I'm Sorry."

*Billboard* 200: *Az Yet* (#60)
*Billboard* Hot 100: "Last Night" (#9); "Hard to Say I'm Sorry" (#8)

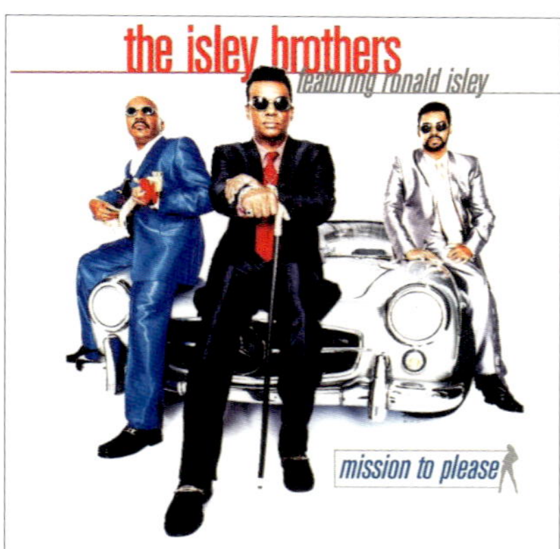


**The Isley Brothers** continued to make the pop and R&B charts four decades after their first hit, aided by R. Kelly, Babyface, Keith Sweat and Angela Winbush.

*Billboard* 200: *Mission to Please* (#31)
*Billboard* Hot 100: "Let's Lay Together" (#93); "Floatin' on Your Love" (#47); "Tears" (#55)

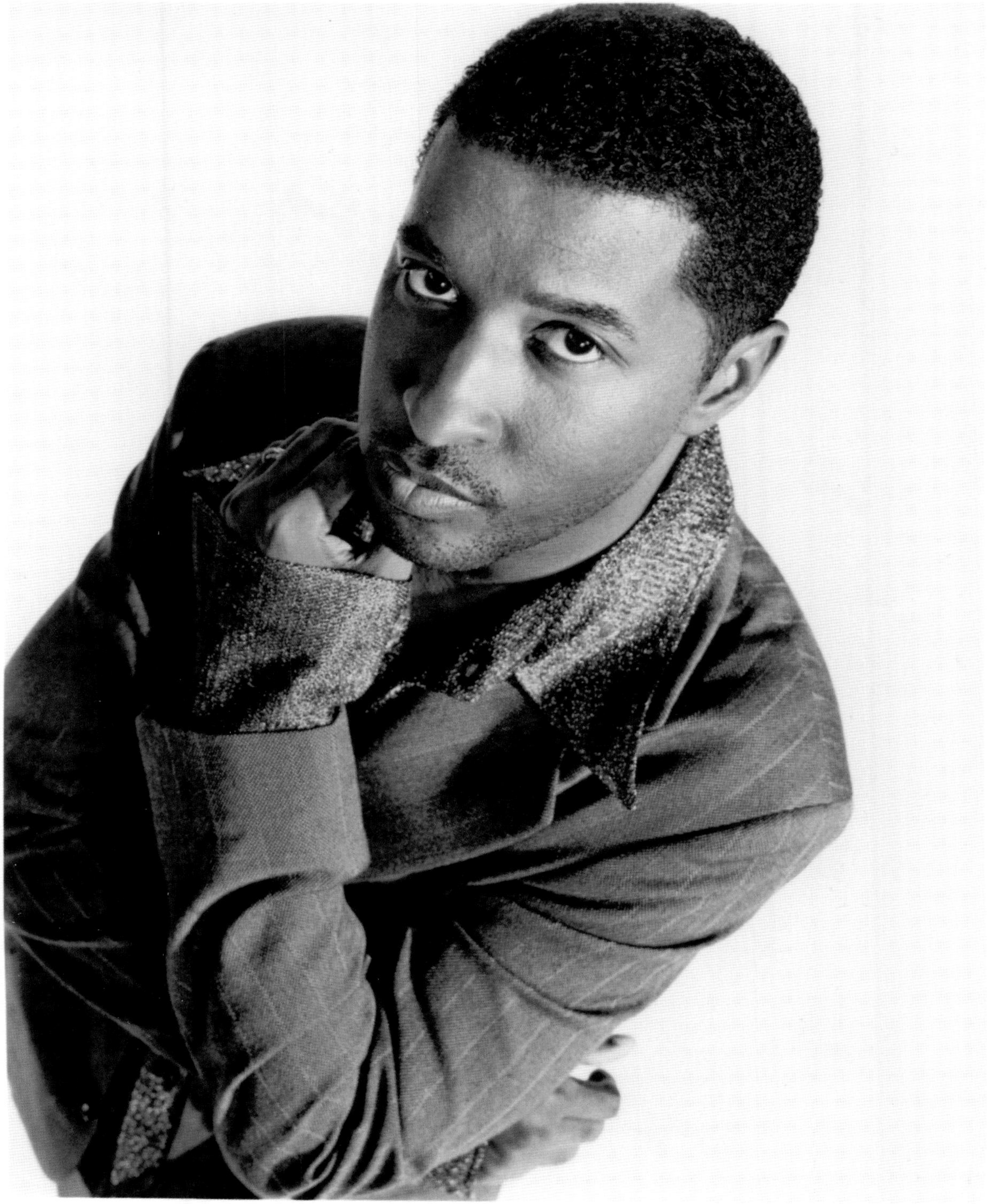

Photo credit: REISIG & TAYLOR

BabyFace

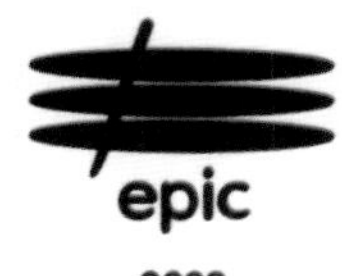


9609

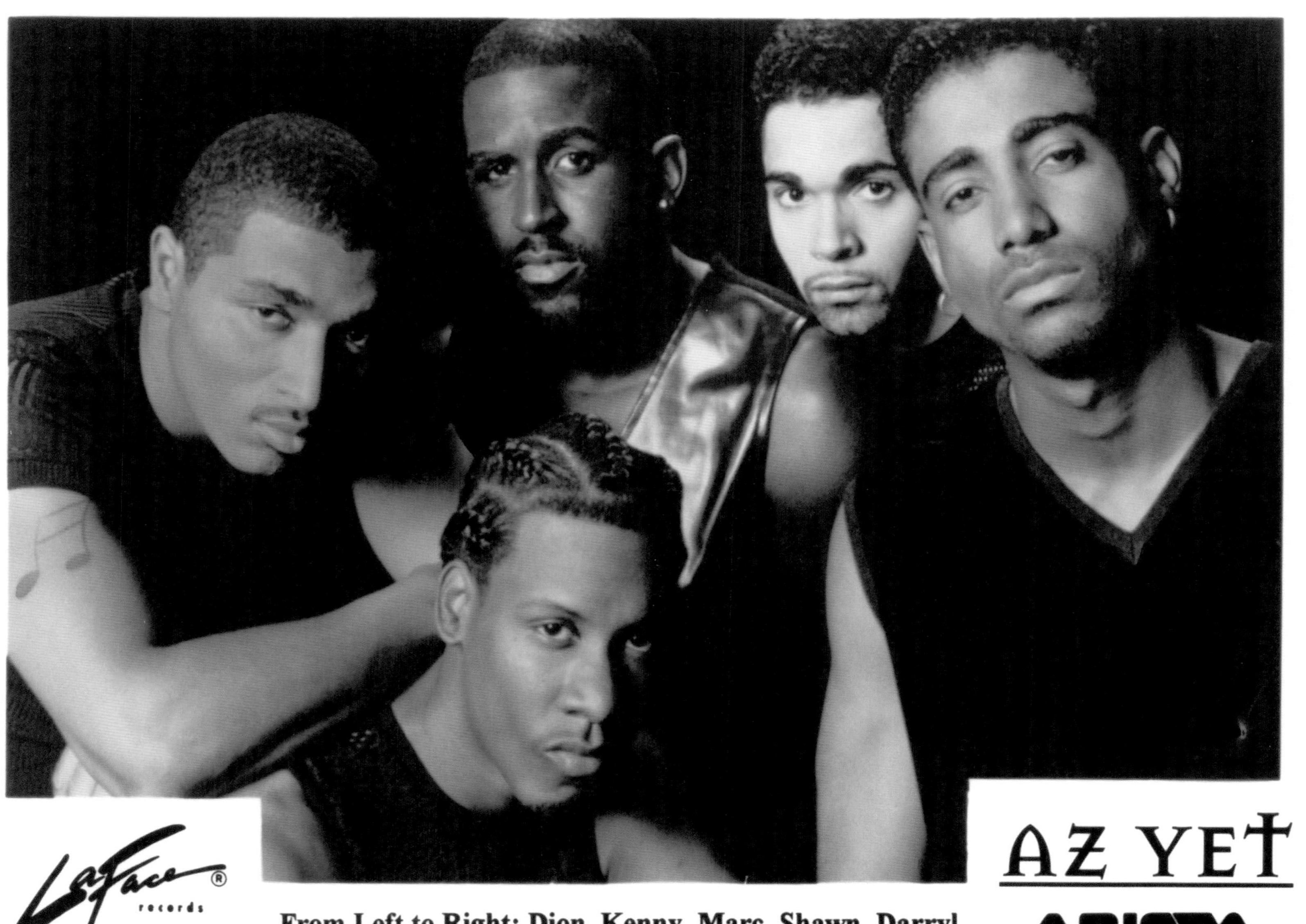



From Left to Right: Dion, Kenny, Marc, Shawn, Darryl

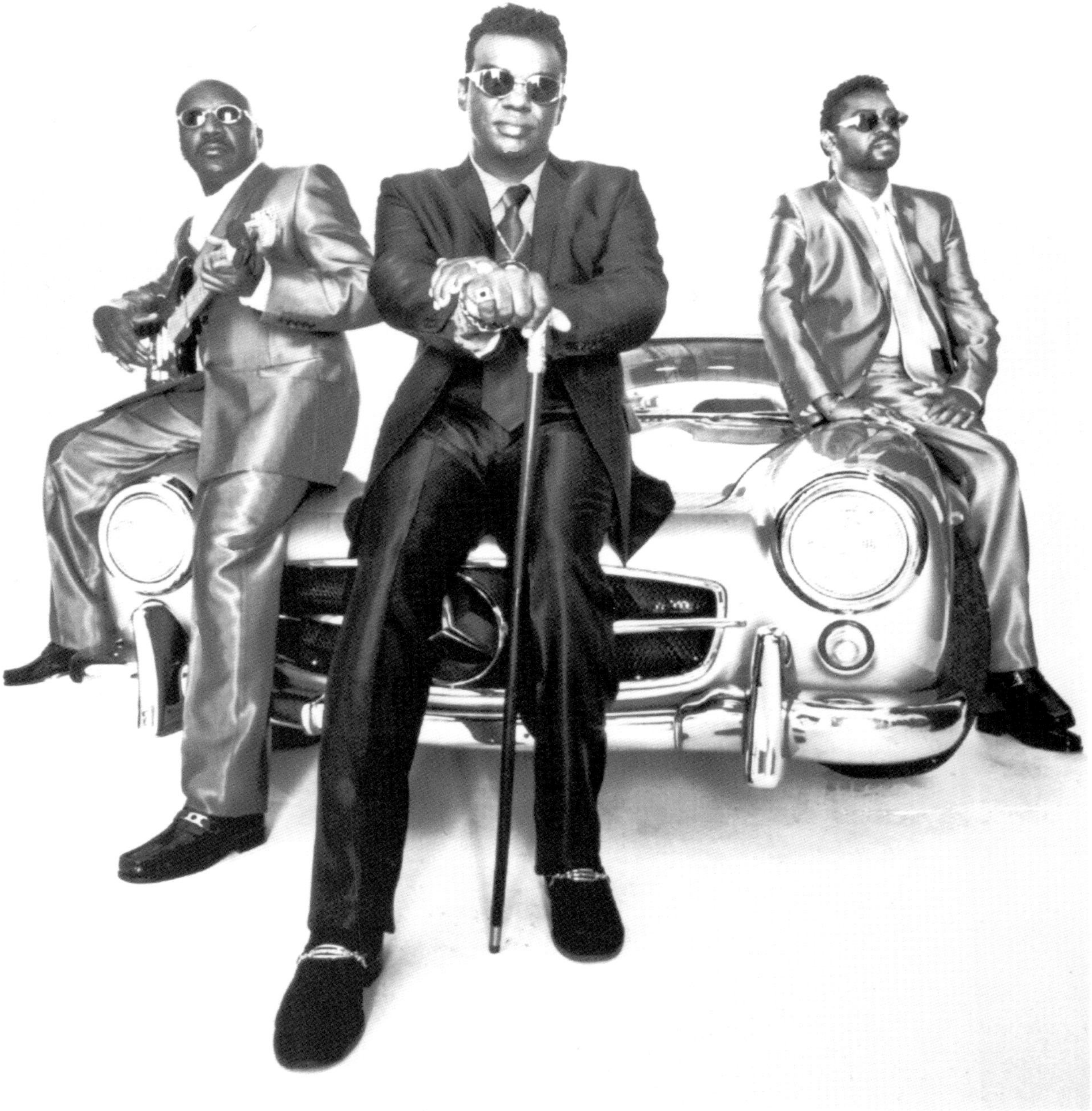

PHOTO CREDIT DAH - LEN

# THE ISLEY BROTHERS

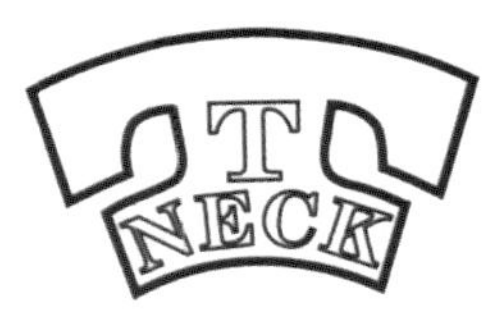


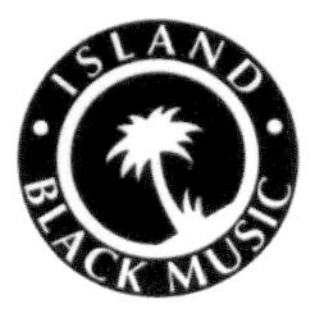

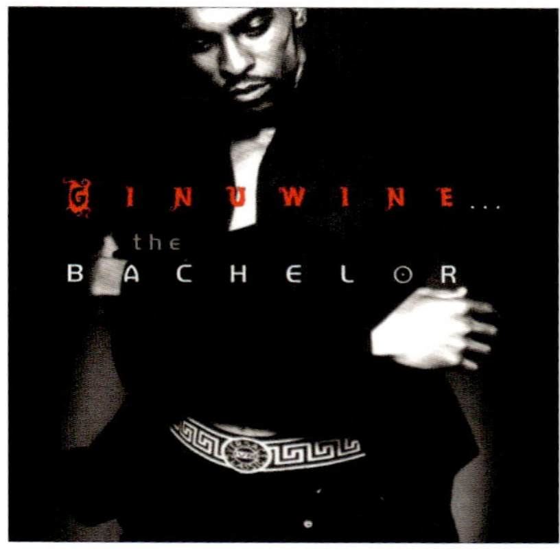


With its throbbing synth riff, amusingly sensual lyrics and a smooth tenor vocal, the No. 1 R&B smash "Pony" denoted **Ginuwine** as a gifted new loverman.

*Billboard* 200: *Ginuwine...The Bachelor* (#26)
*Billboard* Hot 100: "Pony" (#6); "Tell Me Do U Wanna" (#55)

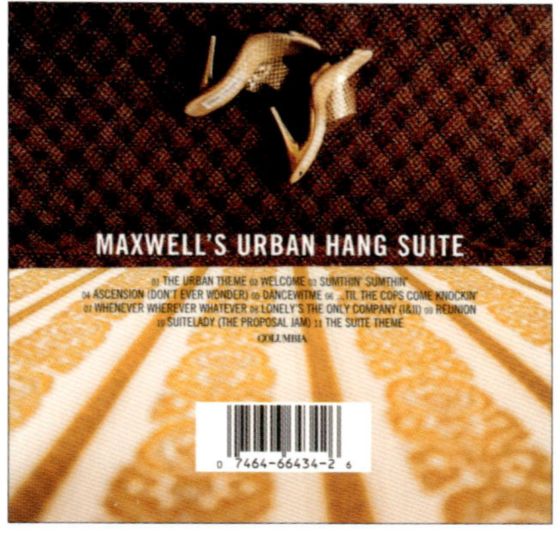


An architect of the neo-soul movement, **Maxwell** wrote and produced the critically and commercially succesful debut album, *Maxwell's Urban Hang Suite*.

*Billboard* 200: *Maxwell's Urban Hang Suite* (#37)
*Billboard* Hot 100: "Ascension (Don't Ever Wonder)" (#36)

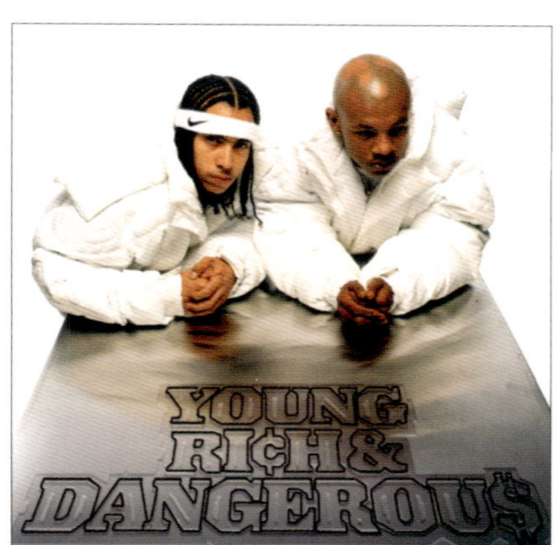


*Young, Rich & Dangerous* included a postpubescent **Kris Kross**' "Tonite's tha Night," the hip-hop duo's fourth single to peak at No. 1 on the rap charts.

*Billboard* 200: *Young, Rich & Dangerous* (#15)
*Billboard* Hot 100: "Tonite's tha Night" (#12);
"Live and Die for Hip Hop" (#72)

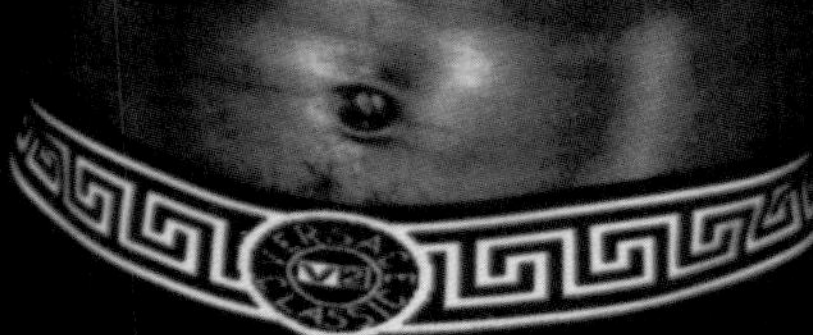

PHOTOGRAPHY · CARL LESSARD

Ginuwine

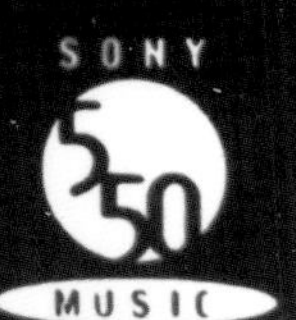

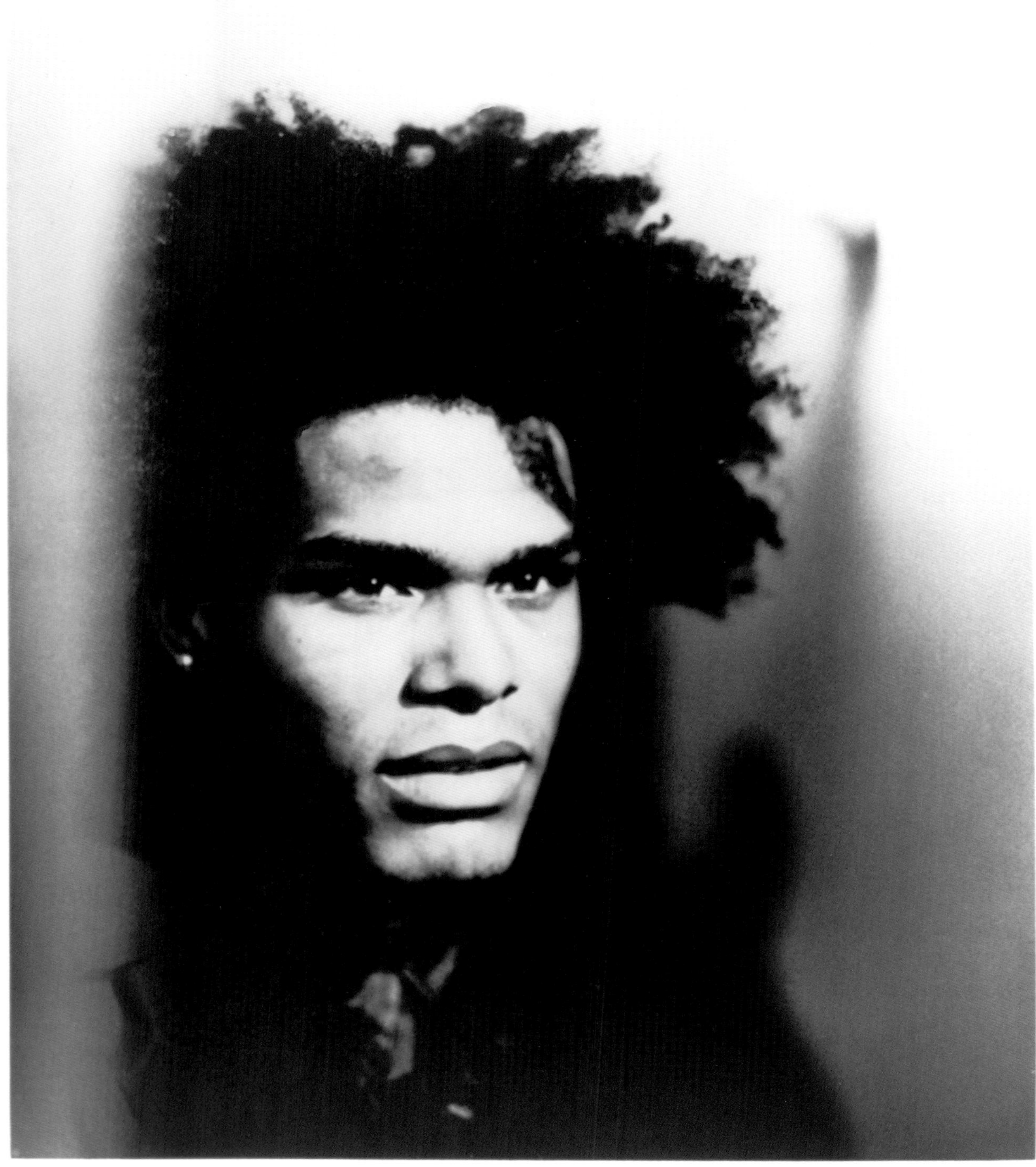

PHOTOGRAPH: ERIC JOHNSON



MAXWELL

COLUMBIA
9512

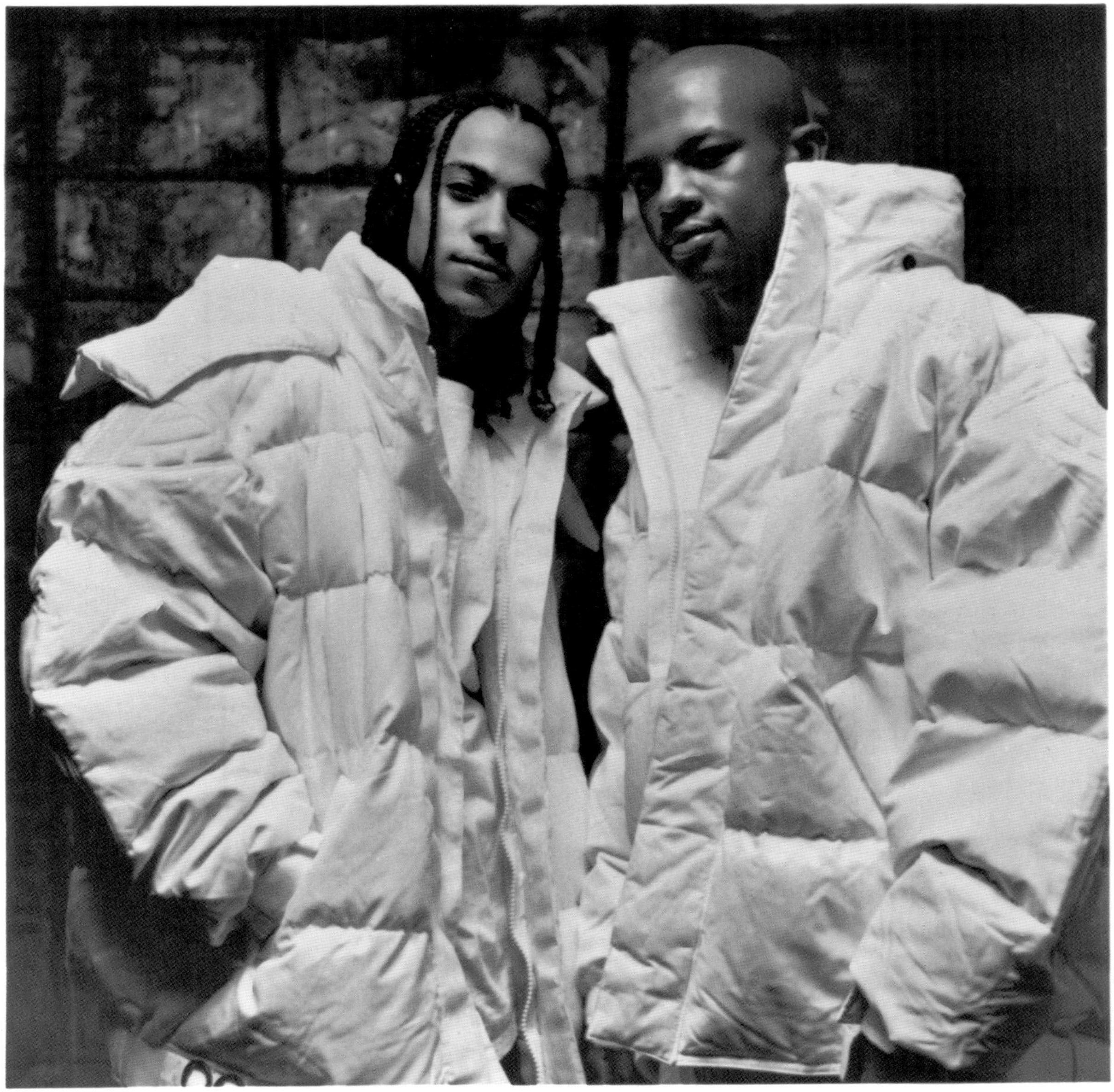

PHOTOGRAPH: MARC BAPTISTF

Chris Smith Chris Kelly

# KRIS KROSS

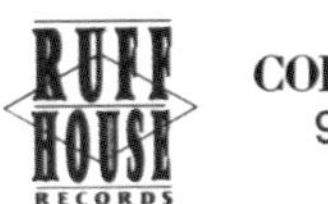


COLUMBIA
9510

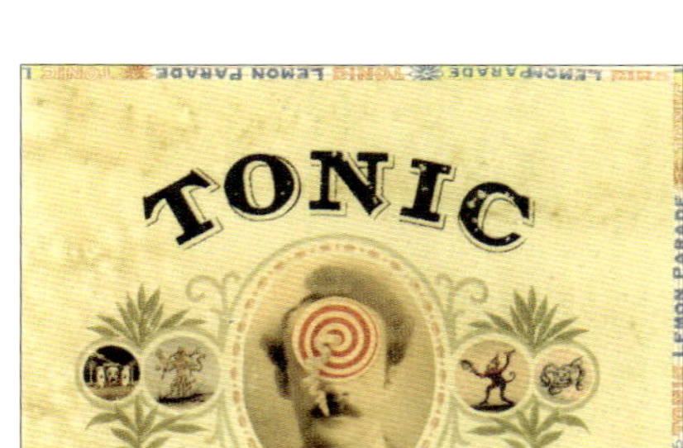


"If You Could Only See" received a staggering amount of airplay, and the melodic, muscular guitar rock of **Tonic**'s *Lemon Parade* reached platinum status.

*Billboard* 200: *Lemon Parade* (#28)

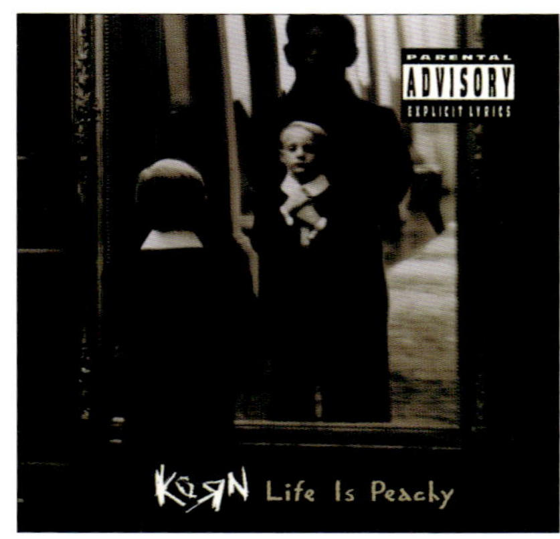


**Korn**'s *Life Is Peachy* thrust the Bakersfield rockers from the lower reaches of the charts to platinum certification, triggering the ferocious nu-metal genre.

*Billboard* 200: *Life Is Peachy* (#3)

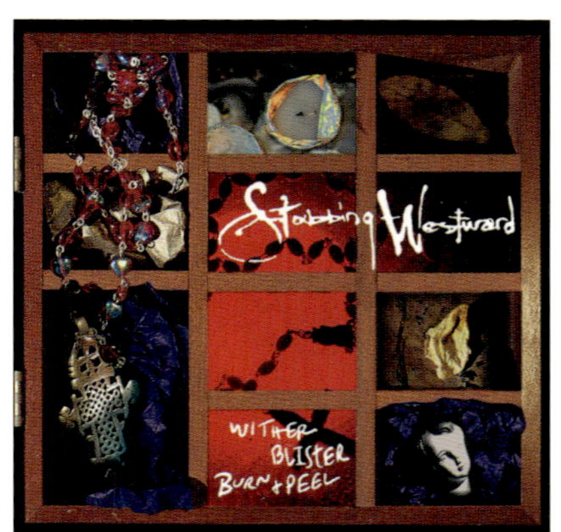


With *Wither Blister Burn + Peel*, industrial rockers **Stabbing Westward** landed a gold album, buoyed by clever videos for "Shame" and "What Do I Have to Do?"

*Billboard* 200: *Wither Blister Burn + Peel* (#67)

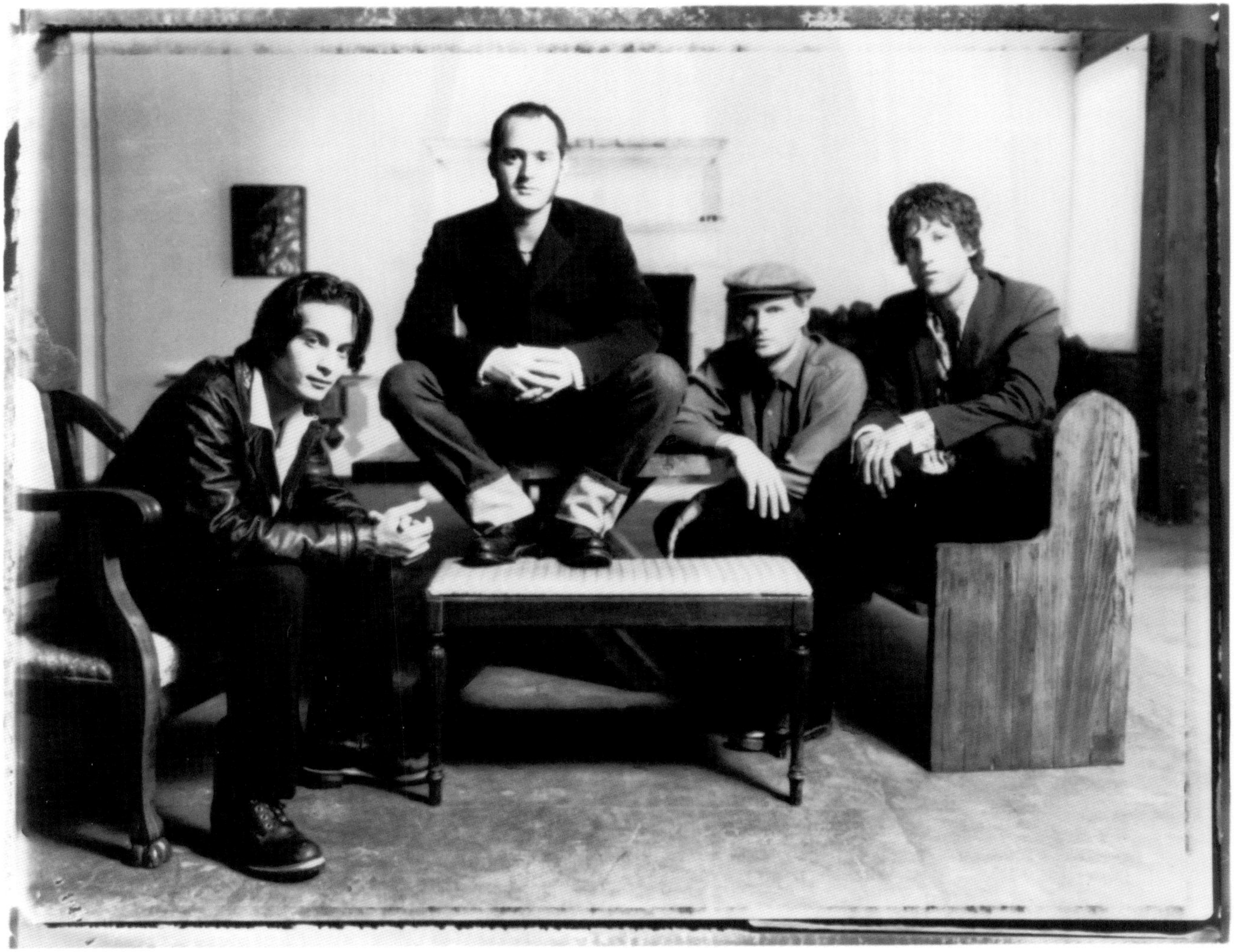

Photo: Danny Clinch 6/96

Jeff Russo Emerson Hart Kevin Shepard Dan Rothchild

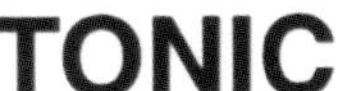

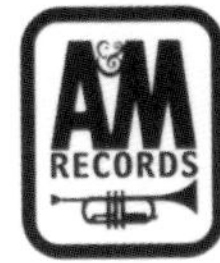

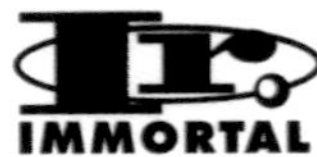


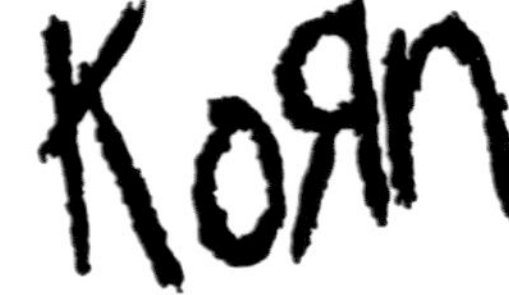

Photo Credit: Dean Karr

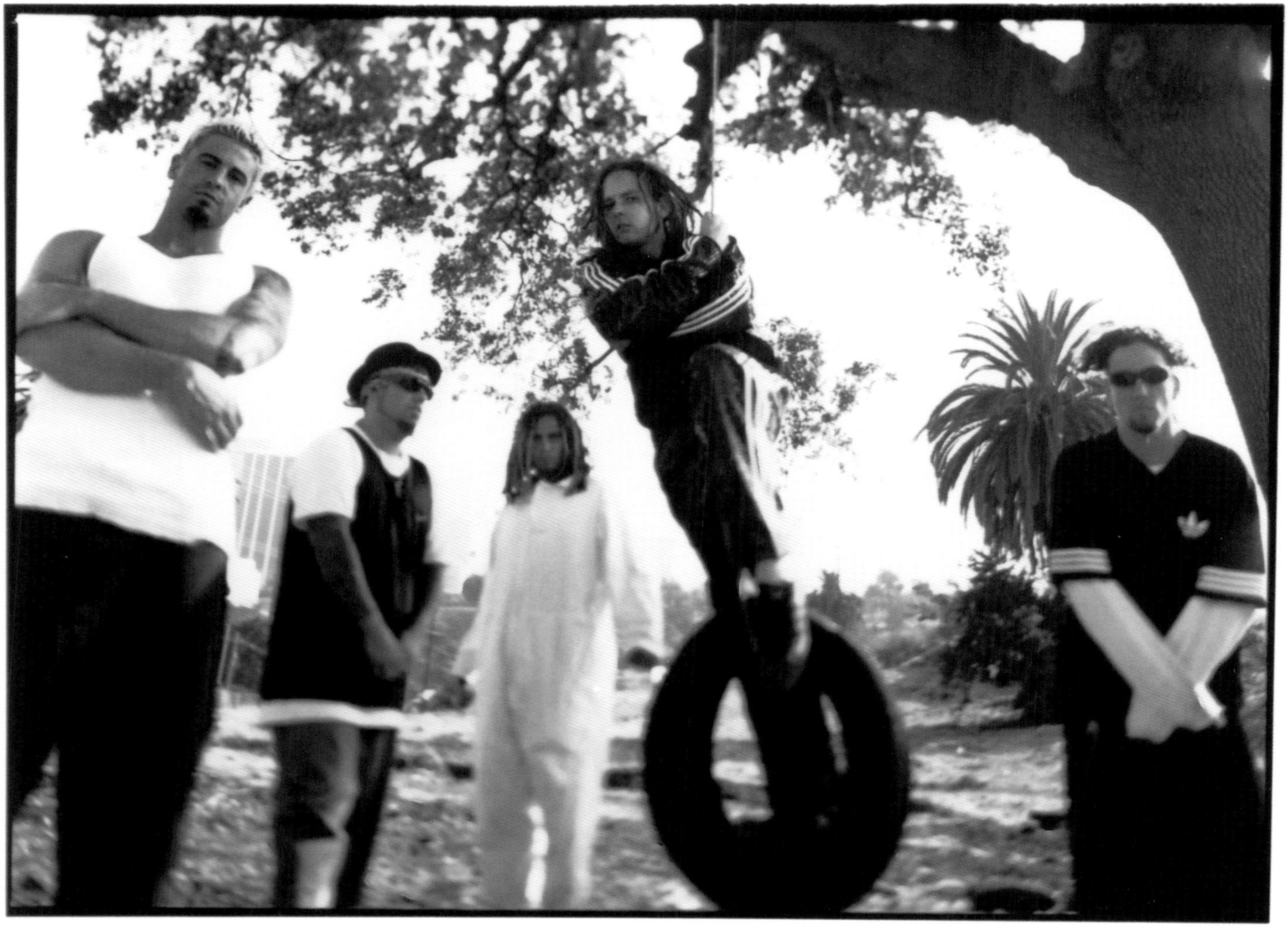

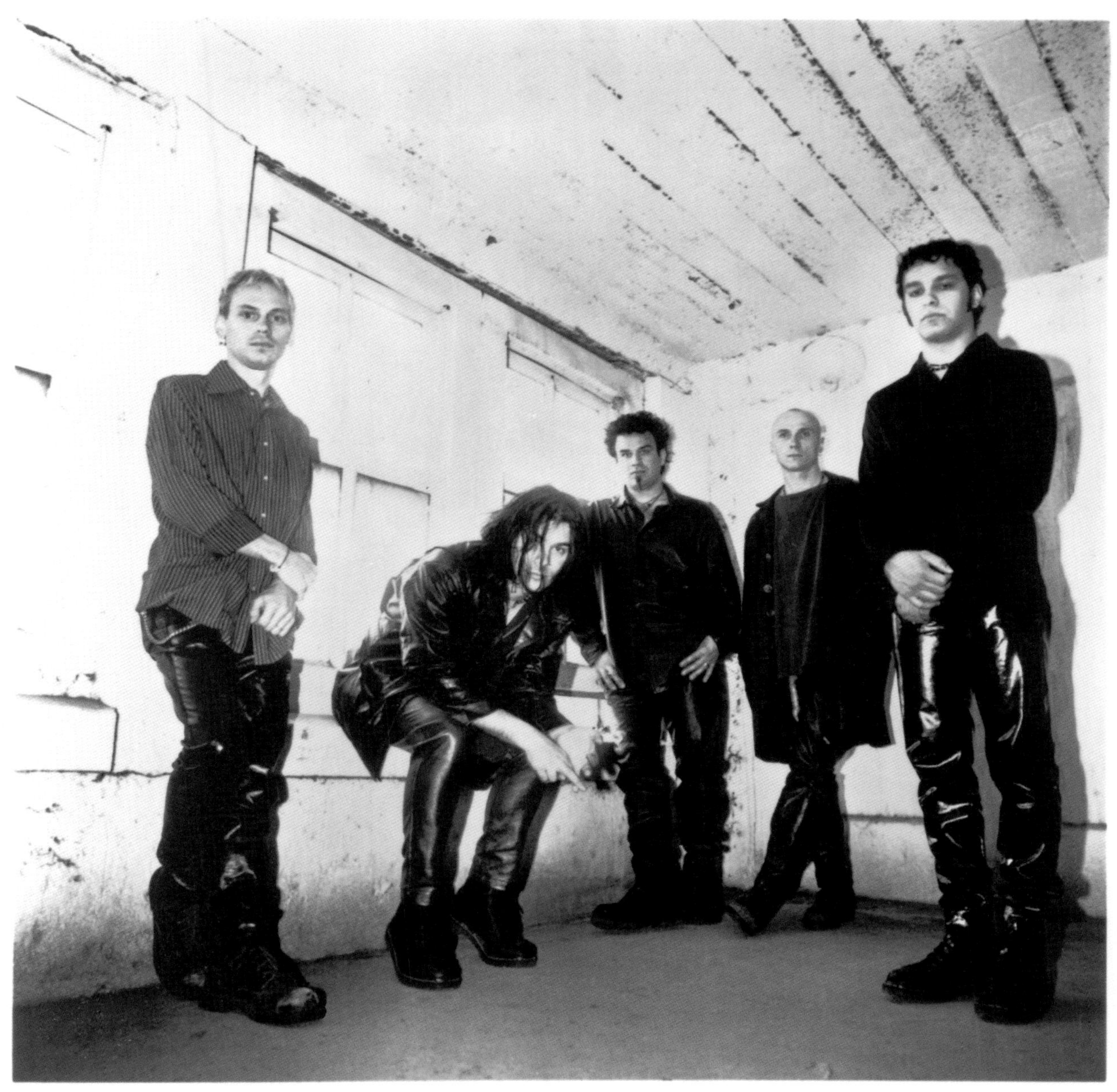

WALTER FLAKUS CHRISTOPHER HALL JIM SELLERS ANDY KUBISZEWSKI MARK ELIOPOULUS

**STABBING WESTWARD**

COLUMBIA
9603

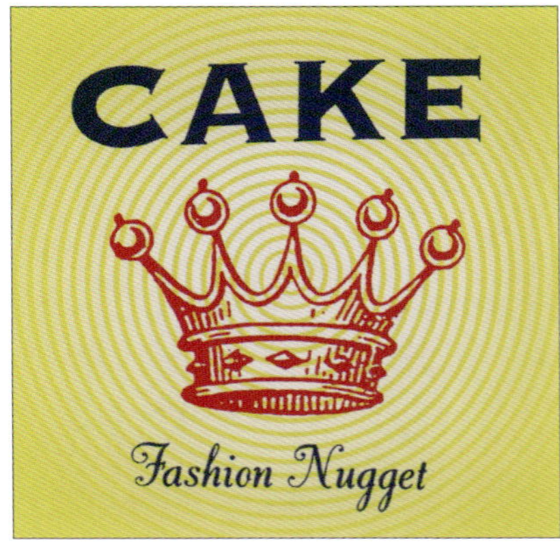


On *Fashion Nugget*, Sacramento band **Cake** intensified its ironic detachment with "The Distance" and a cover of Gloria Gaynor's classic "I Will Survive."

*Billboard* 200: *Fashion Nugget* (#36)

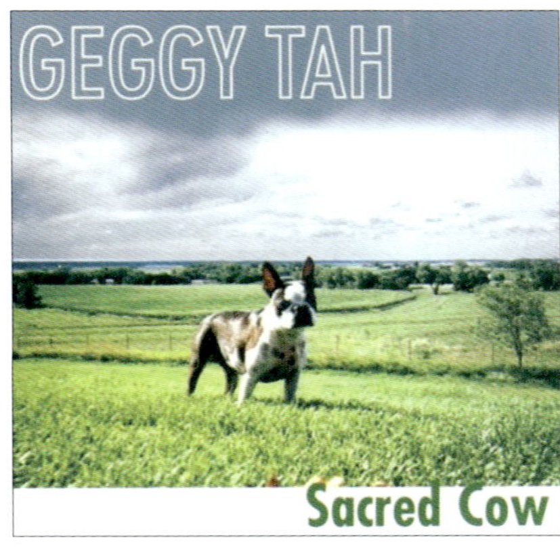


With a three-piece lineup, **Geggy Tah** meshed countless disparate elements into the sound of *Sacred Cow*, landing the modern-rock hit "Whoever You Are."

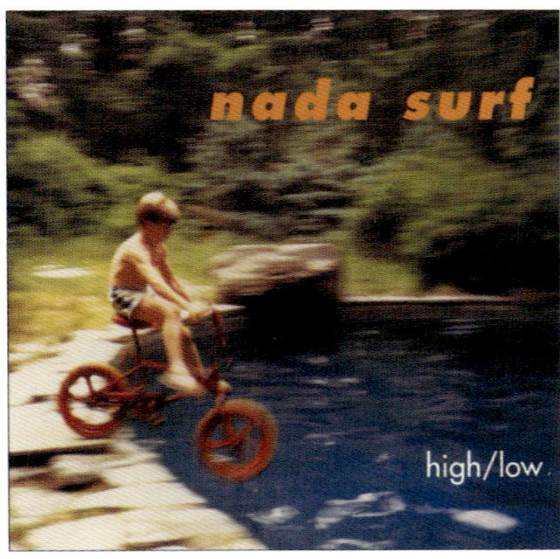


Pulling lyrical influence from early Sixties etiquette books, the alternative-rock song "Popular" blossomed into a surprising summer anthem for **Nada Surf**.

*Billboard* 200: *High/Low* (#63)
*Billboard* Hot 100: "Popular" (#51)

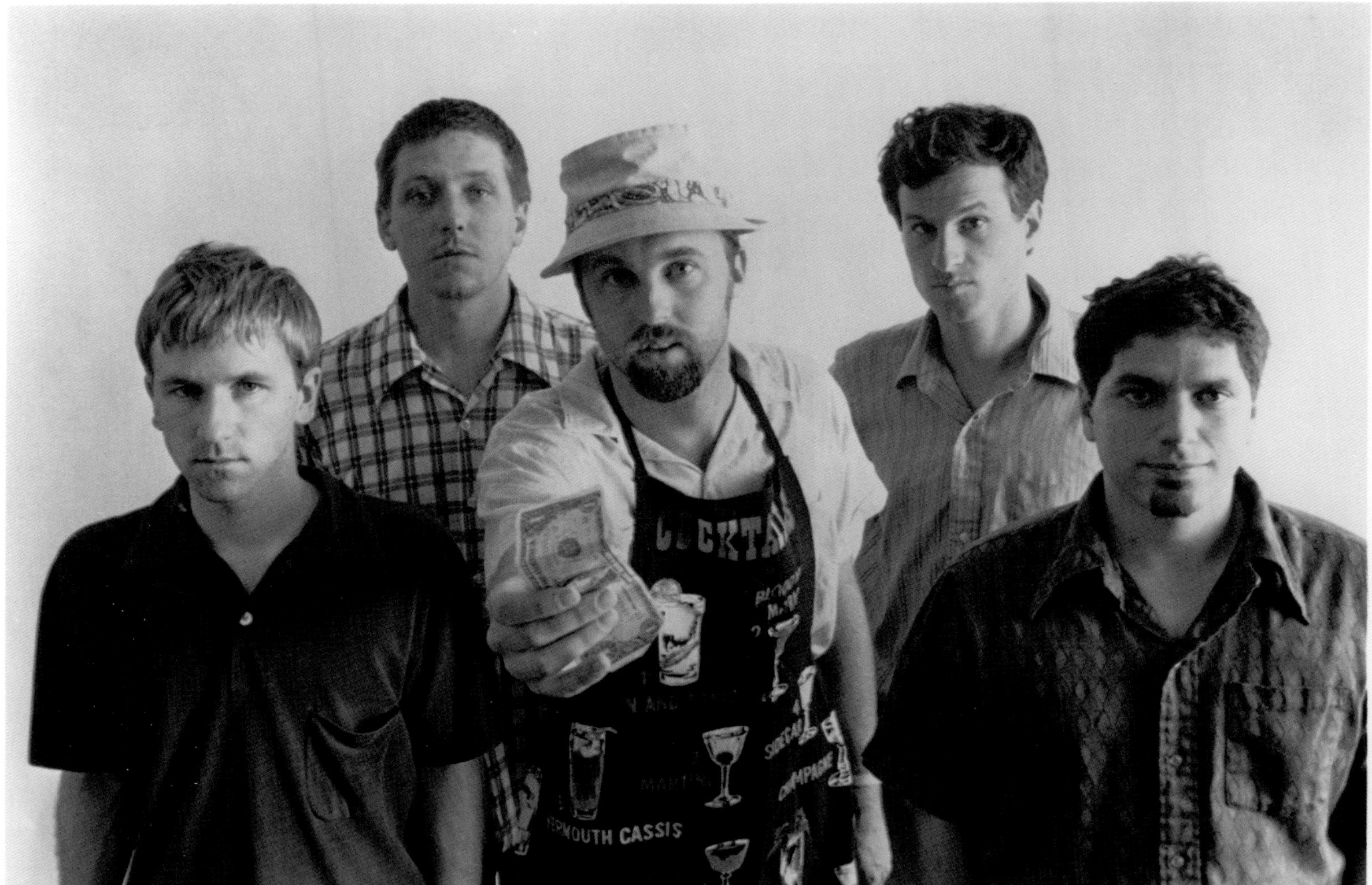


Photo: NOEL NEUBERGER (01)

GREG BROWN TODD ROPER JOHN McCREA VINCE DiFIORE VICTOR DAMIANI

# CAKE

Capricorn
2205 STATE STREET
NASHVILLE, TN 37203
(615) 320-8470

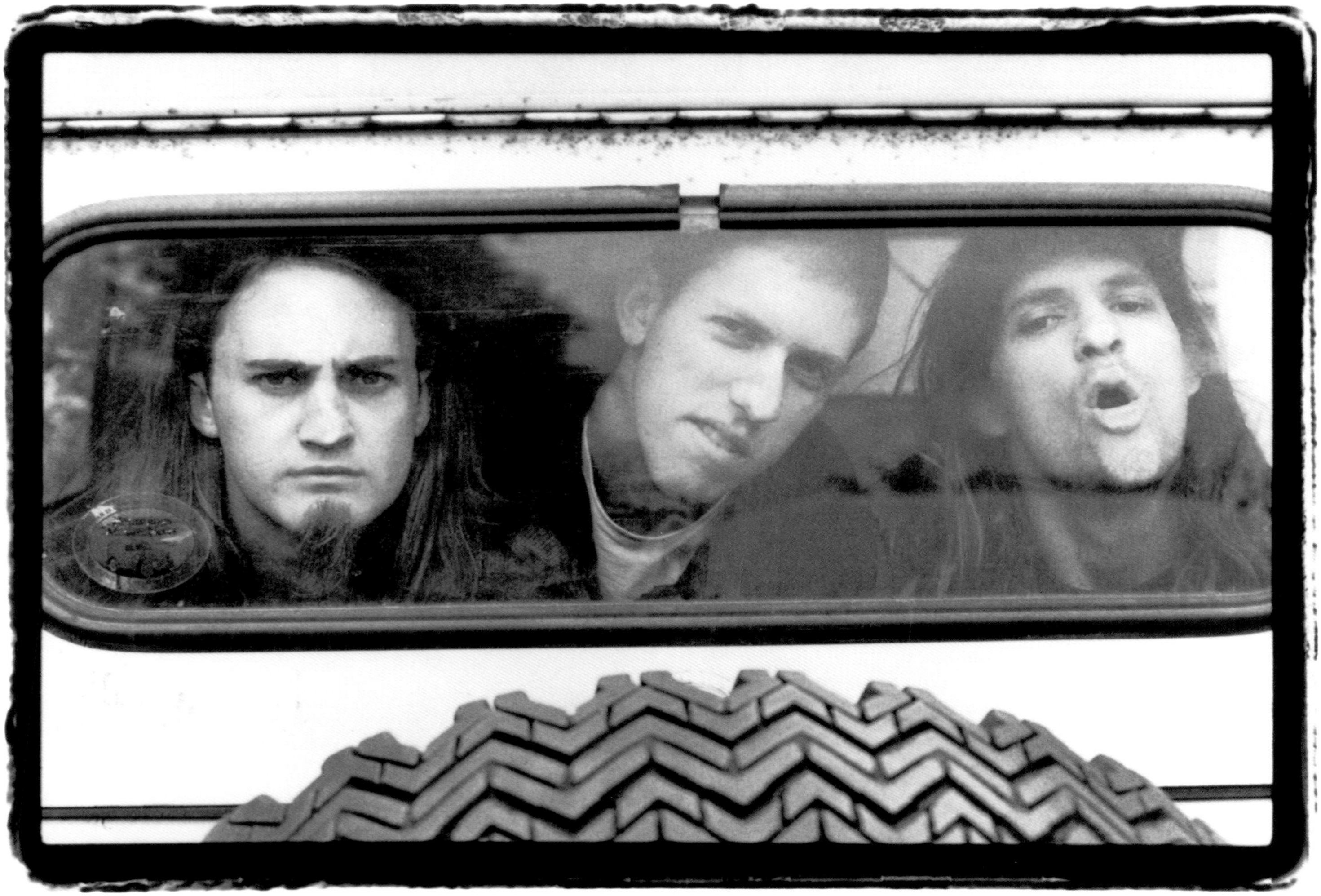

Photo Credit: Max S. Gerber

# GEGGY TAH

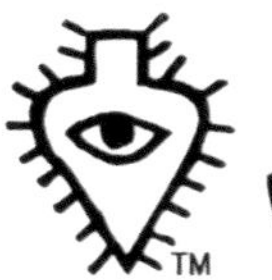

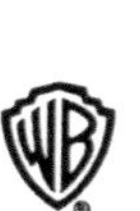

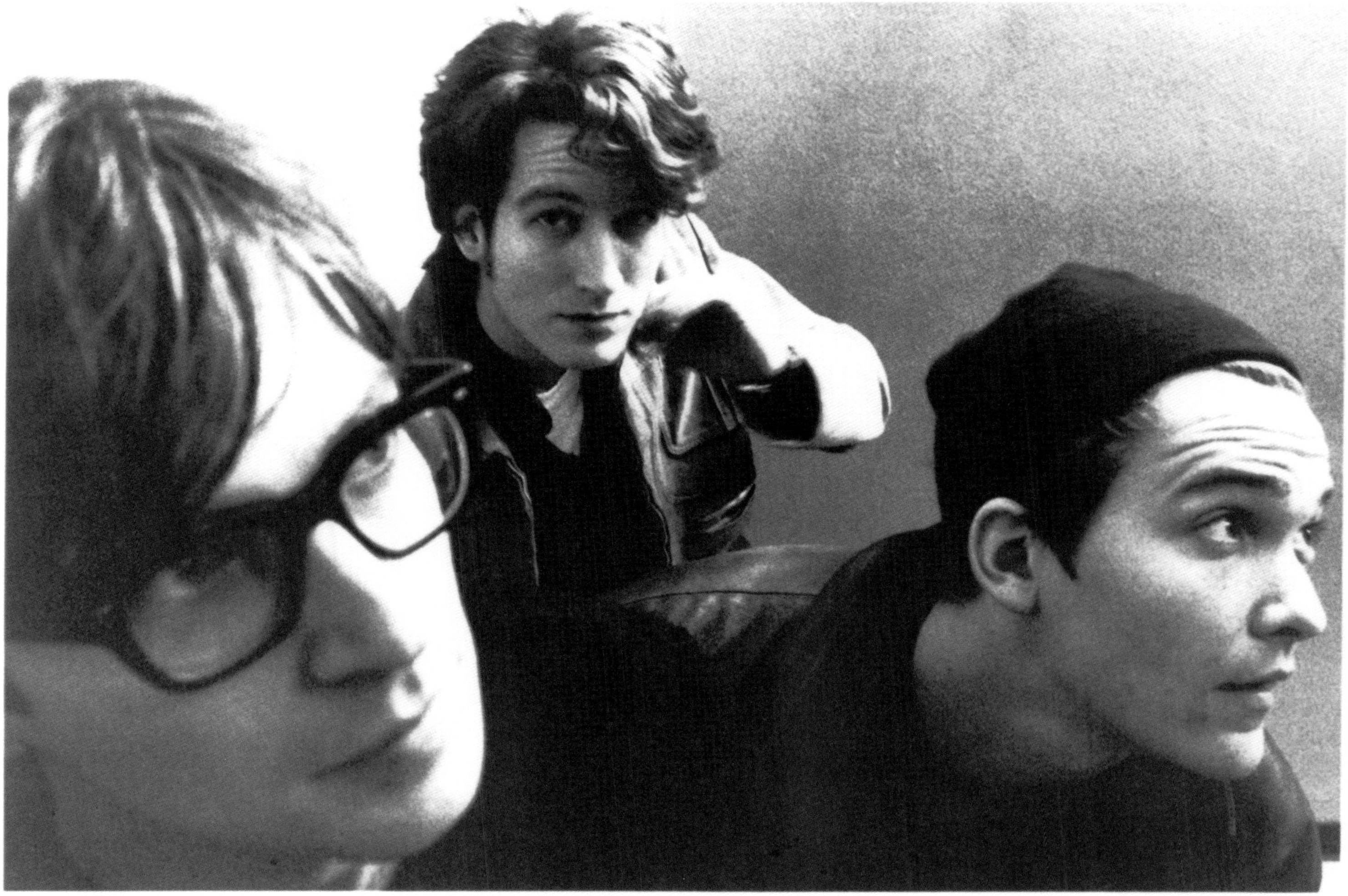

PHOTO CREDIT CHERYL DUNN

L R : MATTHEW CAWS, IRA ELLIOT DANIEL LORCA

# nada surf

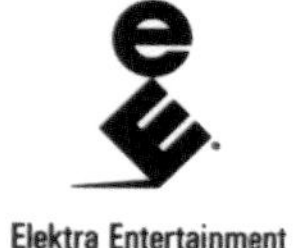

Elektra Entertainment

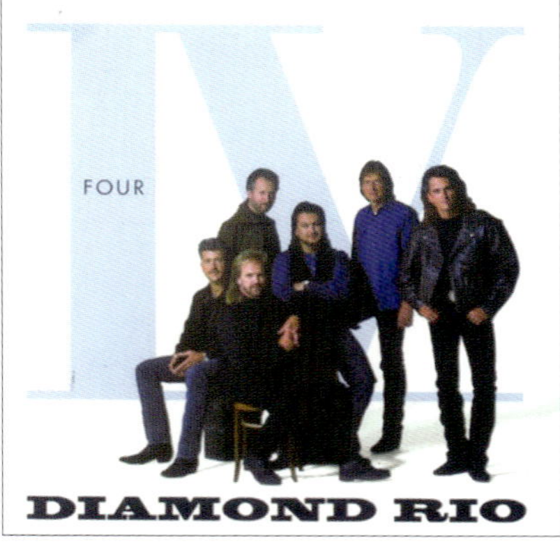


**Diamond Rio**'s *IV*, another showcase for the celebrated six-man band, made use of modern country musicianship, bluegrass roots and rock comportment.

*Billboard* 200: *IV* (#92)

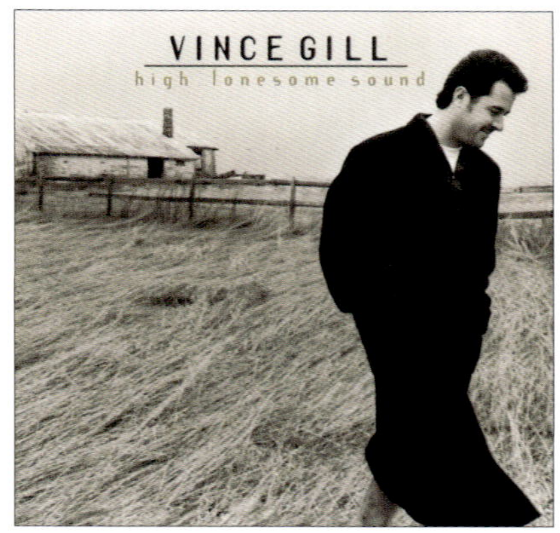


Country star **Vince Gill** stepped up with *High Lonesome Sound*, a set of traditional music that sold platinum and earned its maker three Grammy Awards.

*Billboard* 200: *High Lonesome Sound* (#24)

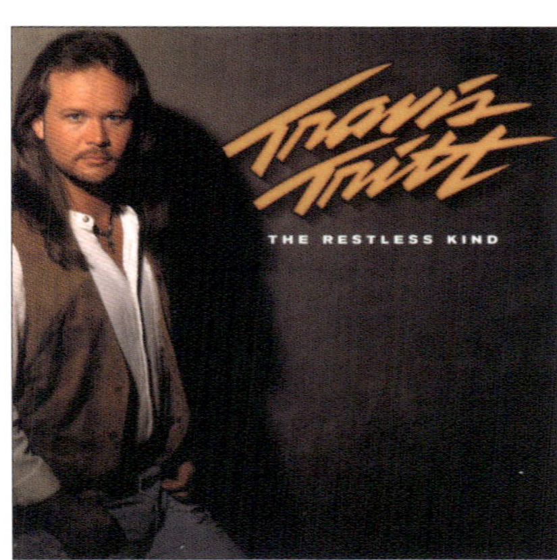


Following a greatest hits release, singer **Travis Tritt** took charge of his recordings, sharing production responsibilities with Don Was on *The Restless Kind*.

*Billboard* 200: *The Restless Kind* (#53)

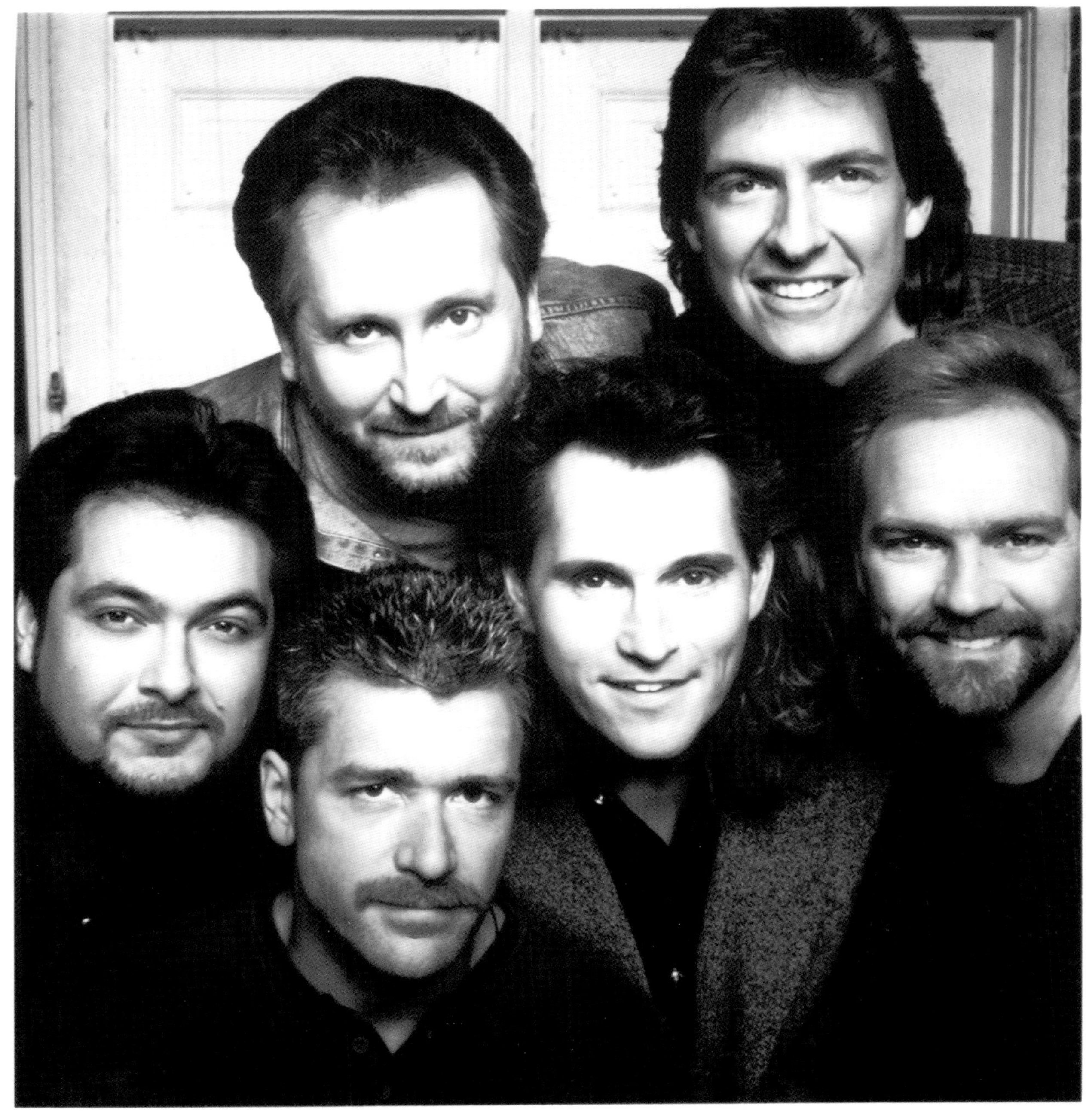

photo: John Scarpati

Gene
Johnson

Dan
Truman

Dana
Williams

Jimmy
Olander

Marty
Roe

Brian
Prout

**DIAMOND RIO**

ARISTA™
NASHVILLE
7 MUSIC CIRCLE NORTH
NASHVILLE, TN 37203
(615) 780-9100

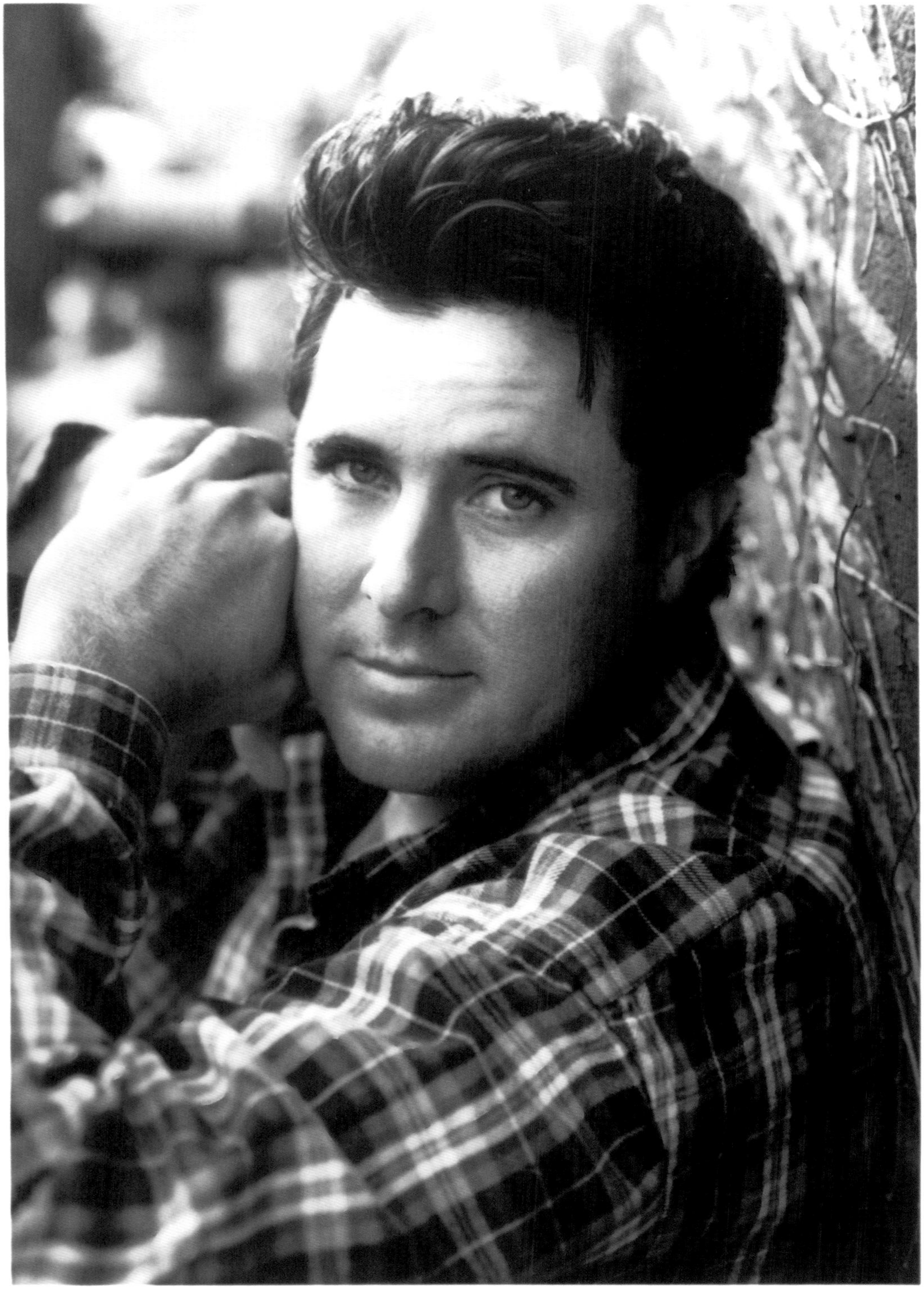

VINCE GILL

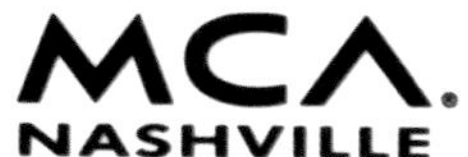


photo: Victoria Pearson 0495A

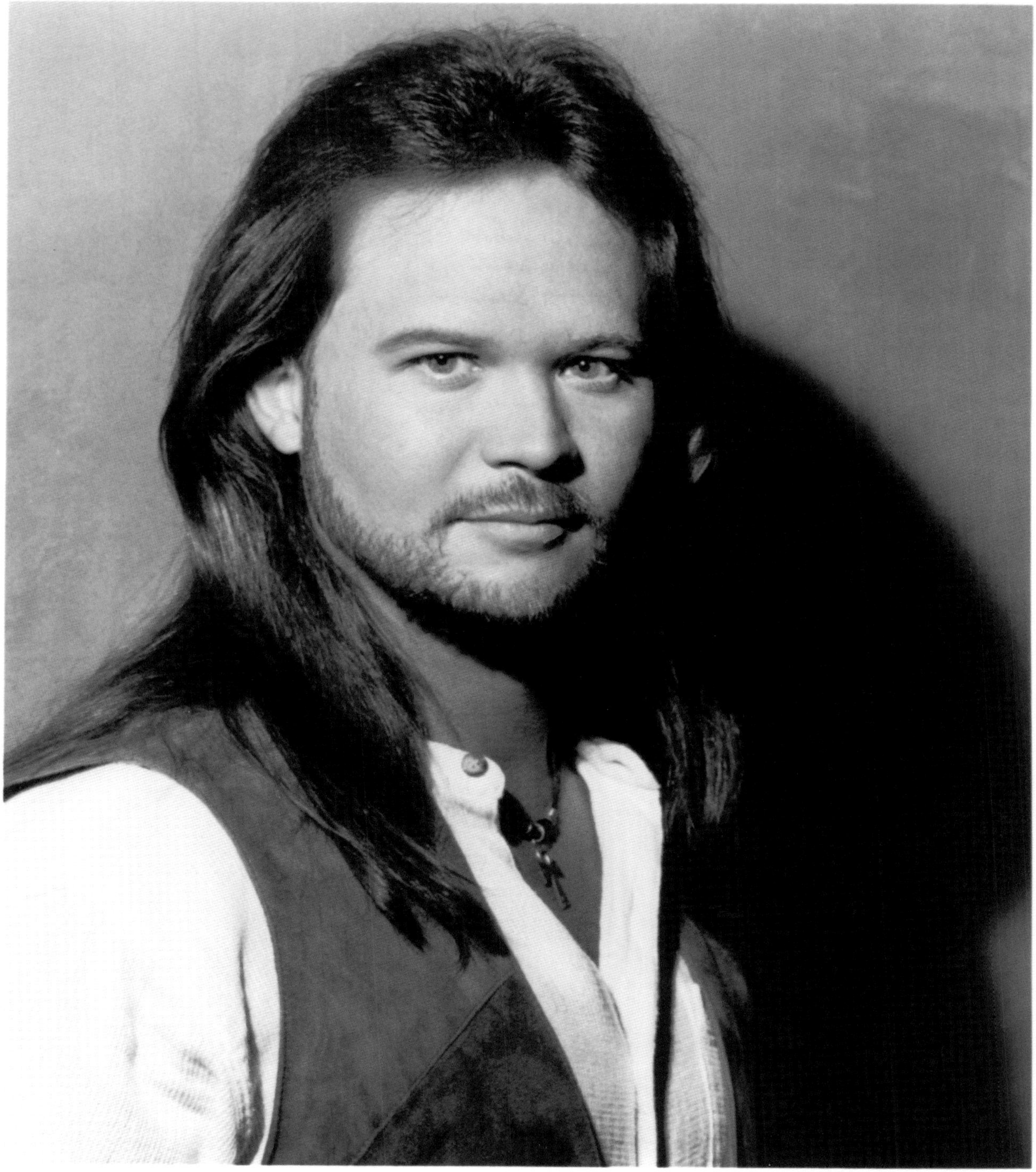

photo: Greg Gorman

# TRAVIS TRITT

Irresistible renditions of Tom T. Hall's "Little Bitty" and "There Goes" propelled **Alan Jackson**'s *Everything I Love* album to triple-platinum status.

*Billboard* 200: *Everything I Love* (#12)
*Billboard* Hot 100: "Little Bitty" (#58)

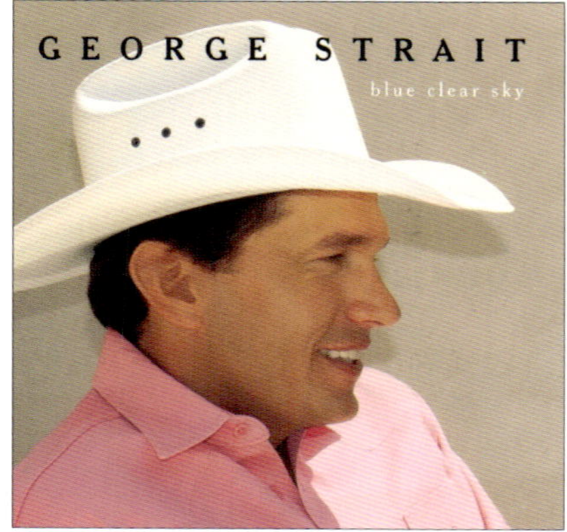


*Blue Clear Sky*, **George Strait**'s 10th album to reach the top of the country charts, offered his 28th and 29th No. 1 hits, the title track and "Carried Away."

*Billboard* 200: *Blue Clear Sky* (#7)

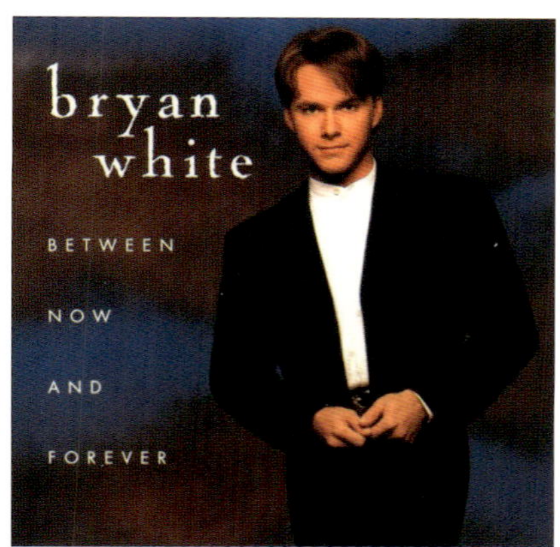


**Bryan White**, country music's youngest star, scored four hit songs, including "I'm Not Supposed to Love You Anymore" and "So Much for Pretending."

*Billboard* 200: *Between Now and Forever* (#52)

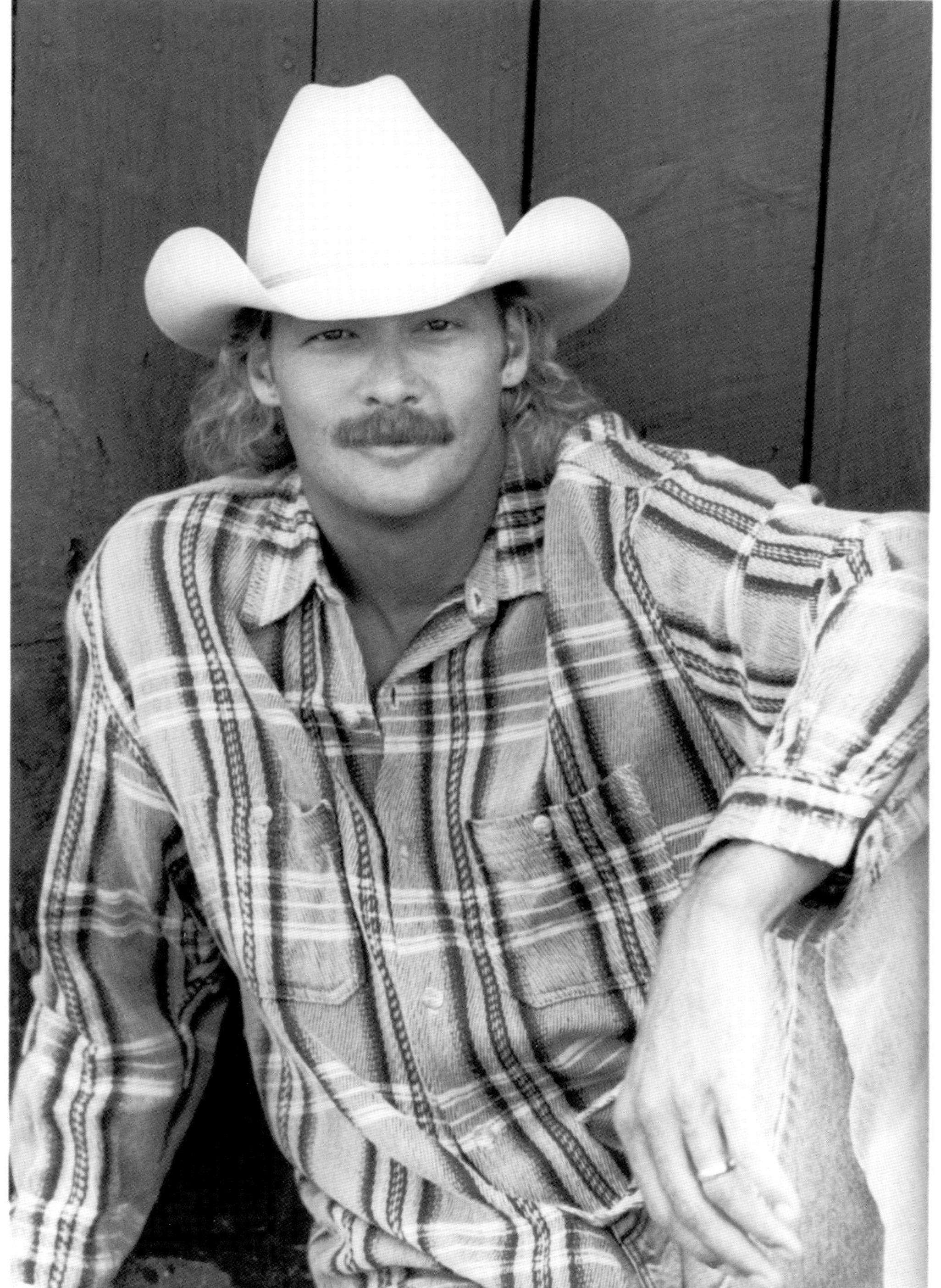

photo: Pamela Springsteen

# ALAN JACKSON

ARISTA NASHVILLE
7 MUSIC CIRCLE NORTH
NASHVILLE, TN 37203
(615) 780-9100

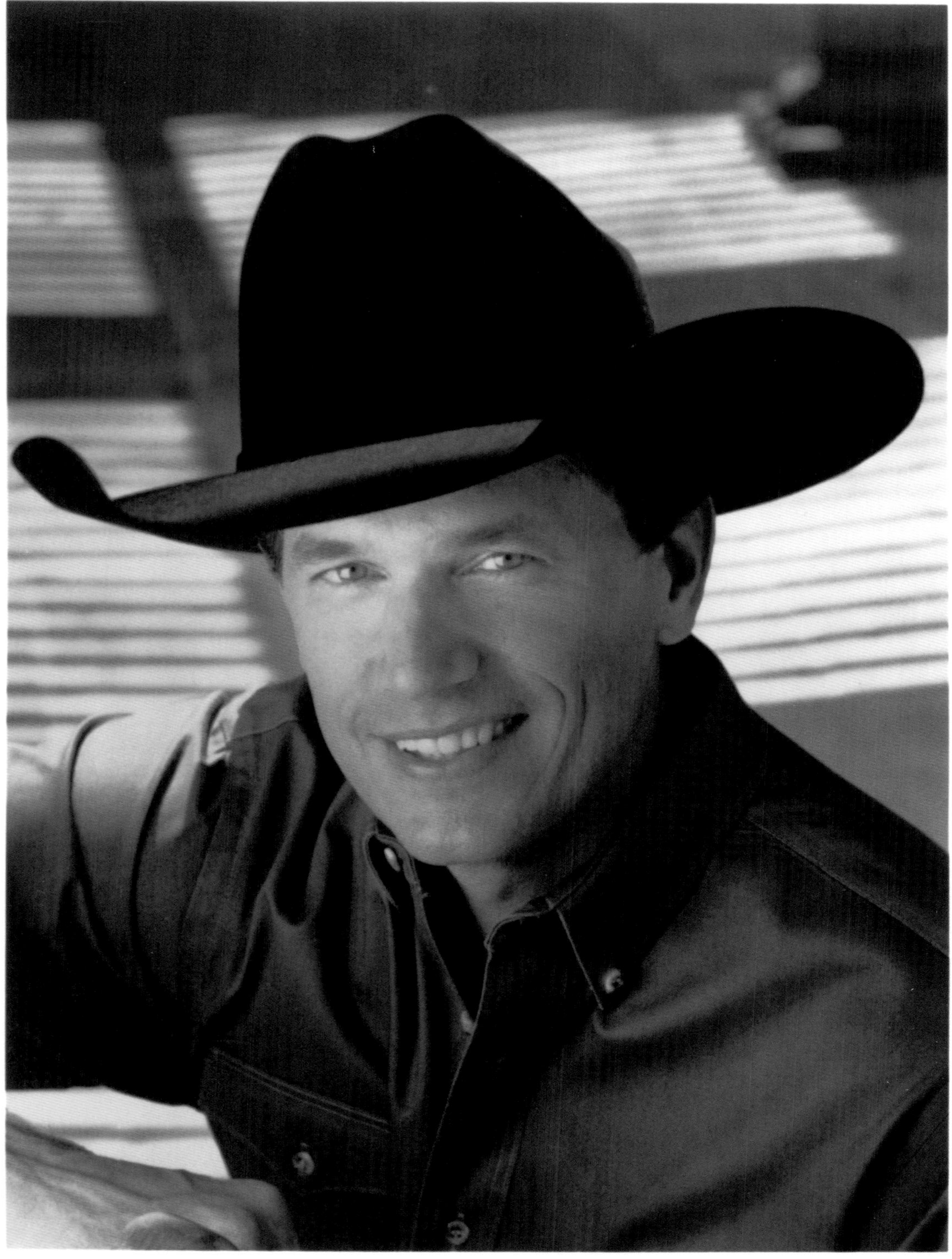

photo: Mark Tucker 0895A

GEORGE STRAIT

MCA.
NASHVILLE

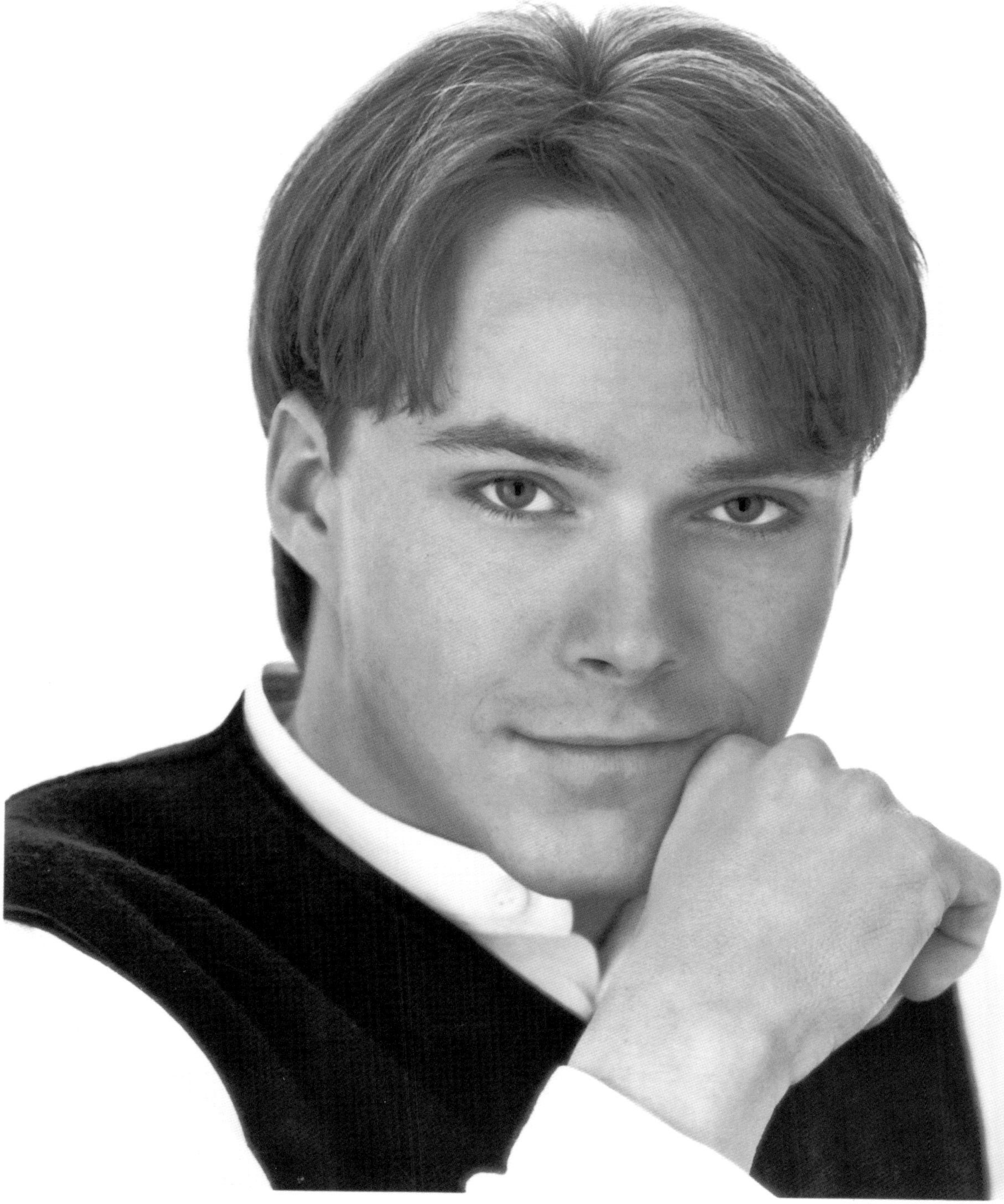

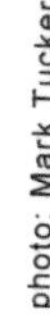


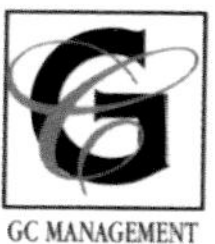


Marty Gamblin and Stan Schneider
(615)329-9886 (310)552-0960

Publicity: Holley & Harman
Summer Harman & Debbie Holley
(615)460-9550
Booking: William Morris Agency
Rick Shipp/Rob Beckham
(615)963-3337

# BRYAN WHITE

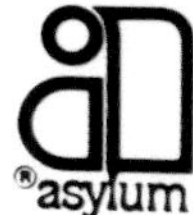

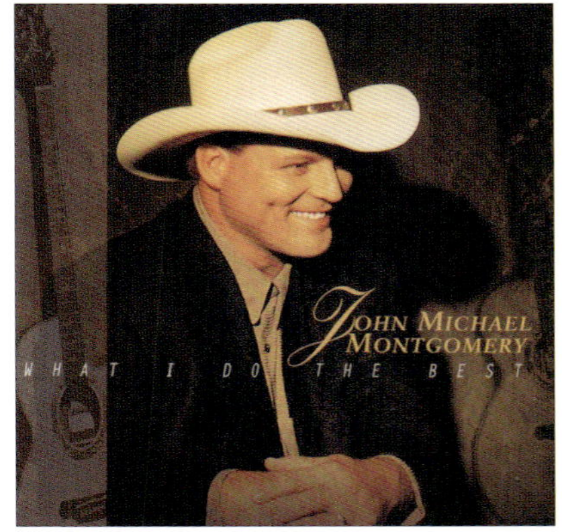


A king of country power ballads, **John Michael Montgomery** ruled the roost with the loyalty of "Friends" and the emotional solidity of "I Miss You a Little."

*Billboard* 200: *What I Do the Best* (#39)
*Billboard* Hot 100: "Friends" (#69)

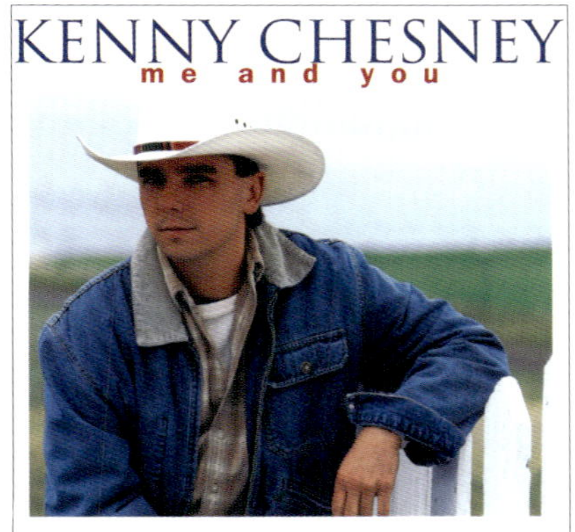


Thanks to the sentimental "When I Close My Eyes" and the title track, *Me and You* became country troubadour **Kenny Chesney**'s first gold-selling effort.

*Billboard* 200: *Me and You* (#78)

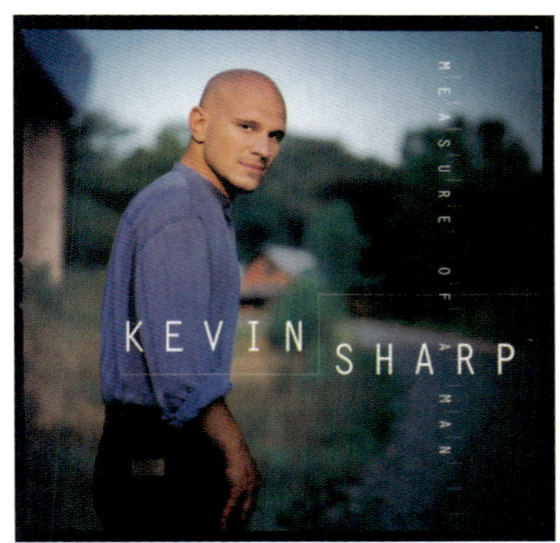


**Kevin Sharp** arrived on the country scene with *Measure of a Man*, and the cancer survivor scored a blockbuster hit with his first single, "Nobody Knows."

*Billboard* 200: *Measure of a Man* (#40)

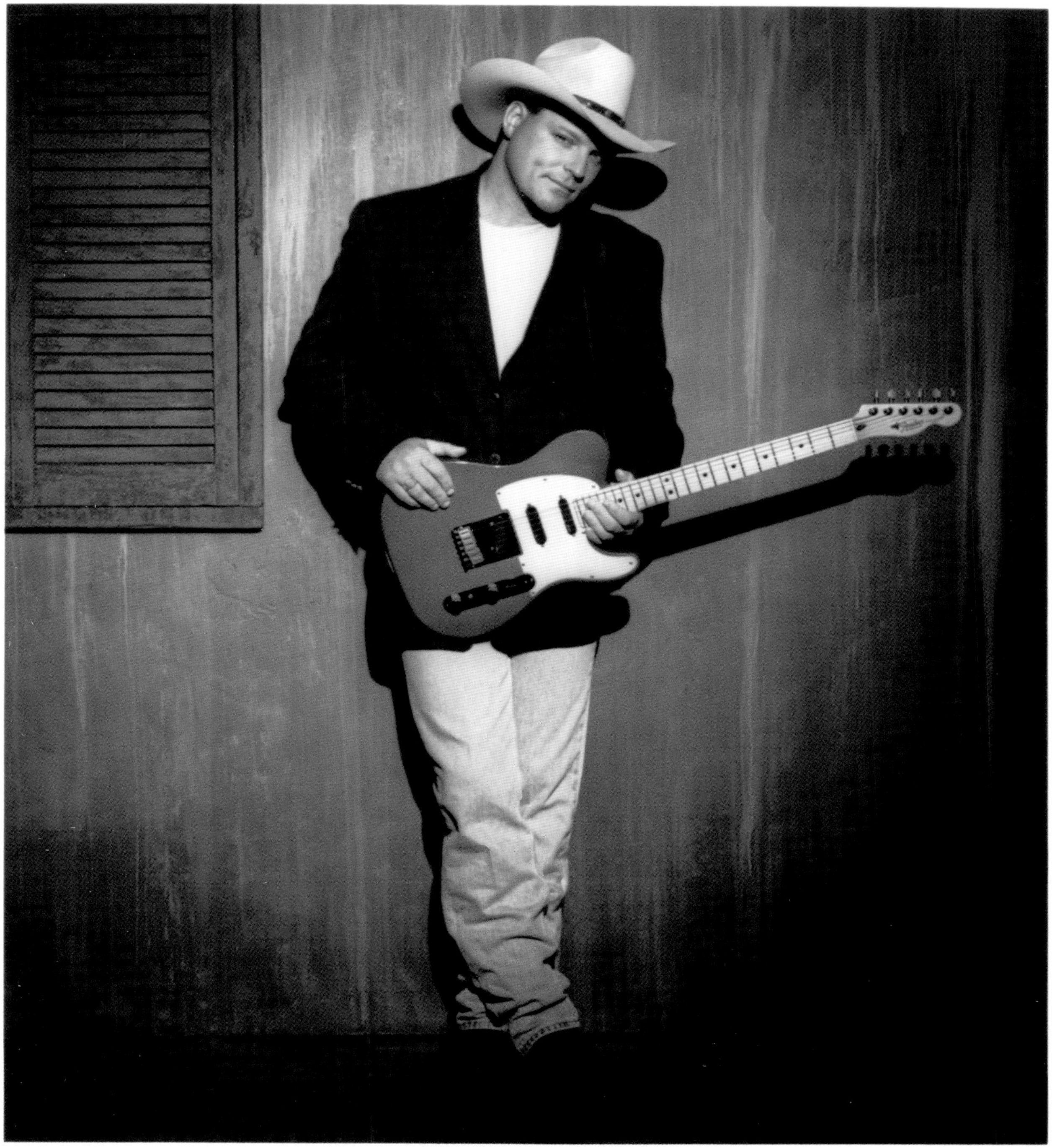

photo: Jim McGuire 9/96

JOHN MICHAEL MONTGOMERY

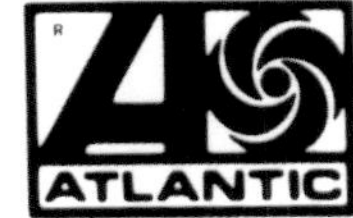

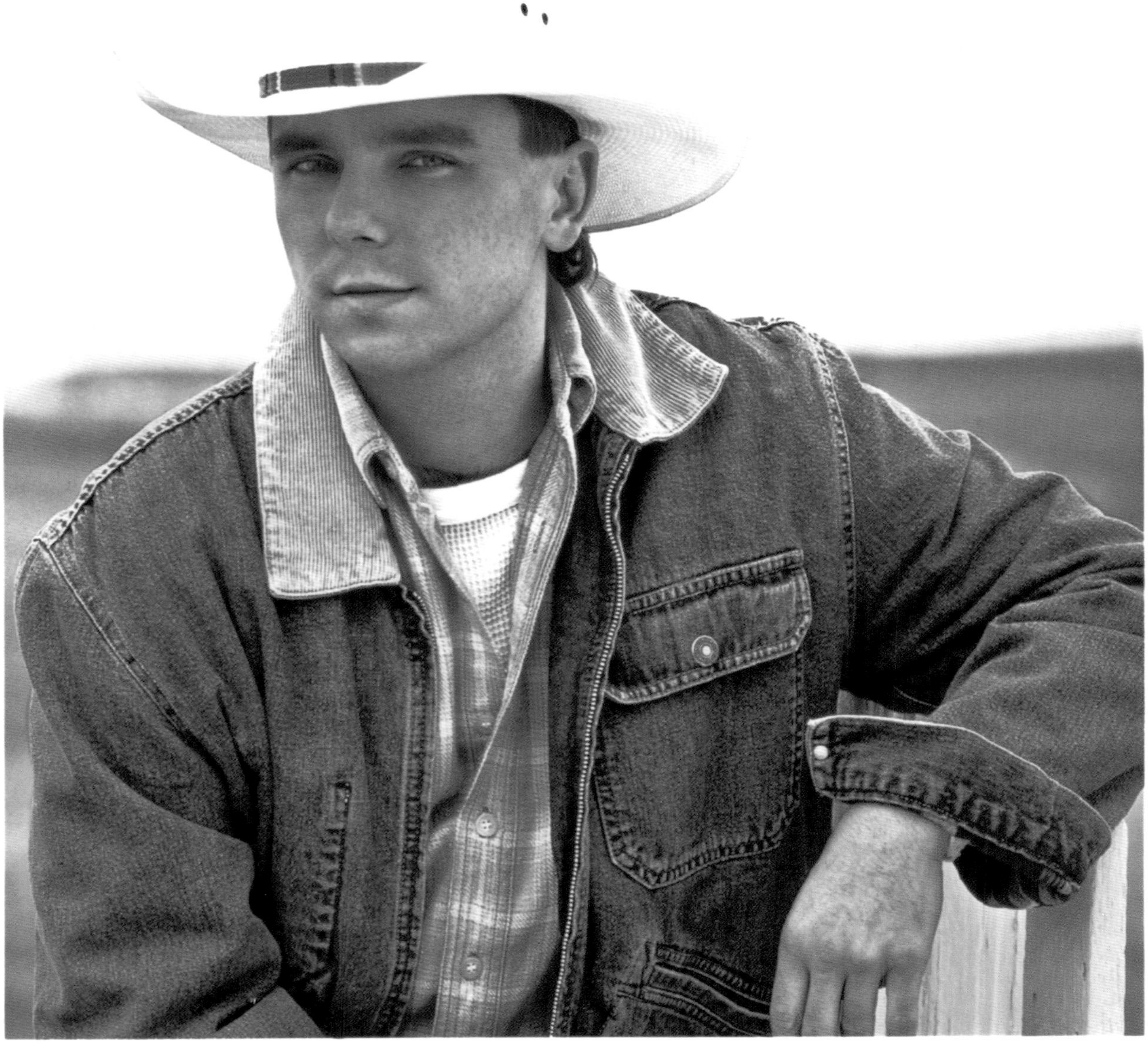

photo: Chuck Kuhn

KENNY CHESNEY

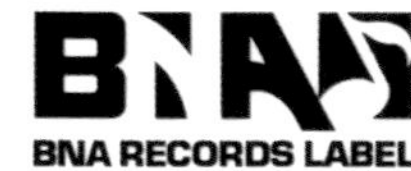

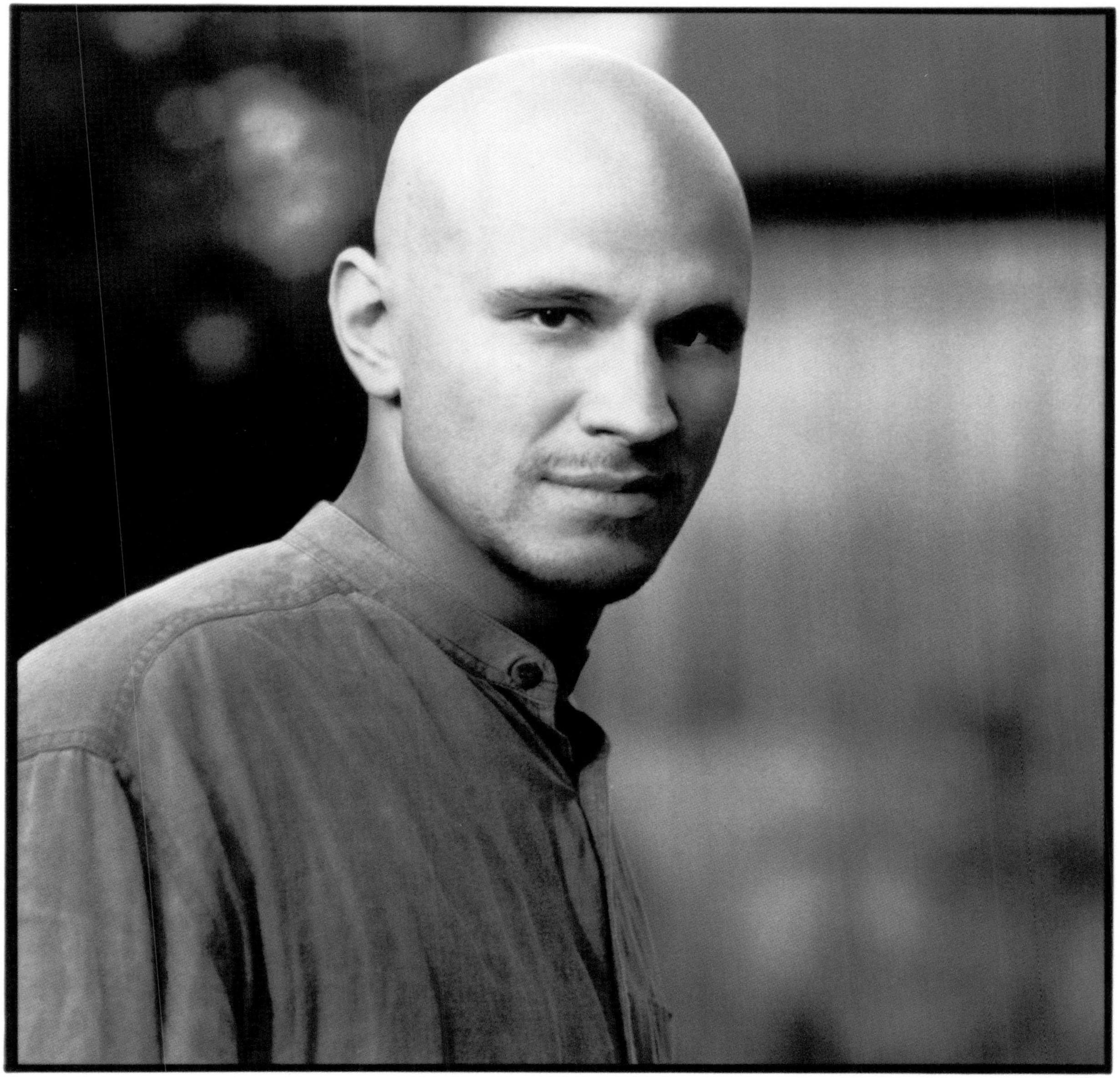

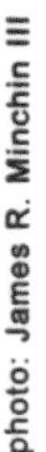


*SOUND & SERENITY MANAGEMENT*
P.O. Box 22105
Nashville, TN 37202
phone 615-731-3100
fax 615-731-3005

# KEVIN SHARP

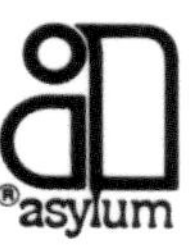

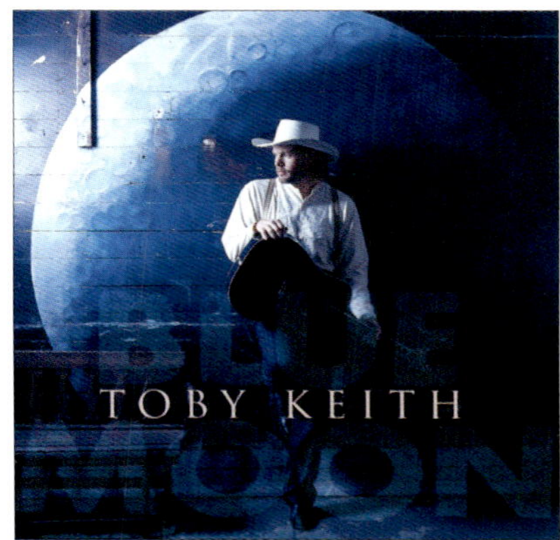


**Toby Keith**'s *Blue Moon* album offered three country singles, the No. 1 hit "Me Too," "Does That Blue Moon Ever Shine on You" and "A Woman's Touch."

*Billboard* 200: *Blue Moon* (#51)

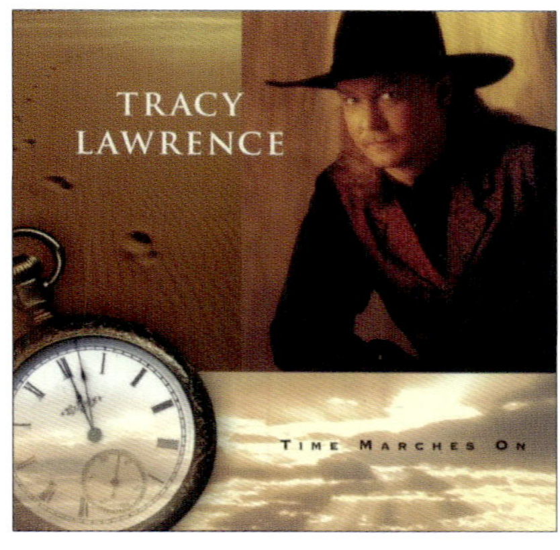


*Time Marches On* adapted the traditional styles **Tracy Lawrence** had picked up during his honky-tonk upbringing, and the title song scaled the country charts.

*Billboard* 200: *Time Marches On* (#25)

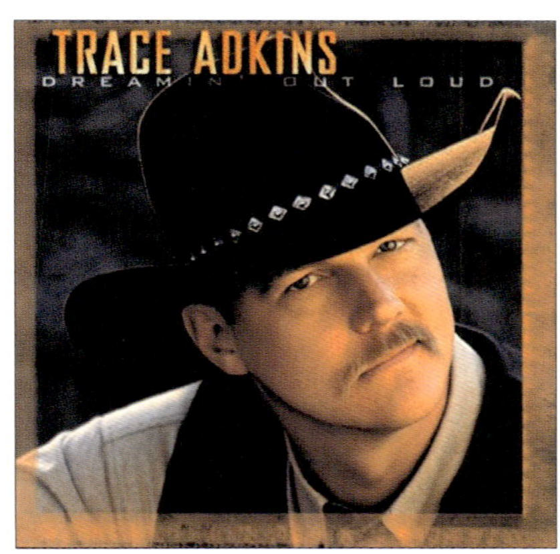


*Dreamin' Out Loud* ushered in **Trace Adkins**' booming baritone on two country hits, "Every Light in the House" and the No. 1 "(This Ain't) No Thinkin' Thing."

*Billboard* 200: *Dreamin' Out Loud* (#53)
*Billboard* Hot 100: "Every Light in the House" (#78)

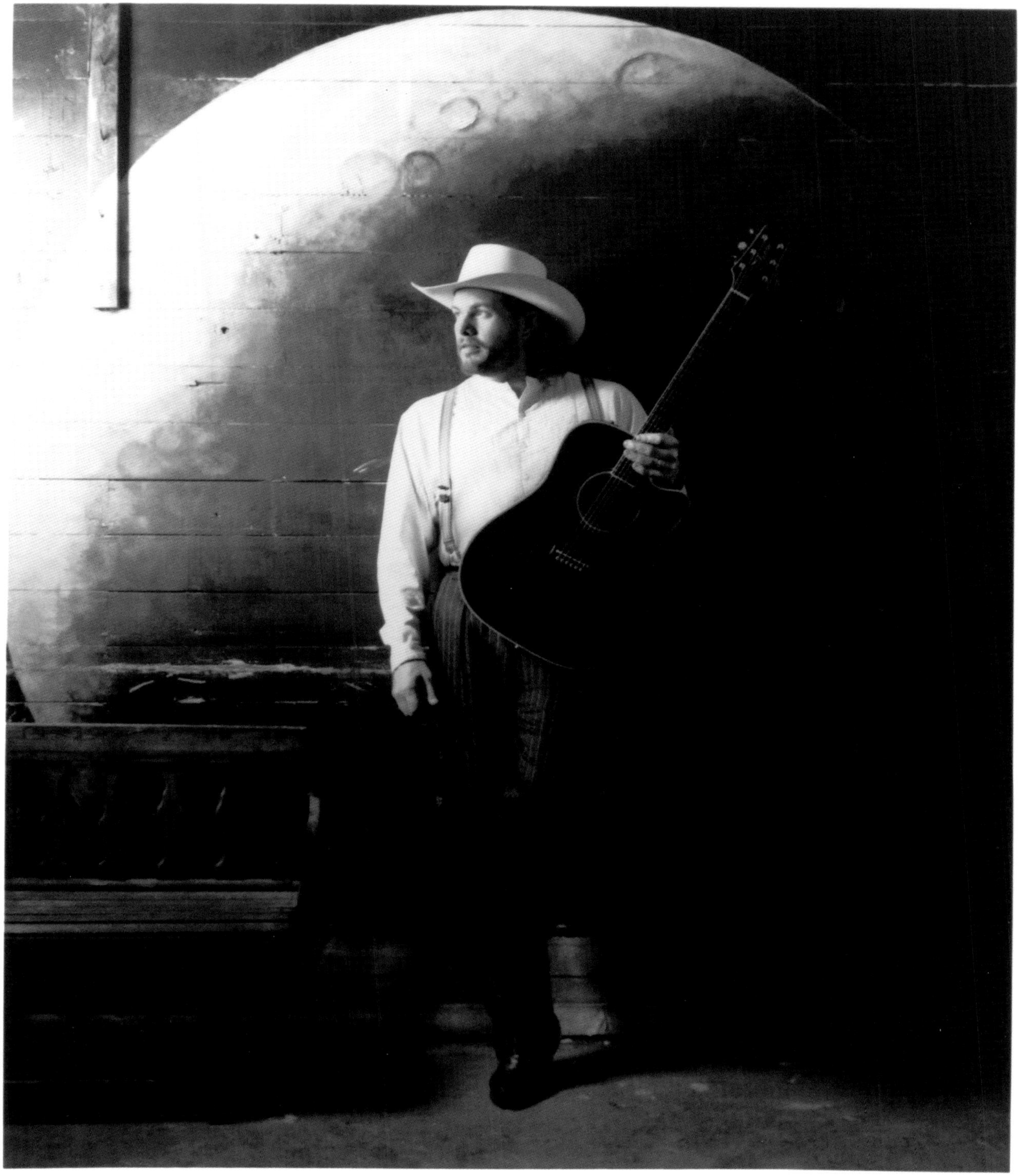

Evelyn Shriver Public Relations
1313 16th Avenue South
Nashville, TN 37212
615/383-1000
fax 615/383-1966

# TOBY KEITH

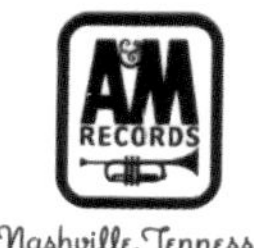


Nashville, Tennessee

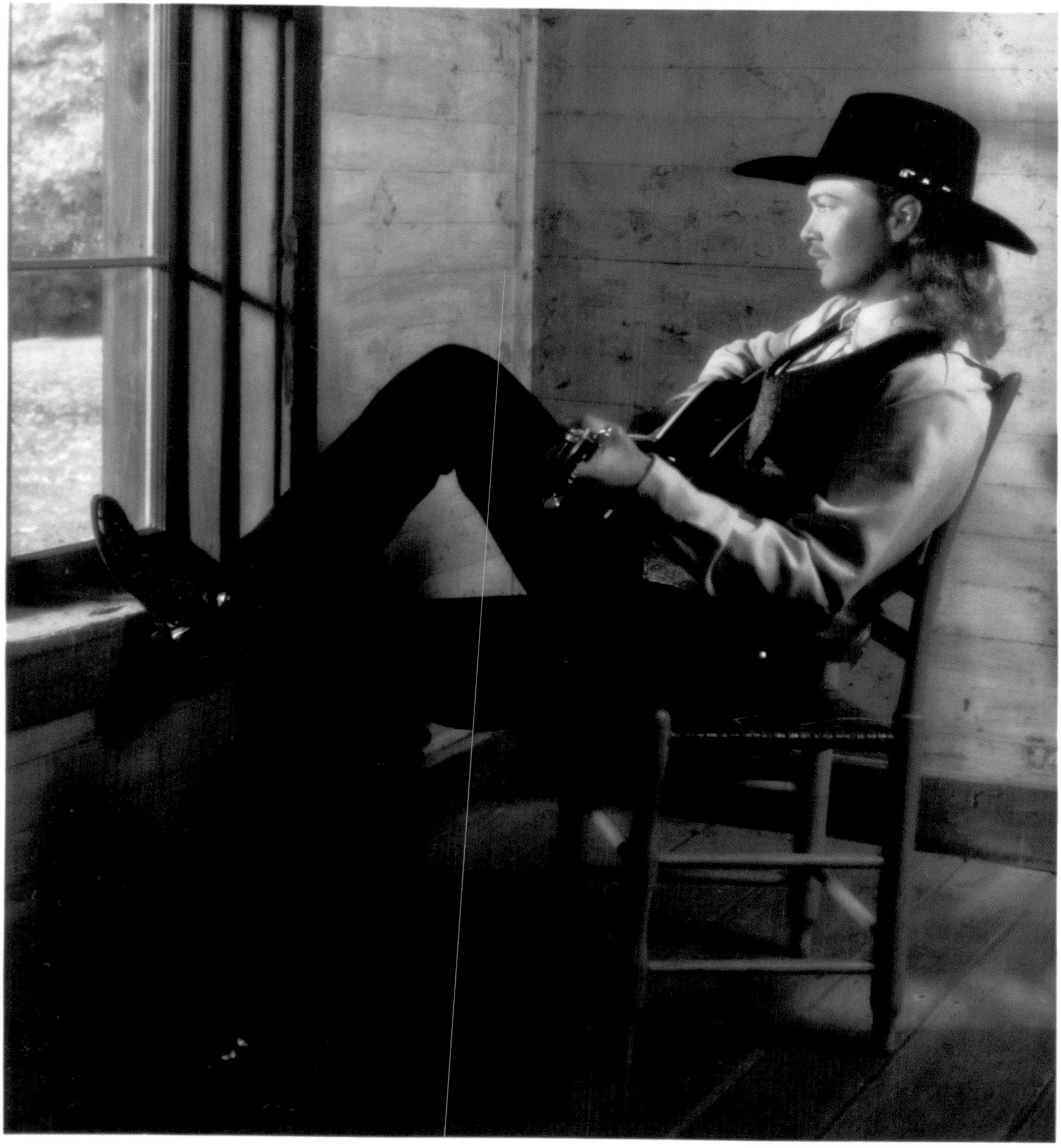

TLE Management, Inc.
1100 17th Avenue South
Nashville, TN 37212
(615)329-0900
(615)329-0977 fax
Web sitE-HTTP://songs-com/TLE

# TRACY LAWRENCE

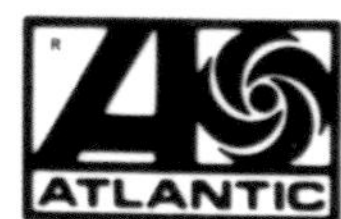


WILLIAM MORRIS AGENCY, INC.
TALENT AND LITERARY AGENCY

2100 West End Ave., Ste 1000, Nashville, Tennessee 37203
Tel (615) 963-3000

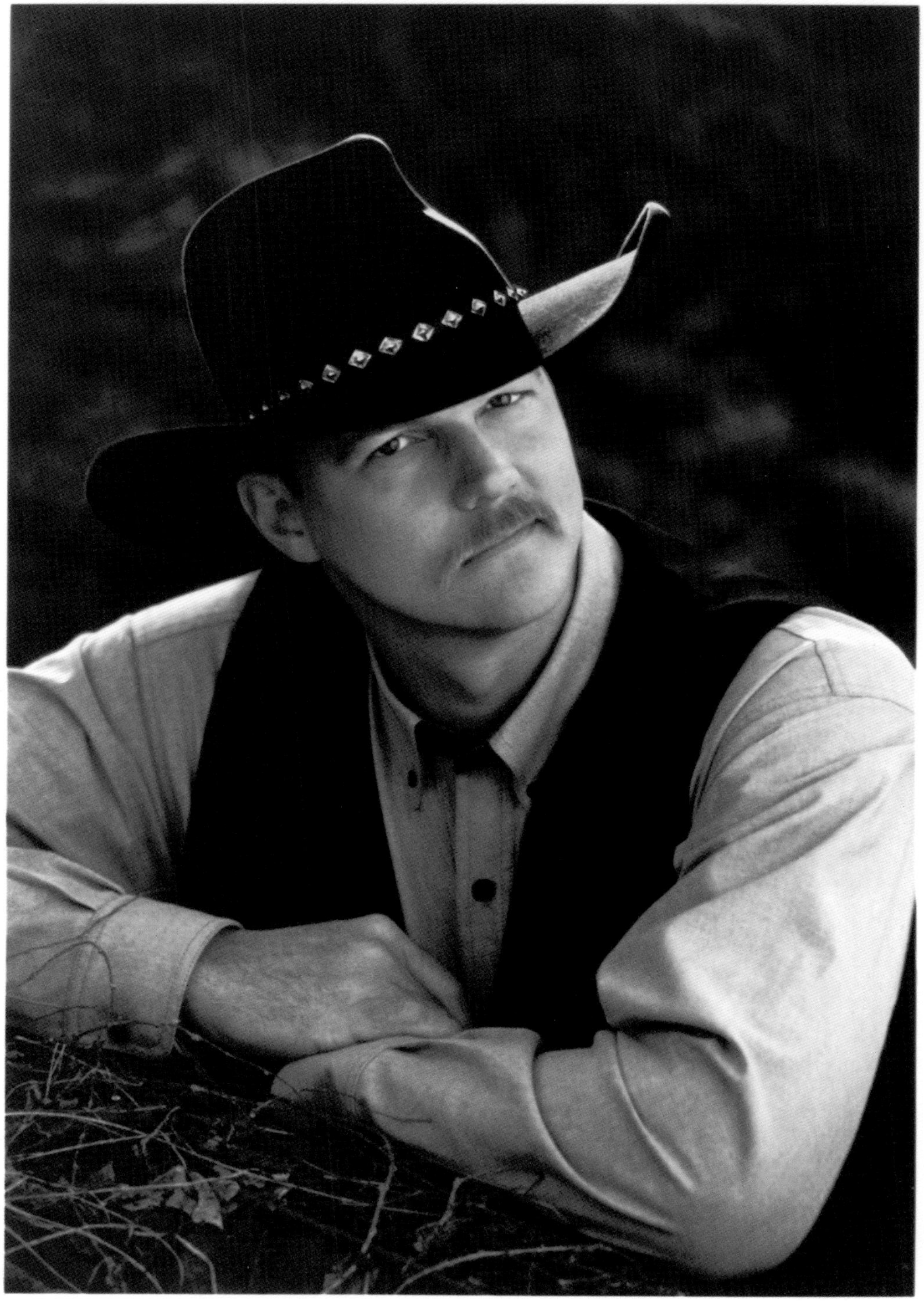

photo: Mark Tucker 3/96A

TRACE ADKINS

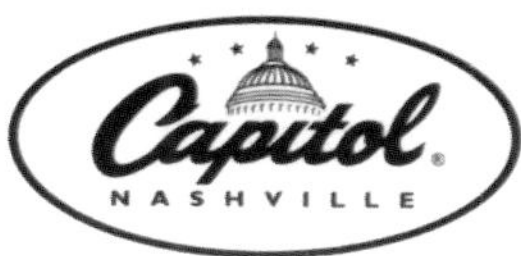

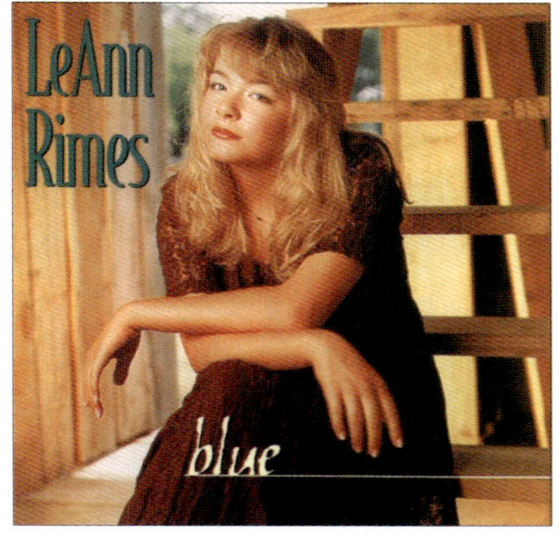


Only 13 years old, singer **LeAnn Rimes** shot to overnight stardom as a country-music chanteuse with the song "Blue" and a debut album of the same name.

*Billboard* 200: *Blue* (#3)
Billboard Hot 100: "Blue" (#26)

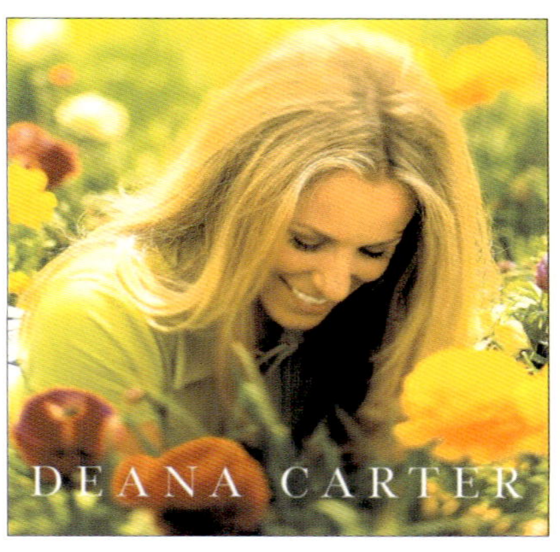


The daughter of one of Nashville's most in-demand session guitarists, country artist **Deana Carter** climbed the charts with *Did I Shave My Legs for This?*

*Billboard* 200: *Did I Shave My Legs for This?* (#10)
*Billboard* Hot 100: "Strawberry Wine" (#65); "We Danced Anyway" (#72); "Did I Shave My Legs for This?" (#85)

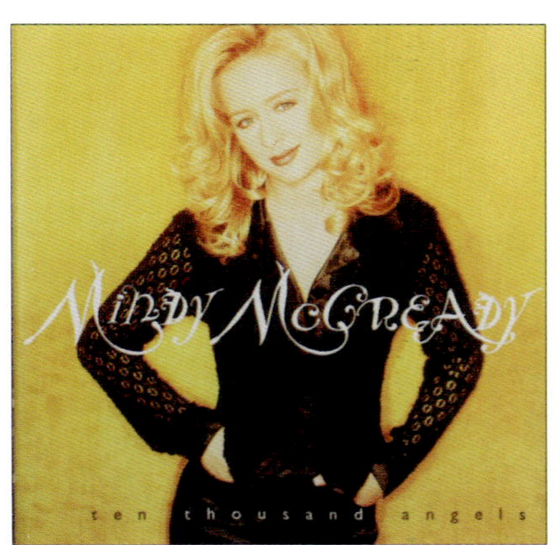


**Mindy McCready**'s first album bore the witty "Guys Do It All the Time," a No. 1 hit on the country charts that boosted her into Nashville's front ranks.

*Billboard* 200: *Ten Thousand Angels* (#40)
*Billboard* Hot 100: "Guys Do It All the Time" (#72)

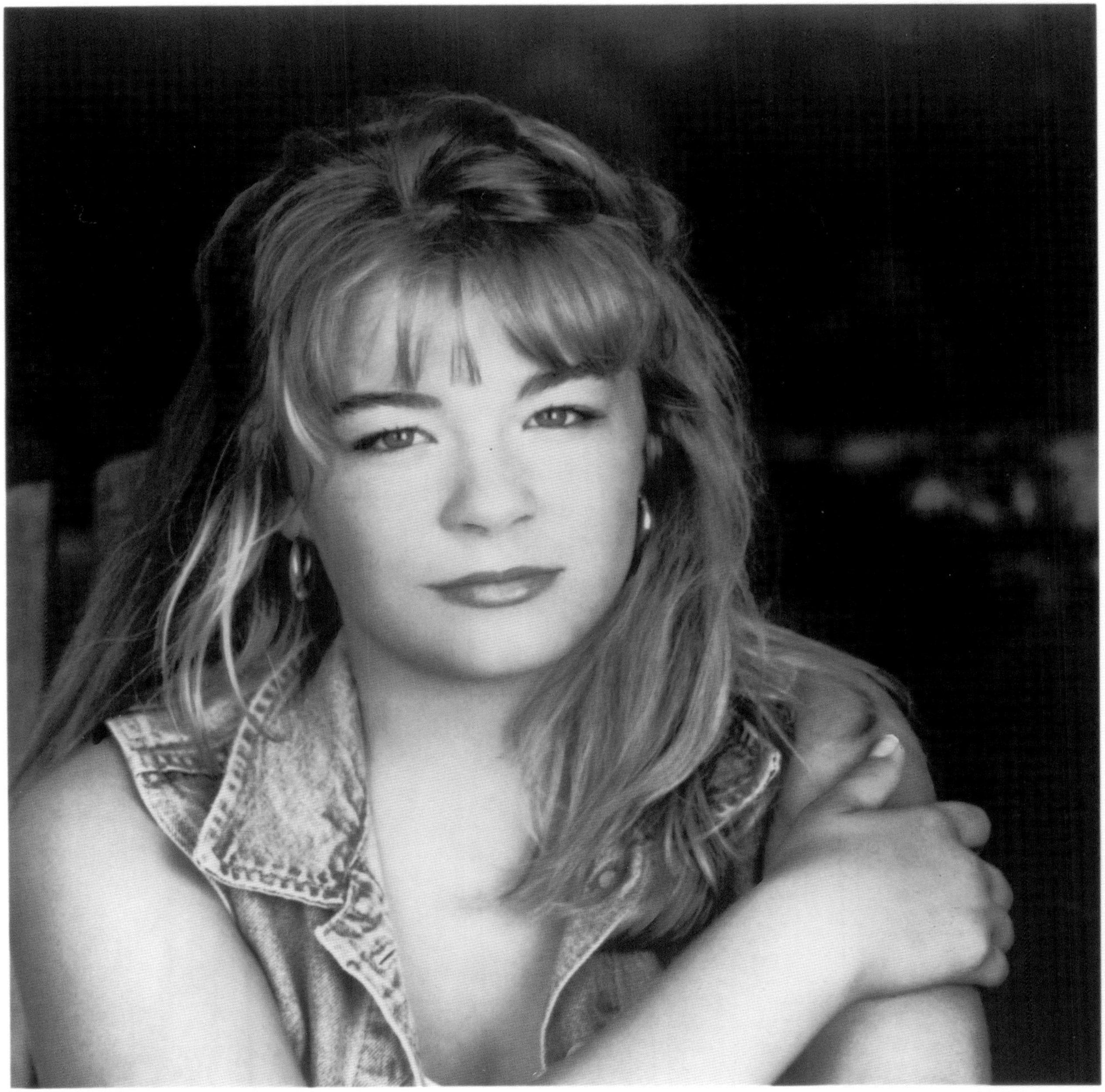

photo: Peter Nash

LeAnn Rimes

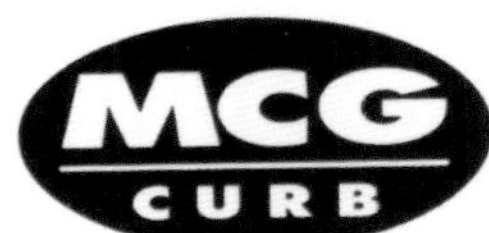

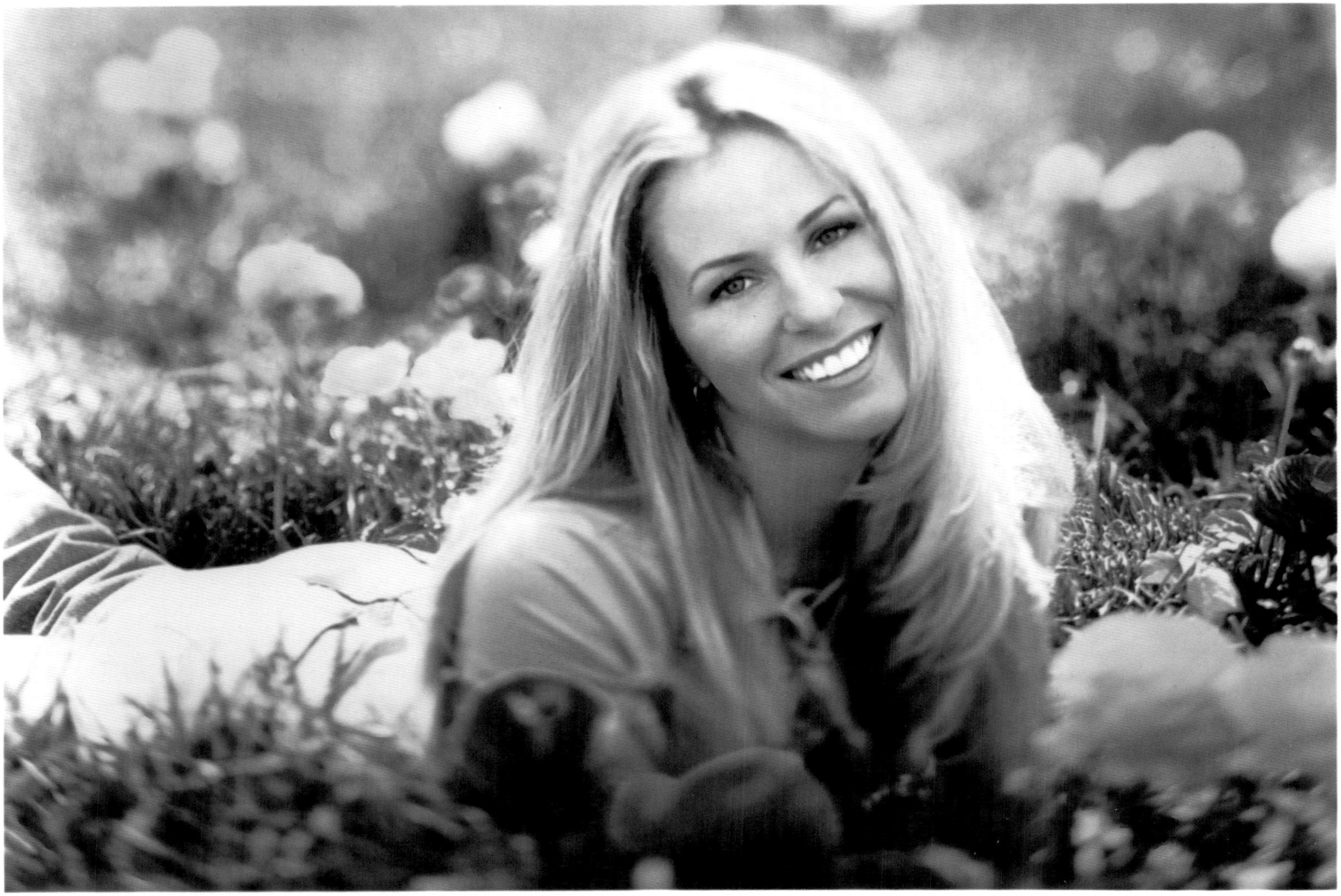

photo: Mark Tucker 7/96A

DEANA CARTER

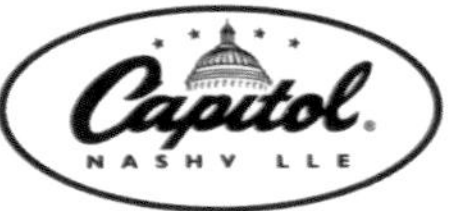

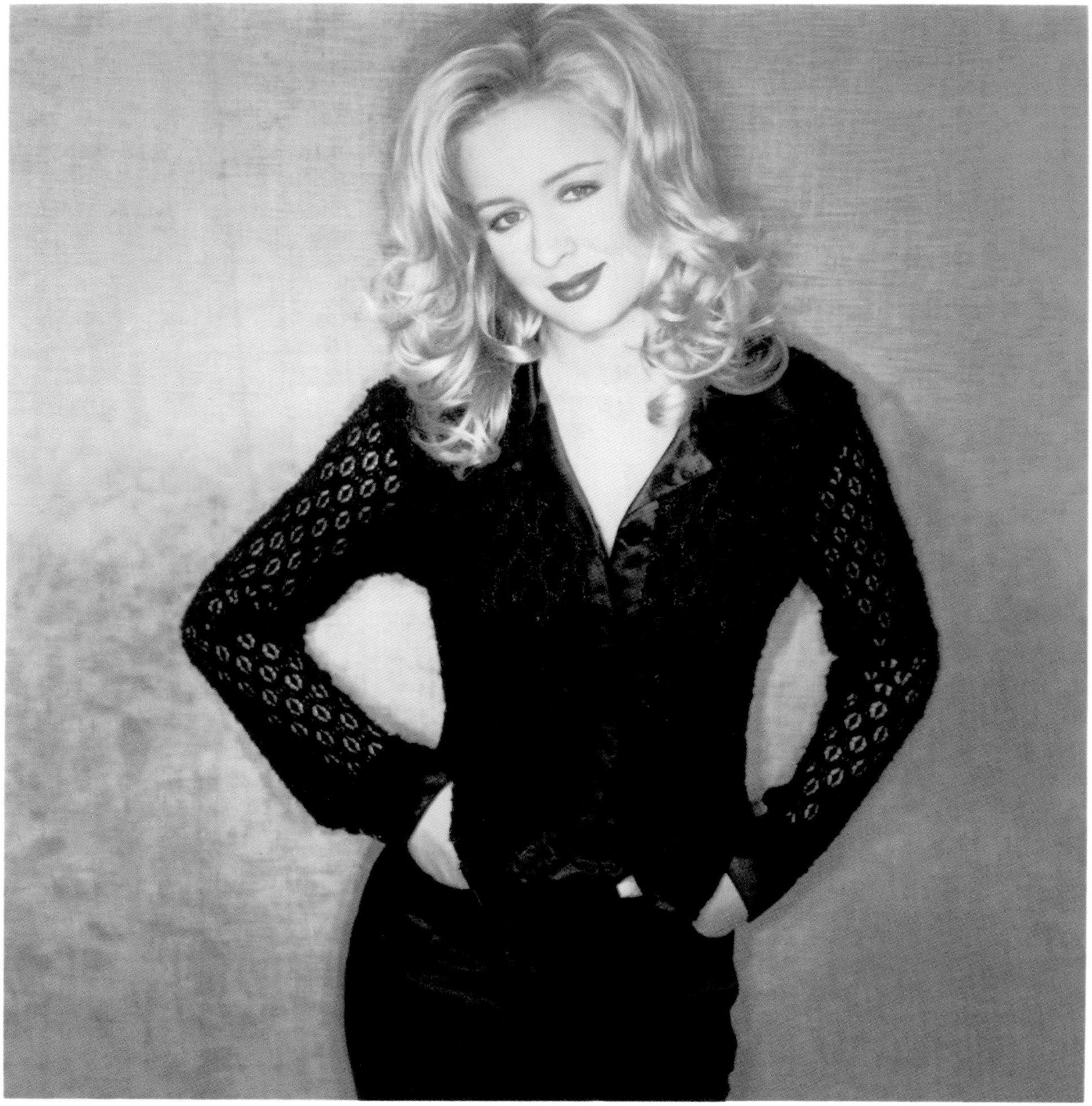

MINDY McCREADY

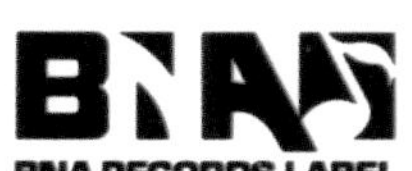


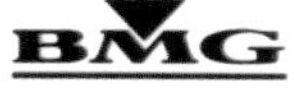

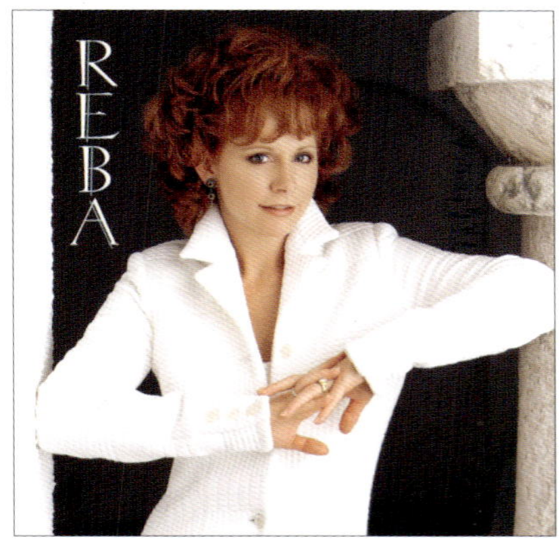


**Reba McEntire** marked another chart-topping country album with *What's If It's You*, fueled by the hits "Fear of Being Alone" and "How Was I to Know."

*Billboard* 200: *What If It's You* (#15)

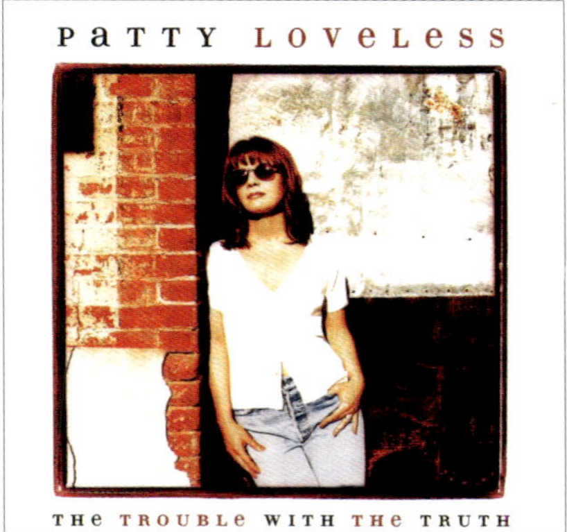


*The Trouble with the Truth* powered **Patty Loveless**' resurgence on the country charts with two No. 1 smashes, "You Can Feel Bad" and "Lonely Too Long."

*Billboard* 200: *The Trouble with the Truth* (#86)

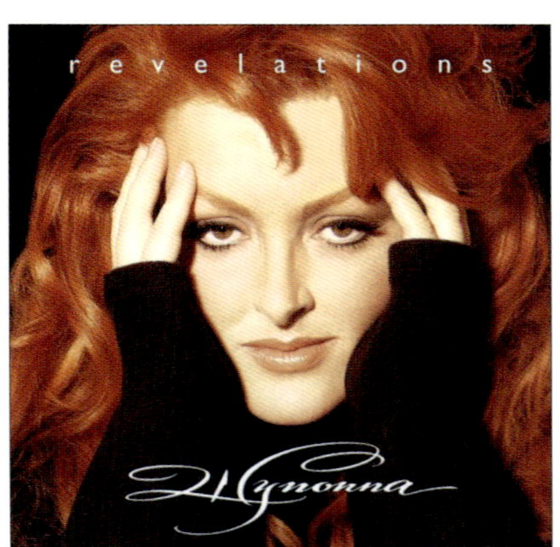


Pregnant and delaying marriage, **Wynonna** rendered songs related to her experience, and "To Be Loved by You" turned into the country singer's fourth No. 1.

*Billboard* 200: *Revelations* (#9)

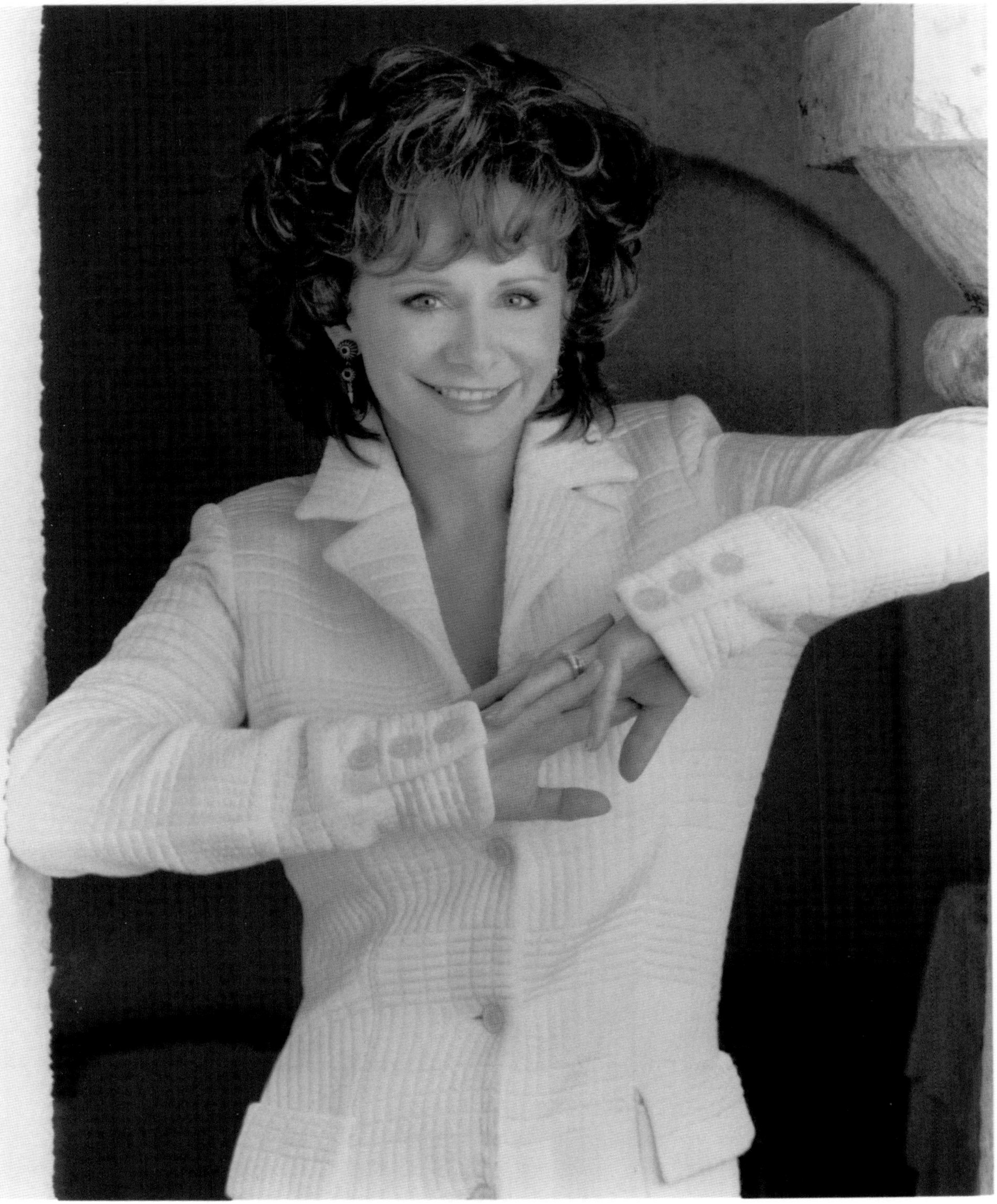

photo: Mark Tucker 1096A

REBA McENTIRE

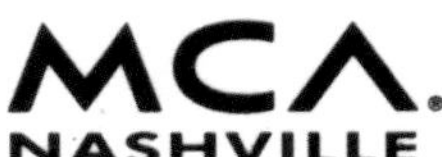

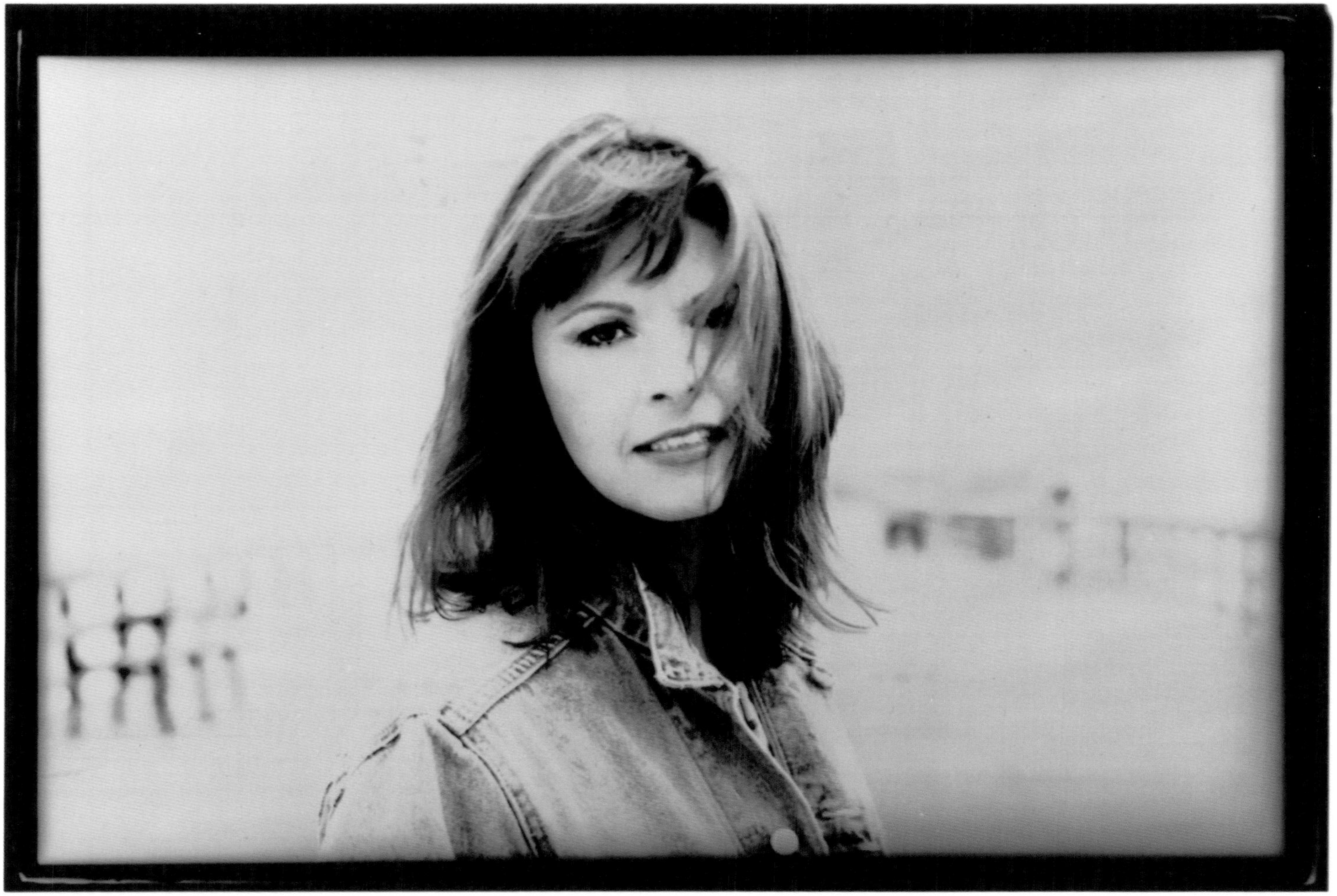

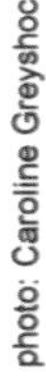


# PATTY LOVELESS

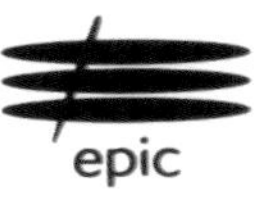




9512

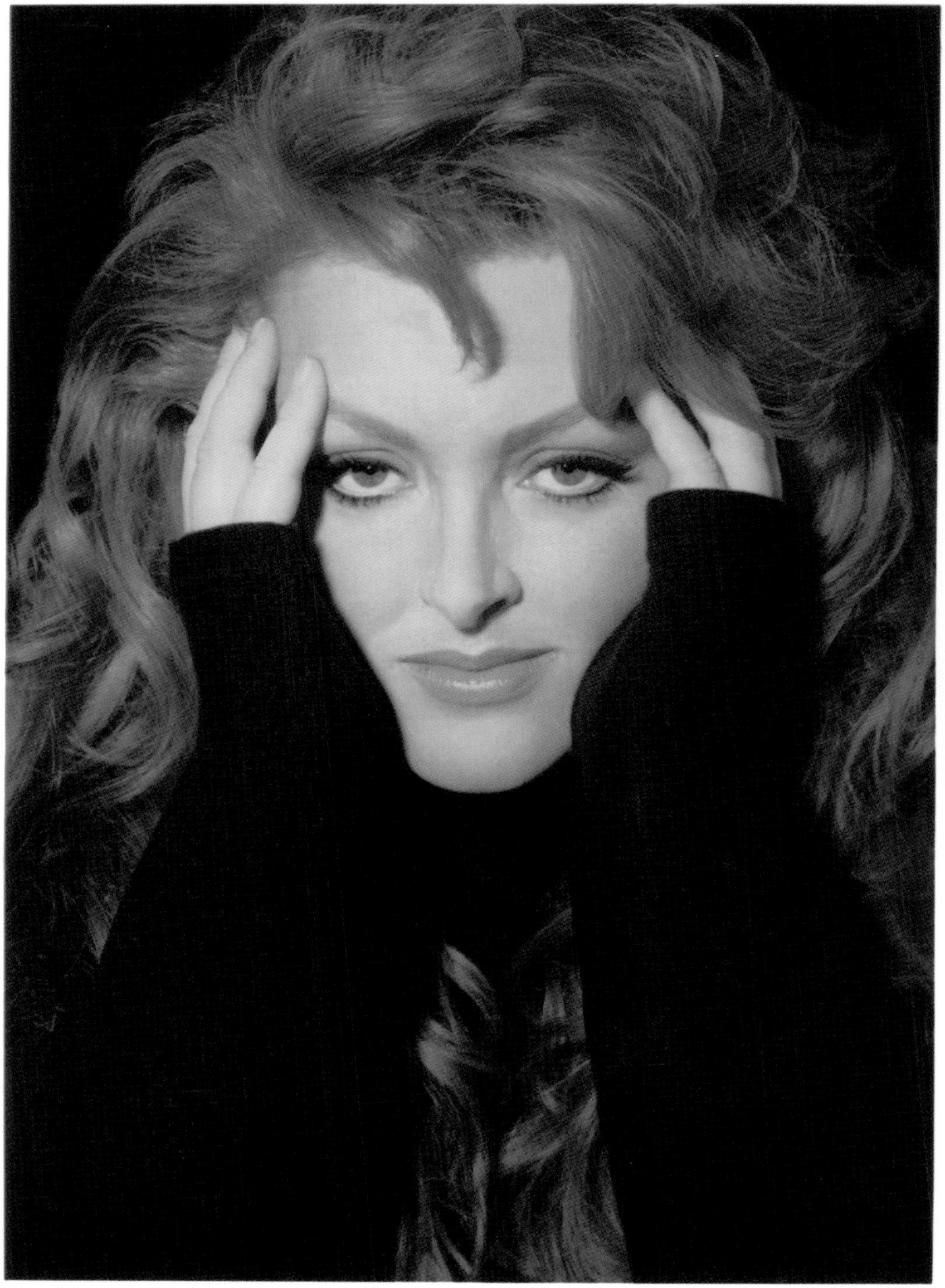

photo: Randee St. Nicholas 0196A

WYNONNA

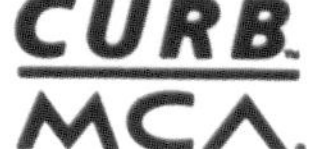

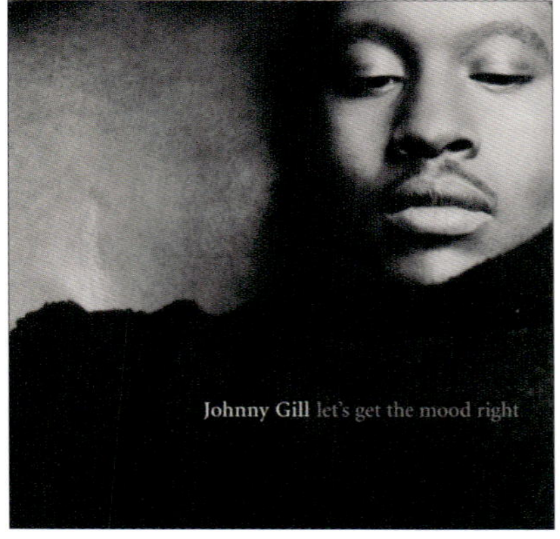


After participating in a reunion with New Edition, R&B singer **Johnny Gill** released *Let's Get the Mood Right*, further connecting him with his female fans.

*Billboard* 200: *Let's Get the Mood Right* (#32)
*Billboard* Hot 100: "Let's Get the Mood Right" (#53); "It's Your Body" (#43)

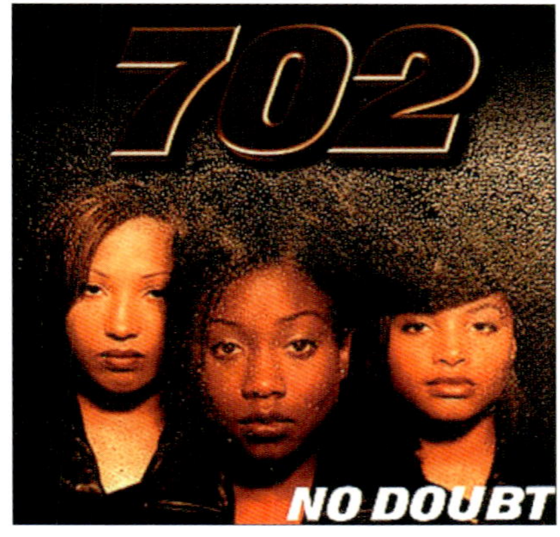


A teenage girl group from Las Vegas discovered by Michael Bivins of New Edition, **702** issued a debut single, "Steelo," followed by the *No Doubt* album.

*Billboard* 200: *No Doubt* (#82)
*Billboard* Hot 100: "Steelo" (#32); "Get It Together" (#10); "All I Want" (#35)

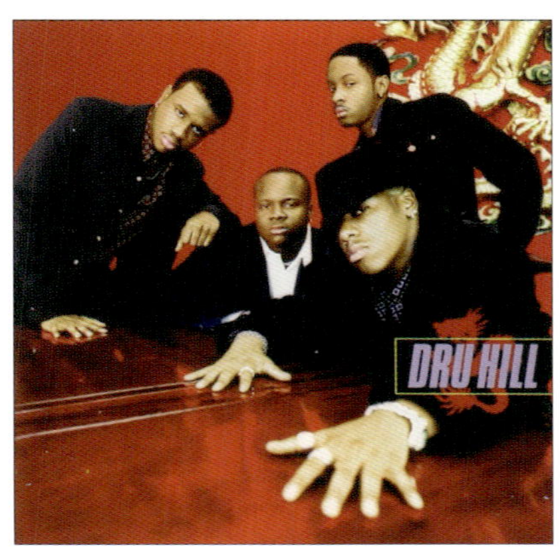


The Baltimore-based quartet **Dru Hill** earned plaudits for two No. 1 R&B smashes, the hot-blooded "In My Bed" and the fervent "Never Make a Promise."

*Billboard* 200: *Dru Hill* (#23)
*Billboard* Hot 100: "Tell Me" (#18); "In My Bed" (#4); "Never Make a Promise" (#7)

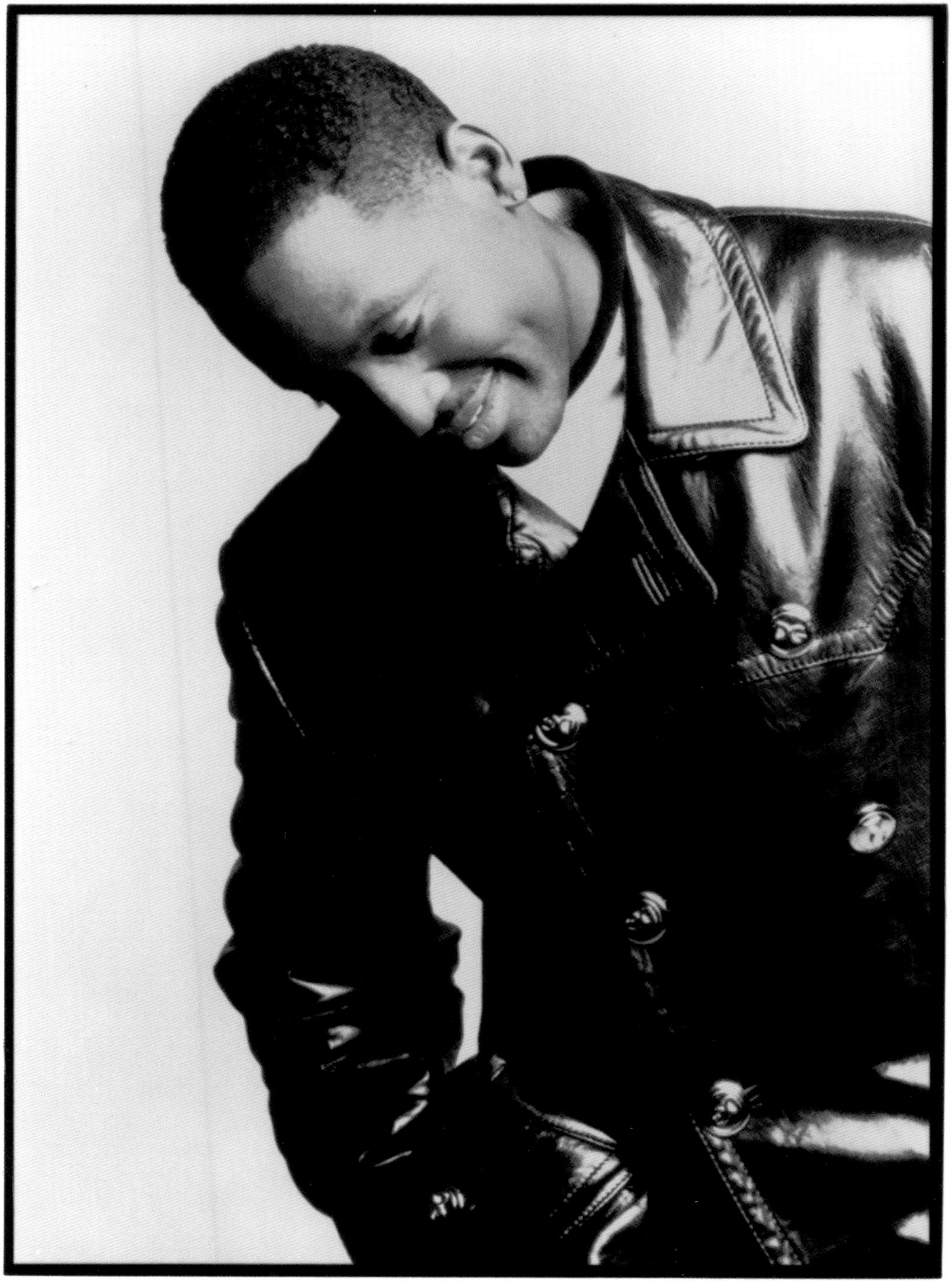

Photo credit: Carol Friedman 9/96

# JOHNNY GILL

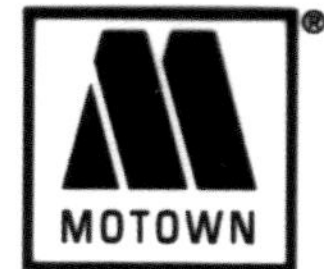

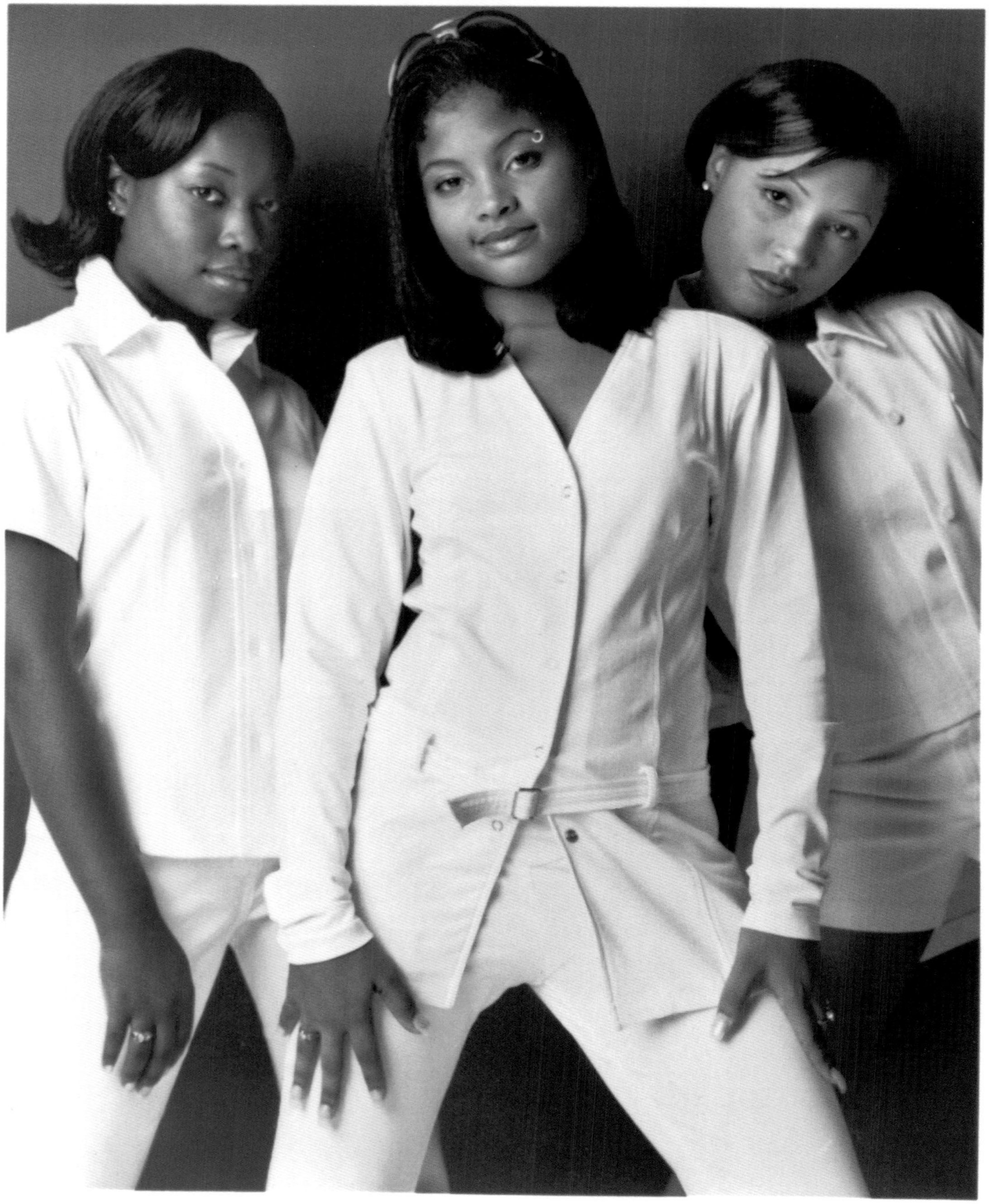

Photograph by Daniela Federici 7/96

KAMEELAH IRISH LEMISHA

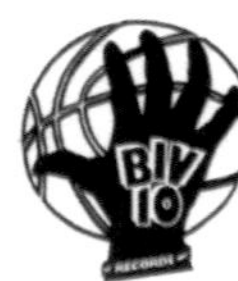


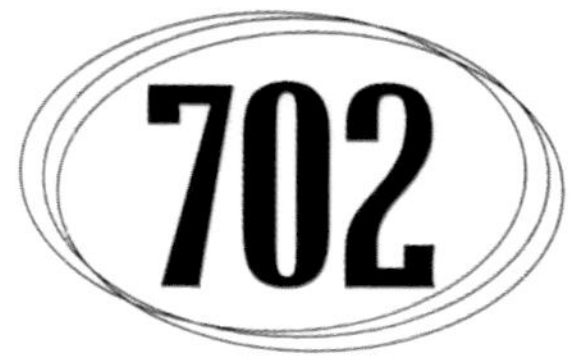


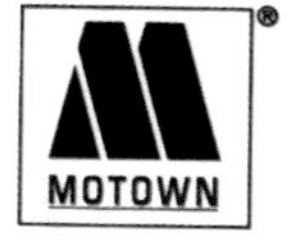

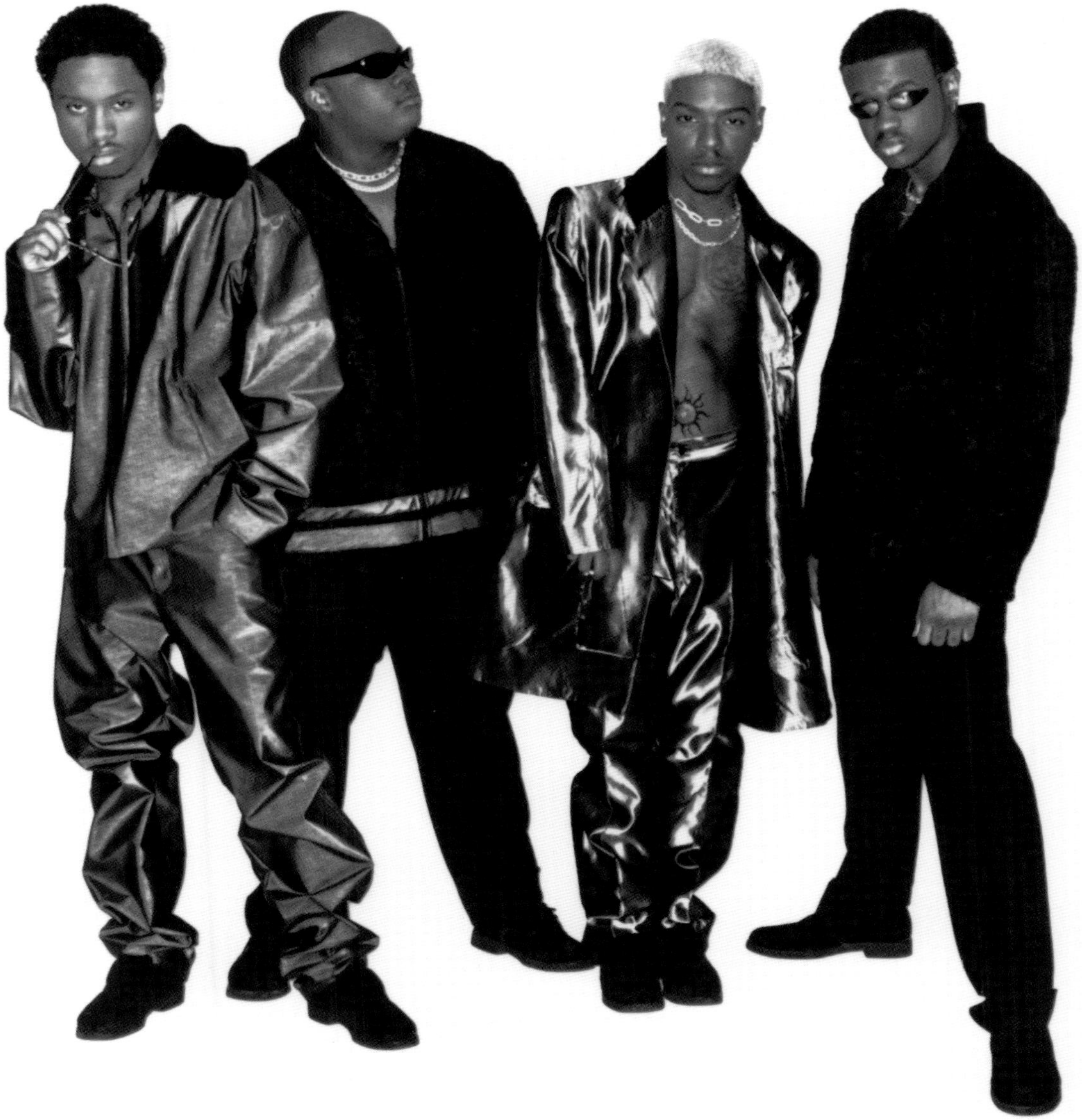

NOKIO JAZZ SISQO WOODY

PHOTO CREDIT ELI HERSHKO

# DRU HILL

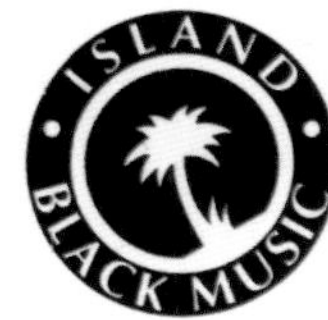

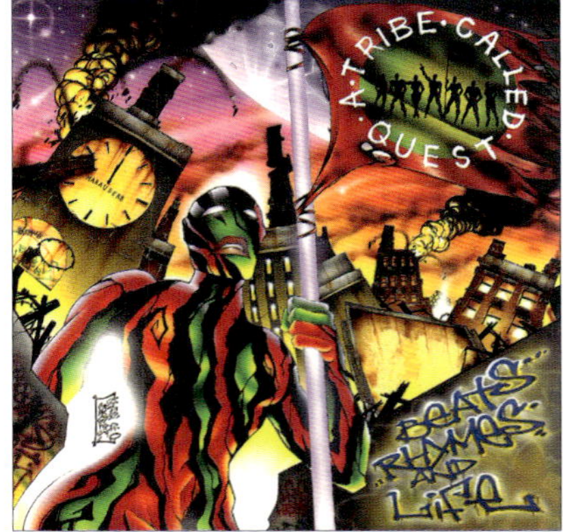


*Beats, Rhymes and Life*, **A Tribe Called Quest**'s fourth album, mined a jazz-flavored, R&B-fueled stylistic flow and debuted at No. 1 on the album charts.

*Billboard* 200: *Beats, Rhymes and Life* (No. 1)

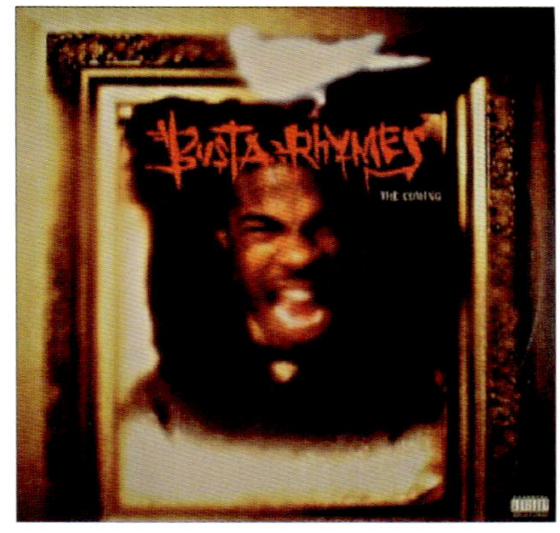


Rapper **Busta Rhymes** broke out with "Woo Hah!! Got You All in Check," a rowdy hit from his debut album that earned him his first Grammy nomination.

*Billboard* 200: *The Coming* (#6)
*Billboard* Hot 100: "Woo Hah!! Got You All in Check" (#8);
"It's a Party" (#52)

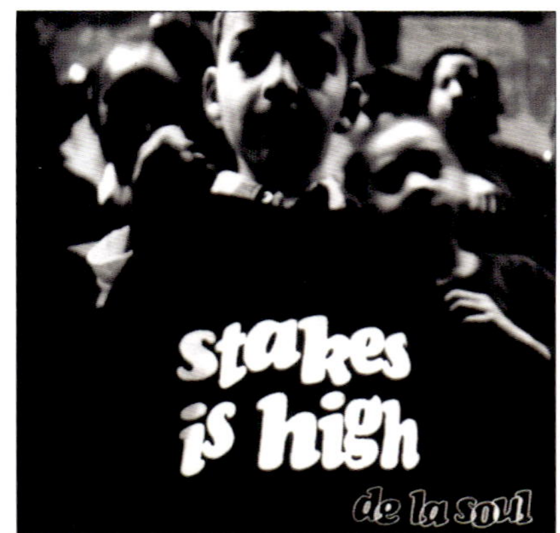


**De La Soul**'s fourth album, *Stakes Is High*, was lauded for its overarching theme, the group's consternation over the way hip-hop culture was trending.

*Billboard* 200: *Stakes Is High* (#13)

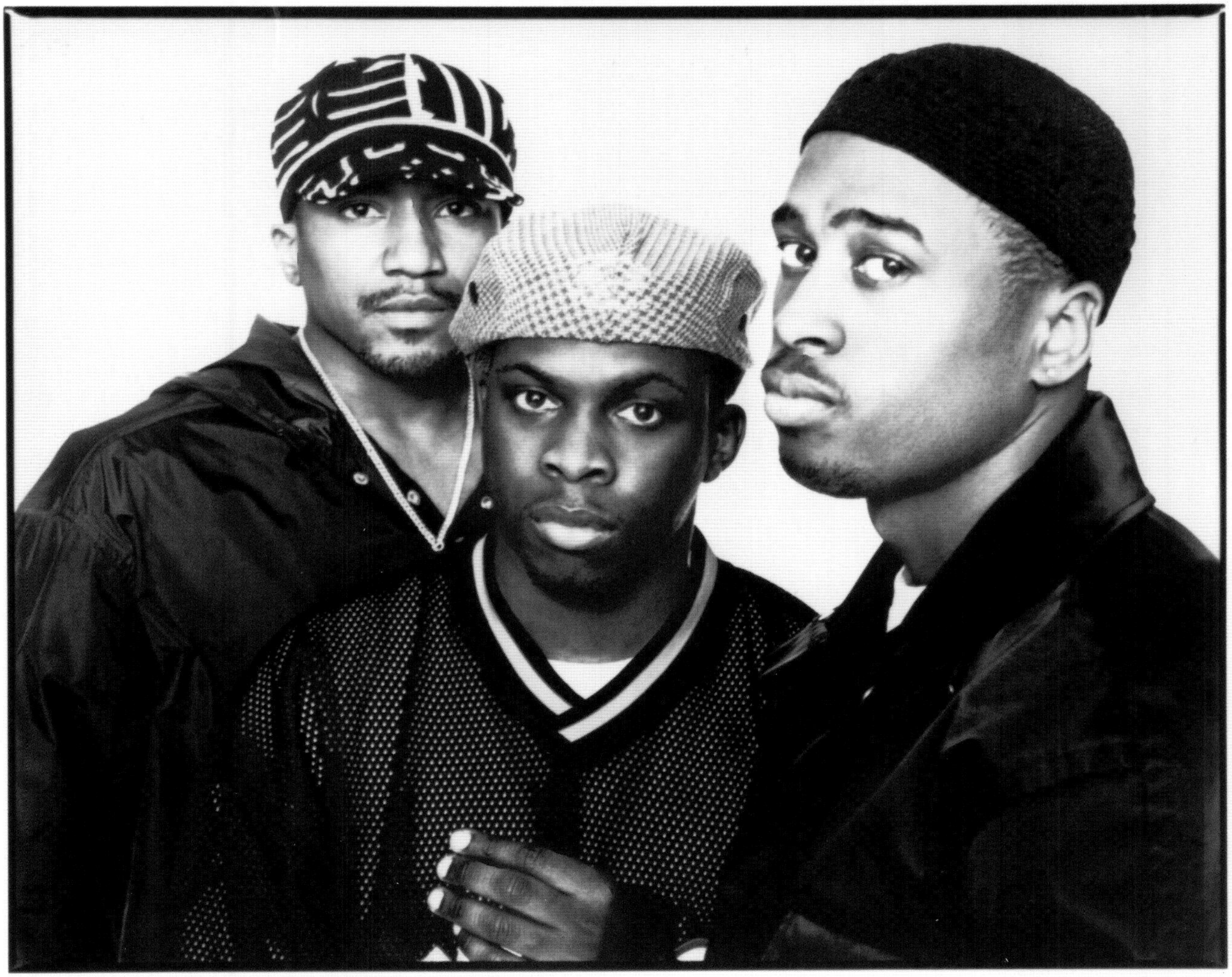

L R Q-TIP, PHIFE, ALI SHAHEED MUHAMMAD

PHOTO CREDIT CHRISTIAN LANTRY

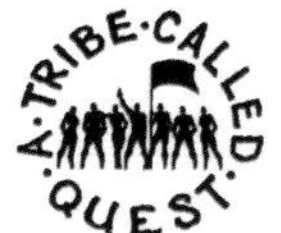


# A Tribe Called Quest

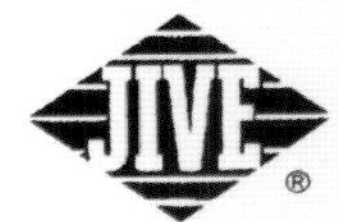

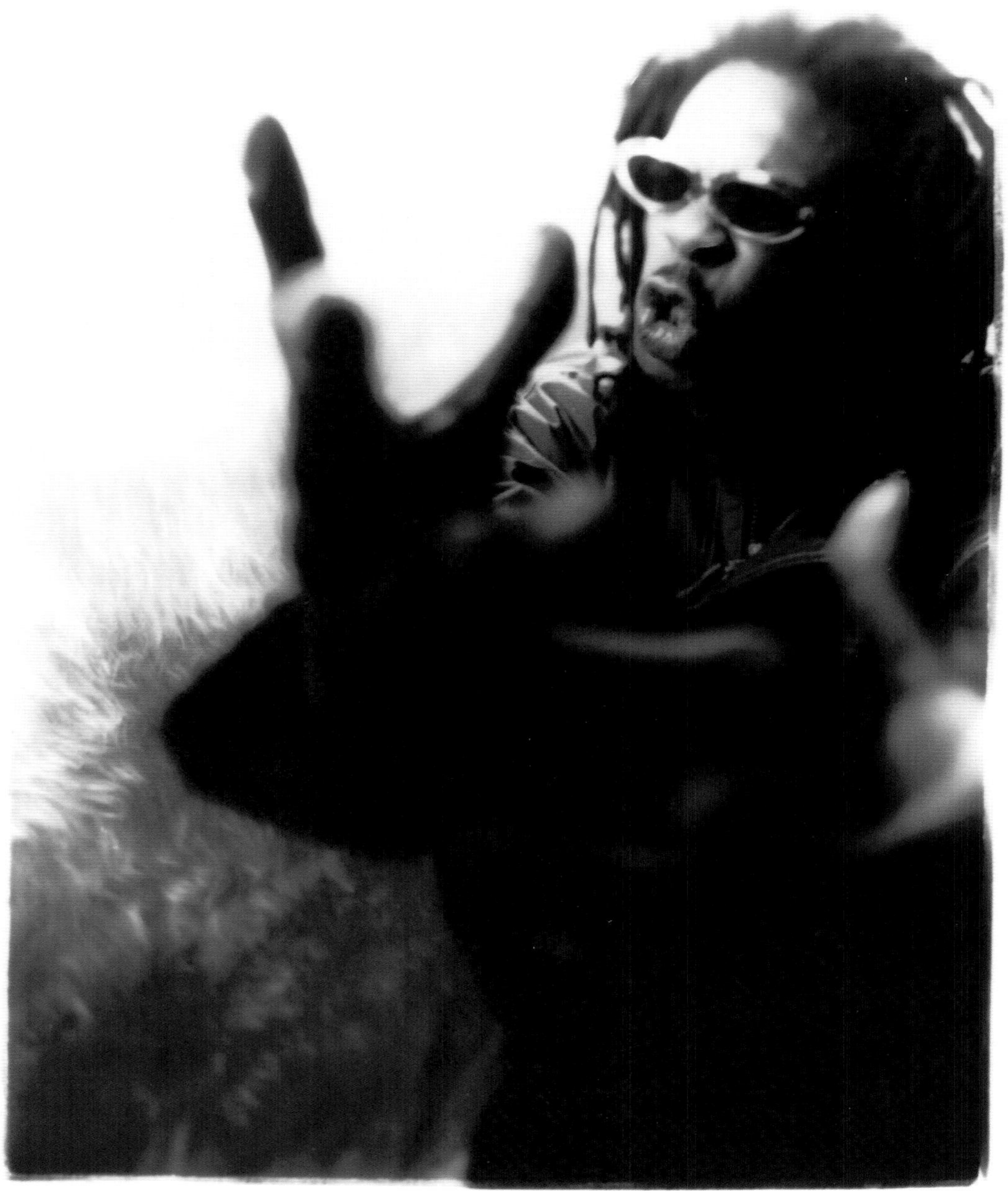

PHOTO CREDIT DEAN KARR

BUSTA RHYMES

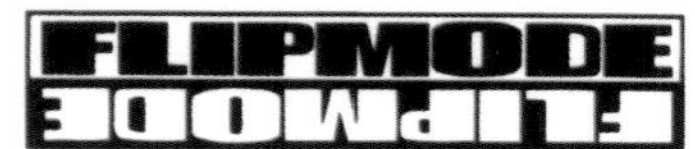


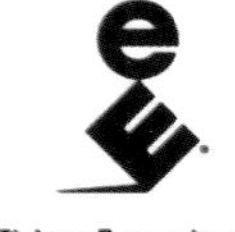

Elektra Entertainment

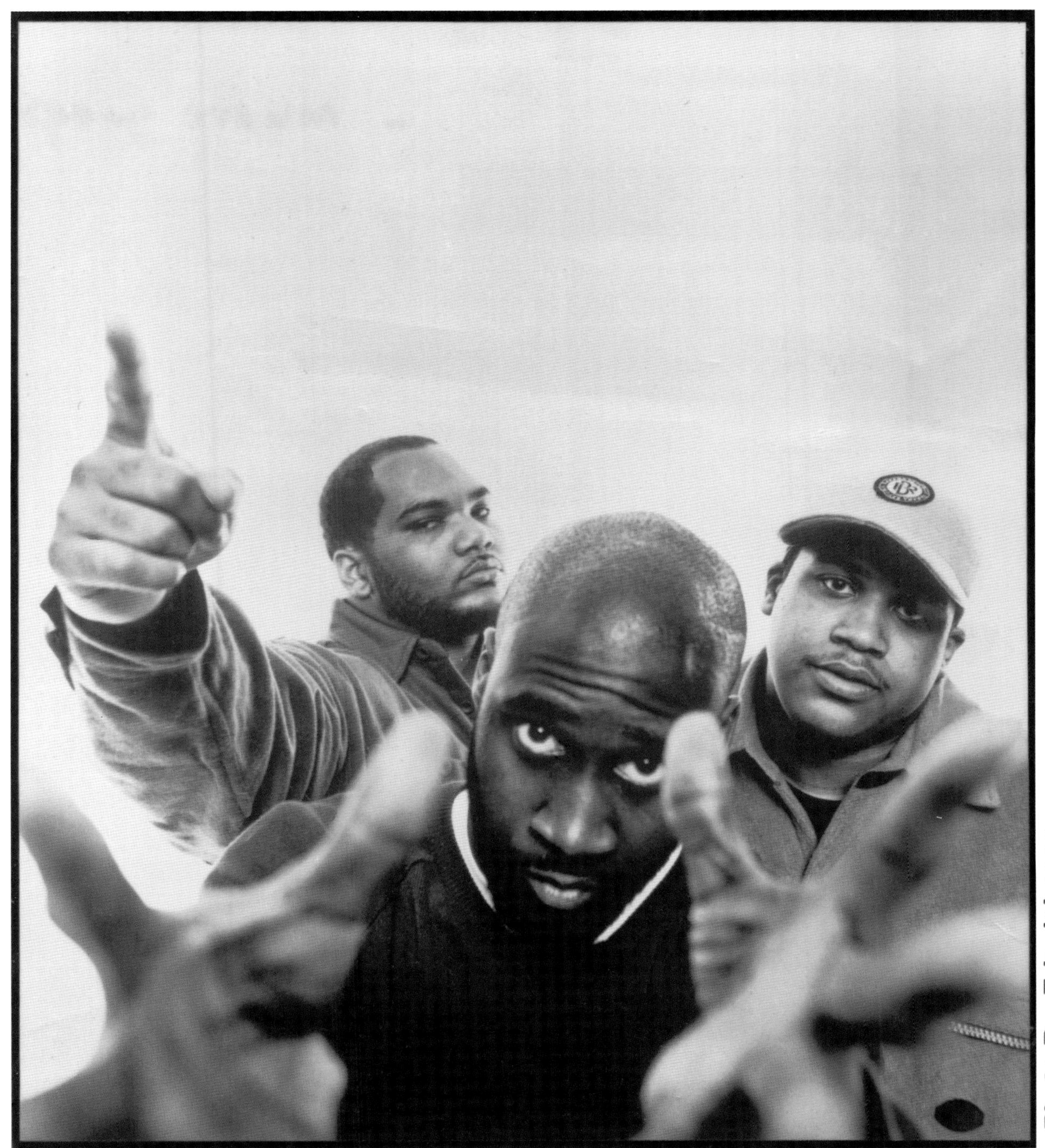

Photo By: Eric Johnson

de la soul

Tommy Boy

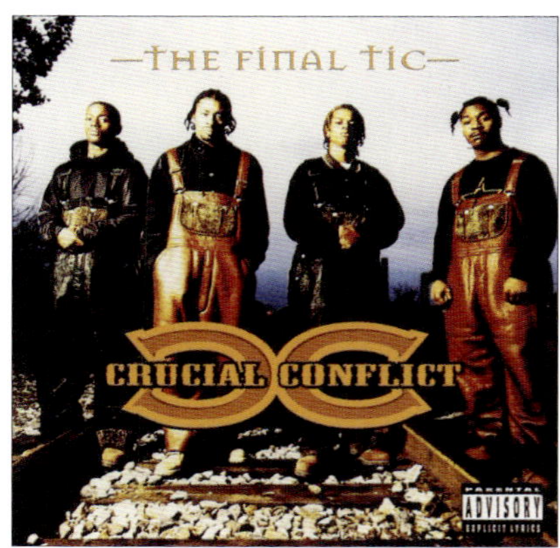


A hip-hop outfit from urban Chicago professing to an Old West vibe, **Crucial Conflict** lauded the pleasures of marijuana with "Hay," a breakthrough hit.

*Billboard* 200: *The Final Tic* (#12)
*Billboard* Hot 100: "Hay" (#18)

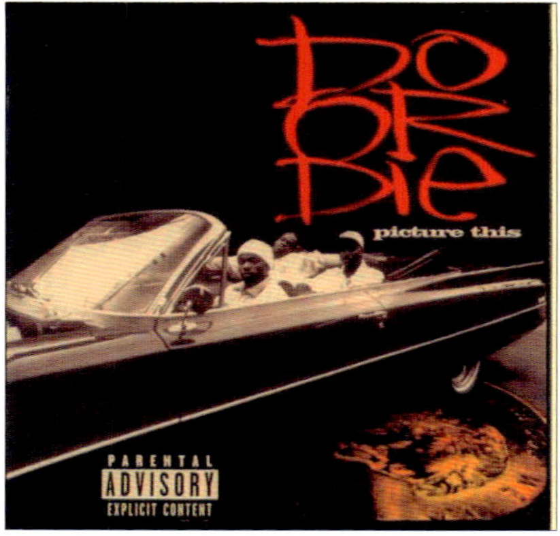


Originally issued on a tiny label in **Do or Die**'s native Chicago, the single "Po Pimp" became a mainstream hit for the rap trio with its nationwide release.

*Billboard* 200: *Picture This* (#27)
*Billboard* Hot 100 "Po Pimp" (#22)

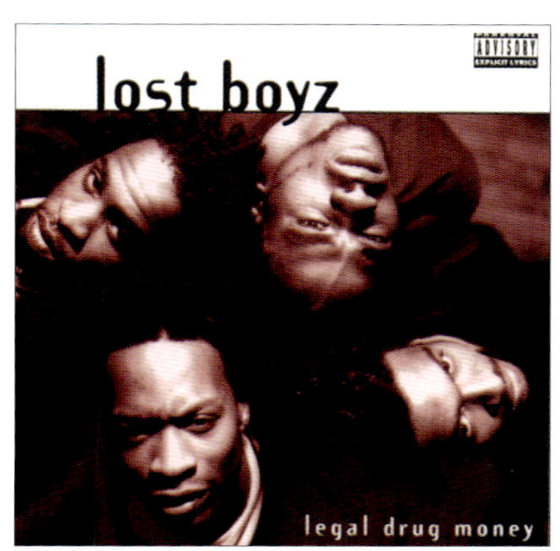


A crew from South Jamaica, Queens, **Lost Boyz** materialized with a debut album that yielded five hit singles, notably the hip-hop narrative "Renee."

*Billboard* 200: *Legal Drug Money* (#6)
*Billboard* Hot 100: "Lifestyles of the Rich & Shameless" (#91); "Jeeps, Lex Coups, Bimaz & Benz" (#67); "Renee" (#33); "Music Makes Me High" (#51); "Get Up" (#60)

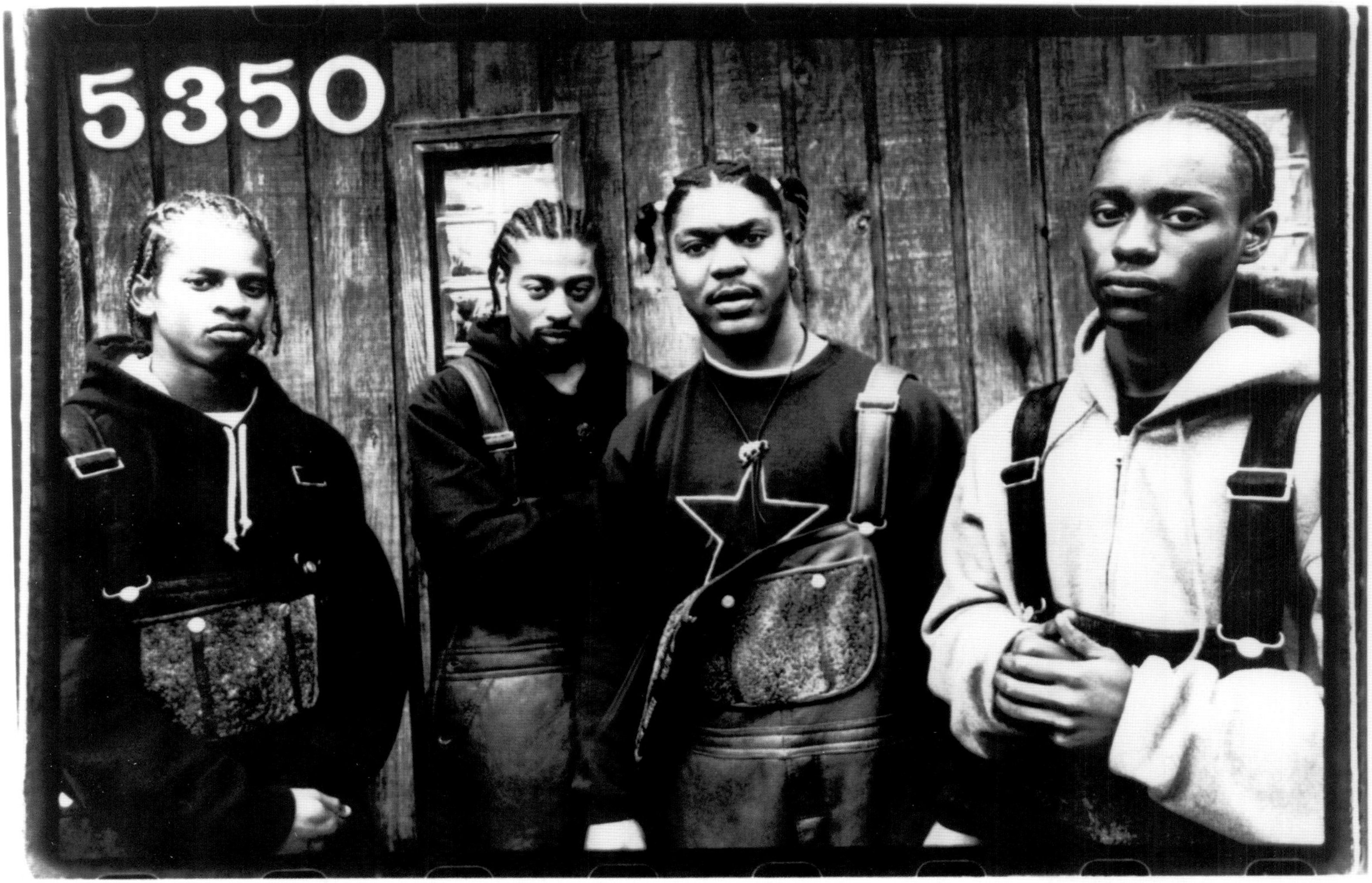

5350

Photo by DANIEL HASTINGS / CARTEL

WILD STYLE KILO COLD HARD NEVER

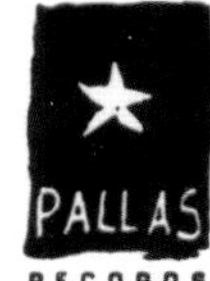


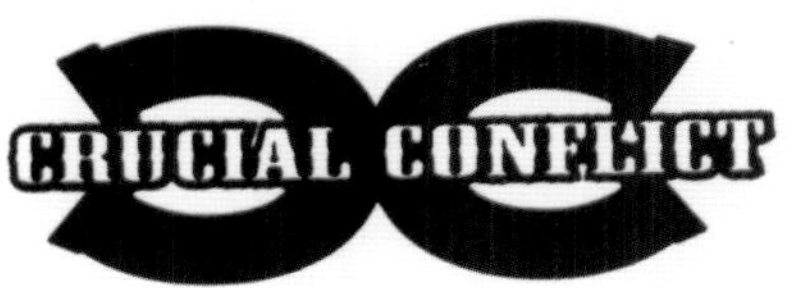

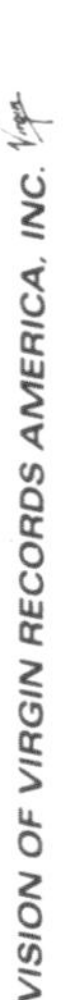

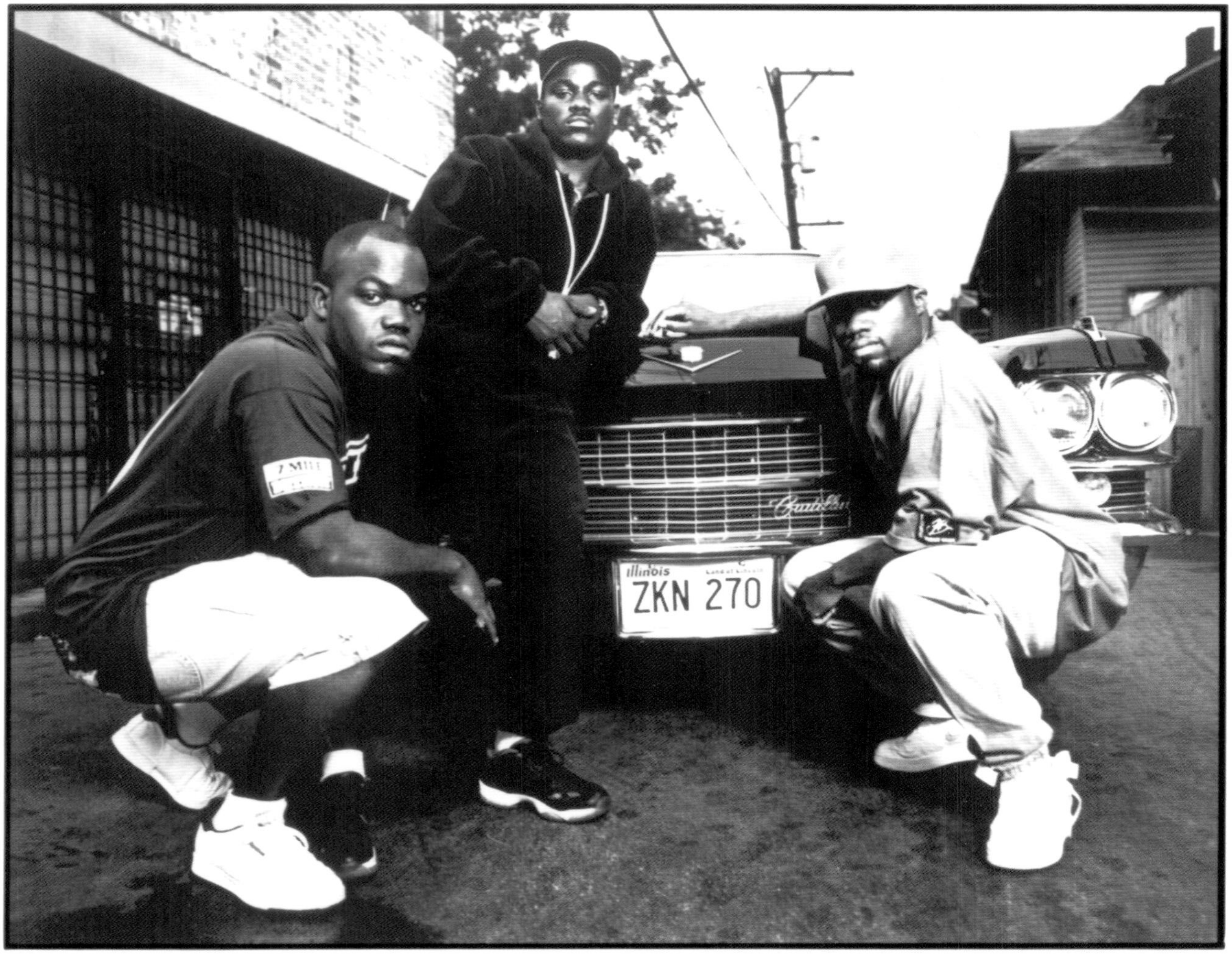

Photo Credit: Denise Milford 7/96

# DO OR DIE

neighborhood
watch records

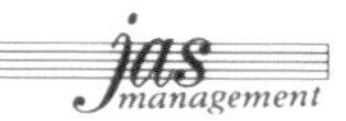


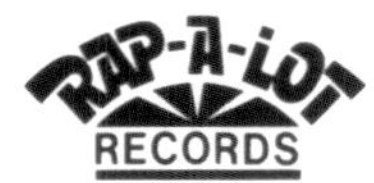


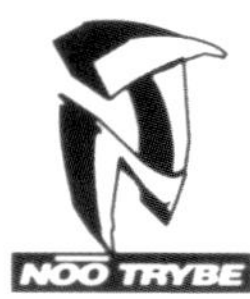

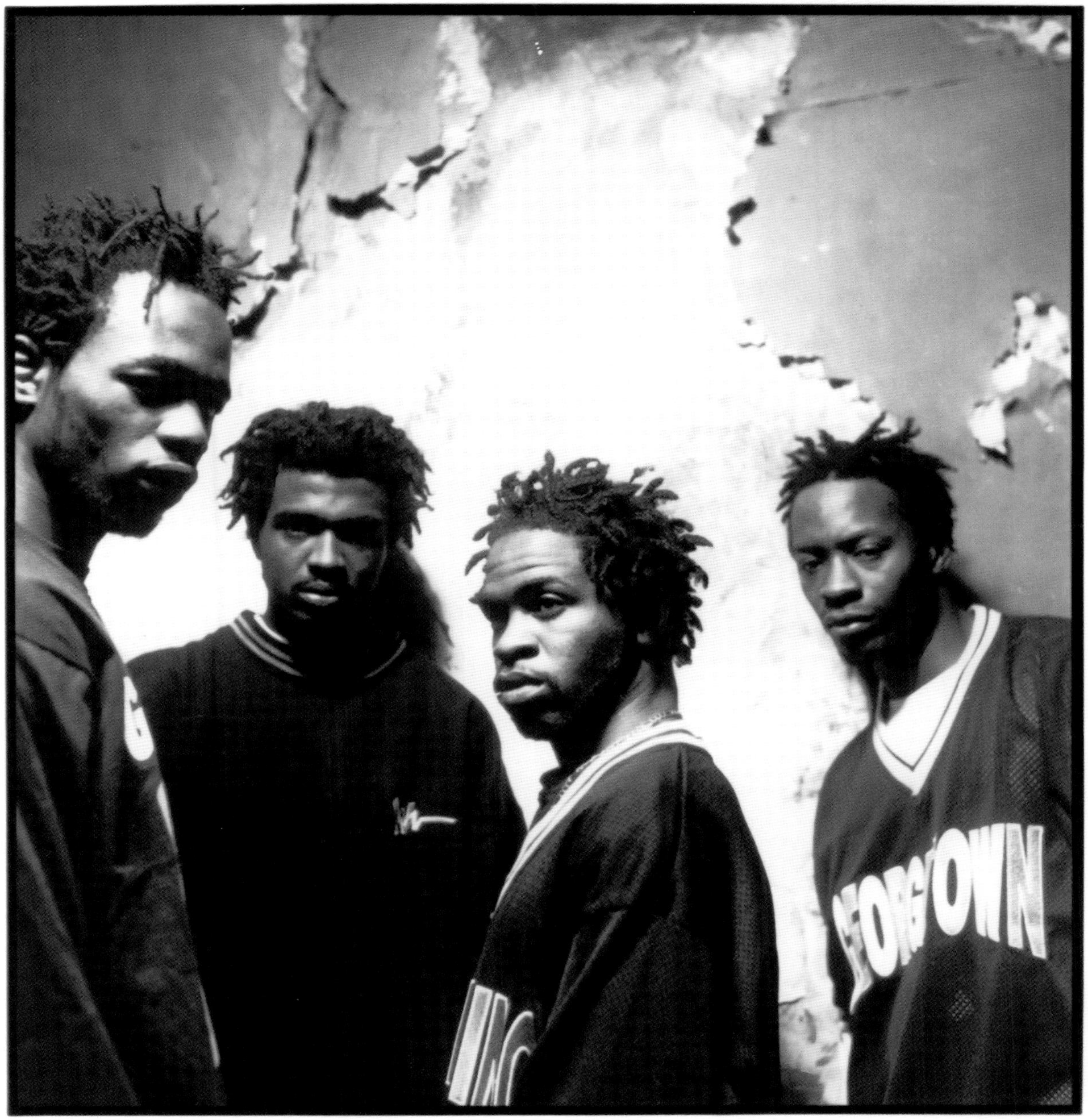

Photo credit: Danny Clinch

FREAKY TAH PRETTY LOU DJ SPIGG NICE MR. CHEEKS

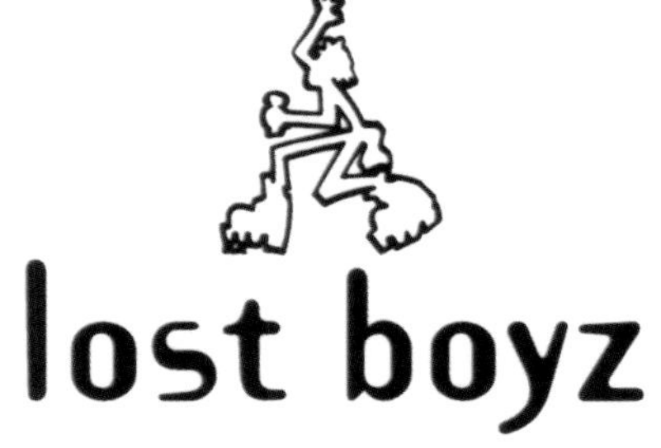


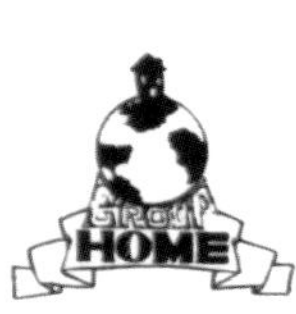


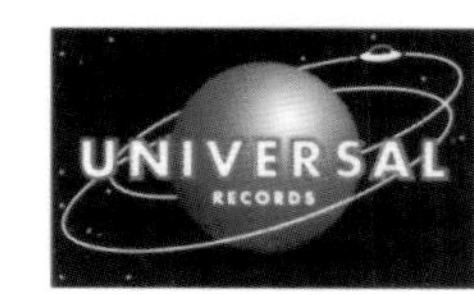

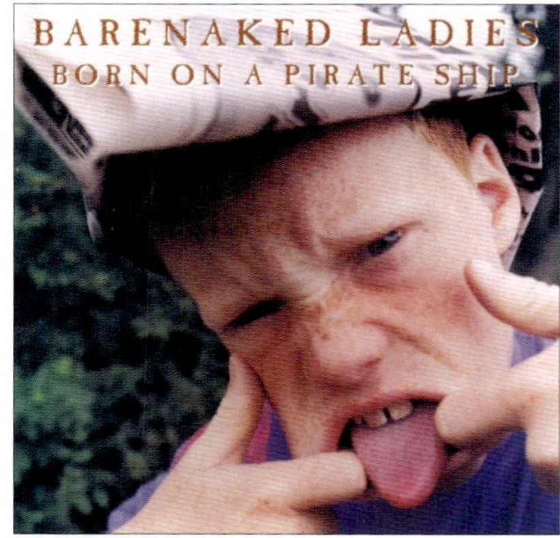


Lifted by a charting single, the wistful "The Old Apartment," **Barenaked Ladies**' fame spread from their native Canada to the US with *Born on a Pirate Ship*.

*Billboard* 200: *Born on a Pirate Ship* (#111)

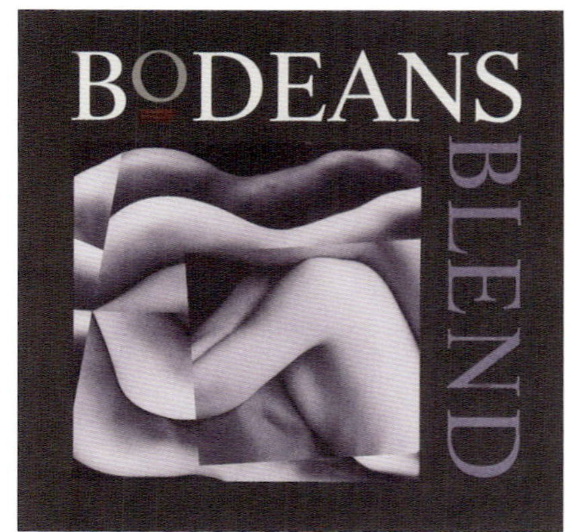


With "Closer to Free" becoming a hit three years after its initial release as the theme song for the TV show *Party of Five*, **Bodeans** retrenched on *Blend*.

*Billboard* 200: *Blend* (#132)

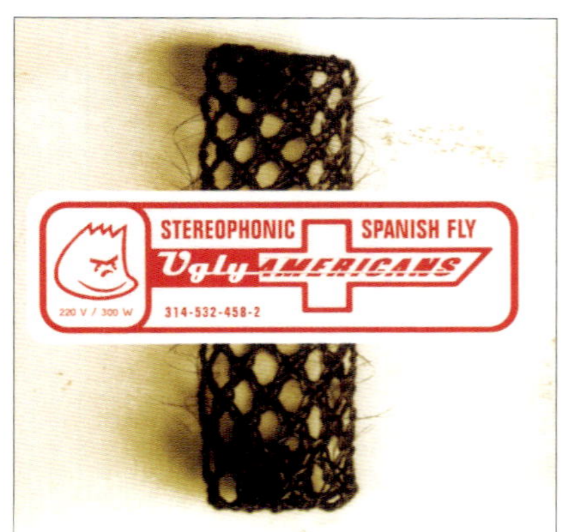


Fronted by the magnetic Bob Schneider, Austin-based **Ugly Americans** flashed rock, soul and funk elements, impressing with the hooky "Vulcan Death Grip."

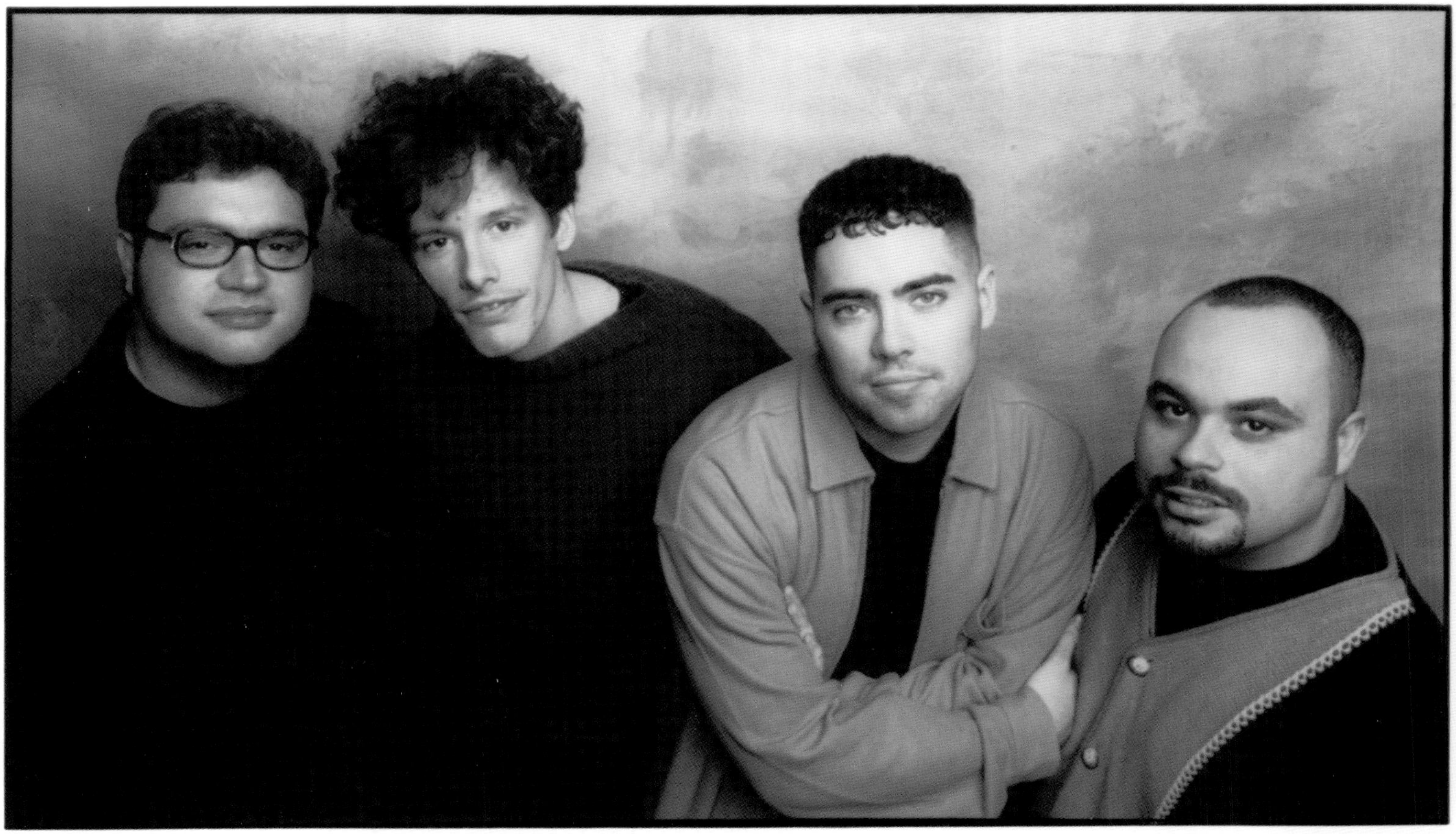

PHOTO CREDIT: Andrew MacNaughtan

# BARENAKED LADIES

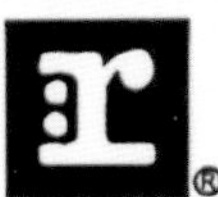

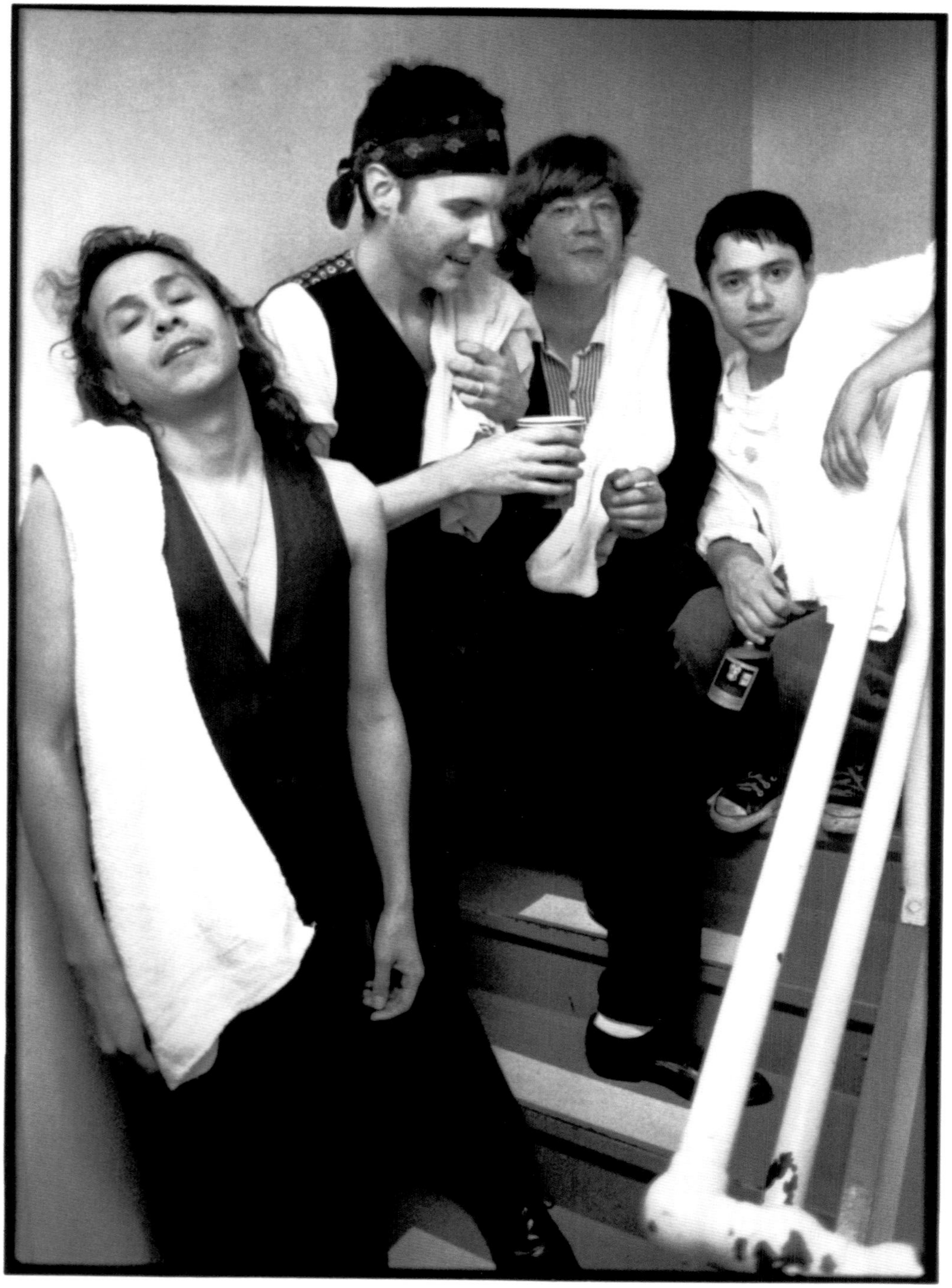

Photo Credit: John Unger

# BoDEANS

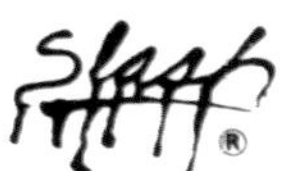

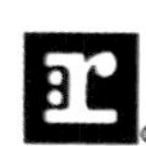

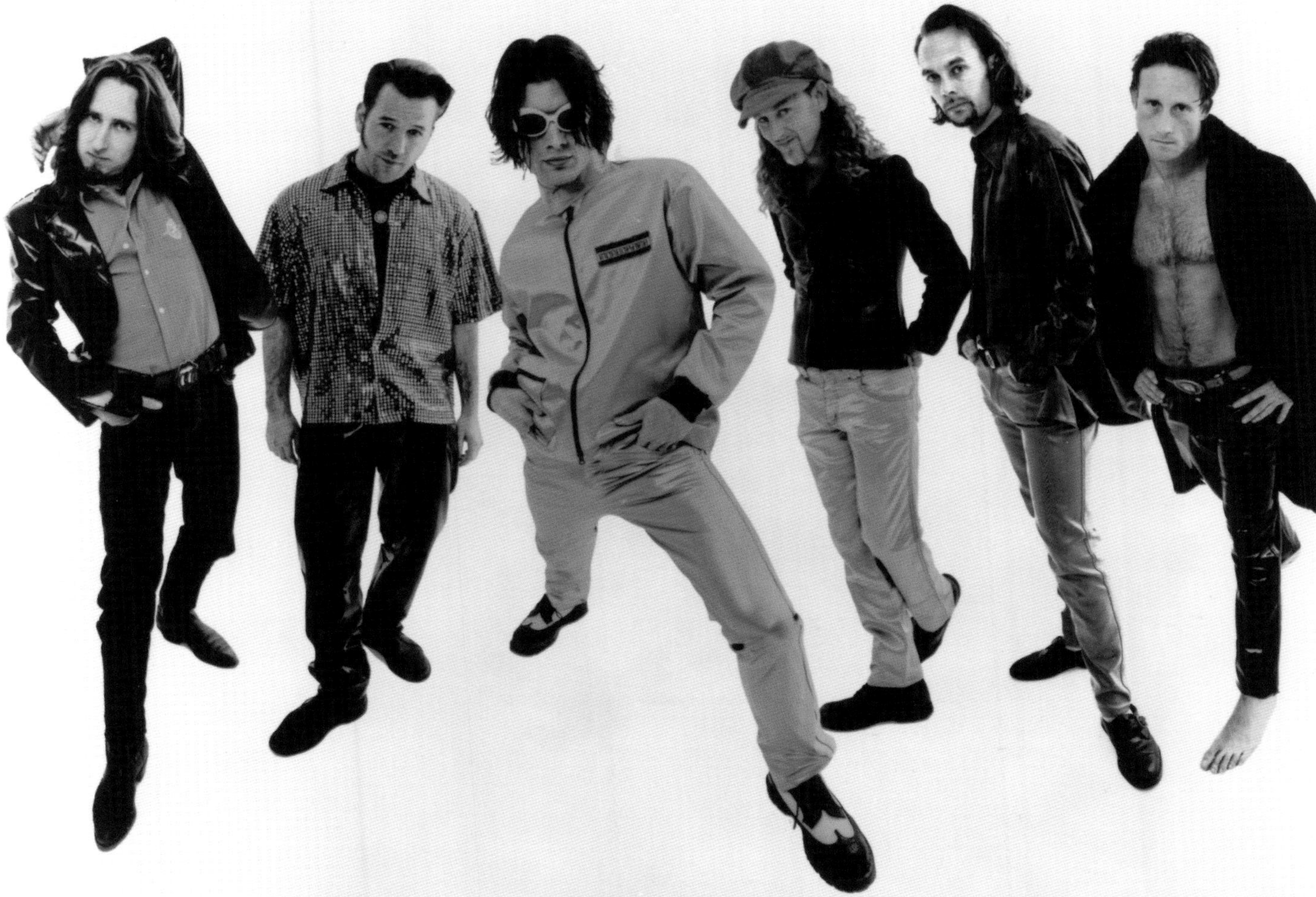

Photo: JIMMY BRUCH (01)

DAVID BOYLE MAX EVANS BOB SCHNEIDER BRUCE HUGHES SEAN McCARTHY DAVE ROBINSON

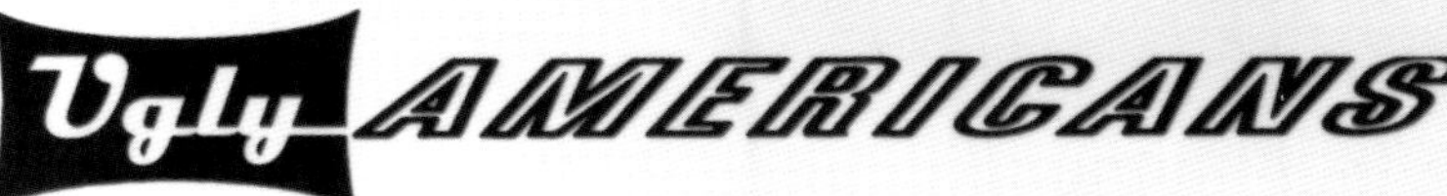


2205 STATE STREET, NASHVILLE, TN 37203 (615)320-8470


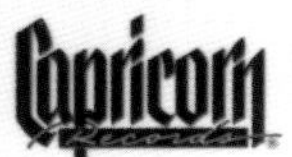

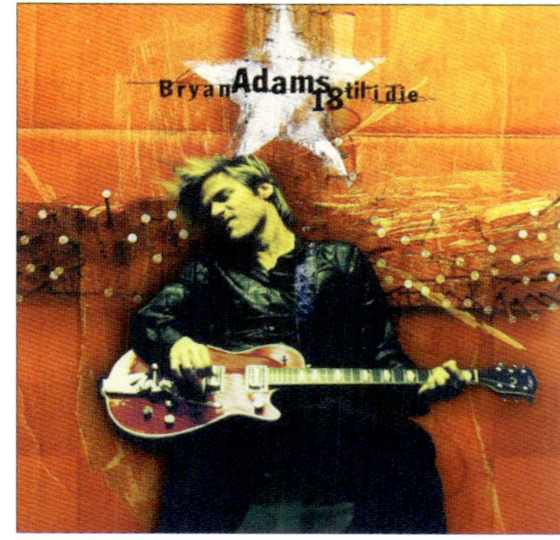


*18 Til I Die* featured yet another movie soundtrack hit for **Bryan Adams**, the No. 1 "Have You Ever Really Loved a Woman?" from *Don Juan DeMarco*.

*Billboard* 200: *18 Til I Die* (#31)
*Billboard* Hot 100: "Have You Ever Really Loved a Woman?" (No. 1);
"The Only Thing That Looks Good on Me Is You" (#52);
"Let's Make It a Night to Remember" (#24)

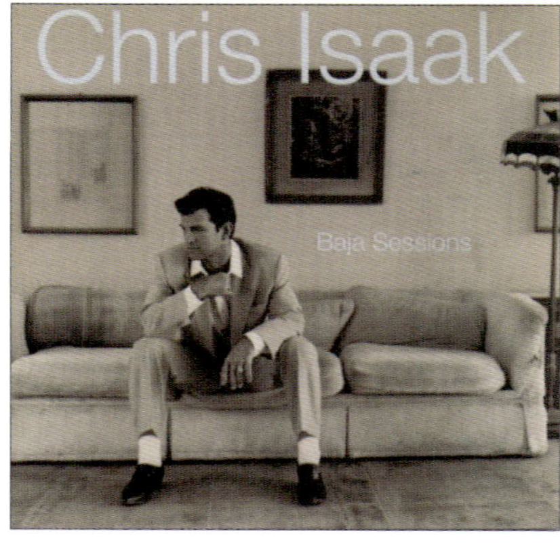


A sunny, sentimental musical travelogue, **Chris Isaak**'s *Baja Sessions* tackled cover songs, reworked versions of his early material and a few new originals.

*Billboard* 200: *Baja Sessions* (#33)

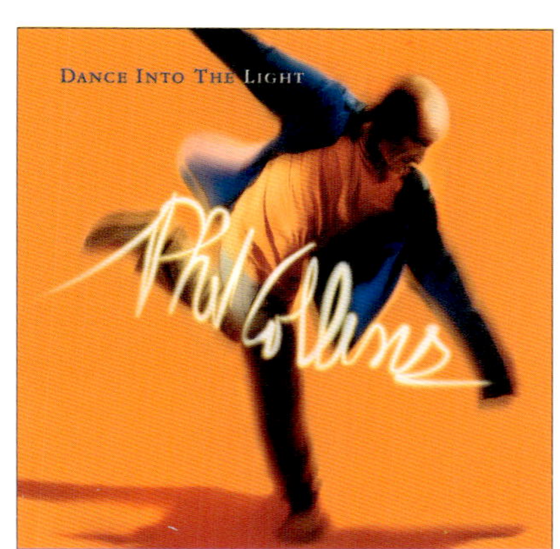


**Phil Collins**' sixth album, *Dance into the Light*, was the British musician's first as a full-time solo artist, having closed out his 25-year tenure in Genesis.

*Billboard* 200: *Dance into the Light* (#23)
*Billboard* Hot 100: "Dance into the Light" (#45);
"It's in Your Eyes" (#77)

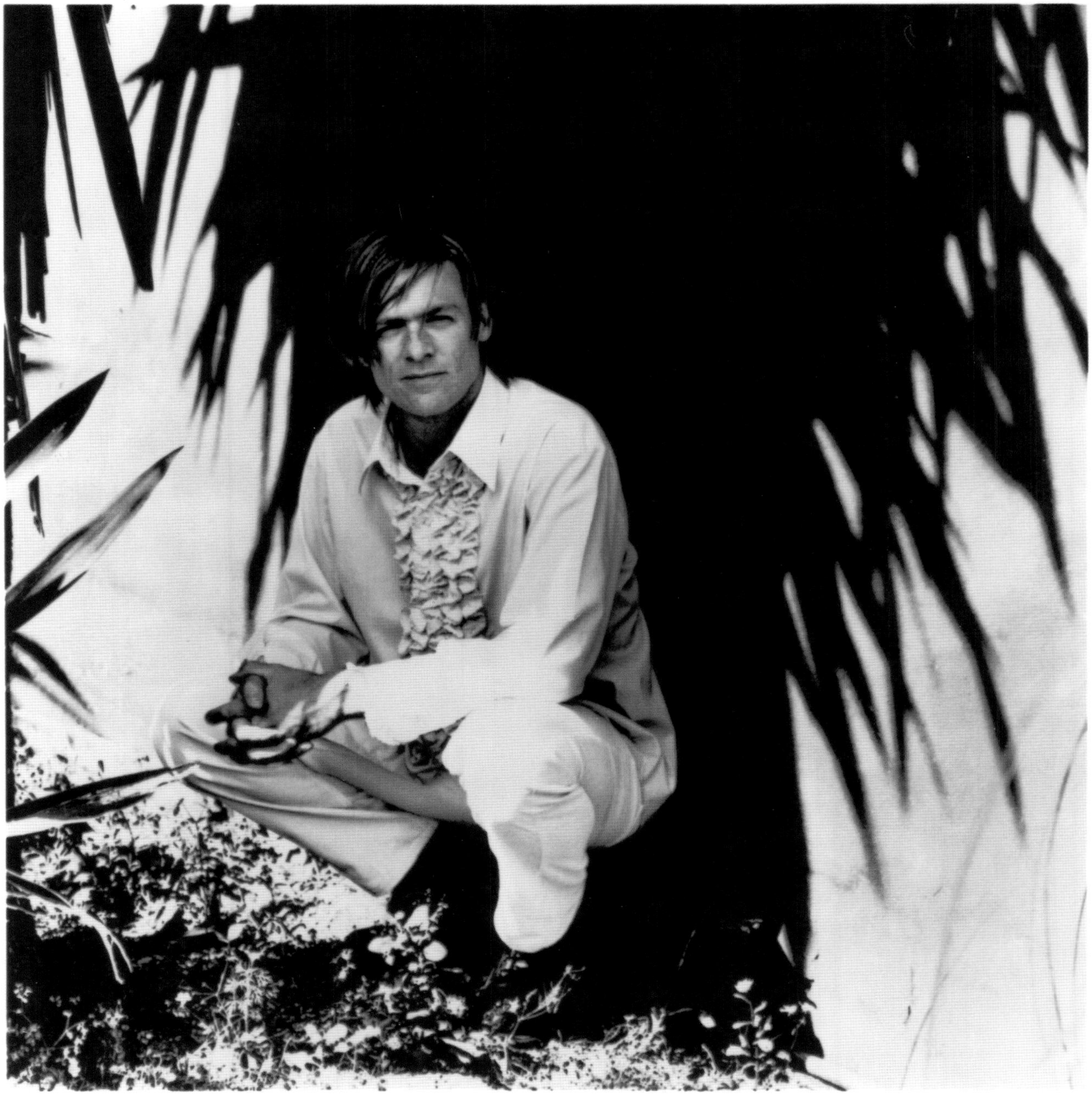

Photo: Anton Corbijn 5/95

**BRYAN ADAMS**

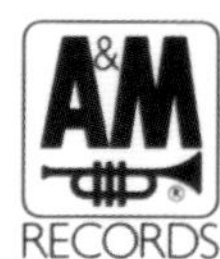

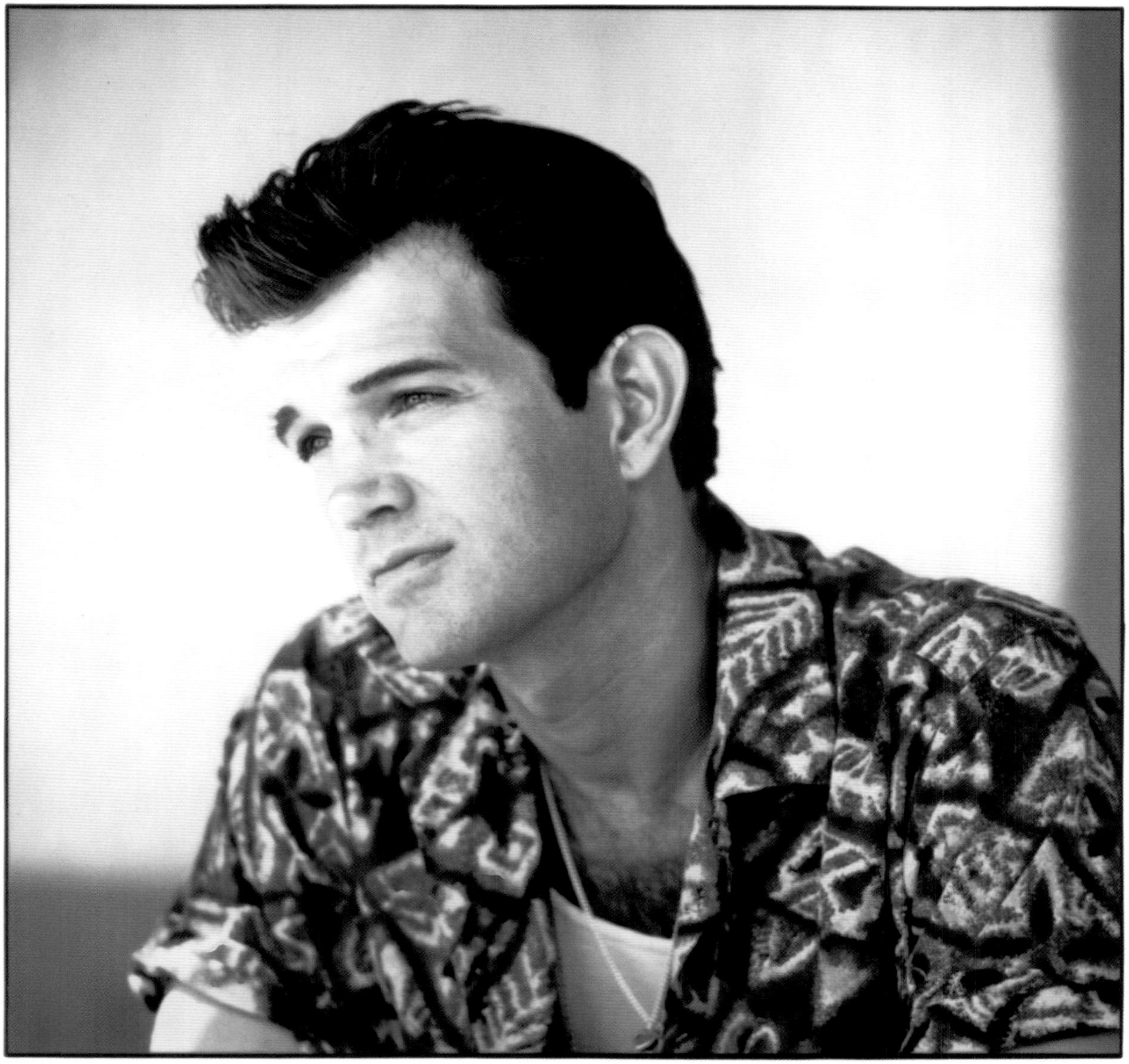

Photo Credit: Aaron Chang

# Chris Isaak

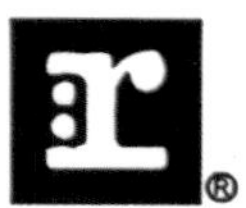

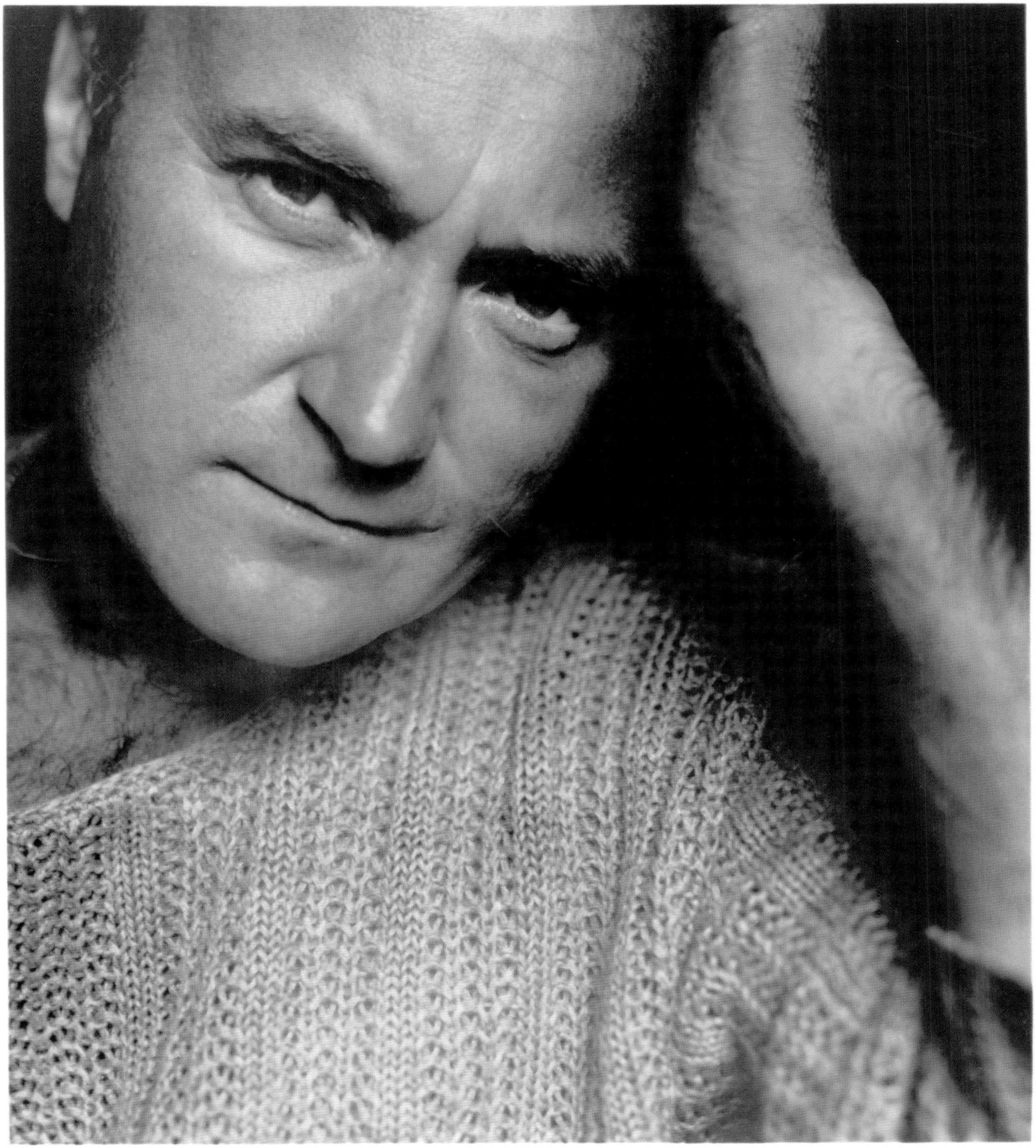

Photo Credit: Julian Broad

# phil collins

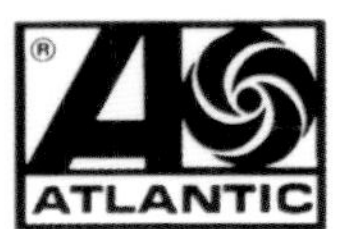

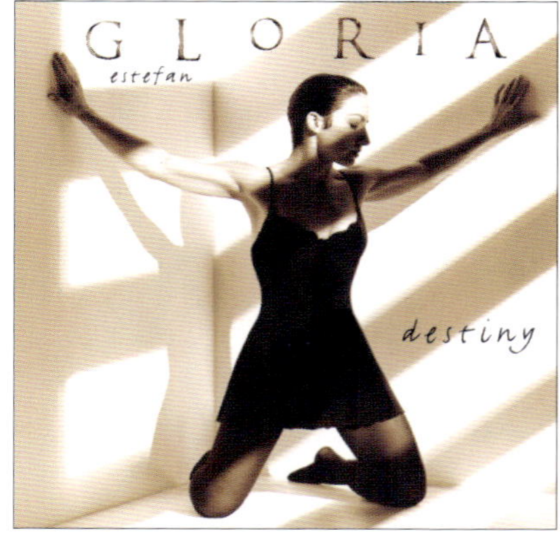


**Gloria Estefan**'s "Reach," selected as the theme of the 1996 Summer Olympics in Atlanta, was performed by the Latin pop star at the closing ceremony.

*Billboard* 200: *Destiny* (#23)
*Billboard* Hot 100: "Reach" (#42);
"You'll Be Mine (Party Time)" (#70); "I'm Not Giving You Up" (#40)

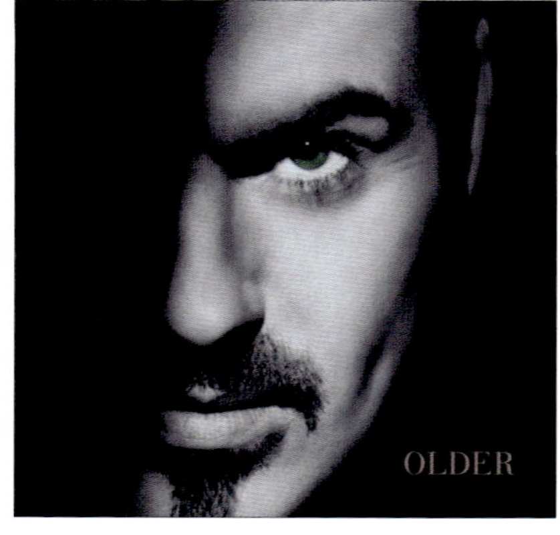


Subsequent to a long legal battle with his former record company, **George Michael** produced the somber *Older* and several international hit singles.

*Billboard* 200: *Older* (#6)
*Billboard* Hot 100: "Jesus to a Child" (#7); "Fastlove" (#8)

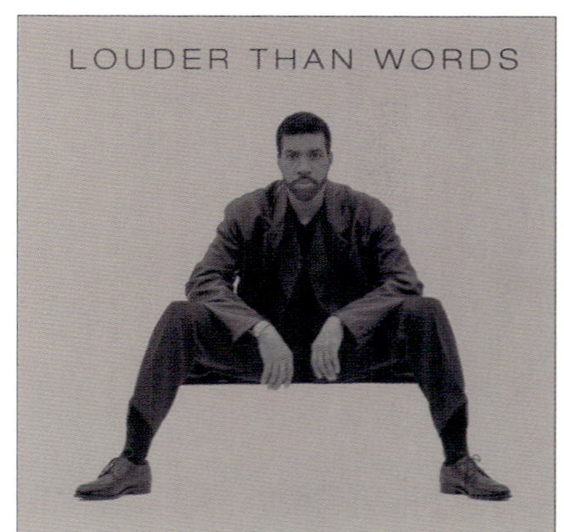


Following a hiatus involving the passing of his father, a divorce and the death of a friend to AIDS, **Lionel Richie** broke the silence with *Louder Than Words*.

*Billboard* 200: *Louder Than Words* (#28)
*Billboard* Hot 100: "Don't Wanna Lose You" (#39)

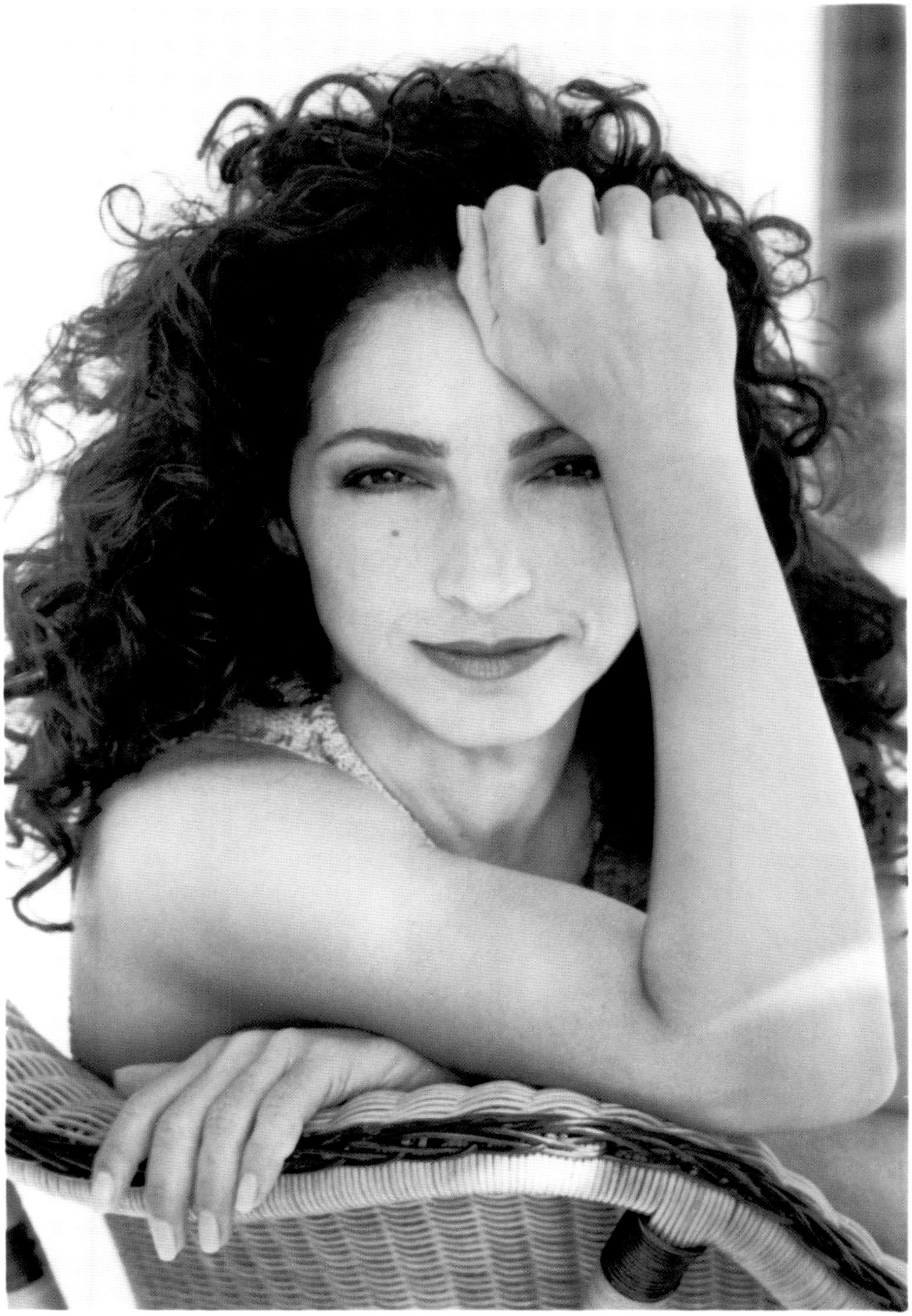

PHOTO CREDIT ANDREW MELLICK

GLORIA
estefan

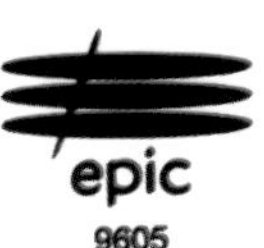

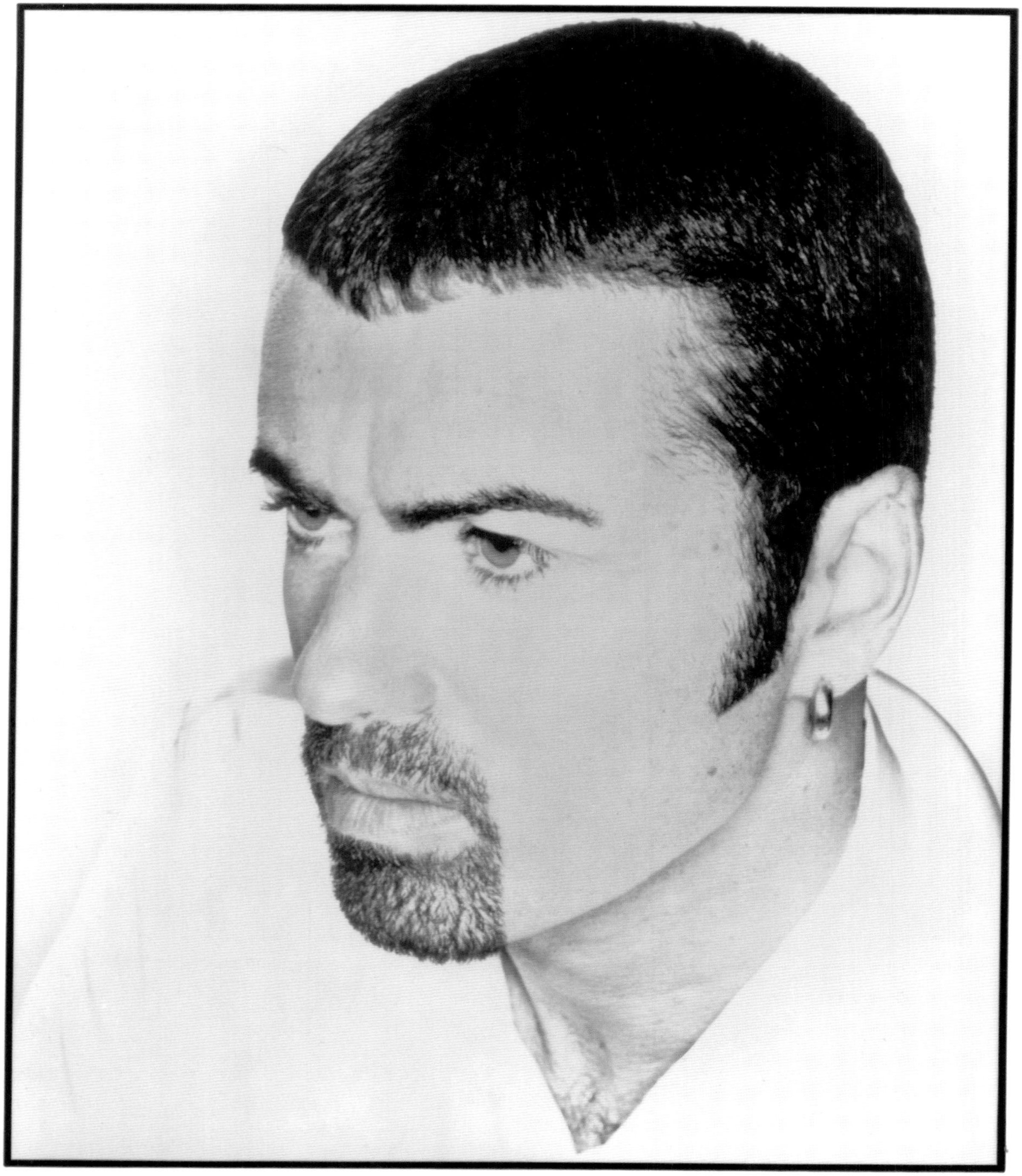

Photo Credit: Nick Knight

GEORGE
MICHÆL

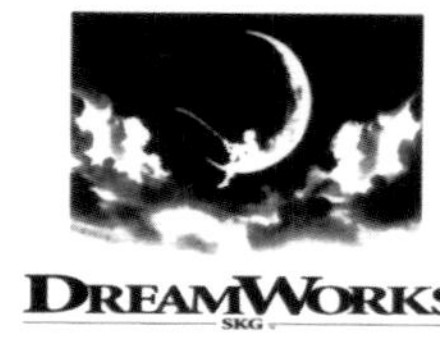

DREAMWORKS
SKG

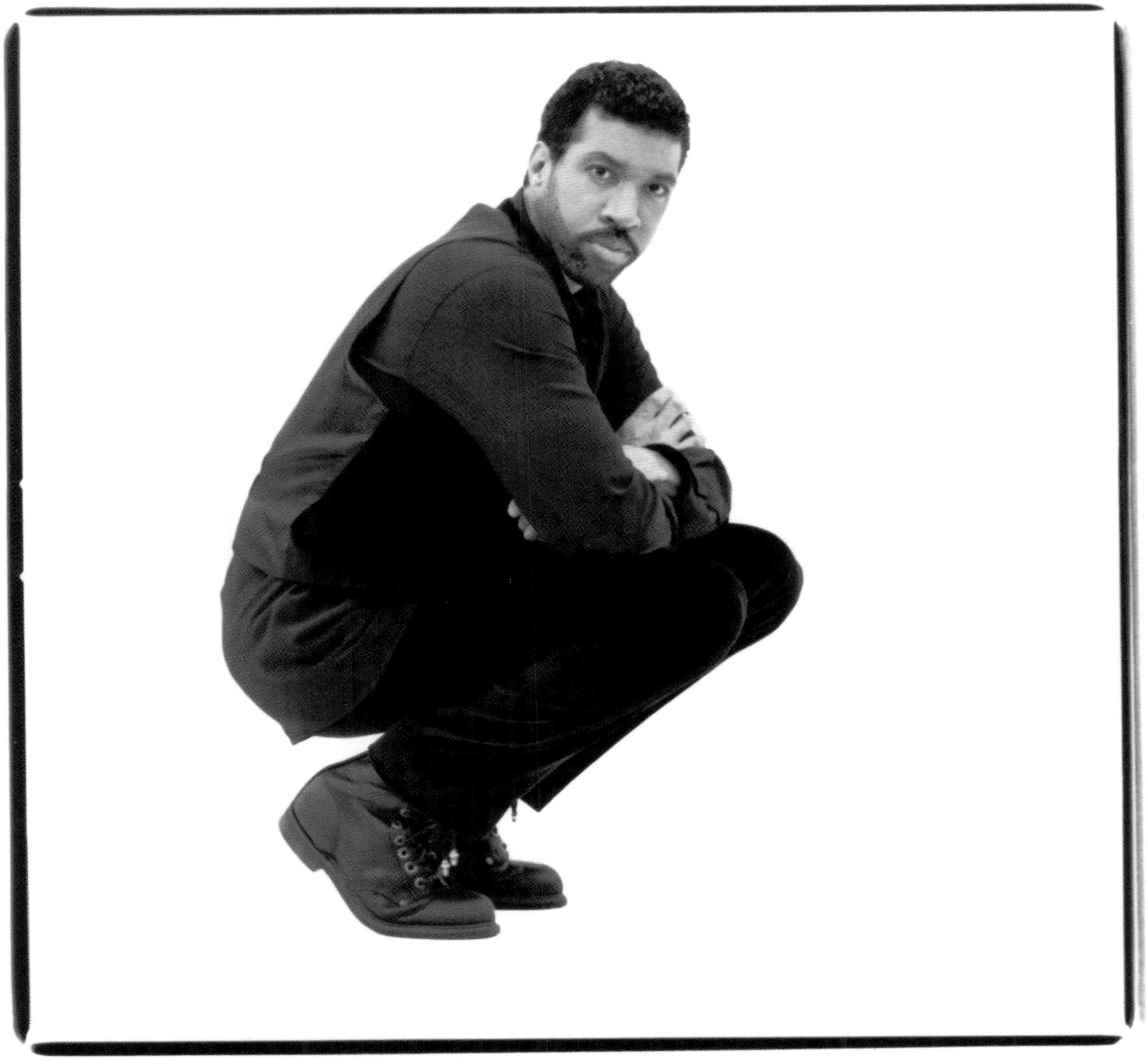

Photo Credit: Alan Silfen

# LIONEL RICHIE

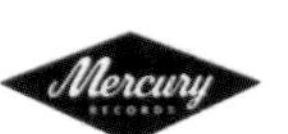


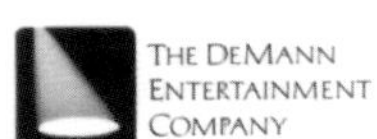

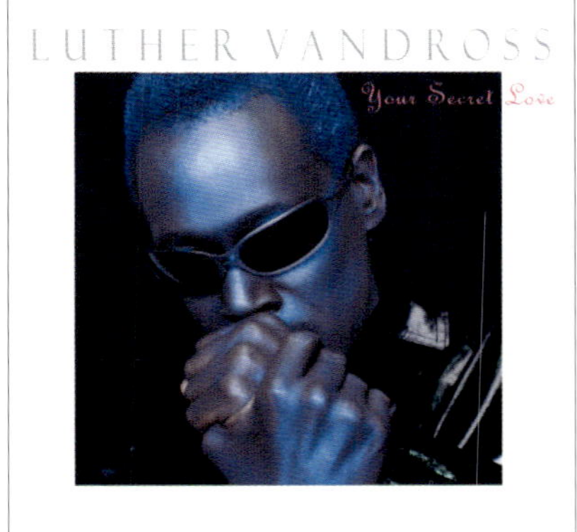


The midtempo title track from **Luther Vandross**' *Your Secret Love* won the pop-soul master another Grammy Award for Best Male R&B Vocal Performance.

*Billboard* 200: *Your Secret Love* (#9)
*Billboard* Hot 100: "Your Secret Love" (#52);
"I Can Make It Better" (#80)

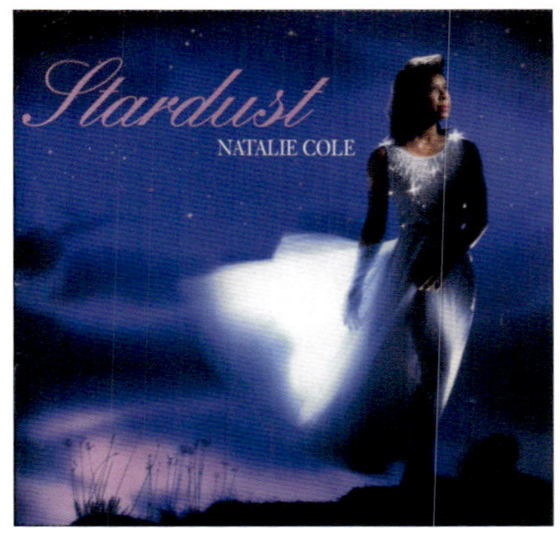


**Natalie Cole** sang a standard, "When I Fall in Love," as a virtual duet with her late father, pop legend Nat King Cole, and their version won two Grammys.

*Billboard* 200: *Stardust* (#20)

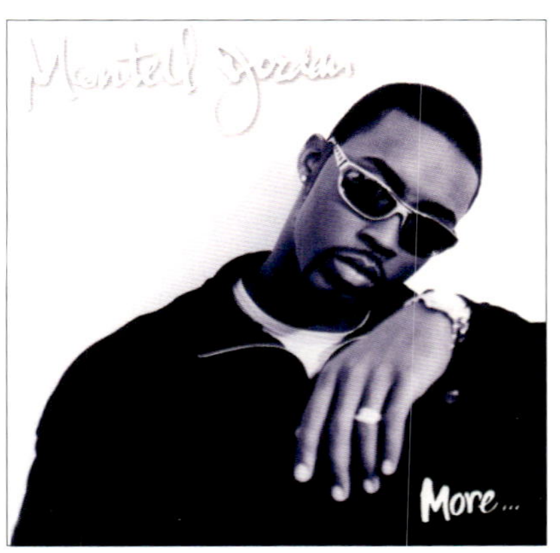


*More...* by **Montell Jordan**, the R&B singer, songwriter and producer's second effort, spawned two gold-certified singles, "Falling" and "What's on Tonight."

*Billboard* 200: *More...* (#47)
*Billboard* Hot 100: "I Like" (#28); "Falling" (#18);
"What's on Tonight" (#21)

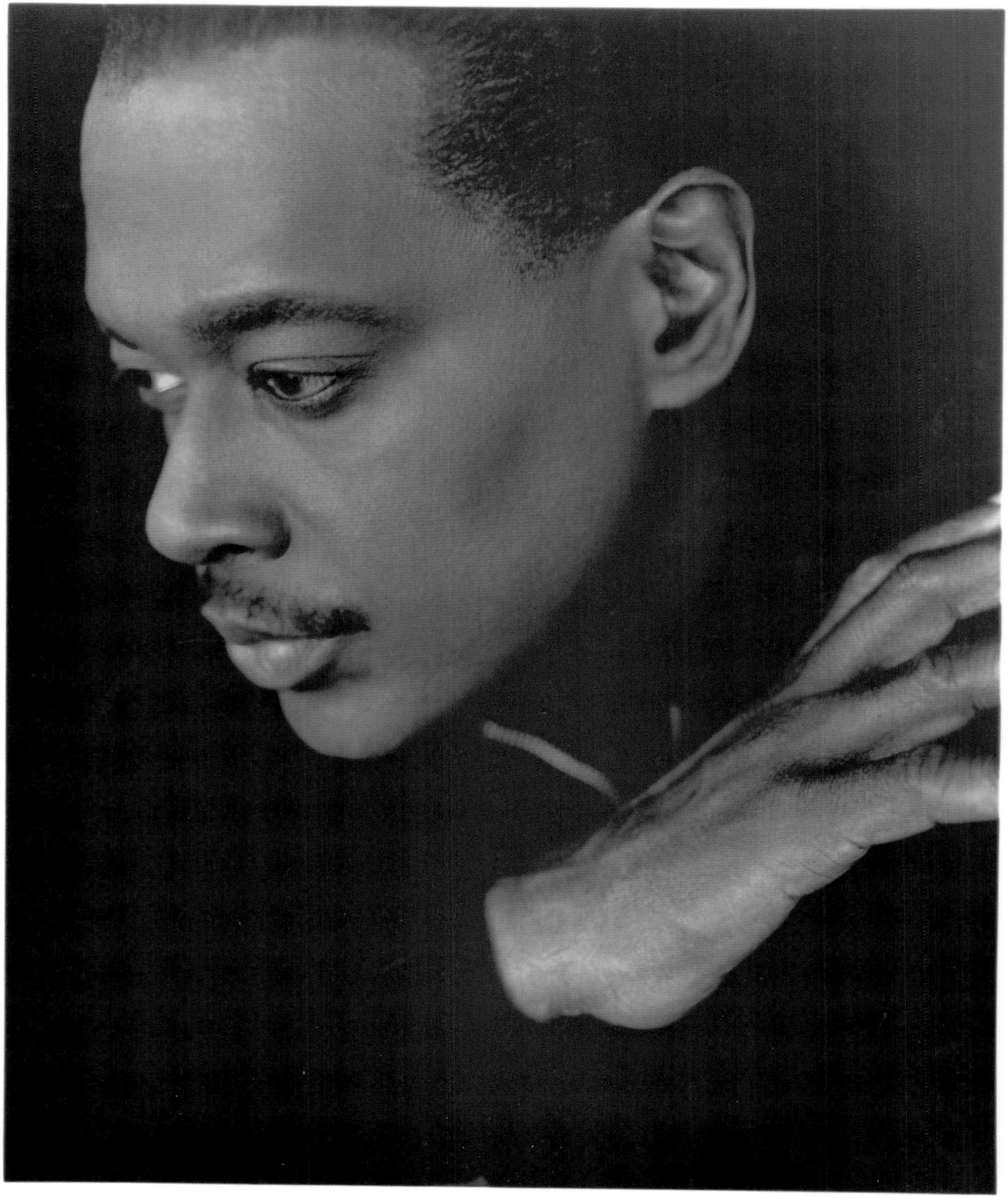

Photo Credit: Norman Jean Roy

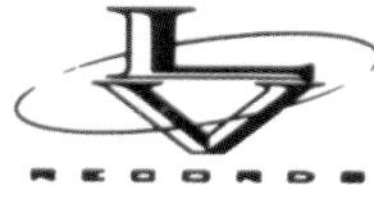

# Luther VANDROSS

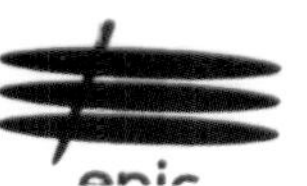

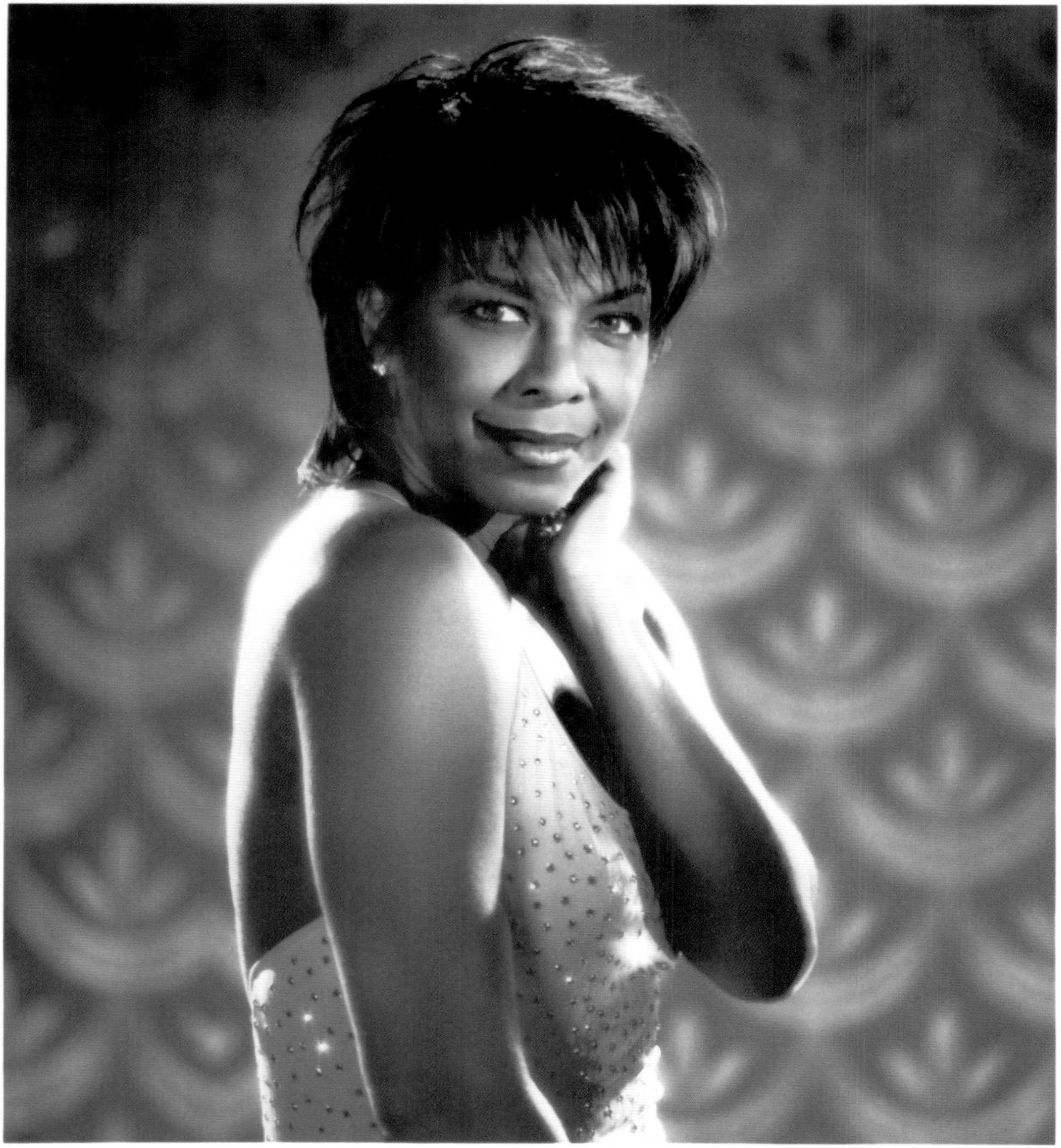

PHOTO CREDIT ROCKY SCHENCK 1996

# NATALIE COLE

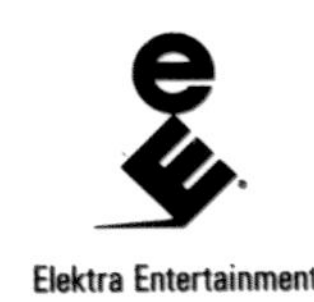

Elektra Entertainment

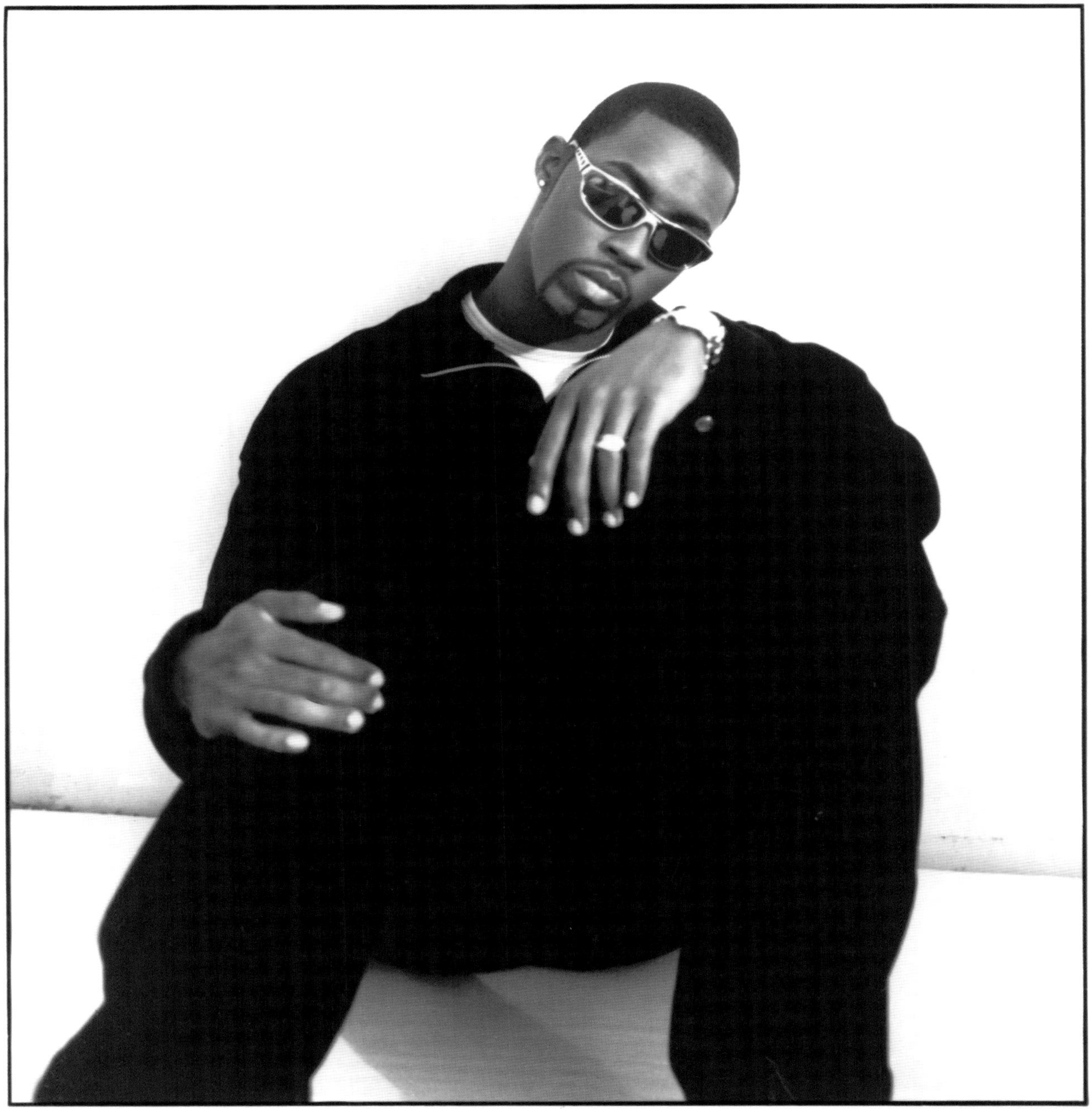

PHOTO CREDIT GUZMAN

Montell Jordan

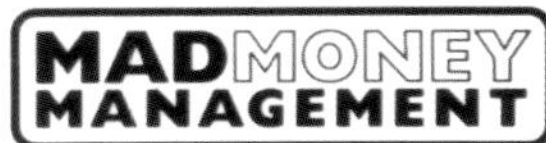


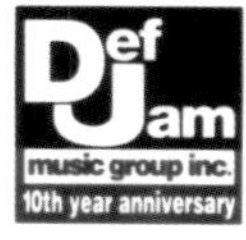


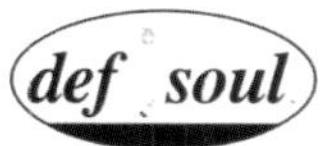

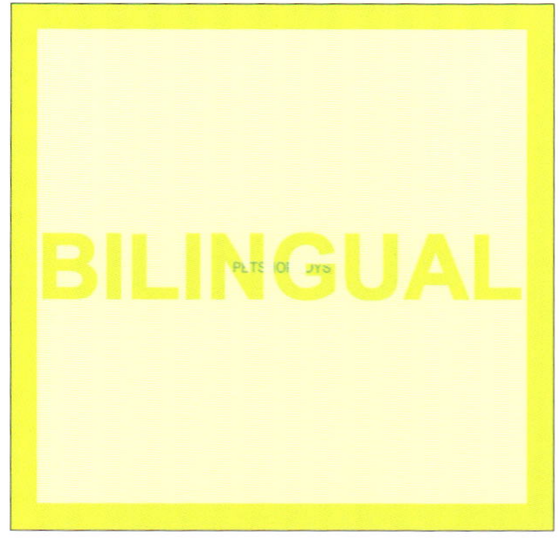


The title of **Pet Shop Boys**' *Bilingual* reflected the album's Latin influence, and the British duo topped the dance-club charts with the single "Before."

*Billboard* 200: *Bilingual* (#39)

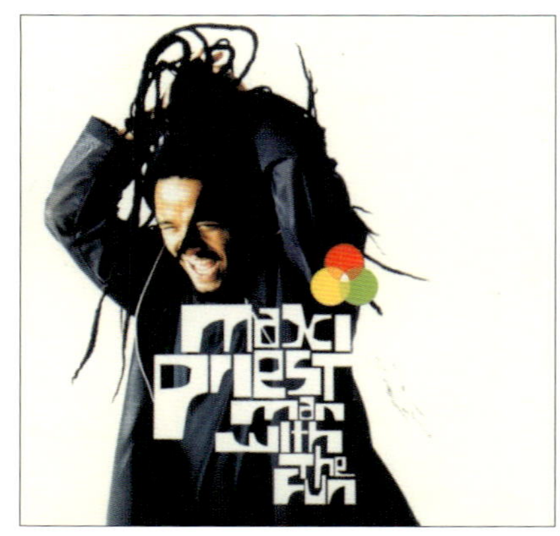


A bouncy duet with Shaggy from **Maxi Priest**'s *Man with the Fun* album, "That Girl" became an international smash hit for the British reggae singer.

*Billboard* 200: *Man with the Fun* (#108)
*Billboard* Hot 100: "That Girl" (#20)

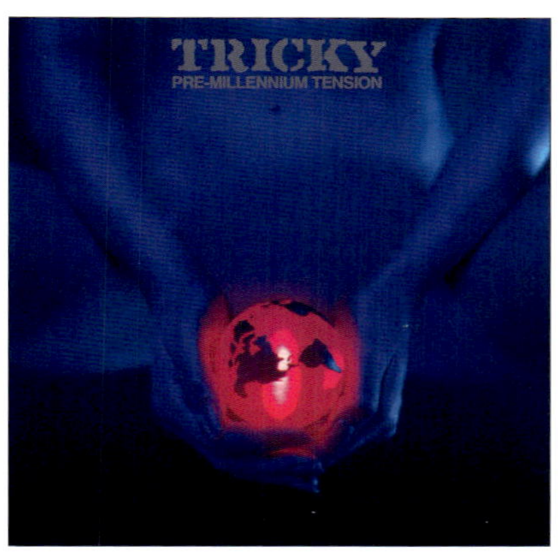


Enigmatic trip-hop star **Tricky** earned a burgeoning cult status in the US with stark, creepy electro-guitar grooves from his *Pre-Millennium Tension* release.

*Billboard* 200: *Pre-Millennium Tension* (#140)

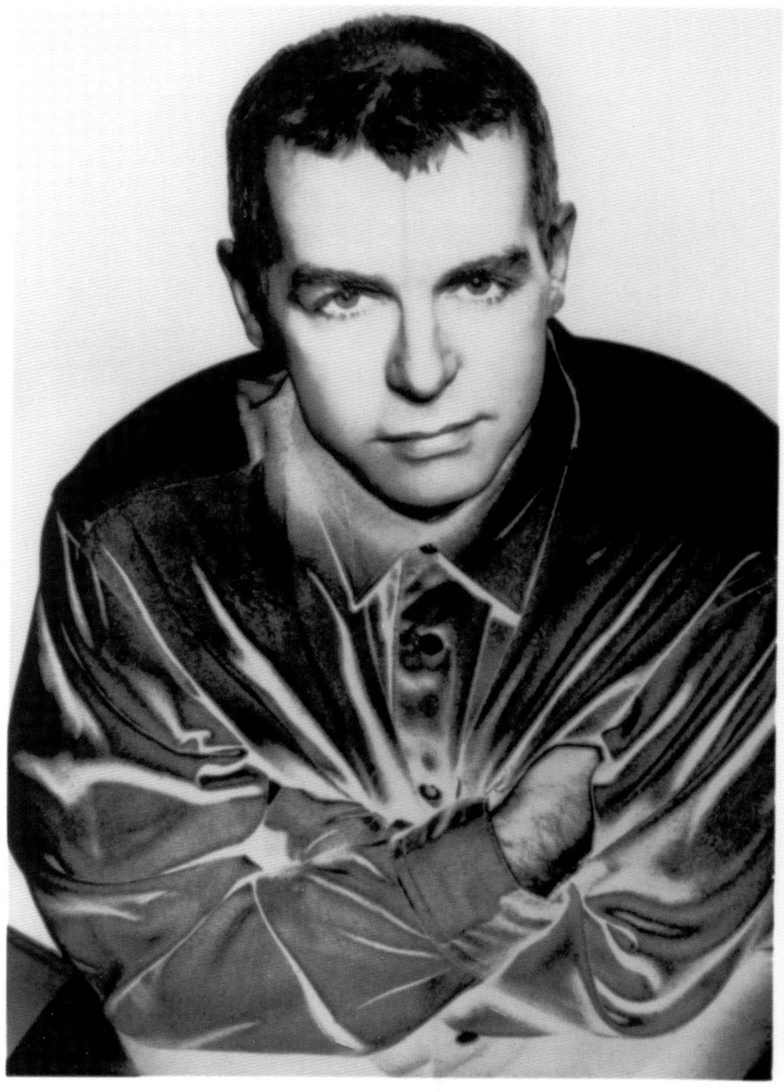

Neil Tennant

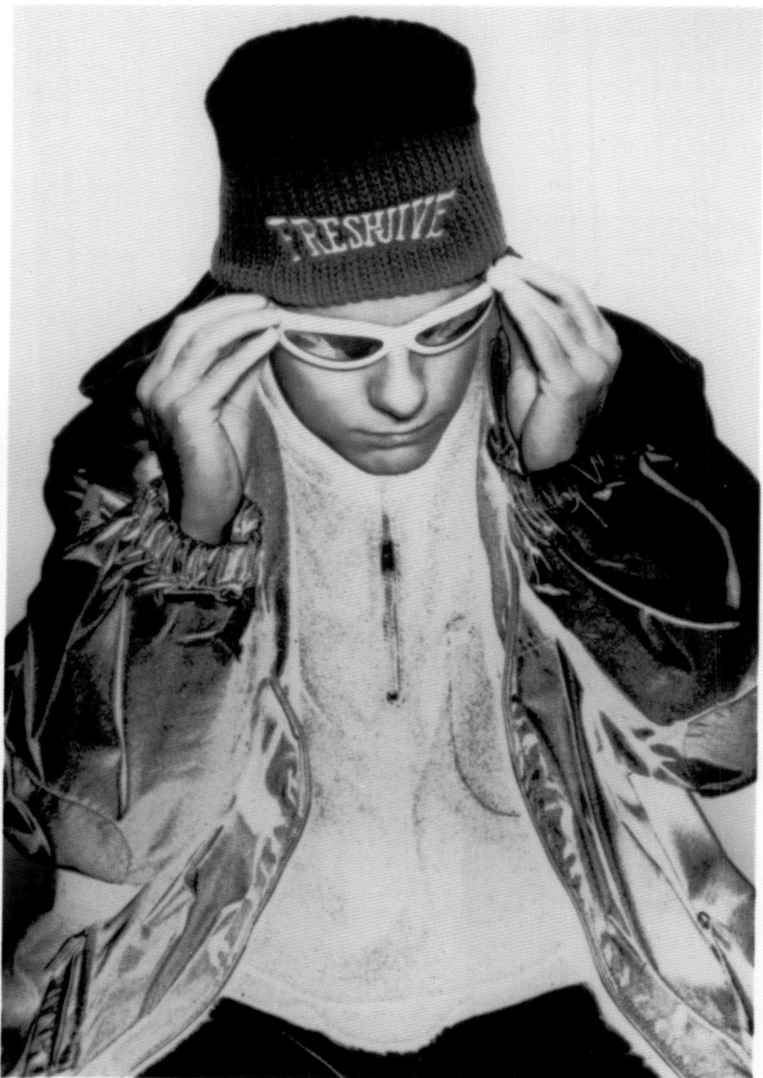


Chris Lowe

Photo Credit: Brad Branson

Pet Shop Boys

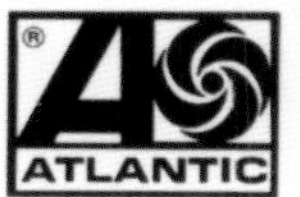

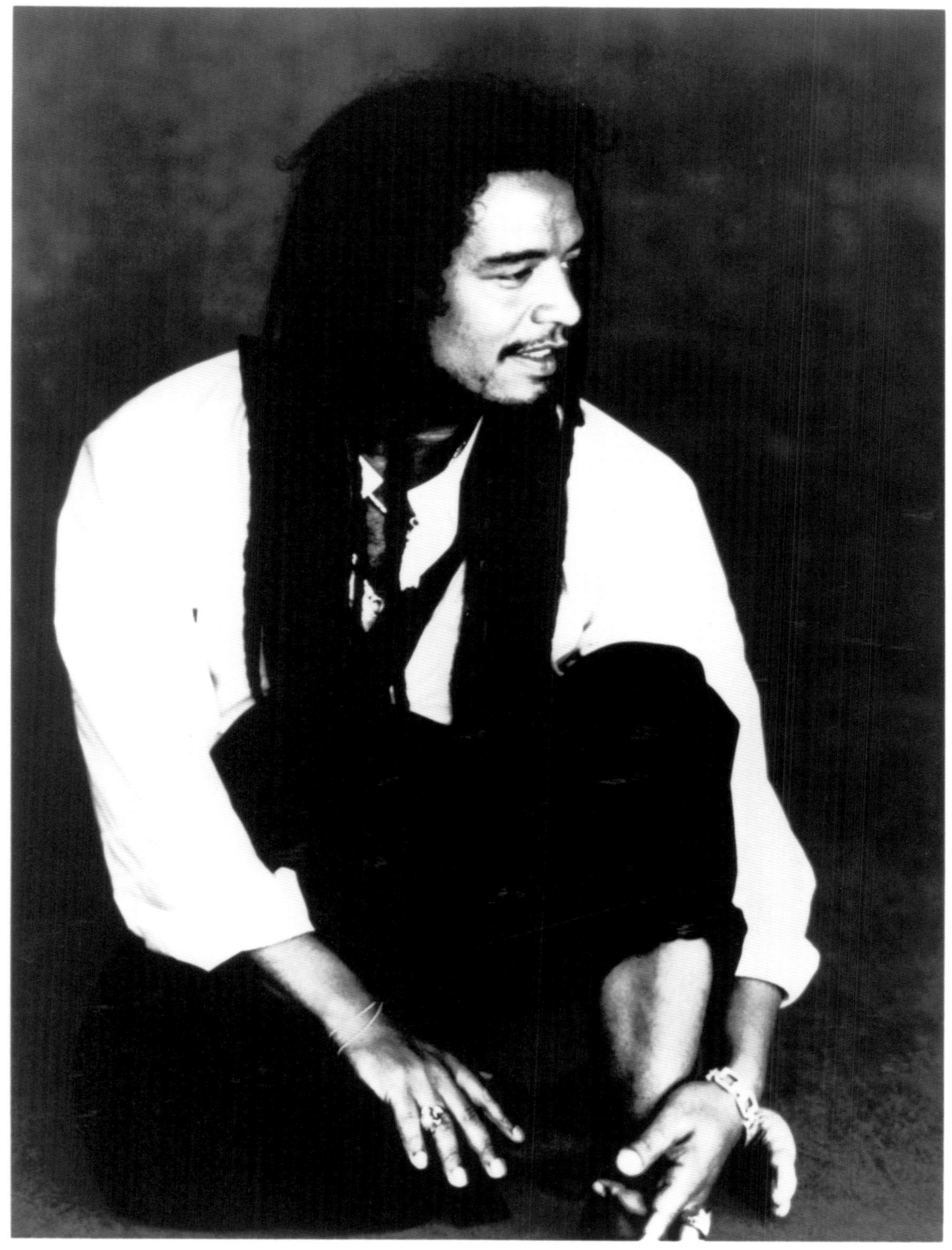

Photo Credit: Hideo Oida 4/96

# MAXI PRIEST

Virgin

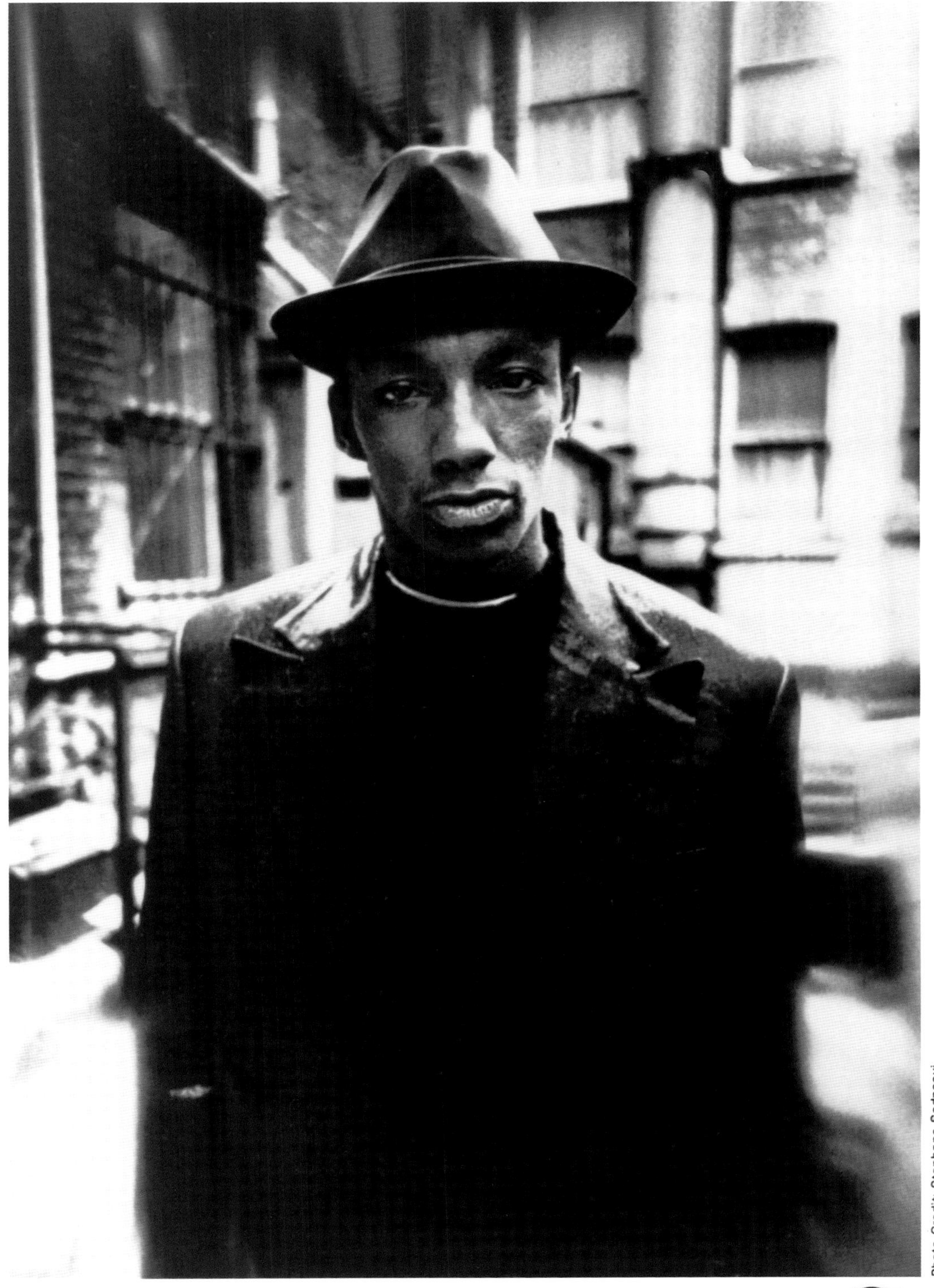

Photo Credit: Stephane Sednaoui

**Tricky**

ISLAND

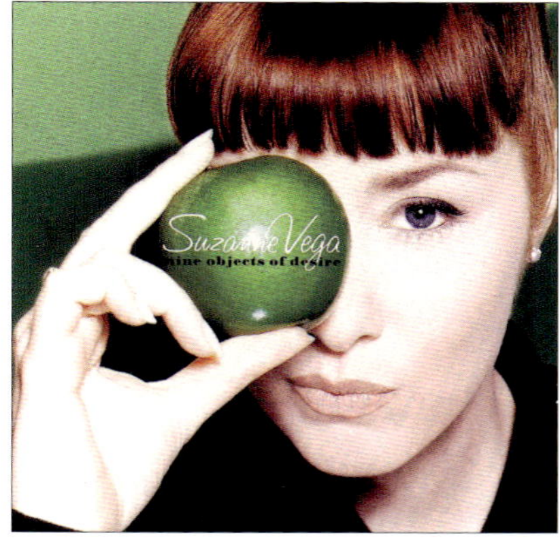


Adopting a coolly knowing look and attitude, once-folkish **Suzanne Vega** returned with *Nine Objects of Desire*, another flurry of unexpected sonic twists.

*Billboard* 200: *Nine Objects of Desire* (#92)

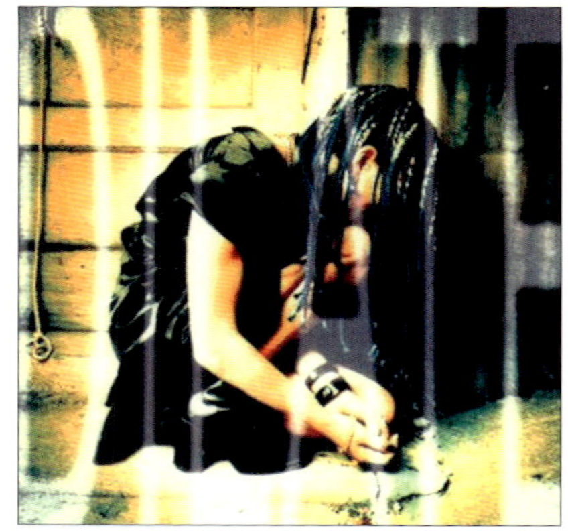

As with all her albums of alternative-folk music, *Dilate*, **Ani DiFranco**'s seventh, was released on the singer-songwriter's own record label, Righteous Babe.

*Billboard* 200: *Dilate* (#87)

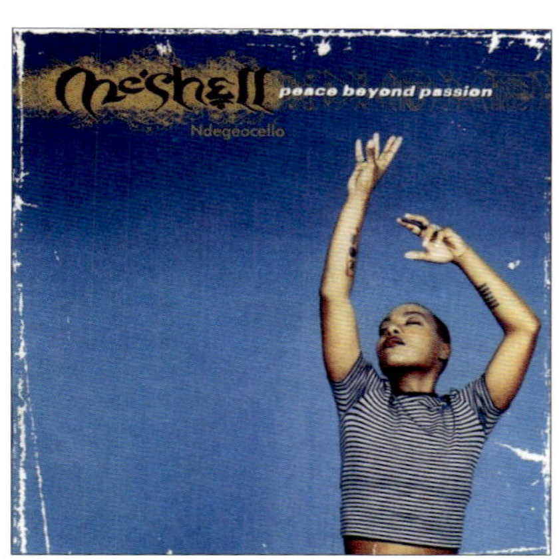


With "Who Is He and What Is He to You," her rendition of a Bill Withers song from the Seventies, **MéShell Ndegéocello** reached No. 1 on the club charts.

*Billboard* 200: *Peace Beyond Passion* (#63)

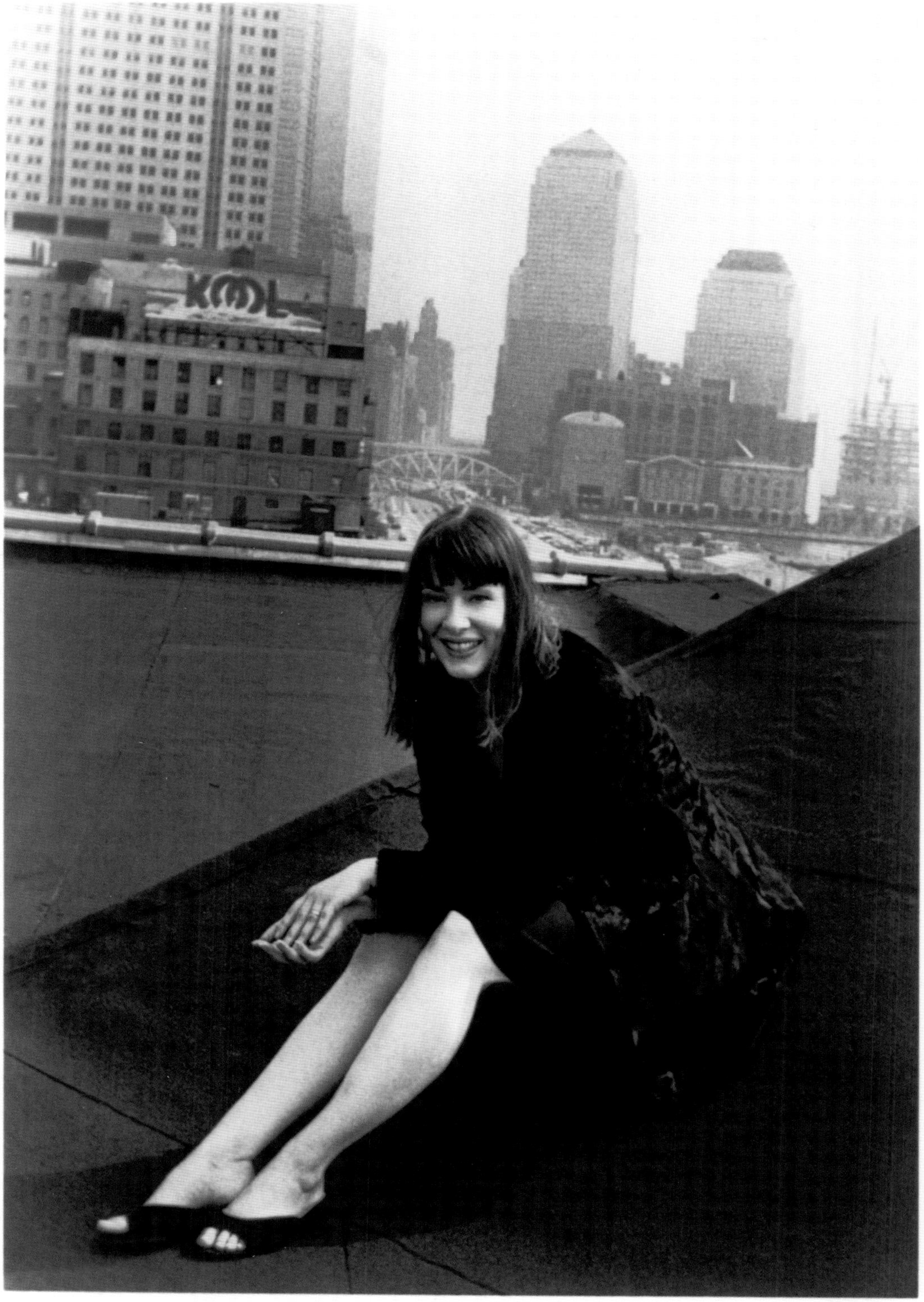

PHOTO: David Seltzer 10/96

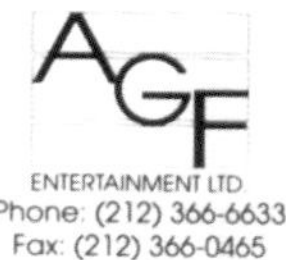


ENTERTAINMENT LTD
Phone: (212) 366-6633
Fax: (212) 366-0465

Suzanne Vega

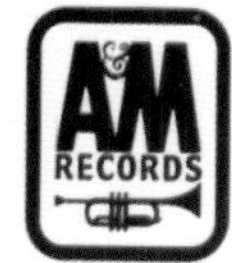

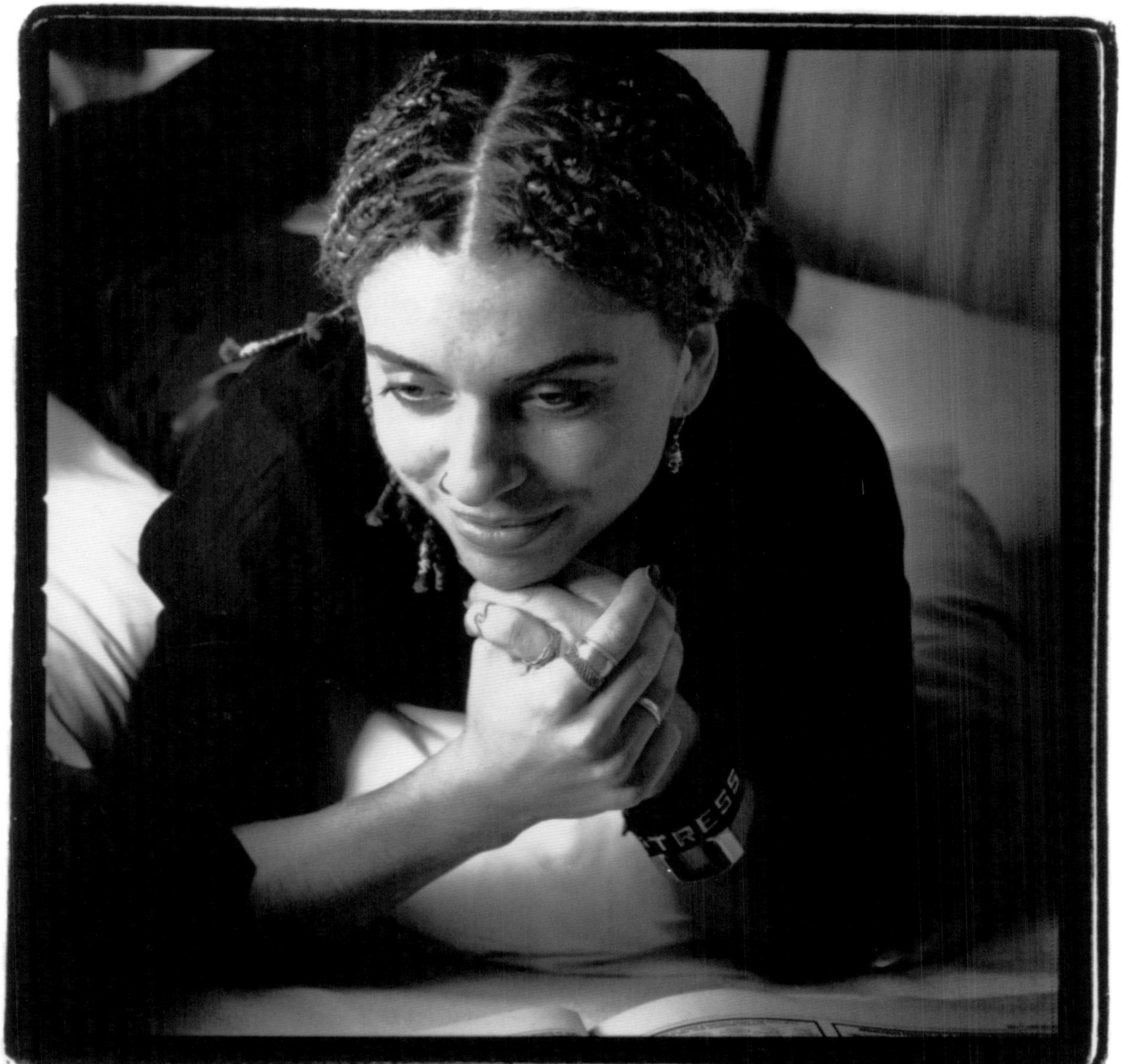

FLEMING
TAMULEVICH
& Associates Inc.
Artist Representatives • (313) 995-9066

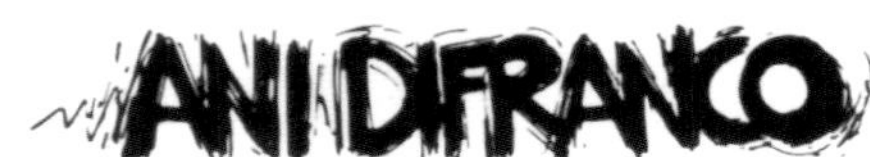


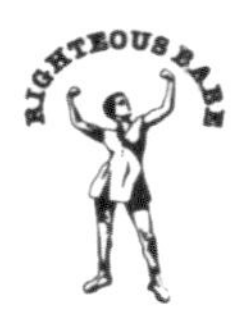

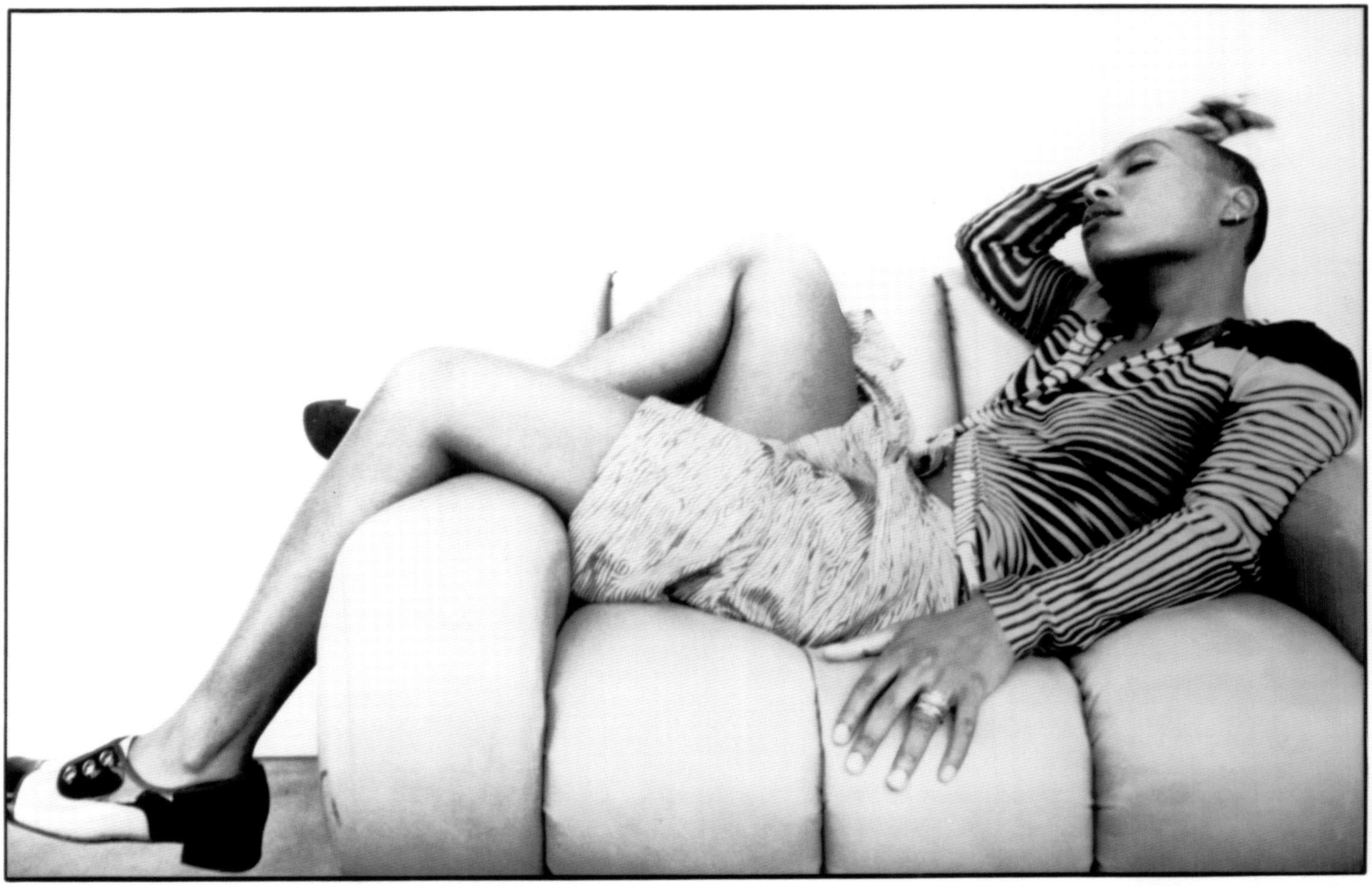

PHOTO CREDIT: Guzman

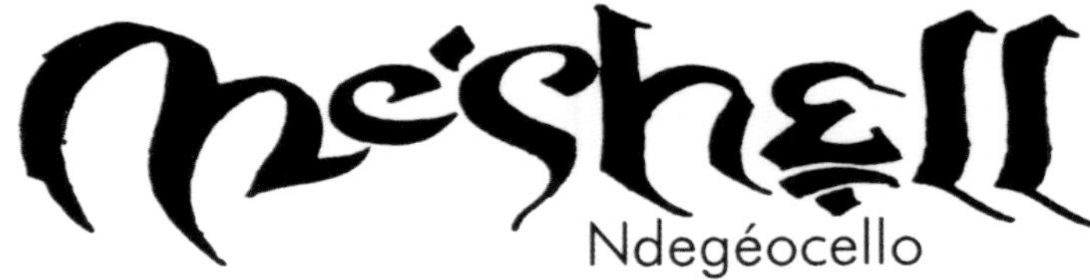


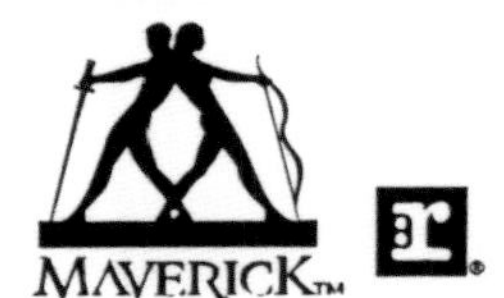

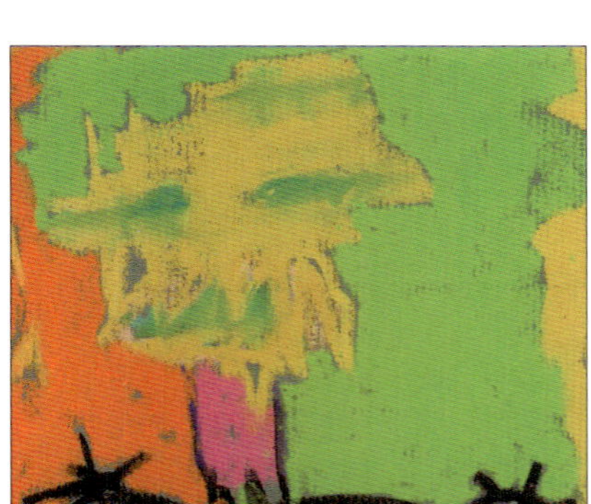

Hewing to soul-jazz grooves, **Medeski Martin & Wood** forged *Shack-man* in a remote Hawaiian shanty, with power supplied by solar panels and a generator.

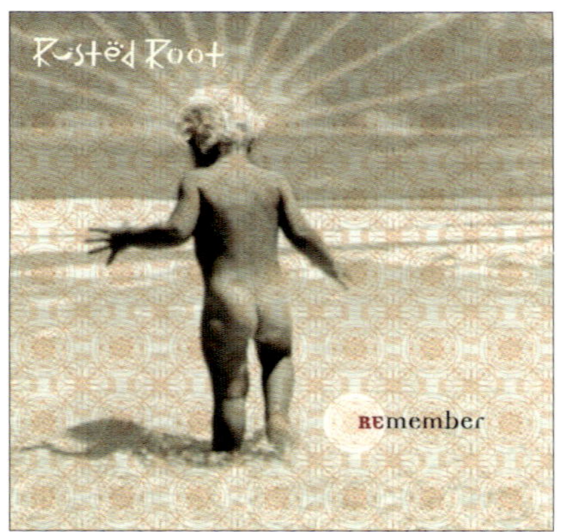


Rhythm-intensive jam band **Rusted Root** added more international influences and mainstream electric settings to *Remember*, produced by Jerry Harrison.

*Billboard* 200: *Remember* (#38)

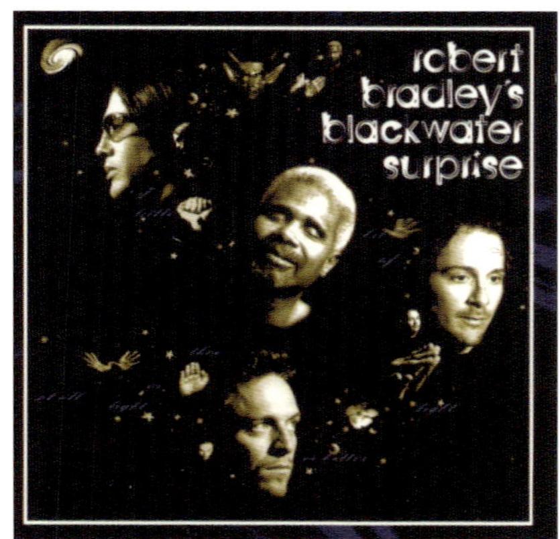


The self-titled debut album by **Robert Bradley's Blackwater Surprise** cast an alliance between a blind street performer and a Detroit alternative-rock band.

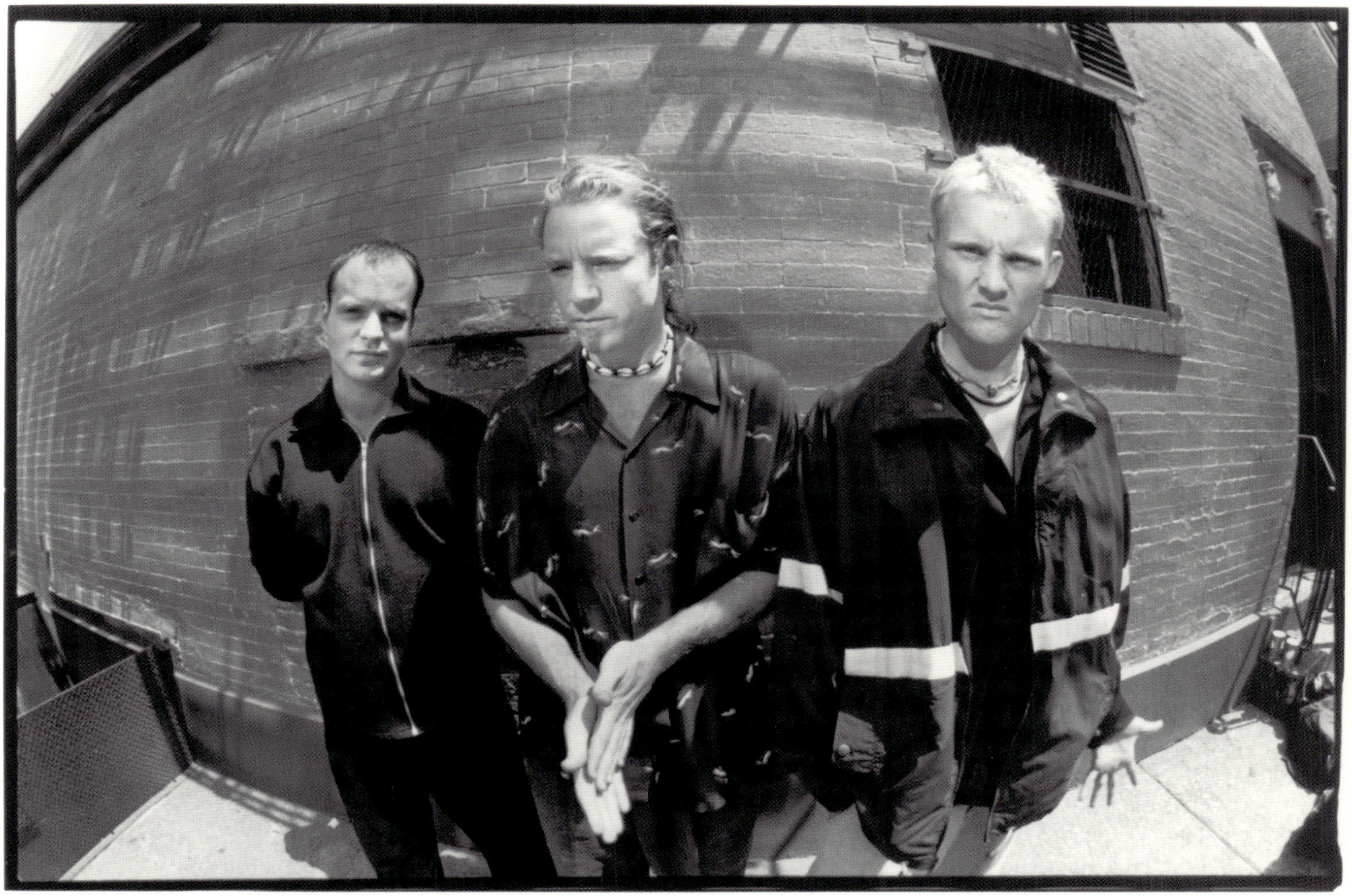

Photo Credit: Micheal Macioce

# MEDESKI MARTIN AND WOOD

GRAMAVISION

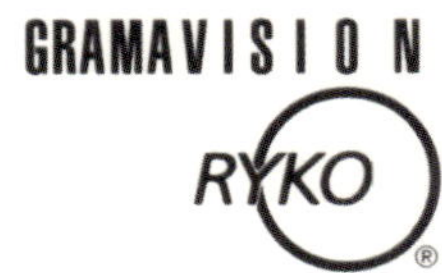

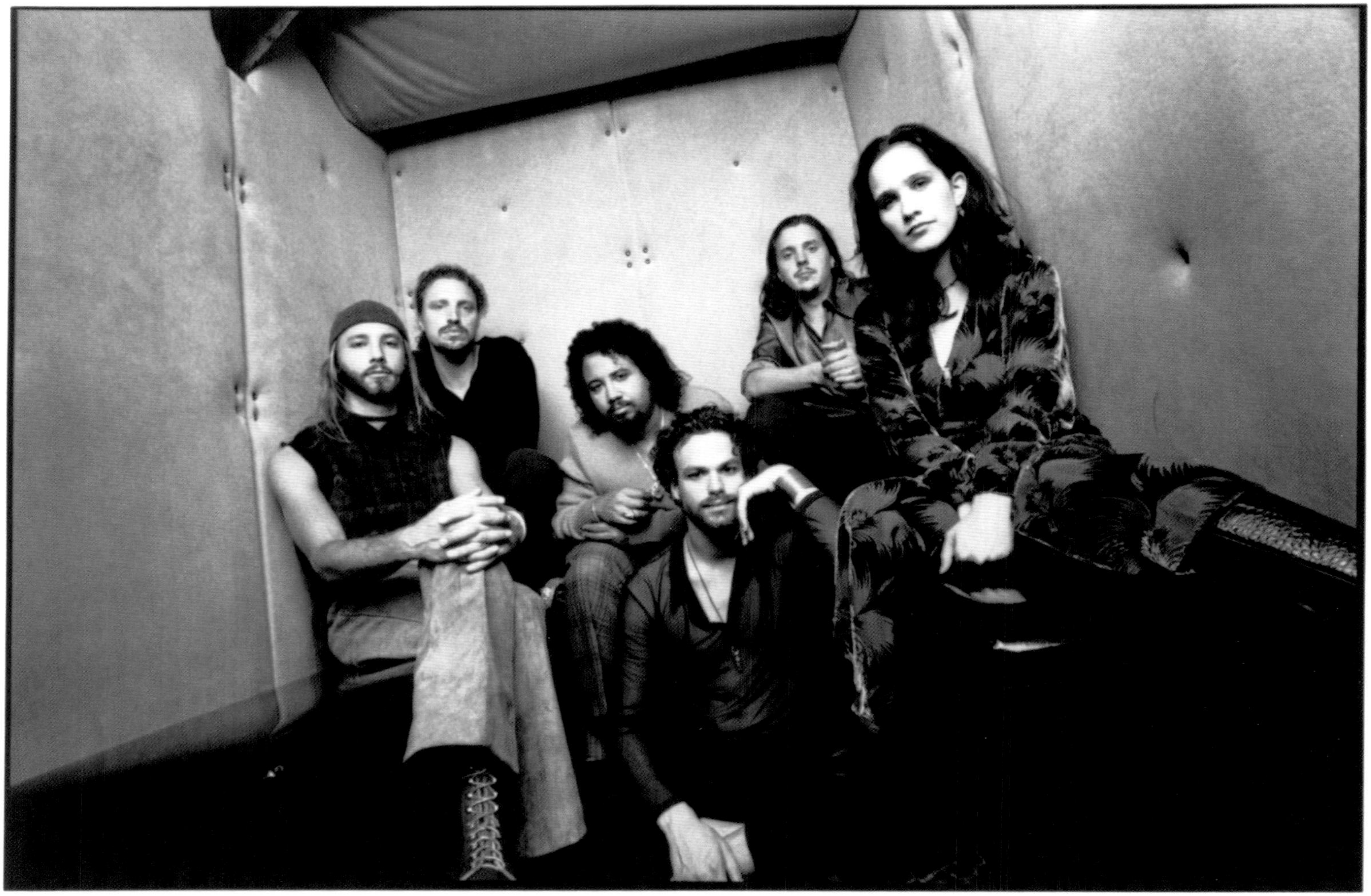

PHOTO CREDIT DANA TYNAN 1996

L R : JOHN BUYNAK, JIM DISPIRITO, PATRICK NORMAN, MICHAEL GLABICKI, JIM DONOVAN, LIZ BERLIN

# Rustëd Root

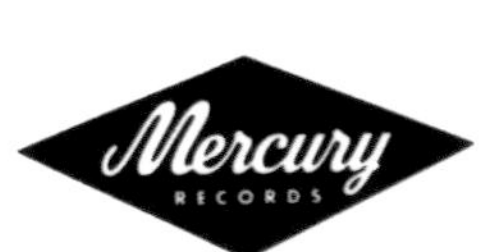

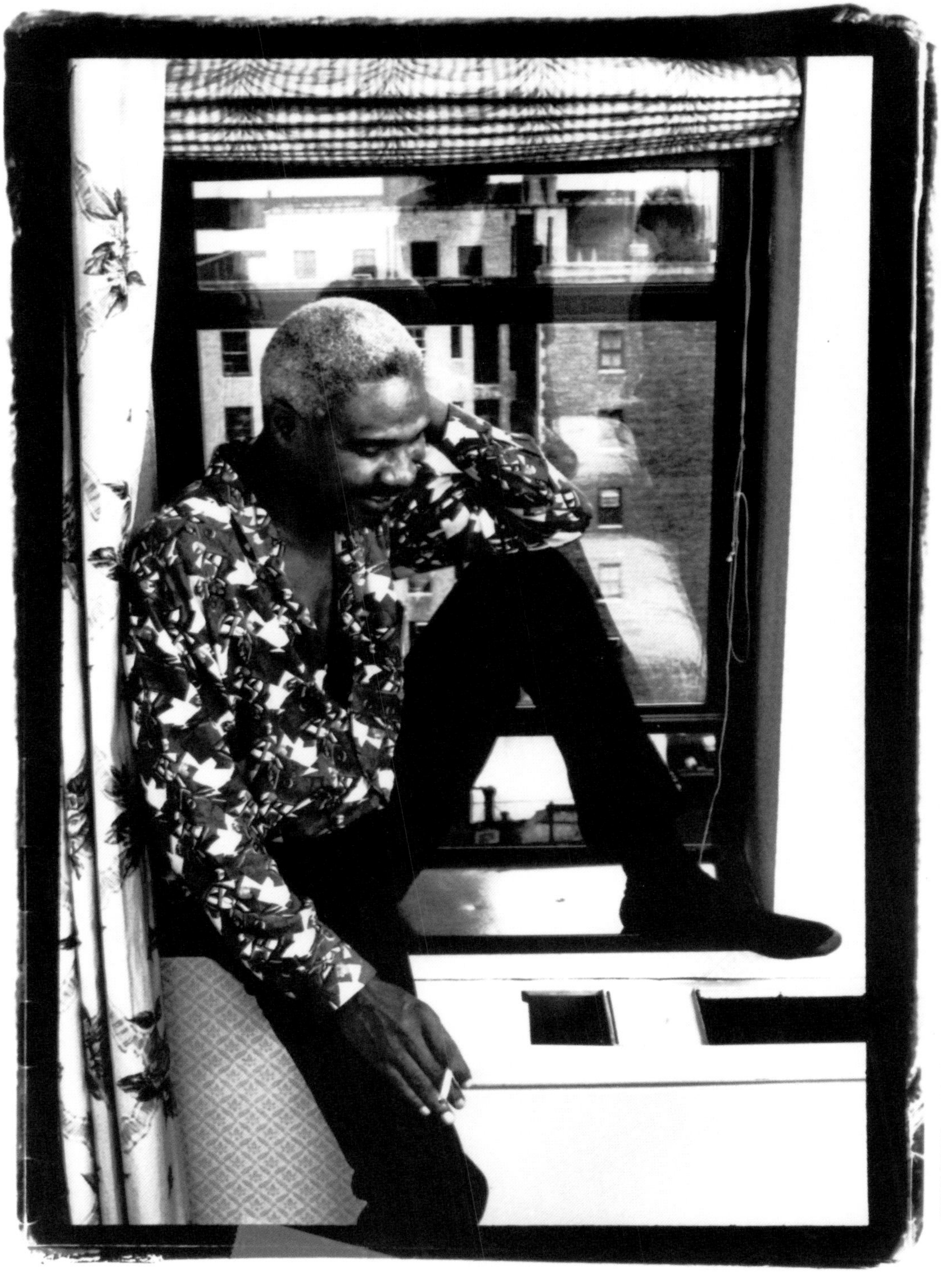

PHOTO CREDIT: IAN GLITTER

**Robert Bradley**

Management:
Vinny Rich
For It's A Gas Mgmt.
(908) 929-0456

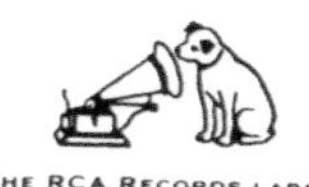

THE RCA RECORDS LABEL

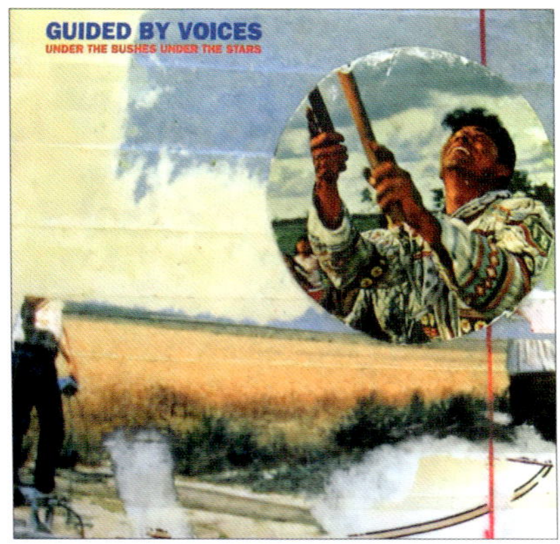


Noted for a lo-fi aesthetic, indie-rock act **Guided by Voices** took a stab at recording in a 24-track studio to bang out *Under the Bushes Under the Stars*.

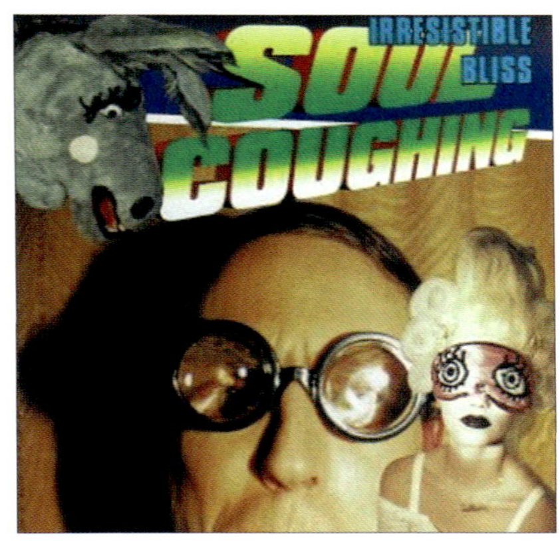


Led by M. Doughty, New York's **Soul Coughing** enjoyed alternative-rock hits with the spirited "Super Bon Bon" and the polyrhythmic "Soundtrack to Mary."

*Billboard* 200: *Irresistible Bliss* (#136)

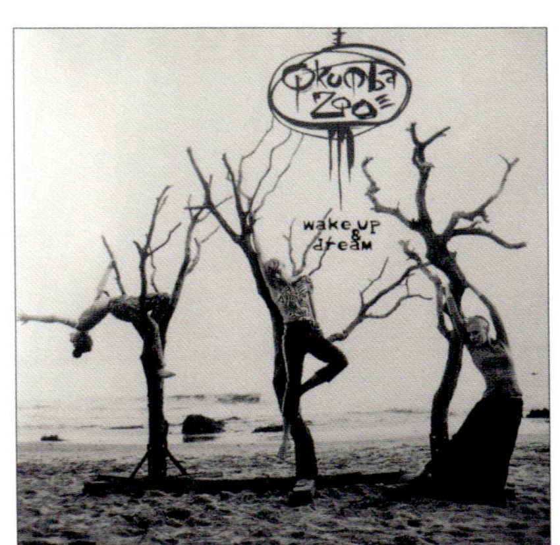


South African trio **Qkumba Zoo** combined tribal rhythms with a vibrant pop melody, rising to No. 1 on the US dance-club charts with "The Child (Inside)."

*Billboard* Hot 100: "The Child (Inside)" (#69)

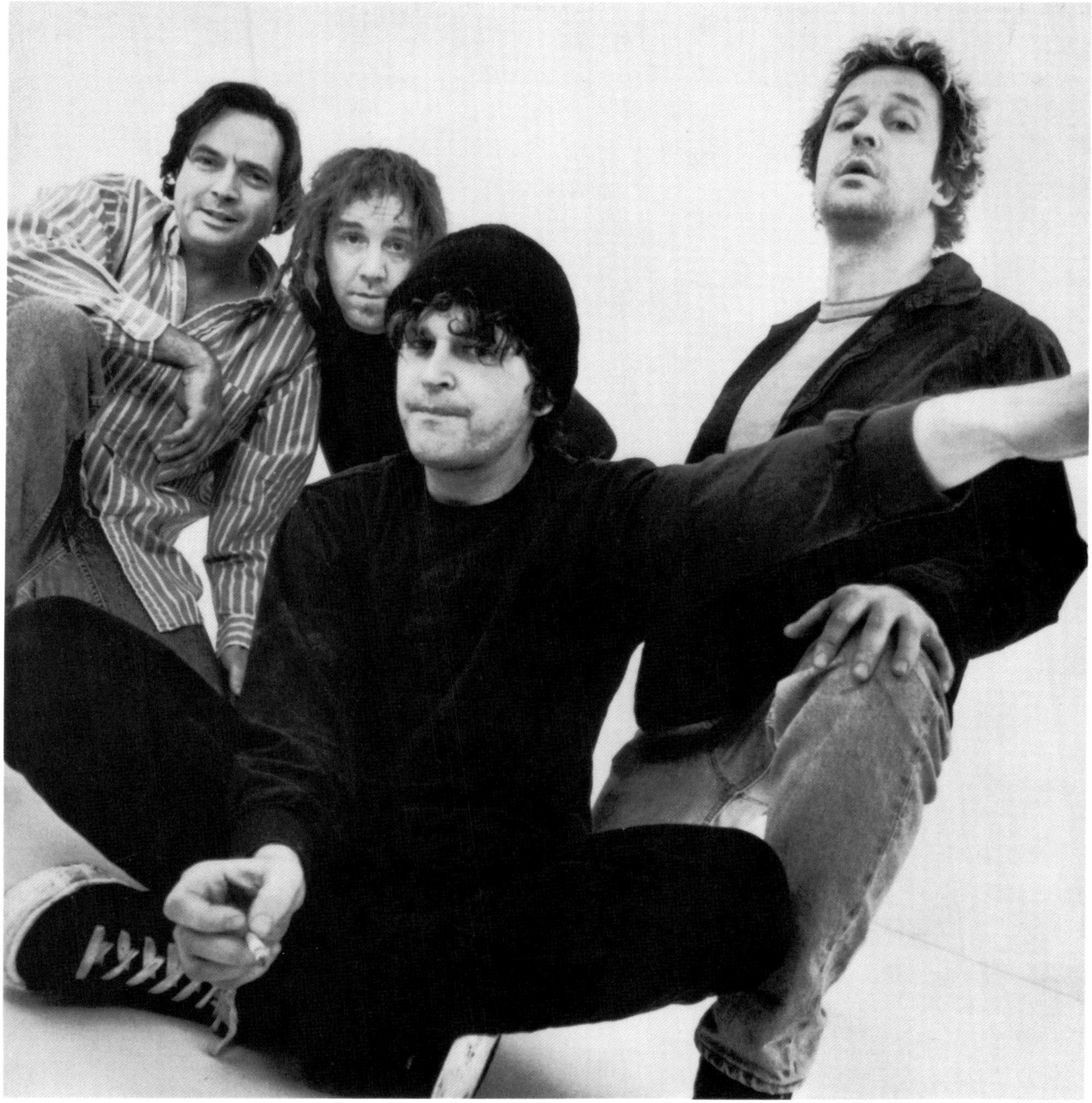

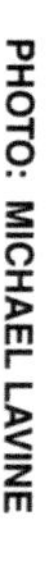


# GUIDED BY VOICES

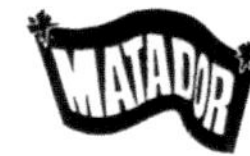

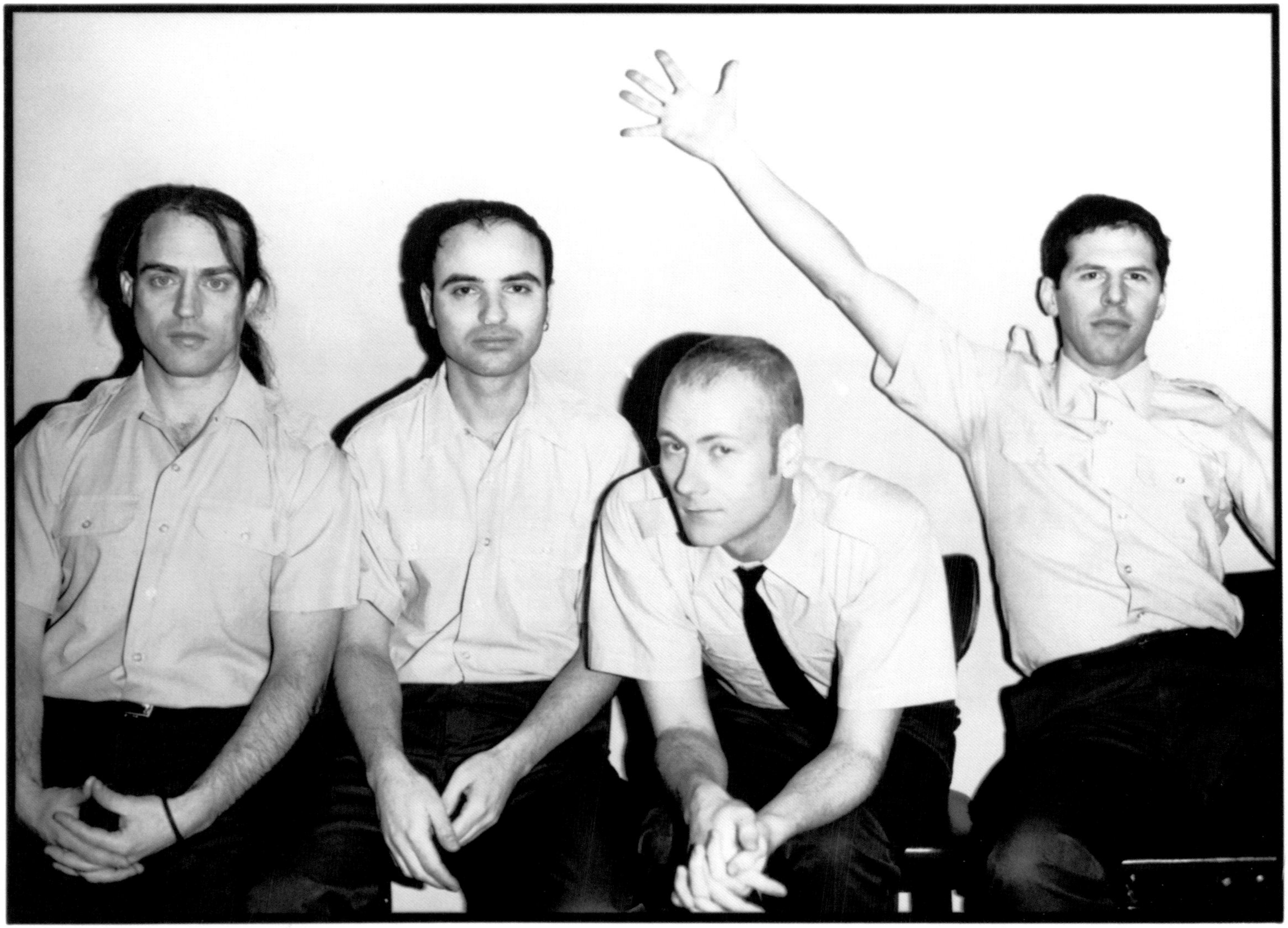

Photo Credit: Marcelo Krasilcic

# SOUL COUGHING

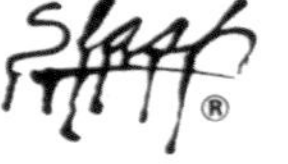

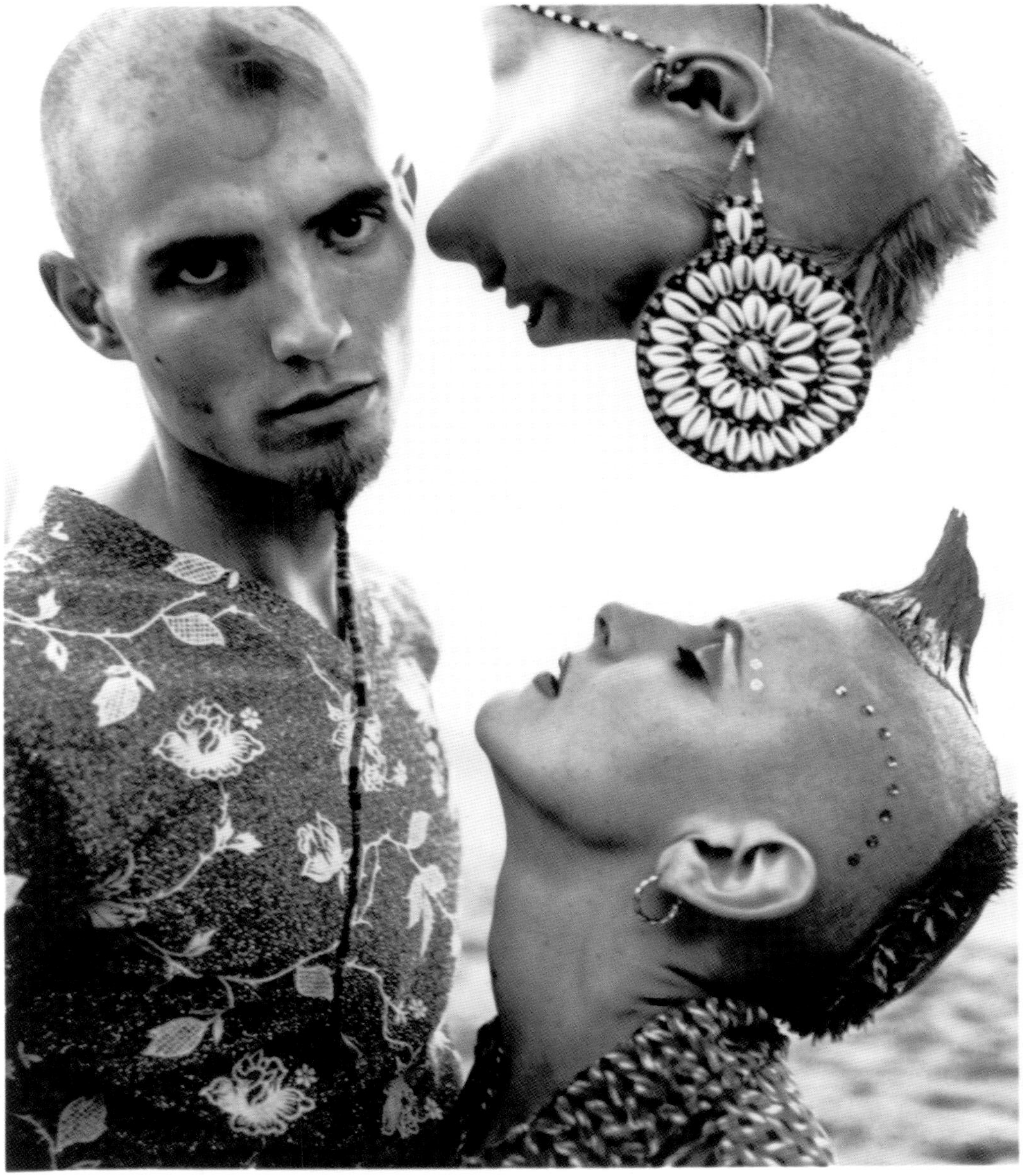

PHOTO: RUVEN AFANADOR

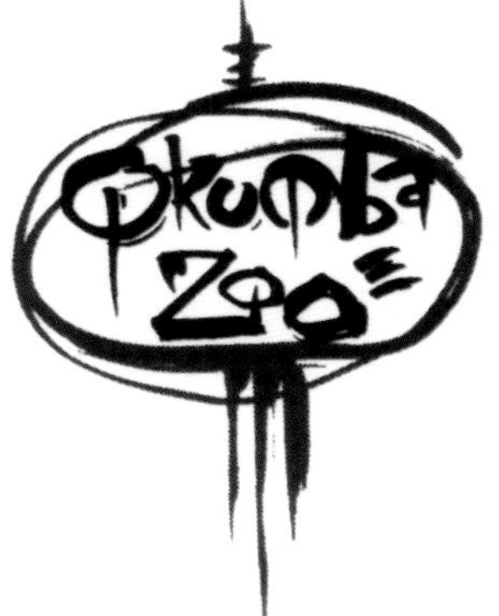

ARISTA™

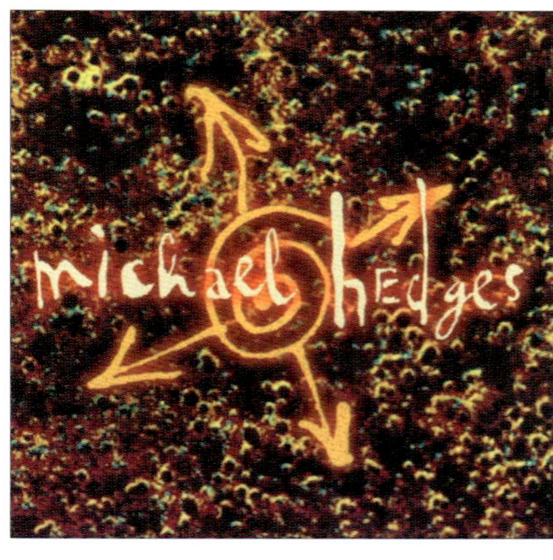


After his death in a single-car accident, guitarist **Michael Hedges**' final record, the mostly instrumental *Oracle*, won the Grammy for Best New Age Album.

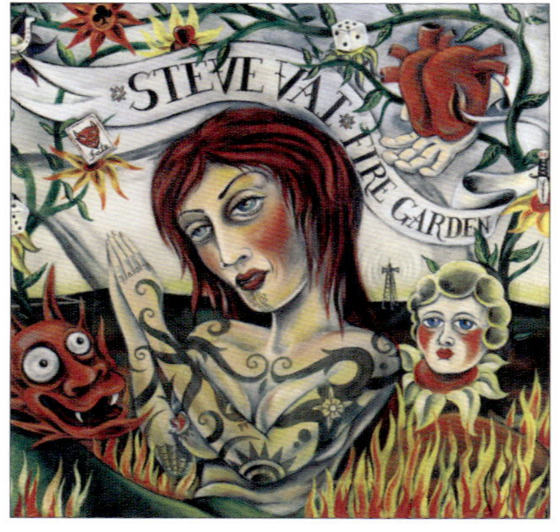


Rock-guitar virtuoso **Steve Vai** undertook the ambitious *Fire Garden*, with a first phase of instrumental tracks and a second phase of tackling vocals.

*Billboard* 200: *Fire Garden* (#106)

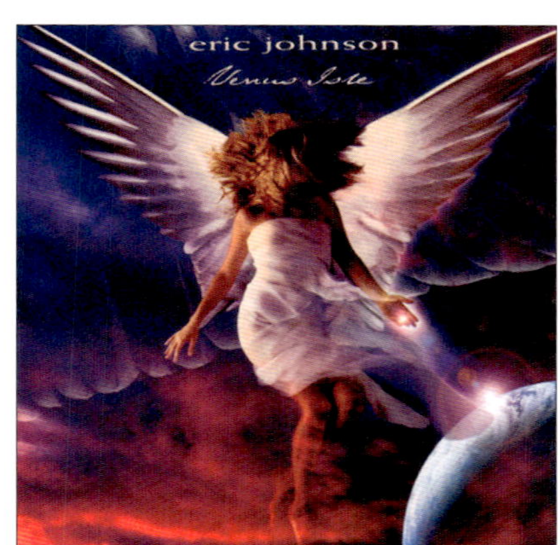


Not one to rush the creative process, Austin-based guitar icon **Eric Johnson** took six years to send out *Venus Isle*, the followup to 1990's *Ah Via Musicom*.

*Billboard* 200: *Venus Isle* (#51)

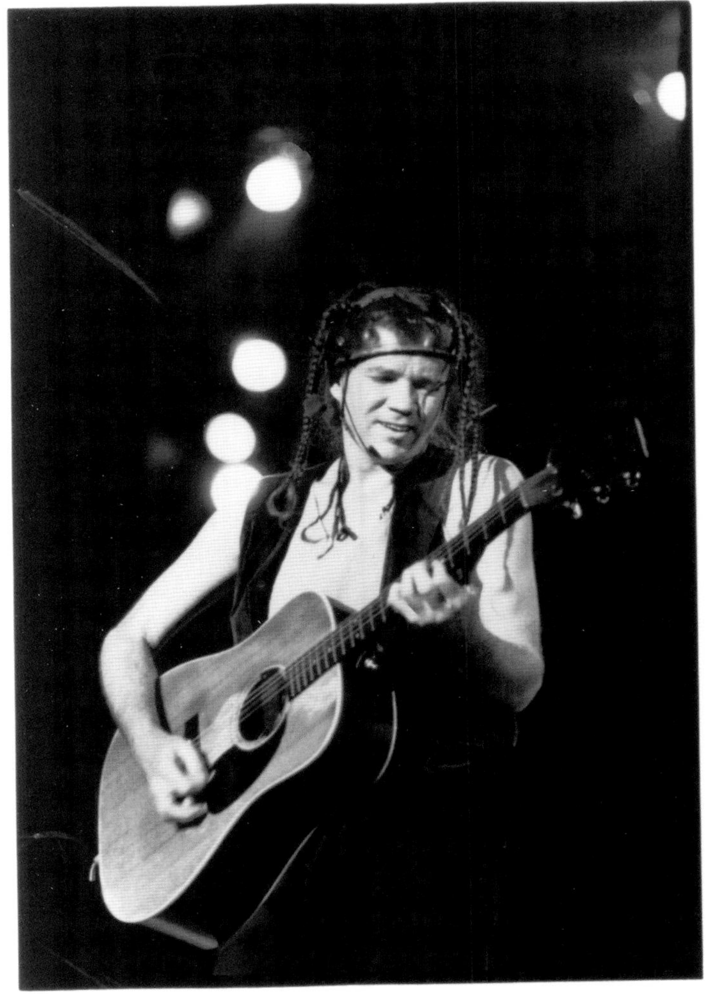

Photo Credit: Ebet Roberts

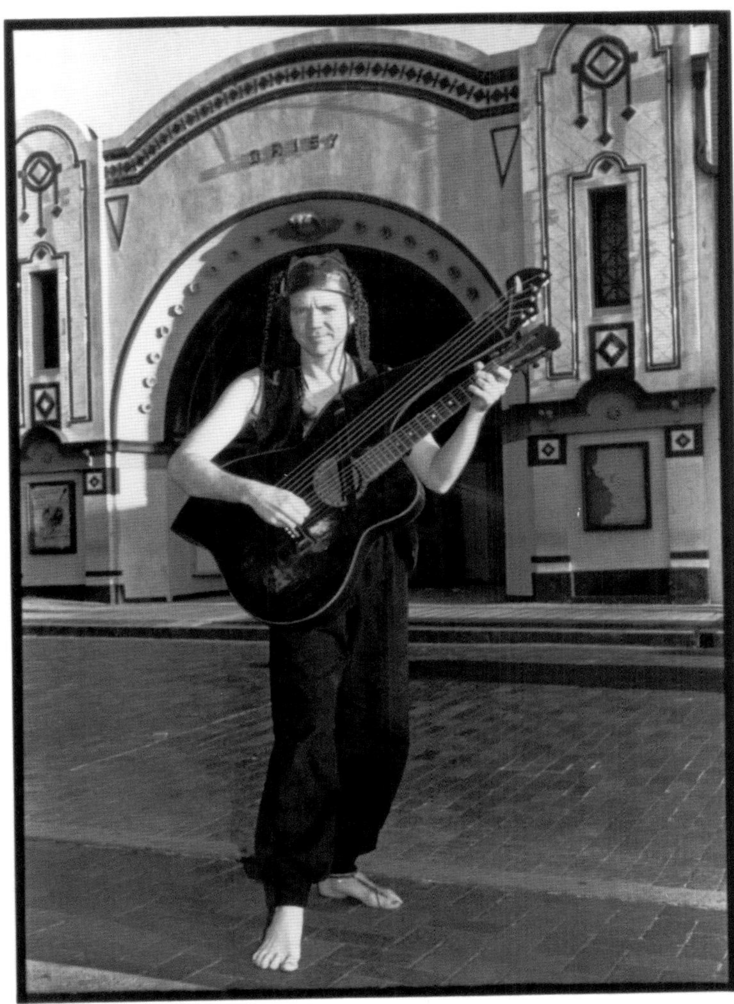

Photo Credit: Ebet Roberts

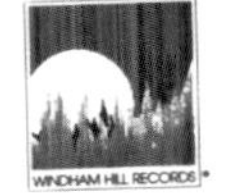


Windham Hill Records
8750 Wilshire Boulevard
Beverly Hills, CA 90211
(310) 358-4800

Windham Hill Recording Artist

# MICHAEL HEDGES

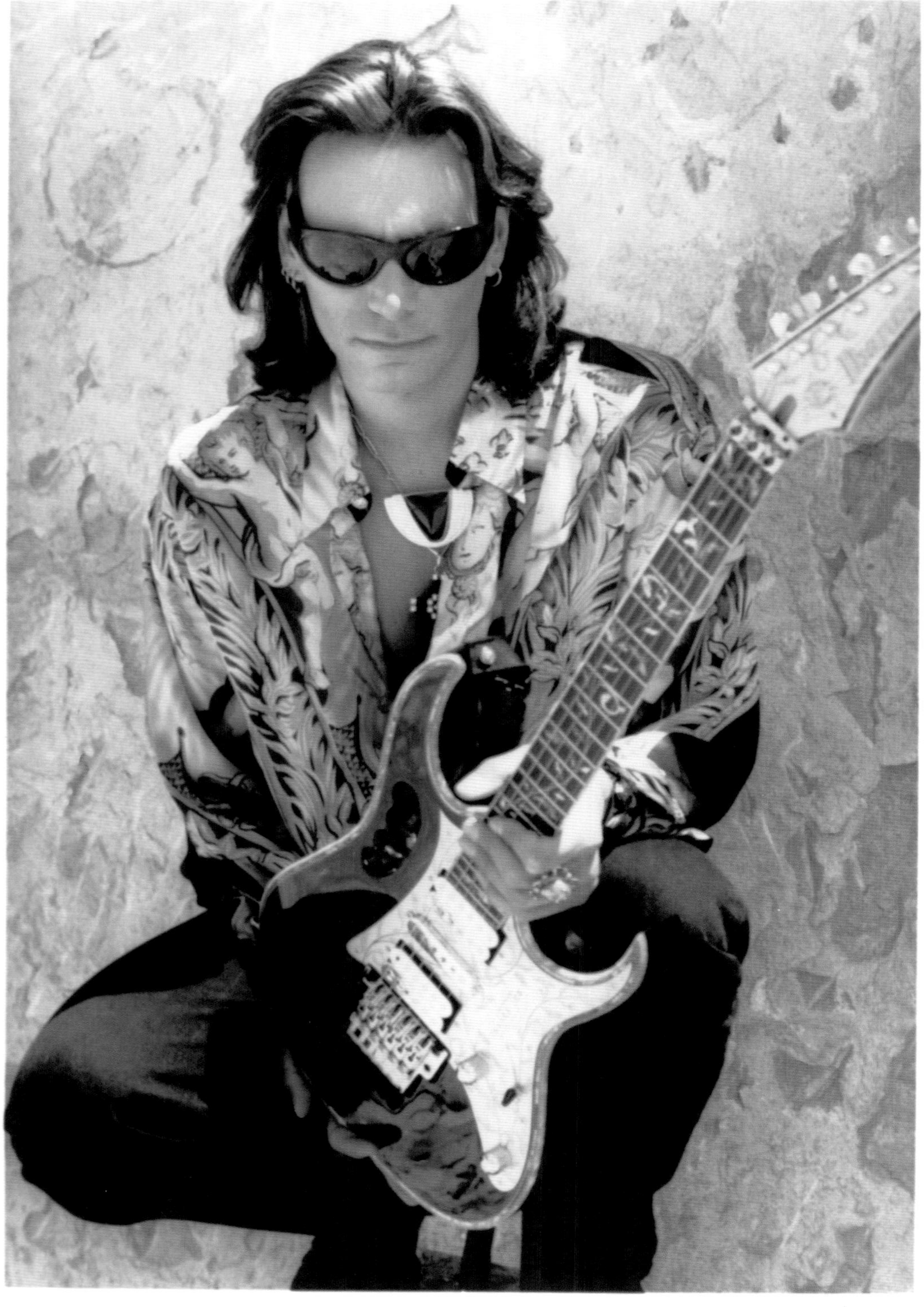

Photo Credit: Ross Pelton

Management By:
SEPETYS ENTERTAINMENT GROUP

# STEVE VAI

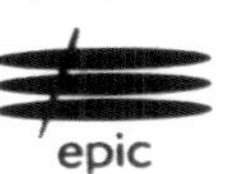

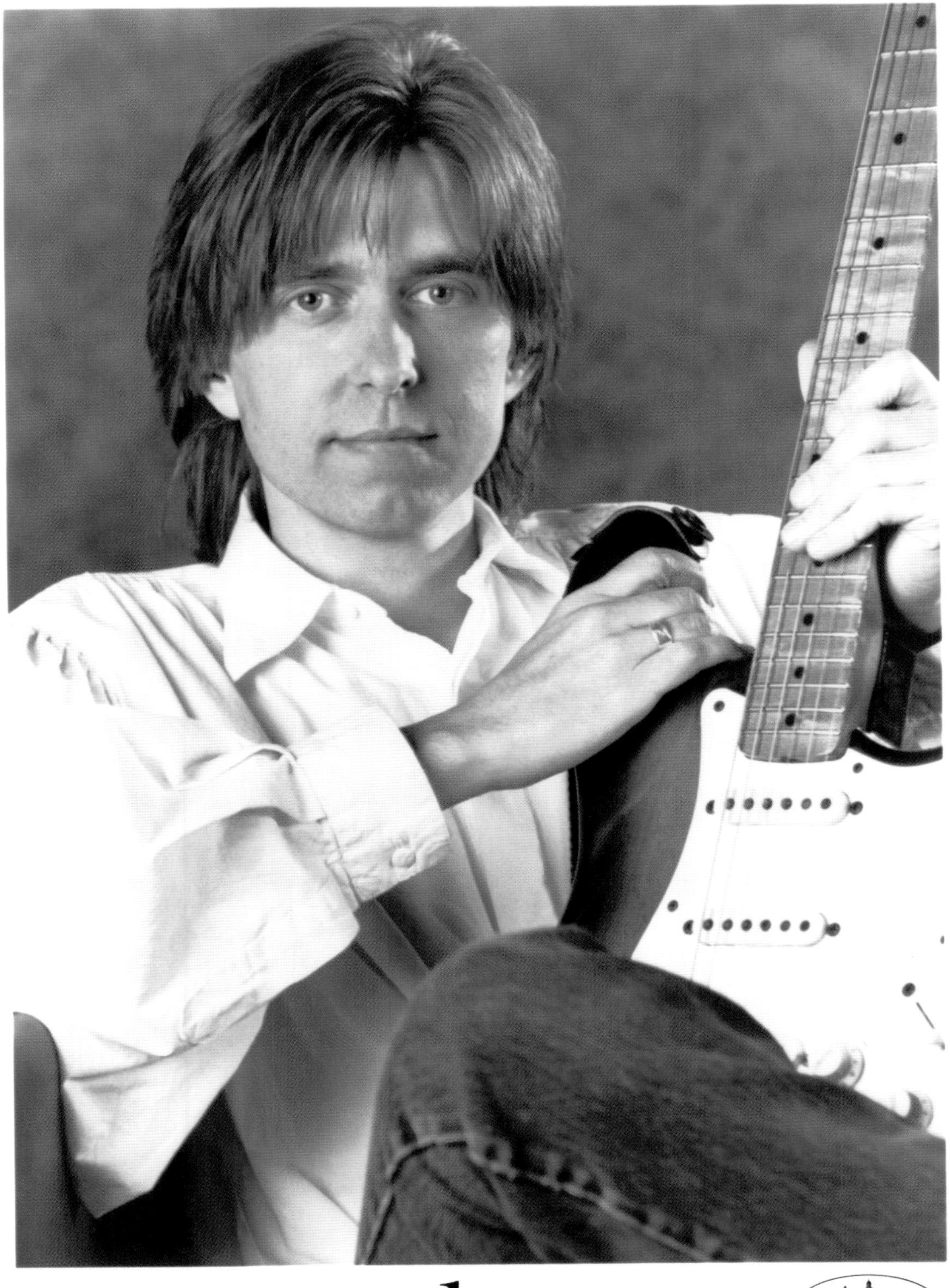

Photo Credit: Max Crace/1996

eric johnson

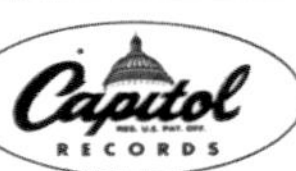

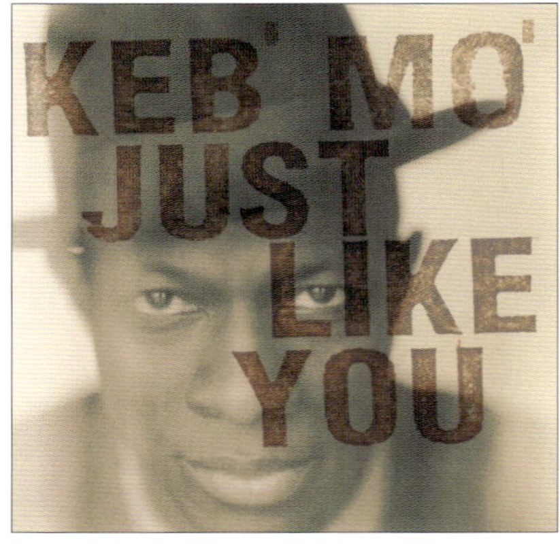


Contemporary bluesman **Keb' Mo'** won his first Grammy for *Just Like You*, featuring vocals by friends Jackson Browne and Bonnie Raitt on the title track.

*Billboard* 200: *Just Like You* (#197)

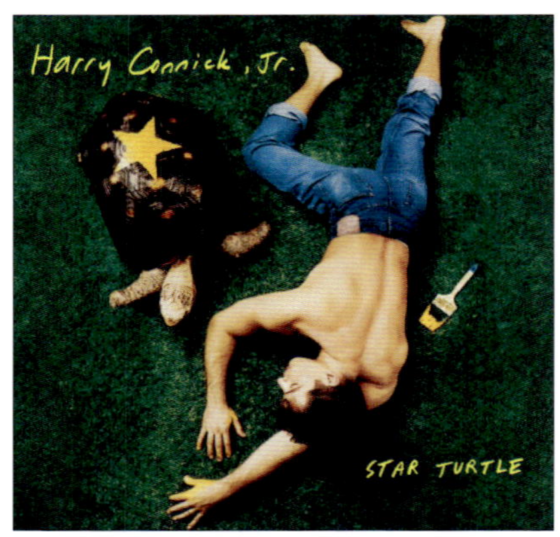


On *Star Turtle*, **Harry Connick, Jr.** treated fans to a second album of New Orleans funk, weaving the bodacious tale of a cosmic reptile seeking salvation.

*Billboard* 200: *Star Turtle* (#38)

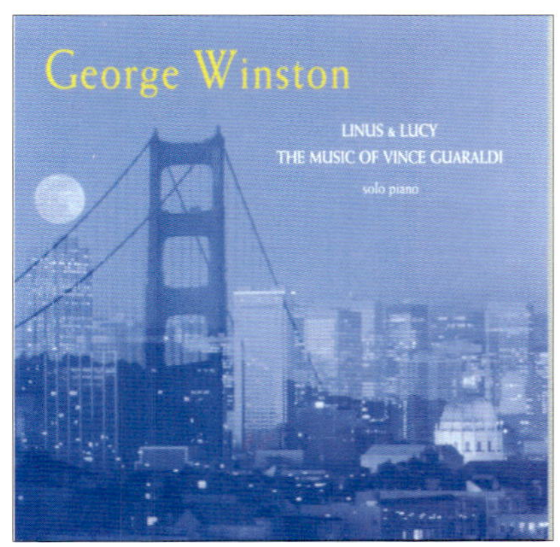


Pianist **George Winston** recorded *Linus & Lucy: The Music of Vince Guaraldi*, paying tribute to the theme music composed for *Peanuts* animated TV specials.

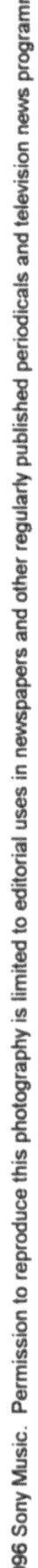


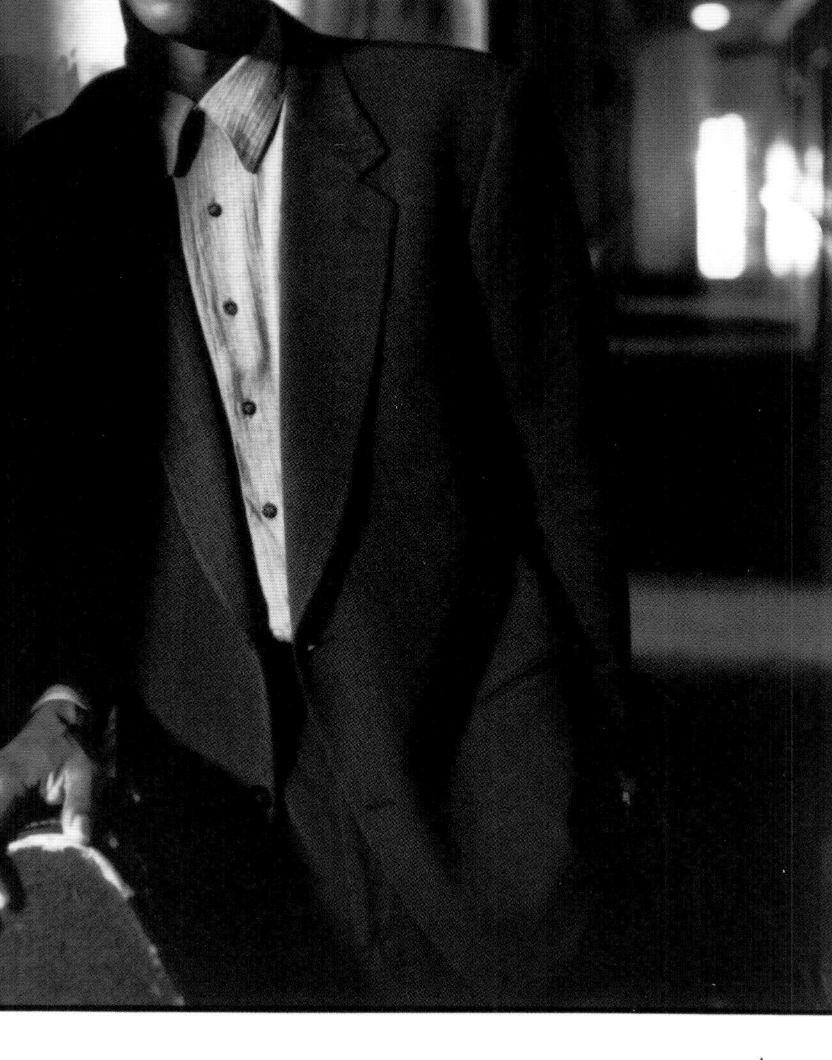

PHOTO CREDIT FRANK OCKENFELS[3]

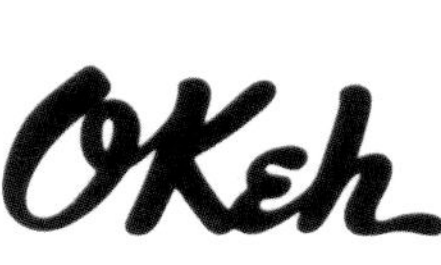


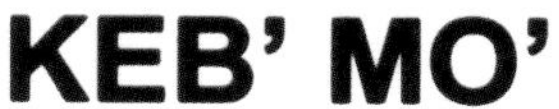

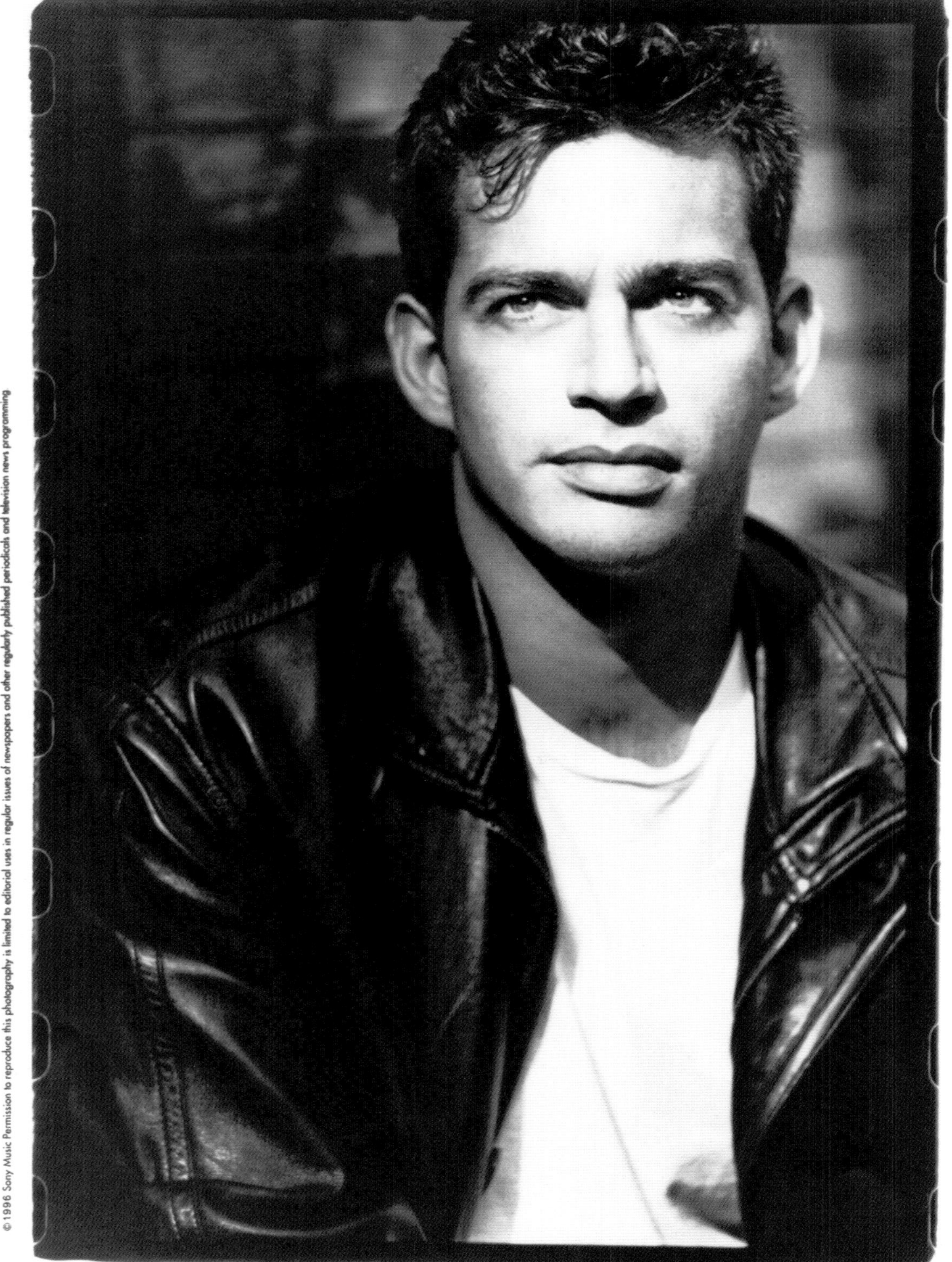

PHOTOGRAPH: PALMA KOLANSKY

**HARRY CONNICK JR.**

COLUMBIA
9605

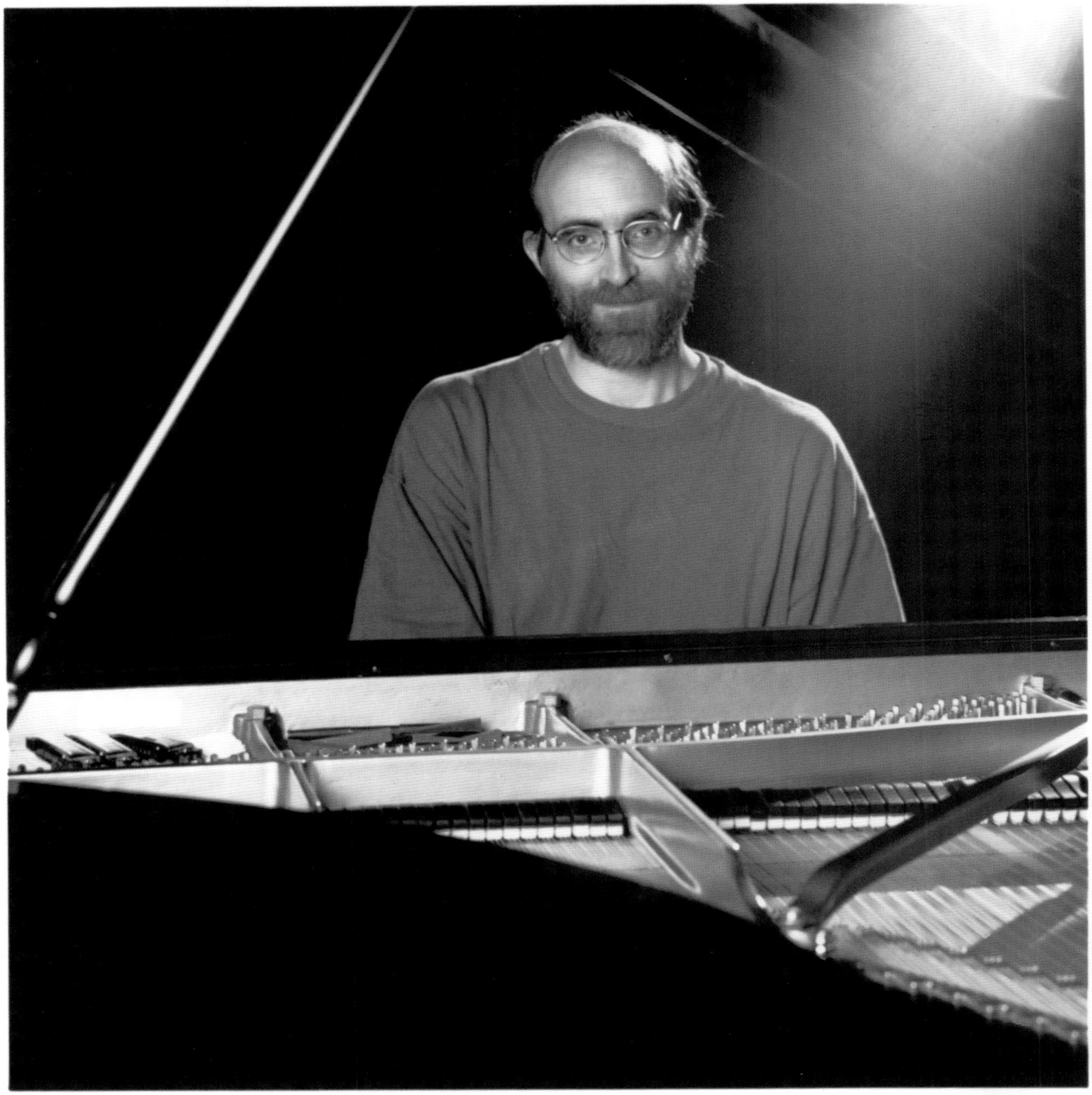

Photo Credit: Lester Cohen

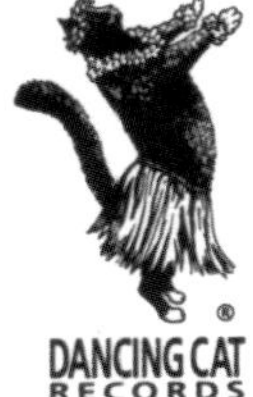


George Winston

8750 Wilshire Boulevard
Beverly Hills, CA 90211
(310) 358-4800

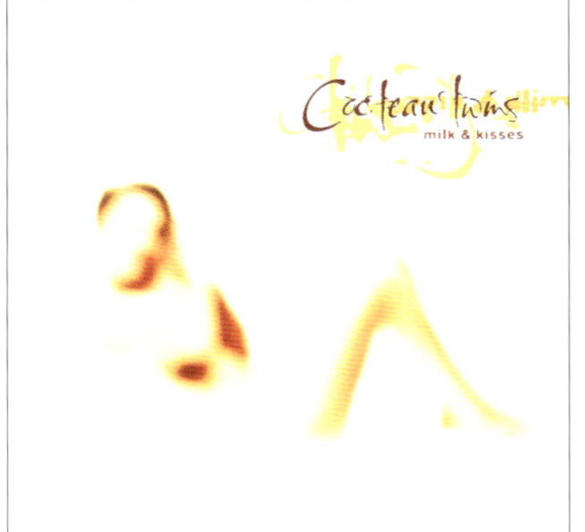


*Milk & Kisses* returned to **Cocteau Twins**' alluring style, grounded in textured guitar work and Elizabeth Fraser's indeterminate lyrics and intoxicating voice.

*Billboard* 200: *Milk & Kisses* (#99)

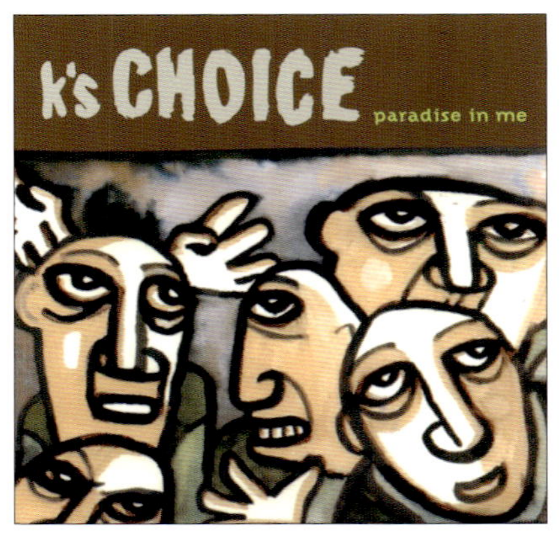


A Belgian quintet centered around a brother-sister duo, **K's Choice** drew attention in Europe and America with "Not an Addict," a lulling modern-rock hit.

*Billboard* 200: *Paradise in Me* (#121)

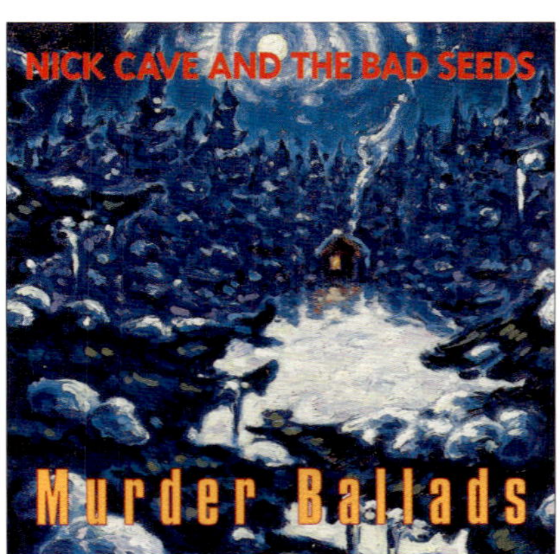


Inspired by death, **Nick Cave & the Bad Seeds**' *Murder Ballads* featured a dark duet with Australian pop idol Kylie Minogue, "Where the Wild Roses Grow."

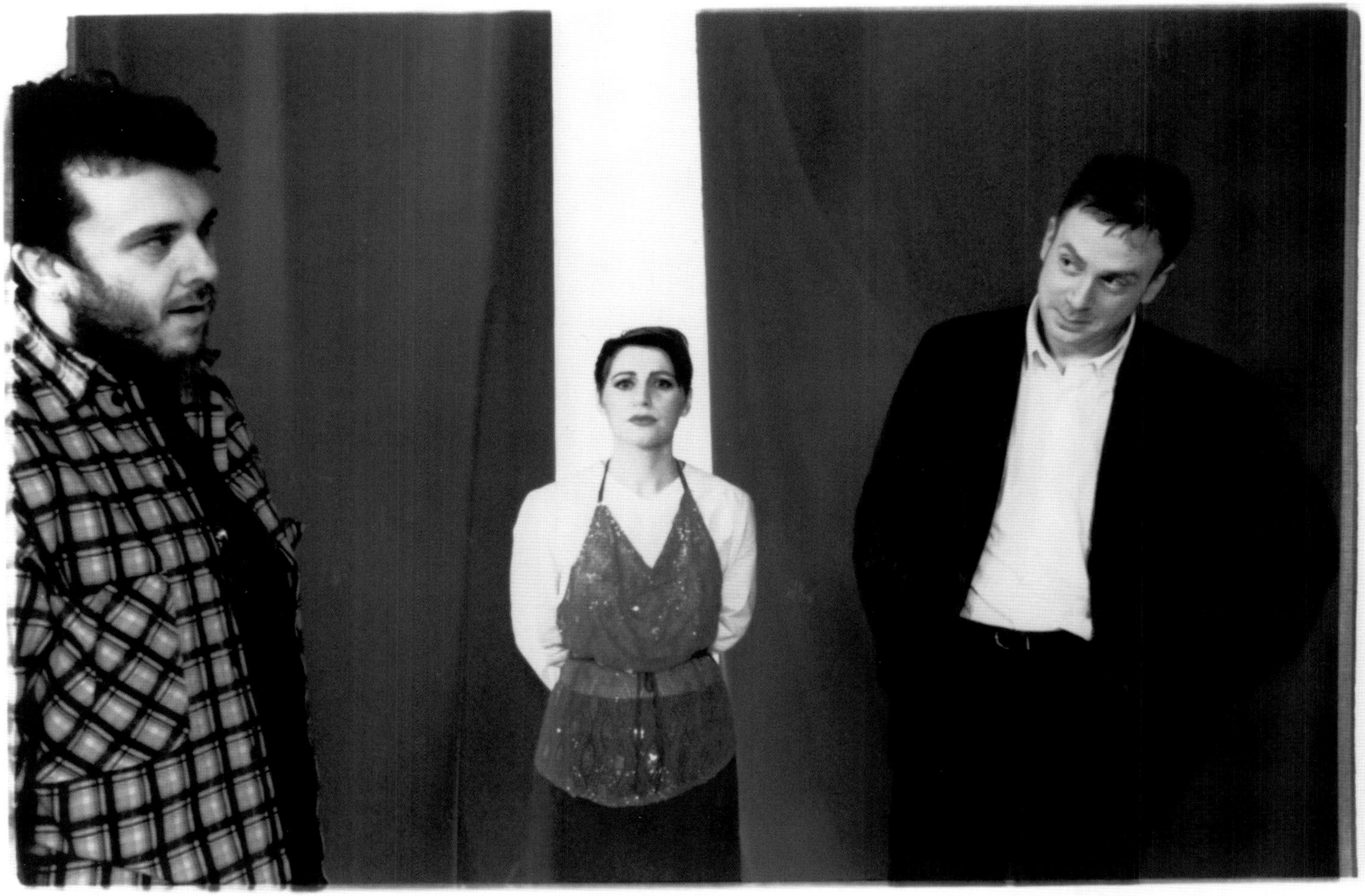

Robin Guthrie

Elizabeth Fraser

Simon Raymonde

PHOTO CREDIT: PAV/1996

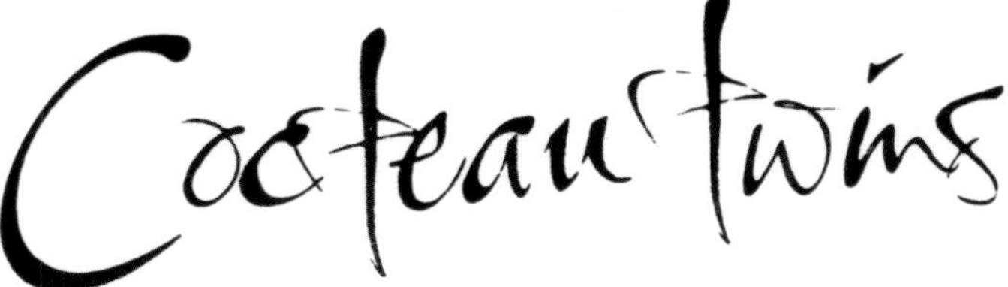


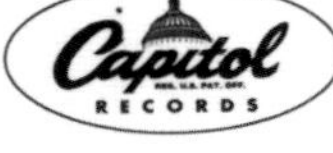

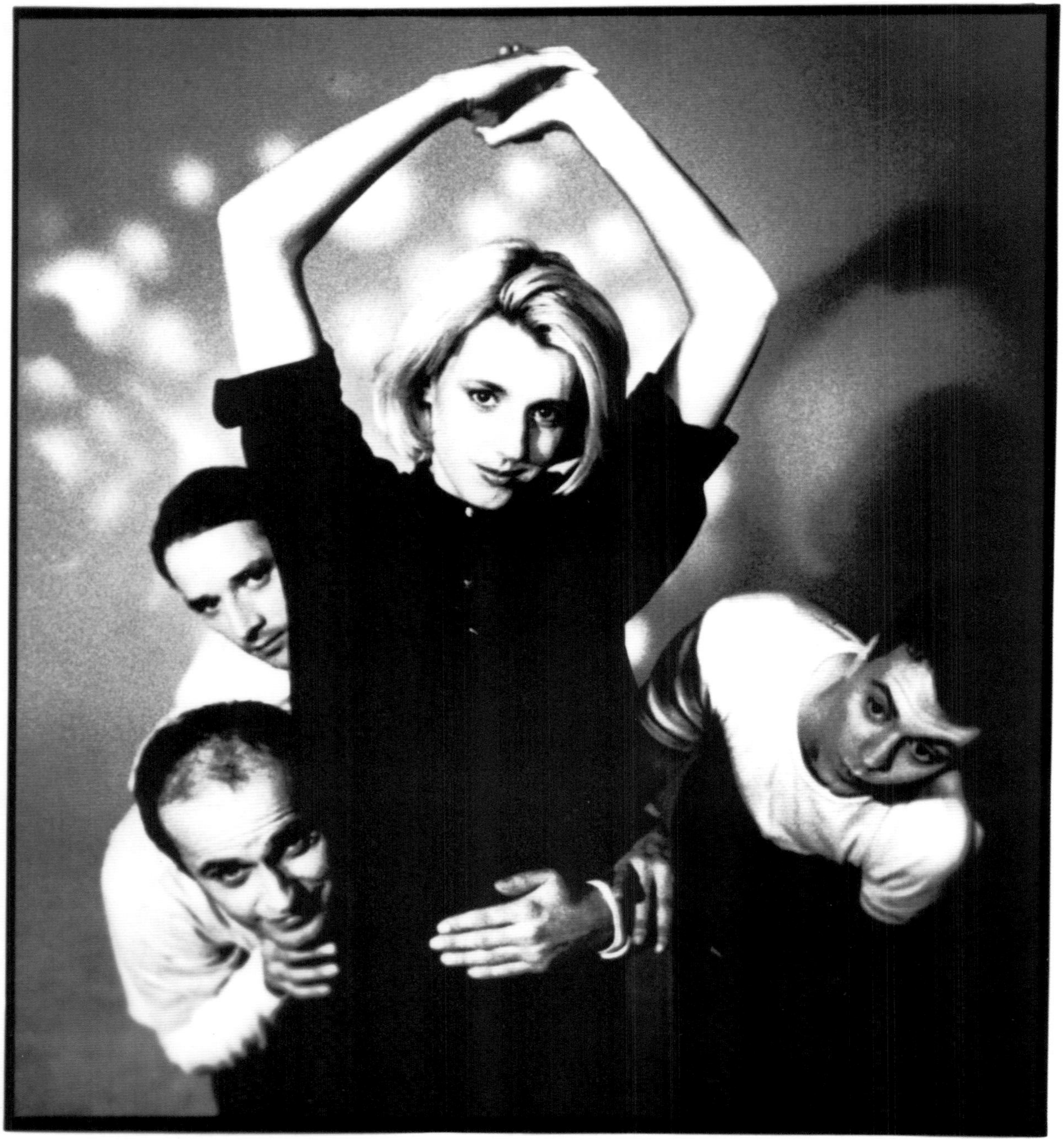

Photo Credit: Stefan Bastelier

Bart Van Der Zeeuw
DRUMS

Sarah Bettens
VOCALS, GUITAR

Jan Van Sichem Jr.
GUITAR

Gert Bettens
VOCALS, GUITAR

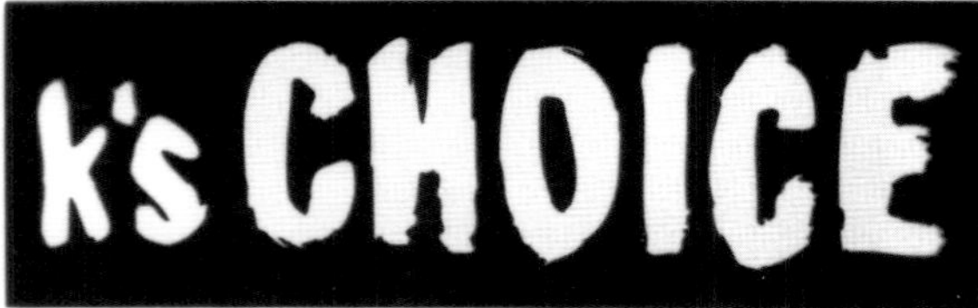


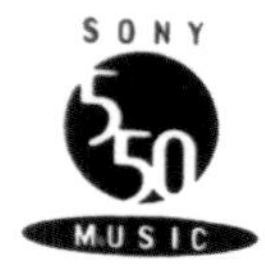

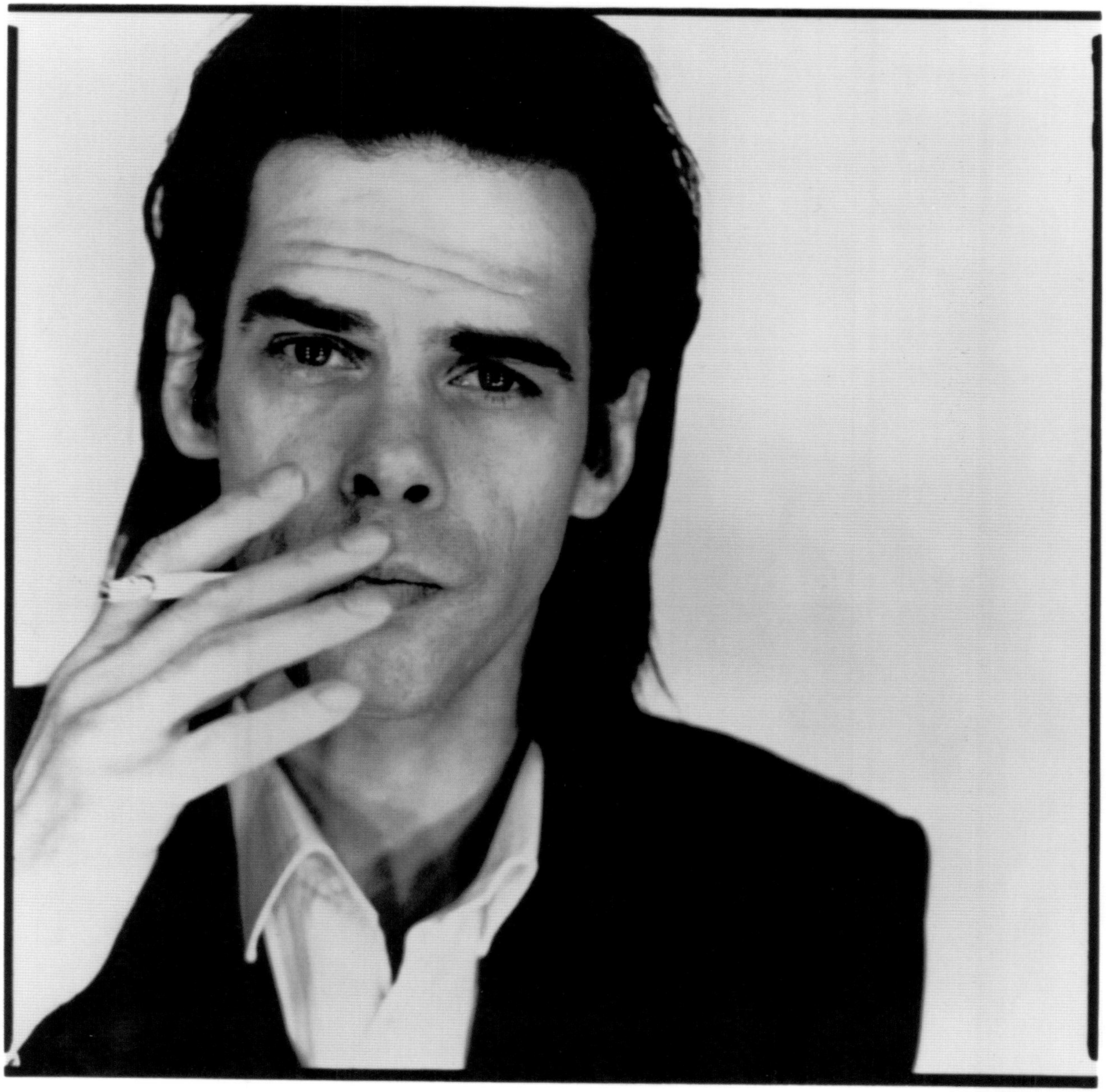

PHOTO CREDIT: Steve Double

# NICK CAVE AND THE BAD SEEDS

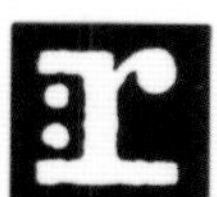

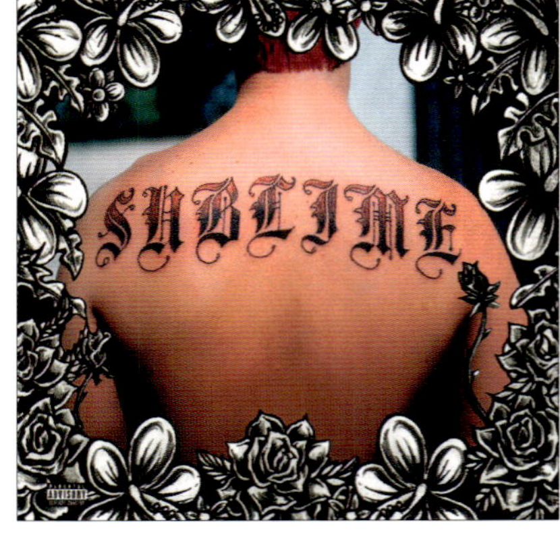


Released two months after leader Brad Nowell died of a heroin overdose, **Sublime**'s self-titled third album triggered a No. 1 modern-rock hit, "What I Got."

*Billboard* 200: *Sublime* (#13)
*Billboard* Hot 100: "Doin' Time" (#87)

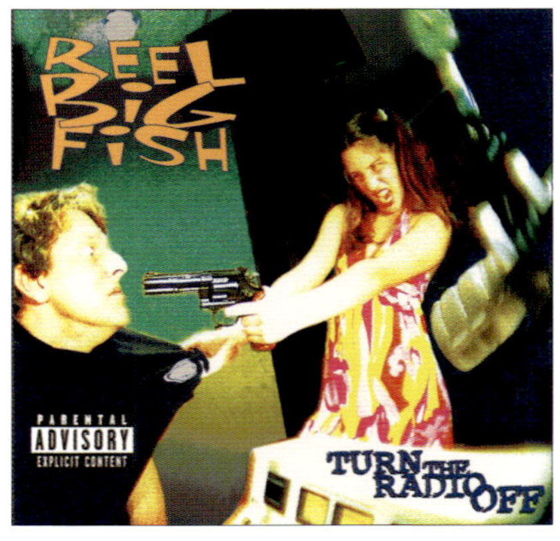


Jump-started by ample radio and MTV play, alternative-rock act **Reel Big Fish** rode a ska-punk wave with "Sell Out," from the album *Turn the Radio Off*.

*Billboard* 200: *Turn the Radio Off* (#57)

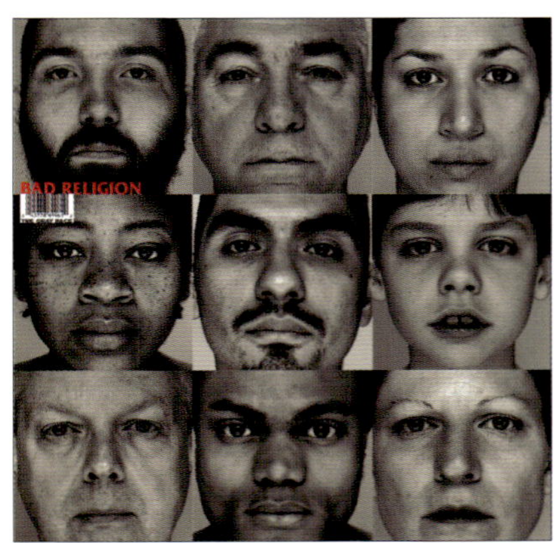


Absent original guitarist Brett Gurewitz, punk band **Bad Religion** cut *The Gray Race* and scored with "A Walk," a fan favorite written by singer Greg Graffin.

*Billboard* 200: *The Gray Race* (#56)

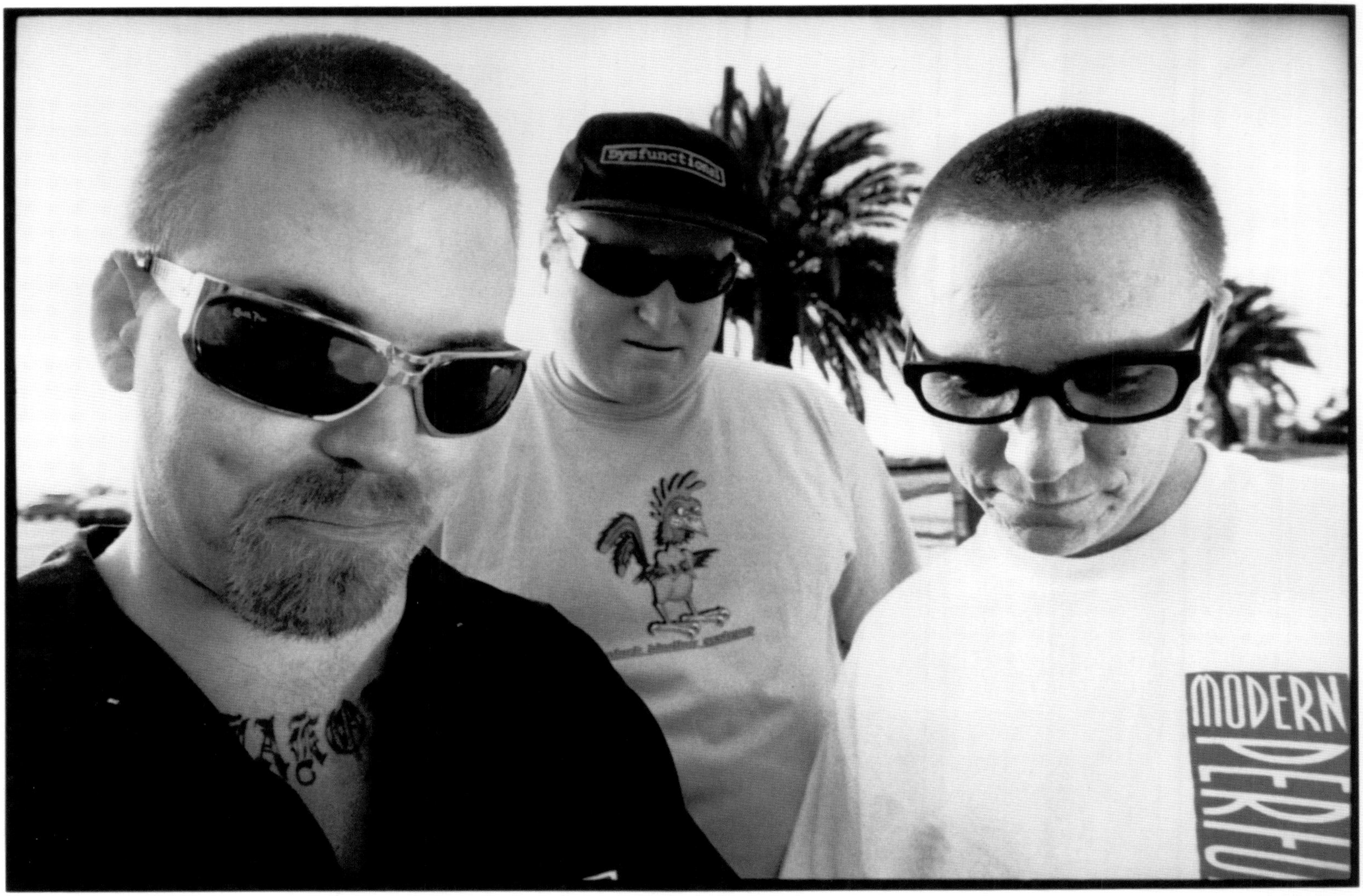

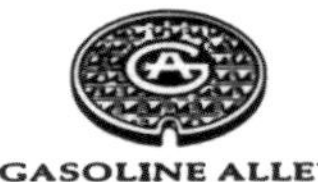


# sublime

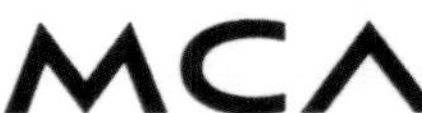

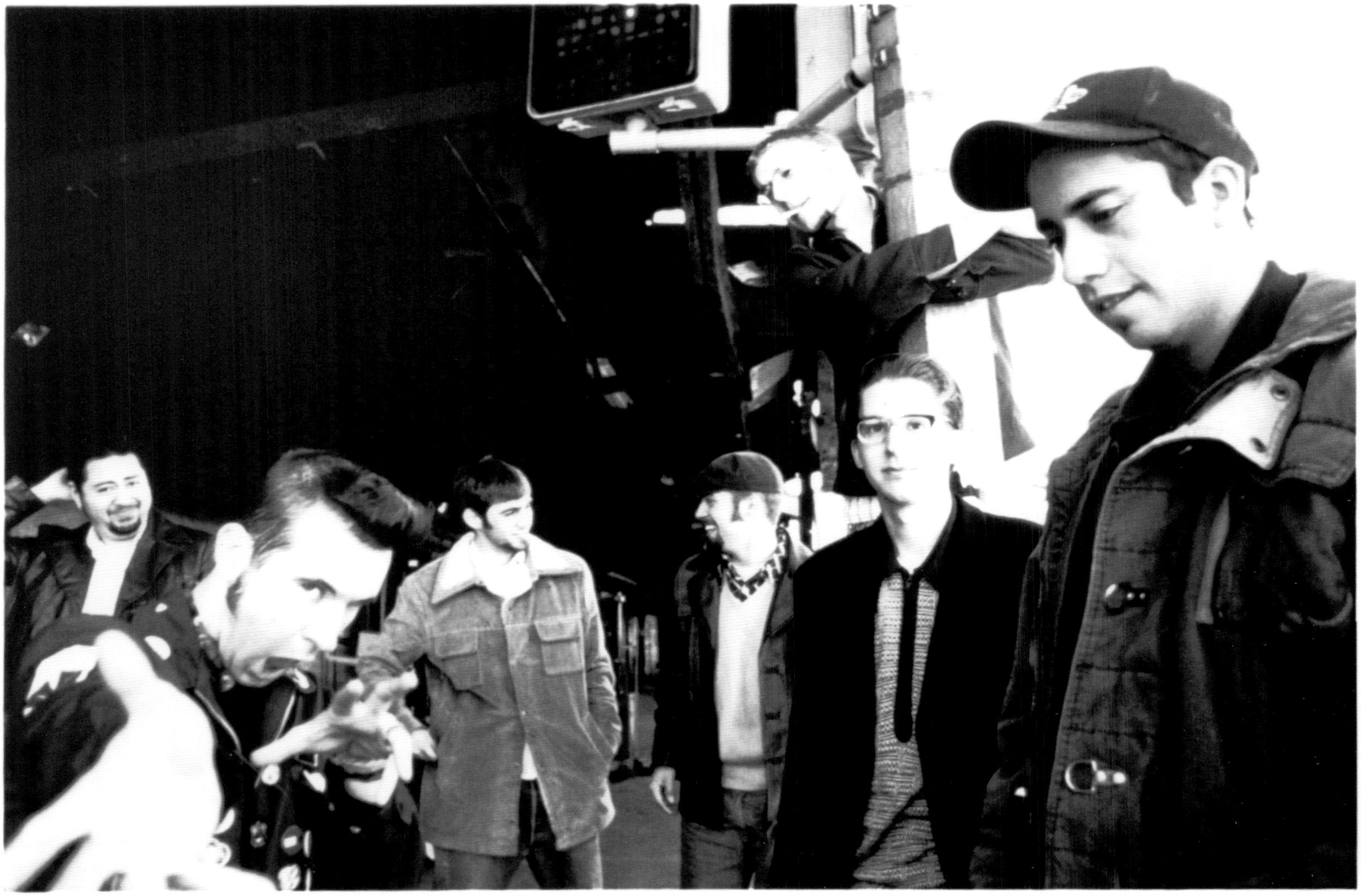

Photo Credit: Paul Whicheloe

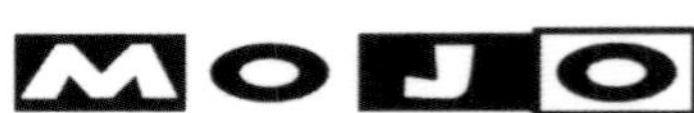


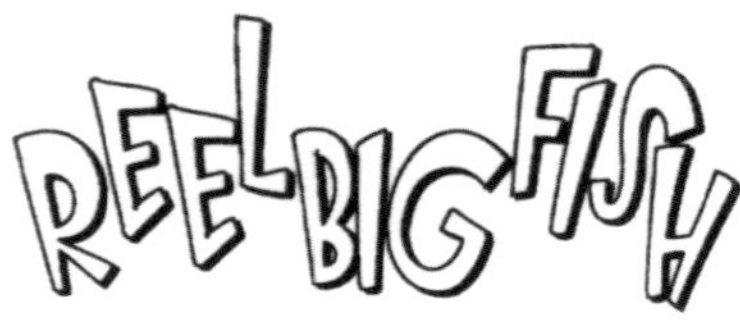


Contact:
Vince Pileggi-Milano Music-714-997-0919
Jenny Bendel-Plain Jane PR-206-324-7447

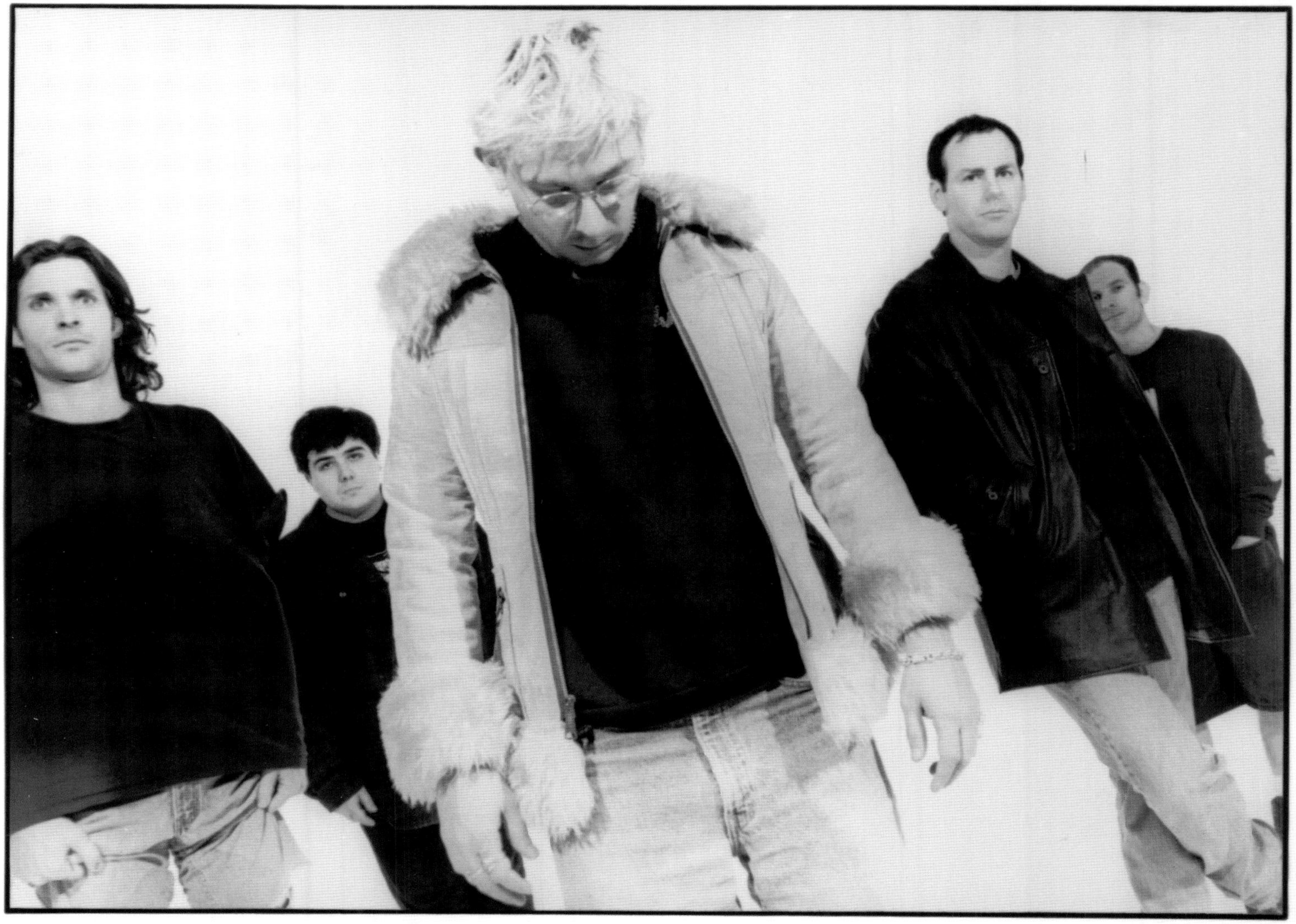

Photo credit: Sheryl Nields

Jay Bentley Bobby Schayer Brian Baker Greg Graffin Greg Hetson

# BAD RELIGION

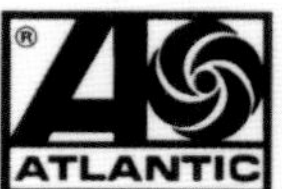

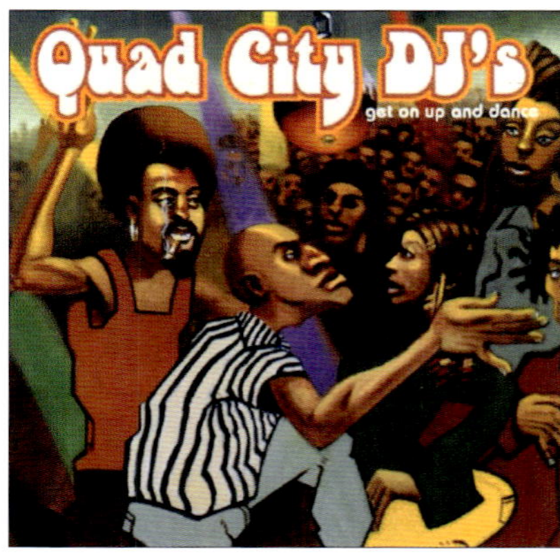


The video clip of the **Quad City DJ's** smash "C'mon N' Ride It (The Train)" drove a dance sensation in the clubs, on college campuses and at NBA games.

*Billboard* 200: *Get on Up and Dance* (#31)
*Billboard* Hot 100: "C'mon N' Ride It (The Train)" (#3)

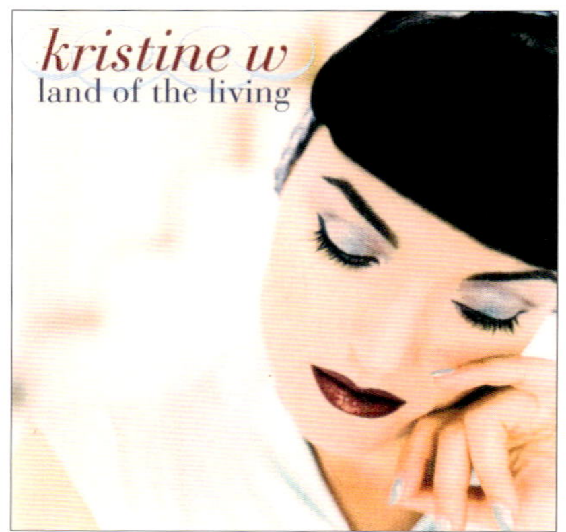


Singer **Kristine W** placed three No. 1 singles on the dance-club charts, the anthemic tracks "Feel What You Want," "One More Try" and "Land of the Living."

*Billboard* Hot 100: "One More Try" (#78)

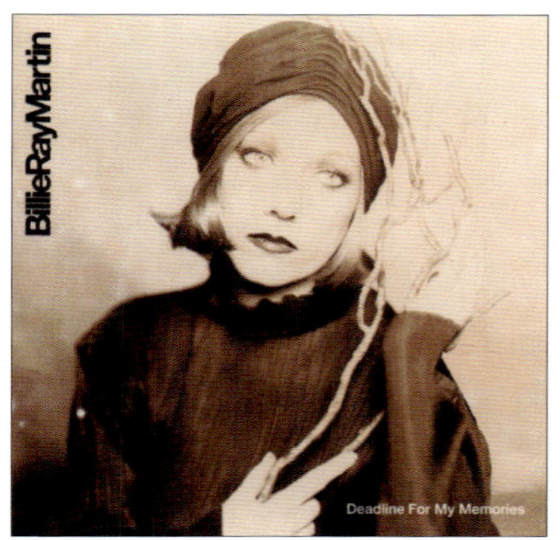


German-born and London-groomed, techno singer and songwriter **Billie Ray Martin** achieved a No. 1 dance-club track in America with "Your Loving Arms."

*Billboard* Hot 100: "Your Loving Arms" (#46)

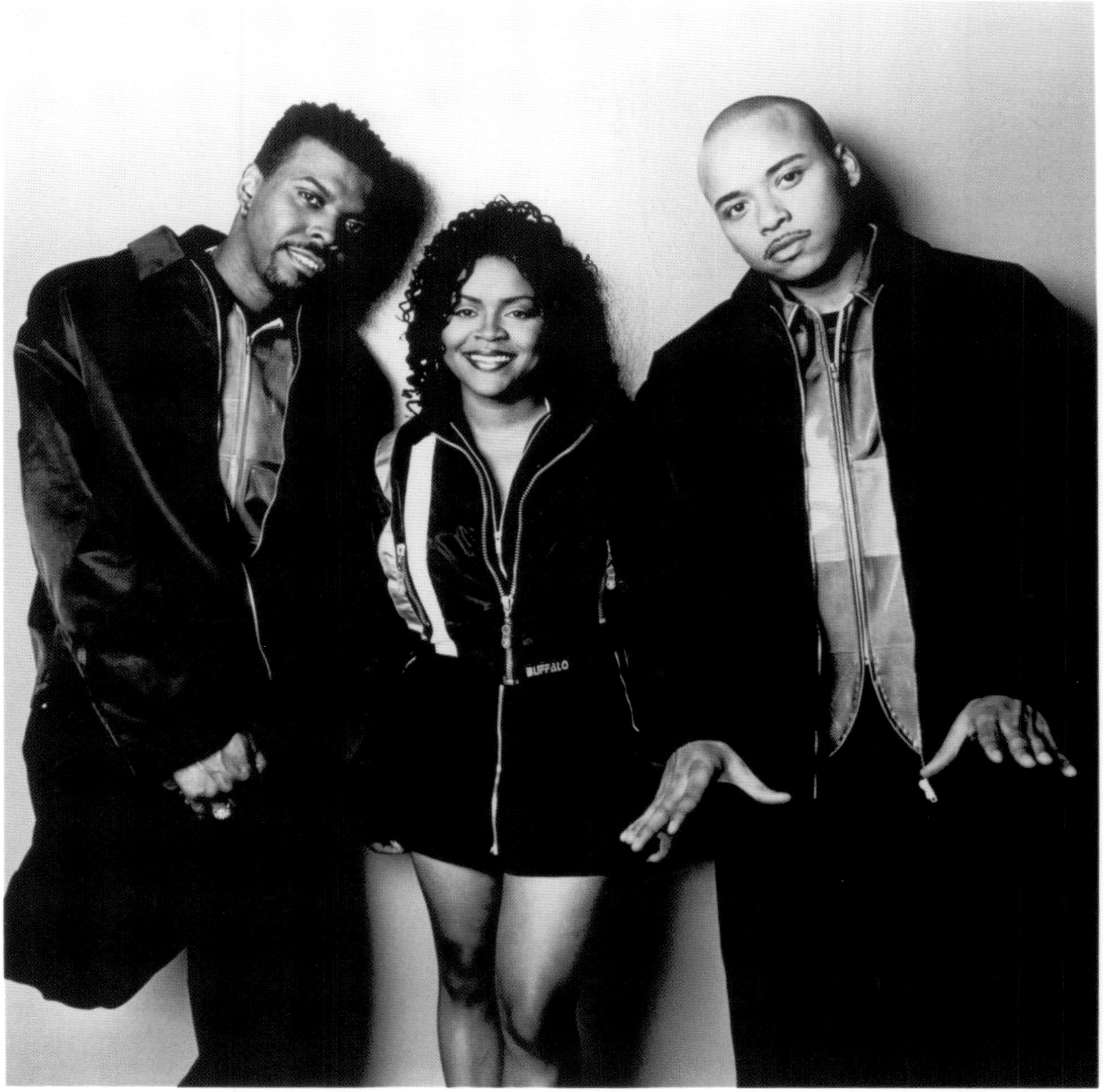

Photo Credit: Angelika

# QUAD CITY DJ'S

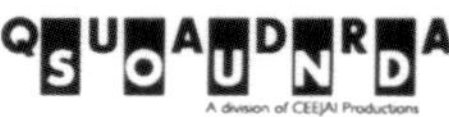


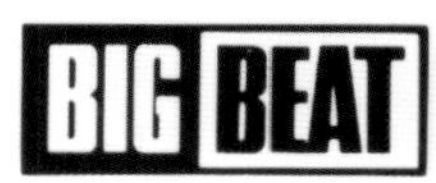


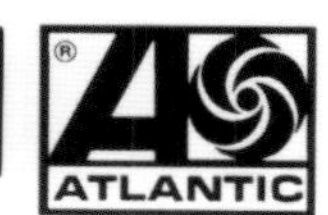

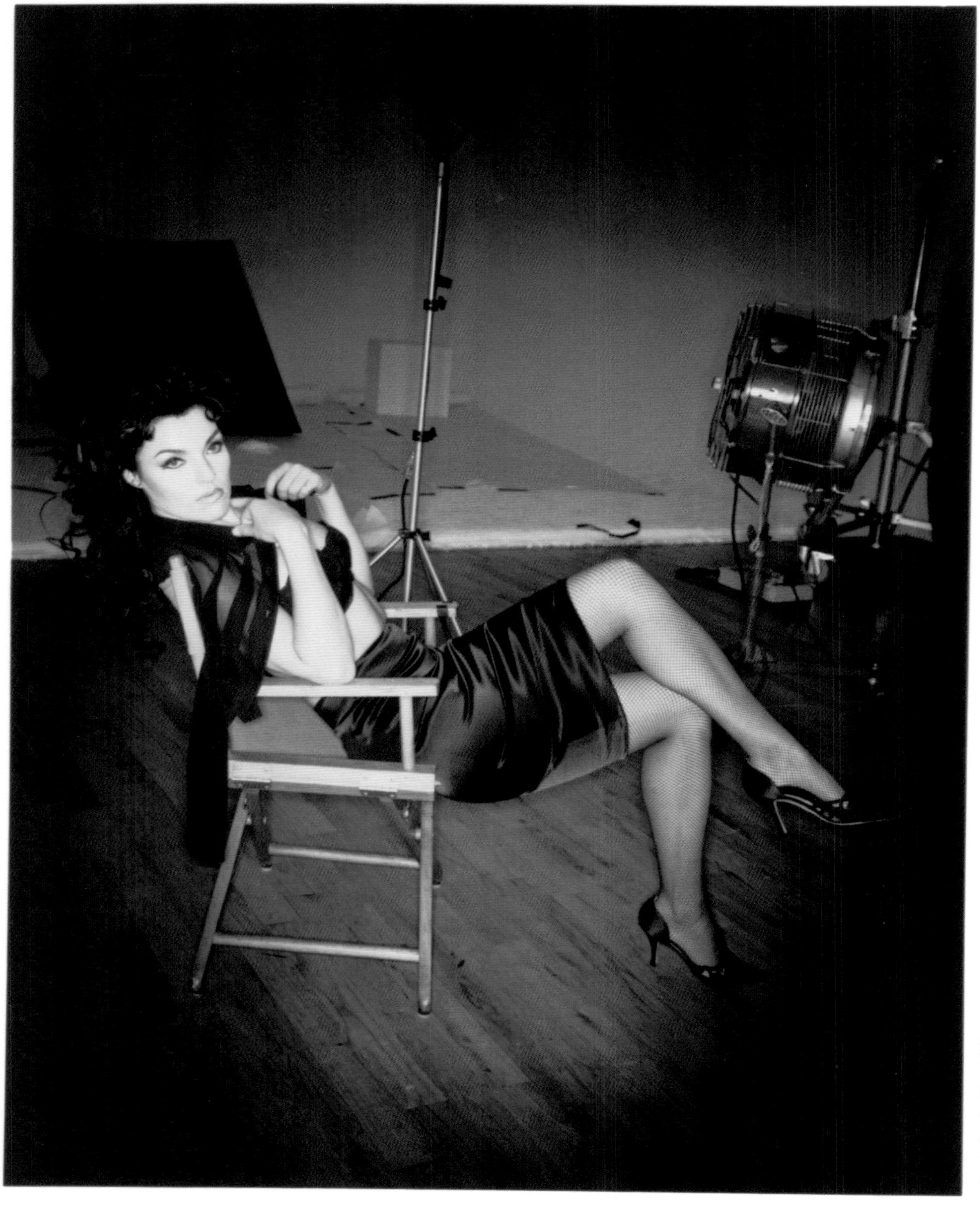

Photo Credit: Naomi Kaltman

# KRISTINE W

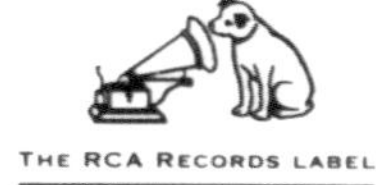

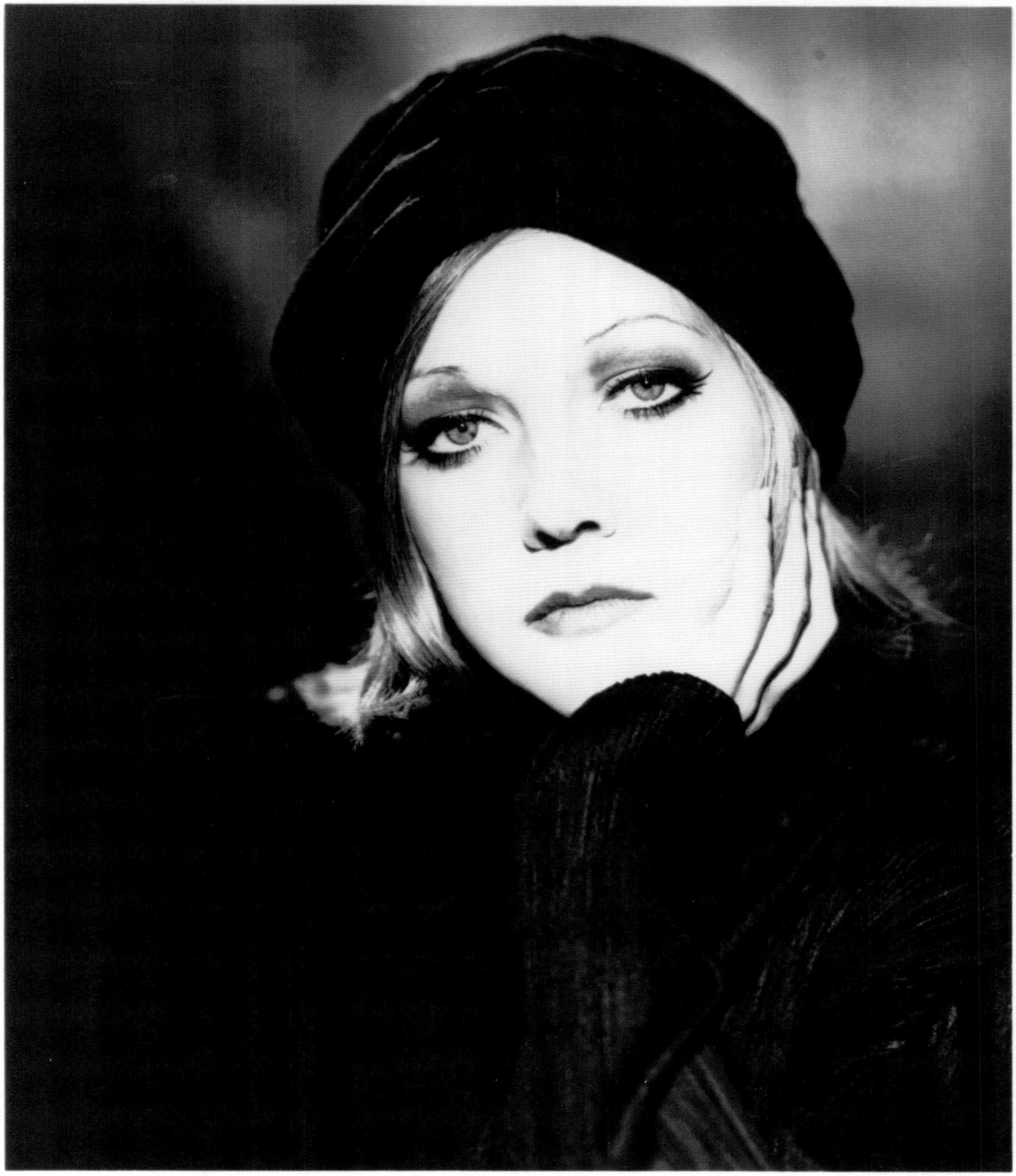

BillieRayMartin

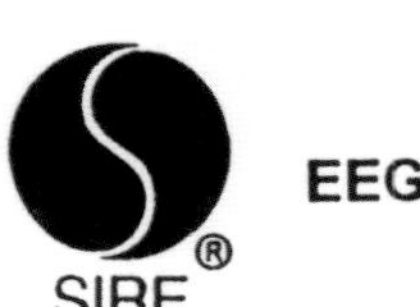


EEG

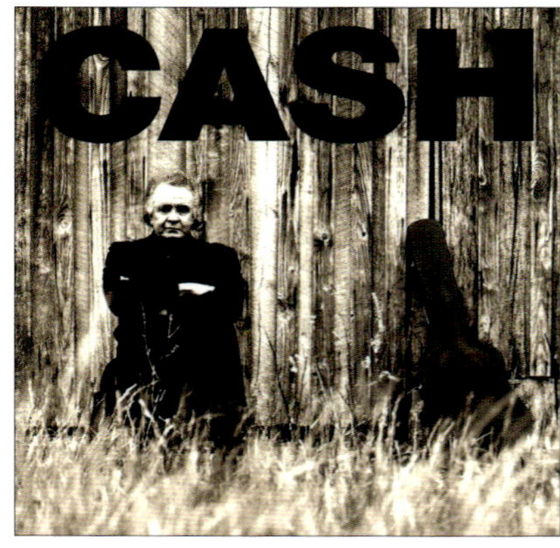


In the late stage of his career, **Johnny Cash**'s determination to experiment resulted in *Unchained*, featuring support from Tom Petty & the Heartbreakers.

*Billboard* 200: *Unchained* (#170)

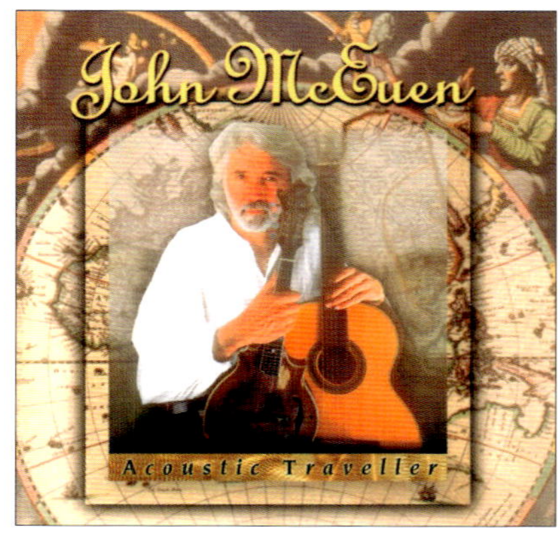


A cofounder of the Nitty Gritty Dirt Band, **John McEuen** dazzled with his wizardry on vintage stringed instruments for *Acoustic Traveller*, a solo sojourn.

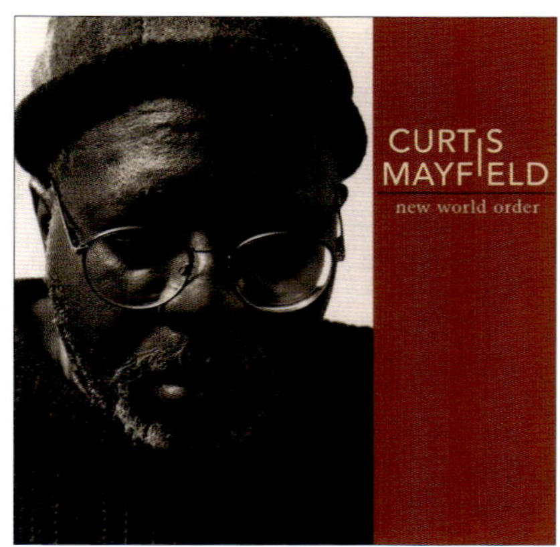


Left paralyzed from the neck down by a 1990 stage mishap, the great **Curtis Mayfield** continued to write songs and sing, reemerging with *New World Order*.

*Billboard* 200: *New World Order* (#137)

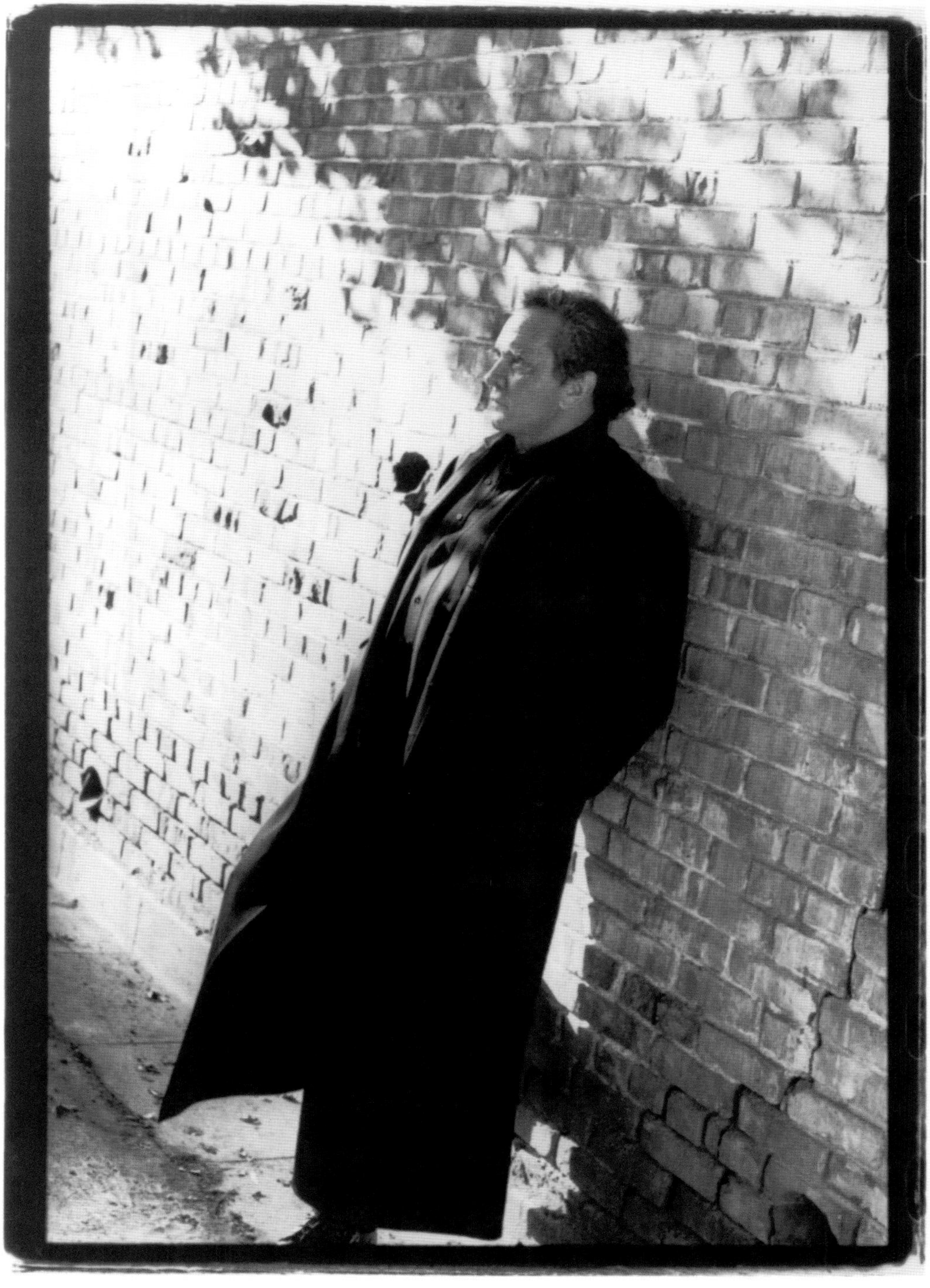

Photo Credit: Dana Tynan

# JOHNNY CASH

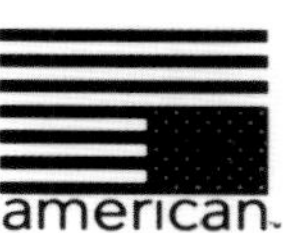

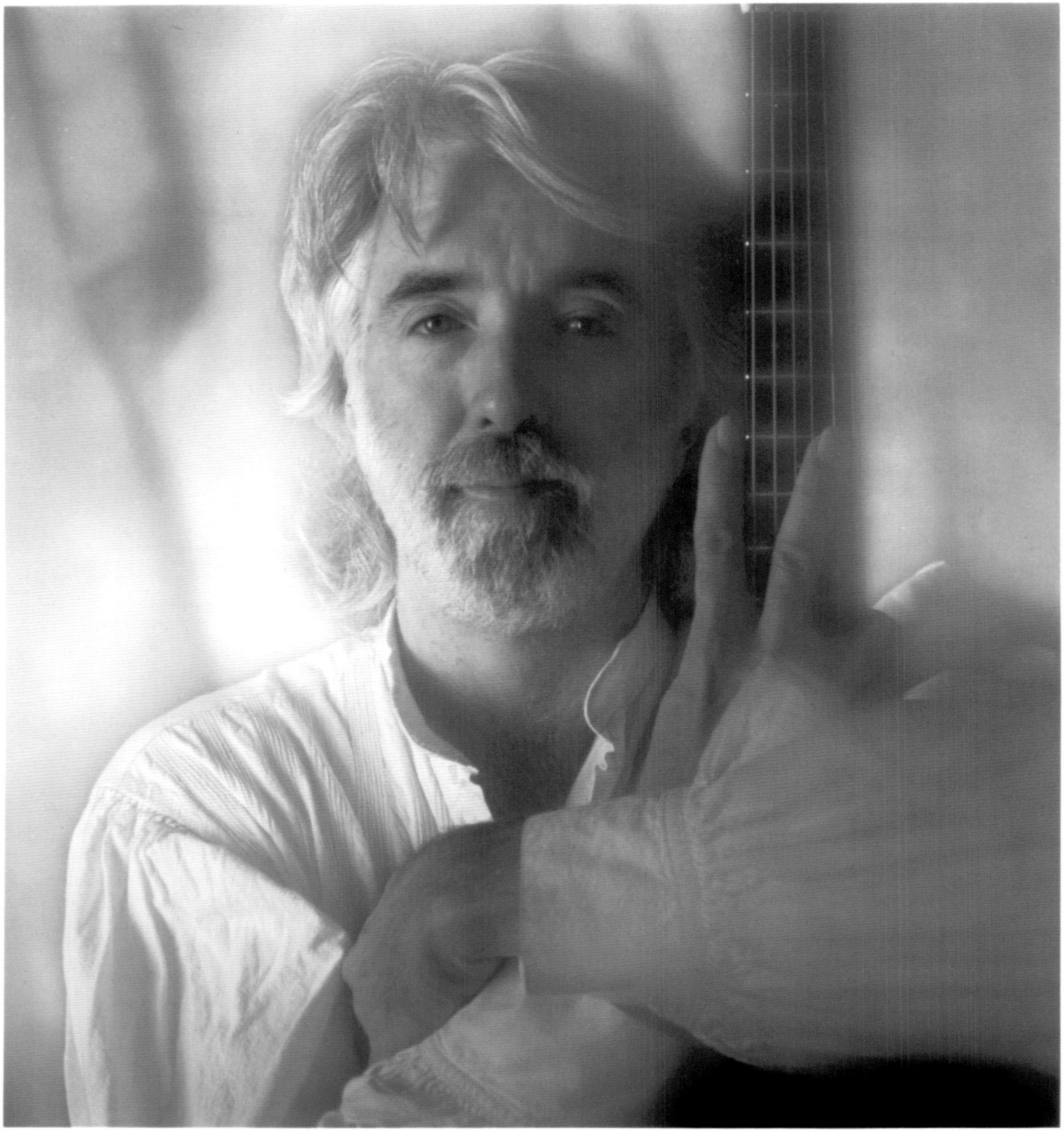

photo by: Gary Regester

# JOHN McEUEN

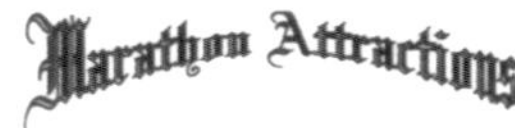


Lee Farmer
(615)248-8500

VANGUARD

**VANGUARD RECORDING SOCIETY**
VANGUARD RECORDS, A WELK MUSIC GROUP COMPANY
1299 OCEAN AVENUE, SANTA MONICA, CA 90401
PHONE 310-451-5727 FAX 310-394-4148
Email: Vangardrec@aol.com

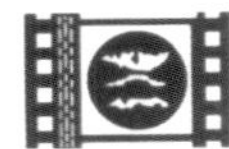

Aspen Management
(801)265-8486
(800)895-2984
(805)684-7778

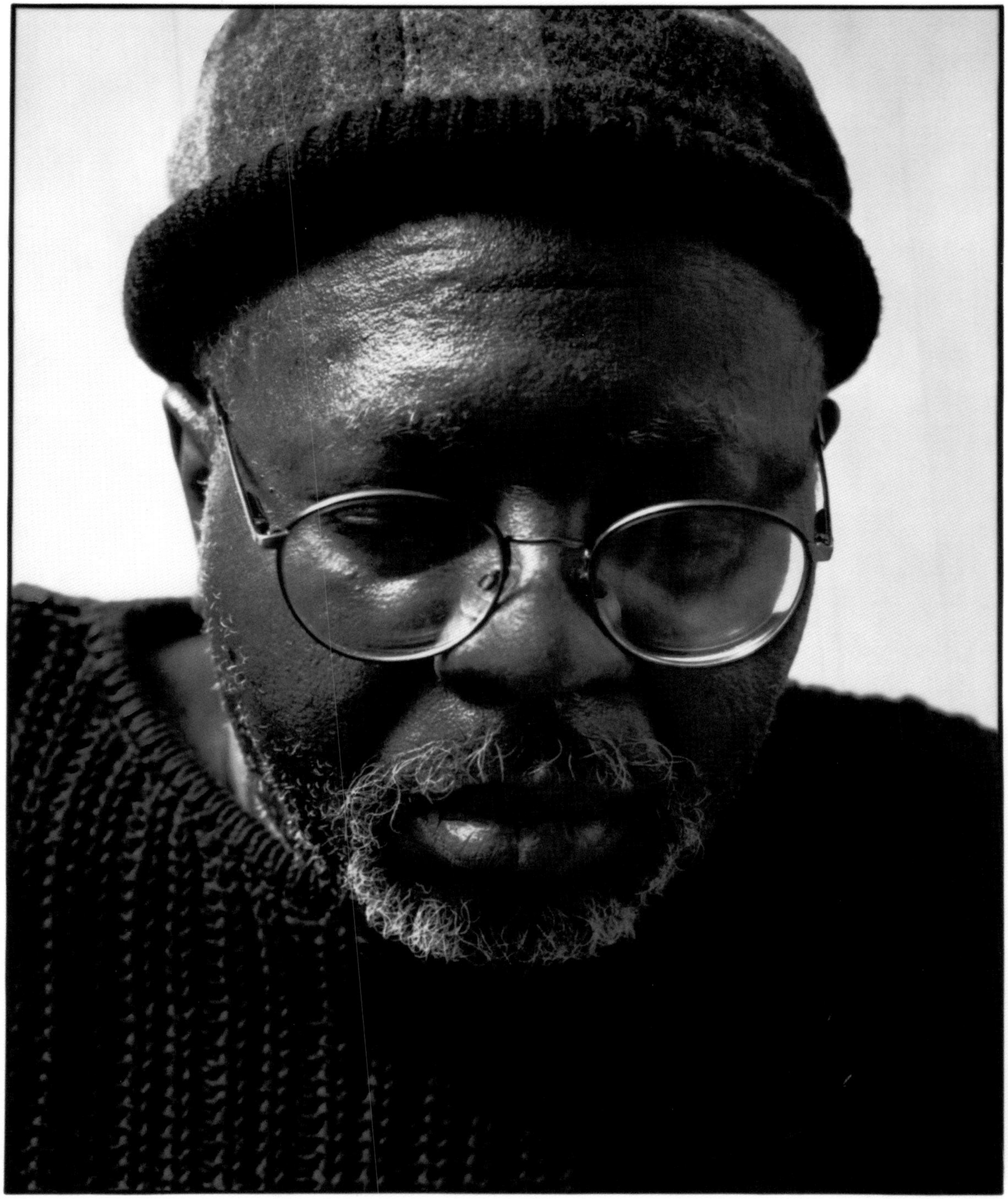

Photo Credit: Dana Lixenberg

CURTIS
MAYFIELD

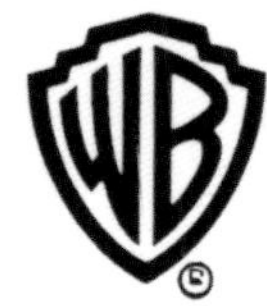

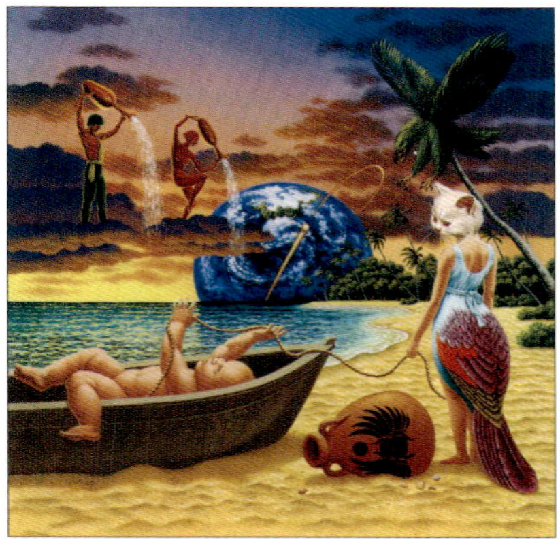

**Journey**'s classic Eighties lineup reunited after a 10-year lull, recording the album *Trial by Fire* and a Top 20 hit, the ballad "When You Love a Woman."

*Billboard* 200: *Trial by Fire* (#3)
*Billboard* Hot 100: "When You Love a Woman" (#12)

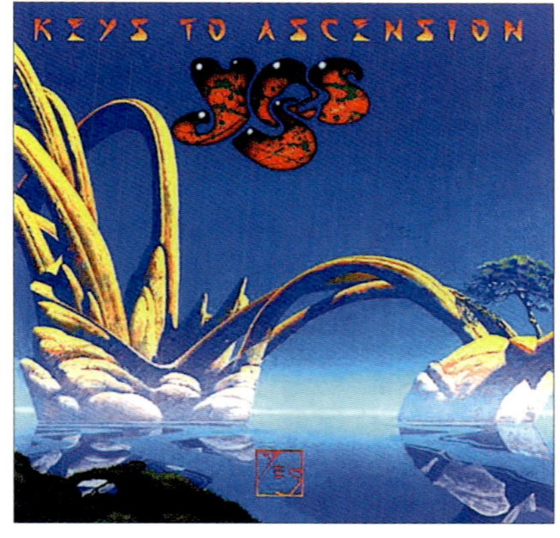


Members of **Yes** from the mid-Seventies recorded live shows in California and two longform studio tracks, released as *Keys to Ascension*, a double album.

*Billboard* 200: *Keys to Ascension* (#99)

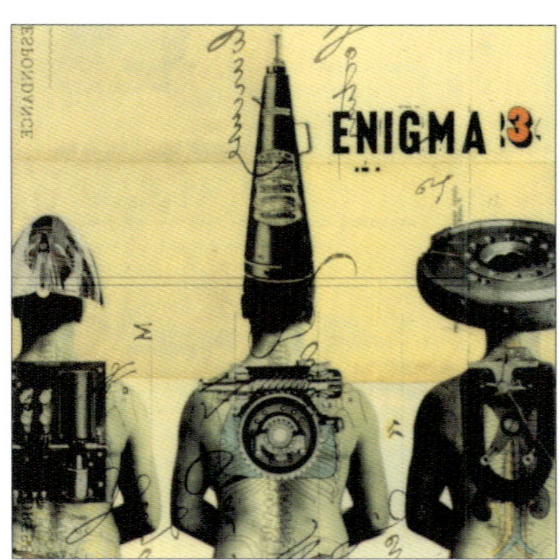


*Le Roi Est Mort, Vive Le Roi!*, **Enigma**'s third album, bore producer Michael Cretu's familiar sonics, Gregorian chants with pan-cultural atmospherics.

*Billboard* 200: *Le Roi Est Mort, Vive Le Roi!* (#25)

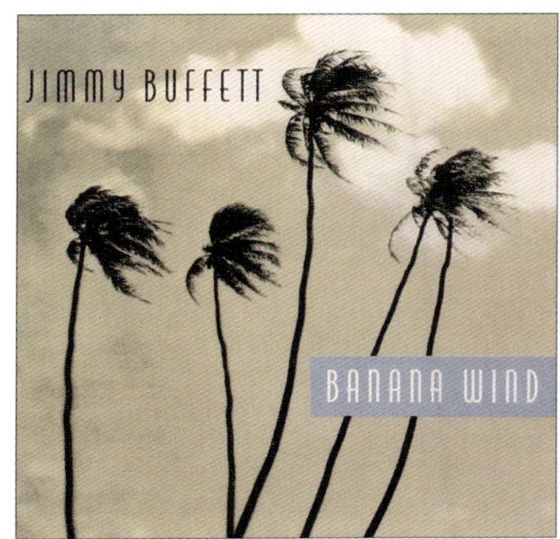


**Jimmy Buffett** penned "Jamaica Mistaica" when his personal seaplane was shot at by Jamaican police, who mistook the craft for a smuggling operation.

*Billboard* 200: *Banana Wind* (#4)

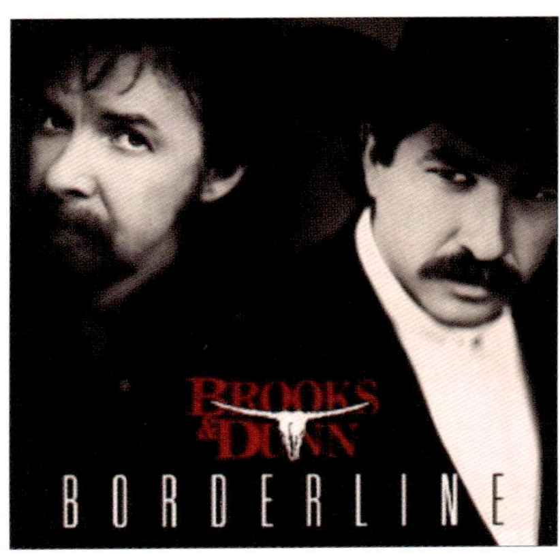


**Brooks & Dunn** reached No. 1 on the country music charts and earned a Grammy with "My Maria," a cover version of B.W. Stevenson's 1972 pop hit.

*Billboard* 200: *Borderline* (#5)
*Billboard* Hot 100: "My Maria" (#79)

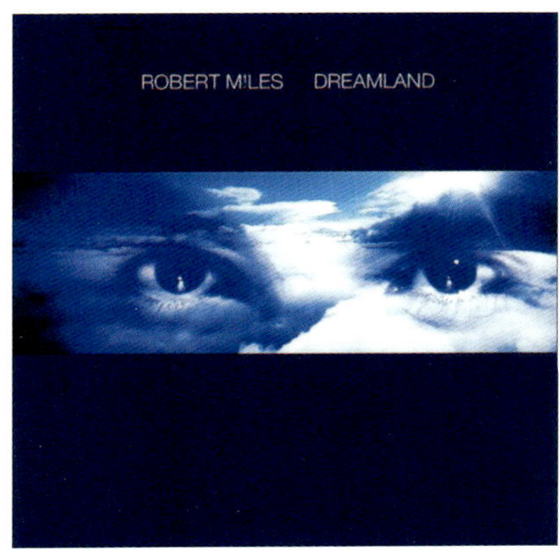


With "Children," an instrumental composition in the "dream house" genre, Italian DJ **Robert Miles** topped the charts in more than 12 countries worldwide.

*Billboard* 200: *Dreamland* (#54)
*Billboard* Hot 100: "Children" (#21); "One and One" (#54)

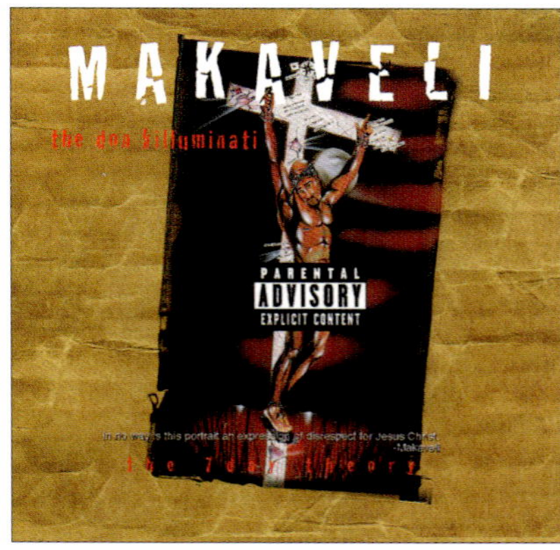


*The Don Killuminati: The 7 Day Theory*, a posthumous album by rapper Tupac Shakur and issued under the stage name of **Makaveli**, debuted at No. 1.

*Billboard* 200: *The Don Killuminati: The 7 Day Theory* (No. 1)
*Billboard* Hot 100: "Toss It Up" (#28); "To Live & Die in L.A." (#33); "Hail Mary" (#24)

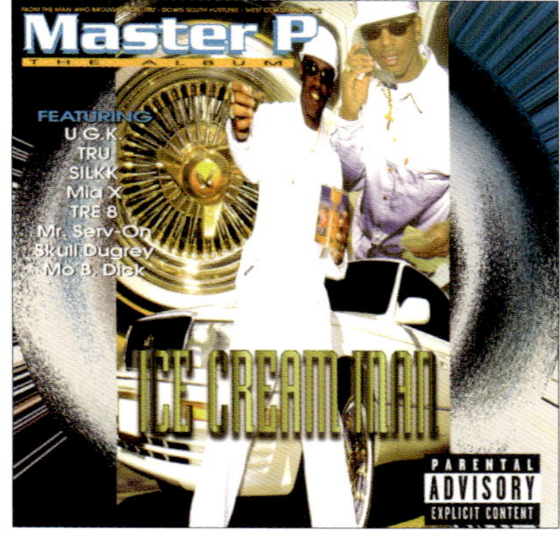


**Master P**, his No Limit label and the Beats by the Pound production team gained fame with *Ice Cream Man*, the New Orleans rapper's fifth solo album.

*Billboard* 200: *Ice Cream Man* (#26)
*Billboard* Hot 100: "Mr. Ice Cream Man" (#90)

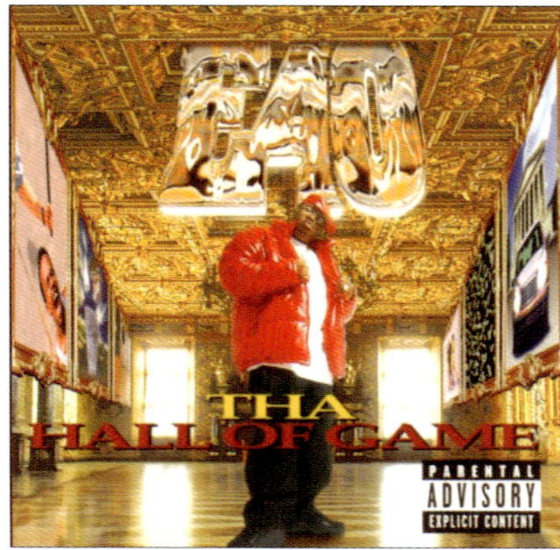


"Things'll Never Change," a single from Bay Area rapper **E-40**'s *Tha Hall of Game*, revised Bruce Hornsby's "The Way It Is" as a reminder of ghetto life.

*Billboard* 200: *Tha Hall of Game* (#4)
*Billboard* Hot 100: "Things'll Never Change"/"Rapper's Ball" (#29)

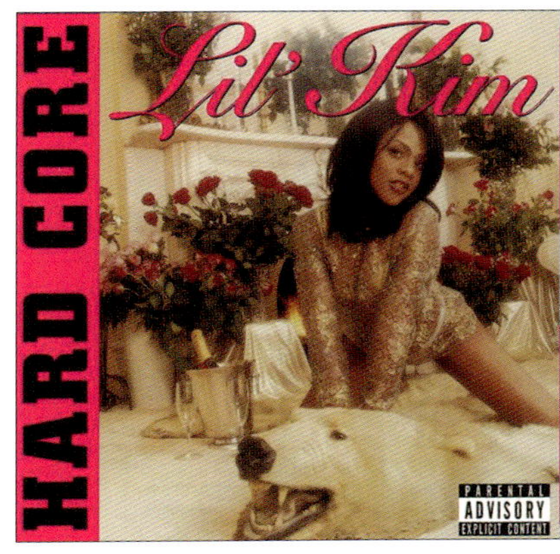


After getting ahead with Junior M.A.F.I.A., **Lil' Kim** put out her salacious solo album, *Hard Core*, and "No Time" and "Crush on You" topped the rap charts.

*Billboard* 200: *Hard Core* (#11)
*Billboard* Hot 100: "No Time" (#18); "Not Tonight" (#6)

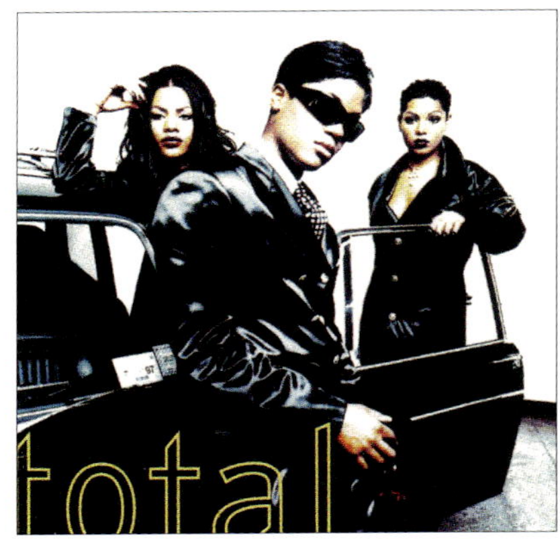


Having caught on as backing vocalists for the Notorious B.I.G., the girl group **Total** released a self-titled album, primarily produced by Sean "Puffy" Combs.

*Billboard* 200: *Total* (#23)
*Billboard* Hot 100: "Can't You See" (#13); "No One Else" (#22); "Kissin' You" (#12); "Do You Think About Us" (#61)

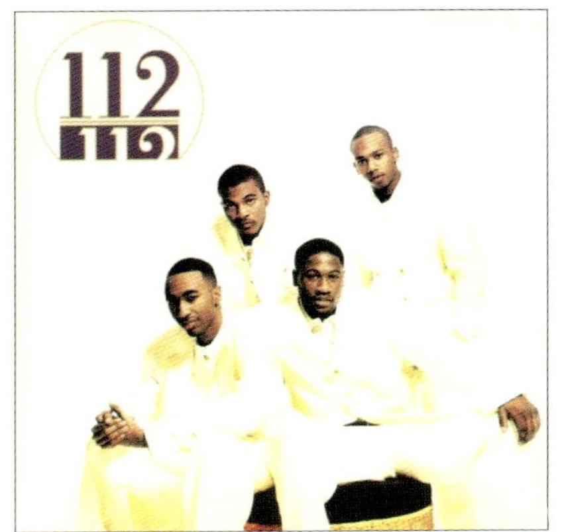


Issued on Sean Combs' Bad Boy label, **112**'s eponymous debut yielded "Only You," featuring the Notorious B.I.G., and the romantic soul ballad "Cupid."

*Billboard* 200: *112* (#37)
*Billboard* Hot 100: "Only You" (#13); "Come See Me" (#33); "Cupid" (#33)

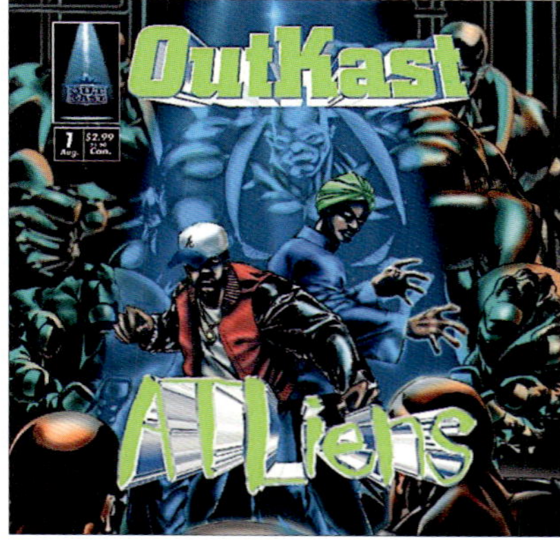


*ATLiens* by Southern hip-hop duo **Outkast** marked the production debut of members Big Boi and Dré, who crafted a No. 1 rap hit, "Elevators (Me and You)."

*Billboard* 200: *ATLiens* (#2)
*Billboard* Hot 100: "Elevators (Me and You)" (#12); "ATLiens" (#35); "Jazzy Belle" (#52)

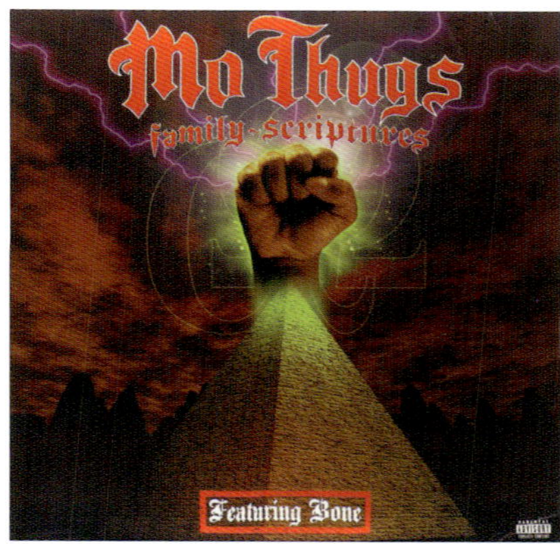


One of the multifarious acts signed to rap crew Bone Thugs-n-Harmony's own label, the collective **Mo Thugs** reached platinum status with *Family Scriptures.*

*Billboard* 200: *Family Scriptures* (#2)

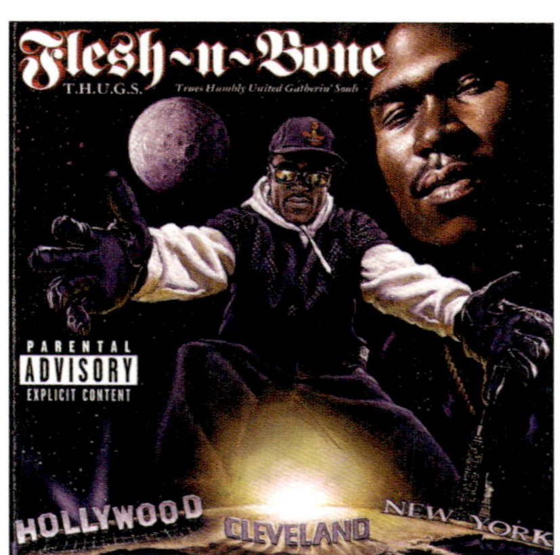


A member of Cleveland hip-hop group Bone Thugs-n-Harmony plagued with various problems, **Flesh-n-Bone** prepared his debut solo album, *T.H.U.G.S.*

*Billboard* 200: *T.H.U.G.S.: Trues Humbly United Gatherin' Souls* (#23)

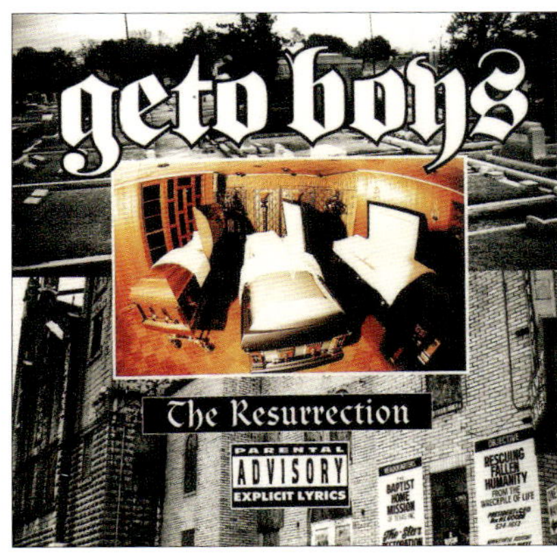


Following a three-year disengagement, the original **Geto Boys** lineup returned for *The Resurrection*, reuniting Willie D with Scarface and Bushwick Bill.

*Billboard* 200: *The Resurrection* (#6)
*Billboard* Hot 100: "The World Is a Ghetto" (#82)

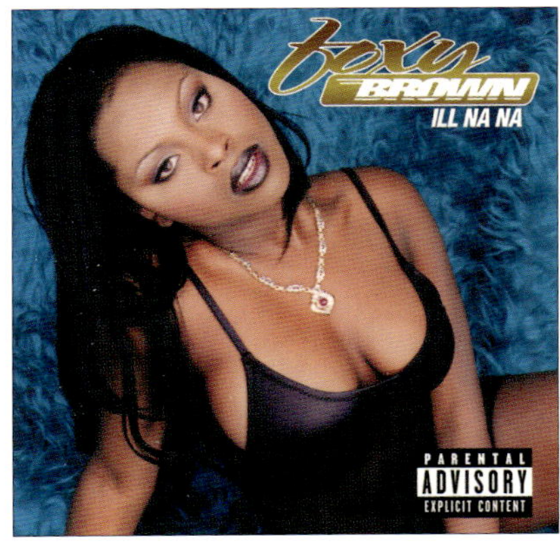


The rising raunchy rapper **Foxy Brown** scored with *Ill Na Na*, her debut release, collaborating with Brooklyn's Jay-Z on the monumental single "I'll Be."

*Billboard* 200: *Ill Na Na* (#7)
*Billboard* Hot 100: "Get Me Home" (#42); "I'll Be" (#7); "Big Bad Mamma" (#53)

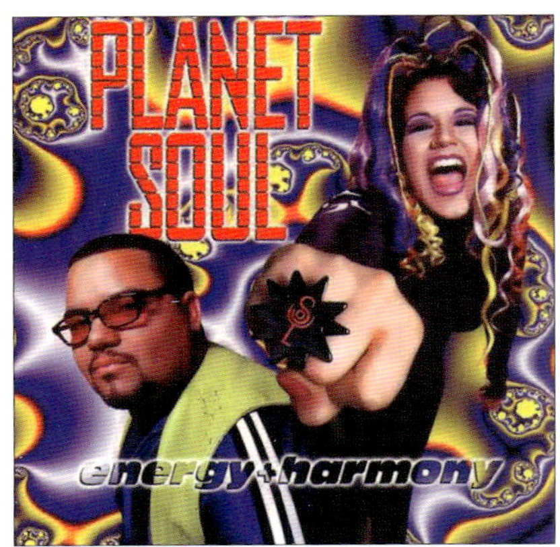


Singer Nadine Renee teamed with Miami DJ George Acosta and attained worldwide recognition with "Set U Free," released under the moniker **Planet Soul**.

*Billboard* 200: *Energy & Harmony* (#165)
*Billboard* Hot 100: "Set U Free" (#26); "Feel the Music" (#73)

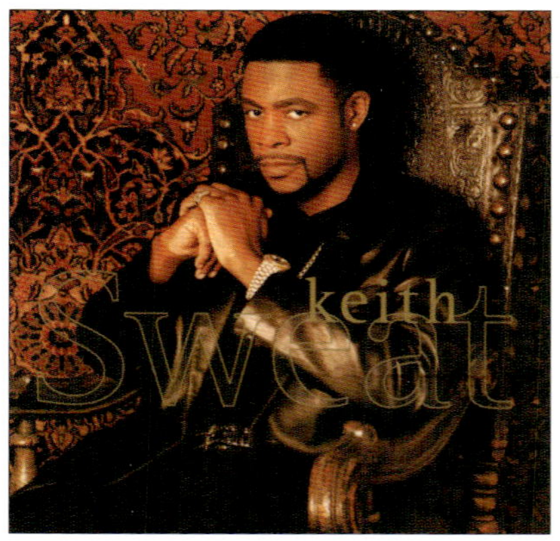


A regular presence on urban radio, singer **Keith Sweat** found crossover success with a self-titled album and two pop and R&B hits, "Twisted" and "Nobody."

*Billboard* 200: *Keith Sweat* (#5)
*Billboard* Hot 100: "Twisted" (#2); "Nobody" (#3); "Come with Me" (#68)

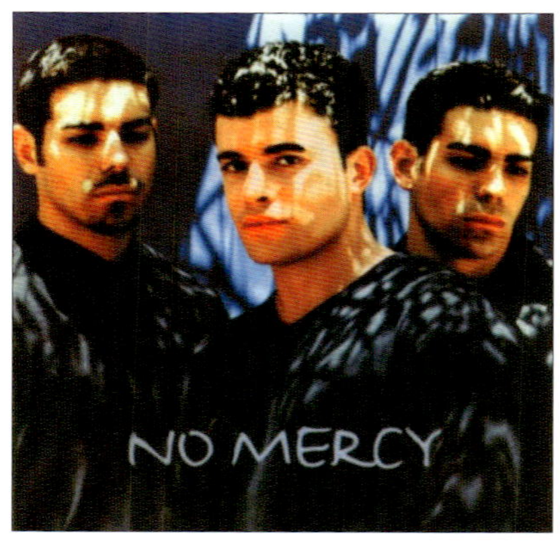


**No Mercy**, a troika of singers brought together by German producer Frank Farian, scored four global hits, highlighted in the US by "Where Do You Go."

*Billboard* 200: *No Mercy* (#102)
*Billboard* Hot 100: "Where Do You Go" (#5); "When I Die" (#41); "Please Don't Go" (#21); "Kiss You All Over" (#80)

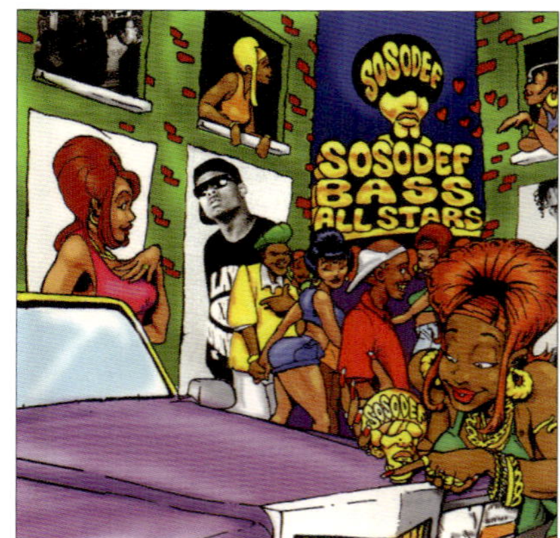


Arriving on Jermaine Dupri's So So Def label, the Miami bass-influenced "My Boo" became a smash for **Ghost Town DJ's**, an Atlanta-based hip-hop group.

*Billboard* Hot 100: "My Boo" (#27)

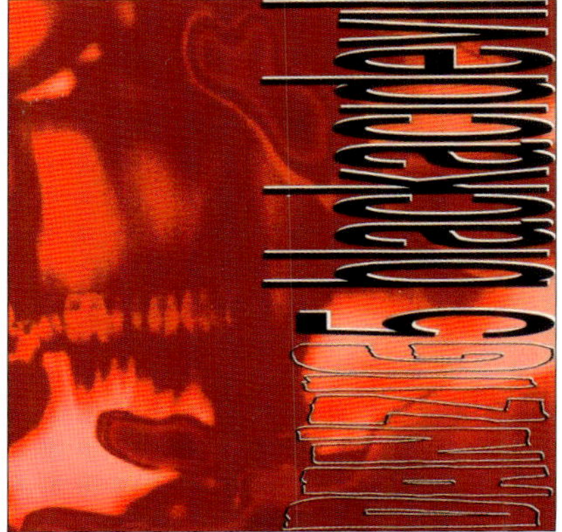


Recorded after the demise of the definitive **Danzig** lineup, *Blackacidevil* was mostly a solo effort by Glenn Danzig, an experiment with industrial sounds.

*Billboard* 200: *Blackacidevil* (#41)

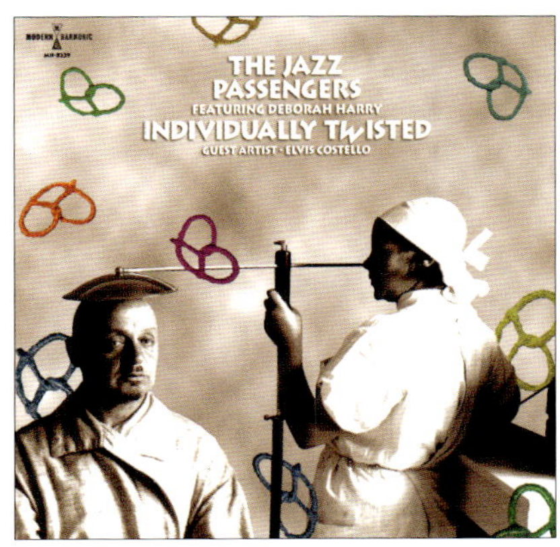


**The Jazz Passengers**' *Individually Twisted* featured vocal input from Deborah Harry, who appeared as a member of the band, along with Elvis Costello.

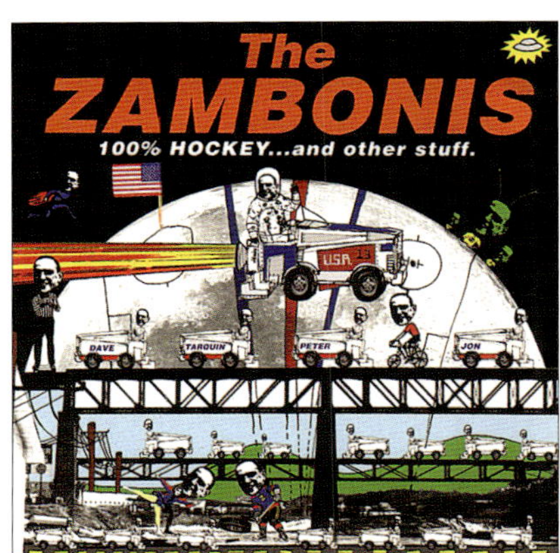


**The Zambonis** generated songs specifically about ice hockey, fostering a following of fellow fanatics with the debut album *100% Hockey...and Other Stuff.*

{ IN MEMORY OF LUCY PUGLIN }


## ACKNOWLEDGMENTS

Many people were essential to the creation of this book. My first thanks go to my amazing publishing team—Jon Rizzi for bringing his special brand of editorial wit and intelligence, and Kate Glassner Brainerd for her design artistry and unflagging pursuit of excellence. Special appreciation goes to the Michael & Patricia Matthews Fund, as well as John Cerullo, Annette Hobbs Magier and our colleagues at Publishers Group West.

Mike Dickson, Chip Garofalo, Jennifer Soulé, Mark Zaremba, Peter Marcus, Matt Rue, Jay Elowsky, Dave Zobl, Mark Lewis and Alexander Hau contributed expertise and resources. I am especially indebted to my dear friend Michael Jensen, as well as Sue Satriano, Janice Azrak, Bryn Bridenthal, Byron Hontas, Kathy Acquaviva, Shelly Selover, Sue Sawyer, Glen Brunman, Rick Ambrose, Bob Merlis, Bill Bentley, Heidi Ellen Robinson, Les Schwartz, Rick Gershon, Jim Merlis, Judi Kerr and Susan Blond—all of whom supported my efforts.

I specifically treasure the beneficence of Dave Rothstein, Greg Phifer, John Tope, Kevin Knee, Dick Merkle, Jeff Cook, Michael Brannen, Zak Phillips, Rich Garcia, Jason Minkler, Burt Baumgartner, Mitch Kampf, Don Zucker, Carl Walters, Charlie Reardon, Robin Wren, Jimmy Smith, Sharona White, John Ryland, Geina Horton, Michael Linehan, Mike Prince and Jeffrey Naumann, who all graciously furnished information and assistance.

I gratefully acknowledge the editing and reviewing skills of Dick Kreck, Tom Walker, Diane Carman, Mike Rudeen, Ed Smith, Jay Whearley, Mark Sims, Jeff Bradley and Peggy McKay.

I also salute David Gans, Leland Rucker, Steve Knopper, David Menconi, Jon Iverson, Gil Asakawa, Mark Bliesener, Butch Hause, Ricardo Baca, John Moore, Justin Mitchell, Michael Mehle and Harvey Kubernik, whose writings formed a vital index for the music-obsessed.

Finally, I would like to acknowledge with gratitude my beloved wife, Bridget, for her constant devotion and kindness. I cherish her—the love of my life.

EDITOR | **JON RIZZI**
ART DIRECTOR | **KATE GLASSNER BRAINERD**





ISBN 979-8-9885329-5-8    PRINTED IN CHINA | Asia Pacific Offset

HARVEY SID FISHER

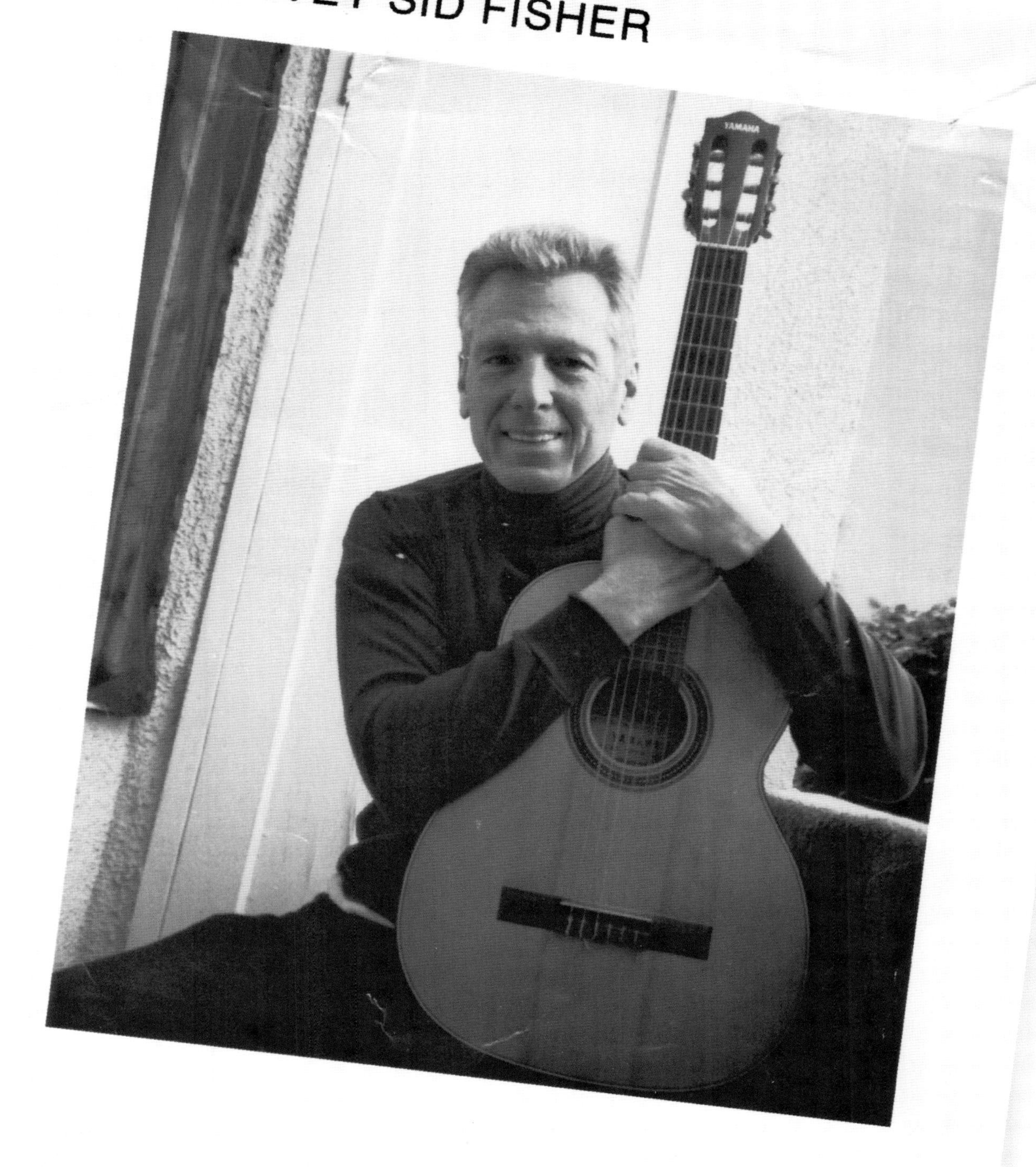

Next in the *ON RECORD* book series

# Vol.13 1980

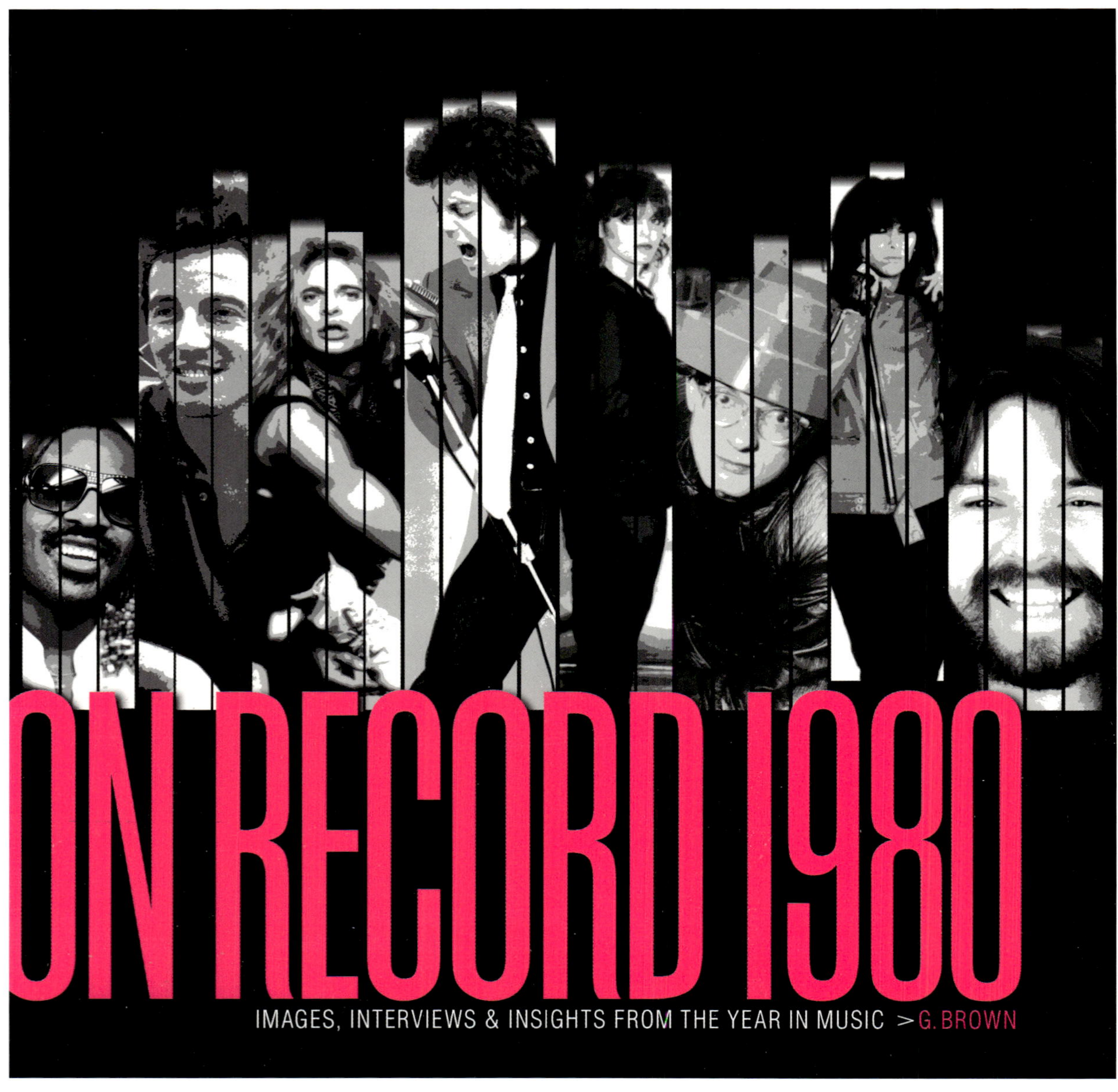